THE LONG PROCESS OF DEVELOPMENT

Douglass North once emphasized that development takes centuries, but he did not have a theory of how and why change occurs. This groundbreaking book advances such a theory by examining in detail why England and Spain developed so slowly from 1000 to 1800. A colonial legacy must go back centuries before settlement, and this book points to key events in England and Spain in the 1260s to explain why Mexico lagged behind the United States economically in the twentieth century. Based on the integration of North's institutional approach with Mancur Olson's collective action theory, Max Weber's theory of value change, and North's focus on dominant coalitions based on rent and military in *In the Shadow of Violence*, this theory of change leads to exciting new historical interpretations, including the crucial role of the merchant-navy alliance in England and the key role of George Washington's control of the military in 1787.

Jerry F. Hough is the James B. Duke Professor of Political Science at Duke University. He has taught at Duke since 1973. He previously taught at the University of Toronto and the University of Illinois at Urbana-Champaign, and he has served as a senior Fellow at the Brookings Institution. Hough received his PhD from Harvard University in 1961. His research has focused on the Soviet Union, the democratization of Russia and America, and nation building in the United States. He is the author of *How the Soviet Union Is Governed*; *Soviet Leadership in Transition*; *The Struggle for the Third World*; *Soviet Debate and American Options*; *Democratization and Revolution in the USSR, 1985–1991*; *The Logic of Economic Reform in Russia*; and *Changing Party Coalitions: The Mystery of the Red State–Blue State Alignment*.

Robin Grier earned her PhD from George Mason University in 1995. She was an assistant professor of economics at Centro de Investigación y Docencia Económicas (CIDE) in Mexico City before joining the University of Oklahoma in 1999. She became an associate professor of economics in 2004 and a professor in 2010. Grier's research has been published in the *Journal of Development Economics*, the *Journal of Law and Economics*, *Economic Development & Cultural Change*, *Review of Development Economics*, the *Journal of Development Studies*, *Economic Inquiry*, *Public Choice*, the *Southern Economic Journal*, *Kyklos*, *Economía Mexicana*, *El Trimestre Económico*, and *Rationality and Society*. Her area of specialization is the political economy of development in Latin America and Mexico.

The Long Process of Development

Building Markets and States in Pre-industrial England, Spain, and Their Colonies

JERRY F. HOUGH
Duke University

ROBIN GRIER
University of Oklahoma

CAMBRIDGE
UNIVERSITY PRESS

CAMBRIDGE
UNIVERSITY PRESS

32 Avenue of the Americas, New York, NY 10013-2473, USA

Cambridge University Press is part of the University of Cambridge.

It furthers the University's mission by disseminating knowledge in the pursuit of education, learning, and research at the highest international levels of excellence.

www.cambridge.org
Information on this title: www.cambridge.org/9781107063693

First published 2015

Printed in Great Britain by Clays Ltd, St Ives plc

A catalog record for this publication is available from the British Library.

Library of Congress Cataloging in Publication Data
Hough, Jerry F., 1935–
The long process of development: building markets and states in pre-industrial England, Spain, and their colonies / Jerry F. Hough, Duke University; Robin Grier, University of Oklahoma.
pages cm
Includes bibliographical references and index.
ISBN 978-1-107-06369-3 (hardback)
1. State, The – Philosophy. 2. Political development. 3. Great Britain – Politics and governmenty – 1066–1485. 4. Spain – Politics and government – To 1479. 5. Great Britain – Colonies – America – Administration. 6. Spain – Colonies – America – Administration. 7. Economic development – United States – History – 18th century. 8. Economic development – Mexico – History – 18th century. I. Grier, Robin M. II. Title.
JC131.H68 2014
338.9–dc23 2014020949

ISBN 978-1-107-06369-3 Hardback

Contents

Tables and Figures

Tables

Figures

Monarchs, 1037–1833

English Monarchs

Saxons	
Edward (the Confessor)	1042–1066
Harold II	1066
Normans	
William I	1066–1087
William II	1087–1100
Henry I	1100–1135
Stephen	1135–1154
Plantagenets	
Henry II	1154–1189
Richard I	1189–1199
John	1199–1216
Henry III	1216–1272
Edward I	1272–1307
Edward II	1307–1327
Edward III	1327–1377
Richard II	1377–1399
House of Lancaster	
Henry IV	1399–1413
Henry V	1413–1422
Henry VI	1422–1461

House of York	
Edward IV	1461–1483
Edward V	1483
Richard III	1483–1485
Tudors	
Henry VII	1485–1509
Henry VIII	1509–1547
Edward VI	1547–1553
Mary I	1553–1558
Elizabeth I	1558–1603
Stuarts	
James I	1603–1625
Charles I	1625–1649
Commonwealth	
Oliver Cromwell	1649–1658
Richard Cromwell	1658–1659
Stuarts (restored)	
Charles II	1660–1685
James II	1685–1688
William III	1689–1702
Mary II	1689–1694
Anne	1702–1714
House of Hanover	
George I	1714–1727
George II	1727–1760
George III	1760–1820

Castilian Monarchs

Jiménez Dynasty	
Ferdinand I	1037–1065
Sancho II	1065–1072
Alfonso VI	1072–1109
Urraca	1109–1126

House of Burgundy

Alfonso VII	1126–1157
Sancho III	1157–1158
Alfonso VIII	1158–1214
Henry I	1214–1217
Ferdinand III[1]	1217–1252
Alfonso X	1252–1284
Sancho IV	1284–1295
Ferdinand IV	1295–1312
Alfonso XI	1312–1350
Peter	1350–1369

House of Trastámara (1479–1555)

Henry II	1369–1379
John I	1379–1390
Henry III	1390–1406
John II	1406–1454
Henry IV	1454–1474

Spanish Monarchs

Isabella I[2]	1474–1504
Ferdinand V[3] (Regent)	1504–1516

House of Habsburg

Charles I	1516–1556
Philip II	1556–1598
Philip III	1598–1621
Philip IV	1621–1665
Charles II	1665–1700

1 The Castilian kings also ruled the region of León from 1230 onward. Prior to then, Castilian kings had only occasionally ruled León.

2 As the text indicates, these dates can be misleading. Henry IV's death ushered in a civil war, and Isabella did not consolidate her power until 1479.

3 Succeeding to the throne of Aragon as Ferdinand II on January 19, 1479, Ferdinand ruled Castile as a regent of Joanna. Ferdinand also went on to rule Granada (1492) and Navarre (1515).

House of Bourbon	
Philip V	1700–1724
Louis I	1724
Philip V	1724–1746
Ferdinand VI	1746–1759
Charles III	1759–1788
Charles IV	1788–1808
Ferdinand VII	1808
House of Bonaparte	
Joseph I	1808–1813
House of Bourbon	
Ferdinand VII	1813–1833

Introduction

American economists and political scientists first began to focus on economic development in the Third World in the 1950s. As time passed, attention shifted from the difficulties of de-colonization to fears about "dominos" after Vietnam, concerns about dependency and economic stagnation in the 1970s and 1980s, hopes for democratization after the fall of communism around 1990, and then fears about Islamic revolution and terrorism after 2001.

In all these cases, American presidents of both parties wanted immediate results. They sought advice from academics with different perspectives from their predecessors and hence who might be more successful. Each wave of advisers faced the demand to over-promise, and many responded. The first were the modernization theorists of the 1950s and 1960s who were members of the New Deal generation and favored government intervention. Progress was slow, and the failure of the Vietnam War sealed the fate of the theory.

The government then turned to neoclassical economists who developed the "Washington consensus" and demanded extremely rapid withdrawal of the state from the economy. As Alan Greenspan, chairman of the Federal Reserve Board, stated in 1997, "some ... supposed" that "the dismantling of the central planning function in an economy [would] automatically establish a free market entrepreneurial system."[1] The "some" were precisely the economists who had responded to the pressure to over-promise or who had been chosen for their preexisting optimism.

Whatever the ultimate validity of the reform package of the Washington consensus, its goals clearly could not be achieved in the short and medium

[1] Alan Greenspan, *The Embrace of Free Markets* (Washington, DC: Woodrow Wilson International Center for Scholars, 1997), p. 2.

run. The results of the Washington consensus in the former Soviet Union and the developing world were highly disappointing and discredited the theory.

Many, of course, were always skeptical during the periodic waves of over-optimism. In the 1990s, both authors of the present book were critical of the Washington consensus, one on the basis of years of studying the Soviet Union and the other Latin America.[2]

The foremost skeptical economist at the time was Douglass North. At the beginnings of the 1990s, North damned what he called "the glib rhetoric of all the neoclassical economist types that have jumped into 'the reform the East Europeans game'." Then he summarized his central argument in sweeping terms in his speech accepting the 1993 Nobel Prize: "Neoclassical theory is simply an inappropriate tool to analyze and prescribe policies that will induce development."[3]

In his Nobel acceptance speech, North attributed the mistakes of neoclassical theorists to "two basic erroneous assumptions." One is "that institutions do not matter," and the other is "that time does not matter."[4] North's warning about the importance of institutions (first of all, informal ones) was widely accepted by economists and became the basis for a school of economic analysis called "New Institutionalism." By contrast, his warning about time was largely neglected, at least by those high in the policy process.

For North, "time" meant that the heritage of the past produced enormous inertia ("path dependence") in the development process. He believes that "it takes a long time" to build "the necessary prerequisites for political and economic development." In 2008, he spoke concretely of 400 years as the amount of time that is needed. Oliver Williamson, another leading economist with a similar approach, said that the change in underlying norms, customs, mores, and traditions requires "centuries or millennia."[5]

[2] For Russia, see Jerry F. Hough, *The Logic of Economic Reform in Russia* (Washington, DC: Brookings Institution Press, 2001). For Latin America, see Robin Grier, "Losing Ground: Economic Growth in Latin America from 1955–1999," *Southern Economic Journal* 74 (2007), 177–203. For the argument that the neoclassical model gets almost nothing right about growth in the developing world, see Kevin Grier and Robin Grier, "Only Income Diverges: A Neoclassical Anomaly," *Journal of Development Economics* 84 (2007), 25–45.

[3] Letter from Douglass North to M. D. Morris, February 24, 1991, Box 2, February 1991 folder. The Douglass North papers are located in the Special Collection Library, Duke University. They were from original. Douglass North, "Economic Performance through Time," *American Economic Review* 84 (1994), 359–68, p. 359.

[4] North, "Epilogue: Economic Performance through Time," p. 343.

[5] For the "long time," see Margaret Levi, "A Model, a Method, and a Map: Rational Choice in Comparative and Historical Analysis," in Mark Irving Lichbach and Alan Zuckerman,

While those with the ear of policymakers argued that the neoclassical model must be supported by "institutions," they often used North's language simply to support the next panacea embraced by policymakers – the belief that democratic institutions were the key to stable development. This was associated with U.S. policy in countries such as Iraq and Afghanistan and also in the general policy of the World Bank. In April 2003, Thomas Friedman, the Middle East expert of *The New York Times* spoke for this view:[6]

> Iraq is the only Arab country that combines oil, water, brains, and secularism. Lebanon has water, brains, secularism and a liberal tradition. The Palestinians have a similar potential.... If Lebanon, Iraq, and a Palestinian state could all be made into functioning, decent, free-market, self-governing societies, it would be enough to tilt the entire Arab world onto a modernizing track.

Once again, expectations were disappointed. Once again, economists tried to warn against over-optimism and the importance of time. Those such as Dani Rodrik wrote about the need to adopt "second best measures" while others wrote about need to understand the difficulties of creating the rational-legal values that the sociologist Max Weber saw as the essence of a modern market. Lant Pritchett and Michael Woolcock[7] labeled this:

> the strategy of "skipping straight to Weber" – seeking to quickly reach service delivery performance goals in developing countries by simply mimicking (or adopting through colonial inheritance) the organizational forms of a particular "Denmark." We call this approach "skipping straight to Weber" because this form did not emerge from an internal historical process of trial and error and a political struggle (as it did in most European and North American countries).

eds., *Comparative Politics: Rationality, Culture, and Structure* (Cambridge University Press, 1997), p. 36. For 400 years, see John Joseph Wallis, "Answering Mary Shirley's Question, or What Can the World Bank Learn from American History?" in Stephen Haber, Douglass North, and Barry Weingast, eds., *Political Institutions and Financial Development* (Stanford: Stanford University Press, 2008), p. 92; Oliver Williamson, "The New Institutional Economics, Taking Stock, Looking Ahead," *Journal of Economic Literature* 38 (2000), 595–613, p. 596. Williamson won the Nobel Prize in Economics in 2009.

6 Thomas L. Friedman, "Roto-Rooter," *New York Times*, April 16, 2003, p. A19.

7 The authors' reference to "Denmark" does not refer to the country but rather to a typical developed country with an effective state and bureaucracy. Lant Pritchett and Michael Woolcock, "Solutions When the Solution Is the Problem: Arraying the Disarray in Development," *World Development* 32 (2004), 191–212, pp. 193 and 201. Some of the best work on historical legacies has been done by Nathan Nunn. Good examples of this include Nathan Nunn, "The Long-Term Effects of Africa's Slave Trades," *Quarterly Journal of Economics* 123 (2008), 139–76, Nathan Nunn and Diego Puga, "Ruggedness: The Blessing of Bad Geography in Africa," *Review of Economics and Statistics* 94 (2012), 20–36, and Nathan Nunn, "Historical Legacies: A Model Linking Africa's Past to Its Current Underdevelopment," *Journal of Development Economics* 83 (2007), 157–75.

Despite the severe problems in Afghanistan and Iraq, the Arab Spring in 2011 once more produced excess optimism – and with predictable results. When North's warnings about time were not heeded during the optimism about democratization, he repeated them in different language in two books published in 2009 and 2013. The first, entitled *Violence and Social Orders,* dealt primarily with developing countries in the decades just before the transition to a democratic political system and market economy, while the second, *In the Shadow of Violence,* dealt with the earlier stage of development found in much of modern Africa, Asia, and Latin America.

In the 2013 preface to *Violence and Social Orders,* North and his co-authors were clear about the events to which they were responding: "The world continues to be full of Arab springs and, unfortunately Arab winters."[8] As David Laitin wrote in his blurb on its back cover, *In the Shadow of Violence* shows "how the World Bank's attempts to transform countries into 'open access orders' [democracies with free markets] typically yield more violence than development."

Having observed the successive waves of optimism, we became convinced that a simple warning about the importance of patience is not enough. Scholars must have concrete advice – or at least a concrete framework – that gives guidance to policymakers about what is to be done, what a patient and gradual policy would entail. For all the faults of the proponents of modernization theory, the Washington consensus, and democratization, they told policymakers what to do. In the words of the old cliché, "you can't beat something with nothing."

North has never provided a theory of change. He openly acknowledged in his Nobel acceptance speech that he "does not provide a theory of economic dynamics.... We do not have such a theory." In 1997, he said that "we simply do not know how to create efficient political markets." North added that this "is essential if we are to implement policies consistent with intentions."[9]

In 2005, North reported that his work both as an author and an editor had had a sobering effect: "As someone who has 'played God' in attempting to

[8] Douglass North, John Joseph Wallis, and Barry Weingast, *Violence and Social Orders: A Conceptual Framework for Interpreting Recorded History* (New York: Cambridge University Press, 2009); Douglass North, John Joseph Wallis, Steven Webb, and Barry Webb, eds., *In the Shadow of Violence: Politics, Economics, and the Problems of Development* (Cambridge: Cambridge University Press, 2013). The quote on the Arab springs and winters is from the 2013 preface to the paperback edition of *Violence and Social Orders,* p. xv.

[9] North, "Economic Performance through Time," p. 359. Douglass North, *The Contribution of the New Institutional Economics to an Understanding of the Transition Problem* (Helsinki: UNU World Institute for Development Economics, 1997), p. 16.

improve performance of transition and Third World economies, I have been made acutely aware of the shortcomings in our understanding of how to set them right, which means in the first instance creating a political-economic structure that will lead to an improvement in their performance."[10]

Neither of the 2009 and 2013 books of North and his co-authors made any substantial attempt to build a theory of change except in the last 50 to 100 years of the process. In a 2014 book on the legacy of North, Claude Menard and Mary Shirley declare that New Institutionalism "needs a better theory of institutional change.... Some aspects of current institutional theory make change seem almost impossible." This point is repeated by John Joseph Wallis in his chapter in the same book.[11]

In recent decades, other scholars have also generally followed North's example in concentrating on the period of the final transition to a modern society. This, however, constitutes only 10% to 15% of the time North and Williamson say is necessary. We decided to concentrate on the more neglected 85% to 90% of the process – the period we call "pre-industrial." This is a crucial period because so many developing countries have progressed no further.

Our research design was based directly on North and Williamson's insight about time. If the development process requires centuries or millennia, a good research design should cover this length of time. We thought that a comparison of at least one "good" case and one "bad" case was required, cases that were truly comparable. They should be subject to the equivalent of loose controls by being in the same geographical area and in the same period with a 1000-year sweep. This history should be well documented in both cases in the scholarly literature that the authors could read.

For an American, Europe is the obvious choice of locale, and England is the obvious choice for the "good case." The most comparable "bad" case is Spain. In AD 800, both England and Christian Spain along the Bay of Biscay were sheep-growing areas dominated by small warlords. The beginning of the English and Spanish states in their most primitive form can reasonably be dated to the same time: the Norman invasion of William the Conqueror

10 Douglass North, *Understanding the Process of Economic Change* (Princeton, NJ: Princeton University Press, 2005), footnote 5, pp. 67–8.

11 Claude Menard and Mary M. Shirley, "The Contribution of Douglass North to New Institutional Economics," p. 28, and John Joseph Wallis, "Persistence and Change in Institutions: The Evolution of Douglass North," p. 48, in Sebastian Galiani and Itai Sened, eds., *Institutions, Property Rights, and Economic Growth: The Legacy of Douglass North* (Cambridge: Cambridge University Press, 2014).

in 1066 and Garcia Sanchez's formation of the Leon-Castilian "kingdom" (a loosely knit coalition of small warlords) in 1038.

Both England and Spain (Castile) had long been Catholic in the mid-1000s and were to remain so for another 500 years. Both exported wool in increasing amounts to Flanders, and both were heavily engaged in foreign trade until the late 1500s. Both created a great colonial empire in the New World that depended on secure transportation across the Atlantic Ocean.

Moreover, the economic development of Spain and England was closely linked. Spain began with a command of the sea that prevented English colonization in the 1500s, and the Tudor creation of an English navy and merchant fleet was the key event that led to the virtual collapse of the Spanish Empire in the 1600s. The Bourbon re-creation of the Spanish fleet in the 1700s restored their control over the Empire. Seemingly, the two countries should have followed similar paths of development, but they did not do so.

The use of England and Spain as our two main cases made it natural and easy to add two more cases: the United States and Mexico. Indeed, one of the two authors had a long special interest in Mexico and the other in the United States. We began the study with a special interest in the role of the colonial legacy in explaining why the United States developed much more rapidly than Mexico. As a result, we decided to end the book roughly a decade after the United States and Mexico became independent. This meant it covered the period from 1000 to roughly 1800 in the American case and 1830 in the Mexican.

But Mexico was a colony for 300 years and the United States for 170. Our acceptance of North and Williamson's insight about time forced us to trace their "colonial tradition" well back into English and Spanish history. Indeed, we came to realize that the different consequences of Henry III's conquest of London in 1265 and Alfonso X's conquest of Cadiz in 1262 made the 1260s a key moment in the colonial legacy to the two countries.

Since the colonial experiences of England and Spain were both heavily shaped by the changing relative capability of their armed merchant fleets, the book provides an interesting – and for economists, quite fresh – sub-case study of the role of armed merchant ships in "peaceful trade" and their crucial importance in commerce, economic development, and domestic politics. We focus on two elements of English domestic political history that are ignored in the American economic literature: the critical role of the Hanseatic League fleet in its late medieval development and the merchant-naval alliance in English politics in the 1600s and 1700s.

The intellectual assumptions of this book rest on the failure of Douglass North and the "New Institutionalists" to put forth a multi-century theory of change. North himself implicitly agreed that the insights of New Institutionalists were not in themselves enough for such a theory. He sought the answers in modern psychology, but he did not find that literature sufficient to solve the problem.[12]

This suggests to us that insights from still other intellectual traditions need to be added to those of New Institutional theory to move in the direction of a theory of change. We think that the place to start is with the work of two great scholars in the 20th century who became central figures in sociology and political science: Max Weber and Mancur Olson.

Douglass North argues that a modern society depends on the development of the appropriate norms, values, mental images, and ideologies (informal institutions, in his phrase). Yet he never says anything about the content of either the informal institutions that are needed or those that have to be overcome. Max Weber's *Economy and Sociology* and his *Politics as a Vocation* concentrate on the difference between the values of village and tribal society on the one hand and those of modern society on the other.

As a result, Weber is a perfect supplement to North. This is particularly the case, as Pritchett and Woolcock point out, because many development economists implicitly think in terms of "skipping straight to Weber" – that is, his image of modern values – without giving their intellectual assumptions much thought.

Mancur Olson was a neoclassical economist who applied neoclassical assumptions about human motivation to individual behavior in the political sphere. As a result, he concluded that it was almost never rational for members of large groups to engage in large-scale collective action simply because they favored the achievement of a collective goal. He argued that such collective action depends on compulsion or selective side payments (rewards that only the individual receives).

Since the role of compulsion (the military) and selective side payments (the tax collection necessary to provide them) are almost never discussed in the social contract and contractarian analyses, Olson naturally was a sharp critic of these arguments that are at the heart of New Institutionalism. Indeed, Olson had been stimulated to develop his theory of the state in the early 1990s by his negative attitude toward the social contract embedded in Douglass North and Barry Weingast's iconic

[12] For a summary of the work, see North, *Understanding the Process of Economic Change*, pp. 23–64.

1989 article on the Glorious Revolution of 1688: "Constitutions and Commitment."[13]

Olson had "Constitutions and Commitment" specifically in mind when he wrote that voluntary collective action simply "*cannot* obtain the gains from a peaceful order [of a state]." Instead, Olson argued, the ruler is the person who "can organize the greatest capacity for violence."[14] North has had a negative attitude toward rulers and bureaucracies, but Olson reminds us that violence is needed to control violence and to provide the framework for cooperative action within society and the economy. Olson, thereby, provides us with insights into a mechanism of change that is quite absent in North's work.

Both Weber and Olson analyzed the earliest forms of society and the state and also the character of modern society. Unfortunately, neither of them analyzed the long period of transition between the two periods. Neither explained how the change takes place. This intermediate period is the main focus of this book, and we think that Olson's analysis leads to a series of new insights – hypotheses, if you wish – that are not found in the literature of American economists.

The fundamental historical question of this book is why it took England so many centuries to develop an effective state and market and why Spain required 200 years longer. A collective action theory that focuses on compulsion and selective side payments gives far greater importance to the direct or indirect impact of factors including military force on key events that mythologists want to discuss in other terms. We suggest – and document at some length – that this includes the three English regime changes in the 1640s, 1660, and 1688 and the Constitutional Convention of 1787 in the United States.

In the last section of this chapter, we discuss those aspects of Weber's and Olson's analyses that we consider most useful to integrate with North's analysis to answer North's question: Why does time matter? Why does development take so long and how is positive change accomplished?

North's 2009 *Violence and Social Orders* and 2013 *In the Shadow of Violence* move partially, but only partially, toward Olson's analysis. We are able to compare these recent books with North's earlier work and with his archived correspondence from the 1970s, 1980s, and 1990s in order to clarify more clearly the difference between a social contract and a collective approach.

[13] Douglass North and Barry Weingast, "Constitutions and Commitment: The Evolution of Institutions Governing Public Choice in Seventeenth Century England," *Journal of Economic History* 49 (1989), 803–32.

[14] Mancur Olson, "Dictatorship, Democracy, and Development," *American Political Science Review* 87 (1993), 567–76, p. 568.

Absorbing the Meaning of "Time" in Development

Probably the most difficult aspect of this book is seemingly the simplest, namely, how to ensure that readers have some understanding – or really some feel – for the real meaning of the phrase "hundreds of years or millennia." Even a year or two of a crisis seems an eternity when we are forced to live through it, but decades seem like years and centuries seem like decades when we look at the past. So do millennia when we talk about the third millennium BC or the like.

As a result, we begin this book with an effort to illustrate this most basic of facts. We use English history as an example, primarily because its history is more familiar to most readers of this book than the history of Spain. In addition, even though we ask why economic development was much slower in Spain than in England, the more basic question is why development took such an incredibly long period in the "good" case of England.

The Norman invasion of 1066 is certainly the point at which to start, all the more since the "English" state and culture are really Franco-English. Consider the chronology in England after the Norman Conquest in 1066. The Magna Carta was signed in 1215; London was established as a capital of a city-state in 1337; London imposed control over all of England in 1485 (really the early 1500s); the Glorious Revolution took place in 1688 and the partial move toward the democratization of Britain in the Reform Act of 1832.

If we do some simple mathematics, we find that the period of time between each of these events was more or less 150 years. The American Civil War was 150 years ago, but it seems part of the ancient past. There were over five such periods between 1066 and 1832 in England. It is harder to believe that the Glorious Revolution occurred 576 years after the Magna Carta of 1212, a period 50 years longer than the time from Columbus's voyage to the present.

Let's think hypothetically. Kabul has still not established control over the interior of Afghanistan, even as the capital of a confederation. But imagine optimistically that that occurs by 2020. The victory of Henry VII in 1485 was the equivalent watershed event in English history. If Afghanistan is on the English time path, it will have its Glorious Revolution in 2323 and full democracy in 2437. Obviously the change in contemporary Afghanistan will come much faster because of the transformation in technology and education, but these dates help us to understand just how slowly England evolved.

Or let's look at the period from 1066 to 1776 in a different way. It was 237 years from 1776 to 2013. All of us are quite aware of the enormous changes that have taken place in the United States socially, economically, and politically since the American Revolution. It turns out that the period from 1066 to 1776 can be divided into three periods, *each* exactly as long as that from 1776 to the present. As much change – or almost as much change – occurred in England during each of these three periods as occurred between 1776 and 2013.

The first of the three periods extended from the Norman Conquest in 1066 to 1302. In the first 60% of the period, the Norman kings and lords lived primarily in France. When the kings came to England for visits, they were itinerant rulers who received most of their revenue from "rent" from peasants living on their land and from looting. King John, who signed the Magna Carta in 1215, was the last of these French kings.

John's son, Henry III, was the first king to identify himself fully with England and its pre-Norman past. He disregarded the Magna Carta by defying the lords and gained full control of London and the surrounding area in 1265. Nevertheless, Henry III and all "English" kings until 1387 still spoke French as their native language.

As one of Henry III's descendants began to establish himself as the warlord of the city-state in London (really in Westminster and the Windsor Castle), the other English warlords consolidated their positions in their castles in the countryside and, of course, retained their military force. The political-economic system in 1300 is rightly called "military feudalism" (warlords with military force, but without classic serfdom).[15] We call it a pre–nation-state.

The second period of 237 years stretched from 1303 until 1539 and also featured drastic changes. In 1303, London still would not be a real capital for 34 years, and a permanent large wool export tax would not be introduced for more than 40 years. The latter was the first major tax that the kings were able to collect other than rent from their own estates. Yet they did so only by allying with the greatest naval power of the time, the Hanseatic League.

The major achievement of the king before 1485 was the gradual creation of an effective government and economy in London, but its economy was based almost entirely on monopoly guilds. The king governed London quite well through a city council composed largely of guild leaders. That is, the king still did not have the military force to control the lords of the interior,

[15] For a discussion of military feudalism, see Charles Wilson, *England's Apprenticeship, 1603–17*, 2nd ed. (London: Longman, 1985), pp. 3–4.

and he had a real authoritarian system only within the city-state of London. As the power of the Hanseatic League weakened in the 1400s, the kings had to defer more to the regional warlords in order to receive revenue from them. That increased the power of the representatives of the rural elites in Parliament.

Then in 1485, the Tudor Henry VII seized the throne and began to consolidate control over all of England. By 1538, Henry VII and especially his son, Henry VIII, had destroyed much of the military power of the feudal lords. By that time the Tudors had for the first time in English history introduced what Daron Acemoglu and James Robinson call "political centralization" of London vis-à-vis England as a whole – what we call a "minimally effective state." Yet Lawrence Stone, the foremost authority on the military power of the aristocracy, asserts that the decisive period in the whole process was the years from 1570 to 1620 – a century after Henry VII came to power.[16]

At the beginning of the third period from 1540 to 1776, London had a population of only 75,000 people. Henry VIII was the greatest tyrant in English history, and he had largely eviscerated the power of Parliament. Economic growth was accelerating, but 90% of England's exports still consisted of wool and woolen cloth. Both were sent across a narrow channel to Calais where export taxes were collected.

The period from 1540 to 1776 was enormously complex and contained a number of sub-periods. It featured the authoritarian reigns of Henry VIII and Elizabeth I, 150 years of religious wars, the Puritan Revolution in 1640, the Restoration of the Stuart monarchy in 1660, the Glorious Revolution in 1688, and then three-quarters of a century of what John Brewer labels a "fiscal-military state."[17]

It was not until the beginning of the Hanover dynasty in 1714 that England first had what we call a truly effective state. By 1776 the economy of England had been utterly transformed. The Industrial Revolution was under way, and London had grown from 50,000 people in 1500 to 200,000 in 1600, 500,000 in 1700, and 900,000 in 1776.

The meaning of all the key economic concepts used in this book also changed enormously over these three periods. In 1991 Douglass North wrote, "I don't know what the word capitalism means and therefore I have

[16] Daron Acemoglu and James Robinson, *Why Nations Fail: The Origins of Power, Prosperity, and Poverty* (New York: Crown, 2012), pp. 186–7; Lawrence Stone, *The Crisis of the Aristocracy*, abridged edition (London: Oxford University Press, 1967), p. 133.

[17] John Brewer, *The Sinews of Power: War, Money, and the English State, 1688–1783* (Cambridge, MA: Harvard University Press, 1990).

never used the term."[18] We too never employ the word, and, if it were possible (which it is not), we would avoid any of the broad economic and political concepts used to cover periods and places distant from each other. The "mercantilism" of 1300, 1500, and 1700 were all starkly different from each other. The mercantilism of 1776, when Adam Smith criticized it in *The Wealth of Nations*, was far more market-oriented than the earlier ones.[19]

To repeat, 237 years is a *really* long period of time. It is as long as the time since the Declaration of Independence, and we know how much technology has changed over that period. If we go back 75 years, there were no antibiotics, jet airplanes, rockets, television, computers, and the multiple means of communication of the last 20 years. That is only one-third of 237 years. Indeed, we know how much the technology of personal communication has been transformed in the last 30 years alone. Earlier generations had that sense of change as well, especially those who lived in urban areas or moved there.

Somehow this enormous length of time must be taken into account in any theory of change. We divide England into four periods within the time frame of this book: 1066 to the early 1200s (the pre–nation-state), the early 1200s to the early 1500s (the early state), the early 1500s to the early 1700s (the minimally effective state), and the early 1700s to 1832 (the truly effective state). The stage of the democratic state of the 19th century is beyond the scope of this book. Yet even the enormous difference between England of 1550 and 1750 – the period when a minimally effective state evolved into a truly effective one – must be informally subdivided.

From this perspective, the striking difference between England and Spain was that the Spanish pre-state lasted some 250 years longer than the English. It came to an end only when Isabella ascended to the throne in 1480. Then we date the Spanish early state to the period from 1480 to the early 1700s, the minimally effective state from the early 1700s to the late 1800s and the truly effective state until 1975. There is a strong case to be made for treating Franco's forty years as the first truly effective state and recognizing its more limited character after the 1930s.

Our first task – and it is the primary question of Chapter 2 – is to explain why this was so. Many older scholars thought that Spain's economic

[18] North to Mike Haupert, September 15, 1992, North Papers, Box 3, Correspondence September 1992. He makes the same point in a letter to Pavel Pelikan, April 2, 1992, North Papers, Box 3, Correspondence, April 1992.

[19] For a recent survey of changing views of mercantilism, see Philip Stern and Carl Wennerlind, eds., *Mercantilism Reimagined: Political Economy in Early Modern Britain and Its Empire* (Oxford: Oxford University Press, 2013).

backwardness came from its centralized bureaucratic state in the 1500s and 1600s, but modern historians think that the reverse is true. The Spanish rulers simply did not have the administrative capability of the Tudors until the 1700s after the French Bourbons seized control of the Spanish government at almost the same time as the Glorious Revolution of 1688. That evolution may have resulted not from internal evolution but from the Bourbons' experience in France.

Understanding the Mechanisms of Change

Although we focus on England, Mexico, Spain, and the United States from 1000 to the early 1800s, we are interested in a theory of change that applies to the contemporary developing world as well. We, therefore, are not presenting a straightforward historical analysis but organize the first half of the book on England and Spain by levels of development, very loosely defined.

Obviously any transfer of "lessons" from the past to the present is fraught with extreme peril. The past, especially one that extends over 450 years from the Magna Carta of 1212 to the Glorious Revolution of 1688, is multifaceted. It is easy for any analyst to find some sequence of events supporting any "lessons of the past" that he or she consciously or unconsciously wants.

Thus, prior to World War I, many saw American democracy coming from the democracy of medieval German towns, not from the French Norman lords of 1212 and afterward. Before Franco's coup in 1936, many saw the instability of Spain coming from a frontier psychology produced by centuries of war against the Muslims. The instability of Mexico could be explained by its silver-seeking "Klondike" psychology. After Franco came to power, pieces of evidence were easy to find to show the Spanish tradition was authoritarian. It is almost impossible to prove which of these interpretations is more plausible.

While North originally presented a cultural approach, others such as Robert Bates argued that "the study of the political economy of development is the study of prosperity and violence":[20]

> Political development occurs when people domesticate violence, transforming coercion from a means of predation into a productive resource. Coercion becomes productive when it is employed not to seize or to destroy wealth, but rather to safeguard and promote its creation.

[20] Robert H. Bates, *Prosperity & Violence: The Political Economy of Development*, 2nd ed. (New York: W. W. Norton, 2010), 84–5.

As the titles of *Violence and Social Orders* and *In the Shadow of Violence* indicate, Douglass North has now shifted from a focus on informal institutions to agree with Bates about the crucial importance of controlling violence. This is particularly so in *In the Shadow of Violence,* which deals with the contemporary developing world:[21]

> All societies must deal with the problem of violence. In most developing countries, individuals and organizations actively use or threaten to use violence to gather wealth and resources, and violence has to be restrained for development to occur. In many societies the potential for violence is latent: organizations generally refrain from violence in most years, but occasionally find violence a useful tool for pursuing their ends. These societies live in the shadow of violence, and they account for most of human history and for most of today's world population.

Regional warlords and/or central military hierarchies are the ones with the greatest potential to unleash organized violence. Not surprisingly the long experience of Europe allows us to see the forms that violence can take and its varying consequences, at least if we look behind the myths created to hide reality. Clearly the establishment of modern stability depends not on the formation of a government with a nominal preponderance of control of the instruments of violence, but a government of real control.

The military factors obviously were an important factor in Spanish history. The so-called nobles were heads of families who controlled the various city-states throughout the peninsula as warlords. Isabella came to power in 1480 and began – but only barely began – to bring those warlords to heel. Only the victory of France in the long War of Spanish Succession of 1700 to 1713 allowed it to put a French Bourbon king on the throne who could bring the regional warlords under control.

Violence was just as important in English and American development. In medieval times, the English king was able to tax the lords only by offering them the chance to acquire land and other forms of booty in wars against France, Scotland, and Ireland and by allying himself with the fleet of the Hanseatic League to gain export taxes on their wool. Then the military coup of Henry VII in 1485 began the destruction of the feudal lords.

The Tudors and the Stuarts did not have a significant standing army, but their deep-sea merchant fleet was armed and was allied with the growing state navy. The two together played a key role in the Restoration of 1660 and the Glorious Revolution of 1688 and then the establishment of the "fiscal-military regime" of the 1700s.

[21] North et al., *In the Shadow of Violence*, pp. 1–2.

Similarly, the key, if unappreciated, events in the American Revolution were John Adams's failed attempt to overthrow George Washington in 1776–1777, Washington's decision to place his troops at Valley Forge near the capital in order to force Adams into unwilling exile in France, and then Washington's threat of a military coup that produced the Constitutional Convention in 1787.

The 1787 decision to decentralize military power to the state level permitted the effective federalism that was impossible in Mexico because the latter lacked organized provincial governments with organized military force. Development economists who warn about the control of violence in the contemporary developing world need to have a realistic understanding of English and American history that is quite lacking in the American policy elite. No one discusses the fact that it took from 1485 until 1720 to deprive the English lords of military force and change their culture of violence. No one talks about the Second Amendment in discussing policy in the developing world.

Of course, the pace of change in the 21st century clearly will not be as slow as English development, but there was a time when all European countries faced the problem of transforming the personalistic values of the village into the impersonal values needed for a market economy. All European countries faced the collective action problem of creating reliable "agents" in the military and other bureaucracies, notably, the tax-collecting ones. Modern developing countries need to learn from Europe how to achieve these goals, even if more rapidly.

In practical terms, it does not matter if the speed of the transition is greater today than in the European past. The modern problem is to get leaders to take a 30- to 40-year perspective instead of a four-year or eight-year one. The early states in Africa today will not need the 400 to 500 years that it took England and Spain to develop a truly effective state – and nearly another century to develop a stable democracy, but it will take at least 40 to 50 years – and almost surely longer.

A half-century is literally a lifetime, even for a younger policymaker. So long as policymakers assume that a modern government and economy will not develop for a number of decades, they can accept the need to work for partial success. They will be ready to take "second-best" measures.[22]

In this book, we adopt an approach that incorporates four major "lessons" from the 800 years of English and Spanish history that we examine:

[22] Dani Rodrik, *One Economics, Many Recipes: Globalization, Institutions, and Economic Growth* (Princeton, NJ: Princeton University Press, 2007).

(1) the need to recognize loosely defined differences in levels of development; (2) the integration of Max Weber's insights about the difference between village-based and urban-based values into Douglass North's insights about informal institutions; (3) the importance of creating an effective state as a pre-condition of an effective market, and the collective action obstacles to the creation of effective governmental and private bureaucracies; and (4) the importance of accepting and learning how to operationalize Douglass North's new argument that the control of violence requires the acceptance of "dominant coalitions" including the military whose members are enriched by what is normally called corruption.

The Need to Recognize Different Levels of Development

This book says nothing about the proper role of the state in a modern economy, but the sub-title of the book expresses our conviction that an effective market is dependent on an effective government of some type. We fully agree with Douglass North that the construction of such a government takes centuries.

We think that English history from 1300 to 1776 illustrates this point perfectly. From our perspective, it is very fortunate that Adam Smith published *The Wealth of Nations* in 1776. Almost certainly, Smith rushed the book into print because of its hundred-page section that called upon the king to grant the colonies independence. This was almost surely why it became a bestseller.

Smith argued that free trade and colonial independence would give the king more tax revenue from the internal taxation than from colonial trade. We quite agree with him about 1776. The crucial point that we make about English history is that Smith would have been wrong for almost all of English history prior to 1776. At earlier stages, the English government did not have the ability to collect taxes either from free trade or from manufacturers. Indeed, England was not able to levy income taxes until after 1776. If London had introduced free trade much earlier in the century, it surely would have lost tax revenue.

The secret of the development of the city-state of London in the 1300s, we suggest, is that the English kings decided to ally with the Hanseatic League and its fleet in order to compensate for their lack of a merchant marine, a navy, and an effective tax-collecting bureaucracy. This was how the kings acquired the ability to stop smugglers and collect customs duties. A reason for the financial difficulties of the English kings in the 1400s was the decline of the power of the Hanseatic League.

Similarly, in the 1500s, England had no ability to colonize the New World until Henry VIII and Elizabeth I developed a major naval and oceangoing merchant fleet and finally defeated the Spanish Armada in 1588. By the time England began large-scale colonization in the 1620s, it had developed a reasonably effective ability to collect taxes from any English and colonial shippers who traded with or within in the Atlantic empire – at least, if they brought the commodities only to England. Yet England still had to rely on the monopoly of the East India Company for trade with the East until after 1776. When England instituted a molasses tax in 1732 in the colonies, it did not yet have the ability to collect it.

At each period a policy that could not be sustained by the existing government machinery would not have been effective. The same is true in the developing world today. Many policies can profitably be introduced in Mexico and Turkey that cannot profitably be introduced in many less-developed countries. Different policies are needed in Afghanistan than in Pakistan. We need ways of organizing our thinking about such differences, and we hope that our categories are useful first steps.

In this book, we criticize the extreme optimism of the most politically active proponents of modernization theory, the Washington consensus, and the pro-democratization school. Yet, each approach had valuable insights, and they should not be lost. It is particularly important to recover such insights of modernization theory. Some modernization theorists were too rigid, and some let their analysis become "an anti-Communist manifesto," to quote the sub-title of the famous book of W. W. Rostow, the future national security adviser of Lyndon Johnson.[23]

Yet the political atmosphere of the 1960s and 1970s meant that the younger scholars rejected the theory too completely. As a result, too many generations of graduate students received no exposure to its insights. As the last section made clear, anyone who thought the Third World could and should follow the Western model knew full well that development in the West had taken a very long time. When Robert Scott, the top modernization theorist on Mexico, was asked privately in the 1960s for his prediction about Mexico in the 1980s, he answered that he had no idea. He said, however, that he was fairly confident what Mexico would look like in the mid-21st century. Those with that perspective had insights that are worth reexamining.

There are a number of good indicators of development, but per capita income has proven a relatively reliable one, if we exclude some poorer

[23] W. W. Rostow, *The Stages of Economic Growth: A Non-Communist Manifesto* (Cambridge: Cambridge University Press, 1960).

countries whose income is distorted by the high production of petroleum or other commodity that has little impact on the life of the population or other sectors of the economy.

The countries of sub-Saharan Africa, at least those without mineral and oil production, are clearly among the world's poorest and also are at the lowest level of development by any criterion. Nevertheless, many countries in other parts of the world have had only somewhat higher living standards, if that. For instance, in 2012, Afghanistan had a literacy rate of 28% and per capita income of $1,100. Other such countries included Somalia ($600), Haiti ($1,200), Burma ($1,600), Bangladesh ($2,000), and Yemen ($2,300). They almost all are at what we call an early state or minimally effective level of political development.[24]

A second group of countries are at either a minimally effective stage or a very early truly effective stage of development. These include the countries involved in the Arab Spring. All had similar incomes: Syria ($5,100), Jordan ($6,000), Egypt ($6,500), Iraq ($7,000), Algeria ($7,300), and Tunisia ($9,700). Not surprisingly, the rebellion in Tunisia was the most successful. The Philippines ($4,400), Indonesia ($4,900), and Bolivia ($5,000) are at the bottom end of the same category.

Other developing countries are economically more advanced. These include countries such as Brazil ($11,700), Turkey ($14,800), Mexico ($15,400), and Argentina ($18,400). These "more developed" developing countries are, it should be noted, still far from the poor countries of Western Europe: for example, Portugal ($23,000), Greece ($24,300), and Spain ($30,100) – or South Korea ($31,900).

It is dangerous to try to have precise definitions of vague categories because readers may gain the impression that the categories are more precise than they seem. There are no clean dividing points between our categories, even if we define "precise" as involving decades. In general, many scholars may find our categories of pre–nation-state, early state, minimally effective state, and truly effective state easiest to understand if we discuss them in terms of the well-known categories of Max Weber: patriarchal, patrimonial, and rational-legal.

The boundary between pre-state and early state is the most difficult to define. The basic problem is that the pre-state can extend almost indefinitely into the past. So far as the mass of the population was concerned, for example, the Norman regime beginning in 1066 was not that different

[24] *The World Factbook 2013–14* (Washington, DC: Central Intelligence Agency, 2013). https://www.cia.gov/library/publications/the-world-factbook/index.html.

from the Danish regime it overthrew. The Castilian pre-state period really extended further back into the past than 1038, at least to 800.

The problem is not one-sided. National mythmakers choose when a state begins, and they have a tendency to go much too far into the past. If we followed them, we would begin with the mythical King Arthur in England, pre-Muslim Spain, or Kievan Rus in Russia. They could have chosen a later king or queen (for example, Isabella in Spain) as the real beginning of a new state. We have chosen the Norman invasion of 1066 and García Sánchez's creation of the León-Castile Kingdom in 1038 as the beginning of the "pre-state" in England and Castile, primarily because they are reasonable beginning points for a discussion that has to begin somewhere. In Max Weber's terms, the pre-state is characterized by a patriarchal system:[25]

> "Patriarchalism" is the situation where, within a group, which is usually organized on both an economic and a kinship basis, as a household, authority is exercised by a particular individual who is designated by a definite rule of inheritance.... It is crucial that ... there is a complete absence of an administrative staff over which the individual in authority has personal control.

The "early state" by our definition is a still a patriarchal system, but one that is very slowly beginning the transition to what Weber calls a patrimonial system. Patrimonialism was marked by the development of "a personal administrative system, especially a military force under the control of the chief." Yet the first administrative systems often are more corporate than bureaucratic. The key administrative officials were often still primarily employed in the household of the ruler. The "early state" by our definition is a still a patriarchal system, but one that is slowly beginning the transition to what Weber calls a patrimonial system.

England was typical. The key administrative officials were still primarily employed in the royal household, but the household came to be divided into those officials who had more personal responsibilities and those who had more "governmental" ones. "Upstairs" officials became different from "downstairs" ones. Nevertheless, the same people who acquired food for the royal castles were used to acquire food for ships in wartime because they alone had the organizational capability and experience to gather together such a quantity of food. The "navy" was composed of private armed merchant ships mobilized by the monarch in war. But both the navy and the "victualizing" became specialized institutions over the centuries.

[25] Max Weber, *Theory of Social and Economic Organization*, translated by A. M. Henderson and Talcott Parsons (New York: Oxford University Press, 2009), p. 346.

Although definition is difficult, an outside observer can see that something important happened in England when a capital was established in London in the late 1200s and early 1300s and a functioning city-state was established. Similarly, in Spain (Castile) Isabella obviously had a "different" system of rule than the kings who preceded her, even though she had no real government bureaucracy. For us, those changes define the beginnings of an "early state" in England and Spain.

The full-fledged patrimonial state had a more meaningful bureaucracy, but one still marked by personalistic relations. The early construction of such a state marks the transition from what we call an early state to a minimally effective one. Everyone recognizes that something important happened in England under Henry VII and especially Henry VIII in the 1530s. The same is true of Spain under the Bourbons in the 1700s. Daron Acemoglu and James Robinson call this "political centralization," but the phrase can be misleading to a layman because the United States had a fully centralized system in 1787 by their definition. We prefer the phrase "minimally effective."

The truly effective state, and especially the beginnings of such a state, is also hard to define, but the transition essentially involves a country's evolution past the tipping point toward (but not to) a state based on rational-legal values. Again, the difference between the English system in the 1600s and 1700s is hard to define precisely, but it is easy to sense. As we will see in Chapter 6, a truly effective state includes a substantial growth in the size of the bureaucracy and in the degree of specialization within it, a regularized policy process in which the bureaucracy is a key player, a disappearance of a number of types of organized violence of the past, and as our awkward label suggests, greater governmental effectiveness.

This book deals with the lessons of European development. We have no firm opinion about countries such as China, Korea, and Japan that often had failed-state interludes but that usually maintained some kind of bureaucracy or sense of one. We do not know enough about Korea to judge whether we would agree with Andrew Mwenda, a prominent Ugandan intellectual, that Korea had more than 600 years with a strong and centralized state. Yet Mwenda surely is right that the comparison of sub-Saharan Africa with East Asia is an unfair one:[26]

> By 1960, South Korea had been in existence as a nation for over 600 years with a strong and centralised state, a common language and a shared consciousness of

[26] Andrew Mwenda, "Africa versus East Asia: Why South Korea Succeeded Where Uganda Failed," *Independent*, April 28, 2012. http://www.independent.co.ug/the-last-word/the-last-word/5667.

nationhood. There had been a brief interruption of Japanese colonialism from 1910 to 1945. Therefore, the challenge facing Syngman Rhee and later Park Chung Hee, the military rulers in Seoul, was not nation or state building but economic reconstruction after the devastation brought about by the war. On the other hand, Ghana by 1960 had been born three years earlier, Uganda two years later. The immediate challenge facing Kwame Nkrumah and Milton Obote was to mould a nation from tens of disparate nations and tribes with different languages, cultures and sometimes hostility to each other.

One should, of course, recognize that Ghana was not born in 1957 and Uganda in 1958. Studies of colonial legacy show that both the length of colonial rule and the nature of that colonial rule matter a great deal. The United States was not born in 1776 or Mexico in 1821.

England did build a more effective state in its colonies than Spain did in its colonies. Moreover, Ghana and Uganda surely would have been far more successful if England had begun ruling them in the 1600s, as it did in India with the East India Company, and not in 1874 and 1888, respectively. Not surprisingly, the least effective former colonies – Somalia and Libya – were owned by Italy for only a short time and received little interest from Mussolini.[27]

The prolonged 200-year period required for England to make the transition from minimally effective to truly effective is especially important today. The great majority of the contemporary developing countries are somewhere in the course of this evolution. If we understand that England and Spain took several hundred years at that stage and each were at different points of their own development in 1530, 1630, and 1730, it may be easier to grasp how different today's countries are from each other. And, of course, countries can take different amounts of time as did England and Spain. Then we may really appreciate that the same policy, whatever its nature, cannot be profitably applied throughout the developing world. In the words of Dani Rodrik, there may be one economics, but there are many recipes.

[27] See, for instance, Robin Grier, "Colonial Legacies and Economic Growth," *Public Choice* 98 (1999), 317–35; Robin Grier, "The Effect of Religion on Economic Development: A Cross National Study of 63 Former Colonies," *Kyklos* 50 (1997), 47–62; Nathan Nunn, "Historical Legacies: A Model Linking Africa's Past to Its Current Underdevelopment," *Journal of Development Economics* 83 (2007), 157–75; Daron Acemoglu, Simon Johnson, and James Robinson, "The Colonial Origins of Comparative Development: An Empirical Investigation," *American Economic Review* 91 (2001), 1369–401; and Stanley Engerman and Kenneth Sokoloff, "Factor Endowments, Institutions, and Differential Paths of Growth among New World Economies," in Stephen Haber, ed., *How Latin America Fell Behind: Essays on the Economic Histories of Brazil and Mexico* (Stanford, CA: Stanford University Press, 1997), 260–304.

Operationalizing the Importance of Informal Institutions in Light of Max Weber's Insights

We started this study trying to answer Douglass North's questions: Why is "time" so important? Why does the development process take so long? How is change finally effected? From the beginning, we agreed with North that the transitional and developing economies do not have the structure of norms, values, and habits that was necessary for a rapid transition to a modern economy. In the words of Alan Greenspan, former chairman of the Federal Reserve Board:[28]

> Much of what we took for granted in our free market system and assumed to be human nature was not nature at all.... There is a vast amount of capitalist culture and infrastructure underpinning market economics that has evolved over generations: laws, conventions, behaviors, and a wide variety of business professions and practices that have no important functions in a central planned economy.

Nothing in our research shook our belief that North was right to emphasize the importance of informal institutions. In fact, in our opinion, North did not sufficiently emphasize them in his own historical work and should have given them major attention as a source of violence in his most recent two books. When North's writings and voluminous correspondence are examined closely, it turns out that he always makes quite a narrow point: a modern economy cannot function effectively unless self-interest is restrained by the proper "human construct of rules, norms, conventions, and ways of doing things that define the framework of human interaction."[29] Moreover, North has been absolutely insistent that modern transitional and developing countries have not yet developed such a construct. We agree with both points.

Beyond this, however, North has never said much about the role of informal institutions in the development process, except in the last 50 years or so of the transition to a fairly modern state. He has never even specified the nature of the old ideas, norms, and habits that interfere with an effective market or the nature of the new ideas and norms that must replace them. That makes a theory of change impossible.

This is why we have always believed that the insights of the great sociologist Max Weber must be added to North's analysis of informal institutions. Weber argued that mankind from its earliest days had a set of norms and values that severely restrained self-interest – but values and norms that were optimal for the survival of small family-based tribal units and then villages.

[28] Greenspan, *The Embrace of Free Markets*, p. 2.
[29] North, *Understanding the Process of Economic Change*, p. 11.

These norms emphasized behavior based on personalistic (especially family- and clan-oriented) restraints, reward by ascribed social position, and decisions based on tradition. People were not supposed to treat strangers in the same way that they did insiders. These norms do not restrain self-interest in the ways needed in a modern economy.[30]

Unlike North, Weber also specified the norms and values that he saw essential in modern society: the treatment of people by impersonal and impartial rules, decision-making based on rationality, professionalism, and merit-based rewards. These are the opposite of the norms that had become ingrained in humans for several million years. Moreover, this new definition of moral restraints on self-interest has to be inculcated at a time when people are being told for the first time that the pursuit of individual economic self-interest is the best way to achieve the common good.

Such a profound change in the definition of what is moral is inherently slow and difficult, but it is made even slower by the fact that it takes centuries for peasants and other rural personnel to move into the city. Migrants to the city often arrive in their late teens or early twenties when their values have already been formed. By the time their children and grandchildren begin to absorb the values appropriate for the city, new rural inhabitants have arrived in the city and replenished it with traditional values.

The absolute size of the rural population keeps growing long after the percentage of the urban population begins to rise. In 2010, only 19% of the American population lived in rural areas, but the total rural population was 59.5 million compared with 52 million in the 1920 census, the first that reported 50% urban population. By the 1920 definition of urban and rural, the number would be higher.

It is vital to understand the rural origins of the personalistic norms that bedevil developing countries today. When many scholars observe old values that retard development in places such as Spain and Latin America, they label them as culture or national character – the old phrase for culture. To a comparative scholar, however, it is striking how often historians of a Spain, a North Africa, or a Russia talk about the culture or national character of their area and then describe the same characteristics that Weber attributed to village and tribal society.

[30] For the way this worked in a modern African tribe, see Robert Bates, "The Preservation of Order in Stateless Societies: A Reinterpretation of Evans-Pritchard's *The Nuer*," in Robert H. Bates, *Essays on the Political Economy of Rural Africa* (Berkeley: University of California Press, 1983), pp. 7–20.

The failure to discuss rural and urban values has two negative consequences for an understanding of violence and development. First, peasants who come to the city with traditional values often react violently to the educated elites with secular, rational-legal values. The dates of the "great" revolutions of England, Russia, Italy, Spain, China, and Iran are the dates when the flow of peasants into the city reached a critical mass and rulers lost control of the emotions. Indeed, many think that the Hidalgo rebellion in Mexico was a cleric-led revolt in response to the modernization of Charles III of Spain. One wonders if it was weak because it was so early and the revolution a century later was stronger because of its timing.[31]

Second, everyone recognizes that a stable state and a productive economy ultimately rest on government's monopoly of force and its willingness to use it, yet it is also clear that Jean Jacques Rousseau was right in his 1762 *Social Contract* when he wrote that "the strongest is never strong enough to be always the master, unless he transforms strength into right, and obedience into duty." In Mancur Olson's words, "public opinion obviously has some importance even in a totalitarian environment – if it did not, regimes would not bother with propaganda and indoctrination."[32]

The crucial question for development analysts is sequence: Does might or right usually come first? Does the development of long-range stability begin with "laying down the law" (obedience based on military force) or the "winning of the hearts and minds of people" (creating the proper norms and values)?[33] Aristotle argued that the force came first, and Mancur Olson agreed. In the past at least, Douglass North thought that "the place to begin is with the beliefs held by the members of a society."[34]

Max Weber, in his early *The Protestant Ethic and the Spirit of Capitalism*, argued that the elite acquired a belief in the need to save and work from their acceptance of Protestantism. Few American economists know that

[31] Will Fowler, *Mexico in the Age of Proposals, 1821–1853* (Westport, CT: Greenwood Press, 1998).

[32] Mancur Olson, "The Logic of Collective Action in Soviet-Type Societies," *Journal of Soviet Nationalities* (1990), 8–27, pp. 26.

[33] Susan Collins of the University of Houston used this language in discussing Aristotle's position at "Homo Politicus and Homo Economicus," 7th Annual Conference of the Gerst Program in Political and Economic Studies, Duke University, April 27–28, 2006, Durham, NC.

[34] Douglass North, "Response to Geddes and Keohane," in James Alt, Margaret Levi, and Elinor Ostrom, eds., *Competition and Cooperation: Conversations with Nobelists about Economics and Political Science* (New York: Russell Sage Foundation, 1999), p. 252.

Weber's classic critic, R. H. Tawney, argued that Weber had cause and effect reversed. Calvinism was popular, Tawney argued, because it was attractive to a business class that was already developing. In Tawney's view, Calvinism allowed them to legitimate themselves, including to themselves, by saying that they were among God's elite, that the poor were condemned by God to eternal damnation, and that phenomena such as interest rates that others considered immoral actually had been pre-determined by God in order to glorify Him.

Tawney's critique of Weber is crucial to keep in mind in any comparison of Spain and England. If the Protestant ethic was a first cause, then its chance acceptance in England is an important explanation for English capitalism. Yet, if the Protestant ethic was accepted by a rising capitalist class because Calvinism corresponded to that class's interests, then the failure of the Reformation in Spain was not a cause of its backwardness, but a result of its lack of a rising middle class.

Weber himself pointed in the same direction in his more important *Economy and Society*. In this work, Weber suggested that the personalistic values of the tribal unit and village developed because of the imperatives of small-scale tribal and village life. The survival of the tribal unit and village, he suggested, depended on personalistic norms. By the same token, exposure to the large city forces people (or their children or grandchildren) to adjust to the need of more impersonal values and norms. They could not survive if they did not adapt. But the transition can be wrenching.

Because North did not distinguish between rural-based and urban-based values and the tension produced during the evolution from one to another, he never dealt with the political conflicts and violence associated with the transformation of values during the transition. His article with Barry Weingast on the 1600s in England never mentions religion, despite the fact that the three regime changes in the 1640s, 1660, and 1688 were all fought on religious battle lines. The article also never mentions the development of desirable informal institutions during the 1600s – what Weber called rational-legal norms. His recent two books on violence do not mention value-caused violence at all.

We, by contrast, devote 30% of our discussion of England in the 1600s and 1700s to the modern values that developed from the Age of Discovery onward and to the norms, values, ideologies, and emotions of the religious conflicts of the 1600s. This, we think, is crucial both for an understanding of English development and the creation of a theory of change for the modern world.

An understanding of the religious conflicts of the 1600s is also crucial for an understanding of the development of the United States. Each colony was based on one of the warring English religions of the 1600s in England, and hence this religious conflict was built into the structure of the colonies in the New World and then the states of the United States. These religious conflicts were still of great importance in the U.S. Civil War from 1861 to 1865. To say, as many do, that the United States was stable because of its common values is to ignore this fact. We give great attention to this factor in Chapters 6, 7, and 9.

The Importance of the State in Development and the Collective Action Analysis of Mancur Olson

Max Weber is known for two major arguments in *Economy and Society*. One is the difference between the values of traditional village and tribal society and the impersonal rules, merit-based employment, and professionalism of modern society. The other argument is the critical importance of a well-functioning, professional bureaucracy for a modern society.

The two points come together in Weber's analysis of the values that are needed in a rational-legal bureaucracy and a society dominated by public and private bureaucracies. Americans often refer to "rule of law," but Weber suggested it would be more precise to say "rule of laws" or "rule of rules." The modern market is basically a system of laws and rules that is created by the state. An ineffective state can neither establish an effective system of such laws nor enforce their impartial application.

This point is often obscured by careless language. The creation of the modern market in Europe did not really involve de-regulation, as is sometimes said, but the replacement of personalistic subsidies, monopoly guilds, privileges, and decrees of early rulers by impersonal laws, rules, and regulations that should be applied impartially. De-regulation is impossible unless regulation already exists. De-regulation cannot end all regulation but selectively removes or modifies specific regulations that are counterproductive.

A key element in modern society, according to Weber, is the dominance of specialized bureaucracies, both governmental and non-governmental. This point, we argue, is crucial for distinguishing between England and Spain, but precisely in the opposite direction than suggested in the American economic literature. It was England that was developing effective bureaucracies in the 1500s, 1600s, and early 1700s, not Spain.

The evolution from a minimally effective state to a truly effective one from the early 1500s into the 1600s in England largely involved more an evolution toward a more effective executive branch than growth in the power of the legislature. We agree with John Brewer that the development of the executive branch was also the key development after 1688. We especially agree that the most important new role was to provide an institutional framework that forced the growing bureaucracies and the interest groups around them to develop and coordinate the flood of information necessary for a sophisticated policy process,

Spain was very different until the 1700s. Modern historians now agree that the slow economic growth of Spain and Latin America, whatever its cause, was not produced by the Spanish "bureaucratic" tradition or its excessive centralization. Rather, most have concluded the opposite is true. In the words of William Summerhill, a prominent historian on Latin America, "the old association of centralization with negative [economic] outcomes has ... been turned on its head."[35] That also corresponds to the results of our research. It is dramatically shown in Spain's inability to control its colonies in the late 1500s, 1600s, and early 1700s.

Indeed, we would go further and agree with Weber that bureaucracy is a key element in restraining the real power of the ruler. Rulers cannot achieve the advantages of bureaucracy if they intervene to override the rules and the predictability that these rules introduce. Moreover, the ruler is aware that the specialists in the bureaucracies know more about their subject than he or she does. A wise ruler overrides such policy advice only for a good reason. The leading historian on the English Treasury in the second half of the 1600s notes that this was already true of English monarchs at that time: "The business of Treasury [gradually] became too complicated for the sovereign to grasp or control and the office assumed a measure of independence."[36]

We argue that the collective action problems of creating effective bureaucracies – private as well as those of the military and the civilian government – represent a key factor that makes the process of creating an effective government and market so prolonged.

It is striking to reread Samuel Huntington's 1968 *Political Order in Changing Society* about the central problem in development: early

[35] William Summerhill, "Fiscal Bargains, Political Institutions, and Economic Performance," *Hispanic-American Historical Review* 88 (2008), 219–33, pp. 221 and 227. Also see Alejandra Irigoin and Regina Grafe, "Bargaining for Absolutism: A Spanish Path to Nation-State and Empire Building," *Hispanic-American Historical Review* 88 (2008), 173–209, pp. 173–4.

[36] Stephen Baxter, *The Development of the Treasury, 1660–1702* (Cambridge, MA: Harvard University Press, 1957), p. 4.

developing governments often "simply do not govern" – and cannot.[37] What is surprising is how many of his examples of ineffective developing governments are still in that category after a half century. We observe exactly the same problem in the creation of effective governments in Europe at different times in different countries.

But why is it so hard for rulers to establish effective control over key organs of the government, especially the military commanders and the tax-collecting bodies? Why do they often not function in a professional manner or apply impersonal rules impartially? As already indicated, we use the collective action theory of the neoclassical economist Mancur Olson as our leading answer to these questions.

Mancur Olson's collective action theory, we would emphasize, is different from many others, especially the game theory that is most utilized in economics.[38] The problem of using game theory in analyzing development is that an outside scholar sets firm rules of the game and the players are forced to follow them rigidly in playing the game.

By contrast, the very essence of economic development is the gradual introduction of the rules of the game of a market – often vague and ambiguous rules – over many generations. Moreover, the "players" themselves have a major role in writing the rules. As a result, game theory with its fixed rules of the game assumes away the core problem of economic and political development: How are the proper rules of the game created, how do they evolve over time, and how are they enforced?

Mancur Olson began his analysis with the assumption that people follow the same neoclassical rules of rational behavior in the political sphere as in the economic. He then looked at the narrow cost-benefit calculations of individuals as they decided whether to participate in the achievement of collective public goods. Since the contribution of one individual to the achievement of the collective goal is so minuscule, it is, Olson argued almost always outweighed by the costs of participation. Hence, the individual normally has the rational self-interest not to participate – to be a "free rider."

Yet people obviously do engage in political activity, and Olson sought to explain this fact within the rational-actor assumptions of the neoclassical

[37] Samuel Huntington, *Political Order in Changing Societies* (New Haven, CT: Yale University Press, 1968).

[38] Pamela Jakiela, "Using Economic Experiments to Measure Informal Institutions," in Sebastian Galiani and Itai Sened, eds., *Institutions, Property Rights, and Economic Growth: The Legacy of Douglass North* (Cambridge: Cambridge University Press, 2014), 248–65, pp. 250–3.

model. He saw compulsion and "selective side payments" (benefits that participants receive but not non-participants) as the rational reasons that induce participation. When Olson began to analyze the state in the late 1980s, he used the same assumptions and naturally reached the same conclusions. "Selective side payments" (first of all, government salaries to make participation in the collective action of government rational) depend primarily on tax revenue. Since taxes cannot be collected without the threat of punishment, Olson emphasized control of military force.

Olson analyzed the state on many levels: the problems of rulers in controlling the military and tax collectors, the logical impossibility of mass revolution, and, finally, the difficulty the ruler has in preventing his or her own officials from being free riders. Modern government itself is the largest collective action of all, and, therefore, it has the greatest collective action problems. Olson addressed the point very directly:[39]

> Why do the operatives of a regime carry out the dictator's orders? This takes us right back to the difficulties of collective action – and especially to the need for selective incentives.... Just as it does not normally pay a typical individual to rebel, so it also does not pay for the typical policeman or soldier or bureaucrat who happens to believe in the regime to go out of his way to help the regime survive simply because he favors the regime. It does not pay the typical official of the regime to carry out the orders of the leadership unless there is some incentive for him to do that *separate from* his belief in the established system....
>
> If a government's operatives, and especially those in the police and the military, believe that they will be punished if they fail to carry out their orders and rewarded if they do, an autocracy is secure.... Yet a regime whose power rests on nothing more than a shared perception [that it can reward and punish] can lose all its power once perceptions change.... Perceptions can change in the blink of an eye.

This analysis was intended to explain the failure of governments in Eastern Europe, and it certainly applies to the government in Baghdad in 2003. The logic also applies to the period when governments are being formed. When rulers are strong enough to punish and reward, they usually can keep the self-interest of officials enough under control to keep government functioning, at least ineffectively. When they do not have the money to pay the troops, they are overthrown. This was a key fact in the English Civil War and the Mexican war of independence.

But the ruler faces a circular problem. The ability to pay salaries depends on having tax collectors who can collect enough taxes, and the ability to punish depends on paying salaries to the military and police who will

[39] Olson, "The Logic of Collective Action in Soviet-Type Societies," pp. 14–16.

enforce the punishment. Yet why should tax collectors, the military, and the agencies controlling them not follow a path of self-financing when they do not have adequate and reliable salaries? Similarly, a military commander should have the self-interest and ability to overthrow the ruler and gain control of all tax revenue. The way these collective action problems are solved is the question we address in our four cases over an 800-year period.

Douglass North's New Emphasis on the Dominant Coalition

One element of our current approach was not present at the beginning of our project. We were quite aware that a coalition of urban-based elites had to replace a rural one during the process of development. Political scientists largely came to take for granted the argument of Maurice Duverger in 1962 and then Giuseppe Di Palma in 1990 that democratic society emerged from a basic agreement by a plurality of elites based on bureaucratized organizations. But since our book ended around 1800, arguments about democratization were really not relevant for it.[40]

Then Douglass North thrust the issue of elites to the fore when he and the co-authors of his recent books unexpectedly de-emphasized informal institutions and representative institutions in all but the last stage of the development process. They argued that the developing countries of the present and past were what they called "natural states." Such states, they argue, are based on a "dominant coalition" that "limits access to valuable resources – land, labor, and capital – or access to and control of valuable activities – such as trade, worship, and education – to elite groups. The creation of rents through limiting access provides the glue that holds the coalition together."[41]

Unfortunately, North's analysis of a dominant coalition does not provide any operational guidance for a theory of development. He defines a dominant coalition as a collection of "members who specialize in a range of military, political, religious ... and economic activities," but there is little indication of who they are.[42] He recognized that they change over time, but only because their relative power position changes. This is a very abstract judgment except *ex post facto*.

In fact, the definition has an even more basic problem because of the use of the word "specialize." The creation of powerful specialized elites occurs

[40] Maurice Duverger, *Political Parties: Their Organization and Activities in the Modern State* (London: Methuen, 1962), and Giuseppi Di Palma, *To Craft Democracies: An Essay on Democratic Strategies* (Berkeley: University of California Press, 1990).

[41] North et al., *Violence and Social Orders*, p. 30.

[42] Ibid., p. 18.

relatively late in the development process. As we will see in Chapters 2 and 3, the members of reasonably defined early dominant coalitions are predominantly unspecialized regional warlords. They have variously been called feudal lords, families, Spanish nobles in charge of city-states, tribal leaders, caudillos in Latin America, or just plain warlords.

Whatever the language used, the power of the warlords was based on their control of the local military force and the land that it allowed them to control. The "king," whatever he was called, normally was simply the warlord who could organize the greatest military power – a fact that often was determined on the battleground, especially in the succession struggle when the old king died. He ruled through members of his family who commanded the family troops, collected revenue, and controlled the church – which played important economic roles for him.

As North and his co-authors implicitly recognized in their 2013 preface to the paperback edition of their 2009 *Violence and Social Orders*, that book focused on "the transition from a natural state to an open access order [a modern democracy and free market economy]," a period that they called the mature natural state. This transition often takes only some 50 years at the end of the development process. "Less central to our focus," they continued in the preface, "was the 'second development problem,'" the multi-hundred-year transition prior to the final stage. This preface notes that their new book, *In the Shadow of Violence,* is devoted to an examination of "the 'second development problem'" – that is, to the evolution within and between the types of the earlier natural state.[43]

Our book never dealt with the last 50 years of the development process when democratization was under way, but with what they called "the second development problem" – really the first. It also was always focused on change. *Violence and Social Orders* did mention the rise of a "new source of wealth from commerce and trade" in the 1600s, but it did not analyze the new elites or the struggles between them. It said nothing about the military being a powerful member of the elite and only discussed the transformation of the navy into an effective fighting force in the mid-1700s as evidence of the effectiveness of the English government.[44]

We agreed that the professionalization of the navy was evidence of the transition to a truly effective state, but we were primarily engaged in a

[43] "Preface to the Paperback Edition," North et al., *Violence and Social Orders*, p. xii.

[44] North et al., *Violence and Social Orders*, pp. 77–110. See pp. 105–6 on the dating of the mature natural state in England and the new economic forces. For the navy, see pp. 181–7 and 242–3.

collective action analysis of the politics of the 1600s and early 1700s. As we asked Olson's question: Who could "organize the greatest capacity for violence?" we were much attracted to the historians who all said the navy was crucial in the Restoration of 1660 and, at a minimum, was a key actor in the revolution of 1688.

We were also much attracted to the contrasting interpretation of the consequences of the Glorious Revolution that was published in the same year (1989) as North and Weingast's article, "Constitutions and Commitment." Written by John Brewer, it was entitled *The Sinews of Power* and emphasized the rise of the executive and a "fiscal-military state" in the 1700s, not the power of rural-based Parliament. Brewer's analysis fit much better with a collective action approach than the social contract analysis of North and Weingast, and we naturally gave it prominence.

As a result, we read the 2013 *In the Shadow of Violence* with great interest. It deals only with the contemporary developing world and it does not talk about written constitutions or representative institutions as key variables until the mature natural state near the end of the development process. Rather, *In the Shadow of Violence* brought violence among elites sharply to the fore. Violence was to be controlled by the granting of rent to elites, notably the military and government officials.

European development is almost never mentioned in *In the Shadow of Violence*, but the book implicitly changed the analysis of 1688 from that presented by North and Weingast in 1989 and even 2009. The key change was implied indirectly when Mexico was called a basic natural state or order from the 1940s to the 1980s. Mexico's transition to a mature natural state is said to have occurred in the 1990s.[45]

The comparison of different countries far removed in time is always fraught with peril, but one thing is certain. England from the 1580s to the 1680s was at a much lower level of political and economic development than Mexico in the 1980s. At a minimum England did not change into a mature natural state order until it evolved into a fully developed state in the mid-1700s.

The 1600s in England did, indeed, look very much like the natural basic state described in *In the Shadow of Violence*. England was extremely violent in that century, and the Revolution of 1688 was the third violent regime

[45] Unfortunately, North and his co-authors changed their labels between the two books. In 2009, the two types of regime were called a basic natural state and mature natural state, respectively. In 2013, they were called a limited-access basic order and a limited-access mature order, respectively. The definitions were not changed, and we decide to use the 2009 categories throughout for reasons of simplicity.

change in 40 years. All of them involved the decisive use of military forces in the support of the new social and elite forces that were rising in the 1600s. The major military force was the naval-armed merchant alliance.

In short, England of the 1600s and early 1700s did seem to be ruled by the dominant coalitions found in the contemporary developing world, one in which the elite included the military and in which stability was bought by rent to the various elites. Parliament had largely been excluded from the dominant coalition in the 1640s and only partly restored in 1660. The Revolution of 1688 brought the rural land-owning elite into the dominant coalition, but only as a lesser member. There was an excellent reason that John Brewer called England of the 1700s a "fiscal-military state."

The implications of a collective action approach and the insights of *In the Shadow of Violence* for the emphasis on representative institutions in "Constitutions and Commitment" will be the subject of an entire chapter (Chapter 6).[46] Prior to that chapter, however, we first discuss the theories of North, Olson, and Weber in the next chapter, and then we turn to the evolution of the pre-states, early states, and minimally effective states in England and Spain. That will allow us to look at the problems of early development when powerful specialized elites usually do not exist, when the members of the dominant coalition are regional warlords with military force at their disposal. Specialists on sub-Saharan Africa and some of the least developed countries in Asia will find the discussion familiar in a number of respects.

[46] Chapter 6 also discusses the findings of a new book published just as this manuscript went into production. It too seriously questioned "Constitutions and Commitment." D'Maris Coffman, Adrian Leonard, and Larry Neal, eds., *Questioning Credible Commitment: Perspectives on the Rise of Financial Capitalism* (Cambridge: Cambridge University Press, 2013).

1

The Collective Action Difficulties of Creating an Effective State

Since ancient times, the most eternal questions for political thinkers have been "Why are human societies stable?"and "Why do people obey?" The two polar answers have been compulsion and consent. The debate is eternal because both answers are right, and the interaction of the two is extraordinarily complex.

On the one hand, compulsion is ultimately impossible unless army officers tell soldiers to fire their weapons and unless the soldiers obey orders. There have many cases in human history when either officials or soldiers have failed to consent. Officers do not want to fire on student demonstrators when their own children are among the students. Soldiers do not want to fire on members of their own ethnic group who are demonstrating against repression of that group by a regime of another ethnic group. Regimes must take the strength of these feelings into account when they make decisions on when and how to use force.[1]

On the other hand, people never simply withhold consent if they think that a situation is not ideal. They must consider reality and decide how to adjust to it. They often give their "consent" to the lesser evil even when it is still quite great. Many Americans may have the most critical attitude imaginable toward Washington, but at the same time they want to suppress anyone who favors a change in the form of government. Which is "consent?"

In the vast majority of cases, all of us obey the law without thinking about it (that is the real meaning of consent). We seldom reflect on the fact that compulsion is crucial in the collection action of tax payment, but in no area is there more of a reason to be a free rider. A scholar who went to the Soviet Union over many decades was struck by the degree to which

[1] Jerry F. Hough, "The Logic of Collective Action and the Pattern of Revolutionary Behavior," *Journal of Soviet Nationalities*, 1 (1990), 34–65.

many liberal, anti-regime Soviet scholars accepted what they considered inevitable and lived a relatively contented life, if the regime gave them choices that they thought meaningful. How does all of this fit into a theory of consent?

In game theory, the players do not have the freedom to change the rules of the game that limit and define their freedom of action. This book deals with the way in which the rules of the game are developed that result in a reasonably effective political and economic system. In particular, we are concerned with the economic rules of the game. They too limit and define freedom of action. Government rules obviously limit freedom of choice, but, although few are conscious of it, the rules of the game of a spontaneous market also strictly limit freedom of action.

In this book, and especially in this chapter, we focus on two facts about the societal rules of the game. First, governments are crucial both in writing legally enforceable rules and in enforcing them. Second, economic actors and government officials have the self-interest to modify these rules to their advantage, to influence the way in which they are modified, and to violate them themselves. This includes the rules of the game if there is little threat of punishment and no individual "selective side payment" reward for obeying them.

In this chapter, we do not examine the ancient debate about compulsion and consent, but concentrate on the way several leading economists have participated in it. Douglass North is the most prominent economist of recent decades who has argued for the centrality of consent. Since he most forcefully raised the issue of the length of time required to build an effective state and market, we were delighted that he had developed a consent theory over a prolonged period. The fact that North's correspondence has already been made available to scholars greatly increases the attractiveness of basing our analysis on his work.

James Buchanan was a neoclassical economist who explicitly focused on the issue of the rules of the game, even in the titles of many of his books. Yet while Buchanan most frankly posed the question of the maintenance of the rules of the game, he never gave an empirical answer to his question. Instead, he frankly admitted that he could only analyze what ought to be.

We begin with Buchanan's analysis because his failure to say what explains restraints on self-interest was a factor that led North to emphasize the limits of a rational actor explanation and to follow Friedrich Hayek in using norms as the answer. Mancur Olson published his own major book only three years after Buchanan's espousal of a contractarian approach in *The Calculus of Consent* and also had it in mind. We also briefly discuss the work of Friedrich Hayek because North rested his own analysis so heavily on Hayek. Finally, we explore the analysis of Max Weber, since he was the major scholar who best introduced a developmental perspective into the study of norms and values.

Mancur Olson is the best economist in recent decades to read on the need of compulsion because he was quite frank. He demonstrated that an individual's participation in the collective promotion of a policy he or she wants, even intensely, is irrational by the assumptions of the neoclassical definition of rationality. Olson accepted those assumptions and concluded that the only rational explanation for mass participation must be compulsion or a selective side payment (a reward that only the participant receives.)

Olson is also the perfect economist to use as a counterpoint to North because his sophisticated work on the state was written in direct response to an article that North published in 1989 with Barry Weingast, "Constitutions and Commitment." North believed that the rules of the games are created and maintained by consent, a social contract. He, Summerhill, and Weingast argued, that the central requirement for a stable state was "a shared belief system about the legitimate ends of government and the extent of citizen rights [and] a credible commitment that citizens [will] react in concert when officials violate their rights."[2]

Olson believed that a shared belief could never form the basis for political action to establish a state, let alone protect one against a ruler with military force who tries to overthrow a government with the support of the governed. Voluntary collective action, Olson wrote, simply "cannot obtain the gains from a peaceful order [of a state]." The ruler, he thought, is the one who "can organize the greatest capacity for violence."[3] North takes the opposite position. He understood that "might" must ultimately be supported by "right," but for him, like Aristotle, "laying down the law" had to come first.

The Maintenance of the Rules of the Game: Social Contract or Norms

Douglass North and Mancur Olson have one thing in common. Each used few footnotes, and each only rarely acknowledged intellectual debts. Yet

[2] Douglass North, William Summerhill, and Barry Weingast, 'Order, Disorder and Economic Change: Latin America vs. North America,' in Bruce Bueno de Mesquita and Hilton Root, eds., *Governing for Prosperity* (New Haven: Yale University Press, 2000), p. 24.

[3] Mancur Olson, "Dictatorship, Democracy, and Development," *American Political Science Review* 87 (1993), 567–76, p. 568.

both North and Olson clearly were greatly influenced by James Buchanan, a Nobel Prize–winning economist with a deep belief in the "spontaneous order of the [unregulated] market." However, North and Olson each implicitly tried to deal with a major inconsistency in Buchanan's analysis, but in different ways.

As Buchanan noted in his autobiography, New Deal economists focused on what they called "market failure." Buchanan acknowledged much of the New Deal argument, but he contended that the same self-interest that led economic actors into unfortunate actions also made government officials biased "referees." He was convinced that "the spontaneous order of the [pure] market" was the lesser enemy.

Even more basically, Buchanan saw the market performing important political functions. The market, he said, is a mechanism that "coordinates the separate activities of self-seeking persons, *without the necessity of detailed political direction*." It serves "a political function, which is to minimize the need for politicized control over and decisions concerning resource use." He called this the "coordinating principle" of economics.[4]

Buchanan began his analysis with the definition of rationality in the neoclassical model. He assumed that *homo politicus* was a human being and hence must be driven by the same motivations as *homo economicus*. If both economic and political actors are driven by the desire to maximize profit, then both should cooperate in "rent-seeking" behavior, resulting in great harm to the economy.

Buchanan recognized that a spontaneous market order cannot function properly unless the economic actors operate within "an appropriate 'constitutional context' – a proper structure of rules, along with some arrangement for their enforcement."[5] Buchanan believed these rules should be consciously introduced and that they should take a written form. He even wanted taxes to be embodied in constitutional rules to prevent them from being raised, and the role of the government to be limited to reduce the opportunity for rent-seeking.

Dennis Mueller has explained quite clearly the reason a "constitutional context" is needed. Classical and neoclassical economic models assume that

[4] James Buchanan, *Economics from the Outside In: "Better than Plowing" and Beyond* (College Station: Texas A & M Press, 2007), pp. 71–2 and 97. The emphasis is his. For an appreciative evaluation of Buchanan's contribution on this point on the 50th anniversary of his seminal *Calculus of Consent*, see Michael Munger, "Coercion, the State, and Obligations of Citizenship," *Public Choice* 152 (2012), 415–21.

[5] Geoffrey Brennan and James M. Buchanan, *The Reason of Rules: Constitutional Political Economy* (Cambridge: Cambridge University Press, 1985), p. 6.

economic actors will follow the rules of the game and engage in free competition, observe contracts, protect each other's property rights, and so forth. Yet Dennis Mueller points out that the rational actor of the neoclassical model should not follow the rules of the game.

Mueller begins with a conventional point: "probably the most important accomplishment of economics" is to demonstrate "that individuals with purely selfish motives can mutually benefit from exchange." Then, he makes the awkward point that theft is more profitable than exchange:[6]

> If A raises cattle and B corn, both may improve their welfare by exchanging cattle for corn.... [However], the choices facing A and B are not merely to trade or not, as implicitly suggested. A can choose to steal B's corn, rather than give up his cattle for it; B may do likewise.... In an anarchic environment, the independent choices of both individuals can be expected to lead both to adopt the dominant stealing strategy.

By Buchanan's assumptions, this should be true both of economic man and political man. It should be true both of day-to-day laws and the rules of game – the "constitutional context." Unlike Mancur Olson, however, Buchanan did not use the neoclassical definition of rational self-interest to try to explain how the adherence of officials to constitutional norms is guaranteed.

Instead, Buchanan shifted to a "social contract" when he tried to explain the durability of constitutional rules. A social contract is an implicit informal contract about rules of the game that people have accepted in order to live together peacefully and fruitfully. When introduced into economics, it included the agreement to live together in a market economy that best promoted efficiency and economic growth.

Unfortunately, the social contract was not developed by Thomas Hobbes and John Locke to describe reality, but rather to legitimate a particular type of government or economic system. This is true not only of the philosophers of the past, but also of those who take a contract approach today. In the words of Christian Muller,[7]

> Modern contractarians emphasize that the social contract is a metaphor rather than an historical fact. [John] Rawls, for instance, states that any agreement reached by

[6] Dennis Mueller, *Public Choice II* (Cambridge: Cambridge University Press, 1989), pp. 9–10. The identical language is retained in the third edition, published in 2003. This book is a classic encyclopedic volume on public choice theory.

[7] Christian Müller, "The Methodology of Contractarianism in Economics," *Public Choice* 112 (2002), 465–83, p. 468. Muller cites John Rawls, "Justice as Fairness: Political, Not Metaphysical," *Philosophy and Public Affairs*, 14 (1985), 223–51, p. 236, and James Buchanan, *Freedom in Constitutional Contract: Perspectives of a Political Economist* (College Station: Texas A & M University Press, 1977), p. 82.

the parties in a so-called original position "must be regarded as both hypothetical and nonhistorical." In the same vein [James] Buchanan states, "We know, factually and historically, that the 'social contract' is mythological, at least in many of its particulars. Individuals did not come together in some original position and mutually agree on the rule of social intercourse.... The contract is a myth designed in part to rationalize existing institutional structures of society.

When Stergio Skaperdas and Constantinose Syropoulous focused on the contractarian approach in economics alone, they stated that it explains "a wide variety of organizations and institutions by the fact that the agents involved make a self-enforcing contract to cooperate:[8]

Social norms, institutions and organisations have come to be seen by economists and other social scientists as primarily cooperative or efficient arrangements; firms are viewed as minimizing transaction costs, with their most important component associated with durable, relationship-specific assets; legal institutions economize on information in enforcing efficient trading arrangements; norms of cooperation in general arise when the future is important in long-term relationships.

The crucial line in this paragraph is the last one. In pure contractarianism, the norms of cooperation and the cooperation itself arise almost automatically.

James Buchanan was the economist who introduced contractarianism into modern economics in 1959 by translating an 1896 article of Knut Wicksell into English.[9] Then he emphasized the point in his first major book, *The Calculus of Consensus*, which was co-authored with Gordon Tullock and published in 1962.[10] Buchanan pointed to "the contractarian tradition" as "the bridge between the individual-choice calculus and group decision."[11] He repeated this in his autobiography: "Almost by definition,

[8] They are critical of this approach. Stergio Skaperdas and Constantinose Syropoulous, "Gangs as Primitive States," in Gianluca Fiorentini and Sam Peltzman, eds., *The Economics of Organised Crime* (Cambridge: Cambridge University Press, 1995), pp. 69, 72–3. As illustrations, they refer to Robert Axelrod, *The Evolution of Cooperation* (New York: Basic Books, 1984); Paul Mildgrom, Douglass North, and Barry Weingast, "The Role of Institutions in the Revival of Trade: The Law Merchant, Private Judges, and the Champagne Fairs," *Economics and Politics* 2 (1990), 1–23; and Oliver Williamson, "Transaction Cost Economics," in Richard Schmalensee and Robert Willig, eds., *Handbook of Industrial Organization* (New York: Elsevier Science, 1989).

[9] Knut Wicksell, "A New Principle of Just Taxation," in Richard A. Musgrave and Alan T. Peacock, *Classics in the Theory of Public Finance* (London: Macmillan, 1958), pp. 72–118. We owe this information and the citation to Michael Munger.

[10] James Buchanan and Gordon Tullock, *The Calculus of Consent: Logical Foundations of Constitutional Democracy* (Ann Arbor: University of Michigan Press, 1962). Buchanan wrote the sections that took a contractarian approach.

[11] Ibid., pp. 96, vii.

the economist who shifts his attention to political process while retaining his methodological individualism must be contractarian."[12]

In explaining the binding force of constitutional rules, Buchanan simply says that they are needed for economic performance. An effective constitution exists because "it is rational to *have a constitution*."[13] It is, in fact, quite rational to have a constitution, but "rational" in this context refers to the collective interests of the society and its members, not necessarily the rational self-interest of the individual of the neoclassical model.

The very titles of some of Buchanan's best-known books reflect his preoccupation with the question of constitutional rules.[14] Yet Buchanan was quite aware that by his own assumptions, officials should follow their self-interest and should seek to violate and overturn the rules of the game – the social contract or a strong constitution. In his first major book, he and Gordon Tullock wrote with absolute frankness, "We are not directly interested in what *the* State or *a* State actually is, but propose to define quite specifically, yet quite briefly, what *we think* a State ought to be."[15]

In this book, we are not engaged in political philosophy but empirical analysis – in what "actually is" instead of what "ought to be." That is what is crucial for development theorists. So too were Douglass North and Mancur Olson. Olson's response to Buchanan is quite apparent to anyone familiar only with the short analysis of Olson in the introduction. Olson wholeheartedly accepted Buchanan's neoclassical definition of self-interest, but he was convinced that self-interest could not be meaningfully restrained by any social contract.

Douglass North, by contrast, was deeply attracted to social contracts all his life, but he rejected Buchanan's definition of individual self-interest. Yet he realized that a social contract, let alone one reached in a formal document several centuries ago, surely was not strong enough to restrain self-interest. Instead, self-interest has to be constrained by contemporary norms and values.

North derived his view of norms from the other major proponent of the "spontaneous order of the market" position in the 20th century, Friedrich Hayek. As Steve Fleetwood discussed, Hayek had always seen "conceptions, ideas, beliefs, attitudes, and so forth" as important constraints but had

[12] James Buchanan, *Economics from the Outside In*, pp. 14–15.

[13] Buchanan and Tullock, *The Calculus of Consent*, p. 81.

[14] Ibid., Buchanan, *Freedom in Constitutional Contract*; Brennan and Buchanan, *The Reason of Rules*; James Buchanan, *Constitutional Economics* (Oxford: Blackwell, 1991).

[15] Buchanan and Tullock, *The Calculus of Consent*, p. 3. The emphasis is in the original.

emphasized the centrality of the price mechanism.[16] But then around 1960, Hayek begin to emphasize more strongly the importance of an integrated "underlying structure of rules" in underpinning the price mechanism and the market process. Hayek himself expressed the point most clearly in his *Rules and Order* in 1973:[17]

> Man is as much a rule-following animal as a purpose-seeking one. His thinking and acting are governed by rules which have by a process of selection been evolved in the society in which he lives, and which are thus the product of the experience of generations.
>
> Many of the institutions of society that are conscious aims are in fact the result of customs, habits or practices which have been neither invented nor are observed with any such purpose in view. We live in a society in which we can successfully orientate ourselves ... not only because our fellows are governed by known aims or known connections between means and ends, but because they are also confined by rules whose purpose or origin we often do not know and of whose very existence we are often not aware.

It is possible that Hayek's receipt of the Nobel Prize in 1974 led North to read Hayek's recent work more carefully. In any case, North in the late 1970s began to argue that self-interest was controlled by what he later called "a human construct of rules, norms, conventions, and ways of doing things that define the framework of human interaction." He argued that this "construct" affects their behavior – their very definition of self-interest – and that the neoclassical model does not recognize this.[18]

Douglass North's Institutions and the Functioning of the Economy

Douglass North did not begin as a person trying to explain the state, but as a person deeply hostile to it – and especially to rulers, the executive branch, and the bureaucracy. Like Buchanan and Hayek, North was always interested in economic performance and in an economy in which compulsion was not necessary. He began as a Marxist, but certainly not one attracted to the Soviet Union. He likely was strongly attracted to Marx's vision of a stateless future.

[16] The words are Fleetwood's. Steve Fleetwood, *Hayek's Political Economy: The Social-Economics of Order* (London: Routledge, 1995), pp. 5, 29, 73–75, 83–6, and 98–100. The key book in 1960 was Friedrich A. Hayek, *Constitution of Liberty* (Chicago: University of Chicago Press, 1960).

[17] Friedrich Hayek, *Law, Legislation, and Liberty* (Chicago: University of Chicago Press, 1973), p. 9.

[18] Douglass North, *Understanding the Process of Economic Change* (Princeton, NJ: Princeton University Press, 2005), p. 11.

As Claude Menard and Mary Shirley wrote, World War II had a major impact on North.[19] North had to think profoundly about violence and societies when he decided to join the merchant marine because, as he put it, "I didn't want to kill people." Later he was exposed to the ideas of Joseph Schumpeter, who had a strong influence on North's thinking. From our perspective, the crucial fact about Schumpeter was his insistence in 1942 that stable democracy rested, first of all, on a political class with "traditions that embody experience ... a professional code ... a common code of views."[20]

In the early 1950s North became what he called "a Chicago School neoclassical theorist" – "gung ho on neoclassical economics ... holier than the Pope."[21] A former student recalls North's "long-term love affair with price theory."[22] North never used the term, but he was much attracted to the general assumptions of a "social contract."

In much of the 20th century, American scholars treated ideas primarily as a reflection of concrete interests. Marxists focused on the interests of the ruling class, but most political scientists emphasized conflict between interest groups or different elites – or in international relations, between the interests of different nations. Yet they all saw ideas of subsidiary importance.

When the influence of Marxism declined in the 1980s and 1990s, the pendulum swung back in the other direction. Scholars began to treat culture and ideas as a powerful autonomous force. Douglass North was one of them. Before the late 1970s, North gave little attention to culture and norms. His first book to deal with world economic development, *The Rise of the Western World: A New Economic History*, was co-authored with Robert

19 Claude Menard and Mary Shelly, "The Contribution of Douglass North to New Institutional Economics," in Sebastian Galiani and Itai Sened, eds., *Institutions, Property Rights, and Economic Growth: The Legacy of Douglass North* (Cambridge: Cambridge University Press, 2014), p. 18. This attitude was the decisive evidence that North was not a Marxist even mildly attracted to the Soviet Union. Once the Soviet Union was attacked in 1941, any such Marxist was wholly dedicated to fighting the war.

20 Joseph Schumpeter, *Capitalism, Socialism, and Democracy* (New York: Harper and Brothers, 1942), pp. 290–1.

21 Transcript of interview with North, October 2, 1993, attached to letter of John Lyons to Douglass North, October 2, 1993, North papers, Box 3, Correspondence October 1993 (Part 2). The interview was published many years later in John Lyons, Louis Cain, and Samuel Willington Jr., eds., *Reflections on the Cliometrics Revolution: Conversations with Economic Historians* (London: Routledge, 2008), p. 199.

22 Jonathan R. T. Hughes, "Douglass North as Teacher," in Roger Ramsom, Richard Sutch, and Gary Walton, eds., *Explorations in the New Economic History: Essays in Honor of Douglass C. North* (New York: Academic Press, 1982), pp. 4–5.

Paul Thomas and had a fully contractarian perspective. North and Thomas essentially described political systems as informal social contracts between societal actors and rulers who were absorbed with promoting efficiency. They even applied the analysis to the Middle Ages and asserted that "the contractual arrangement of the classic manor can now be seen as an efficient arrangement for its day." The manor and local baron, they said, served "the functions of providing justice and protection."[23]

Published in 1973, *The Rise of the Western World* declared that the decline in population associated with factors such as the plague changed the price ratio between land and labor in medieval society and reduced the traditional sources of feudal income. This, North and Thomas argued, produced profound economic change that North treated as virtually automatic.

Thus, the evolution of the military in the early modern period simply reflected the changing ratio of the price of land and labor. This change, the authors asserted, "dictated fewer military units overall, each of a larger size, than previously, and required a contraction in the number of governmental units.... The decline in the number of independent military units was inevitable." North and Thomas also treated the rise of the nation-state as "probably the inevitable result of the development of a money economy and the expansion of trade."[24]

This view of dictation and inevitability is breathtaking. Many areas (even "civilizations") from ancient times to modern experienced similar declines of population at different times, but this usually did not produce North and Thomas's "inevitable" results." Instead, the number of armed militias often increased and anarchy ensued.

North and Thomas also gave little attention to state capability. In their words, "a set of property rights once specified can be extended almost indefinitely to other areas at little additional cost."[25] This showed no awareness that the collective action problems in collecting taxes, controlling an army, or building a bureaucracy multiply as the territory becomes larger.

By the late 1970s, North recognized the shortcomings of *The Rise of the Western World*. The book drew a barrage of criticism for asserting that the serf and lord had entered into an informal social contract. In his 1981 *Structure and Change in Economic History*, North acknowledged that "we did not lay sufficient stress on the one-sided nature of the relationship." He

[23] Douglass North and Robert Paul Thomas, *The Rise of the Western World: A New Economic History* (Cambridge: University Press, 1973), pp. 11 and 32.

[24] North and Thomas, *The Rise of the Western World*, pp. 80–1.

[25] Ibid., p. 94.

now saw the feudal warrior class as "analogous to the Mafia in extracting income from the peasantry."[26]

More basically, North began in the late 1970s to face up to the fact that similar conditions often lead to differences in economic performance and rates of growth in different places. He declared in his speech accepting the Nobel Prize in 1993 that "it is necessary to dismantle the rationality assumption underlying economic theory." By 2005, he was making the point in sharp language: "The uncritical acceptance of the rationality assumption is devastating for most of the major issues confronting social scientists and is a major stumbling block in the path of future progress."[27]

Most who embrace the neoclassical economic model "solve" Dennis Mueller's problem of the rationality of theft by assuming that the model has a "loose" definition of rationality that includes ethics and/or that makes violation of the rules of the game a deep taboo, especially for people working in government. North, by contrast, took the assumptions of the neoclassical model seriously. He thought analysts needed to separate the assumption of rationality from ethical and other informal restraints in order to make progress.

In the late 1970s and early 1980s, North searched for the best way to discuss what he had in mind. He first used "ideology" to describe the "construct that must be added to the neoclassical model." Over time, he abandoned "ideology" in favor of "belief system," because he had discovered that the word "ideology" often conveyed "the Marxist notion of false or incorrect beliefs."[28]

North meant the opposite. He chose "belief system" as a less confusing equivalent; he said, "I mean that everybody has belief systems. Belief systems enable us to interpret that part of reality that we are trying to understand and build into models for ourselves a positive and always a normative perspective on that world."[29]

[26] Douglass North, *Structure and Change in Economic History* (New York: W. W. Norton, 1981), pp. 129–31; Douglass North, "Institutions and Economic Growth: An Historical Introduction," *World Development* 17 (1989), 1319–32, p. 1326.

[27] Douglass North, "Epilogue: Economic Performance through Time," in Lee Alston, Thrainn Eggertsson, and Douglass North, eds., *Empirical Studies in Institutional Change* (New York: Cambridge University Press, 1996), p. 346; North, *Understanding the Process of Economic Change*, p. 5.

[28] Douglass North letter to Moses Abramovitz, September 26, 1979.

[29] Douglass North, "Response to Geddes and Keohane," in James Alt, Margaret Levi, and Elinor Ostrom, eds., *Competition and Cooperation: Conversations with Nobelists about Economics and Political Science* (New York: Russell Sage Foundation, 1999), p. 250.

North then moved to the word "institutions" to make clearer that the belief system actually created incentives to which individuals responded as much as they did to self-interest. Over time North has used somewhat different words to define "institutions," but all are basically consistent. A recent definition is comprehensive:[30]

> Institutions are the "rules of the game" ... the patterns of interaction that govern and constrain the relationships of individuals. Institutions include formal rules, written laws, formal social conventions, informal norms of behavior, and shared beliefs about the world, as well as the means of enforcement. The most common way of thinking about institutions is that they are constraints on the behavior of individuals as individuals.... However, institutions also structure the way individuals form beliefs and opinions about how other people will behave.

North, we reemphasize, did not include governmental bodies among "formal institutions." Rather, "formal institutions" are constitutions that restrain government and written laws and rules that government enacts. The state and political organs are "organizations." Others define "institution" more conventionally, and this introduces great confusion into the debate. Thus, in 2011 when Joseph Stiglitz criticized the "mainstream view that institutions don't matter," he was not repeating North's insight, but rejecting it. Stiglitz was speaking about the role of the state. We agree with Robert Bates when he commented sharply, "If, as some proclaim, 'institutions rule' ... one would think it better not be because institutions can be anything." He clearly thinks this is the case.[31]

All scholars would agree with North that "rules, norms, conventions, and ways of doing things" have a great impact on human behavior, including economic and political behavior. The problem is that people have always operated within "human constructs". Hence, North's general statement means nothing unless one can distinguish concretely among human constructs

[30] Douglass North, John Joseph Wallis, and Barry Weingast, *Violence and Social Orders: A Conceptual Framework for Interpreting Recorded History* (New York: Cambridge University Press, 2009), p. 15.

[31] Leslie Norton, "The Dangers of Lessons Unheeded: Interview with Joseph Stiglitz," *Barrons,* March 21, 2011, p. 40. Acemoglu and Robinson are a bit more ambiguous, but they are close to Stiglitz when they say that they "will refer to political institutions that are sufficiently centralized and pluralistic as inclusive political institutions." Daron Acemoglu and James Robinson, *Why Nations Fail: The Origins of Power, Prosperity, and Poverty* (New York: Crown Business, 2012), p. 81; Robert Bates, "The New Institutionalism," in Sebastian Galiani and Itai Sened, eds., *Institutions, Property Rights, and Economic Growth: The Legacy of Douglass North* (Cambridge: Cambridge University Press, 2014), p. 56.

and belief systems. It is simply a tautology to say people are constrained by constitutions, laws, and informal institutions that actually constrain them.

We believe that that Margaret Levi was right in suggesting that North was simply "treating ideology as a residual category for those situations in which self-interest is clearly not explanatory."[32] North himself has been acutely aware of this difficulty. As he wrote in 1983, he knew he was "not going to convince the Gary Beckers of the world without some empirical measurement."[33] Yet North never seriously addressed the problem of measurement. Indeed, he has never even tried to describe the institutions that he thinks are a pre-condition of an efficient economy, not even by referring to those that Max Weber posited. That made measurement impossible.

In short, North has basically been concerned with warning development economists that the countries with which they deal do not yet have the norms needed for a more or less spontaneously organized economy. In practice, he focused in his work on those countries that are beginning to approach modern societies. A large number of neoclassical economists have come to write in general terms about the need to adopt the right institutions, and this implies that they too have been thinking about relatively advanced developing countries.

This too is a reason why North has never really had a concrete explanation for why hundreds of years are needed for development. Like Daron Acemoglu and James Robinson, he has concentrated on the period when the state is already built, as it was by the 1750s in England – that is, the last 50 to 100 years of development. North had relatively little to say about the prior period until *In the Shadow of Violence*. That is the period to which this book is dedicated.

Douglass North and the State

At the same time North started emphasizing the importance of informal norms, values, and assumptions, he also began to say that an efficient market depended on an effective government. This was a major theme in his letters in the 1980s, as he sharply distinguished himself from those embracing contractarianism, rent-seeking, or self-enforcing constraints. A 1987 letter to a libertarian economist, Donald McCloskey, was typical:

[32] Margaret Levi, *Of Rule and Revenue* (Berkeley: University of California Press, 1988), p. 51.

[33] Letter to Jack Hirshleifer, February 8, 1983, North papers, Box 50. Gary Becker was a Nobel Prize–winning economist.

"Certainly in my view, though probably not in yours, the development of a judiciary and a system of law or third party enforcement of contracts has played an overwhelmingly important role in the development of western economies."[34]

Nevertheless, if we look at North's view of the state with perspective, something seems wrong. From the late 1970s until the end of the mid-1990s, North was a frequent participant in the workshops of the libertarian Liberty Fund.[35] Frequently invited participants to these workshops are seldom proponents of government involvement in the economy.

In 1981, North provided a definition of the state which we find extraordinarily useful and which we utilize throughout this book: "an organization with a comparative advantage in violence, extending over a geographic area whose boundaries are determined by its power to tax constituents."[36] Yet he has never talked about tax collection or how a comparative advantage in violence is achieved.

In particular, North has never discussed the obvious issues that arise from this definition – the problems with which this chapter began. How do rulers gain a stable comparative advantage in violence or the power to tax constituents? How do they prevent their administrative and military officials from maximizing their income through corruption of various types or even through conducting a coup d'état? How do they develop a basic ability to govern that Samuel Huntington rightly said is so lacking in the developing world today, in medieval and early modern Europe, and elsewhere in the world in the past?

When North emphasized the importance of a state to Donald McCloskey, we should note that his letter specifically referred to the judiciary. This is true of other letters at the time. The same phenomenon is found in North's published comment on a long paper by Joseph Stiglitz on the functions of government. North's comment had a section entitled "What Government Should Do," but instead of analyzing many functions as Stiglitz did, North referred only to the government's role in establishing ill-defined rules and

[34] Letter to Donald McCloskey, July 27, 1987, North Papers, Box 1, Correspondence July 1987. Also see North's letters to T. N. Srinavasan (September 4, 1985), Terry Anderson (April 18, 1986), Donald McCloskey (January 17, 1987, and July 27, 1987), David Feeny (November 18, 1987), and Daniel Bromley (December 14, 1987). North papers, Box 1. Younger scholars may know McCloskey only as Deirdre McCloskey and they will realize that her views have evolved over a quarter of a century.

[35] The first reference in the archives is in 1979. The latest reference is to a 1999 session reported in Bruce Caldwell, *Hayek's Challenge: An Intellectual Biography of F. A. Hayek* (Chicago: University of Chicago Press, 2007), p. 352n.

[36] North, *Structure and Change in Economic History*, p. 21.

then in serving as a third-party referee in contract disputes.[37] Again, this was the judiciary – and implicitly the civil courts and civil law rather than the criminal courts and criminal law.

By contrast, North's treatment of the executive branch has been basically as negative as James Buchanan's. Nowhere in his work is there anything that even hints that North accepted Acemoglu and Robinson's belief that "a lack of, or weak, political centralization" is a major "barrier to the spread of industry" and that "the centralization of state institutions [under Henry VII and Henry VIII from the 1485 to the 1540s] meant that, for the first time inclusive political institutions became possible."

Instead, when North commented on Stiglitz's paper on the functions of government, he asserted that "the State has not provided a framework conducive to economic growth.... A State that is self-consciously concerned with the performance of the economy is a relatively modern phenomenon ... [primarily] associated with the rise of 'representative' government." In an earlier letter, he wrote that "it probably is true that governments by and large have been bad for growth.... Throughout history it has not been in the interests of those who ran governments to promote efficient property rights."[38] As will be seen later, North explicitly told Mancur Olson that this was the main issue between them.

Even North's recent books *Violence and Social Orders* and *In the Shadow of Violence* do not suggest that government is necessary to control violence. Instead, they focus on a dominant coalition of elites who distribute rent among themselves, implicitly by negotiations. The analysis contains no ruler to help negotiate the conflicting interests of those in the coalition, to decide how to divide and provide the necessary side payments (rent), let alone to be a stationary bandit who suppresses violence.

This is Robert Bates's major criticism of new institutionalism. He writes of "the unwarranted reluctance of those who subscribe to the new institutionalism to pursue the implications of the basic insight ... that coercion can be socially productive."[39]

[37] Douglass North, "Comments 2," in Joseph Stiglitz and Arnold Heertje, eds., *The Economic Role of the State* (Oxford: Basil Blackwell, 1989), pp. 109–10.

[38] Ibid., p. 108. Letter to Donald McCloskey, January 16, 1987.

[39] North et al., *Violence and Social Orders;* and Douglass North, John Joseph Wallis, Steven Webb, and Barry Weingast, eds., *In the Shadow of Violence: Politics, Economics, and the Problems of Development* (Cambridge: Cambridge University Press, 2013); Robert Bates, "The New Institutionalism," in Galiani and Sened, eds., *Institutions, Property Rights, and Economic Growth*, p. 55.

Similarly, North never shared Max Weber's belief that bureaucracy is crucial for modern society or for the development of constraints on the ruler. Indeed, despite his definition of a state and the obvious lesson of developing countries, he never has mentioned the need for an effective tax-collecting bureaucracy. He has never discussed Oliver Williamson's emphasis upon the importance of a Weberian bureaucracy in creating the efficiency of the modern corporation.

When North does refer to bureaucracy, it is only in a negative sense. For example, his main explanation for poor economic growth in Latin America (and implicitly for that in Spain) was "the centralized, bureaucratic traditions carried over from its Spanish/Portuguese heritage."[40] His most recent discussion of Latin America in 2005 refers only to the impact of the 1500s and 1600s when Spain did not have strong governmental capability. He never discusses the last 50 years of the Bourbon regime when the bureaucracy did, in fact, become more effective – and policy became much more market-oriented.

Although North rejected a pure contractarian doctrine in 1981, he never adopted the opposing view that government is ultimately based on force. Instead, he substituted societal forces for the demands of efficiency as the factor that is necessary to compel government to promote economic growth. In 1981, he came to see politics as a bargaining process between rulers and their "constituents," a word that no longer included peasants, but remained ill defined:[41]

> The state trades a group of services, which we shall call protection and justice, for revenue.... The state is constrained by the opportunity cost of its constituents since there always exist potential rivals to provide the same set of services.... Constituents may, at some cost, go over to a competing ruler ... or support a competitor for ruler within the existing state organization.... The ruler's own agents may be able [to] attract supporters from among the constituents by offering a better division of the existing rents.

By the late 1980s, North was moving to emphasize representative institutions. This was seen in his criticism of Stiglitz cited earlier, but more famously in his 1989 article on the Glorious Revolution of 1688 with Barry

[40] Douglass North, *Institutions, Institutional Change and Economic Performance* (Cambridge: Cambridge University Press, 1990), pp. 116 and 102.

[41] North, *Structure and Change in Economic History*, pp. 23 and 27. This theme is particularly strong in a major book, *Of Rule and Revenue*, that was written by his colleague Margaret Levi in the 1970s. Levi and North taught a seminar together at the University of Washington.

Weingast. North and Weingast asserted that "a constitution must arise from the bargaining context between the state and constituents."[42]

North and Weingast also saw such bargaining as the key to tax collection. They attributed the ability of the English government to gain more revenue after 1688 to the fact that "the wealth holders gained a say in each of these [financial] decisions through their representatives in Parliament. This meant that only if such changes were in their own interests would they be made."[43]

The bargain between the state and constituents, North and Weingast asserted, "must be *self-enforcing* in the sense that the major parties to the bargain must have an incentive to abide by the bargain."[44] Writing separately, Weingast elaborated the argument and stated that a coup d'état or usurpation of power could be prevented if people have "a shared belief system about the legitimate ends of government and the extent of citizen rights [and] a credible commitment that citizens [will] react in concert when officials violate their rights." North continued to use similar language in later work. Then in 2014, Weingast expressed the argument more clearly than ever and summarized it bluntly: "the principal mechanism in enforcing constitutional rule is citizen resistance."[45]

North and Weingast's 1989 article on the Glorious Revolution clearly reflected the argument of John Locke about "consent of the governed" presented exactly 300 years earlier in his 1689 *Two Treatises on Government*. Locke proclaimed his intention to present an alternative to the theory that "all government is merely the product of force and violence" and began with a quite mythical state of nature. North himself acknowledged his debt to Locke in a letter to a correspondent who criticized him for not recognizing it in his work. "I certainly owe Locke a great deal," North declared, "but at times I don't know when I'm talking Locke and when I'm talking North since I'm sure that I have absorbed him through my pores for a long time."[46]

[42] Douglass North and Barry Weingast, "Constitutions and Commitment: The Evolution of Institutions Governing Public Choice in Seventeenth Century England," *Journal of Economic History* 49 (1989), 803–32.

[43] Ibid., p. 829.

[44] Ibid., p. 806.

[45] Barry Weingast, "The Political Foundations of Democracy and the Rule of Law," *American Political Science Review* 91 (1997), 245–63. For a later North statement, see, for example, North, *Understanding the Process of Economic Change*, p. 107. Gillian K. Hadfield and Barry Weingast, "Constitutions and Coordinating Devices," Sebastian Galiani and Itai Sened, eds., *Institutions, Property Rights, and Economic Growth: The Legacy of Douglass North* (Cambridge: Cambridge University Press, 2014), 121–50. The quotation is from p. 137.

[46] North to Donald Nichols, May 23, 1991. Nichols's letter was dated May 16. North Papers, Box 2, Correspondence May 1991.

But what did North and Weingast mean? It must always be remembered that North uses the word "organization," not "institution," for concrete bodies such as the Congress and Parliament. When North and Weingast said that the main lesson of their article was that "the fundamental institutions of representative government ... are intimately related to the struggle for control over governmental power," this statement had a meaning that the casual reader would not notice.

North and Weingast did not say, it must be emphasized, that "the fundamental organizations of representative government" are crucial as they would have if they had Parliament and Congress in mind. "Institution," as has been seen, has a very different meaning – the formal and informal norms and rules that constrain individuals and organizations. The statement referred to the norms of governance, not concrete governing bodies.

Nothing indicates that North was any more attracted to real legislatures than to rulers or bureaucracies. Adam Smith opposed Parliament because he knew that merchants and manufacturers used it to gain the special privileges he opposed – that is, to engage in rent-seeking in modern language. Smith knew that the Hanover kings had succeeded in controlling Parliament by bribing its members. This is how Secretary of the Treasury Alexander Hamilton controlled the Congress for George Washington. Development agencies actually prefer weak legislatures because they allow strong rulers to introduce unpopular market measures. North knows all this and is repelled by the way that real legislatures actually work.

North's most recent work, *Violence and Social Orders* and *In the Shadow of Violence*, can be interpreted in a number of ways. It says little about representative institutions and bodies until the last stages of development and instead, emphasizes the necessity of rule by a dominant coalition. This could be seen as no more than a clarification of North and Weingast's 1989 praise of a written constitution that gave a veto to the wealthy or wealth-holders.

Now North sees the wealthy to be differentiated and to be self-interested in receiving "rent." Implicitly he recognizes the military to be a key element of the ruling coalition that demands being given its share of the rent. Indeed, to some extent, the vague concept of a dominant coalition is a return to the pre-1989 North attraction to an informal social contract, not one embodied in a written constitution such as that of 1689.

North's emphasis on violence and self-interest (rent) in his recent books is, we think, a step forward, but it is not complete. North's view of the military, the ruler, and the bureaucracy remains unchanged. Basically they continue to play no positive role and are hardly even discussed at all. While

North recognizes that the military is a source of violence, he does see that it is necessary to suppress violence. This means that he does not explore the crucial contradiction between the need for a strong military to suppress violence and the threat of a strong military to order, property rights, and the protection of liberty. The difficulty of resolving this contradiction is a key reason that development takes so long.

North also does not discuss the mechanisms needed to solve the critical problem of tax collecting and adequate financing – a continual problem in development both of the past and present. The difficulty in financing the states as territory grows and the complexity of governing increases obviously is another factor that explains the length of the development process that cannot be ignored.

Mancur Olson is a perfect corrective to the incomplete discussion presented in Douglass North's theory. His model clearly exaggerates the role of compulsion and selective side payments – as he himself surely would have readily agreed. Like North, who was reacting to the over-simplified neoclassical model, Olson deliberately simplified his model to illuminate the logic of a crucial problem in large-scale cooperative human behavior, including a market. We turn to an examination of that logic in the section on Olson's theory of collective action.

Introducing Dynamics into the Analysis: Max Weber and the Evolution from Personalistic to Impersonal Norms

The sociologist Max Weber is often described as the alternative to Karl Marx – a man who emphasized the impact of ideas on social development instead of economics. Weber's only book well known to modern economists, *The Protestant Ethic and the Spirit of Capitalism*, attributes the "spirit of capitalism" and the Industrial Revolution to the ideas of the Protestant Reformation.[47] Weber's far more important book on values in development is *Economy and Society*. American sociologists voted it the most important sociology book of the 20th century, and it has had a far greater impact.

In *Economy and Society*, Weber emphasized the importance of the difference between values in tribal, foraging, and village societies and those in modern society. He did not, however, treat the difference in the moral codes

[47] Max Weber, *The Protestant Ethic and the Spirit of Capitalism*, translated by Talcott Parsons (London: Scribner, 2013). For a discussion of this thesis and of the classic counter-argument by R. H. Tawney, see Chapter 5. R. H. Tawney, *Religion and the Rise of Capitalism* (New York: Harcourt, Brace, 1926).

of early and modern society as autonomous, but he attributed it to the different functional needs of those kinds of societies.

When North discusses ideological restraints on individual self-interest in concrete terms, he usually goes no further than phrases such as "moral and ethical judgments about the fairness of the world," "equity," and "legitimacy." He argues that "strong moral and ethical codes" are the pre-condition of reducing "the costs of enforcing the rules and property rights" to acceptable levels. In his words, government "investment for legitimacy is as much a cost of economic organization as [anything else]."[48]

These statements are accurate, but they assume that norms about fairness, equity, and legitimacy are universal. In fact, Weber insisted it is not. He argued that the definitions of morality in place as marketization began were very different from those needed for a modern market.

For several million years, humans lived in small hunting and foraging groups where a different conception of right and wrong was required. Offspring were so helpless and took so long to mature that the human race would not have survived had it not learned how to live in small cooperative groups.

The moral codes that early small groups needed were those that constrained individual self-interest and subordinated them to the interests of more or less extended families. Early government, broadly defined, was also infused with the values of the tribal unit and village. This was true of chiefdoms in the tribal societies studied by anthropologists and of early "kings" who were no more than very small warlords.

Weber called the first larger governments "patriarchal" and "patrimonial" after the Latin word for father, "pater." Patrimonial governments, including those in England and Spain during most of period covered by this book, began with a "court politics" that were deeply personalistic in nature. Lower officials were not "civil servants" of the state but the ruler's personal retainers who were "paid" through a percentage of booty, through a percentage of taxes and other fees collected, and/or through self-enrichment by personal participation in economic activities.

Rulers could place brothers and sons in different elite structures, appoint friends from their hometowns to important administrative positions, and have their sons, daughters, and siblings broaden personal ties through intermarriage. All these officials and their retainers normally were heavily influenced by strong moral and ethical codes, but these codes were not those needed for modern markets and states.

[48] North, *Structure and Change in Economic History*, pp. 44 and 47–54.

International relations were just as personalistic. Isabella strengthened her position in the Civil Wars of the 1460s and 1470s by marrying Ferdinand of Aragon and thereby assuring the Castilian elite that her victory would mean the acquisition of Aragon. Similarly, when Henry VII of the House of Lancaster seized power in 1485 and consolidated power over York and the rest of England, he facilitated his conquest by agreeing to marry Elizabeth of York. Later, Henry married his heir to Isabella's daughter, Catherine of Aragon, in order to form an alliance with Spain.

Modern society requires norms of fairness based on impartiality, impersonality, and professionalism: the norms that Weber attributes to rational-legal society. An increasingly complex specialization of labor implies the development of a high degree of trust in strangers and ability to deal with them.

The Weberian image of pre-industrial governance has major implications for explaining the development of the constraining values needed for the modern government and market. For millions of years people had different conceptions of right and wrong, and the old ones had to be rejected. Officials had been *supposed* to treat people according to personalistic criteria. They were *supposed* be paid by a share of the taxes and fees they collected and were *supposed* to earn profits from economic activities. Wholly legitimate activities had to become illegitimate.

The problem was not simply to inculcate norms that constrain individuals. Rather, it was to change norms that already did constrain them. Moreover, officials were to adopt the new norms at the very time when they were supposed to learn that the pursuit of individual self-interest is good. They had to learn that profit maximization and interest rates are not sinful or unethical, but are necessary for markets.

The question is how the family-oriented values necessary in village and tribal society are changed into the impersonal and individualistic values that are necessary in modern market society. North does not discuss the issue, but he seems to think that the changes must arise first – and more or less autonomously – in the realm of ideas and norms. As has been seen, North has emphasized that "it is beliefs, ideas, dogmas, and ideologies that ultimately shape polities and economies. The place to begin," he says, "is with the beliefs held by members of a society."[49]

[49] Douglass North, William Summerhill, and Barry Weingast, "Order, Disorder and Economic Change: Latin America vs. North America," in Bruce Bueno de Mesquita and Hilton Root, eds., *Governing for Prosperity* (New Haven, CT: Yale University Press, 2000), p. 22.

Most analysts who have looked seriously at the actual formation of states have agreed with Aristotle that "laying down the law" must precede the "winning of the hearts and minds of people." Modern scholars usually say that the European nation-states were created by military force, which was made possible by a revolution in military technology. Then the winning warlord created a national language and national culture. This scholarly consensus only repeats an ancient witticism: a language is simply a dialect with the strongest army behind it. Or, perhaps as in England, it may be an amalgamation of one of the English dialects and one of the Old French ones.

The question is whether the kings were also crucial in creating the rational-legal values needed for a modern market. Max Weber said little about the transition from a traditional society and patrimonial government to a rational-legal one, other than in the unique case of the Protestant work ethic. Nevertheless, he clearly believed that the secret of the efficiency of modern society is the creation of a rational-legal bureaucracy in both the public and private sectors. The following excerpt refers to private, military, and civilian government bureaucracies alike. In Weber's words:[50]

> The fully developed bureaucratic apparatus compares with other organizations exactly as does the machine with the non-mechanical modes of production. Precision, speed, unambiguity, knowledge of the files, continuity, discretion, unity, strict subordination, reduction of friction and of material and personal costs – these are raised to the optimum point in the strictly bureaucratic administration, and especially in its monocratic form.
>
> It is primarily the capitalist market economy that demands that the official business of public administration be discharged precisely, unambiguously, continuously, and with as much speed as possible. Normally, the very large modern capitalist enterprise are themselves unequalled models of strict bureaucratic organization.

The first sentence in the second paragraph of this quotation deserves very special attention. No "economy" can "demand" that a bureaucracy function as Weber and Williamson suggest. If it could, the public administration and the private bureaucracies in the developing world would function in the way that the economy "demands" immediately and not require centuries or millennia to develop, including with effective corporate bureaucracies as well.

[50] Max Weber, *Theory of Social and Economic Organization*, translated by A. M. Henderson and Talcott Parsons (New York: Oxford University Press, 1947). The quotation is from Max Weber, *Economy and Society: An Outline of Interpretative Sociology*, edited by Guenther Roth and Claus Wittich (Berkeley: University of California Press, 1978), pp. 973–4.

It is not "the economy" that demands government bureaucrats to function in the way Weber says they should, but rulers who must use rewards and punishments to try to ensure that they do so. It is those who own and manage corporations who must demand that employees act the way that Weber suggests.

Yet, a bureaucracy cannot function with the precision and predictability that rulers want if the rulers themselves behave arbitrarily. Weber's functional argument really implied that imperfect bureaucracies must be created first. As their work involves more specialization of labor, rulers are driven to restrain themselves if they want to maximize the tax base.

Weber has many implications for a theory of change during the development process. First, of course, the fact that the desired norms must replace norms that have been in place for hundreds of thousands and millions of years inevitably means that the process must be prolonged.

Second, the "second-best" and "third-best" and "fourth-best" measures necessary during different stages of the long transition must involve the use of the village and tribal values already in place.[51] Indeed, one of the purposes of this book is to illuminate precisely how this happened in European history.

Thus, as a reader of Weber would expect, the first more-regularized taxation was based on personalistic ties. The guilds began as relatively small groups whose leaders had personal ties to the king and who could control their members through personal contact. The "aldermen" of the city council of London were usually guild leaders.

Another semi-personalistic solution often illustrated in this book was to obtain revenue by using private agents to perform what we consider governmental functions – for example, merchants who lent their ships to act as naval vessels, church clerics who served as government "clerks" without pay, and business monopolies that collected taxes, served as commercial courts, and built infrastructure.

[51] There are economists who recognize the importance of looking at second-best policies. See Lant Pritchett and Frauke de·Weijer, "Fragile States: Stuck in a Capability Trap?" Background Paper for World Development Report 2011. For other examples, see Merillee Grindle, "Good Enough Governance: Poverty Reduction and Reform in Developing Countries," *Governance: An International Journal of Policy, Administration and Institutions* 17 (2004), 525–48, Dani Rodrik, "Second-Best Institutions," *American Economic Review: Papers and Proceedings* 98. 2 (2008), 100–104, and Dennis Rondinelli, *Development Projects as Policy Experiments: An Adaptive Approach to Development Administration* (New York: Routledge, 1993), and Nicholas van de Walle, "The Paths from Neo-Patrimonialism: Democracy and Clientelism in Africa Today," Cornell University, Center for International Studies, Working Paper No. 3–07, 2007.

As Thomas Ertman noted, the use of these "private bodies" often also provided the expertise needed for government. The collection of customs duties required knowledgeable officials who understood the value of goods being traded.[52] Legal maritime issues were difficult to understand, and the constant movement of ships made the legal resolution of disputes difficult. Monarchs originally relied on merchants and their guilds that had the expertise, the personal contacts, and the ability to impose sanctions outside the port area.

We think that many rulers through history, including today in the developing world, have been quite willing to restrain themselves to create a well-functioning bureaucracy and permit economic growth. They could not, however, solve the problem of transforming values and they could not solve the collective action problems of bringing civilian and military bureaucrats under control and turning them into their real "agents." In the next section, we explore Mancur Olson's analysis of these collective action problems.

Introducing Dynamics into the Analysis: Mancur Olson and His Collective Action Theory

There is no single collective action theory or rational actor model in modern scholarship. Unfortunately, the most popular collective action theory in the scholarly community – game theory – is not well suited for analyzing how an effective state develops. While game theory analyzes the response of actors to fixed and precise rules of the game, the key to the development of an effective state and market is to change the rules of the game of the past to control government officials, military officers, and economic actors who have the self-interest to ignore them and/or change them in ways advantageous to themselves.

Few New Institutionalists discuss this problem. Most use game theory and are reassured by the near universal result:[53]

> The robust conclusion of all experimental studies is that human behavior is almost never consistent with the "standard" model of self-interest. Across a range of contexts, many individuals are willing to reduce their own payout to help or cooperate with others.

[52] Thomas Ertman, *Birth of the Leviathan: Building States and Regimes in Medieval and Early Modern Europe* (Cambridge: Cambridge University Press, 1997).

[53] Pamela Jakiela, "Using Economic Experiments to Measure Informal Institutions," in Sebastian Galiani and Itai Sened, eds., *Institutions, Property Rights, and Economic Growth: The Legacy of Douglass North* (Cambridge: Cambridge University Press, 2014), 250–3. The quotation is from p. 250.

The great majority of people are probably risk averse and are either conformists or semi-conformists. The problem is that this is not true of everyone and that those driven to maximize power and wealth seek out the places in society where this is most possible. The question is how to constrain them. The New Institutionalists who deal most explicitly with this problem develop coalition theory on the basis of relatively small groups such as the U.S. Senate and House of Representatives where collective action problems are not as great – and where party leaders do, after all, have important means of providing selective side payments.[54]

Mancur Olson was a neoclassical economist who wrote his seminal *The Logic of Collective Action* in the 1960s. Perhaps influenced by James Buchanan, whose *The Calculus of Consent* was published in 1962, Olson began with the same assumptions as Buchanan about the identical motivation of *homo economicus* and *homo politicus*. Olson took the narrow definition of rationality in the neoclassical economic model and applied it to the calculations of a rational individual trying to decide whether or not to participate in political action.[55]

Olson thought that informal pressure exerted by rewards and punishments from peers and family is sufficient to compel collective action in small villages and tribal units of up to 200 people – and in modern small group situations. He concluded, however, that it is almost never rational for individuals to participate in mass collective action – joining interest groups, voting, marching in demonstrations, defending constitutions from usurpers – at least, if the individual's purpose is simply to achieve a collective goal, even one that he or she strongly desires.

Olson began his collective action analysis of politics by emphasizing a difference between the economic and political spheres that all economists would recognize – the difference between a private good and a public good. In the economic sphere, people receive a concrete benefit (for example, a product, wages, the prospect of profit) in exchange for a concrete expenditure of time and/or money. They receive the benefit only if they pay the cost.

A public good is defined as one whose benefits (or harm) are received by everyone regardless of whether he or she participates in providing it. A national park or museum without an admittance charge is a public good.

[54] For a sophisticated discussion of changing the rules of the game, see Kenneth Shepsle, "The Rules of the Game: What Rules? What Games," in Sebastian Galiani and Itai Sened, eds., *Institutions, Property Rights, and Economic Growth: The Legacy of Douglass North* (Cambridge: Cambridge University Press, 2014), especially pp. 69–73.

[55] Mancur Olson, *The Logic of Collective Action: Public Goods and the Theory of Groups* (Cambridge, MA: Harvard University Press, 1965).

So are national defense, election results, and revolutions. All citizens benefit (or suffer) whatever the level of their political participation in trying to create it or block it.

Olson emphasized that rational individuals should not decide whether to participate in political action simply because they wanted some outcome. Rather, they should participate only if the impact of their individual participation on the benefit to themselves personally would outweigh the personal cost of the participation. If not, they should be a "free rider" and receive the benefit without effort.

The cost-benefit relationship of participation is often favorable for wealthy or politically powerful persons in a modern society. A large campaign contribution may lead to the public good of a tax loophole, but the contribution is rational if enactment depends on it and if the benefit to the contributor is more valuable than its cost. Influential persons may also make a phone call to a policymaker and change an outcome at low cost.

The average individual will find that his or her participation in elections, interest groups, demonstrations, or revolutions can almost never have the slightest influence on the outcome. Casting a single vote, paying membership dues, or marching in a demonstration will never be noted. Yet in all these cases the individual will have to pay a cost in time, including the information cost of learning enough to participate intelligently. In most cases, the individual also faces a financial cost as well, and in some cases a potential cost of death or injury.

As a result, Olson argued the cost of participation for the average citizen always outweighs the zero benefit. Since average persons always have the incentive to be a free rider, the only pressure for the creation of public goods should come from special interests that have a different cost-benefit ratio from that of the average citizen. Mancur Olson analyzed the implications for self-interest domination of the state in his 1982 *The Rise and Decline of Nations*.[56]

But why does mass participation take place, as it obviously does? Olson knew that non-rational emotion and sense of duty can be a factor, but he was analyzing rational considerations. He pointed to two such reasons: (1) compulsion, and (2) selective side payments – rewards that go only to those who participate.[57]

[56] Mancur Olson, *The Rise and Decline of Nations: Economic Growth, Stagflation, and Social Rigidity* (New Haven, CT: Yale University Press, 1982).

[57] For a brief acknowledgment of the role of emotion, usually ephemeral, see Mancur Olson, *Power and Prosperity: Outgrowing Communist and Capitalist Dictatorships* (New York: Basic Books, 2000), p. 3.

The clearest example of compulsion is the threat of imprisonment if people do not pay taxes to support the collective action of government. Olson illustrated selective side payments with the incentives to join interest groups. He argued that individuals join organizations such as the American Association of Retired Persons (AARP) not to promote favorable laws for older people but to obtain concrete side payments such as motel discounts. As a result, even though the AARP sells health insurance and really represents the interests of insurance companies in negotiations for legislation such as the Affordable Care Act, older people who join only for the selective side payments have no incentive to quit in protest.

In the late 1980s, Olson began to discuss issues of political development seriously. The 300th anniversary of the Glorious Revolution of 1688 focused attention on John Locke and his theory of consent of the governed, and Olson thought that Locke's theory was utterly unrealistic. It was North and Weingast's 1989 "Constitutions and Commitment" based on Locke's views that provoked him to elaborate his views on the subject.

Anyone with the slightest familiarity with Olson's analysis knows how he reacted to the view that usurpation of power could be prevented if people have (in the words of Barry Weingast) "a shared belief system about the legitimate ends of government and the extent of citizen rights [and] a credible commitment that citizens [will] react in concert when officials violate their rights."[58]

Olson thought that a commitment to "react in concert" could never be credible because of the logic of collective action. He believed that participation of individuals to act in concert to defend a constitution against a ruthless ruler with soldiers at his disposal had the worst conceivable ratio of costs and benefits. It was this analysis that led Olson to conclude that voluntary collective action simply "*cannot* obtain the gains from a peaceful order [of a state]." At one point, Olson made his point starkly:[59]

> Political outcomes do not mainly depend on the hearts and minds of the people – on what the various populations or nationalities want.... Unpopular governments – and even despised alien regimes can stay in power for very long periods [because] the logic of collective action keeps the huge number of people who don't like a regime from taking the actions that would overthrow it.

When Olson began to try to explain the state, he concentrated for analytical reasons on the creation of the first, most basic "state." He went back to the

[58] Weingast, "The Political Foundations of Democracy and the Rule of Law," pp. 245–63.
[59] Mancur Olson, "The Logic of Collective Action in Soviet-Type Societies," *Journal of Soviet Nationalities*, 1 (1990), 9–10.

key factors that he emphasized in his general analysis of political collective action: compulsion and selective side payments. In analyzing the origins of the state, Olson basically reversed the argument of Karl Marx on the relation of force and property. According to Marx, the owners of the means of production created a state to defend their property against the non-owners. From Olson's perspective, the basic flaw in Marx's argument is that armed men whom owners hire to protect their property have a stronger incentive to seize it than to defend it. Hence, the main danger to major property owners should not be class revolution (a collective action in which it is irrational for rank-and-file people to participate), but military coups and armed militias both from inside and outside. History confirms this.

Olson believed that "property rights" arose when men with sufficient armed force seized land and then established a state to create – and then defend – such property rights for themselves and their chief lieutenants. Olson began his analysis of government with men he called roving bandits – the leaders of marauding gangs or militias. In Olson's view, one roving bandit defeats others in an area and creates a monopoly of force that allows him to become a "stationary bandit" (a government):

> Bandit rationality ... induces the bandit leader to seize a given domain, to make himself the ruler of that domain, and to provide a peaceful order and other public goods for its inhabitants, thereby obtaining more in tax theft than he could have obtained from migratory plunder.

Indeed, in Olson's words, the gang leader is led to such behavior "as though by an invisible hand."[60] The phrase "stationary bandit," it should be noted, is a bit misleading. Many of the first warlords whom Olson was discussing remained quite mobile and ruled a small territory from horseback. The crucial requirement was that they provide enough security for peasants to plant valuable crops and to raise valuable animals with some expectation that they would not be stolen.

Olson went further. He did recognize that a ruler may take a short-term view of his or her interests and seek to maximize short-term revenue at the expense of economic growth, but he mainly saw the state as a positive force for growth.[61] The ruler, Olson argued, has a powerful incentive to promote economic growth in order to increase his tax base. If one roving

[60] Mancur Olson, "Dictatorship, Democracy, and Development," *American Political Science Review* 87 (1993), 567–76, p. 568.

[61] Margaret Levi discussed the difference between short-term and long-term interests in more technical terms as variations in the rulers' discount rate. Levi, *Of Rule and Revenue*, pp. 2, 13 (including n. 3), and 32–3.

bandit defeats the others and takes only a set percentage of production in taxes, people have the incentive – and the security – that they need to be productive. The more they produce, the more tax revenue he receives:[62]

> If he steals only through regular taxation, then his subjects know that they can keep whatever proportion of their output is left after they have paid their taxes.... The victims of the theft can expect to retain whatever capital they accumulate out of after-tax income and therefore have an incentive to save and invest, thereby increasing future income and tax receipts.... It will also pay [the warlord] to provide other public goods whenever the provision of the good increases taxable income sufficiently.

While North saw static per capita income over many millennia as evidence that government did little to promote growth, Olson focused on the growth in world population and overall world economic production, and especially on the rise of urban civilization as evidence of the opposite. Unlike North, Olson thought that government had been crucial for the economic growth and rise of civilization over the last 12,000 years.[63]

Olson emphasized "the great superiority of stationary banditry over anarchy and the advances of civilization that have resulted from it." It was the utter fragility of the state resulting from internal divisions (not popular pressures) that made it difficult to maintain the state and prevent its periodic collapse that held back growth.

This argument was Olson's answer to James Buchanan's failure to explain constitutional restraints and to North and Hayek's use of norms to explain them. Olson began from the same starting point as Buchanan (both *homo economicus* and *homo politicus* pursue the narrow self-interest of the neoclassical model), but he argued that rulers who desire to maximize long-term tax revenues will find themselves constrained by their own-self interest as they seek to increase efficiency, predictability, and, thus, tax revenue.

Indeed, this argument was implicit in Olson's analysis of the first stationary bandit. The stationary bandit not only had to suppress other roving bandits but to operate on the principle of the Mafia and offer protection for himself as well as others. This was the start of the self-restraint that Olson thought was endemic to the state.

62 Olson, "Dictatorship, Democracy, and Development," p. 568.

63 Ibid., pp. 568–9. In 2014 John Joseph Wallis noted that the argument about static per capita income had been reemphasized in *Violence and Social Orders* in 2009. John Joseph Wallis, "Persistence and Change in Institutions: The Evolution of Douglass North," in Sebastian Galiani and Itai Sened, eds., *Institutions, Property Rights, and Economic Growth: The Legacy of Douglass North* (Cambridge: Cambridge University Press, 2014), pp. 40–1

Olson basically was appropriating Adam Smith's argument to George III in *The Wealth of Nations* about the reason to grant independence to the American colonies and permit free trade. Smith said that if George would give up the power to intervene in the colonies, he would gain more tax revenue from taxing the growth of production created by free trade than from the controlled colonial trade. Olson's argument also fits well with Weber's argument that the creation of an efficient bureaucracy restrains ruler behavior.

In 1993, when Olson sent North a manuscript version of "Dictatorship, Democracy, and Development," North was very explicit in rejecting Olson's basic conception of the relationship of the state and economic growth. The "key issue [between us]," North wrote, is "where you are asking why a roving bandit when he settles down ... only takes part of the take [percentage of income]." North argued that Olson should take seriously Margaret Levi's argument that rulers are predatory.

Olson retorted that he had already rejected Levi's thesis at a conference session with her "some time ago." "It was at that session that I first argued that a rational autocrat, no matter how selfish and brutal, would never be a predator [since] he had an encompassing interest in the productivity of the domain from which he took his exactions."[64]

When Levi used the word "predatory," she was saying that rulers tried to maximize tax revenue in the short run, even at the expense of economic growth. That was also what North had meant when he asserted, as mentioned earlier, that "throughout history it has not been in the interests of those who ran governments to promote efficient property rights." Olson was saying that a rational "stationary bandit" did, indeed, have an interest in promoting efficient property rights – at least after his original seizure of property for himself and his men.

Obviously any realistic analysis of government must rest on a great multiplicity of factors. Rulers can be driven by a desire for glory or power. They can vary greatly in their intelligence, their energy, and their ability to lead. Some are clinically depressed or otherwise mentally ill. They can misjudge their interests, and they sometimes face a 50–50 choice where there is no "rational" decision. All of this is also true of subordinates such as military commanders contemplating a coup against the ruler. All models are meant to illuminate the driving forces of action, and, therefore, they all oversimplify.

[64] Douglass North to Mancur Olson, February 17, 1993; Mancur Olson to Douglass North, February 24, 1993, North Papers, Box 3, Correspondence, February 1993.

Olson died at the age of 66 only five years after his article on the stationary bandit appeared. He spent the intervening years primarily turning the article into a book. His argument about the creation of the small "state" of the warlord is quite convincing. Nevertheless, a state of this size was not durable. The fate of the stationary bandit of Jericho was typical when its stone walls were breached by Joshua and his roving band from across the Jordan River.

Unfortunately, Olson never addressed the collective action problems of the transition from the small personalistic warlord to the ruler of a large territory with its large armies, huge bureaucracies, and rational-technical market. They are immense. Selective side payments (especially salaries) are crucial to induce people to participate in the collective action of governing a territory. Yet those in a tax-collection bureaucracy (a collective action) had to be paid before they could collect the taxes necessary to pay themselves. This was one reason Olson thought that force – not consent of the governed – was originally required to collect needed tax revenue. But, of course, the military had to be paid. The problem was circular.

This book is dedicated to building on this early work of Mancur Olson. We use Olson's collective action analysis to try to explain why the process requires so many centuries. We suspect that Olson would have found the extrapolation of our work very congenial, but, alas, we shall never know.

2

The Pre-State of England and Spain

The Importance of Manmade Geography

An understanding of pre-states must begin with a realistic understanding of "primitive" society. Humans want to dream about a peaceful, idyllic, pre-urban community to which they can return. Alas, it did not exist. Mancur Olson was right that a stationary bandit, however he was selected or self-selected, was vital to provide protection for peasants so that they could produce. Otherwise, hunters and gatherers would find their storage areas and animals too attractive a place to hunt and gather.

The ancient word in Canaan for city came from the word for stockade, but even people in a walled city such as Jericho were not safe. A roving bandit such as Joshua in the Old Testament could cross the Jordan from the wilderness into Canaan, utterly destroy the walled city of Jericho, and kill all the women and children. The leading figures of the Bible may have been mythical, but the Old Testament often was brutally frank about the normal way of life in the pre-state of Canaan before the time of Christ.[1]

As Douglass North emphasized in his recent books, the dominant problem in human history has been the control of violence. So it was in the period of European history covered in this book. Even after the modern state and market were created in Europe, the centuries-long wars to define the territory of the political unit continued until 1945 – and even until the 1990s in the Balkans. The wars of the 20th century killed far more people than all the wars involving the creation of the nation-states in Europe. The issue still is not resolved in places as diverse as Ukraine, Scotland, and Catalonia.

[1] Book of Joshua, Chap. 6, Verse 21. For a discussion of the emphasis in the book on violence and for the major challenge this poses for modern theologians, see Jerome F. D. Creach, *Joshua: Interpretation* (Louisville, KY: John Knox Press, 2003).

In this book, we concentrate on the problems of creating effective government bureaucracies – first and foremost, military and fiscal ones – as warlords gain control of larger and larger territories with correspondingly larger collective action problems. Douglass North is right when he asserts that dominant coalitions of some kind are essential to bring violence under control. Yet he gives no attention to the changes in the dominant coalition that are inevitable and necessary as governments gain dominance over regional warlords and try to rule by law from a distant capital.

The creation of a stable dominant coalition in an urbanizing society is especially difficult because it must solve a circular problem. On the one hand, the dominant coalition of a modern society must be composed largely of elites based in the city. To have effective power, such elites without military power must have a solid organized base – one with a large private bureaucracy. On the other hand, the attempts to form professional private bureaucracies encounter the same collective action problems as governmental bureaucracies.

Indeed, the collective action problems in forming the first private bureaucracies may be worse. The property rights in such large organizations are far more difficult to protect than those in a simple economy of farms, mines, and small factories. The protection of complex property rights depends on the existence of a more effective modern government than one required for the protection of simple property rights – but, to repeat, such a government depends on the existence of private bureaucracies. This is one of many reasons that so much time is required for their development.

This chapter deals with England and Spain when they were pre-states (the phrase we will use as short hand for pre–nation-state.) This was the conflict-filled period when the warlords who called themselves kings were trying to expand the territory they controlled. Yet they had no effective governmental or private bureaucracies – and really, no ineffective ones either. Max Weber asserts that bureaucracies first developed in the 1300s and 1400s in Europe and then only in some of the developed city-states of Italy.[2]

By our definition, the Castilian pre-state lasted from the formation of the León-Castile "kingdom" in 1038 until 1480 when Isabella consolidated her power after a long Civil War. The Norman pre-state in England lasted from 1066 until the late 1200s or early 1300s when Edward I (1272–1307) was trying to consolidate a London city-state.

We are quite confident in our dating of the end of the pre-state of Castile. The kings prior to Isabella had no meaningful state. Although Isabella

2 Max Weber, "Politics as a Vocation," in David Owen and Tracy Strong, eds., *Max Weber: The Vocation Lectures* (Indianapolis, IN: Hackett, 2004), p. 44.

herself did not have meaningful bureaucracies or a capital, she did create or centralize corporate organs and brought them under her control. These included the Catholic Church, the sheep-grazers' guild (the Mesta), and the foreign trade merchant guilds in the major ports (the *consulados*). Their functions were similar enough to those of bureaucracies to say that an early state began in Castile during her reign.

The definition of the pre–nation-state of Norman England is more problematic. England began forming a city-state of London in 1265. It was completed by 1337 when Edward III began to turn the city (or its suburb of Westchester) into a real and well-governed capital. From that perspective, England had an early state from then onward.

Yet London did not gain effective control over England as a whole and did not become a large nation-state until 1485, when Henry VIII seized power. Even then, England was smaller than the present U.S. state of North Carolina. From that perspective, England did not have what characterizes an early state, but had "military feudalism" until the early 1500s. The warlord of London had relatively little control over the inland warlords, except in being able to force them to pay a substantial wool export tax. That required an alliance with the great armed fleet of the Hanseatic League.

We have decided to call England from 1300 to 1485 an early state because it is like many contemporary developing countries. They too typically begin with a government in reasonably firm control of the capital and a city-state around it – actually one much larger than the London city-state – and with tenuous control outside the inner core.

In addition, the development of a reasonably effective system of governance in the city-state of London prior to 1485 meant that the Tudors required only some four decades to develop a minimally effective state to rule over all of England. Spain had no such experience before Isabella, and over 200 years were needed before a minimally effective state could be established in Spain in the 1700s.

Ultimately, of course, we are interested in contributing to a theory of change, not simply to a classification of types of states. The interesting theoretical question is why it took Castile 450 years to form an early nation-state after 1038, but England only some 225 years after 1066. As we have emphasized, both were Catholic, rural, sheep grazing, and wool-exporting areas, and the foreigners' view of English national character around 1500 was similar to our present view of Spanish national character at that time.

This chapter presents a collective action explanation of the reason it took longer to form an early state in Castile than in England – primarily, the greater difficulty in solving collective action problems in governing a large territory than a city-state. Rulers in both Castile and England still had to use largely personalistic methods of rule until 1500, and even the English monarchs retained them for many purposes into the 1600s. The collective action problems in doing so are relatively minor in a small area, but enormous in an area the size of Castile.

There is a theoretical corollary to this point that is seldom, if ever, mentioned. Many say that geography in a physical sense is a major explanation for the difference in English and Spanish economic growth. In particular, many scholars emphasize the multiplicity of rivers and ports in England and the lack of rivers on the Castilian plateau.

England did, of course, have many rivers, but that is misleading. The many ports in England actually made it difficult for London to become a major commercial center. London – a town of some 40,000 in the 1200s, half the size of Seville at the time – was by no means certain to occupy the place it eventually assumed.

The assertion that the Castilian plateau had no major rivers is simply incorrect. The plateau had two major rivers that empty into the sea, one at Porto in Portugal and the other in Lisbon. The physical geography of Castile "dictated" either that the Castilian kings acquire the mouths of "their" rivers or that the Portuguese kings acquire the plateau. In either case, the port cities should have been major economic centers of the plateau. For inexplicable reasons, they never achieved this status. An early Castilian king even abandoned Porto, which was already in his territory.

The geography that resulted from the failure of the Castilian kings to try to conquer the mouths of the Duero and Tagus Rivers became an important economic factor in Spanish history, but the geography was man-made. Much politically and economically relevant geography in the world today was also man-made, a general point that needs to be emphasized more in the development literature.

The Problem of the Pre-Nation-State

Douglass North's definition of the state is quite precise and seemingly quite simple: "an organization with a comparative advantage in violence, extending over a geographic area whose boundaries are determined by its power to tax constituents."[3] We prefer it to Max Weber's similar and more famous

[3] Douglass North, *Structure and Change in Economic History* (New York: W. W. Norton, 1981), p. 21.

definition, because it illuminates some of the key problems in the formation of an effective state.

The reader should be warned once again that North uses the word "organization" idiosyncratically. He does not necessarily mean an organized government with bureaucracies. The kings of the Old Testament had no bureaucracies, and King Solomon had to decide the custody of a disputed baby himself because he had no judges or courts. Yet these kings were "organizations" by North's definition. A militia leader or a "dominant coalition" is an "organization." Indeed, so is a simple nuclear family.

The first important substantive point about North's definition is the two-word phrase: "geographic area." It seems clear, but a modern reader may assume that it implies the area of a modern state. If you read the definition closely, it becomes apparent that it does not.

A geographic area is one "whose boundaries are determined by [the organization's] ability to tax constituents." North may disagree with Mancur Olson about the origins of the state, but Olson's stationary bandit who controls a small area certainly has a state by North's definition. The definition also covers a large feudal estate over which a lord has a comparative advantage in violence. A valley in Afghanistan that is controlled by a military warlord (we usually say "tribal leader") is also a state if the leader collects revenue from its inhabitants, even if informally from opium trade.

More important, however, the reader may assume from North's definition that the territory of the modern state is the territory indicated on the map. In fact, North's definition refers to an "area whose boundaries are determined by its power to tax constituents." He estimates in his recent co-authored book *In the Shadow of Violence* that the capitals of only 12 developing countries really control all of their territory. There are many places in Africa, Asia, and even Latin America where the nominal government cannot impose its usual taxes, but where taxes are levied, perhaps informally, by a local militia or "Mafia" leader or local warlord.

The more typical situation is that found in what James Scott calls Zomia: the "nonstate space" from Vietnam to northeastern India that is above the altitude of 300 meters and part of the periphery of nine countries. It contains around 100 million people and covers 2.5 million square kilometers, essentially equal to the territory of Western Europe. Scott says that "not so very long ago … such self-governing peoples were the great majority of humankind."[4]

[4] James Scott, *The Art of Not Being Governed: An Anarchist History of Upland Southeast Asia* (New Haven, CT: Yale University Press, 2009), p. ix.

Scott is romanticizing when he says "self-governing." The central government in each of these countries has poured major resources into trying to bring their part of Zomia under control. Clearly, force is needed to resist the armies of the central governments, and, hence the "self-governing" areas must have warlords of one type or another. Local leaders with military force must be major tax collectors if they are to finance their armies.[5]

Nevertheless, the central government has some involvement in Zomia – even in northern Pakistan on the Afghan border or in tribal enclaves in African states. Schools are established and some infrastructure is built. The central government collects some taxes in one way or another – perhaps sales or value-added taxes imposed on goods brought into the area or exported. When the central troops are in the interior, they are like American troops in Afghanistan who were in control when they entered a territory with overwhelming military force. But also like the American troops, they find out that local rebels reemerge when they pull out.

This kind of conditional comparative military advance was found throughout Europe in the medieval and early modern period. The situation is well described in one of the best summaries of medieval Europe, Norman Cantor's *The Civilization in the Middle Ages*:[6]

> When the king, with his chancery, court, and army, was in a given area, there was no problem in obtaining the loyalty of the local population. But given the bad communications and the atomized nature of society ... how were the duke [the local military official] and the count [the king's local representative in matters of law and finance] to be controlled in the areas away from the immediate influence of the royal court? This problem had bedeviled the Merovingians, and their inability to solve it greatly contributed to the collapse of royal power in the sixth and seventh century. It remained a stumbling block to the Carolingians. Indeed, it may be said to be the most continuous, difficult problem of medieval monarchy.

By North's definition, what is the state in such cases? The reasonable answer is both. The leaders of the two military forces both had a comparative advantage of violence in the same territory in different circumstances, and both were able to impose taxes against the will of the other.

Many talk about a revolution in military technology being a key factor in the creation of the state in the late medieval and early modern period.

[5] For an excellent description of the powerful Kachin militia in this area in the Myanmar section of Zomia, see Thomas Fuller, "Ethnic Groups in Myanmar Hope for Peace, but Gird for Fight," *New York Times*, May 10, 2009, A4.

[6] Norman Cantor, *The Civilization of the Middle Ages* (New York: HarperCollins, 1993), p. 192.

This literally cannot be true by North's definition of a state. The revolution in military technology obviously did not lead to the creation of the state, but to the destruction of a large number of states and the creation of a smaller number of large nation-states.

The scale of this "state-destroying" activity is suggested by the number of state-like institutions that the sociologist Charles Tilly counted in late medieval Europe. In Tilly's judgment, Europe as a whole had 1,000 state-like institutions in the 14th century and some 500 in 1500.[7] Tilly probably did not include the territories of the important English lords and the key Castilian city-states in this number. He should have, but even the reduction from 1,000 states to 500 took 200 years, and the 500 state-like units in 1500 were still 10 times the present number in Europe.

In any case, we should not think of 1,000 autonomous billiard balls on the table of Europe in 1300. Instead, most were located inside some larger state, kingdom, or federation (for example, the Holy Roman Empire). At a minimum, the king of such a larger territory laid claim to the territory of the smaller states and tried to demand some payment from them.

The reduction in the number of state-like units took place in a variety of ways. Sometimes, as in the case of Castile and Aragon, two countries were brought together by a dynastic marriage in the midst of a Civil War or a succession crisis. In some cases, a more powerful ruler simply conquered a neighboring state and absorbed its territory. Or perhaps outside powers defined the borders, as was to happen after World War I.

The modern developing world should be understood in similar terms. Forty years ago, Walker Connor wrote a famous article about the current developing world that he entitled "Nation-Building or Nation-Destroying?" Although "nation-building" was the standard phrase used by modernization theorists at the time, Connor thought nation-destroying was more accurate.[8] Fifteen years later, Myron Weiner found that this was still true:[9]

> Hegemonic rather than accommodative ethnic politics characterize the new states. In country after country, a single ethnic group has taken control over the state and used its powers to exercise control over others.... There has been far less

[7] Charles Tilly, "Reflections on the History of European State-Making," in Charles Tilly, ed., *The Formation of National States in Western Europe* (Princeton, NJ: Princeton University Press, 1975), pp. 15, 76.

[8] Walker Connor, "Nation-Building or Nation-Destroying?" *World Politics* 24 (1972), 319–55.

[9] Myron Weiner, "Political Change: Asia, Africa, and the Middle East," in Myron Weiner and Samuel P. Huntington, eds., *Understanding Political Development* (Boston: Little, Brown, 1987), pp. 35–6.

"nation-building" than many analysts had expected or hoped, for the process of state building has rendered many ethnic groups devoid of power and influence.... Ethnic hegemony has been exercised in a variety of ways, from the repression of ethnic and religious minorities to the more benign use of state power to give preferences in education and employment to the dominant ethnic group.... Several newly independent governments have even expelled economically successful minorities they considered alien.

Just as we are looking at the development process in Europe to help to illuminate the contemporary developing world, so we can also utilize the experience of the modern developing world to convey a more concrete sense of what happened in Europe before the formation of a larger state. We try to do both in this section.

An understanding of the transition of the pre-state to an early state should begin with the recognition of an indisputable flaw of Olson's model of a stationary bandit. This is the suggestion that there is only one stationary bandit who introduces peace and creates the conditions for economic growth.

The Old Testament makes clear that there were countless stationary bandits and would-be stationary bandits even in a tiny area such as Canaan in the first millennium BC. Each was trying to introduce peace in his own area but was in frequent conflict with his neighbors and roving bandits (militia leaders) from the outside.

This has been a ubiquitous problem in world history. In 2003, the United Nations' Expert Panel on Liberia described contemporary Africa in terms that could have been used in most of the world for 15,000 years:[10]

The chaotic conflicts of Africa ... today are not conventional civil wars. Rather, they are part of a lethal, internecine web that has ensnared every country on this suffering patch of the continent, as guns proliferate across the bush, hardened fighters roam in search of work and rebel armies flourish with the succor of neighboring heads of state.... Millions of ordinary people ... must live in this bedlam.

The level of violence in such areas varies in intensity as local warlords gain temporary control and introduce order. The order can be maintained for years and even decades, especially when there is little worth stealing, but it is always fragile. Lethal violence can erupt suddenly and escalate into chaos. It seems almost permanent in areas such as the Congo and Sudan that have large mineral or oil deposits.

[10] Somni Sengupta, "Chaos in West Africa: Unending Wars," *New York Times*, May 5, 2003, p. A7.

The following statement deals with the Civil War in Sudan in 2008:[11]

> While the government and militia attacks on straw-hut villages that defined the earlier years of the conflict continue, Darfur is now home to semi-organized crime and warlordism, with marijuana-smoking rebels, disaffected government militias and anyone else with an AK47 taking part.... There were two rebel groups, but now there are dozens ... and the struggle in the desert these days is less about liberating oppressed Darfurians than about acquiring the means to power: money, land, trucks.

In fact, as we will see in the Mexican War of Independence beginning in 1810, several processes almost always overlap. The majority of bandits in Mexico during the war were simply seeking loot (theft). Other leaders hoped to become the boss of a city or perhaps a few villages that could provide the base of some kind of estate. A few hoped to obtain control of a province or city where their tax income could be greater. A few even had the more grandiose dream of control of the taxation in the capital.

A collective action theorist would caution against assuming those in leadership positions in, say, Iran and the Taliban are dedicated to large collective goals such as spreading Islam or undermining the West. They may use such appeals for tactical reasons to gain support, and they, no doubt, hope for such an outcome. If Olson is right, however, the great majority of Taliban leaders is seeking – or certainly would be satisfied with – the side payment of loot, a salary, or a secure share of the "taxation" on the local opium trade.

Sometimes, of course, the dreamers win. A coalition of warlords marched on the Chinese capital under Chiang Kai-Shek in 1927, and another such coalition under Alfonso VI captured Toledo in 1085. A leader may get control of a small territory in the hinterland and expand it. For example, Mao Zedong built a mini-state in the Hunan-speaking area in inland China in the 1930s and 1940s. It was based on the army he organized there and on his ability to tax and provide "government" services that gave him the resources to pay for an army large and strong enough to defeat the central army. A person who spoke Mandarin with a heavy accent came to rule the Mandarin city of Beijing.

Hezbollah organized a similar mini-state in Shiite areas in Lebanon in recent decades. Hezbollah too has wanted to become an integrated part of the Lebanese political system. Hezbollah leaders say that they simply want to be a large democratic party. While many believe this, others fear that Hezbollah seeks to create a dictatorial theocracy. The important fact for

[11] Stephanie McCrummen, "A Wide-Open Battle for Power in Darfur," *Washington Post*, June 20, 2008, p. A1.

us, however, is that Hezbollah's militia began providing police, educational, and other "government" services in the Shiite areas and won the support of this majority group within the population. Hamas followed a similar strategy of providing government-like services in areas not being served.[12]

Normally a country such as Afghanistan has a government that has a strong comparative advantage of violence in the capital and the area around it. Yet the outlying territory is still a pre–nation-state. Rulers or contenders for power hope that over time, the outlying regions can be brought under control without the excessive use of force.

For example, when Iraq was formed in 1921, multiple "tribal leaders" continued to control the irrigation systems along the Tigris and Euphrates Rivers as they had done for centuries under the nominal control of various outside rulers. These tribal leaders became impotent in the 1960s not because Saddam Hussein used force, but because he built roads and promoted policies that led to rapid urbanization. Villagers simply abandoned the tribes and their leaders and moved to the city to improve their living standards. There they became the base of radical movements in an alien city with an alien secular elite with alien rational-legal values.[13]

Such an evolution was also a key part of the lengthy transition from a London city-state to a real English state dominated by London. As we will see, the kings built canals and roads from the interior to London so that traders would use what was otherwise an inconvenient port for them. The dialect of London changed to that of the sheep-grazing area of East Anglia as the kings allied with the Hanseatic League and its huge armed fleet to ensure that London became the dominant merchant center instead of the East Anglian ports.[14] The key final event was the victory of Henry VII in 1485, which he sealed by marrying Elizabeth of York. All this is the subject of the next chapter.

England Prior to the Formation of the City-State of London

Around AD 800, the English Isles were dominated by small militia leaders or warlords. The literature refers to "Anglo-Saxon kingdoms," but we should not be misled. These pre-Norman kingdoms were really confederations

[12] See Eli Berman and David Laitin, "Religion, Terrorism, and Public Goods: Testing the Club Model," *Journal of Public Economics* 92 (2008), 1942–67.

[13] Elizabeth Warnock Fernea and Robert Fernea, *The Arab World: Forty Years of Change* (New York: Doubleday, 1997).

[14] Eilert Ekwall, *Studies on the Population of Medieval London* (Stockholm: Almquist and Wiksell, 1956), pp. xi, lxiv–lxv.

(coalitions) of men who controlled small fiefdoms. The borders of the fiefdoms often extended only a day's horse-ride from their center.[15] The historian Bede made it clear in his eighth-century *Ecclesiastical History of the English People* that the king was the strongest warlord who received tribute from lesser rulers through conquest.[16] These kings gained support through gifts to their supporters – gifts that almost surely included a share in the treasure that they and their supporters seized during looting raids.

The pre-Norman kingdoms are not a major concern of this book. The previous paragraph is, however, important in pointing to a crucial modification of Mancur Olson's distinction between a roving and a stationary bandit. In the real world, there are many stationary bandits. The early ones do, as Mancur Olson said, finance themselves by taxing the peasants and imposing various kinds of tolls on passers-by. Yet they still engage in looting in neighboring areas. They also try to extract "tribute" by promising to abstain from looting in exchange for a regular payment. In his role as an outsider, the stationary bandit is himself a roving bandit.

Because it had a more temperate climate than much of Europe, England became a major producer and exporter of wool in Roman times. This continued afterward, and Flanders used the nearby wool to develop a rapidly growing woolen cloth industry. As a result, the history of England early became intertwined with the evolution of the military balance of power in the northern trade area.

The combination of roving bandit and stationary bandit was also found in ocean commerce. In the days before state navies, merchants needed to carry an armed force on their ships for self-defense, but this armed force could also be used to attack. As a result, those engaged in early long-distance trade were a kind of roving bandit.

The great seafarers of ancient times, the Phoenicians, were typical. They had "a long and well-founded marine reputation as both merchants and pirates." In Homer's words, they were "fine sailors but rogues." Indeed, "in very ancient times, there was no fundamental difference between the two professions of merchant and pirate."[17]

15 For "Anglo-Saxon kingdoms" and "tribes and loosely knit confederacies," see Peter Hunter Blair, *Roman Britain and Early England, 55 B.C.–A.D. 871* (New York: W.W. Norton, 1963), pp. 33 and 43.

16 For a good sense of this, see Ann Williams, *Kingship and Government in Pre-Conquest England c. 500–1066* (London: Macmillan, 1999), pp. 32–6 and 40–1.

17 Jean Rouge, *Ships and Fleets of the Ancient Mediterranean* (Middletown, CT: Wesleyan University Press, 1981), p. 141. For a good analysis of the Phoenicians during Homeric times, see Maria-Eugenia Aubet, *The Phoenicians and the West: Politics, Colonies, and Trade* (Cambridge: Cambridge University Press, 2001), pp. 102–7, and 135.

Medieval Europe was similar. The city-states of Venice and Genoa were major commercial powers, but Venice's armed fleets gave it a crucial military role vis-á-vis Byzantium. Genoa carried Castile's Mediterranean crops from Seville and served also as its navy.[18] In the early Middle Ages, Viking territory was the northern counterpart of the Italian city-states: "The Vikings drew no distinction between trade, piracy, and raiding, turning from one to the other as the occasion offered."[19] Indeed, since booty often is not as valuable at home as to others, looting and trade inevitably were linked.

The Danes – or rather the Danish branch of the Vikings – replaced the northern Vikings as the dominant power, and they conquered England in the late 900s. "Conquered" should not, however, be misunderstood. Much of the conquest involved looting or establishing tribute relations. In addition, Danes shared the general Viking practice of marrying into the local population and adopting its language and culture. Since the Saxons and Danes were already closely related culturally and linguistically, they quickly intermarried after Danes settled in East Anglia.

The Normans were Vikings who had settled in Normandy in the 800s and 900s and who had assimilated into the local French culture and language. Most of the 8,000 Normans who acquired land in England also lived there and intermarried with the local inhabitants. Nevertheless, until 1204, the top Norman rulers and barons also continued to have land in Normandy and spent the majority of their time there. William the Conqueror naturally gave himself more and better land than his lieutenants, and the best land was in the south just across the narrow channel from England in Flanders. London was 300 miles from York and 400 miles from Edinburgh.

By 1200, the Normans had built 500 castles in England to defend their lands. The kings received their main tax income from the land they controlled in what we would call rent and what historians call domainal income. It could either be in cash or in kind. Since the kings had the most land and peasants, they could assemble and finance more troops than the

[18] Archibald Lewis, "Mediterranean Maritime Commerce, A. D. 300–1000. Shipping and Trade," in Archibald Lewis, *The Sea and Medieval Civilizations: Collected Studies* (London: Variorum Reprints, 1978), pp. 1–21; R. H. Bautier, *The Economic Development of Medieval Europe* (New York: Harcourt, Brace, Jovanovich, 1971), pp. 96–118; Frederic Lane, *Venice and History* (Baltimore, MD: Johns Hopkins University Press, 1966).

[19] T. H. Lloyd, *The English Wool Trade in the Middle Ages* (Cambridge: Cambridge University Press, 2005). For a book that emphasizes this fact and includes pictures, see Martin Dougherty, *A Dark History: Vikings: Raiders, Pillagers, and Traders – The Truth Revealed* (New York: Metro Books, 2013).

other warlords. As in Bede's day, they used their superior military force to extort tribute from those with lesser force.[20]

In the past, economic historians of medieval England focused on the agricultural sector and often debated whether English feudalism was really based on serfdom. Traditional political histories of the period focused on the battles of various kings and lords, but with a grandeur that hid the fact that the "lords" as well as the "kings," were what we would call warlords today. They all lived in a culture of violence.[21]

We need not discuss these matters, except to mention that the politics of England prior to 1265 cannot profitably be visualized in terms of dominant coalitions of any durability. As we noted in Chapter 1, North and his co-authors define a dominant coalition as a group of "economic, political, religious, and education leaders [elites] whose privileged positions create rents that ensure their cooperation with the dominant elite."[22] In our opinion, however, this definition does not apply to the first half of the development process. In the pre-state and early-state stages there are no specialized elites. The creation of that specialization is the first major step in development.

As we will see, a major historian of Spain, Henry Kamen, argues that Isabella's system of rule was like the diplomacy of international relations. This is even more accurate of pre-1265 England or pre-1480 Castile. Sometimes the alliances or truces lasted for some time, sometimes they were fragile, but they were the alliances of repeated – and sometimes continual – wars.

As Mancur Olson emphasized, the first task of the kings was to learn to rule their own large landholdings in a way that maximized their taxes. This entailed self-restraint. The retinue of Henry I (1100–1135) plundered the countryside so much in his early years as king that the peasants ran from them. Henry had to order his men not to bother the peasants so they could produce more and he could collect rent from them. No doubt, the other lords, who lived in France as well, also had to bring their men in England under control.[23]

[20] For the Normans in England, see David Carpenter, *The Struggle for Mastery: Britain 1066–1284* (Oxford: Oxford University Press, 2003), pp. 4–11.

[21] For a vivid description as it continued into the 1500s, see Lawrence Stone, *The Crisis of the Aristocracy, 1558–1641* (Oxford: Oxford University Press, 1967).

[22] North et al., *Violence and Social Orders*, p. 18, and Douglass North, John Joseph Wallis, Steven Webb, and Barry Webb, eds., *In the Shadow of Violence: Politics, Economics, and the Problems of Development* (Cambridge: Cambridge University Press, 2013), p. 5.

[23] In this book, when we put dates in parentheses after a monarch's name, we are referring not to the person's life span but to the years of his or her reign. Carpenter, *The Struggle for Mastery*, p. 149.

Gradually the kings and lords began to build stronger castles on their different pieces of land in England and to use them as their residences and, therefore, more stable bases of rule. The result by 1300 was that, in the words of Charles Wilson, England became "a military society ... a society stratified for war ... a system of 'military feudalism.'"[24] The king was just one of the warlords, but the one based in London. This continued until Henry VII's victory in 1485.

With their land in the south, the kings first based themselves in Winchester but in 1156 they moved the Treasury to Westminster. Yet they continued to move continually through their "realm." Like other medieval kings discussed by Norman Cantor, they depended on the presence of their troops – or the threat of their presence – to collect taxes. Indeed, the local warlord had to feed and care for the king's entourage when he was in their area. This basically was a tax-in-kind.

When the lords were meeting the king and his troops, they were not giving consent in the sense the word implies. They were discussing how to distribute the burden of a forthcoming or continuing war in the face of the king's superior force or, perhaps, how to divide the land and other booty that they hoped would be acquired during the war. If the issue was a foreign war, the question was who would provide what amount of money, troops, and, supplies – and who would receive what share of booty in return.

In addition, when the king assembled a larger army for a foreign war, he was able to obtain a larger amount of tribute because he had more troops to use against the lesser warlords. Michael Prestwich describes one set of negotiations over the provision of food to the troops: "Although these negotiations in 1301 were genuine, it is striking that in all cases it was agreed to provide the quantities suggested by the government."[25]

The Anglo-Saxon kings had appointed provincial "governors" called sheriffs, and the system was maintained by the Normans. Yet the sheriffs were not paid salaries, and they did not remotely function as effective bureaucrats who enforced central policy. Normandy was the primary base of the kings and greatest lords until they were expelled in 2004. They needed ambassadors in the provinces of England, and, in a world without banks and bank accounts, they needed people who physically collected and transported tax payments. The sheriffs oversaw this activity.

[24] Charles Wilson, *England's Apprenticeship, 1603–17*, 2nd ed. (London: Longman, 1985), pp. 3–4.

[25] Michael Prestwich, *War, Politics and Finance under Edward I* (Totowa, NJ: Rowman and Littlefield, 1972), p. 132.

As time elapsed, the king gradually spent more time in the palace in Westminster outside of London or in Windsor Castle, somewhat further away. This was particularly true of Henry III, who ruled from 1216 to 1272. Henry strongly identified with the pre-Norman past and especially the last great pre-Norman king, Edward the Confessor. Edward based himself at Westminster and built an abbey as a burial place. Nevertheless, only Henry's great-grandson, Edward III, actually began to establish a capital there in 1337.

The word "parlement" first appeared during the reign of Henry III, but it did not have its present meaning. It was simply the French word for discussion. Prior to the establishment of London as the capital, it referred to ad hoc council meetings held in the regions where the king was visiting with his troops.

Another way for a king to obtain revenue or its equivalent was to use private agents to perform what we consider governmental functions. For example, merchants lent their ships to act as naval vessels and business monopolies that collected taxes, formed commercial courts staffed by merchants, and built infrastructure. Church clerics served as government "clerks" without pay. The very word "clerk" correctly signifies that church clerics performed this governmental work without pay for the government.

Modern historians may say these practices were inefficient and unduly enriched private individuals or bodies, but they were better at serving their governing functions than the alternatives. When customs agents were later appointed, they often came from merchant families. "The modern state," Max Weber stated, "begins to develop wherever the monarch sets in train the process of replacing such autonomous, 'private agents.'"[26]

Since the export of wool was always a major source of income for the lords and the king, the taxation of this wool was a major issue. The various towns strove to charge tolls for the wool and other products passing through them.[27] This gave international commerce a crucial political importance from the beginning. Even the invasion of William the Conqueror in 1066 was supported by a warlord in Flanders who hoped to obtain a preferential position in wool trade. In fact, the Flemish became the major cross-channel merchants who handled wool trade for 200 years.

Nevertheless, the multiplicity of rivers in England meant that lords had a nearby river they could use to export their wool and import goods from

[26] Weber, "Politics as a Vocation," pp. 37–8.

[27] James Masschaele, "Toll and Trade in Medieval England," in Lawrin Armstrong, Ivana Elbl, and Martin M. Elbl, eds., *Money, Market and Trade in Late Medieval Europe: Essays in Honour of John H. A. Munro* (Leiden: Brill, 2007), 146–78.

abroad. Each of them wanted to impose taxes on this wool trade – and did so. Ships of the Hanseatic League, a monopolistic association of the merchants in some 70 German cities, had long come into eastern ports such as Hull, Boston, and Yarwich to take wool to ports north and east of Flanders.

The Flemish merchants had worked closely with the domestic merchants and guilds of London, and when Henry III took over London and wanted loyal guild leaders, he expelled the Flemish merchants. Nevertheless, English foreign trade was still so dominated by different foreign merchants that the leading historian of medieval London claimed England was still in its "colonial phase" in 1300. The same was true of products other than wool. England still obtained most of its wine from France, and as late as 1300, 75% of the merchants engaged in this trade between Gascony and England were natives of Gascony.[28]

The Italians were a major naval power in the Mediterranean with their galleys and had had an important role in delivering wool and especially crude woolen cloth from England to the cloth manufacturers of the Italian city-states. Henry III and Edward I installed the Italians in the dominant position in the wool trade. From 1272 to 1322, they almost continuously relied on the Italians for financial assistance. They retained a major role in Mediterranean trade, even when their general power declined.[29]

The role of the Hanseatic League in English trade became progressively stronger in the 1200s. This role did not simply rest on the League's monopoly position and the commercial skills of its merchants. In the 1100s, the League acquired larger sailing ships armed with cannons for self-defense – and for attack. As a result, its merchants "got all the trade [of the North Sea] with the eastern ports of England into their hands."[30] They gradually drove the Italians out of all the non-Mediterranean trade.

One should not, however, see this process simply as the result of developing skills in commercial activity, habits of peaceful trade, and informal

[28] Gwyn Williams, *Medieval London: From Commune to Capital* (London: Athlone, 1963), pp. 10 and 65; Pamela Nightingale, *Trade, Money, and Power in Medieval England* (Aldershot: Ashgate, 2007); Margaret Labarge, *Gascony, England's First Colony, 1204–1453* (London: H. Hamilton, 1980), pp. 46, 86.

[29] Eileen Power, *The Wool Trade in English Medieval History* (Oxford: Oxford University Press, 1965), pp. 53–4; Adrian Bell, Chris Brook, and Paul Dryburgh, *The English Wool Market, c. 1230–1327* (Cambridge: Cambridge University Press, 2007), p. 114; E. B. Fryde, *William de la Pole, Merchant and King's Banker* (London: Hambledon Press, 1998), p. 2; Richard Kaeuper, *Bankers to the Crown: The Riccardi of Luca and Edward I* (Princeton, NJ: Princeton University Press, 1973), esp. 141–51.

[30] Philippe Dollinger, *The German Hansa* (New York: Macmillan, 1970), pp. 23, 49–50, and 55–8.

institutional restraints and trust. This was the eventual outcome, but the first step often was the imposition of some order by the merchant guilds and their armed fleet. In the words of N.A.M. Rodger,[31]

> It is always a mistake to look at medieval naval warfare with the modern distinction between warships and merchantmen too much in mind. Not only were the two hardly distinct in design but "peaceful trade" was almost a contradiction in terms. The sea was widely regarded as lying beyond laws, treaties and truces; even in peacetime foreign ships were always in danger, and in wartime the distinction between enemies and neutrals was difficult to observe on the rare occasions when English seamen tried.... Even in peacetime, there was not much peace at sea. Unprovoked attacks were common, torture was often used to extract information, and prisoners were usually drowned unless they were worth a ransom.

As discussed in the next chapter, the Hanseatic League became a key element in Edward III's consolidation of power in the 1330s, primarily because these seamen became the major instrument that enabled him to collect high wool export taxes. The League was also powerful enough to introduce some regularity into the trade under its control, and hence the royal alliance with the League was essential in establishing London as a quite effective city-state.

Castile from 800 to 1262: "A Society Organized for War"

During the 700s, the Muslims drove the Christians to the mountains just south of the Bay of Biscay or to the narrow coastal area beyond the mountains. Like the Anglo-Saxons in England at the time, the Iberian Christians were ruled by a large number of small mobile warlords. Despite the emphasis in the general literature on the Christian-Muslim conflict, the Christian warlords fought each other more than they did the Muslims.[32]

The ports along the Bay of Biscay shipped wool and other materials to northern Europe, but they never became a center of political power. One reason is that there were many such ports, not just one major one. Instead of building a city-state on a northern port, the Christian warlords began to move southward into the plateau and founded the town of Burgos in 884 on its northern edge. It became the major merchant center of the north.

31 Nicholas A.M. Rodger, *The Safeguard of the Sea: A Naval History of Britain, 660–1649*, Vol. 1 (New York: W.W. Norton, 1998), p. 115.

32 For a readable description of Castile at this time, Richard Fletcher, *The Quest for El Cid* (London: Hutchinson, 1989), 58–73, especially pp. 58–62.

Many of the nearby fortified settlements officially were monasteries, but their leaders had the military force to defend them and the land they controlled. Even the bishops were often overlords of cities and/or fortified monasteries. In Galicia in northwest Iberia, fourteen great monasteries became the main landowners between 1142 and 1225, and their leaders possessed the necessary military force to defend them.[33]

In 1038, García Sánchez III of Navarre conquered Castile and created the large kingdom of León-Castile, a loose political unit of smaller warlords, like the kingdoms of England. He hoped the small warlords would be a source of tribute and/or would provide troops for his looting expeditions against the Muslims. Around 1050, one of his sons reached the Duero River, some 100 miles south of Burgos, and in 1085, a grandson conquered the ancient capital of Toledo. Toledo was 300 miles from the port of Bilbao on the Bay of Biscay.[34]

The Muslim states to the south had never settled the plateau; they had only sent raiding parties into it, often in search of slaves. The southern movement of the Christians gave these raiding parties more targets. In response, the Castilian kings awarded city charters and created new garrison cities in the area to protect the Christians and acquire more revenue. Each became the center of an inland city-state. The nobles from the agricultural and animal-raising sectors lived behind the walls of the city-state along with those having urban occupations.

The climate was too dry to produce exportable agricultural crops, especially before population growth began to outpace the growth in grain production in Europe in the 1700s. Hence, the Castilian kings could not have the same kind of revenue-producing estates on the plateau as the English kings. They had to rely on something else. Raising sheep and shipping wool to Flanders was one source of revenue, but the original disorder on the plateau meant that this source of revenue was too small. The kings turned to looting as an alternative.

Since the kings did not have a standing army in the modern sense of the word, they had to organize looting parties with the warlords of local cities. Like the Islamic leaders, the Castilian ruler demanded 20% of the material taken, but the raids also gave local inhabitants an economically profitable occupation and provided the city-states with a regularized source

[33] Sharif Gemie, *A Concise History of Galicia* (Cardiff: University of Wales Press, 2006), p. 25.

[34] Thomas Glick, *Islamic and Christian Spain in the Early Middle Ages* (Princeton, NJ: Princeton University Press, 1979), pp. 42–50; Bernard Reilly, *The Kingdom of Leon-Castilla Under King Alfonso VI, 1065–1109* (Princeton, NJ: Princeton University Press, 1988).

of income. The central role of looting in the economic role of the plateau is the reason scholars refer to Castile prior to 1262 as "a society organized for war."[35]

The relationship of the king to the forces he mobilized remained precisely what a collective action theorist would predict:[36]

> There was every probability that many contingents would desert at the outset, if the campaign did not meet with their approval, or if the prospect of booty was small; indeed, the monarch would have reason to think himself fortunate if none of his forces were ultimately found in the ranks of the foe.

Nevertheless, success could bring great rewards. When the king and allied forces defeated the Muslims in 1212 at the great battle of Las Navas de Tolosa, the Castilians required over 2,000 mules to take away the booty from the battle.[37] This victory led directly to the conquest of Córdoba, Seville, and other cities to the south in Andalusia, primarily for purposes of looting and seizing land.

The previous paragraph points to the crucial why-not question about Castile. If observers look at the geography of Iberia with fresh eyes, it is quite clear that the physical geography "dictated" quite different state borders for Iberia than the battle of Las Navas de Tolosa produced. Much of Andalusia was in the Mediterranean climate zone, and it was an unnatural partner for the dry northern plateaus whose main cities were hundreds of miles away. It would have been more normal for a southern state to be formed that united the eastern Mediterranean ports of Barcelona with Andalusia.

The plateau also "should" have been the hinterland for a much different state. It had two major rivers that flowed to the Atlantic: the Duero and the Tagus. The Duero River enters the Atlantic at Porto (Oporto), a major economic and commercial port city of modern Portugal. The Tagus River reaches the Atlantic at Lisbon, one of the most important ports in Europe in the 1400s and 1500s.

35 James Powers, *A Society Organized for War: The Iberian Municipal Militias in the Central Middle Ages, 1000–1284* (Berkeley: University of California Press, 1988), pp. 1–3 and 52–63; Derek Lomax, *Reconquest of Spain* (London: Longman, 1978), pp. 16, 27, 53, and 145; Simon Barton, *Aristocracy in the Twelfth Century León and Castile* (Cambridge: Cambridge University Press, 2002); Miguel-Ángel Ladero Quesada, "Castile in the Middle Ages," in Richard Bonney, *The Rise of the Fiscal State in Europe, c.1200–1815* (Oxford: Oxford University Press, 1999), p. 181.

36 Roger Merriman, *The Rise of the Spanish Empire in the Old World and in the New*, Vol. 1 (New York: Macmillan, 1918).

37 Robert Burns, *Islam under the Crusaders: Colonial Survival in the Thirteenth Century Kingdom of Valencia* (Princeton. NJ: Princeton University Press, 1973), pp. 8–9.

Porto originally was part of Galicia, a province of the Castile and León kingdom. Valladolid, a city located on the Duero, was the pre-Madrid base of the Castilian kings, while Toledo was built on the Tagus. It seems absolutely inevitable that the rivers would have become part of the same state as the mouths of the rivers.

In particular, the Castilian kings seemingly would have wanted to make conquering the mouths of the Duero and Tagus rivers a top priority, but they never acted as if control of Porto and Lisbon were crucial. Indeed, Alfonso VI had conquered Toledo in 1085 with the help of French knights. He gave one of them the area of Porto, and his son expanded southward to create the first kingdom of Portugal.[38] Even later when Philip II became king of Portugal in 1580 by right of succession, neither he nor his successors tried to integrate Portugal into Spain. In 1640, it regained its independence without resistance.

Other than looting, the economy of the plateau had to be based on grazing animals – primarily, migrating sheep. From the beginning, wool had been sheared on the northern plateau and was carried across the Cantabrian Mountains to the ports on the Bay of Biscay. It was a long and tortuous route, and two historians, Carla and William Phillips, emphasize that the east-west routes for the delivery of wool to the coasts were economically preferable. They think it would have been more natural for wool merchants in the north to ship their wool through Porto, and, perhaps, the wool from the sheep of the southern regions down the Tagus River to Lisbon.[39]

Richard Fletcher agrees. In his view, the Castilian kings should have established a modus vivendi with the Muslims to the south, perhaps even a profitable tribute relationship, and concentrated on consolidating a state in a manageably sized area. This seemed economically advantageous, and it certainly would have eased the collective actions problems caused by expansion to the south.[40]

Lisbon became the most important city and capital in Portugal, and perhaps it would also have been the capital of Castile if it had included the mouth of the Tagus River. In many ways, however, Porto seems the more natural city-state capital of early Castile because it was closer to the area

[38] William Phillips Jr. and Carla Rahn Phillips, *A Concise History of Spain* (Cambridge: Cambridge University Press, 2010), p. 69.

[39] Carla Rahn Phillips and William Phillips Jr., *Spain's Golden Fleece: Wool Production and the Wool Trade from the Middle Ages to the Nineteenth Century* (Baltimore, MD: Johns Hopkins University Press, 1997), pp. 210–14.

[40] Richard Fletcher, "The Early Middle Ages 700–1250," in Raymond Carr, ed., *Spain: A History* (New York: Oxford University Press, 2001), p. 81.

where the sheep were sheared near Valladolid. Moreover, the name of port wine comes from the area along the Duero River near Porto where the grape for the wine is grown. It was an important export product. Castile could have exported both wool and port from Porto.

The reasons that the Castilian kings drove south below Toledo in the 1000s rather than consolidated a more natural state is not well explored in the literature. Most take for granted the drive for the "Reconquest" emphasized in Spanish mythology. Two other explanations seem more plausible. One is that the migratory sheep economy was not well-enough established in the early centuries to provide sufficient income either for the king or the northern city-states. Perhaps the kings and the northern city-states felt that economic necessity required them to go south to obtain loot.

A second explanation is theoretically more interesting. In today's age of globalization, economists usually emphasize the positive effects of international commerce and often even treat it as the main engine of economic growth. In fact, England had a very primitive international commerce until the time of Elizabeth I. As late as the early 1500s, England had no deep-sea merchant fleet, and some 90% of its exports were wool and woolen cloth, most of it going to Flanders. Except for wool and woolen cloth carried to Calais in France within sight of the cliffs of Dover, English trade was conducted by armed foreign ships.

Iberia had a much more complex role in international commerce. The Basque ports on the Bay of Biscay traded with England and Flanders. Porto and Lisbon at the mouths of the Duero and Tagus also traded with England and northern Europe. Barcelona and Valencia of the Aragon Federation were major ports in Mediterranean trade. Seville in the south had been a major Moorish port and had 75,000 people in 1250, nearly twice the population of London. It remained a great port after its capture by the Castilians in 1248. From 1516 to 1713 the Spanish kings also controlled Antwerp as a colony, and they owned Naples for much of the period from 1442 to 1861.[41]

The multiplicity of major ports may actually have been an obstacle in the economic development of Castile. The Castilian kings may have found it difficult to turn one of the ports into a political center – a city-state based on commerce – because the merchants of other ports would oppose anyone who tried to do so. The merchants serving the Bay of Biscay ports certainly did not want Porto or Lisbon to be the capital.

41 For a comprehensive survey of the complex Iberian trade connections and merchant networks, see Phillips and Phillips, *A Concise History of Spain*, pp. 85–9.

The political problem became even worse when Ferdinand III conquered the major southern port of Seville. When Philip II finally established a capital at Madrid in 1561, he felt that he had to choose a "neutral" small town midway between Barcelona and Lisbon on the east-west route and the Biscay ports and Seville on the north-south one.

Whatever alternatives might have been chosen, the Castilian kings did continue south after 1085 rather than consolidate their position north of Toledo. The creation of the city-states with warlords in the interior reduced the danger of Muslim raiding parties and gradually introduced peace on the plateau. In 1147, however, the peace in the north was threatened when a fanatical Berber sect from North Africa captured Muslim Andalusia in southern Iberia. The new Muslim rulers vigorously attacked the Christians and even threatened Toledo.

To improve the defense of the plateau from the new threat, the Castilian kings helped to create or to strengthen militarized religious orders along the general frontier line from Portugal to Aragon. Eventually three military-religious orders absorbed or dominated the others in central Castile: Alcántara on the Portuguese border to the west, Calatrava south of Toledo, and Santiago in La Mancha to the east.[42]

The term "religious order" does not imply a collection of monks or a powerful, centralized Catholic Church, let alone one under the control of the state. The founders of the religious orders were encouraged to occupy huge pieces of land in the expectation that the military forces they created to defend their own land would also guard the city-states to the north. They needed little encouragement, and, as we will see, the heads of these orders became extremely wealthy.

The troops of the big militarized religious orders, like those of the city-states, became part of the "royal" forces that attacked the Muslims to the south. After the 1212 battle of Las Navas de Tolosa, nearly all of Andalusia fell to the Castilians: Córdoba, Seville, the Guadalquivir River valley, and the south Atlantic coast at Cadiz. Only Granada remained under Muslim control, and it became a vassal state that had to pay tribute.

The conquest of the south was quite unlike a modern war. The battle of Las Navas de Tolosa largely destroyed the Muslim defensive capability, and the Castilians had the military ability to roll rather quickly to the sea.

[42] Probably the most comprehensive English-language summary of these orders is Desmond Seward, *The Monks of War: The Military Religious Orders* (London: Eyre Methuen, 1972), pp. 135–93; Clara Estow, "The Economic Development of the Order of Calatrava, 1158–1366," *Speculum* 57 (1982), 267–91; Joseph O'Callaghan, *The Spanish Military Order of Calatrava and Its Affiliates* (London: Variorum, 1975).

Instead, it took 50 years. The key reason was that the Castilian kings were not primarily seeking territory to build a great state. The land was distributed as booty to members of the coalition in proportion with their role in the victory, and hence the king received only a slice of it. It was more profitable for the armies to move south one city a year because they had to stop in order to take the mobile booty home from the conquered cities.

The capture of Cadiz in 1262 was, however, the end of the era. Alfonso X attempted to continue looting in Granada, but his forces were repulsed. Members of the great families of the northern city-states had received land in the Guadalquivir valley and wanted to build estates there. Now the kings had to find a new source of revenue. That will be the subject of the concluding section.

The Consolidation of the Spanish City-States

James Lockhart and Stuart Schwartz argued that the "basic [political] entity" in Mediterranean civilization "from time immemorial" was the city-state and that Spain and its colonies were no different.[43] Yet while most of the famous city-states of the past such as Athens, Genoa, and Venice (and London as well) were dominated by port cities and their urban elite, the great majority of the city-states in late medieval Spain were true urban-rural amalgamates. The rural elites lived in walled cities rather than in rural castles. Their wealth was based on their sheep flocks in the north and on agricultural estates and cattle ranches in the south.

In a study of Spain in the 1600s, Helen Nader found that the "implicit legal reality" was that "every noble estate was a town," whether the owner of the estate was a private noble, a church body, or the king. It was the same before the 1600s. Indeed, except for some subdivision over time, the basic boundaries of the urban-rural units in the 1600s had remained very much the same as they had been for centuries.[44]

The size of the rural area (*término*) of the city-state outside the formal city limits varied with the density of the population, but it included villages and small towns. In 1500, the city of Ciudad Real, the capital of La Mancha, included 47 square kilometers *inside* its city limits, enough to farm and raise animals. The territory of the *término* of the city was 48,000 acres

[43] James Lockhart and Stuart Schwartz, *Early Latin America: A History of Colonial Spanish America and Brazil* (Cambridge: Cambridge University Press, 1983), pp. 3–4.

[44] Helen Nader, *Liberty in Absolutist Spain: The Hapsburg Sale of Towns, 1516–1700* (Baltimore, MD: Johns Hopkins University Press, 1990), pp. ix.

or 194 square kilometers.[45] The small "city" of Madrid was so large that it included the nearby mountains where the sheep grazed in the summer.

The ruling organ of the city-state was the *concejo* – a word usually translated as "city council" or "municipal council," but really more like a "city-state council." When Helen Nader wanted to write a dissertation on the agricultural strategy of the Castilian agricultural elite in the 1500s and 1600s, she discovered she could not because there was no agricultural elite.

As we noted, the semi-arid climate on the plateau and its distance from ports meant that the economic base of the rural elite on the plateau could not be agriculture, but had to be the raising of cattle and especially migrating sheep. The cattle produced leather and the sheep produced wool. Both were exported. As a result, the agricultural elite was engaged in "foreign trade," whether or not they so desired. Unlike the English lords, they had to be their own "shippers," carrying the wool to market on the backs of their own sheep.

The city-state councils made all the concrete decisions on agriculture and focused overwhelmingly on the supply of food to the city. Indeed, they engaged in heavy regulation of the supply and prices of agricultural goods. Craft guilds were almost never formed in medieval Castile, a fact that Pablo Sancho Leon attributes to the dominant role of the municipal government in the economy.[46]

The concept of "family" plays a larger role in the general English-language literature on Castile than that on England. Indeed, it is a prominent part of the discussion of the court politics of Spain in the 1500s and 1600s and of city-state politics of colonial Mexico. Clearly, elite family ties were highly important in England, but the rural areas in Castile were far more integrated with the urban areas than in England. This made family ties between the urban and rural elite more important in Castile. As a Spanish scholar wrote, there was often no clear distinction between the urban and rural spheres in Castile:[47]

[45] Carla Rahn Phillips, *Ciudad Real, 1500–1750: Growth, Crisis, and Readjustment in the Spanish Economy* (Cambridge, MA: Harvard University Press, 1979), p. 8.

[46] Nader, *Liberty in Absolutist Spain*, p. ix; Pablo Sanchez Leon, "Town and Country in Castile, 1400–1650," in S. R. Epstein, ed., *Town and Country in Europe, 1300–1800* (Cambridge: Cambridge University Press, 2001), pp. 277–8 and 286–7.

[47] Miguel-Ángel Ladero Quesada, "Monarquía y ciudades de realengo en Castilla siglos XII-XV," *Anuario de estudios medievales* 24 (1994), 719–74. For more on the comparison between medieval lives in Castile and across Europe, see Máximo Diago Hernando, "El papel de los linajes en las estructuras de gobierno urbano en Castilla y en el Imperio alemán durante los siglos bajomedievales," *En la España medieval* 20 (1997), 143–78.

The urban society was linked in many ways to rural society, and at times there was not a legal distinction between them, which made the development of a clearly differentiated bourgeoisie difficult. This arrangement stimulated the maintenance of links and mixed economic interests and encouraged the development of social groups with activities, interests, and ways of life converging with those of the landed aristocracy, whose members, on the other hand, often had urban residences.

In societies with a rural elite and primogeniture, the second and third sons often were placed in the church and the army. This was all the more important in Castile because monasteries and religious orders were centers of military power. In the words of Bernard Reilly, "kings, nobles, and burghers continued to vie eagerly for the ability to find income for their families and retainers by placing them in church office."[48]

Jaime Vicens Vives, a Spanish economic historian, concurred: "Every noble aspired to providing the lieutenancy of a castle, or a commandery in one of the military orders, or perhaps some abbey lands, to his second son." Other sons needed to be provided with similar, if perhaps, lesser offices.[49] These sons managed the military force to defend family interests and could rely on family wealth to keep these military forces strong.[50]

The regionalization of Castile was furthered by the lack of a strong centralized Catholic Church with massive independent property. The Muslims would not permit Christian churches to be formed in their territory. As the Christians moved south, they had to introduce religious life and cathedrals. Naturally the founders of the city-states installed bishops and other high religious officials who were subordinate to them. The subsequent placement of sons into these posts continued the pattern.

One indicator of the failure of the Catholic Church to develop as a powerful centralized institution is that Latin had a lesser role in Castile than elsewhere in Europe. Since the elite did not develop a pervasive knowledge of Latin, Castilian political authorities had to use the vernacular language in their official documents. The leaders of regional religious orders and monasteries did become important landlords and even warlords, but the

48 Bernard Reilly, *The Medieval Spains* (Cambridge: Cambridge University Press, 1993), pp. 181–2.

49 Jaime Vicens Vives, *An Economic History of Spain* (Princeton, NJ: Princeton University Press, 1969), pp. 245–6.

50 Brian Catlos, *The Victors and the Vanquished: Christians and Muslims of Catalonia and Aragon, 1050–1300* (Cambridge: Cambridge University Press, 2004), p. 91; Richard Fletcher, *The Episcopate in the Kingdom of Leon in the Twelfth Century* (Oxford: Oxford University Press, 1978), p. 3.

church's base in fortified monasteries ensured its integration with regional family elites from the beginning.[51]

Indeed, because of the city-states' involvement in the transportation of "wool," the leading families of the city-states also had to have close relations with those who drove the sheep to market at the shearing points and who engaged in the trade of wool for European consumer goods at the nearby fairs.

The financial relationship of the king and the city-states is a central issue that is poorly illuminated in the literature. A century ago, Roger Merriman reported that "the number and variety of the revenues to which the king was in one way or another legally entitled were enormous." Many scholars have assumed that the tax codes represented reality, and, as a result, many have concluded that the Spanish bureaucracy was more centralized and effective in tax collection than the English. As we will see, the English tax historian, Gerald Harriss, took the opposite view.

Merriman himself added that "the poverty of the Castilian monarch was a jest in the mouths of their subjects."[52] Castile gradually developed an elaborate tax system based on the *alcabala* (sales tax), but it was largely a fiction. The "sales tax" that was collected by the Mesta on the wool was basically an export customs duty, while that on internal trade was collected by a tax-farming system that was bought by the wealthiest families and nobles.

But what does this mean? The city-states were the dominant political units and, whatever language one wants to use, they were ruled by warlords (heads of families) who operated through members of their families placed in different elite posts or occupations or through daughters married to men in those positions. This makes the real meaning of the tax-farming system unclear. Since the wealthiest families were those who controlled the city-states and their military force, this seems to mean that the tax farms were a type of tribute that the city-states were expected to give the king.[53]

In England of this period, taxes were often paid in the form of troops and supplies for war, and this must also have been true in Spain in the 1500s. In Spain, taxes often were also paid in sophisticated expenditures

[51] For an example of the mixing of the church and politics – and the impossibility of judging the direction of flow of informal pressures – see Peter Linehan, "The Economics of Episcopal Politics: The Cautionary Tale of Bishop Severo Pérez," in Peter Linehan, *The Processes of Politics and the Rule of Law: Studies on the Iberian Kingdoms and Papal Rome in the Middle Ages* (Aldershot: Varorium, 2002), 1–29.

[52] Merriman, *Rise of the Spanish Empire*, p. 247.

[53] Ruth Pike, *Aristocrats and Traders: Southern Society in the Sixteenth Century* (Ithaca, NY: Cornell University Press, 1972), p. 138; Ladero Quesada, "Castile in the Middle Ages," p. 190.

on infrastructure rather than in cash. In medieval Castile, we simply do not know what percentage of taxes was paid in cash.

Ladero Quesada makes it clear, however, that the relationship between the city-states and the Crown was precarious and shifting prior to 1500: "The complexity is apparent in the geography of taxation, which differed from one source of revenue to the next, and even from one subdivision or 'branch' of the same source of revenue to another." Maria del Carmen Carlé finds that the powers of the *concejo* relative to the Crown waxed and waned throughout the medieval period.[54]

Indeed, the literature on the 1400s implies that the weak kings of that time, while they might have called themselves absolute, had only the most tenuous power. Thus, Merriman states that the kings often made large financial grants to a number of the major families and cities.[55] Yet the kings had no money to use in making grants unless they were collecting taxes from families and cities.

Conceivably the kings were engaged in regional income redistribution between supporters and opponents, but the kings of the 1400s are always described as weak and uninterested in the exercise of royal power. It is likely that many regions were refusing to send their tribute to the king and that he was making them a "grant" of the money they were refusing to send.

The kings' economic relationship to the city-states in the medieval period is very hard to judge, but the Crown surely wanted a share of the taxation imposed on the migrating sheep in the north. Whether officially based on the *alcabala* (sales tax) or not, the city-states were responsible for collecting it. As we noted earlier, much of the farmed tax must have come from the wool moving northward on the backs of sheep until the sheep-grazers' organization, the Mesta, was created to collect taxes. The farmed tax may still have been paid in kind.

Castile after 1262: A Society "Disorganized by War"

Economists often treat the medieval period in Europe as a seamless era. In fact, as we have seen, both England and Castile changed dramatically during this time. Statements that are quite accurate about the 11th and 12th century often are not true of the 15th century, and vice versa. In the Castilian

[54] Ladero Quesada, "Castile in the Middle Ages," p. 185. Miguel-Ángel Ladero Quesada, "Los primeros pasos de la *alcabala* castellana, de Alfonso X a Pedro I," *Anuario de estudios medievales*, Vol. 22 (1992); Maria del Carmen Carlé, *Del Concejo Medieval Castellano-Leones* (Buenos Aires: Instituto de Historia de España, 1968).

[55] Merriman, *Rise of the Spanish Empire*, pp. 254–5.

case, an integrated economy that had largely been based on raising sheep, exporting wool, and looting lands to the south became bifurcated when the Castilian king conquered the Guadalquivir valley that produced crops such as olives, olive oil, figs, and wine. The new lands in southern Castile had the Mediterranean climate that permitted formation of large agricultural estates.[56] Such estates or plantations that grew commercial crops inevitably looked to foreign markets to be economically viable. In the words of David Ringrose:[57]

> The essential elements of export-oriented agrarian capitalism were all in place in Andalusia in the eighteenth century.... The regional elites were well on the way to a liberal concept of landed property long before the nineteenth century and ... they showed great sensitivity to the possibilities of capitalist, export-oriented production throughout the era in question.

The labor force consisted of landless peasants who worked as day laborers. Scholars emphasize the unequal distribution of the income and the impoverished state of the peasantry in Andalusia. Yet, while this is true, impoverishment is a relative concept. Peasants moved voluntarily from the subsistence agriculture in the north to the more fertile southern estates, surely because the standard of living was better there.[58]

The literature on Spain gives surprisingly little attention to the huge area south of Toledo. We think a major reason is that the king's power did not extend into the south in a significant manner. It is unclear how much real tax revenue the south remitted to the king until Seville began receiving silver from the colonies in the 1500s and Spain had created an early state. Even then it is unclear how much non-silver revenue it paid in cash.

As we see in the next chapter, even after Isabella came to power, the city-states often paid their "taxes" in the form of expenditures made on infrastructure or the like. It seems probable that this occurred even more frequently when the monarchs were weaker, especially in the south. From

56 Manuel González Jiménez, "Frontier and Settlement in the Kingdom of Castile (1085–1350)," in Robert Bartlett and Angus MacKay, eds., *Medieval Frontier Societies* (Oxford: Clarendon Press, 1989), pp. 60–61; Lomax, *The Reconquest of Spain*, pp. 107–11; Charles Bishko, "The Castilian as Plainsman: The Medieval Frontier in La Mancha and Extremadura," in Archibald Lewis and Thomas McGann, eds., *The New World Looks at Its History* (Austin: University of Texas Press, 1963).

57 David Ringrose, *Madrid and the Spanish Economy, 1560–1850* (Berkeley: University of California Press, 1983), p. 296.

58 For a summary of the region, see Ringrose, *Madrid and the Spanish Economy*, pp. 291–309; Richard Herr, *Rural Change and Royal Finances in Spain at the End of the Old Regime* (Berkeley: University of California Press, 1989).

the 1260s onward, the southern commercial centers used the Genoa fleet to carry its olives, leather, figs, and wine to northern markets, and this fleet also served as Castile's navy. Genoese merchants dominated the merchant community in Seville.

As the fleet of the Hanseatic League became less dominant in the 1400s, the Castilian fleet together with the forces of Genoa became the leading naval power in northern and southern Europe – or, at least, it "shared [this leadership] in some measure" with the Netherlands. Castile defeated the English navy in 1372 and the fleet of the Hanseatic League in 1419. Castile also was a leader in the technological revolution in shipbuilding that occurred at this time.[59]

One assumes that the king did not pay full value, if any, for this protection, and it is probable that the real "taxes" from the south took the form of naval protection for ships going from the northern ports of the Bay of Biscay, and perhaps free or subsidized products such as olive oil and wine for the plateau and especially for the king's household. The payments for the Genoese naval production were likely built into the monopoly prices being charged.

The reason that the king maintained his base in the north near the sheep-shearing areas around Valladolid rather than in Toledo or Seville almost surely was because that was where he collected most of his revenue. Nevertheless, as the sheep moved between their winter and summer grazing grounds, they had to pass through a number of city-states twice a year. Each of these states wanted to collect taxes that the kings wanted for themselves, and the problem became worse after the 1250s because the distance between the winter and summer grazing grounds increased.

If we are going to understand how the state and market developed in Castile, we need to look at the world of the 1250s and 1260s through the eyes of Alfonso X. Rulers do not think with the broad sweep of the historian about "the 13th century." They think of the immediate problems that confront them in the short run. Seen from this perspective, several of Alfonso's key steps are not fully appreciated in the English-language literature. This

[59] Peter Russell, *The English Intervention in Spain in the Time of Edward III and Richard II* (Oxford: Clarendon Press, 1955), 227–37; Angus MacKay, *Spain in the Middle Ages, from Frontier to Empire, 1000–1500* (New York: St. Martin's Press, 1977), pp. 124–5; Archibald Lewis, "Northern European Sea Power and the Straits of Gibraltar, 1031–1350 A.D.," in Archibald Lewis, *The Sea and Medieval Civilizations: Collected Studies* (London: Variorum Reprints, 1978), 141–62; Archibald Lewis and Timothy Runyan, *European Naval and Maritime History, 300–1500* (Bloomington: Indiana University Press, 1985), p. 144.

is especially true of his creation of the "non-noble knights" in 1255 and his formalization of the Mesta as a royal agent in 1273.[60]

The timing of the creation of the non-noble knights and the Mesta was not accidental. Alfonso faced two major problems following the conquest of Andalusia, and the non-noble knights and the Mesta were attempts to solve them. As we discuss in the next section, the first was a security problem not unlike the one faced by the English kings when military action in France during the Hundred Years' War or along the Scottish border ceased temporarily or permanently. The large number of troops employed by local warlords in obtaining booty from Muslims could now obtain it only from each other or from the king. Indeed, demobilized soldiers could act on their own.

In addition, much of the new land seized south of the Tagus River was semi-arid and suitable only for sheep grazing. The sheep living on it had to travel farther to reach their summer grazing grounds. The owners in the south needed more troops to guard them. The owners of the northern flocks, for their part, wanted to use the new high-quality and warmer winter grazing grounds. The powerful forces in the south – notably those of huge militarized religious orders – wanted to prevent this migration. Both the northern and southern owners needed more troops, and both could use them against the king.[61]

The second problem for Alfonso X was an increased challenge to his collection of taxes. Everyone in medieval trade within Europe or with Asia had to worry about a multiplicity of tolls and fees imposed along the way. At one time traders had to pay tolls 18 times as they went along 80 miles of the Seine River approaching Paris and 30 tolls on the Rhine River between Mainz and Cologne.[62] The owners of the migrating sheep were no different, and any increase in the distance of the migration increased the potential number of collectors. Alfonso X thought this tax revenue should go to him.

Alfonso created the non-noble knights (*caballeros villanos*) in 1255, only three years after he came to power. The knights were members of a

[60] For a discussion of the timing, see Bishko, "The Castilian as Plainsman," pp. 60–4.

[61] Charles Julian Bishko, "The Castilian as Plainsman: The Medieval Ranching Frontier in La Mancha and Extremadura," in Archibald Lewis and Thomas McGann, eds., *The New World Looks at Its History* (Austin: University of Texas Press, 1963), pp. 47–50 and 61–3.

[62] The most popular tourist cruises on the Rhine River today go between those two cities, and tourists can view the ruins of many of the toll-collecting fortresses. Norman J. G. Pounds, *An Economic History of Medieval Europe* (London: Longman, 1974), p. 392. For the same phenomenon on the overland route from Asia, see Janet Abu-Lughod, *Before European Hegemony: The World System A.D. 1250–1350* (New York: Oxford University Press, 1989), pp. 177 and 182.

militarized merchant class in the north who were exempted from personal taxation if they owned horses and weapons and supported the king militarily and provided him with income from foreign trade.[63]

Teofilo Ruiz argues that the knights had the same role in defending trade that we have seen in oceanic commerce but that also was needed in land trade throughout Europe at the time. In Ruiz's words, "the military role of the so-called bourgeoisie [the merchants] is a well-known aspect of the history of urban medieval Europe and is by no means unique to Castile." The armed force that allowed the merchants to protect trade also allowed them to dominate the political life of their city. Like the Phoenicians, Venetians, and Hanseatic League, they could also use their military force to try to conquer other areas.[64]

When Alfonso created the Mesta in 1273, only eleven years had passed after the capture of Cadiz. Alfonso had hoped to continue his old policy of obtaining booty, this time in Granada, but by the early 1270s he realized that his plan had failed. He understood that his revenue had to come through an expansion of wool production. The Mesta had been a loosely organized group of sheep grazers created to defend migrating sheep, but in 1973, Alfonso transformed it into a heavily armed Castile-wide body that all wool producers in the kingdom had to join. It was under his strict control and probably was his major base of power.

As in the case with all corporate monopoly guild bodies in England and the rest of Europe, the Mesta performed a number of governing functions, notably the resolution of legal disputes between the grazers and agricultural interests over whose land the sheep passed. Nevertheless, the section on taxation in the Mesta charter was larger than all the other sections combined.[65]

The tax section focused on the regulation and control of locally imposed taxes. The section specified in great detail the types of taxes and fees that could be imposed by localities on the migrating shepherds and those that

[63] Teofilo Ruiz, *The City and the Realm: Burgos and Castile, 1080–1492* (Aldershot: Ashgate, 1992), pp. 5–16; Teofilo Ruiz, *Crisis and Continuity: Land and Town in Late Medieval Castile* (Philadelphia: University of Pennsylvania Press, 1994), pp. 237–42.

[64] Ruiz, *Crisis and Continuity*, p. 237. He refers to Henri Pirenne, *Economic and Social History of Medieval Europe* (New York: Harcourt, Brace, 1937). Helen Nader emphasizes the potential aggressive role of the knights. Helen Nader, *The Mendoza Family in the Spanish Renaissance, 1350 to 1550* (New Brunswick, NJ: Rutgers University Press, 1979), pp. 36–7.

[65] J. N. Hillgarth, *The Spanish Kingdoms, 1250–1516*, Vol. 2 (Oxford: Clarendon Press, 1978), pp. 32–3; Julius Klein, *The Mesta: A Study in Spanish Economic History, 1273–1836* (Cambridge, MA: Harvard University Press, 1920), pp. 176–7.

were forbidden, but its purpose, of course, was to increase the king's revenue. In the words of Ekelund and Tollison, the Crown considered the Mesta to be "a 'cash cow,' which in return for secure geographic and other property rights, was a lucrative source of revenues."[66]

Alfonso X had to make domestic political alliances to form the Mesta, but two facts mentioned earlier put him in a dominant position. First, the migrant sheep owners were being subjected to multiple tolls and fees, and Alfonso was able to be the classic stationary bandit who could tell those being robbed multiple times that he could introduce order at a price, but reduce the overall cost to them.

Second, the city-states were both the robbers and the robbed. They all had sheep going through the territory of others, but they also tried to tax the others' sheep going through their land. All of them also faced independent bandits and wasted time and resources both as the taxed and the collectors. In a "social contract" situation, each had an interest in being a free rider unless someone could use compulsion and side payments to solve the collective action problem that many wanted to have solved. The benefits of the old system may have outweighed the cost for some city-states, but it was easy for Alfonso to build a coalition against them.

The creation of the Mesta and the non-noble knights gave Alfonso X precisely what he wanted. He obtained a military force that essentially was loyal to him and that allowed him to monopolize most of the taxation on the export of wool and on imported European goods for which the wool was exchanged. In addition, the king now had a force that acted as a balance against the new military force in Andalusia and those of the individual northern warlords.

One could imagine that the arrangement would be quite stable and lead to a gradual demilitarization of Castile and the basis for the creation of the state. So long as the king maintained reasonable levels of taxation – and that seemed guaranteed by the existence of an armed force in the control of the various warlords – the reduction in the local taxes on migrating sheep was a collective good that no one seemed to have an interest in challenging.

[66] Robert Ekelund and Robert Tollison, *Politicized Economies: Monarchy, Monopolies, and Mercantilism* (College Station: Texas A & M Press, 1997), p. 136. For the debate on the economic role of the Mesta in the economic literature, also see Jeffrey Nugent and Nicolas Sanchez, "The Efficiency of the Mesta: A Parable," *Explorations in Economic History* 26 (1989), 261–84; Robert Ekelund, D. R. Street, and Robert Tollison, "Rent Seeking and Property Rights Assignments as a Process: The Mesta Cartel of Medieval-Mercantile Spain," *Journal of European Economic History* (Spring 1997), 9–35; Mauricio Drelichman, "License to Till: The Privileges of the Spanish Mesta as a Case of Second-Best Institutions," *Explorations in Economic History* 46 (2009), 220–40.

There was one major problem, however: kings are not immortal. Power was decentralized to armed city-states with highly diverse interests in a Castile that was roughly the size of California. A new ruler might make decisions that were highly advantageous to one region but not to another. The issue during the long Civil War that Isabella finally won in 1480 was whether Castile should ally with (really, merge with) Aragon on the Mediterranean to the east or Portugal on the Atlantic to the west. The issue had fundamental economic and security ramifications.

In addition, the Mesta forces that provided stability for one king were a destabilizing force in a succession. Many potential kings wanted the revenue the Mesta produced, while the Mesta leaders had their own interest and army with which to defend them.

All of these factors changed the character of the Castilian political system after 1262. Prior to then, the reliance of the city-states on loot in the south as a main source of revenue meant that the post of king was not as valuable. This meant, as we have seen, that Castile prior to 1262 had been "a society organized for war." The changed calculus of costs and benefits in the succession increased the chance of Civil War at that time. In the words of Peter Linehan, "A society organized for war [before 1262] ... was [then] disorganized by war."[67]

In fact, Castile experienced two centuries of chaos and anarchy after Alfonso X's death in 1284. Indeed, it began earlier as the conflicting city-states looked forward to the succession to Alfonso. The identity of a new ruler often had to be resolved on the battlefield, and defeat could mean the loss of life and property for the losing warlords and their extended families.

There were interludes of peace, but few reigns in this long period lasted as much as 20 years, and the kings died at the average age of 38. The one king with a long reign, John II, is considered one of the least capable in Castilian history, and perhaps he survived so long because he challenged no one.[68] The kind of integrated economy that, as we see, was being formed around London during these centuries was quite lacking. In the words of Angus MacKay, Castile in the 1400s "was a series of regions and 'markets'

67 Peter Linehan, *Spain, 1157–1300: A Partible Inheritance* (Oxford: Blackwell, 2008), p. xi.

68 A reader who wants a sense of the continual conflict can look at the biography of Alfonso X in Wikipedia's online encyclopedia and follow the short biographies of his successors until Isabella. This was a period more than 200 years long.

rather than a coherent economic unit," and, of course, the non-Castilian areas of the peninsula added to the diversity.[69]

The result, to quote Teofilo Ruiz, was a kingdom that "tilted perilously on a knife edge" in 1300 and moved toward stability only periodically in the next 50 years. There was, he said, a replay of "the chaos and disorder" in the second half of the 14th century "with a vengenance." Then came 50 years of "John II's long, tormented, and fairly incompetent rule" from 1406 to 1454; Henry IV's 20-year reign that "was as chaotic or even more so"; and a six-year civil war Isabella finally ended in 1480. Yet Ruiz emphasizes that the kingdom hung together and a sense of community and a political structure developed. That set the stage for Isabella's reign.[70]

Geography in Economic Development: A Collective Action Analysis

In many respects, Castile and England were not that different in their political systems in the mid-1250s. The English kings received most of their regular revenue from their land, but the wars between England and Scotland were essentially aimed at obtaining loot, much like the attacks on the Muslims by the Castilians.

By 1485, however, England had become far more effectively governed than Castile and economically more advanced. London had become a thriving city-state while Isabella was driving out the Jews and Moors who played such an entrepreneurial role in the southern cities. In 1485, Henry VII gained control of a quite effective government at the city-state level, one that had served as the capital city for 150 years prior to 1485. Henry was able to use it to take over and rule effectively all of England. Castile was to acquire a capital only in 1561 when Isabella's great-grandson created one in Madrid.

A major cause of this difference between English and Castilian development from 1265 to the 1480s, we have argued, was that the man-made geography created by 1265 by English and Castilian rulers was very different. The English rulers had chosen a model that made it relatively easy to consolidate and then gradually expand a state. The Castilian rulers had formed a territory too big to rule effectively.

[69] Angus MacKay, "A Pluralist Society: Modern Spain," in John Elliott, ed., *The Spanish World: Civilization and Empire: Europe and the Americas, Past and Present* (New York: Harry N. Abrams, 1991), p. 22. The regions are described on pp. 5–23 of this book.

[70] Teofilo Ruiz, *Spain's Centuries of Crisis* (Oxford: Wiley-Blackwell, 2007), pp. 199, 78 87, 94. For the developing political structure, see pp. 110–38.

The Normans had largely ruled England from France until 1204. Henry III had seen the problems of his father, John, that had culminated in the Magna Carta of 1215, and he decided to identify himself with the pre-Norman English past. Ignoring the Magna Carta, Henry engaged in a war with the lords that won him total control of London in 1265. His successors turned their efforts to transforming London into a city-state as their base of rule. In 1337 Henry III's great grandson, Edward III, turned it into a real capital.

The Castilian kings of the 1000s moved southward across the plateau until Alfonso VI captured Toledo, over 250 miles south of the ports on the Bay of Biscay. As we have discussed, they did not try to capture the mouths of the two great rivers of the plateau, the Duero near the sheep-shearing center of Valladolid and the Tagos near Toledo. Instead, they drove southward another 350 miles to capture Cadiz on the South Atlantic in 1262. Hence, instead of having a manageable area to rule based on Porto at the mouth of the Duero or even at Lisbon, the Castilian kings "controlled" an area much larger than Great Britain as a whole. London did not even succeed in incorporating Scotland until another 450 years had passed from 1265.

Alfonso X's capture of Cadiz in 1262 gave him nominal control of a territory three times the size of England. He did not have any port for his capital, but was an itinerant ruler who centered his activities around Valladolid on the northern plateau near where the migrating sheep were sheared. The area was simply too big to govern, as was the area to the south that centered on Seville.

Our thesis is that the size of the territory the early rulers of England and Castile attempted to rule makes these countries ideal case studies for a book that tries to add collective-action analysis to development theory. So long as a "stationary bandit" rules a small number of people and uses people whom he knows well as lieutenants, he can use personal rewards and threats of punishment, as well as personalistic values, to control them. This chapter has mentioned many techniques in passing. The situation becomes very different when a territory is so large that more impersonal mechanisms of control are needed to rule it effectively. The latter require an enormous amount of time to build.

There are two reasons we consider the 1260s to be an important part of the colonial tradition of the United States and Mexico. First, the resulting difference in the level of the effectiveness of the government in the England and Spain of the 1500s and 1600s was inevitably reflected in the effective or ineffective governance from which the colonists learned how to rule.

Second, the Spanish Philip II of the 1550s and the English kings of the 1600s consciously or unconsciously chose to repeat the geographical history of their own countries in their colonies. England created colonies in North America that were city-states. Each had a capital city on the Atlantic seaboard and had its own governor. These units all remained city-states until the mid-1700, were well governed, and developed the ability to govern in their elites.

By contrast, Spain established two viceroys in ruling the New World, one essentially for North America and the other for South America. Neither viceroy had significant staff, and neither had a centralized bureaucracy. Until the 1770s, Madrid did not even create an orderly set of provincial governments at the level of the future American states. Power was decentralized to the city-state level as in Spain, but Madrid's fear of a coup led it to insist that the city-states remain relatively unarmed. Even when the Bourbon rulers began to create an effective structure of government in the 1770s, this structure was swept away in the chaos of the independence period. Mexico returned to semi-anarchy outside the Mexico City city-state for 60 years.

3

The Early State in England and Spain

This chapter examines the period when more effective states began to be established in England and Spain. Henry III began the formation of the city-state of London in 1265, 200 years after the Norman invasion. Isabella began to construct such a Castilian state in 1480, 450 years after García Sánchez created the Castilian-León "kingdom." A further difference, an important one we argued at the end of the previous chapter, was that Spain provides a model of the evolution of a reasonably large territory that began with centuries of partial semi-anarchy, while England had the familiar modern pattern of a country that began with a stable capital that gradually extended its control over more remote areas.

Castile after 1265 was nearly the size of California and became 20% larger when Isabella acquired Aragon and Granada. It also was geographically and economically as diverse as California. The Castilian warlords lived in walled cities, but their migrating sheep and the unsettled succession crises meant they had to maintain large, mobile armies. The size of the territory of Castile provides a better sense of the problems in contemporary developing countries than an England that was the size of North Carolina.

Spanish development is particularly important for American economists to understand. The English rebellion against the Catholic Church in the 1530s and the conflict that culminated in the attempted Spanish invasion of England in 1588 left a strong residue in English-American thinking: a highly negative view of Spain, the so-called Black Legend. This view was reenforced by the 40 years of Franco's dictatorship from 1936 to 1975 and by Franco's claim that he represented a highly centralized Spanish tradition. As a result, in the words of Alejandra Irigoin and Regina Grafe: "[In the old interpretation], Spain was absolutist, interventionist, centralist, statist, bureaucratic and constitutionally disinclined to grant its subjects much local government."[1]

The old descriptions of Spain faded after Franco's death in 1975 and the subsequent 40 years of Spanish democracy and integration into Europe. A fresh generation of scholars working on Spain and Latin America reexamined Spanish history closely and, again in the words of Irigoin and Grafe, produced "a large, exciting historiography that has shown that in both peninsular Spain and its American possessions reality was very different from this simplistic portrayal."

William Summerhill goes further: "the old association of centralization with negative [economic] outcomes has ... been turned on its head."[2] Summerhill reached this conclusion from his own study of Brazil in the 1800s. This work convinced him that economic development was not possible until it solved "the imperatives of political centralization" and state-building in the second half of the century.[3] We agree and argue that Castilian economic difficulties in the 1500s and 1600s resulted not from over-centralization but from the lack of political centralization that Daron Acemoglu and James Robinson say was also crucial for growth in Tudor England.

The reinterpretation of Spanish and Latin American history by modern historians has not been reflected in the comparative analysis of European economic history. Instead, Spain has simply disappeared from books such as Douglass North's *Violence and Social Orders* and Daron Acemoglu and James Robinson's *Why Nations Fail*. Moreover, "remnants" of the old thinking still remain in analysis of Latin America or in widespread broader preconceptions about the relationship of centralization and economic growth. It is important to look at Spanish history in detail to understand how far removed Franco-age generalizations about Spain are from modern understanding.

In one respect, however, the English model of development is more relevant for developing countries today. Modern former colonies began with a

[1] Alejandra Irigoin and Regina Grafe, "Bargaining for Absolutism: A Spanish Path to Nation-State and Empire Building," *Hispanic-American Historical Review* 88 (2008), 173–209, pp. 173–4. They point specifically to Douglass North and quote his "Institutions and Economic Growth: An Historical Introduction," *World Development* 17 (1989), 1319–32, p. 1328.

[2] Irigoin and Grafe, "Bargaining for Absolutism," p. 174; William Summerhill, "Fiscal Bargains, Political Institutions, and Economic Performance," *Hispanic-American Historical Review* 88 (2008), pp. 221, 227.

[3] William Summerhill, *Order against Progress: Government, Foreign Investment, and Railroads in Brazil, 1854–1913* (Stanford, CA: Stanford University Press, 2003), p. 2.

capital, and except in cases such as the United States and Canada that were largely populated by Europeans, the colonial powers often made little effort to penetrate into the interior for a quite substantial period. The colony quickly became an early state or a minimally effective state in the capital and other large cities but largely remained a pre–nation-state in most of the rest of the colony.

England had a path of development similar to this later colonial model. Medieval London was quite unlike the London of today or even that of the 1600s and 1700s. Some think it had as many as 100,000 people in 1300 before the plague and famine reduced it to the 40,000 to 50,000 range in 1400, but Pamela Nightingale is more convinced that the population was never much larger than it was in 1400. A historian of London in the late 1300s said that it still seemed "a busy but small market town."[4] London still had only some 50,000 people in 1500.

In 1400, the territory of London was still largely contained within the old city walls of London and totaled less than one square mile. The open countryside was less than a 30-minute walk from anywhere in the city. One of London's small "suburbs" was a small village where Trafalgar Square is now located. There "the main road swung to the right ... but a muddy side road on the left led to Westminster" where the abbey and palace were located.[5]

Since the city-state of London was, indeed, a city-state and a capital, it could be more effectively governed than the usual early state. We argue that a crucial step was Edward III's ability to induce the Hanseatic League to join his coalition and become the taxing agent for the wool and woolen cloth exports to Flanders. The power of the Hanseatic League explains why the kings were able to obtain the lords' "consent of the governed" to customs duties but not to internal taxes when a strong royal army did not exist.

As a result, Henry VII and Henry VIII had a real financial and institutional base from which to build a nation-state when they came to power in 1485. London had slowly expanded the area of its effective control in the 1300s and 1400s, and the Tudors quickly extended it to all of England after 1485. They ruthlessly forced the warlords to abandon their military forces except in foreign wars. If local lords began to mobilize troops for their own purposes, the Tudors were quite willing and able to accuse them

4 For a survey of the literature, see Pamela Nightingale, "The Growth of London in the Medieval English Economy," in Pamela Nightingale, *Trade, Money, and Power in Medieval England* (Aldershot: Ashgate, 2007), 89–106. For her estimate, see pp. 97–8; Alec Myers, *London in the Age of Chaucer* (Norman: University of Oklahoma Press), p. 3.

5 Myers, *London in the Age of Chaucer*, pp. 3–8, and 12.

of treason and execute them. Henry VIII was particularly brutal and killed some 70,000 political opponents during his reign.

By the 1530s, Henry VIII was able to build a much more effective state that no longer deserved the label of "early." Acemoglu and Robinson call it "politically centralized." We call it "minimally effective." Spain did not reach that level of government effectiveness for 200 years, and its slow pace of economic development reflected this fact.

Chance always plays a role in historical development, and the quality of a country's rulers is one such important chance element. The Union of South Africa was extremely fortunate in having Nelson Mandela as its first leader, while Rhodesia (Zimbabwe) was unfortunate in having Robert Mugabe. Fidel Castro's length of rule clearly was a negative factor for Cuban development. England had above-average rulers – most of them truly first class – during the period from 1485 to the 1750s, but five of the six kings between Isabella's death and 1700 were grossly inadequate.

Indeed, it is unclear what would have happened in Spain in the 1700s if Bourbon France had not imposed the grandson of Louis XIV as the ruler of Spain in 1700 and if he had not used experienced French advisers to transform the government. Even then, most would date the formation of a minimally effective Spanish state to the second half of the 1700s, maybe even to Charles III and his reign from 1759 to 1787. In our opinion, the first quarter of the 1700s is more equivalent to the early Tudor period.

The City-State of London

Before 1204, the English kings had lived primarily on the continent and had not been able to rule England effectively. Every king had rivals who tried to overthrow him to get control of his income-producing land, and the death of a king usually brought bloody battles to determine his successor. The kings tried to buy support by gifts of land, but this only weakened the income base of their successors and limited their effective rule.

King John died in 1216, shortly after defeat in war forced him to sign a Magna Carta that turned him into a figurehead. His son, Henry III, repudiated the Magna Carta and quickly moved to restore and even strengthen the stature of his office. He was determined to create an image for himself as a true English king by linking himself with the pre-Norman past. In particular he tried to identify himself with the last major pre-Norman king, Edward the Confessor, by locating his main base of power in Westminster and building a new abbey there as his and Edward's burial place.

Henry III is generally considered a mediocre king because he spent most of his 55-year reign engaged in war and violent conflict throughout Britain and Europe. Nevertheless, his acquisition of full control over London in Civil War in 1265 was a historic moment in English history. This action provided the base for the formation of a city-state of London and a much more manageable base for an effective state than the huge territory of Castile. Henry III was the real father of the Industrial Revolution.

Once Henry III's successors established a city-state, they moved to strengthen the city's position as a foreign trade center. The east coast port of Boston had been the main port for the export of wool in the last quarter of the 1200s, but by 1400, London was exporting between 30% and 40% of England's wool exports and 45% of its woolen cloth. The kings created a variety of incentives for those in the interior to send other goods to London, and the knights who originally guarded the wool going to London often became merchants.[6]

Edward I, Henry's son who ruled from 1272 to 1307, actively engaged in war to retain land in France or regain land lost by his grandfather in 1204. The Normans considered France their basic homeland, and, in fact, the land between London and Paris was a more natural and compact economic unit than that between London and Scotland. Wars were a continual part of English life from the 1100s into the 1500s, and they were the similar to Castile's wars to expel the Muslims from Iberia. They also served the same revenue purposes.

The scholarly literature takes for granted that the regional warlords agreed to higher wartime taxes, but it does not explain why. The basic reason is that the English lords were like the heads of the Castilian city-states who joined the kings to obtain land and booty from the Muslims. During war, the added English taxes were often in kind – men and supplies – and, as in Castile, they often were not so much taxes in the modern sense of the word, as they were an investment made in the effort to obtain future wealth. The real income for the king, if he received any, was part of the booty that was collected.[7]

6 G. L. Harriss, *Shaping the Nation: England, 1360–1461* (Oxford: Clarendon Press, 2005), p. 302; Myers, *London in the Age of Chaucer*, p. 20; Pamela Nightingale, "Knights and Merchant Trade, Politics and the Gentry in Late Medieval England," in Pamela Nightingale, *Trade, Money, and Power in Medieval England* (Aldershot: Ashgate, 2007).

7 Because of his reliance on private ships as his navy, the king received very little from the ships and cargos that were captured. Shipowners usually got one-third, shipmasters one-sixth, and the crews half. Maryanne Kowaleski, "Warfare, Shipping, and Crown Patronage: The Impact of the Hundred Years War on the Port Towns of Medieval England," in Lawrin Armstrong, Ivana Elbl, and Martin Elbe eds., *Money, Markets, and Trade in Late Medieval Europe: Essays in Honour of John H. Munro* (Leiden: Brill, 2007), p. 253. See Nicholas A.M.

Edward I centered his domestic policy on a concerted effort to improve the English legal and administrative system. The military actions and administrative reforms went together. As Michael Prestwich emphasizes, the provision of food to the troops was a major administrative task even when troops were not living off the land. The sheriffs provided food to soldiers in lieu of wages through "compulsory purchases." "Though hardly spectacular, the achievement of Edward I's servants in building up so efficient a victuallizing service was very considerable," Prestwich said. "Without it, the king's military ventures could never have taken place."[8]

Edward's successors continued these efforts, but they too involved little bureaucratic control. The sheriffs were still more the ambassadors to the interior than real governors, and they usually were local officials. In 1327, Edward III established justices of the peace as the king's men to administer the local areas as well as serve as judges. In reality, they were local officials, usually members of the gentry, and they ruled with relative autonomy and little central control. They were meant to counterbalance the lords.

The bishops of the Catholic Church were appointed by the king and usually from the king's own administrative staff. They often controlled huge estates and still performed administrative duties for the king. They also were tax collectors. The monasteries seemed close to the dominant family in the region – and, as in Spain, may often have been staffed by its members. There was a reason that Henry VIII destroyed the abbeys whose ruins today dot the English landscape.[9]

Although the kings from Henry III in 1216 onward spent an increasing amount of time in Westminster, they did not create a real capital there until Edward III came to power. Even then Edward III from 1327 to 1337 remained an itinerant ruler like Isabella in Castile. Only in the latter year did Edward begin to move his court to London and build government buildings in which bureaucracies were located.

One of the clearest indications of the creation of a capital was the change in the locale where the kings and the lords assembled in their various

Rodger, *The Safeguard of the Sea: A Naval History of Britain, 660–1649*, Vol. 1 (New York: W.W. Norton, 1998), p. 127.

8 Michael Prestwich, *War, Politics and Finance under Edward I* (Towota, NJ: Rowman and Littlefield, 1972), 114–36. The quote is from 136. See also Michael Prestwich, *Edward I*, 2nd ed. (New Haven, CT: Yale University Press, 1997).

9 Thomas Tout, *The English Civil Service in the Fourteenth Century* (Manchester: University of Manchester Press, 1916), pp. 11–12 and 16; W. M. Ormrod, *The Reign of Edward III: Crown and Political Society in England, 1327–1377* (New Haven, CT: Yale University Press, 1990), pp. 155–160. For the church, see Harriss, *Shaping the Nation: England, 1360–1461*, pp. 311–27.

councils and Parliament sessions. Until 1337, the kings convened most of the sessions of councils and parliament outside the London area. This was true of 16 of the 24 councils and parliaments that assembled under Edward from 1327 to 1337, but 48 of his 51 sessions after 1337 met in the London area.[10] Some attribute the movement of the Parliament meetings to London to the increased power of Parliament, but the key fact was the ability of Edward III and his successors to summon the lords. This was a sign of the growing power of the king, not of the lords.[11]

Yet even when the warlords were compelled to pay a substantial wool export tax, they were still able to consolidate their own power over their regions outside the city-state of London:[12]

> Great lords . . . reigned in their counties "like Petty Kings," with Jura regalia, and gallows within their liberties when they could try, condemn, and hang and draw. Only an annual visit to London, to sit in Parliament or do homage to the King, [took] them away from their broad acres of retainers, from the feasting and jollification.

In England as a whole, the regional lords were, in North's words, the men with a comparative advantage in violence and the power to tax constituents. By North's definition, England really consisted of a number of mini-states centered on castles whose owners could assemble military force. One of them was the king's mini-state of London. This was the essence of the military feudalism discussed in the previous chapter. The decentralized nature of military force was the major constraint on the king prior to Henry VIII, not Parliament as an institution.

Most scholars do not use the phrase "city-state" to refer to London, but historians describe a reality that is quite compatible with the phrase. Some are explicit and use the label. For example, Gary Walton and Roger Miller correctly write about "the traditional city-states of northern Italy, Germany, England, and Holland" in the 1300s and 1400s.[13] London drew immigrants from a radius of 120 miles, but much of that area was not part of the original city-state. Nevertheless, its size gradually increased as the transportation network converging on London expanded and the king could introduce order over a broader area.

[10] May McKisack, *The Fourteenth Century, 1307–1399* (Oxford: Clarendon, 1959), p. 154; Scott Waugh, *England in the Reign of Edward III* (Cambridge: Cambridge University Press, 1991), p. 170.

[11] Harriss, *Shaping the Nation*, pp. 14–16.

[12] Charles Wilson, *England's Apprenticeship, 1603–1763* (London: Longman, 1971), pp. 3–4.

[13] Gary Walton and Roger Miller, *Economic Issues in American History* (New York: Harper and Row, 1978), p. 17.

Some describe England prior to 1500 as a slow growing, economically backward country, but this can be misleading. London contained only 2% of the population of England – and less of the population of England, Scotland, and Ireland together. Even though the economic growth of England as a whole may have been unimpressive, London had better economic performance. It had 2% of England's assessed lay value in 1334, but 8.9% in 1515.[14] The small size of London's population meant that the city had little impact on the country's per capita income. London was to be the base of English economic growth, and its growth was the most relevant factor for the movement toward an effective market and government.

The kings basically ruled the city-state of London through the aldermen and the guilds the aldermen supervised. The city council was essentially a collective organ of the guild leaders. The mayors, chancellors (chief financial officers), and aldermen of the city council usually came from the ranks of guild leaders, and the kings gave the London guild leaders a great deal of autonomy if they served his general purposes and provided him with the loans he desired.[15]

The foreign trade merchant guilds were, of course, especially crucial because they played such an important role in ensuring that the king received customs revenue and "loans." Yet we should not exaggerate their power. The one realm of London's economy in which the kings involved themselves was the relations of the English and foreign merchants, especially those of Hanseatic League, Italy, and Gascony. The kings often overrode the wishes of the English merchants in this crucial area because they could play foreign merchants against local ones.

In addition, the London merchants played an important role in providing revenue to the kings. They made loans that surely were an advance on customs duties that they had had a role in collecting in increasing amounts. Before the consolidation of London as a capital, the tariff on the shipments of wine from Gascony in France consisted of casks of wine given to the king. The French wine may have been the model for much future taxation because the king's palaces at Westminster and Windsor required enormous amounts of food and other supplies.

Many scholars have criticized the king for using his personal household in providing naval ships with food and supplies for war, but N.A.M. Rodger

[14] Nightingale, "The Growth of London," p. 89.

[15] See the long discussion in Myers, *London in the Age of Chaucer*, pp. 86–146. An earlier generation of scholars wrote a large number of works on the guilds, individually and collectively. For a bibliography, see pp. 218–20.

cautioned that supplying Windsor and Westminster with food was a comparable task and no other group had similar administrative experience in this realm.

The domestic guilds functioned in the same way as the better-known foreign trade guilds. Each was offered a monopoly position in the economy at the wholesale level in return for performing government functions such as collecting taxes, maintaining some price controls, policing the behavior of their own members, and providing police protection for their own businesses. They also built infrastructure and adjudicated disputes within and between the guilds. Again, it is unclear how much of the taxes from London took the form of supplies provided to Windsor, Westminster, and the navy as a tax in kind.

It is important to remember the reality of the city-state when we generalize about England and its dominant coalitions prior to the Tudor period. The king did not have a single dominant coalition as he tried to govern. Inside the city-state, his dominant coalition was composed of guild leaders, the leaders of neighboring towns, a few major landowners, key local bishops of the Catholic Church (themselves and probably the main landlords), and, most of all, the main Italian and Hanseatic merchants.

The city-state was ruled by a real stationary bandit, as defined by Mancur Olson. Inside of it, the king had a predominance of force and the ability to tax that was maintained by personalistic methods. The lands to the north of London were a different matter and are discussed later, but in England outside the city-state, the dominant coalitions of the different kings centered on groupings of regional warlords.

The Hanseatic League as a Key Member of Edward III's Dominant Coalition

As we will see, the kings of the city-state of London had quite limited power vis-à-vis the warlords in the interior prior to 1485. Their vaunted ability to tax these lords during wartime was, we have argued, little more than trying to persuade the lords to send troops and supplies to seek booty with them in France, Scotland, and Ireland.

Yet we still are left with a mystery about the London city-state. Although many comparative scholars think that the Castilian kings of this period were more successful in raising taxes than the English, the great specialist on pre-Tudor finances, G. L. Harriss, disagrees. He argues that England shifted from "domainal to tax revenues" in the period from 1290 to 1340. While Harriss acknowledged that "the tax state was also emerging in other

European kingdoms," he concluded that "England was notable for both the volume and proportion of its tax income and its sophisticated system of public finance."[16]

Harriss's judgment about the English tax system does not, in fact, contradict what has been said in the first paragraph of this section. He is not referring to the ability of the kings to collect inland taxes from the lords. Rather, he is talking about the kings' successful collection of customs duties, especially on exported wool and woolen cloth. The export tax on raw wool was quite high.

Yet how did the king collect the export tax? If all the major rivers of England converged on London and emptied into the Atlantic as they do at Buenos Aires in Argentina, this would be easy to understand. In reality, London is an inland port, and England is a land of many rivers. London was well-placed vis-à-vis the Rhine, the main route for luxury goods from the Mediterranean. That is why the Romans established a capital there.[17] It was not, however, the normal route to Flanders from most areas of England. Geography "dictated" that most producers should use rivers other than the Thames to ship their wool directly to Flanders. In fact, they continued to do so after the king imposed the high export taxes.

But since the king did not have enough force (or "consent," if you will) to extract large internal taxes, how did he get the "consent" of the lords to pay large wool export taxes? How did he prevent them from evading the wool export duties with smuggling? The answer, we argue, is the alliance that the kings made with the strongest armed fleet in the area, the Hanseatic League. Products for Italy went through southern ports.

Originally, Edward III created "staples" in different places in England (fixed places to which goods had to be brought for taxation). In 1348 he then created a single staple for tin, lead, and woolen cloth in Calais, the last piece of land that England owned on the continent. In 1363, raw wool was added to the products that had to be delivered to the Calais staple.[18]

The merchant guild for the export of wool and woolen cloth was formalized as the Company of the Staple and that for woolen cloth as the Company

[16] Harriss, *Shaping the Nation*, p. 58. This book is Harriss's summary work, published when he was 80.

[17] Nightingale, "The Growth of London," pp. 91–2.

[18] For more on the Company of the Staple, see Ephraim Lipson, *The Economic History of England* (London: A. & C. Black, 1956), Vol. 1, pp. 560–72; for the Merchant Adventurers, Vol. 2, pp. 196–269. See E. M. Carus-Wilson, *Medieval Merchant Ventures: Collected Studies* (London: Metheun, 1954), pp. 149–50; George B. Hotchkiss, "Introduction," in John Wheeler, *A Treatise of Commerce* (New York: New York University Press, 1931), 18–21.

of Merchant Adventurers of London. When the amount of woolen cloth exported was small, the Company of the Staple often handled it as well, but the expansion of the wool cloth trade produced a sharp differentiation between the two.

The king still faced an obvious problem. Especially when he insisted on a very high export tariff, producers and shippers had a strong self-interest to trade directly with Flanders across the English Channel to avoid taxation. He would have called this trade smuggling. How did the monarch in his inland capital of London gain control over the flow of wool and woolen goods to Flanders from the estates of powerful warlords who also controlled the ports of England's other rivers?

Indeed, even small shippers near the mouth of the Thames who sailed in the English Channel had an interest in carrying untaxed wool to the continent. When the Crown raised tariffs to high levels after the Glorious Revolution of 1688, this introduced "the grand adventurous epoch of the smuggler." Even the Royal Navy engaged in smuggling, and techniques used by the smugglers near the mouth of the Thames are described at length in E. Keble Chatterton's *King's Cutters and Smugglers*.[19]

The first answer is that the king came to let independent shippers carry wool from a variety of ports to the town of Calais where it was taxed. But this only begs the question: how did the king force the shippers to go to Calais instead of some port where they could have avoided the tariff?

The instinctive answer is that the king must have had a navy that prevented smuggling. The surface evidence seemingly supports this answer: Henry III mobilized 288 ships for military action in 1230, Edward I 305 ships in 1297, and Edward III 300 ships in 1340, 224 ships in 1341, and 738 ships in 1347.[20]

Yet England did not have a state navy of any size. A leading historian of the British navy began his book with an unambiguous statement: "Medieval England was not a sea power."[21] The Crown's "navy" was composed of the fishing ships and other small ships that carried goods across the Channel, precisely the ships most likely to engage in smuggling. How were they controlled in peacetime?

[19] E. Keble Chatterton, *King's Cutters and Smugglers: The Revenue Service and the War against Smuggling* (Philadelphia: J. B. Lippincott, 1912), pp. 1, 38, and 40. The techniques of the smugglers are found on pp. 40–5.

[20] Archibald Lewis and Timothy Runyan, *European Naval and Maritime History, 300–1500* (Bloomington: Indiana University Press, 1985), pp. 119, 123–4, and 130.

[21] David Loades, *England's Maritime Empire: Seapower, Commerce, and Policy, 1490–1690* (Harlow: Longman, 2000), p. 1.

As we have seen, sea trade was conducted in armed ships that were capable not only of defending themselves, but also of attacking others. The Hanseatic League followed a similar path in the 1100s after its members acquired the larger sailing ships needed for trade away from the shore. These ships were armed with cannons for self-defense – and for attack. By the end of the 1300s, the Hanseatic League had a shipping capacity of 60,000 tons, 20,000 of it in the Baltic Sea and 20,000 in its North Sea trade with Flanders and England. This made it "the leading naval power of the period."[22]

With naval power came a broader political role. As Douglas Bisson notes, the Hanseatic League "attained the diplomatic status usually reserved for a sovereign power."[23] Although the League was originally and ostensibly for mutual production, it naturally happened that the members sometimes used their power for aggression as well. They were in a position to dictate – and *did* dictate – to Scandinavian princes, and they aimed to exercise a monopoly of trading along the northern coasts.

In the process, the League used its ships to protect the ports with which it was trading and to strengthen the domestic political role of the leaders with whom it had a close and profitable relationship. In the 1200s, the Hanseatic League's dominance of trade in the North Sea gave it the same role in English trade to the north of Europe, especially that through the eastern ports that were closest to the Baltic Sea. These were precisely the ports whose wool trade Edward III had the greatest difficulty in taxing. He solved his problem by making an alliance with the Hanseatic League, in the form of a two-part agreement.

First, they would play a key role, direct or indirect, in the collection of the export duty on wool and wool cloth sent to Flanders from the staples at Calais. Calais was 70 miles from Bruges, the commercial center of Flanders that was dominated by the Hanseatic League. Like the Italians, who handled trade with Italy, the Hanseatic merchants made "loans and gifts to needy English kings" in pre-payments that were secured by future customs payments.

The Hanseatic League would use its powerful fleet to ensure that small English ships would sail their ships only to Calais where the wool and woolen cloth would be unloaded and taxed. The League had every incentive to do so. Smugglers would undercut the League's monopoly profits, and the League merchants surely were somehow given a portion of the duties they

22 Philippe Dollinger, *The German Hansa* (New York: Macmillan, 1970), pp. 23, 49–50, and 55–8.

23 Norman J. G. Pounds, *An Economic History of Medieval Europe* (London: Longman, 1974), p. 384; Douglas Bisson, *The Merchant Adventurers of England: Company and the Crown, 1474–1564* (Newark: University of Delaware Press, 1993), p. 48.

were collecting. In return, the League was given "an exceptionally strong position from the thirteenth to the fifteenth century" in English commerce. In the words of George Hotchkiss:[24]

> Their commercial influence may be judged from the fact that they occupied the Steelyard ... a place of commanding importance in the commerce of the City.... They obtained special privileges. The most important was the privilege of exporting and importing at a very low rate which was less than other merchants, even English merchants, had to pay. With this privilege the Hanseatic merchants naturally acquired an increasing proportion of England's commerce.

In short, Edward III solved his major collective action problem by creating a strong economic incentive for the most powerful military force in the area to protect him, help him collect his taxes, and increase his income-producing commerce. Of course, the Hanseatic League had no interest in spending resources to help the king impose and collect internal taxes, but this only gave the king an interest in concentrating his attention on the city-state and its foreign trade.

The kings naturally wanted to satisfy the major domestic interests if the cost was not too high. The two most important interests with respect to the export tariff on wool and woolen cloth were the landlords and the domestic merchants and shippers. Members of the domestic elite were deeply concerned about one key question. Who was really going to pay the largest share of the export customs duty – the sheep owners through lower prices they received for their wool, the merchants through lower profits, or the foreign purchasers?

Edward III took several steps to try to reassure these domestic interests. First, he denied the export-import merchants a monopoly in the domestic purchase of wool and woolen cloth. Hence the profits of this trade were spread broadly among domestic traders and ensured that competitive market pressures among them determined the prices for the producers.

Second, Edward let small-scale English shippers and merchants participate in the transportation of wool and woolen cloth across the Channel. Not only were English merchants and shippers given control of the internal wool trade, but small English shippers usually performed the physical task of carrying the wool across the Channel once Calais became the major staple.

In the 1300s and 1400s, Englishmen dominated the merchant community in sheer numbers, but this fact can be misleading. Most were the small shippers who were always required to bring the wool and woolen cloth to Calais, and they were not the dominant ones.

[24] Hotchkiss, "Introduction," pp. 15–17.

Third, Edward III reassured the producers by charging a nominal export duty of only 2% on woolen cloth and by establishing a prohibitive import duty to protect English cloth producers from foreign competition. The tariff meant that woolen cloth had 5.5 times the value of wool for the producers. If the rural lords thought the tariff was lowering the price of wool excessively, they could always turn it into woolen cloth on their estates and pay almost no export tariff.[25]

In the past, historians thought that Parliament – that is, the representatives of the rural elite – was deeply involved in the negotiations about the export duties, but modern historians believe these negotiations actually took place in meetings of merchants. The negotiations did not prove that the king had to yield to the merchants on crucial questions. Negotiations and compromises are always part of politics, as are rulers' decisions that accommodate the interests and desires of others. Power matters in the determination of outcomes reached in negotiations. It matters in determining what people "consent" to. When the kings were backed by the ships of the Hanseatic League, they had power vis-à-vis the lords, but only on issues that mattered to the League.

It would be misleading to characterize the outcome as the result of the "consent of the governed" or of negotiations within a "dominant coalition" (unless perhaps between the League and the king). The lords who did not consent to pay internal taxes did not suddenly embrace a high wool export tax willingly. Domestic merchants surely would have preferred to have no export tax, and they absolutely did not want foreign merchants to have such a dominant role in the London commercial community.

The English King and the Lords of the Interior

England, as we have seen, was really composed of two "countries" from the 1260s to 1485, and they each had different dominant coalitions. One England was the city-state of London. It had a strong king based on a coalition of guild leaders, including Italian merchants and especially Hanseatic ones in London, and it was gradually becoming quite well governed.

[25] For a succinct summary of the changes under Edward III, see Ormrod, *The Reign of Edward III*, pp. 181–94. For the short-term changes between 1350 and 1383, see Alice Beardwood, *Alien Merchants in England 1350–1377: Their Legal and Economic Position* (Cambridge: Medieval Academy of America, 1931), p. 28. There is a debate on whether Edward III had a protectionist purpose as well as a revenue one. See Lipson, *The Economic History of England*, p. 455, footnote 6.

The other England comprised the rest of England and Wales. It was ruled by a dominant coalition of regional warlords of mini-states. The warlord of the mini-state of London was the strongest, but outside the city-state he still was a weak king, except on the issue of export taxes. The larger England essentially remained a pre–nation-state with continued conflict and war over who would be king and obtain the income from the export tariffs, the king's lands, and the city-state. That changed only with Henry VII's victory over Richard III in 1485.

It is striking how different this bifurcated image of England is from the traditional political histories of England. The historians of England say almost nothing about the role of the king in ruling London, but treat the capital as if it were somehow ruled by itself. Instead the historians focus on the king's relations with the lords and the various pretenders. The pages of their books are filled with conflict, intrigues, murders, executions, and land confiscation.

As John Gillingham emphasizes, this is particularly true of the 1400s, a century whose difficulties have often been exaggerated because of the Tudor propaganda that was expressed in Shakespeare's plays.[26] In the 1300s and 1400s the government was gradually becoming stronger, and the legitimacy of the king's rules and taxes was becoming more accepted. An article on the religious taxes noted that they were regularly collected no matter what battles were occurring at the top.[27]

As was the case in Castile, the power of the king varied with the distance over which it had to be exercised. The Castilian king in the northern plateau had less power in the areas 300 to 400 miles to the south than in the northern plateau. In like manner the English king was at his weakest 200 to 300 miles to the north of London. Frequent wars and mini-wars, both offensive and defensive, were fought along the border with Scotland (and also with Wales to the west). As a result the lords on the borders needed to be able to mobilize substantial military force against the Scots. They could also use it against each other and against the king, and they did both.

Scholars emphasize that the legend of Robin Hood, even if not true, accurately depicts the reality of the English political system of the time:

[26] John Gillingham, *The Wars of the Roses: Peace and Conflict in Fifteenth-Century England* (London: Weidenfeld and Nicolson, 1981), pp. 1–8.

[27] A. K. McHardy, "Clerical Taxation in Fifteenth Century: The Clergy as Agents of the Crown," in Barrie Dobson, ed., *The Church, Politics, and Patronage in the Fifteenth Century* (Gloucester, UK: Alan Sutton, 1984), pp. 168–89. For the explicit statement about the lack of impact of changes either in kings or dynasties, see p. 178.

"the problem of the north [of England]; at first of maintenance and misgovernment at their worst, of border and baronial warfare; later of medieval survivals."[28]

The internal evidence of our version of the legend of Robin Hood allows it to be dated to 1323. Robin Hood met king "Edward," but Edward I and Edward III never visited Nottingham. Edward II visited the area only once in his life – in 1323. Edward's governor, the sheriff, clearly had no real control over Nottingham at that time. The three Edwards ruled from 1274 to 1377, and Nottingham, although only 125 miles from London, was too remote to be administered effectively – or even to be visited more than once in a century.[29]

The situation remained much the same in the 1400s, especially in areas still farther north. The houses of Lancaster and York in the 1400s were both based in northern regions, and Gerald Harriss casually wrote of "the remote and lawless north and west" in 1450.[30] Even the English Civil War of the 1640s began when a Scottish army invaded to prevent Charles II's attempt to impose a prayer book on the Scottish church. The northern armies did not resist.

Without a large standing army or even a significant armed merchant fleet, the king did not have the power to prevent a coalition of lords from trying to overthrow him and gain control of his lands and customs revenue. That changed only after Henry VII and Henry VIII systematically reduced the military power of the lords and killed almost any conceivable claimant to the throne from competing genealogical lines. As we will see, however, the process was completed only in the first decades of the 1700s.

The historians who studied the governing process from 1265 to 1485 – and especially from 1377 to 1485 – traditionally provided an extremely detailed account of the struggles for power among individual lords or royal favorites. The books were organized decade by decade – or reign by reign – and the authors focused on the reasons for the rise and fall of particular kings. This older literature also devoted a great deal of detailed attention to the issue of taxation. Scholars generally agreed that the king was able to raise more taxes during war, primarily for the struggles to

[28] J. C. Holt, "The Origins and Audience of the Ballads of Robin Hood," in Stephen Knight, ed., *Robin Hood: An Anthology of Scholarship and Criticism* (Woodbridge: D. S. Brewer, 1999), p. 212.

[29] For the dating, see Joseph Hunter, "Robin Hood," in Knight, *Robin Hood*, pp. 187–91.

[30] Harriss, *Shaping the Nation*, p. 632.

conquer Wales, Ireland, and Scotland and to regain the old Norman lands in France.[31]

We would, however, reemphasize the point with which we began the introduction to this book. The 220 years from 1265 to 1485 were a very long time. That is the length of time from George Washington's second term in office to 2014. It would be foolish to generalize about the structure of power in America over that period as a whole or even assume that a generalization about one president applied to another only a few decades earlier or later. Yet generalizations about late medieval England often are based on evidence drawn from different years that are many decades or even centuries apart.

We need to remember that the tax revenue system and different merchant groups, foreign and domestic, could vary from year to year.[32] The same is true of regional conflict. As a result, the literatures both on taxes and on regional conflict usually correspond to the cliché about the forest and the trees. A comparative scholar who tries to summarize the changing patterns over this long period requires the mastery of a level of detail that is impossible for a comparative book of this time span.

As a result, we limit ourselves in this book to several broad generalizations about the relationship between London and the inland provinces from 1265 to 1485, and we can advance several of them only as hypotheses. Our most basic hypothesis is that, except for its city-state capital, medieval England seems much more like medieval Spain than the literature suggests – or that we ourselves appreciated well into our research. It may be recalled that we accepted the judgment of Peter Linehan that Castile was "a society organized for war [before 1262] … [which then] was disorganized by war."[33] The same generalization applied to England in the 1300s and 1400s.

The Castilian provincial city-states built up military force in order to drive the Muslims out of the Iberian Peninsula. The regional Castilian warlords who joined the king's war paid for their own forces and supplies, and they gave 20% of the loot to the king. If one so desires, both the warlords' self-financing contributions to the war and the king's booty could be visualized

[31] Scholars in recent decades have concentrated far more on social and cultural history. For an excellent survey of the history of this period based on this new literature, see Miri Rubin, *The Hollow Crown: A History of Britain in the Late Middle Ages* (London: Penguin Books, 2006). As an example of the change in focus, Rubin's book, the book on this period in a multi-volume Penguin books series on the history of England, discussed the reign of Edward III without even mentioning the wool export tax or the Hanseatic League.

[32] For an excellent sense of this variation in the foreign trade realm over just a few decades, see Beardwood, *Alien Merchants in England, 1350–77.*

[33] Peter Linehan, *Spain, 1157–1300: A Partible Inheritance* (Oxford: Blackwell, 2008), p. xi.

as taxes to support his war effort, but no one tries to visualize Castilian history in that way.

Even after the looting of the Muslims became impossible after the 1260s, the city-states retained their military force and used it against each other and the king. The fighting could be especially fierce and prolonged during succession crises. This was what Linehan meant when he said that a society organized by war led to a society disorganized by it.

It is not at all conventional to "see" English history in these terms. The financing of English forces in France, Scotland, and Ireland are always described as additional taxes paid to the king during wartime. It would be just as appropriate – and probably more realistic – to say that, as in Castile, the lords were usually investing in troops and supplies in hopes of gaining more booty (including land) than they expended to obtain it.

One of the major English historians of a half-century ago, Ernest Jacob, asserted that "to the 15th century the inducement of immediate gain by successful warfare was always more compelling than remoter considerations of economic security or political achievement." The kings received their share.[34]

More recently, historians have focused more on the myths, rituals, and legitimization associated with war. Miri Rubin, for example, concludes that war "could become a way of life, a quite intoxicating one. There was just enough glory and self-approbation in the wars in France to encourage those who needed it to seek justification in the culture of chivalry fostered in and around knightly families." Yet, Rubin was quite aware of the other goals of war and described some of them in detail:

> To be sustainable the French wars had to meet some of the expectations of the political communities of England and Wales. Rewards came in the form of war spoils, booty which flowed into the coffers and pockets of captains, and which also trickled down to lesser men. The booty had a way of making itself seen and known in the regions from which fighting men originated. Women boasted cushions, garments, hangings and jewellery which had previously adorned the persons or the chambers of French matrons.

A chronicler wrote that "a woman who did not possess spoil from France – garments, furs, bed covers, silver vessels and cloth of linen – was of no account."[35] The troops not only seized movable property but also

[34] E. F. Jacob, *The Fifteenth Century, 1399–1485* (Oxford: Oxford University Press, 1961), p. 202 (paperback).

[35] Rubin, *The Hollow Crown*, pp. 82–3. The chronicler statement is found in Barbara W. Tuchman, *A Distant Mirror: The Calamitous 14th Century* (New York: Knopf, 1978), p. 186. The statement is in an entire chapter on the looting and hostage taking by both sides.

personnel of the enemy for purposes of ransom. In the mid-1300s, King Jean of France was held for a fortune, and the ransoms for lesser French officers and men were proportionately lower. The ransom paid for an archer was two pounds. Geoffrey Chaucer was in France in the household of the second son of the king when he was captured. His ransom was 16 pounds. A lord ransomed his dead horse for 6 pounds, 13 shillings, and 4 pence, presumably for the equipment on it.[36]

When Henry V won the great battle of Agincourt in 1415, he captured more prisoners than there were soldiers in his own army. Thinking that French reinforcements were coming, he ordered that his prisoners, including a large number of noble officers who awaited distribution to English units, be killed. "There were cries of protest in the army at the loss of so many valuable ransoms."[37]

If seen in these terms, a broad difference between the 1300s and 1400s in England is much more explicable. Successful phases of the Hundred Years' War were quite profitable, but, even in the 1300s, peace meant that men who had enriched themselves in looting came home. They often did not want to return to the life of the poor. Tuchman describes the situation after the peace treaty of 1360:[38]

> The plunderers of France brought home the habit of brigandage. Many in the invasion forces had been outlaws and criminals to begin with who had joined up for a promised pardon. Others were made lawless and violent by the approved daily practice in France. Returning home, some formed companies in imitation of their fellows who had stayed in France. "Arrayed as for war," they robbed and assaulted travelers, took captives, held villages for ransom, killed, mutilated, and spread terror.

Even though Edward II was eventually overthrown by troops supporting his wife and son, an outsider has the impression of a fair amount of stability from 1265 to 1377 when Edward III died. Henry III lived until 1272, when he died a natural death after a 56-year reign, and his son Edward I ruled for 35 years. Even the murdered Edward II was king for 20 years, while his son, Edward III, had a 50-year reign. All these successions were natural and uncontested.

Then in the slightly more than 100 years from Edward III's death in 1377 until Henry VII's military victory in 1485, there were seven kings, but nine

[36] Tuchman, *A Distant Mirror*, pp. 187–93.

[37] Jacob, *The Fifteenth Century*, p. 156. On the previous page, Jacob reports that the French had plundered the English baggage.

[38] Tuchman, *A Distant Mirror*, p. 195.

reigns, as two overthrown kings were restored. Four of the kings seem to have been murdered, while a fifth was rumored to have been poisoned. A sixth died on the battlefield in France.

Only one of the kings from 1377 to 1485, Edward IV (1461–1483), had a long and productive reign, but even his reign was interrupted for ten months when Henry VI was returned to the throne in a coup. Whatever the causes and effects, the successions were quite unsettled. Different lords, most famously those associated with the Lancaster line and the York line, respectively, engaged in continuous plots, rebellions, and battles to gain power – and the property of those who were defeated and often executed.[39]

A scholar who tries to look at these micro-events from afar is drawn to two facts. The first is the already-mentioned distance between London and the north where the warfare with Scotland and Ireland was centered. Lancaster and York were both in the north and had major landholdings that would support the necessary military forces.[40]

The second obvious fact about the 1300s and 1400s is the Hundred Years' War with France from 1337 to 1453. When the war was going well for Britain (or was replaced by successful wars on the northern and western borders), the domestic conflicts inside England seemed to diminish. They seemed to increase during periods of peace or of English losses.

Without any doubt, the 1400s were a period of financial difficulty for the Crown. Part of the problem was the decline in the export of raw wool on which a high export tax was imposed and a rise in the export of wool cloth on which a much lower export tax was imposed (see Table 3.1). The decline in the power of the Hanseatic League also limited the power of the king until Henry VIII and Elizabeth I began to build a navy and merchant fleet.

But another part of the answer was the course of the war or wars. If a war was going well, those who financed the war were gaining booty and potential booty. The war itself became inexpensive because the troops lived off the land by seizing what they wanted from the local population. Henry V (1413–1422) was having substantial success when he died of dysentery in France on the battlefield. If he had lived, the map of Europe might have

[39] For a good summary of the conflicts between the House of Lancaster and the House of York in the 1400s, and on the background of these conflicts, see S. B. Chrimes, *Lancastrians, Yorkists, and Henry VII* (London: Macmillan, 1966). For Edmund's property and its fate, see pp. 15–20. Also see Anthony Tuck, *Crown and Nobility 1272–1461* (Oxford: Blackwell, 1986).

[40] Anthony Goodman and Anthony Tuck, eds., *War and Border Societies in the Middle Ages* (London: Routledge, 1992).

Table 3.1. *Export of wool and wool cloth, 1371–1500, bags of wool and equivalent cloth, selected decades*

Decade	Wool	Wool cloth
1371–1388	23,241	3,432
1401–1410	13,922	7,651
1441–1450	9,398	11,803
1491–1500	8,149	13,891

Source: A. R. Bridbury, *Economic Growth: England in the Later Middle Ages* (London: G. Allen & Unwin, 1962), p. 32.

been quite different, and the English lords might have received a great deal of land in present-day France. When the war went badly, however, the war in Normandy would cease to be self-financing. If so, enthusiasm for the war faded and complaints about the king's "taxes" increased.[41]

Peace could also produce financial difficulties for the king because of the lack of revenue from a successful war. This was one of the problems both when Henry IV overthrew Richard II and when he himself tried to rule. Unrest faded when Henry V became king and was successful against the French, but after he died, the French reversed the course of the war. In 1353, the Hundred Years' War finally ended. In 1355, the War of the Roses began.

When war was replaced by peace, the lords who were hoping for loot and booty abroad now had to obtain it from each other. If the lords had had a single estate with a strong castle, England might have been stable, but the property of a family was often widely scattered as the family acquired land from the king or other lords. In addition, the lords began to build elegant mansions instead of easily defended castles, and they could not defend their land if they were defeated in battle.[42]

The end of the Hundred Years' War also meant that there were large numbers of soldiers and knights who had been on salary and/or had been paid through booty, and who were now without employment and income. The result was similar to what Barbara Tuchman saw in the 1300s. After 1453, as David Loades states, "no trouble-maker, great or small, had any difficulty in raising an armed and turbulent following."[43]

41 Jacob, *The Fifteenth Century*, pp. 205 and 256. Jacob quotes Richard Ager Newhall, *The English Conquest of Normandy 1416–1424: A Study in Fifteenth Century Warfare* (Westerham, UK: Russell & Russell, 1971), pp. 150–1.

42 Gillingham, *The War of the Roses*, p. 1.

43 David Loades, *Politics and Nation, England 1450–1660*, 5th ed. (Oxford: Blackwell, 1999), p. 53.

The most surprising thing about the late 1400s was that Henry V's 1485 military coup brought this conflict to an end. Many did not expect it at the time, and many tried to overthrow Henry in his first years in office. Part of the answer is that Henry tried to create a broader coalition of regional lords by distributing patronage to a number of families rather than just relying on a few families on one side or another. This was symbolized by his agreement as a Lancastrian to marry Elizabeth of York.

More basically, however, the Tudors were gradually able to disarm the lords or at least ensure that their force would not be used in domestic wars. This, first of all, resulted from the transformation of war that the Hundred Years' War produced. The knights and military armaments that the lords had used became ineffective as guns became more widespread. The lords could no longer afford the new weapons and defensive measures that were necessary.

Nevertheless, as we see in the next two chapters, it took a century for the Tudors to gradually reduce the power and influence of the old feudal magnates and their families. They increased the power of the lesser rural elite (the gentry) during the 1500s and 1600s and began building a powerful, armed navy-merchant alliance. It still took more than 200 years before England of the 1700s began to have a modern-appearing dominant coalition that included elites based on government, military, and non-government bureaucracies. Douglass North is right. Time matters, and development takes an enormous number of decades and even centuries.

Isabella's Creation of an Early Corporate State

Precisely at the same time as Henry VII was ending the combination of a well-governed city-state of London and a pre-state in England as a whole, Isabella was beginning to create Castile's first real state. Isabella consolidated her power in Castile in 1480, and like Henry VII, she came to power in the wake of a military victory. Her victory, however, came at the end of five years of Civil War in which she had the military support of Aragon and her opponent had that of Portugal.

Henry VII and Isabella shared something else in common. Henry wanted an alliance with Spain, and in 1501 he pursued this goal by having his heir apparent marry Isabella and Ferdinand's daughter, Catherine of Aragon. Henry VIII's unsuccessful attempt to have the pope annul his marriage with Catherine in the 1520s led to his break with the Catholic Church.

This book does not, however, try to compare Isabella and Henry VII. In broader historical perspective, Isabella and her successors in the 1500s and

1600s had a political role and power more like Henry III (1216–1272) and his immediate successors. This book compares her with the men who were building an early state in London.

Henry VII and his heir were able to consolidate London's control over the rest of England in relatively few decades. Isabella was ending a century of repeated near-chaos and trying to create a state in a "country" that still had no capital or meaningful government bureaucracy. She did very well in her 24-year reign, but another 200 years would elapse before Spain was ready to create a minimally effective government.

In Castile, the leaders of the city-states had become accustomed both to great autonomy and to deep involvement in prolonged succession struggles. Isabella came to power with the support of the city-states in the northern sheep areas, the Mesta, and the city-states associated with Aragon in the east. Her chief opponents were to the south, including the three major military-economic religious orders south of Toledo, and they wanted a policy oriented toward Portugal. Perhaps they ultimately wanted the union of Castile with Portugal and, therefore with the Tagus River, which ran from Toledo to Madrid.

After her victory, Isabella strengthened the Mesta and, perhaps most important, took over the three religious orders and placed them under Ferdinand's control. This ensured that the couple would receive the income from these lands.

We have argued that the size of Castilian territory was a major obstacle to the formation of an effective state, especially since there was not a city-state capital with easy access to the sea. Isabella only worsened the problem. Since Ferdinand continued to rule Aragon as an autonomous unit while Isabella was queen of Castile, the alliance of the two did not increase her problems of domestic governance. Nevertheless, Aragon's control of Sicily and Naples to the west thrust the Spanish kings into the international relations of the Mediterranean. The Turkish fleet became a special concern.

In the long run, however, the Spanish kings could not create a minimally effective Spanish state until they created a bureaucracy that brought Aragon under their administrative control. This posed much greater problems for her successors than for Isabella. Aragon was not subjected to a bureaucracy in Madrid until the early 1700s, and the kings did not consider it wise even to create a common flag until 1785.

Isabella also made her own task of governing Castile more complex by several decisions that extended Castilian responsibilities south of Toledo and beyond. The Castilian monarchs had based themselves in the northern plateau where the migrating sheep were sheared and where their wool was exchanged for European consumer goods. Yet this base of power gave the monarchs only tenuous control over the great port of Seville and the estates in the valley of the Guadalquivir River 400 miles to the south.

Isabella expanded her territory by conquering Granada, the last Muslim outpost on the Iberian Peninsula, and by attacking the Jews and Moors who were particularly strong in that area. She completed this task in 1492 and expelled all the Jews and Moors in Spain or forced those permitted to stay to convert to Catholicism. This served to emphasize that Catholicism that was one of the few bases of national unity for the city-states, but it also gave her only real bureaucracy, the Catholic Church, greater power in the south.

Isabella's decision to send Columbus on his voyage in 1492 also likely had national implications: if he found a new route to India, the discovery would help to create a sense of national identity and pride. Instead, she created a new administrative problem, since the resulting and unanticipated colonies became the personal property of the sovereign. Isabella herself did not give much attention to the colonies, nor did the next two monarchs. This changed when major silver deposits were discovered in the 1540s what are now Mexico and Bolivia.

By 2005, Douglass North had abandoned his argument that the pre-1480 Castilian kings had established bureaucratic control over Castile prior to the victory of Isabella. Nevertheless, he still believed that Isabella had succeeded in creating "a centralized monarchy and resultant bureaucracy." He thought that this "centralized political control of the economy and monopoly privileges" was a major cause of poor economic performance or even ultimate economic decline in the 1500s and 1600s.[44]

Whatever the cause of Castile's poor economic performance, modern scholars agree that Isabella did not actually create "a centralized monarchy and resultant bureaucracy." Without doubt, however, she did reintroduce order, and the troops that supported her in the Civil War could be ruthless against her opponents.[45] Although she formed specialized councils that included more lawyers (*letrados*), she did not create a real bureaucracy or a capital in which bureaucratic headquarters could be placed.

Instead, Isabella continued to rule as an itinerant monarch. She "did not stop her peregrinations even during her pregnancies. Her workdays became slower and shorter when she was close to giving birth, but they were not

[44] Douglass North, *Understanding the Process of Economic Change* (Princeton, NJ: Princeton University Press, 2005), pp. 134 and 143.

[45] See Marvin Lunenfeld, *Council of Santa Hermandad: A Study of the Pacification Forces of Ferdinand and Isabella* (Miami, FL: University of Miami Press, 1970).

interrupted. Only the gravest illnesses stopped her travels."[46] Since Isabella did not have a capital in which to build important bureaucracies, she began by relying on and strengthening corporate organs like the Catholic Church, the Mesta, and the foreign trade merchant guilds (*consulados*). Each was a specialized tax collector – the church for the tithe, the Mesta for the de facto tariffs on the migrating sheep, and the *consulados* for other tariffs. In effect, Isabella was using these corporate organs as tax farmers.

The most successful corporate organization built by Isabella was a more centralized Catholic Church. She created the Inquisition in 1480, the very year in which she brought the war for succession to an end. Stanley and Barbara Stein report that "although operating with some autonomy . . . [the Inquisition] exercised its authority in tandem with the state." The Steins saw this continuing into the 18th century.[47]

The Inquisition was probably less intended to intimidate heretics than to frighten the regional bishops into a more submissive posture. Isabella was able to force Rome to give her the power to appoint the top church officials, including those in the colonies. As we saw, she gained personal control of the three great "monasteries" that stretched across central Castile from west to east – Alcántara, Calatrava, and Santiago.[48]

The Mesta had been one of Isabella's major pillars of support in the Civil War, and it continued to be a principal collector of taxes on the migrating sheep and their wool. It regulated relations between the migrating sheep owners, the city-states, and individual agricultural communities. Some used to see the Mesta as a great spoiler of agriculture, but this view was much exaggerated. The city-state nobles had a self-interest both in sheep migration and the land that produced food for their cities. This led them to be sensitive to both interests and to build well-defined paths for the sheep in their migration. Too many stereotypes about the Mesta came from court cases that arose when the normal accommodation broke down. As Mark Kishlansky warned in quite another context, "Studying marriages by concentrating on divorce [records] might lead to the conclusion that the basic

46 Patricio de Forteza, Norah Ramos, and María Estela González de Fauve, "Desplazamientos de la corte castellana: Notas para su estudio," *Estudios de historia de España* 3 (1990), p. 31.

47 Henry Kamen, *The Spanish Inquisition: A Historical Revision* (New Haven, CT: Yale University Press, 1998), pp. 45 and 55; Stanley Stein and Barbara Stein, *Apogee of Empire: Spain and New Spain in the Age of Charles III, 1759–1789* (Baltimore, MD: Johns Hopkins University Press, 2003), p. 32. See Benzoin Netanyahu, *The Origins of the Inquisition in Fifteenth Century Spain* (New York: Random House, 1995).

48 See Helen Rawlings, *Church, Religion, and Society in Early Modern Spain* (New York: Palgrave, 2002).

tenets of matrimony are extreme mental and physical cruelty."[49] The sheep usually followed well-established trails.

Isabella also continued to use the city-states to collect the "sales taxes" that seem so impressive when they are described on paper in the legal codes but unimpressive when they are examined in the real world. As mentioned, Henry Kamen rightly describes Isabella's relations with the city-states in the language of international relations. In his words, she was forced to construct "an impressive series of alliances that achieved political stability without altering the traditional structures of power":[50]

> The civil wars had ended, but the kingdoms [of Castile and Aragon] continued to be beset by instability. The countryside was effectively in the hands of the nobles, warlords who controlled the rural economy and enjoyed the allegiance of thousands of vassals.... [Ferdinand and Isabella] made laws, but only through the traditional *Cortes* [parliament]; they raised taxes, but always with the consent of the [city-state] taxpayers; they punished crime, but only through the machinery that existed in the towns.... They ... diverted the militant spirit of the nobles into foreign war.

The last sentence really meant that Isabella and her successors had the nobles (city-states) send their troops abroad rather than leave them at home where they might be more of a threat. Yet, as Kamen emphasizes in mentioning "the traditional structures of power," the Castilian warlords, unlike their counterparts in England after 1485, retained their military force. This force constrained the kings until the 1700s.

In any case, the existence of the corporate organs did not show that Isabella had formed a centralized authoritarian state in the modern sense of the word. In fact, they showed the opposite. As one indicator of the continuing decentralization, the leaders of the key corporate organs were scattered in different cities of Castile. The church leadership was located in Toledo in the middle of the country while the Mesta headquarters were in Valladolid or Burgos in the north. The foreign trade *consulados* (guilds) were not organized by product or destination as in England, but each port had its own *consulado*. The one dealing with the colonies was centered in Seville to the south.

The role of the foreign trade *consulados* is difficult to judge, because Seville acquired such an important role in the colonies in the mid-1550s that English-language scholars concentrated their attention overwhelmingly on it. The *consulados* in the Mediterranean ports handled trade with

[49] Mark Kishlansky, *Parliamentary Selection: Social and Political Choice in Early Modern England* (Cambridge: Cambridge University Press, 1986), p. 76.

[50] Henry Kamen, *Empire: How Spain Became a World Power: 1492–1763* (New York: Harper Perennial, 2004), pp. 6–9, 11.

the central and eastern Mediterranean. Those in the ports on the Bay of Biscay and Burgos were in charge of trade with northern Europe. If exports and imports to northern Europe were taxed in the form of sales taxes on the northern plateau, it is possible that tariffs collected in northern *consulados* were mainly levied on other goods.[51]

The Early State of the Hapsburg Dynasty, 1521–1700

Isabella died in 1504, long before she could finish creating a strong state. Her husband, Ferdinand, continued to serve as king of Aragon, but he could not become more than regent in Castile. This severely limited what he could do in building a Castilian state or even in collecting taxes. In 1518, Ferdinand's successor "demanded a 'loan' from the Mesta of 3,500,000 maravedies and the following year demanded a direct subsidy after confiscating Mesta revenue records." This almost surely meant that the Mesta had not been paying full taxes to Ferdinand because of his regency status and that Charles, in effect, was demanding back taxes.[52]

Isabella and Ferdinand's grandson, Charles I, succeeded Ferdinand in 1516, but he was a Hapsburg heir on his father's side. He already ruled in the Netherlands and was soon elected emperor of the Holy Roman Empire. He concentrated his attention on his duty as emperor and spent most of his time outside Spain. Indeed, Charles usually is called Charles V, his title as emperor, because that was the role he emphasized.

Charles I gave little attention to the American colonies, and two figures in his budget indicate the meager attention he gave to Spain itself. The total annual salary of his counselors, treasury officials, and judges inside Castile was 38,000 ducats a year. The annual salary of his local officials was 4,300 ducats. In contrast, his embassies and diplomatic missions abroad cost 50,000 to 60,000 ducats a year.[53] Charles sometimes acted as if Castile and Aragon were the dowry his Spanish mother brought to the marriage to be a source of money for his wars in the Holy Roman Empire.[54]

[51] Robert Sidney Smith, *The Spanish Guild Merchant: A History of the Consulado, 1250–1700* (Durham, NC: Duke University Press, 1940), pp. 1–8 and 25–6. For Seville, see pp. 91–111; for the Mediterranean ports, pp. 46–56; and for the northern ports, pp. 67–90.

[52] Robert Ekelund and Robert Tollison, *Politicized Economies: Monarchy, Monopolies, and Mercantilism* (College Station: Texas A & M Press, 1997), p. 141.

[53] William Maltby, *The Reign of Charles V* (New York: Palgrave, 2002), p. 13 and 65.

[54] Marc Boone and Marisa Demoor, eds., *Charles V in Context* (Ghent: Ghent University, 2003); Glenn Richardson, *Renaissance Monarchy* (New York: Oxford University Press, 2002); Alain Saint-Saens, ed., *Young Charles V, 1500–1531* (New Orleans: University Press of the South, 2000).

Charles's son, Philip II, was brought up in Castile within the Castilian court. He learned Castilian as his native language and came to feel comfortable within Castilian culture. In 1543, his father made him regent of Castile, and he held that position until his father abdicated in 1556. When Charles I abdicated, Philip II's brother inherited his position in central Europe, and Philip became king of Spain, which at the time included the Low Countries.

Scholars agree that Philip II was far more of a transformative ruler than either his father or his three successors in the 1600s. When Philip came to power in 1556, he soon began to create a state by establishing a capital. In 1561, he chose the small town of Madrid. He invested a great deal of money in constructing buildings in the capital, and he staffed these buildings with bureaucrats.

Madrid had nothing to recommend it economically or geographically except that it was midway between Bilbao in the north and Granada in the south, and between Barcelona in the East and Lisbon in the West. Philip obviously did not think that he could put the capital in any of the major ports without alienating the others, and he chose Madrid as a "neutral site." In this respect, Philip's decision was similar to that of the American founders when they elected to create the new capital of Washington, DC.

Until 1700, Madrid was really only the capital of Castile. Neither Philip II nor his successors in the 1600s tried to administer Aragon from Madrid or even to integrate Castile and Aragon into a single common market. Castile and Aragon had separate laws, taxes, and languages. Tariffs were imposed on trade between the two regions. A trip between Madrid and Barcelona to the east required two weeks, while the trip between Madrid and Seville to the south took ten days. Mules were virtually the only form of transportation, and they could travel only 30 to 35 miles a day.[55]

Historians praise Philip II for his dedication to duty and for the scale of his involvement in the policy process. In understanding Philip, however, we need to distinguish between power exercised vis-à-vis others at the top and power exercised vis-à-vis the provinces. Philip was quite autocratic in his relations with those in Madrid, although not with the brutality of Henry VIII. Yet Philip did not really have autocratic powers over the city-states and the *Cortes* (parliament) that represented them. He had the ability to give orders, but he did not inherit or really develop an effective bureaucratic machinery to put these orders into effect.

One example of the lack of bureaucratic capability during the 1500s and 1600s is found in a realm especially important for a comparison of Spain

[55] James Casey, *Early Modern Spain: A Social History* (London: Routledge, 1999), pp. 12–14.

with England: the military realm. Most historians criticize Philip for spending too much time and treasure on wars abroad – and rightly so. When his subjects revolted in the Low Countries in 1568, he only tried prolonged military repression. He launched a major war to expand his territorial holdings in Italy, and he waged repeated war against the Ottoman Empire in the Mediterranean. He tried to conquer England with the Spanish Armada.

Yet until the 1580s, Philip's "defense department" had only one secretary assisted by a handful of clerks, and none with military experience. As he prepared to launch the Spanish Armada to try to conquer England, he doubled the number of responsible defense officials to two – one for the army and one for navy![56] The ships were largely rented from Genoa. Although many of them were sunk in the failed attack, Philip did not try to build a merchant fleet of his own to match Elizabeth's rapid expansion of her armed merchant fleet at the same time.

The army generals, who were not professional soldiers, were responsible for obtaining their own supplies. They could pay their troops with their own money and then be reimbursed by the king. When the king encountered financial troubles, however, the generals might not be paid and the debts became "loans." When Philip II died, the commander of the troops in the Low Countries took the money sent to pay the troops as "repayment" of his loans and left the field.

Even the revenue system lacked an effective bureaucracy. Spain did not have any real Ministry of Finances. In the 1500s, the Council of Finances negotiated the terms of the agreements with the tax farmers and the city-states, but it left all day-to-day functions to the Council of Accounting (*Contaduría Mayor de Cuentas*). In 1602, the two were formally merged but remained grossly understaffed. The council had only 24 auditors:[57]

> [The] auditors had the task of auditing all of the records of income and expenditure of the vast Castilian monarchy in Europe, including accounts kept by tax farmers, contractors of all descriptions, treasury officials and commissariat officers, and the *asentistas* in Castile, as well as by the paymasters for naval and armed forces in the Low Countries and in Germany, and His Majesty's ambassadors. Naturally, audits were late, often coming decades after accounts ceased being active.... Often as not, accounts would never be audited.

Philip II's lack of an effective bureaucracy had another negative effect. As discussed at length in Chapter 6, the British Parliament played a different

[56] I. A. A. Thompson, "The Armada and Administrative Reform: The Spanish Council of War in the Reign of Philip II," *English Historical Review* 82 (1967), 712–22.

[57] James Boyajian, *Portuguese Bankers at the Court of Spain, 1626–1650* (New Brunswick, NJ: Rutgers University Press, 1983), p. 155.

role in the English policy process in the 1700s than is usually appreciated. Its real power was more limited than usually supposed, and it often was ratifying basic polities made in the executive branch.

Yet, as John Brewer emphasized, the requirement that Parliament pass all laws and budgets meant that the budgets had to be carefully prepared, even when the Parliament basically was ratifying decisions made in the executive branch. In the 1700s, the preparation of laws required reports from increasingly specialized bureaucratic sub-divisions, inter-agency committees and consultants, specialized policy interest groups, and members of Parliament with specialized knowledge. This was a major step forward.

It was precisely the lack of specialization in the Spanish bureaucracy that deprived Philip II of the rich inter-agency consultation that would have allowed different interests and knowledge to be brought together in an integrated policy. This is the highest cost of having one "secretary" and a few clerks handling all defense questions prior to the mid-1580s and two clerks afterward. The extremely broad span of questions and areas about which the king made decisions cried for a complex policy process, but it did not exist.

Thus, Philip II faced a revolt in the Netherlands and needed to assimilate the newly acquired Portugal in 1580 at a time when Elizabeth was using pirates and private merchant ships to disrupt Spanish trade with its colonies. Moreover, as will be discussed at length, the silver being sent to Spain required so little space in the ship holds that only a few ships were necessary. These ships did not have enough space to carry the bulkier consumer goods to the New World that the colonists needed, and it obviously was necessary to find something bulkier that the ships could bring back to Europe.

In retrospect, Philip II should have produced commodities such as sugar, cocoa, and tobacco in the Caribbean islands for export and should have used Dutch and Portuguese ships to bring them to Europe and return consumer goods to the colonies. Indeed, Portugal was already growing sugar in Brazil. This would not only have produced a great deal of revenue for the king, but it also would have given him enough ships to combat Elizabeth's illegal acts. It would have given the Dutch and the Portuguese an incentive to remain tied with Spain.

Yet this was never done. Philip II took an unusually active role in all government decisions, but his policies seemed unconnected to each other. One of Philip's central problems was that he dealt with a separate group of advisers in each policy realm, and, like those in the military and the Council of the Indies that dealt with the colonies, these advisers had little first-hand knowledge or expert staff. Philip never seemed able to make complex policies that took the problems of the Netherlands and Portugal into account at the same time as the problems with Elizabeth and the New World.

The reader should remember Philip II when we discuss the work of the British Parliament in the 1700s. We agree with Adam Smith that the Hanover kings dominated Parliament through bribery and other patronage. We agree with John Brewer and many English comparative scholars that the major government development in England in the 1700s was the growth of the power of the executive branch, not the Parliament.

But we also agree with Brewer that the mere fact of the development of a complex legislative process, coupled with the rapid growth of a specialized bureaucracy in the 1700s, allowed the kind of systematic discussion and consideration of complex inter-related policy alternatives that were lacking in Spain in the 1500s and 1600s. This is a crucial insight when examining policymaking in developing countries today.

The Return of Court Politics in Spain

After Philip II died in 1598, the Castilian bureaucracy gradually became more competent in the 1600s, but progress was quite slow. The building of an early state is always difficult, especially when a territory the size of Castile is involved, but, in addition, Philip II's successors were largely content to reestablish the fully personalistic court politics characteristic of a pre-modern king. They ruled through favorites who themselves operated through their own network of favorites. This sharply reduced the pressure within the top ruling circles for a professionalization of the bureaucracy.

A Spanish historian whose book is entitled *The Golden Age of Spain, 1516–1659*, calls Philip III (1598–1621) "a disaster as a king" and describes the reign of Philip IV (1621–1665) as "one of the most unfortunate" in the history of Spain. The last king of the century, Charles II (1665–1700) had such severe mental problems and was so ineffectual that he has no major English-language biography.[58]

The policies of the three Spanish rulers of the 1600s would be difficult to defend either by long-term or even short-term criteria, had the three rulers

[58] Antonio Domínguez Ortiz, *The Golden Age of Spain, 1516–1659* (New York: Basic Books, 1971), p. 22. The mere titles of the leading biographies of Philip III express this consensus. See, for instance, Antonio Feros, *Kingship and Favouritism in the Spain of Philip III, 1598–1621* (Cambridge: Cambridge University Press, 2000); Patrick Williams, *The Great Favourite: Duke of Lerma and the Court and Government of Philip III of Spain, 1598–1621* (Manchester: Manchester University Press, 2006). Ruth Mackay summarizes the century well in *The Limits of Royal Authority: Resistance and Obedience in Seventeenth Century Castile* (Cambridge: Cambridge University Press, 1999).

not managed to rule for 23, 35, and 44 years, respectively. This occurred during a period of turmoil throughout Europe that included the Thirty Years' War from 1618 to 1648 and three major revolutions in England.

Presumably the Spanish kings of the 1600s prevented being overthrown by allowing government officials and powerful nobles to enrich themselves and pay relatively low taxes. These kings did, however, leave Spain so weak in 1700 that the succession to Charles II was decided in a war between France and the Hapsburg Empire – the War of the Spanish Succession.

Likely because of its mediocre rulers, Spain had relatively stagnant growth both in its population and the economy in the 1600s. The major Spanish economic historian of the Franco period, Vicens Vivens, thought the Spanish economy actually declined during the 1600s. He believed that the population fell, agriculture "collapsed" because of the power of the Mesta, industrial development did not occur because of wage-price differentials, and the economy as a whole suffered because of excessive taxation and regulation. In explaining these changes, Vicens gave "considerable emphasis" to the norms and values he saw as dominant in Spain: theological prejudices toward commerce, the elite mentality, the lack of a capitalist spirit, rentism, and a "puerile pride in indolence."[59]

Vivens's view became standard in the Franco era. Yet, I.A.A. Thompson and Bartoloma Yun Casalilla reported in 1994 that "little of [Vicens's interpretation] survives." According to the new interpretation, the population was only stagnant or even grew slowly. The Mesta "was really no more than a bit player" in the 1600s, and agriculture may not have declined as much as reported. Instead of excessive taxation, Thompson and Yun Casalilla wrote about "the limits of the effectiveness of the fiscal system."[60]

Thompson and Yun Casalilla generally rejected Vivens's cultural interpretations and gave greater weight to economic factors. Yun saw the difficulties in large part as "a consequence of the working of the political and institutional systems." Their book includes 14 chapters that express the new

59 The summary of Viven's views and the words in quotation marks come from I.A.A. Thompson and B. Yun Casalilla, "Introduction," in I.A.A. Thompson and Bartolomé Yun Casalilla, eds., *The Castilian Crisis of the Seventeenth Century: New Perspectives on the Economic and Social History of Seventeenth-Century Spain* (Cambridge: Cambridge University Press, 1994), p. 8.

60 Thompson and Yun, "Introduction," pp. 6–7. B. Yun Casalilla, "Spain and the Seventeenth-Century Crisis in Europe: Some Final Considerations," both in Thompson and Yun, *The Castilian Crisis of the Seventeenth Century*, pp. 318–19. In a private conversation with Hough early in the research on this book, John Elliott pointed to I.A.A. Thompson as a man who had a major role in reinterpreting Spain of the 1600s in ways that had convinced him and the rest of the field.

scholarship. Typically, none of them deals with the central government or with cultural factors.

From 1640 to 1652, Catalonia revolted, and Philip IV responded by further decentralizing power to non-Castilian states and by giving members of the elite important posts in the central government. John Elliott argued that much the same policy was followed in all "the various provinces of the Monarchy, including Castile and Italy:"[61]

> The principle of scrupulous regard for provincial rights ... was carefully maintained for the rest of the [17th] century. The weakness of Castile, in fact, made the reign of Charles II a golden age for the privileged classes in the various provinces of the Monarchy. In Spain and Italy, provincial liberties were given a fresh lease of life.... The half century which saw the consolidation of royal power in France was thus for the Spanish Monarchy an age of continuing decentralization – a period during which the "Aragonese" federal system was perhaps more wholeheartedly accepted than at any other moment during the government of the House of Austria. This, however, was not federalism by conviction but federalism by default ... no more than ... administrative and political stagnation in a changing world.

All modern historians make the same point in different ways. Regina Grafe speaks of "jurisdictional fragmentation" as a defining characteristic of the period. Juan Gilbert writes that "no one in the royal administration had an exact idea of income and expenditure ... [and that] ... financially speaking, the Crown worked in almost complete darkness." David Ringrose concludes that "it is not clear that either Philip III or Philip IV had a policy of administrative centralization" and that by 1700, "the countryside was firmly in the hands of local government."[62] As will be seen in Chapters 8 and 10, the same was even truer of the Spanish colonies.

Philip IV imposed a long list of internal taxes, and it is easy to look at tax data and believe they show that the Castilian kings were more powerful than the English monarchs, at least until the 1700s.[63] A recent example is Richard Lachmann, who aggregated the data on English and Spanish

[61] John Elliott, *Imperial Spain, 1469–1716* (New York: St. Martin's Press, 1964), pp. 357–8. See also John Elliott, *The Revolt of the Catalans: A Study in the Decline of Spain, 1598–1640* (Cambridge: Cambridge University Press, 1963).

[62] Regina Grafe, *Distant Tyranny: Markets, Power, and Backwardness in Spain, 1650–1800* (Princeton, NJ: Princeton University Press, 2012), p. xv; Henry Kamen, *The War of Succession in Spain, 1710–1715* (London: Weidenfeld & Nicolson, 1969), pp. 35–41; Juan Eloy Gelabert González, "La evolución de la monarquía hispánica entre 1598 y 1650: Asientos de Filipe III y Filipe IV," *Studia histórica, Historia moderna* 18 (1998), p. 273; David Ringrose, *Spain, Europe, and the "Spanish Miracle," 1700–1900* (Cambridge: Cambridge University Press, 1998), p. 352.

[63] For more on taxation under Philip II, see Pablo Fernández Albaladejo, "Cities and the State in Spain," *Theory and Society* 18 (1989), p. 728.

taxation from 1515 to the 1780s and concluded that Spanish taxation was much more effective.[64]

Modern historians of Spain agree that most of the taxes were collected by the city-states and the nobles (families) associated with them. The assessed amounts were somehow negotiated with the central government, and then, as Alejandra Irigoin and Regina Grafe warn, the city-states largely decided the source of the income, whatever the tax codes might say:[65]

> Castile is often portrayed as the more unitary element of the crown [in comparison with Aragon].... [Yet,] in the fiscal sphere the [Castilian] crown had almost no control over how taxes were levied, even when they had been agreed upon with the cities and councils.... The actual shape of taxes and the goods taxed were largely determined at the local level, though again often in negotiation with the king's councils.

We do not even know how much of the tax revenue was actually remitted to the king. Ringrose reports that, as in late medieval England, the Spanish monarchy regularly contracted with merchants, bankers, and the landed elite who were engaged in tax farming to perform tasks that we usually associate with a salaried bureaucracy: they collected "royal and municipal taxes, organized urban supply, cleaned the streets, recruited troops, provided fleets for the Navy, and supplied logistical support for the Army."[66] It is likely that the "payments" to others were subtracted from the taxes that were due.

According to Clarence Haring, the nobles of the city-states preferred not to think of themselves as tax farmers. They demanded that the contracts they signed with the Crown not be called an "*arrendamiento* (i.e., a lease, renting, or 'farm'), an ignoble term implying rather the status of tradesman." Instead they saw their actions as "merely the administration of a branch of the royal service, which the signatories engaged to manage with the aid of their private fortunes, and as such it must in no way detract from their claims to '*nobleza*.'"[67]

This does sound like provision of services that Ringrose described. As suggested in the previous chapter, Seville and the surrounding area may well have provided the "fleets for the Navy" that Ringrose mentioned as the main form of their taxation. The collapse of the navy in the 1600s may well

[64] Richard Lachmann, "Greed and Contingency: State Fiscal Crises and Imperial Failure in Early Modern Europe," *American Journal of Sociology* 115 (2009), 39–73, especially pp. 47–8.

[65] Irigoin and Grafe, "Bargaining for Absolutism," pp. 177 and 179.

[66] Ringrose, *Madrid and the Spanish Economy*, p. 348.

[67] Clarence Haring, *Trade and Navigation between Spain and the Indies in the Time of the Hapsburgs* (Cambridge: Harvard University Press, 1918), p. 80.

have resulted from a decision of the Seville *consulado* that it gained more from illegal trade than it would have from legal trade. We do not know, but this is one of many decisions for scholars to study.

We know nothing about the percentage of the assessed taxes that were paid in cash. We do suspect, however, that the negotiations between the center and the city-states dealt in significant part with the price of the non-monetary components of taxation. Perhaps the king received most of his actual money through export and Mesta taxes.

As a result, modern historians have come to recognize that prior to 1700 the role of the Castilian "parliament" – the *Cortes* – was often underestimated in the past. It represented the most important city-states with whom the kings had to negotiate their financing. This surely was done through their representatives in the *Cortes* in Madrid who not only knew central officials but could also negotiate with other city-state representatives on the regional distribution of burden.

A quarter of a century ago, Nicholas Henshall wrote about this informal role of the *Cortes* representatives in a book entitled *The Myth of Absolutism*. In 2012, Regina Grafe reports that this view had become the consensus view in the academic literature:[68]

> It is now widely accepted that the Castilian *Cortes* (estates), which consisted of delegates from the most important towns, were far from powerless. Throughout the 16th and early 17th centuries, they constrained the Crown fairly effectively. Though they had no formal legislative initiative, they exerted increasing control.

Because of the informal character of taxation in Castile and the hidden process of negotiation, any quantitative comparison of English and Spanish taxes is meaningless. The structure of royal income was very different in England. As we will see in the next chapter, Christopher Hill noted that Elizabeth's successor, James I, let alone earlier monarchs, "was still expected to 'live of his own,' to finance government from Crown lands, feudal dues, and the customs: no distinction was drawn between the public and private capacity of the king." This had a major impact on the structure of taxes and makes a comparison of official tax codes and actual tax collections highly unreliable.

Thus, while "tax payments" to the Spanish kings in the form of supplies to Madrid would be counted in his tax revenue, taxes that the guilds collected for the "local" government of the rapidly growing London would not.

[68] Nicholas Henshall, *The Myth of Absolutism; Change and Continuity in Early Modern European Monarchy* (New York: Longman, 1992), p. 185; Grafe, *Distant Tyranny*, p. 13.

As we discuss at length in the next chapter, Elizabeth created her "navy" for attacking Spanish ships and defending against the Armada by having merchants build armed ships. She received large amounts of booty from the "illegal" ships and from her "investments" in the English foreign trade monopolies.

In addition, much of Elizabeth's income came from her own land, which really was a tax on the peasants who worked it. This was not counted as tax income even though it came from the peasants. The Spanish kings had much less income from land, but their tax of Spanish peasants on others' estates was similar, although collected less effectively.

The precise nature of Spanish taxation and the amount of tax collected is not really important for this book. Our task here is to try to provide the reader with a sense of how ineffective an early state often is, especially when it is not a small city-state. This discussion of the 1600s in Spain deals with a period that, it must be emphasized, emerged 125 to 225 years after Isabella unquestionably began to create a state in 1480.

We chose to delve into more detail about Madrid's relations with the regions than about London's relations with the regions in the 1300s and 1400s because the old images of "a centralized [Spanish] monarchy and resultant bureaucracy" have been so persistent among comparative scholars. So was the assumption that this explains the poor economic performance of Spain in the 1500s and 1600s.

The crucial point is that Acemoglu and Robinson's assertions about the importance of the political centralization – we would say, creation of a minimally effective state – under Henry VII and Henry VIII – need to be generalized. Spain is a perfect illustration that Acemoglu and Robinson were right that "a lack of, or weak, political centralization" is ... a major "barrier to the spread of industry."[69]

The lack of a minimally effective state in Spain and thus inevitably in its colonies in the 1500s and 1600s was, in fact, the main barrier to economic development. In the next two chapters we show how the development of a minimally effective state in England in the first half of the 1500s and in Spain in the second half of the 1700s was associated with economic progress both in the homeland and in the colonies.

[69] Daron Acemoglu and James A. Robinson, *Why Nations Fail: The Origins of Power, Prosperity, and Poverty* (New York: Crown, 2012), pp. 186 and 216.

4

The Minimally Effective State

England, Tax Revenue, and Colonization

The first real states are collections of villages, small towns, a port that engages in long-range trade, or perhaps valleys controlled by a militia leader. When a militia leader – a "roving bandit" – gains a "comparable advantage of violence" in such a small territory, he usually has no collective action problem in controlling his military lieutenants and "tax collectors" with personalistic techniques.

A king who wants to rule a larger territory faces a far more difficult task. Such a territory inevitably includes a substantial number of small stationary bandits (warlords) with their own military power. As Norman Cantor notes, the power of such a king ultimately rests on periodic visits into the interior with his troops or the threat of such visits. The important factors in the power equation are the king's relative military force vis-à-vis the regional warlords, the balance of the costs and benefits to each side in a future intervention, and the attractiveness of collective military action in collecting booty.

The early such "kings" can be like the rulers of the "kingdoms" and "empires" of the Bible, or like the Carolingian Empire from 751 to 840 that North cites as the epitome of the fragile natural state.[1] Indeed, Norman Cantor was talking precisely about the Carolingian empire. As we have seen, merchants at one time had to pay tolls 18 times as they went along 80 miles of the Seine River approaching Paris. That is how weak the king in Paris was at that time.

The transition from a pre–nation-state to an early state and then to a minimally effective state and finally a truly effective one is complex. If we

[1] At its peak, the Carolingian Empire covered much of Western Europe. Douglass North, John Joseph Wallis, and Barry Weingast, *Violence and Social Orders: A Conceptual Framework for Interpreting Recorded History* (New York: Cambridge University Press, 2009), p. 55.

date the beginning of the early state in England to the late 1290s, the minimally effective state to the 1530s, and the truly effective state to the 1730s, that entire period encompasses 450 years. The transition from the minimally effective state to a truly effective state alone took 200 years. By our dating, the length of time between these stages in Spain is similar: 1480 for the beginning of the early state, the early 1700s for the beginning of the minimally effective state, and then the late 1800s or the early 1900s for the truly effective state.

We certainly do not want to suggest any fixed amount of time in the development process in different places and different times. If nothing else, contemporary technology and systems of mass education clearly accelerate the process in the 20th and 21st centuries. Instead, we want to make two simple points about the economic and political development in the past.

First, if Henry VIII introduced a system that deserves Daron Acemoglu and James Robinson's label "political centralization," and George II 200 years later was the first king to have the qualitatively more effective bureaucratic centralization needed for the Industrial Revolution, the 200-year evolution must have been very gradual.

Second, as scholars on the Mesopotamian and Roman bureaucracies warn their readers, we must be very careful about reading our own "mental image" of a bureaucracy into the past. In modern America it is not a compliment to call a person or a process "bureaucratic." Nevertheless, that criticism takes Max Weber's "rational-legal" bureaucracy for granted: a reasonable amount of professionalism, impartiality, appointment on the basis of merit, and rule by rules. Indeed, the essence of our negative definition of "bureaucratic" is an obsessive observance of rules.

This is not true of the minimally effective state. In Weber's terms, the minimally effective state remains patrimonial and is highly personalistic. The historian Christopher Hill describes Elizabeth's successor in the early 1600s, James I, in the same way that could be used for monarchs in earlier periods. The following quotation refers to a time 125 years after Henry VII came to power:[2]

> James, like the Tudors before him, chose ministers and favourites as seemed best to him.... James was still expected to 'live of his own,' to finance government from crown lands, feudal dues, and the customs: no distinction was drawn between the public and private capacity of the king. Parliament, summoned at the King's

[2] Christopher Hill, *The Century of Revolution, 1603–1714* (New York: W. W. Norton, 1961), pp. 1–2. On the patrimonial state, see Max Weber, "Politics as a Vocation," in *Max Weber: Essays in Sociology* (New York: Routledge, 2009).

absolute discretion, expected to vote taxes only in an emergency (although here theory already lagged behind practical necessity).... Members of the landed class themselves admitted to being absurdly undertaxed.

Spain and England in the 1500s and 1600s provide excellent examples of different types of an early and minimally effective state, respectively. Spain had the forms of a centralized state, including a highly authoritarian definition of the monarch's power. The forms have convinced many that Spain actually had such a state. Yet, as we have seen, the Spanish monarch never had real control over the Spanish city-states and the colonies in the 1500s and 1600s. The kings had less control in the 1600s than in the 1500s.

In England of the 1500s and 1600s, the Magna Carta was still the law of the land and Parliament had a fair degree of formal power. Yet the real power of Parliament had declined from the 1400s to the 1600s as the military power of the lords declined. When Conrad Russell discussed Charles I's conflict with Parliament in the 1600s, he noted that "[since] peers had no armies, Charles did not need to worry if they sulked in their tents."[3]

Elizabeth I, who ruled from 1558 to 1603, clearly had a more effective government than her exact contemporary, Phillip II of Spain. Nevertheless, Elizabeth I still did not have the administrative ability to tax free trade with the New World as Charles I was to acquire a half-century later. Indeed, Elizabeth still did not have a large enough navy or merchant fleet to overcome Spanish opposition to English colonization of the Americas, at least until the 1590s when she was in her sixties and not interested in a new venture.

In the 1620s, Charles I was the first English monarch who had a sufficiently strong fleet and tax-collecting ability to be able to abandon the monopoly guilds in trade within the Atlantic colonial system. Yet although the tax-collection system was still strong enough to permit any citizen to engage in free trade within the empire, it still was not strong enough to tax foreign ships engaged in colonial trade or English ships that sailed directly from the colonies to continental European ports. Only in 1776 could Adam Smith implicitly argue that England had a tax system effective enough to permit totally free trade. George III did not agree.

We will give disproportionate attention to trade and the development of armed fleets for several reasons. First, they are the central element in the interrelationship of England and Spain and provide a good illustration of the changing administrative capacity in each country and the reason for it.

[3] Conrad Russell, *The Crisis of Parliaments: English History 1509–1660* (Oxford: Oxford University Press, 1971), p. 320.

The navies and armed merchant fleets are also crucial for our purposes because of the vital role they played in the formation of the state and market in our other two cases, the United States and Mexico. Discussion of other aspects of Elizabeth's rule will be postponed until Chapter 6.

The development of the English and Spanish colonial systems is particularly telling in illuminating the difference between English and Spanish governmental effectiveness over time. The development of these systems depended on the ability of the colonial powers to supply its colonists and to obtain the silver or the commodities that they produced. Moreover, the national historians in the United States and Latin America have given an enormous amount of attention to the history of their respective countries in their colonial periods. These historians often do not consider the changing government capacity in the mother country as an explanation for shifts in colonial policy, but they present more than enough detail to illuminate this changing capacity.

Second, the close relationship of the military power of the armed merchant fleet and the navy was a crucial but often ignored factor in the creation of the urban dominant coalition in England in the 1600s and 1700s. In one way or another, the medieval dominant coalition had to be based on regional warlords with their own military forces. The establishment of a minimally effective central government requires the destruction or at least weakening of the regional military forces. The formation of a fully developed modern government depends on the creation of stable urban elites to replace regional ones in the dominant coalition.

The great advantage of a city-state based on a port – or a port-capital of a larger state – was that it had merchants with armed ships from the beginning. It then developed its own navy that was closely allied with the merchants. Thus, even when the warlords were the main element in the dominant coalition, the armed ships of the merchants helped make the man in charge of the largest port the most powerful warlord. In addition, as the alliance of the merchants and navy grew in strength, it became the first key member of a new urban coalition.

The English kings had such an early merchant-naval member of their coalition, but Isabella and her successors in Castile did not. The Castilian kings might have moved their base of operations to Seville either in the 1260s or the late 1400s, but too much of the easily taxable income had to be collected on the northern plateau. This slowed Spanish development. Indeed, Spain might not have developed an even minimally effective state in the 1700s if France had not conquered it. It might have remained stagnant like the other countries in southern and Eastern Europe.

Finally, the relationship of the merchants and the navy in England casts a light on English history from the 1660s to the 1760s that has been largely ignored in the American economic literature: the relation of military power to the politics of the Restoration of 1660, the Glorious Revolution of 1688, and then the creation of a "fiscal-military state" in the 1700s. This connection provides a prime example for Robert Bates's warning about "the unwarranted reluctance of those who subscribe to the new institutionalism to pursue the implications of the basic insight ... that coercion can be socially productive."[4]

The Whig historians explained the success of England in the 1700s by the rise of Parliament in 1688 and John Locke's "consent of the governed." Douglass North and Barry Weingast accepted this interpretation, and New Institutional economists largely followed their lead. This means that they did not ask why a rural-based Parliament which refused to fund Charles I's navy in the 1630s voted for rapidly rising taxes to fund Charles II's creation of a stronger government during the Restoration, and especially John Brewer's "military-fiscal state" half-century of war after 1688.

A collective action interpretation of the prelude to the Glorious Revolution begins with the fact that the naval alliance with the merchants was the only major urban member of the ruler's dominant coalition in England that existed in the second half of the 1600s. The manufacturers were just becoming important; the state bureaucracies were still embryonic; and the Church of England never had an independent power base after the seizure of its land. But to understand the role of the merchant fleet and navy in the second half of the 1600s, we first must understand their development in the 1500s.

We have already discussed Spain during the 1500s and 1600s in the previous chapter on the early state. In this chapter we will "catch up" chronologically. England was passing through its minimally effective stage during these two centuries, and we will analyze most of its development until the mid-1600s in these countries. This allows us to examine the effectiveness of the English government in the framework of its colonial policy in its American colonies from the 1620s into the 1650s. Then we can look at the Spanish colonial policy to show the impact of the transition of Spain from an early state in 1492 to a minimally effective state in the early 1700s.

4 North et al., *Violence and Social Orders;* and Douglass North, John Joseph Wallis, Steven Webb, and Barry Weingast, eds., *In the Shadow of Violence: Politics, Economics, and the Problems of Development* (Cambridge: Cambridge University Press, 2013); Robert Bates, "The New Institutionalism," in Sebastian Galiani and Itai Sened, eds., *Institutions, Property Rights, and Economic Growth: The Legacy of Douglass North* (Cambridge: Cambridge University Press, 2014), p. 55.

Henry VII's and Henry VIII's Destruction of Military Feudalism and the Construction of a Minimally Effective State

When Henry VII defeated Richard III at the battle of Bosworth in 1485, many lords stayed aloof from the battle, perhaps because they were uncertain of the outcome, or perhaps because they hoped Henry's pledge to marry Elizabeth of York would end decades of conflict. The evolution of military technology meant castles no longer provided the same protection as in the past, and the new fashionable mansions were basically defenseless. The cost of weapons was becoming too high for the benefits that military independence brought.

Indeed, the possession of military force had begun to give the lords a greater fear of being beheaded than a sense of security. Edward III had a number of sons who survived to adulthood, and in the troubled 1400s, many of their descendants had claimed a right to the throne. The Tudors were determined to avoid this problem. As Stanley Chrimes said, "descent from Edward III was to be more than dangerous; it was to become practically equivalent to a sentence of death" if a person was in a competing line of descent to the Tudors. As noted earlier, Henry VIII is estimated to have killed at least 70,000 political opponents.[5]

Henry VII had won at Bosworth with mercenary troops supported by France. Such foreign support is, in fact, an ideal solution to a severe collective action problem. As we will see, French covert aid was crucial in solving these problems in George Washington's victory in 1781 at Yorktown. Nevertheless, foreign overt or covert aid is not a long-term solution. Those who finance the original action are seldom willing to continue after their original goal has been accomplished. Those taking the aid do not want to subordinate themselves to those who financed them. Both phenomena were quite visible in the American Revolution.

Henry VII faced the same problem. He did not want to be dependent on France, and he sought an alliance with Spain both to counterbalance France and to gain access to trade in Seville and the Mediterranean. The traditional way to cement an alliance was a dynastic marriage, and Henry sought a marriage of his heir to one of the daughters of Isabella and Ferdinand.

Isabella and Ferdinand were nervous about a marriage to Henry VII's son, fearing that he would share the fate of his predecessors in the 1400s,

5 S. B. Chrimes, *Lancastrians, Yorkists, and Henry VII* (London: Macmillan, 1964). For an excellent and detailed discussion of how the Tudors operated, see Lawrence Stone, *The Crisis of the Aristocracy*, abridged ed. (London: Oxford University Press, 1967), pp. 97–101.

most notably Richard III whom Henry VII had overthrown. Even if Henry VII himself was able to survive a challenge, then perhaps his successor – the husband of Isabella and Ferdinand's daughter – might be overthrown and/or killed in a struggle for power. It was only in 1501 that they agreed to the marriage of their daughter, the famed Catherine of Aragon.

Isabella and Ferdinand were right to be worried. It is clear only in retrospect that Henry VII's victory was a historic turning point in English history. For this reason, scholars looking back at the Tudor period with hindsight need to maintain an appropriate historical perspective.

The first key fact about England when Henry VII came to power in 1485 was that it remained "a military society … a society stratified for war … a system of 'military feudalism.'"[6] The Tudors were determined to destroy this system. Henry VII issued a decree prohibiting the lords from raising private armies as they had in the past, but, in practice, this only applied to armies the king did not want to use in war. After the 1540s the monarchs seldom used them.

Lawrence Stone described the very slow process and the techniques by which the kings achieved their goals in an extraordinarily illuminating chapter. He argued that even in the 1500s the gradual loss of military power did not immediately change a violent culture. "The behavior of the propertied class," he found "was characterized by the ferocity, childishness, and lack of self-control of the Homeric age." There was a "total lack of rules within which such violence as occurred could be confined."[7]

According to Stone, the Tudors had to tolerate much of this atmosphere, but, partly by engaging in a great deal of violence themselves, they slowly struggled against it. One measure of their success was a strengthening of the legal code and an enormous growth of litigation from the 1550s to 1625. Of even more practical significance was the avoidance of wars after the 1540s. Three-quarters of the peers – almost all of the able-bodied men among them – participated in the wars of the 1540s. By 1576, only one-quarter of peers had military experience, and by 1642, this figure had fallen to well below one in five.[8]

The second major change that occurred under the Tudors was the destruction of the Catholic Church and the seizure of the huge landholdings of the church abbots and bishops by Henry VIII and Elizabeth I, respectively. Henry justified his action by Pope Clement VII refusal to let him annul his

6 Charles Wilson, *England's Apprenticeship, 1603–1763* (London: Longman, 1971), pp. 3–4.
7 Stone, *The Crisis of the Aristocracy*, 96–134, pp. 108–9.
8 Ibid., pp. 130–1.

marriage with Catherine of Aragon and marry Anne Boleyn. The American public has been so fascinated with Henry's six wives that non-specialists have usually accepted this explanation without much thought. This is a mistake.

At a minimum, Henry VIII surely was always aware of the financial advantage of seizing church property. In the first decade of the 1500s, the king received 40,000 pounds income a year from his own lands, 40,000 from various customs duties, and 30,000 from the "fifteenths and tenths" tax on property. When Henry seized the property of the monasteries, the income from his own lands remained at 40,000 pounds, but he now was able to impose a tax on clerics that netted an additional 40,000 pounds. The income from the monasteries alone was an additional 136,000 pounds a year.[9] His men stole the jewels and gold from the monastery shrines and the lead roofs of the buildings, and these brought additional funds.

Henry VIII's break with the Catholic Church began in 1527, when he told Catherine of Aragon that he wanted a divorce. Yet he did not proclaim himself the head of English church until 1534. Many see this length of time as evidence that the King was driven to the final action almost in desperation. An earlier generation of historians had a very different view, believing that the seizure of monastery property was in Henry's mind from the beginning.[10]

There are many reasons to suspect that Henry VIII was engaged in long-term planning. In the early years of his reign, Henry VIII was absorbed with very expensive foreign policy adventures in an apparently quixotic effort to win the French crown for himself. In the mid-1520s, the Parliament rebelled and refused to appropriate another major tax for this purpose. When Henry VIII broke with the church, he abolished the monasteries and seized their property.

Although Henry VIII asked for an annulment in 1527, he knew by at least 1529 that the pope could not possibly give him the annulment that

[9] Sean Cunningham, *Henry VII* (Oxford: Routledge, 2007), pp. 133 and 138–9; Claire Cross, *Church and People: England 1450–1660*, 2nd ed. (Oxford: Blackwell, 1999), p. 57.

[10] Geoffrey Elton discussed the different sides of the debate and thought the evidence is mixed. Geoffrey Elton, *The Tudor Revolution in Government: Administrative Changes in the Reign of Henry VIII* (Cambridge: Cambridge University Press, 1953). The problem for historians working in any archive is that competent rulers always use spin. They always prepare their actions in order to make them seem inevitable and give those who are harmed the possibility of blaming "evil lieutenants." Moreover, competent rulers also give themselves paths of retreat regardless of their original intent. Hence, it is extremely difficult to know how determined a ruler was at an early stage. In general, however, if powerful, ambitious, and very close lieutenants vigorously push a policy and are rewarded, it is highly dangerous to assume that they are not responding to powerful signals, if not instructions.

he wanted. Catherine was the aunt of Charles I of Spain, a man who absolutely did not want his aunt treated in this way. Charles also ruled the Holy Roman Empire as Charles V. In a war over control of Italy between France and Charles V, the pope had become Charles's virtual prisoner and had no freedom of action. Henry VIII must have known this.

If Henry had simply wanted the freedom to marry someone else, he could have divorced Catherine and forced the pope or his successors to accept a fait accompli. He could even have had her quietly put to a "natural death" by poisoning or some other means. Yet, Henry persisted. The fact that he lost almost all interest in Anne Boleyn soon after their marriage raises similar questions about the degree of his obsession with her.

Henry VIII obviously was also conscious of the consequences of the attack on the Catholic Church on the power structure in the provinces. The pope nominally appointed the bishops, but they usually were the candidates of the king. The bishops were very much the men of the monarch. They normally combined their administrative duties in the church with similar duties in the state, but their income came solely from the church and its lands.

The other powerful members of the church hierarchy were the abbots in control of the lands owned by their monasteries. The abbots were not normally appointed by the kings; they had closer ties with the local lords.[11] The monasteries owned a fifth of the country's cultivated land, and the land seized from them was largely sold to the rural gentry to help strengthen their position as a counterweight to the nobles in the countryside.[12] Henry's different treatment of the land of the bishops and monasteries is also illuminating. By the 1530s, Henry VIII had had years to place his men as bishops, and he did not seize their land.

By contrast, when Elizabeth came to power in 1558, the bishops had been appointed by her Catholic predecessor, Mary Tudor. In 1559, Elizabeth had Parliament pass the Act of Supremacy under which all government and church officials were required to take an oath that acknowledged the subordination of the church to Crown. The Catholic bishops refused, and she seized their land.[13] The difference in the behavior of the two monarchs was unlikely to have been a coincidence.

[11] William Abel Pantin, *The English Church in the Fourteenth Century: Based on the Birkbeck Lectures, 1948* (Cambridge: Cambridge University Press, 2010); Richard Barrie Dobson, ed., *The Church, Politics, and Patronage in the Fifteenth Century* (Gloucester: A. Sutton, 1984); David Knowles, *The Religious Orders in England*, Vols. 1 and 2 (Cambridge: Cambridge University Press, 1979).

[12] Elton, *The Tudor Revolution*, pp. 247–9.

[13] J. B. Black, *The Reign of Elizabeth, 1558–1603*, 2nd ed. (Oxford: Clarendon Press, 1949), pp. 14–34.

The third major change under the Tudors was the strengthening of state power as the lords became weaker and the Catholic Church was destroyed. Indeed, if Henry VIII and Elizabeth I had not been capable of establishing their power, the country would have slipped toward anarchy as the old system of rule was destroyed.

As has been seen, even Henry VIII started with a quite personalistic system of rule. There never had been a meaningful distinction between the king's extended household and his government officials. Henry had to pay officials out of his own funds, and taxes were his personal property. The bureaucratic staff did not think of themselves as civil servants who served the state, but as servants of the kings. This continued well into the 1500s.[14]

Cardinal Thomas Wolsey was Henry VIII's chief lieutenant until 1530, and he normally worked with men in the royal household with whom he was close. His successor as lord chancellor, Thomas Cromwell, quickly began taking power from the household and putting it in the hands of the governmental administrative organs. He sharply reduced the size of the chief advising body of the king, the Privy Council, and largely limited it to the chief governmental organs.

Geoffrey Elton called Cromwell's action a revolution in government, but Elton's critics see it as an evolutionary continuum that extended back at least to the 1400s and forward into the 1600s.[15] Indeed, a historian of Elton's generation, S.B. Chrimes, emphasized the role of Edward IV, a king who came to power in 1461. Like Daron Acemoglu and James Robinson, we basically agree with Elton about the importance of the governmental transformation that occurred under Henry VIII, and specifically under Cromwell, and we treat it as a watershed. Yet we think the critics are right about the very gradual nature of the process.

Without any doubt, the various Tudor monarchs built a much stronger bureaucratic system than their respective counterparts in Spain. Henry VII

[14] G. L. Harriss, *Shaping the Nation: England, 1360–1461* (Oxford: Clarendon Press, 2005), pp. 16–21; Scott Waugh, *England in the Reign of Edward III* (Cambridge: Cambridge University Press, 1991), p. 171; John Gillingham, "The Early Middle Ages (1066–1290)," in Kenneth Morgan, ed., *The Oxford History of Britain*, rev. ed. (Oxford: Oxford University Press, 2001), pp. 120–91.

[15] Elton, *The Tudor Revolution*. See Christopher Coleman and David Starkey, eds., *Revolution Reassessed: Revisions in the History of Tudor Government and Administration* (Oxford: Clarendon Press, 1986), especially the introduction and conclusion on pp. 1–12 and 199–208. Elton himself came to see the process as more subtle than he originally believed. Geoffrey Elton, *Reform and Reformation, England, 1509–1558* (Cambridge, MA: Harvard University Press, 1977), pp. 211–20.

(1485–1509) was more effective than Isabella and Ferdinand (1480–1516), Henry VIII (1509–1547) than Charles I (1516–1556), and Elizabeth I (1558–1603) than Philip II (1556–1598). On the other hand, the Tudors did not have a state that was at all comparable to the truly effective state of the Hanover kings of the 1700s, let alone the British state of today.

An example of particular relevance for this book is the navy that Henry VIII was intent on building. In the 1520s, Henry named one of the wealthiest merchants of London to oversee the navy and had him report directly to Wolsey and then Cromwell. Because of the prominence of the merchants involved, Wolsey and Cromwell preferred to work through informal contacts on this particular question, but in 1545 and 1546, naval administration became formalized under what came to be known as the Naval Board.[16]

The Naval Board had separate boards and/or officials in charge of finances, rigging, ordinance, and in 1565, food supply (victualling). N.A. M. Rodger calls the creation of a formal administrative structure "the single most important achievement of sixteenth century England in relation to sea power." Yet Rodger correctly saw the appointment of competent officials as just the beginning of a modern bureaucracy. The creation of a formal administrative system was of even more fundamental importance. "Almost at once," Rodger said, the Naval Board "acquired what no settled organization can do without: 'a new house builded at Deptford Strand for the officers' clerks of the Admiralty to write therein.'"[17]

Rodger thought this structure was crucial in giving England the ability to make the needed changes in the future through "continuity, long-term planning and investment [and] institutional memory and support."[18] This was the structure Elizabeth had in place in the 1670s and 1680s when she conducted her decisive struggle in the Atlantic Ocean with Philip II. It mattered that Philip at that time had a single secretary with a few clerks to handle both the army and the navy.

We should not think, however, that the English naval bureaucracy approached the rational-legal model that Weber posited. The Naval Board remained intimately connected with the merchants and the suppliers. Rodger emphasized the quality and expertise of the top officials

[16] Nicholas A.M. Rodger, *The Safeguard of the Sea: A Naval History of Britain, 660–1649*, Vol. 1 (New York: W.W. Norton, 1998), pp. 221–37. For the Naval Board under Elizabeth, pp. 331–3. For the 1557 reorganization, see David Loades, *The Tudor Navy: An Administrative, Political, and Military History* (Leicester, UK: Scolar Press, 1992), pp. 4 and 166–8.

[17] Rodger, *The Safeguard of the Sea*, pp. 223–6.

[18] Ibid., p. 226.

involved – men who "knew as much as anyone about the management of ships in port and at sea":[19]

The new naval administration created at the close of Henry VIII's reign was strikingly more efficient and "modern" than that of any other European state of the day (Venice and perhaps Portugal excepted), but it was not "modern" at all in the way in which it integrated public and private business. The crown co-opted expertise without which it could not have maintained an efficient navy, but private interests gained considerable control over the king's ships. They could, and did, charter them for private voyages, and sell the navy stores and equipment on their private accounts, appearing alternately if not simultaneously as naval captains, admirals and Officers of the Admiralty, or as private merchants, shipowners, and shipmasters, not to say privateers and pirates.

The professionalization of the navy bureaucracy was to occur very slowly. More than 100 years later in the 1660s, Samuel Pepys wrote the most famous diary of English history when he was serving as chief secretary of the Admiralty under Charles II. As we see in the next chapter, Pepys discussed in great detail the personalistic bureaucratic norms and practices he encountered, but obviously the bureaucracy of the 1550s was still quite personalistic.[20]

A concrete example of the personalistic nature of economic management in the mid-1550s is provided by the most famous Tudor adviser, Thomas Gresham. Gresham is known for Gresham's Law ("bad money drives out good"), but from 1543 to 1579 he was the monarch's top adviser on and manipulator of – the exchange rate as he handled the government debt. He also was responsible for creating the Royal Exchange in London where currency dealers could meet. Gresham was, of course, typical for his time in being paid almost nothing for his work, but in being allowed to trade on his own account despite his inside knowledge. As a merchant (presumably, first of all, a currency speculator), he became one of the richest men in London.[21]

Each realm of government obviously was different, and we do not have either the space or the need to be comparative.[22] We are not attempting to present a subtle or balanced view of the precise nature of change under

19 Ibid., p. 226. Kenneth Andrews, *Drake's Voyages: A Re-Assessment of Their Place in Elizabethan Maritime Expansion* (New York: Scribner, 1967), pp. 9–13.

20 C. S. Knighton, *Pepys and the Navy* (Stroud, UK: Sutton, 2003).

21 John William Burgon, *The Life and Times of Thomas Gresham* (London: Robert Jennings, 1839); Black, *The Reign of Elizabeth*, pp. 45 and 259–60.

22 For administrative changes in other sectors of the bureaucracy, see Michael Braddick, *State Formation in Early Modern England, c. 1550–1700* (Cambridge: Cambridge University Press, 2000).

different reigns. Rather, we are suggesting that there is no balanced view. We do agree with Rodger that Elizabeth was a truly exceptional monarch who created the conditions for future English greatness, but even her achievements in building a navy and merchant fleet did not come to fruition until the colonization of the 1620s – a half-century after she made the key decisions. Her creation of a merchant fleet and navy had a crucial impact on the politics of 1660 and 1688, but a truly effective government was not established for nearly a half-century after 1688.

In short, development takes a very long time. Moreover, it is not "consistent" or linear, and, as we discussed in the previous chapter, chance always plays a major role. Henry VIII was succeeded by his 9 year old son, Edward VI, and the latter's six-year reign was featured by a court politics reminiscent of Spain in the 1600s. If that had continued over a long life, England would not have evolved in the same way.

Edward was succeeded by his sister Mary Tudor, who was determined to reestablish Catholicism. That easily could have produced Civil War, but she ruled for only five years. Elizabeth I then ruled for 45 years and was a great ruler. If she had been as mediocre as the Spanish kings of the 1600s, England's fate would also have been very different.

Elizabeth I's Building of a Merchant Marine and the Problem of Silver in Trade with Asia and the Americas

Economists writing about England, Spain, the United States, and Mexico from a comparative perspective have always given special attention to differences in trade and transportation, but this book has taken a broader perspective on these subjects. We have argued that the armed nature of merchant ships and the alliance of merchants with a growing state navy had a profound impact on domestic political development and on international relations. This is the side of transportation and international trade to which we give the greatest attention.

The non-specialized American readers of this book have likely been surprised by our discussion of the weakness of the English merchant fleet and navy prior to the mid-1500s. Americans take for granted that Britannia always ruled the waves. In fact, small English ships long did little more than carry wool and woolen cloth across the narrow English Channel to Flanders. England did not have a significant merchant fleet that could sail on the open sea at the time.

As a result, as we have seen, England relied on foreign merchants and ships for ocean commerce to Gascony, Castile, Italy, and northern Europe.

The kings' changing alliances with owners of European fleets were crucial not only for the collection of customs duties but also for the position of the kings in English domestic politics.

The Flemish merchants supported William the Conqueror in his invasion, and they remained dominant in the wool trade with Flanders for 200 years. When Henry III gained full control of London in 1265, he expelled the Flemish allies of the old city leaders and replaced them with Italian and then Hanseatic merchants. Edward III's alliance with the Hanseatic League was crucial for making London the center of English political and economic life.

But then in the 1400s, the Hanseatic League began to weaken, and the kings gradually lost their protector of English trade and customs collection. This contributed to the financial difficulties that led to political instability in the 1400s and Henry VIII's seizure of monastery land in the 1530s. We argue that the construction of a dominant navy and merchant fleet not only had geopolitical importance, but also had a major impact on English politics in the 1600s.

Spain had a far more complex system of international trade because of its size and national diversity. The migrating sheep were sheared in the northern plateau, and their wool was shipped to Flanders from northern ports on the Bay of Biscay. The fleet of the Basques in these ports carried some of the wool and other goods to northern Europe, and foreign ships carried the rest of it.

Once Castile captured Seville and the Guadalquivir River valley, it sought to export olives, olive oil, wine, and figs to northern Europe. The merchants and ships of Genoa handled most of this trade, and the Castilian government also used Genoese ships as its navy. When Spain created an empire in the Americas, the kings closed the colonial trade to foreign ships, and all Spanish trade with the New World had to go through Seville.

When Henry VIII launched a significant naval program in the first half of the 1500s, he was responding in significant part to the decline of the Hanseatic League. Yet, at the end of his reign, he still had only 28 ships of 100 tons or more. England did not have a significant merchant fleet until the second half of the 1500s. Only this made it possible for England to settle the Americas – and even then a significant colony was not established until 1623. Only by the mid-1650s had Charles I and the Puritan regime built a navy which, in fact, ruled the waves.

It was Elizabeth I who really set the stage for English dominance of the sea. Elizabeth's first task, but by far the least important, was to rebuild Henry VIII's navy. She had a cautious foreign policy, but conflicts of interest with

Spain, the Netherlands, and France meant she needed a stronger navy for defensive purposes.

Wooden ships literally decay over time, and Henry VIII's ships had deteriorated since his death eleven years earlier. Elizabeth restored and modernized the fleet but did not expand it. By the end of her reign, the navy had 31 ships of over 100 tons, only a small increase from Henry's 28.[23]

Although such a navy was important in defending England in war, Elizabeth was determined to achieve access to ocean commerce. When she came to power, nearly 95% of English exports still consisted of wool and especially woolen cloth of medium quality. These exports continued to be important, but their growth was slowing and becoming irregular. Moreover, raising the export tariff on the cloth could reduce its competitiveness abroad. Henry VIII solved his revenue problems by seizing the lands of the abbeys, and Elizabeth followed the same path by seizing the lands of the bishops.

Nevertheless, Elizabeth needed additional income, and this required diversifying the types of goods in English commerce and the range of ports with which English ships traded. To achieve this goal, Elizabeth faced two basic problems.

First, Elizabeth required a large merchant fleet for England, one that had enough ships to be sailing simultaneously across the Atlantic Ocean, to the eastern end of the Mediterranean, and around the Cape of Good Hope. In addition, England had to develop officers and sailors with the skill to sail and navigate on the deep sea. This it lacked. Rodger notes that "in 1558 there was probably not one Englishman capable unaided of navigating a ship to the West Indies, and in 1568, only one."[24]

Second, Elizabeth had to solve a problem that the non-specialist may not imagine. In profitable bilateral trade, the goods that were sent in each direction of a round trip needed to have comparable bulk for their value. If their bulk were not comparable, fewer ships would be required on one leg of the trade than the other.

The Asian silk and spices had high value for their bulk, and the English needed only a few ships to bring them to Europe. Bulky goods of comparable value sent to Asia would require far more ships. It would be unprofitable

[23] Kenneth Andrews, *Trade, Plunder, and Settlement: Maritime Enterprise and the Genesis of the British Empire* (Cambridge: Cambridge University Press, 1984), pp. 22–5.

[24] Rodger, *The Safeguard of the Sea*, p. 244; David Waters, *The Art of Navigation in England in Elizabethan and Early Stuart Times* (New Haven, CT: Yale University Press, 1958), pp. 79–80, 101.

to send so many ships on the long and expensive voyage to the East unless they could bring back goods of comparable bulk.

The obvious item to be exchanged for the Asian silks and spices was silver from Spanish America. It too had great value but small bulk and would require only a few ships to take to Asia. Spain had shown an awareness of this fact when it acquired the Philippines as a colony so that it could use Manila as a midway trading point for an exchange of silver for spices and silk between China and Mexico. Silver would be just as good in trade between Europe and Asia.

Philip II faced the same imbalance between bulk and value in his trade between Spain and the Americas as England did with its trade with Asia. Relatively few ships were necessary to carry the silver to Spain, but the growing number of increasingly affluent colonists demanded more and more consumer goods. The consumer goods were bulky, and transporting them to the colonies required a number of ships. Hence, more ships were needed to send these consumer goods to the New World than were required to bring the silver back.

Philip's ultimate solution to this problem had to be the production of bulky and valuable goods in the colonies so that the number of ships required to take the bulky consumer goods to the colonies would have something to fill their holds on the return voyage. England and France had no such problem because the tobacco and sugar they were producing were bulky, but Portugal had already shown Philip II the way by exporting large amounts of sugar from Brazil from the 1550s onward. Other such products were readily visible: for example, cacao, rawhides, and dyewood logs.

Philip could have built his own merchant fleet, but this would have required time. His optimal solution was to permit his semi-colonies of the Low Countries – and after 1580, Portugal – to engage in commodity production in the colonies or at least in their transportation. Another option was to allow the growing English fleet to trade with Spanish colonies and encourage commodity production as was to occur illegally in the 1600s.

For reasons discussed in the next chapter, Philip adopted neither of these solutions. Scholars explain this by his fear of silver smuggling. More basically, he perhaps felt that he did not have the governmental capability to collect a tax on Portuguese, Dutch, or English profits, or even to prevent these countries from seizing the islands on which they were allowed to grow commodities. He somehow did not seem to realize that if the Spanish colonists did not received consumer goods legally, they would obtain them illegally.

Perhaps Philip was just over-confident. England did not have an ocean-going merchant fleet, and a basic oceanographic fact made trade with the New World very difficult for England. Americans who have flown to Europe know that the trade winds flow from Canada toward Europe; as a result, westward jet flights across the North Atlantic today take some two hours longer than the flight going east. The phrase "trade wind" comes from the reality of a sailing era when ships generally needed to sail with the winds rather than against them. The small sailing ships of the 1500s that tried to follow the modern airplane route from England to Massachusetts and Virginia did so only with great difficulty.[25]

Yet the trade winds flow in a circular direction within each hemisphere, and the trade winds from Europe to North America go far to the south before turning west. The trade winds from England to North America – even New England – pass Iberia and the Canary Islands, turn west toward the Leeward Islands, and then turn once more to the north. The trade winds split just north of Cuba, one stream going east toward Iberia and the other continuing northward. The Canary Islands were owned by Spain, and English ships had to pass them and then stop at small Caribbean islands for food and water. When Spain had naval superiority, it could easily control this route near the Canary Islands and the Caribbean Islands.

Another option at Philip's disposal was simply to sell silver to England at a reasonable price and obtain consumer goods in exchange. The Spanish kings imposed an immediate appropriation of 10% of the silver mined in Mexico and 20% of that mined in South America and enforced this decree through its control of the mercury supply needed for silver refining. The rest of the silver was left in the hands of the colonists themselves and could have been treated as money the colonists could spend. Instead, Philip added an additional tax of 17% both on private silver that was be exported and on consumer goods that were imported. Spanish merchants also charged a high commission on any such trade.

Elizabeth did not want to pay such a high price for silver and began addressing the problem. The first step, whatever Philip did, had to be to encourage the construction of a merchant fleet – a fleet that by the nature

[25] Another problem with the northern route was that Iceland, Greenland, and Newfoundland were often inhospitable because it was the time of "the Little Ice Age," and the 1590s was the coldest decade of the century. Brian Fagan, *The Little Ice Age: How Climate Made History, 1300–1850* (New York: Basic Books, 2000), p. 94. For the impact of the Little Ice Age on the English assumptions about the settlement of Virginia, see Karen Ordahl Kupperman, "The Puzzle of the American Climate in the Early Colonial Period," *American Historical Review* 87 (1982), 1262–89.

of ocean trade at the time would be armed – and the creation of trained personnel capable of sailing such ships.

The queen appointed a Treasurer of the Queen's Majesty's Marine Causes who was a ship captain with military experience against Spain. He oversaw the construction of a new kind of ship that had fewer guns but was fast and maneuverable enough to outsail the bigger ships. Elizabeth took the lead in creating an iron-foundry industry that produced low-cost guns. While not as good as the traditional bronze guns, they were effective and were cheap enough to "become an everyday commodity within the pocket of any would-be pirate or explorer."[26]

A corps of trained personnel to sail a much larger number of ships on the open sea cannot be created quickly. Elizabeth introduced a policy of seeking silver illegally through smuggling and piracy by non-Establishment merchants and shippers. They were more willing to take risks as the price of admission to foreign trade, and they developed officers and crews with more unorthodox skills.

The Development of Illegal Trade with the New World

Rulers wanted their countries to engage in foreign trade so that they could profit from it through the collection of tariffs or through direct participation in its profits. As we have emphasized, the collection of tariffs is highly dependent upon a country's administrative ability to collect it, and this ability developed very slowly in both countries. Elizabeth's policy was skillfully differentiated to correspond to the growing but still limited capability of her early minimally effective state. Clearly, Elizabeth believed that the traditional system of monopoly guilds was still the most effective way of collecting taxes in the second half of the 1500s. The general demand for all products on the Continent was gradually increasing as the population of Europe outside Russia increased from some 70 million in 1500 to about 90 million in 1600. Yet Elizabeth continued to trade with Europe through monopoly trade guilds, only subdividing them on a geographic basis as the scale of trade increased.

In addition, Elizabeth also created a number of new such guilds to trade with Russia and Asia. These included the Muscovy Company, the Spanish

[26] N.A.M. Rodger, "Guns and Sails in the First Phase of English Colonization, 1500–1650," in Nicholas Canny, ed., *The Oxford History of the British Empire*: Volume I, *The Origins of Empire: British Overseas Enterprise to the Close of the Seventeenth Century* (Oxford: Oxford University Press, 1998), p. 86; David Quinn and A. N. Ryan, *England's Sea Empire, 1550–1642* (London: George Allen & Unwin, 1983).

Company, the Turkey Company, and the East India Company that were created to trade with these different areas. (The Spanish Company and the Turkey Company were combined into the Levant Company.)[27] These monopoly companies continued to perform a number of government functions. The Levant Company was even responsible for maintaining the ambassador and consul at Constantinople. Yet the queen was, of course, mainly interested in obtaining revenue. Customs collection was assigned to farmers who were major merchants or politicians, and they often subleased the task to various syndicates. The complex arrangements meant that the queen could shift the farming arrangements in a way that made merchants dependent on her favor for their wealth. Not surprisingly, the farmers often provided loans to Elizabeth, usually as advances on customs to be collected in the future. A lender could, however, also be given some lucrative concession if he forgave one of these loans.[28]

As we will see, Elizabeth received further income from investing her own money in the guilds, definitely the Levant Company and probably others as well. The detailed records of the East India Company that was formed at the end of her life openly acknowledged the importance of the political connections to James I of a number of its investors – of a privy councilor, key ambassadors, the lord chancellor, and other "friends" of the king. In 1619, Prince Charles, the heir apparent, himself invested 6,000 pounds.[29] As late as 1713, Queen Anne "invested" in the English monopoly South Sea Company for trade in Spanish America and was given one-quarter of the shares.[30]

Elizabeth followed a quite different path in developing trade with the Americas. She understood that her fleet was not strong enough to challenge Spain directly in the New World, but she believed that she could challenge it in a partial manner. She actively promoted smuggling in the Spanish Empire and sponsored attacks on Spanish ships by irregular privateers or pirates.

[27] The Muscovy Company was chartered in 1553, but Elizabeth gave it a whaling monopoly in the north. Robert Brenner, *Merchants and Revolution: Commercial Change, Political Conflict, and London's Overseas Traders, 1550–1653* (Princeton, NJ: Princeton University Press, 1993), pp. 3–23; J. Pauline Croft, ed., *The Spanish Company* (London: London Record Company, 1973); T. S. Willan, *The Early History of the Russia Company, 1553–1603* (Manchester: Manchester University, 1968); A. C. Wood, *A History of the Levant Company* (Oxford: Oxford University Press, 1935); K. N. Chauduri, *The English East India Company: The Study of an Early Joint-Stock Company 1600–1640* (London: Frank Cass, 1965).

[28] Robert Ashton, *The City and the Court, 1603–1643* (Cambridge: Cambridge University Press, 1979), pp. 91, 20–8, and 19.

[29] Chauduri, *The English East India Company*, pp. 29–31.

[30] William Fletcher Johnson, *The History of Cuba*, Vol. 2 (New York: B. F. Buck, 1920), p. 3.

Elizabeth began by encouraging English shippers to avoid Philip's high tariffs by dealing with Spanish merchants before the Spanish ships from the Americas reached the tax collectors in Seville. Thus, both the English and Spanish merchants could avoid Philip's high tariffs on consumer goods going to the Americas and on the silver being brought back. The merchants could make the illegal exchange at the mouth of the Guadalquivir River near Cadiz because Philip was too weak to prevent it.

The Levant Company, which had a monopoly on trade with Spain, was already dealing legally with the Spanish *consulados* (monopoly guilds) and seemed a natural choice to engage in the tax-evasion trade as well. Yet its members (and perhaps Elizabeth herself) worried that illegal commercial activity with the *consulados* would jeopardize their normal trade and in any case reduce the deniability of the Crown's involvement in illegal activities that might provoke war.

To avoid this problem, Elizabeth decided to permit any English merchant and shipper to enter freely into the irregular trade with the Americas even though smugglers and pirates were the most difficult types of shipper to tax. She calculated that there were various direct and indirect ways to ensure that she could at least receive more income than she would otherwise obtain – if nothing else, indirectly through customs duties on Asian silk and spices. That was enough to make the innovation worthwhile. In addition, these activities developed needed sailing skills among those in the merchant marine.

The gradual improvement of the government machinery under the Tudors had given Elizabeth the ability to carry out a policy that Philip could not. His inability even to control the Seville *consulado* belies the talk about his centralized bureaucratic state and about the *consulado* being a sign of his great power. This is what we mean when we say that Elizabeth in the 1570s had a minimally effective state, while Philip had only an early state that was not far advanced.

Elizabeth did not, however, permit the free entry of shippers into trade with the East. The low bulk and high value of the silk and spices made it too easy for a merchant to drop off a substantial amount of them illegally on the long trip back to London and undercut the English re-export price in Europe. Hence Elizabeth retained the monopoly merchant guilds – notably the Levant Company – for that trade.

In practice, many domestic traders were quite willing to take the risks of illegal trade under Elizabeth to gain entry into long-range trade. Brenner reports that "literally hundreds of noncompany, nonmerchant traders invaded the Spanish commerce" and that "until 1625 the trade with Spain was the only really dynamic sector of overseas commerce that was open to the City's domestic tradesmen and ship captains."[31] While their profits were hard to tax, they understood that the queen must benefit or she would cut off their freedom to engage in this trade.

The most dramatic of Elizabeth's innovations in American trade was the commissioning of privateers – or, in more popular language, pirates. They had the responsibility of looting Spanish possessions and ships, but within strict rules of the game that would not provoke Spain to declare war. The pirates were relatively few in number – "a few score captains and a few thousand men." Nevertheless, Elizabeth allowed the press to glorify the pirates and their attacks on the Spanish. David Howarth reported that one sport of Elizabethan England was baiting Spaniards. Howarth asserts that "the whole of the rest of the nation followed it precisely as they follow football now: they celebrated its wins and suffered in its losses, and made heroes of its most successful captains."[32]

As David Howarth noted, Elizabeth "would gladly take her share of the booty."[33] In fact, she invested her own personal funds in some of the privateers. Her most spectacular gain came from her investment in Francis Drake's around-the-world pirate trip that netted enormous amounts of silver. The investors made a 4,700% return on their investment, and Elizabeth received 300,000 pounds, more than her usual annual income. She paid off the foreign debt and invested the remaining 42,000 pounds in the Levant Company.[34]

"Pirate," we should note, was not a precise term because the lines between legal trader, smuggler, and pirate continued to be blurred as it had since the time of the Etruscans, Phoenicians, and Vikings. Pirates often carried goods that they could use in contraband trade, while a shipper who was engaged in smuggling or even legal trade could attack and loot a weaker ship. Even admirals of the navy might cooperate with pirates in exchange for some kind of fee that was essentially a bribe:[35]

> [The English navy] was run in ways which blurred and at times obliterated the distinctions between public and private business. The same men who administered

[31] Brenner, *Merchants and Revolution*, pp. 86, 89. Also see Croft, *The Spanish Company*, preface.

[32] David Howarth, *British Sea Power: How Britain Became Sovereign of the Seas* (London: Collins, 1974), p. 132.

[33] Ibid., pp. 131–2.

[34] Andrews, *Drake's Voyages*, pp. 81–3.

[35] Kenneth Andrews, *The Spanish Caribbean: Trade and Plunder, 1530–1630* (New Haven, CT: Yale University Press, 1978), p. 189; Andrews, *Trade, Plunder, and Settlement*, pp. 22–5; Rodger, "Guns and Sails in the First Phase of English Colonization," p. 96. See C. S. Knighton, *Pepys and the Navy* (Stroud, UK: Sutton, 2003).

> the navy as "Officers of the Admiralty" and commanded squadrons at sea as admirals and captains, were also merchants, shipowners, privateers, shipbuilders, and naval contractors. The fleets they put to sea were normally composed of a mixture of royal and private ships, often built by the same shipwrights to the same designs, and many ships passed from one category to the other.... The Navy Royal was so much under the control of private merchants and shipowners that it was in great measure absorbed into their private naval warfare.

Elizabeth's policy had a series of major consequences. First, as trade with Asia and the Americas expanded, the merchant community began investing heavily in merchant ships. In 1582, England had 20 private ships with over 200 tons of capacity, but another 72 were built by the late 1590s. By 1600, the merchant fleet was 20 times larger than the queen's navy. The number of such merchant ships rose to 150 in 1629. The result was "an extraordinary transformation in the English merchant fleet – if 'merchant fleet' is the right term for privately owned men-of-war, which spent the war years pursuing profit by other means than peaceful trade."[36]

As Rodger indicated, the blurred line between the navy and the armed merchant fleet meant that Elizabeth was building an informal navy at the same time that she was building a merchant fleet. When Philip and his successors did not build enough ships or use allied ships to control smugglers and pirates and to ensure the delivery of silver to Seville for taxation, England gained control of the sea. In the 1600s, Spain even lost much of her control of her own colonies. Some 50% of silver production in the 1600s is estimated to have been smuggled to Europe.

The second major consequence of Elizabeth's policy was the acquisition of the silver needed to expand trade with the East. Eventually the amount of silver is estimated to have risen to 75% of the exports to India. Although historians used to think that the discovery of silver promoted economic growth in Europe by expanding the money supply, it was likely that the more important consequence was that silver was the non-bulky product that allowed an expansion of trade with Asia. Indeed, Andre Gunther Frank argued that Asia was economically more advanced than Europe in the 1500s. Trade with Asia was needed for Europe to learn the innovations of Asian civilizations in the late medieval and early modern periods.[37]

[36] Rodger, *The Safeguard of the Sea*, p. 293. This is a summary of Kenneth Andrews, *Elizabethan Privateering 1583–1603* (Cambridge: Cambridge University Press, 1964).

[37] Andre Gunther Frank, *ReOrient: Global Economy in the Asian Age* (Berkeley: University of California Press, 1998). Also see Kenneth Pomeranz, *The Great Divergence: China, Europe, and the Making of the Modern World* (Princeton, NJ: Princeton University Press, 2000).

The third consequence of Elizabeth's decision to permit the free entry of merchants and shippers into the irregular commerce with Spain and its colonies was the creation of a precedent that Charles I was to adopt in the 1620s in the legal trade with his new colonies in the Americas. We discuss this in the next section.

The crucial point to understand is that two first-class rulers – Philip II of Spain in his reign and Elizabeth I – responded very differently to a transformation in world trade that took place in the mid-1500s. The difference illustrates the relationship of state capability, government policy, and the development of a free market – first of all, to the effectiveness of the government that each of the two monarchs headed.

Charles I's Marketization of Legal Colonial Trade

In the literature on the origins of the English Civil War, Charles I is treated not as a striking innovator but as a reactionary figure who represented the classes of the past (North would say the dominant coalition of the past). The work of the naval historians is given short shrift, and the increasing customs income of Charles I is largely ignored. So too are the implications of the slow improvement of the effectiveness of the state in the century from Henry VII to Charles I and its positive impact on marketization.

One of the striking innovations of Charles I was his colonization of the Americas. Even scholars can be misled by the traditional American textbook descriptions of English colonization of the New World. The textbooks begin with the Lost Colony of Roanoke in North Carolina in 1587, which was settled during the reign of Elizabeth I. In fact, Walter Raleigh was doing little more than trying to establish a port for pirate ships. The textbook version then turns to James I's settlements at Jamestown in 1607 and Plymouth in 1620. These settlements too proved insignificant and failed.

The preoccupation with Jamestown and Plymouth creates the impression that Charles I was not all that significant in colonizing the Americas. This obscures the central role of colonization in his effort to achieve financial independence and the result of this policy in generating fears among his opponents. Charles was particularly eager to increase the size of the navy because of the threat of the Thirty Years' War (1618–1648) in Europe and his policy of colonizing the Americas, and Parliament resisted.

Charles refused to call Parliament into session, and he strove to raise money in other ways. A "Ship Tax" was quite successful, but it became increasingly controversial as it was extended past the port cities dominated by the merchants. As Jack Goldstone emphasized, however, the Ship Tax was just one of the ways that Charles raised money:

> A shortage of money led the Crown into policies and projects that created opposition. Many of these projects were highly commercial and progressive – rent increases to market levels on Crown lands, partnerships to enclose and exploit fens and forests, and sale of trading privileges for international and domestic commerce. Other projects were conservative and feudal – tighter rules of wardship to bring revenue to the Crown, requirement of gentry to take up knighthood, and sale of titles and offices.

The astonishing thing about Goldstone's description of Charles I's search for more funds is that, like most modern American scholars writing about England in the 1600s, Goldstone ignores the king's decision to colonize the Americas in order to grow tobacco and impose a duty on it.[38] In fact, annual customs duties increased from 300,000 pounds at the beginning of the 1630s to 500,000 pounds at the end. Revenues almost doubled from 1603 to 1639. This made Charles I independent of Parliament if he did not become involved in war until his colonial revenue grew still larger.[39]

Similarly, Robert Brenner's monumental study of the role of the merchants in the Civil War describes the involvement of non-guild merchants in the Atlantic colonial trade, but only in the passive tense: "After 1625, free trade became the rule in American commerce." Brenner labels such merchants "interlopers," but they were following official policy, as were the monopoly guilds in their areas. Brenner never indicates that this was the intended result of a deliberate and drastic change in policy by Charles I and that it was introduced in a highly successful attempt to raise tax revenue.[40]

This expansion of customs revenue, most of it based on the colonial trade, occurred primarily under Charles I. James I actually had no large-scale colonization plans. When the Frenchman Samuel de Champlain began to explore and colonize the St. Lawrence River valley in 1603, the French seemed likely to form a major colony that would extend into the rich land of the upper Midwest. The creation of Jamestown and then Plymouth was probably just a signal to the French that James was not ceding North

[38] Jack Goldstone, *Revolution and Rebellion in the Early Modern World* (Berkeley: University of California Press, 1991), pp. 80–1. Colonization is also not mentioned in the summary book on English history in the 1600s by the current Harvard professor specializing on English history of the period. Mark Kishlansky, *A Monarchy Transformed: Britain, 1603–1714* (London: Penguin, 1997).

[39] Derek Hirst, *England in Conflict 1603–1660: King, Community, Commonwealth* (New York: Oxford University Press, 1999), pp. 140–3.

[40] Robert Brenner, *Merchants and Revolution*, p. 105.

America to France. He was trying to form an alliance with Spain and did not want to antagonize the Spanish king with large-scale immigration. He may have hoped that Spain would see England as an ally that formed a protective barrier against French movement southward.[41]

Intentional English colonization of the New World only began in 1623 when James I gave his son, the future Charles I, control of colonial policy. In 1624 Charles I created a new Virginia Company to replace the defunct one and established new island colonies on St. Christopher (now St. Kitts) in 1623 and Barbados in 1627. The purpose of the three was to produce tobacco from which a customs duty could be collected – increasingly, two custom duties as ever more of it was re-exported to Europe.

Charles I, who came to the throne in 1625, also chartered the Massachusetts Bay Colony, a unit centered in Boston that was separate from the Plymouth Colony. It had no economic purpose but was a place of exile and a destination after voluntary flight for Puritan political opponents; Oliver Dickerson reported that the monarchs "even assisted or required" Puritan emigration.[42]

Perhaps Charles was also thinking of the New England settlement as a stronger barrier against French migration from Quebec to the south and against Dutch expansion from the Hudson River north, but in any case he forced the Puritans to settle on land that was fit only for subsistence agriculture and that could not produce significant economic revenue for himself.

Charles I also established a third colony, Maryland, as a Catholic counterpart to the Puritan settlements in New England, but Maryland also served economic purposes. Virginia was a large colony that centered on the James River as it emptied into the Atlantic Ocean at Norfolk, but it also included the Potomac River that flowed toward Norfolk and the Chesapeake Bay farther to the north. By creating a separate colony on the Chesapeake Bay, Charles hoped to create better conditions for the colonization in that area.

In any case, the important English colonies for Charles I were Virginia, Maryland, and Barbados. Pro-royal Anglicans were given Virginia and Barbados as a reward for their services. Religious freedom was not a factor.

41 For James I's policy toward Spain, see Paul Allen, *Philip III and the Pax Hispanica, 1598–1621: The Failure of Grand Strategy* (New Haven, CT: Yale University Press, 2000). In 1565, Spain had ruthlessly destroyed Fort Caroline, a fort that France had established the previous year near Jacksonville, Florida. Spain mercilessly killed all the inhabitants. Charles Bennett, *Laudonniere & Fort Caroline: History and Documents* (Gainesville: University of Florida Press, 1964), pp. 17–22 and 37–48.

42 Oliver Dickerson, *The Navigation Acts and the American Revolution* (Philadelphia: University of Pennsylvania, 1951), p. 149.

Instead, the Anglican colonies established the Church of England as the official religion and forced non-Anglicans as well as Anglicans to pay the tithe as a tax.

The primary purpose of the colonies of Virginia, Maryland, and Barbados was to increase the customs revenue of the king, not to stimulate manufacturing. Americans have been misled by Adam Smith's claim in *The Wealth of Nations* that the purpose of colonization had always been to provide a market for manufacturers. Smith was writing in 1776 not to present an objective history of colonization, but to try to persuade George III that he too should focus on taxing manufacturers. Smith argued that the king should realize that he now could obtain more revenue by taxing the increased industrial production promoted by free trade than from retaining the colonies.

The kings of the 1600s were not, in fact, focused on manufacturing but on tax revenue from trade. In 1650, a quarter of a century after Charles I began serious colonization, the colonies still had only 50,000 people, many of them living on subsistence land in New England and lacking the money to buy a significant amount of manufactured goods. The white population in the South was disproportionately composed of former indentured servants, exiled convicts, and their offspring who also had seldom risen above the subsistence level. Hence, the colonies provided a relatively minor market for English manufactured goods. By contrast, London had grown from 200,000 people in 1600 to over 500,000 by the end of the century.[43] That is where the potential market was located.

More important, the kings could collect customs duties if the ships went through London, but they did not have the capability of taxing manufacturers. Yet if they re-exported the tobacco to the Continent, as they increasingly did, they could collect double taxes. As we will see, this practice continued for another century. In the words of Michael Kammen, "the notorious navigation system did not protect British manufacturers so much as it sheltered an extensive reexport trade."[44]

In return for the re-exported tobacco and Asian products, England and its colonies received European goods for consumption at home and in the colonies. They were carried on English ships and had to pass through an

[43] Roger Finlay, *Population and Metropolis: The Demography of London, 1580–1650* (Cambridge: Cambridge University Press, 1981).

[44] Michael Kammen, *Colonial New York: A History* (New York: Scribner's, 1975), p. 172. J. C. Drummond and Anne Wibraham, *The Englishman's Food: A History of Five Centuries of English Diet* (London: J. Cape, 1939), pp. 116–77 and 203–5.

English port to be taxed. Even in the late 1600s and the first part of the 1700s – a century later – English ships delivered more European goods from London to New York City than ones manufactured in England.[45]

From the perspective of a book about the development of the market, the crucial fact about Charles I's colonial policy in the 1620s was his introduction of rules drastically different from those that James I had established for Jamestown and Plymouth. The latter two colonies were originally settled by companies that had the usual monopoly rights with respect to trade. Charles I extended Elizabeth's free-entry rule for smuggling and piracy in the 1500s to legal trade in the colonies in the 1600s.

The reason that Charles I adopted Elizabeth's policy of free entry of merchants and shippers into colonial trade was the failure of monopoly trade in the original Jamestown colony. New World tobacco served the same function of raising customs revenue as imported spices and silk from Asia. Nevertheless, trade with Asia was different from trade with Virginia and Barbados in one key respect. The Asians could produce as much silk and spices as the English could afford, but the English colonies contained far too few Native Americans to grow the desired amount of tobacco. The English proprietors had to send a substantial number of immigrants, free or otherwise, to grow it.[46]

The basic business plan of the original Jamestown settlement seemed sound, but Jamestown could not obtain the investment to create tobacco plantations. Land had to be cleared, a fort had to be built, slaves or the contracts of indentured servants had to be purchased, and the labor force had to be housed and supplied.

The merchant-shipper community that would benefit from the growth of tobacco was the obvious source of investment. The ship captains carried the labor force to the colony as indentured servants. Servants received a free trip to the colonies in exchange for a contract in which they agreed to work for a number of years for a planter to pay off the cost of the voyage. The captains then sold the servants' contracts to planters. In principle, the shippers could cover much of the investment by selling the servant contracts to the planters on credit and receiving repayment from the tobacco that was produced. As plantation owners became successful enough to buy African slaves, the shippers could sell them on credit as well.

45 Kammen, *Colonial New York*, p. 172.

46 Brenner, *Merchants and Revolution*, pp. 92–116. Wesley Frank Craven, *Dissolution of the Virginia Company: The Failure of a Colonial Experiment* (New York: Oxford University Press, 1932); Wesley Frank Craven, *Southern Colonies in the Seventeenth Century, 1607–1689* (Baton Rouge: Louisiana State University Press, 1949).

The merchants in the monopoly trading companies were not, however, accustomed to making long-term investments in land abroad. They were willing to take large risks, but they hoped to send a ship to some destination and make a profit on the sales both at the destination and back in London. They wanted to judge the risks of the investment within the framework of a single round-trip journey. Insurers also wanted to be able to make the same calculation.

Most of the investors in the monopoly companies considered long-term investment in tobacco plantations especially risky. It was possible that tobacco smoking would be a passing fad in Europe. Charles I himself thought it was a disgusting vice but was willing to profit from it. Given his views, Charles was likely to change his mind if profits were minuscule. No one could be certain that the Native Americans or some disease would not kill the colonists. Indeed, there was a major massacre in 1622.

Charles I decided to solve the investment problem by opening trade with and within the Atlantic colonial empire to any English merchant or shipper. Charles calculated that merchants and shippers who had been frozen out of European and Asian trade by the monopoly guilds would be willing to ensure the necessary investment in the New World to win entry into legal international commerce. He was making the same calculation as Elizabeth I had with illegal trade and was surely influenced by her success.[47]

The first merchants and shippers usually recruited friends and relatives to establish the actual plantations. This created the necessary trust for them to finance the labor force and supplies on credit. The partnerships and business relationships in the English-Chesapeake trade were further extended through intermarriage, and the pattern of reliance on personal ties was continued well after the colonies were established.[48]

The Rules of Colonial Trade and the Consequences of the Shift to Sugar Production in the Caribbean

Charles I established a complex set of rules to govern trade in the Atlantic empire, but four were central: (1) The entry of foreign ships into colonial ports was prohibited. (2) Any English subject was free to trade with any Atlantic colonial or English port, at least if the ship and crew were

[47] Brenner, *Merchants and Revolution*, pp. 94–6 and 113–15.

[48] The previous paragraphs are based on Brenner, *Merchants and Revolution*, pp. 92–116; Peter Mathias, "Risk, Credit, and Kinship in Early Modern Enterprise," in John McCusker and Kenneth Morgan, eds., *Early Modern Atlantic Economy* (Cambridge: Cambridge University Press, 2000), pp. 1–35.

English. (3) The term "English subject" included the colonists. Even Dutch merchants and shippers in the conquered New Netherlands (New York) became "English" if they pledged submission to the English king. (4) English ships, including colonial ones, were prohibited from going directly from the colonies to foreign ports. In practice, most tobacco came to be re-exported to the Continent, but ships had to stop and unload in England (usually London) first.[49]

Originally the rules implied that tariffs would be imposed on all products in the Atlantic trade, but the English customs service was not capable of collecting taxes in the colonies. Moreover, during the 1620s and 1630s, Charles did not have to worry about taxing colonial shipping since the colonies did not have ships that were capable of sailing to the Caribbean, let alone to England. New England did not even have ships that could fish on the banks off Newfoundland and had to depend on English ships from the port of Bristol to do so. These ships provided New England with most of its fish. Only when the English Civil War from the 1640s closed the port of Bristol did New England have to build its own fleet to supply itself.

The ships that sailed in the Atlantic were all based in English ports, and England had developed a strong-enough administrative system to impose customs duties on their cargoes when they returned home. Charles was not concerned about minor coastal trade that might develop between the mainland colonies. His major problem in the colonies was smuggling by Dutch ships in the port of New Amsterdam (New York City). This problem was not solved until his son captured the Dutch colony in 1664.

Charles did not, however, have an ideology of free trade. Even besides excluding foreign ships from the colonies and forbidding English colonial trade with foreign countries, Charles I retained the old monopoly companies in areas other than in the Atlantic. Indeed, he had the new monopoly merchants who traded with the East replace the Merchant Adventurers as the dominant economic group through which he ruled London. He was making precisely the calculation that Mancur Olson expected from the stationary bandit. He was trying to maximize commerce in order to maximize his tax income, but he realized that the achievement of this goal depended on his own ability to collect taxes. He, therefore, followed Elizabeth in adopting a different policy.[50]

[49] Charles Andrews, *The Colonial Period of American History: England's Commercial and Colonial Policy*, Vol. IV (New Haven, CT: Yale University Press, 1938), pp. 13–21 and 59–67.

[50] Brenner, *Merchants and Revolution*, pp. 51–82. For the aldermen, see p. 82.

In summary, several key facts about the English administrative system in the 1630s provide the explanation for the nature of the colonial system. First, London's ability to collect internal taxes effectively was still quite limited, and that included taxes from manufacturers. Second, England did not have a customs system that could collect taxes effectively from shippers who sailed freely between the colonies and foreign ports. Third, England had developed a new ability to collect taxes on bilateral trade between the major English ports, especially London at first, and either foreign or colonial ports.

An ideal triangular trade arose: the export of tobacco from the colonies to England, its re-export to Europe, and then the export of European consumer goods to the colonies with a stop in London. It was easy for the king to collect a customs duty on the tobacco as it was brought into the English port, and to collect one on the consumer goods that were brought to an English port from Europe for re-export.

Many have suggested that non-Establishment merchants had the power to force Charles I to open the Atlantic trade to them. As we have seen, Robert Brenner even calls them "interlopers" and focuses on the relatively few New England merchants who, in fact, had been so weak that they were exiled to the New World. This is misleading. Charles I was using colonization to gain revenue to reduce his dependence on Parliament – he succeeded – and he would have used the monopoly guilds if they had been willing.

Charles's rules were based only on his judgment about how to obtain the maximum amount of tobacco produced in the colonies and then to have it shipped to England where it could be effectively taxed. His successors – the Puritans, Charles II, and the post-Stuart rulers – all testified to his wisdom on this point by institutionalizing his rules into formal Navigation Acts with minor changes.

The major change in the formal rules made by the Puritans and Charles II really did nothing more than formalize the informal practice of Charles I. Charles I had been concerned about taxing a limited number of valuable commodities sent to England, and he did not really care about other trade. This distinction was formalized by a division of goods into "enumerated" and "non-enumerated" categories, one to be taxed and the other not.

Enumerated goods included tobacco, sugar, deerskins, and a few other items not relevant to the life of the mainland colonies. The number increased over the decades, and Adam Smith's *Wealth of Nations* has a detailed discussion of those that were in existence in the 1770s. The Crown continued to insist that enumerated goods be sent only to England (later Great Britain) and under the rules established by Charles I.

Non-enumerated goods were allowed to be traded freely. They could even be traded with foreign countries. In practice, this meant little more than the legalization of smuggling of non-enumerated goods into the European colonies in the New World. In the 1700s, however, the growing European population and prosperity led to an increase in the demand for grain that could not be met internally. Grain remained non-enumerated, and shippers from Philadelphia began carrying Pennsylvania grain to Europe.

The development that drastically changed the impact of Charles's rules on the colonies was a discovery by the Caribbean planters that their islands were ideally suited for sugar production, and that sugar was much more profitable than tobacco. In 1647, Richard Vines of Barbados wrote John Winthrop that New England needed to develop trade with Barbados because its planters "are so intent upon planting sugar that they had rather buy foode at very deare rates than produce it by labour soe infinite is the profitt of sugar workes after once accomplished."[51] Winthrop followed Richard Vines's advice and expanded trade with the Caribbean as rapidly as possible.

As a prominent historian wrote, this shift had a major impact on the English colonies: "tobacco was a valuable crop and an important factor in imperial trade [but still was] sugar's poor relation." The importance of sugar was reflected in the trade statistics. In 1700, the Caribbean colonies were responsible for nine percent of the value of total English worldwide imports compared with eight percent for the mainland colonies as a whole. The Caribbean colonies took four percent of English exports, while the mainland colonies took less than four percent.[52]

The important fact for the mainland colonies was that sugar plantations required enormous numbers of slaves and they had to be fed, clothed, and provided with basic supplies. Yet the Caribbean planters did not want to spend expensive slave labor and land on the production of these basic items. Colonial ships that carried non-enumerated products could, however, travel to a foreign port unless it belonged to a country with which England was at war. As discussed in the next section, ships from New England – and

51 John Winthrop, *Journals* (Boston: Massachusetts Historical Society, 1947), vol. 5, pp. 252–3, quoted in Bernard Bailyn, *The New England Merchants in the Seventeenth Century* (Cambridge, MA: Harvard University Press, 1955), p. 85. Also in Stuart Schwartz, *Tropical Babylons: Sugar and the Making of the Atlantic World, 1450–1680* (Chapel Hill: University of North Carolina Press, 2004).

52 J. H. Parry, *Trade and Dominion: The European Oversea Empires in the Eighteenth Century* (London: Weidenfeld & Nicolson, 1971), p. 50; George Beer, *The Old Colonial System, 1660–1754* (New York: Macmillan, 1933), pp. 23ff.

then increasingly from Charleston, New York City, and Philadelphia – went to foreign territories in the New World as smugglers who violated French, Spanish, and Dutch laws. Nevertheless, tobacco from Virginia, sugar from the Caribbean, and the enumerated commodities from Maryland's Charles Town in the 18th century were overwhelmingly handled by merchants located in Great Britain and carried in ships based in Great Britain. Hence London did not worry much about this trade.

Since the rulers wanted the Virginia colonists to concentrate on the production of tobacco, they relied on the New England colonists to supply basic goods and materials to sugar-producing islands, and they were radical Puritans. Even though the Puritans had beheaded his father, Charles II allowed them to engage in market trade. He did not impose taxes on the free trade, even on the sugar molasses that New England received in return or on the rum that was produced from it in New England. He decided simply to maximize trade between the mainland and the islands, confident that the government could collect the tax indirectly from the resulting added sugar production.

Earlier generations of historians treated New England shippers as a major transporter of slaves from Africa to the South. They emphasized a triangular trade in which New England ships brought molasses from the Caribbean to New England, took rum to Africa in exchange for slaves, brought the slaves to the Caribbean, and then returned to New England with molasses.[53]

This triangular trade did occur, but modern historians who studied the port records discovered that it was relatively unimportant. It is not surprising that London wanted New England ships to play another economic role: to deliver goods to Barbados and Jamaica, not to Africa. They were supposed to supply the Caribbean with the basic foodstuffs and non-manufactured materials that the slaves and relatively few whites required. Incentives, such as toleration of trade with foreign colonies, were established to encourage that trade.

Nevertheless, if readers reflect on the logic of two-way cross-Atlantic transportation in a sailing era, they will realize that shippers in England and New England faced three problems as they traded with the Caribbean. First, New England's trade with the Caribbean and production of rum gave it increasing purchasing power to buy European goods, but New England

[53] Richard Pares, *Yankees and Creoles: The Trade between North America and the West Indies before the American Revolution* (Cambridge, MA: Harvard University Press, 1956), p. 157.

had relatively little that England wanted that would fill the holds of ships for the return voyage.

Second, English shippers taking tobacco and sugar back to England faced the opposite problem. They had ample bulky commodities for the return trip to England, but the Chesapeake and especially the Caribbean did not have enough non-subsistence whites to buy the bulk of valuable manufactured goods from Europe. Third, the amount of molasses produced in England's Caribbean empire was not of sufficient size and quantity to fill the holds on the return voyage to New England.

The problems were solved by two triangular trade routes that made more sense than the New England-Africa-Caribbean-New England one. In one triangle, English ships, a large number of them based in Bristol, handled the export of slaves from Africa to the Americas. They brought goods south to Africa, took slaves to the Caribbean, and then brought sugar back to England.

The second triangular trade involved New England. As we discuss in Chapter 7, many New England ships went back and forth between New England and the Caribbean. The shippers would have preferred that this trade simply involved an exchange of New England goods for molasses or, better still, the bills of sale that the planters had received from the English for their sugar. In either case, the ships had insufficient bulk to fill their holds, and they had to be creative in finding items to carry.

Some New England shippers solved this problem by acquiring slaves in the Caribbean and taking them to Norfolk or Baltimore. There they would exchange them for consumer goods that the English ships coming to Virginia from England had brought in exchange for tobacco. The New England ships would then take the consumer goods and some tobacco home. To create the incentives for such trade, the English did not tax the tobacco going to New England even though it was "enumerated." We return to this subject later when we discuss the impact of this trade on the development of an effective state and market in the future United States-but not in Mexico.

5

Spanish Colonial Policy and the Transition to the Minimally Effective State

The literature on European countries and their colonies are usually not well integrated with each other. Even historians who study specific European countries or their colonies seldom look at both in conjunction.[1] Historians of the domestic development of the "metropolis" rarely look in any detail at the controls in the colonies to shed light on the evolving capability of the homeland government. Dependency analysts treat the relationship of the "metropolis" and "periphery" as relatively static, and, by implication, the metropolis usually seems to be a well-developed exploiter.

In fact, whatever the role of England and Spain vis-à-vis their colonies from the 1500s until the 1800s, England and Spain themselves were developing countries during that period and were constantly changing. Spain in particular was quite undeveloped in the 1500s and 1600s. The mutual feedback between the evolution of the homeland and its colonies needs to be better explored.

Historians of the colonies are very knowledgeable about the homeland's colonial policy, but they sometimes lack the same sophisticated understanding about the relationship of that policy to the ruler's domestic policy or political concerns. This has been especially true in Latin America, where scholarly attention in recent decades has shifted from Spain to the Native American past.

The purpose of this chapter is to illuminate the changing government capability of England and Spain by examining their ability to rule effectively at home. What happened in the Spanish colonies themselves is discussed in Chapter 8. That is where we will deal with the legacy that Spain left to Mexico.

1 A rare exception is a recent book written by John Elliott, the great English historian on Spain. John Elliott, *Empires of the Atlantic World: Britain and Spain in America 1492–1830* (New Haven, CT: Yale University Press, 2007).

A close examination of the relationship between Spain and the Spanish colonies is particularly important for a book intended primarily for contemporary economists. Many American economists since the 1970s have believed that the English government was less centralized than the Spanish and had looser control of its colonies. Many thought this explained why England and the United States had better economic growth and marketization. Douglass North was prominent among them.

As we have seen, modern historians have rejected this interpretation of Spain and Mexico in the 1500s and 1600s. Economists, perhaps influenced by the success of Spain since 1975, have implicitly accepted this view of Spain by no longer including Spain in their comparisons, but they often have retained their old views about Latin America. Yet if Latin America failed to develop properly because it had Spanish culture and bureaucratic tradition, why did that culture and tradition not prevent Spain itself from developing so rapidly in the last 40 years?

Our thesis is that Mexico had slower development compared with Spain in the 1800s because of the collapse of its state from 1810 to 1870. This, of course, is just a continuation of our underlying explanation for the slower development of Castile from the 11th century to 1700. Originally Spain only had to worry about the production and delivery of silver from two relatively compact areas in central Mexico and Bolivia, and this was a reasonably simple administrative task. However, as the colonies began to acquire a larger population and more complex economies, Spain did not have the governmental capacity to rule them properly, especially to supply them with European consumer goods.

The Spanish colonial experience is the clearest possible evidence that Spain could not have the kind of centralized bureaucratic system depicted in much of the economic literature. The king's use of monopoly trade guilds (*consulados*) cannot be an example of his great centralized power if he could not prevent them from engaging in illegal, untaxed colonial trade with England right outside Spain's main port.

Similarly, it cannot be said that Spain governed Mexico through a centralized system from Madrid if foreign smugglers conducted virtually all trade with Europe in the 1600s, including much of the exportation of silver. The future Mexico cannot have been governed by a centralized system from Mexico City if silver and other products were being illegally smuggled out and if imports had to be sold by an illegal trade network.

In short, the Spanish Empire illustrates the same close relationship between effective government and a market economy that we have seen in the English organization of foreign trade. When England had a weak government, it had to rely on domestic monopoly guilds and foreign merchants to conduct its foreign trade and collect customs revenue. Even the creation of a minimally effective state in England in the first third of the 1500s did not immediately give it an ability to conduct free trade. England required another century to develop the governmental capability that allowed the king to move to a policy of permitting free entry of merchants into the Atlantic colonial trade. Only at the end of the 1700s were the Spanish kings becoming ready for such a policy.

The smuggling in the Spanish colonies in the 1600s raises another interesting theoretical point about the nature of market economies. After the English seized New Netherlands (New York), British sea power prevented foreigners from trading with English mainland colonies, but the smugglers in the Spanish Empire were primarily foreigners, at least in the Atlantic (although not the Pacific). The smuggling was nearly totally free trade conducted by merchants who lived in countries with more advanced informal institutions.

Yet this did not prepare Latin America for a sophisticated market economy that was to exist in the future United States. When Americans use the phrase "law and order," they put their emphasis on the word "order." In fact, the smuggling in the Spanish colonies became quite orderly and regularized. What was missing in the Spanish colonies was the "law" and the various legal mechanisms and informal legal institutions of a modern market, which could not be developed until the smuggling abated. These are all points we will also emphasize in the discussion of the colonies in Chapters 7 and 8.

The Origins of the Castilian Colonial System

Isabella did not, of course, have any intention of establishing colonies when she sent Columbus westward across the Atlantic. The year 1492 was historic for Castile, and Columbus's voyage was not the most important event for her in that year. In 1492, Isabella completed the expulsion of the Muslims from Granada and thus from the Iberian Peninsula. At the same time, she issued an edict to expel Jews and Moors from Castile. This was also the year in which the first grammar book on the Castilian language was published. Isabella probably gave relatively little thought to her decisions about Columbus.[2]

[2] Henry Kamen, *Empire: How Spain Became a World Power, 1492–1763* (New York: HarperCollins, 2003), pp. xxv, 11, and 6–9.

The four key events of 1492 had one feature in common. They all contributed to the development of a common sense of identity based on Catholicism, language, and national pride. Isabella and her Hapsburg successors were not concerned with creating a sense of identity between Castile and Aragon. Aragon and Barcelona never became meaningfully involved in the colonies, and they were not forced to use the Castilian language until the 1700s. Isabella's concern was to create some sense of national identity among the various Castilian city-states that had long engaged in civil wars.

The Castilian kings had claimed absolute power, and Isabella followed their lead in claiming the colonies as her personal property. In 1492, Columbus landed on what became the Dominican Republic – or what was called Santo Domingo during the Spanish period. The next year, Isabella sent him back there with settlers. Nevertheless, the Queen never showed much interest in the colonies. She never promoted the conquest of the American Continent, and she died in 1504, 15 years before Hernando Cortéz landed in Mexico.

Ferdinand (1504–1516) and his successor, Charles I (1516–1556) also showed relatively little interest in the colonies. Ferdinand was not even the king of Castile and thus was not the owner of the colonies, while Charles served as the emperor of the Holy Roman Empire and was preoccupied with those duties. Charles did not really establish an administrative system in the colonies, but ruled through irregular conquistadors and church orders, notably the Dominicans.

While Charles I was king, the major policy conflicts about Mexico involved these conquistadors and churchmen. The former concentrated on seeking the source of silver used extensively by the Aztecs, and they found some deposits in the vicinity of Mexico City. The Crown rewarded conquistadors for their efforts with distributions of native labor, called the *encomienda* system. Not surprisingly, it was a legal institution that came under frequent attack by Native Americans and some clergymen. The conquistadors essentially wanted to use the indigenous population as serfs on the large pieces of land they claimed.[3] The churchmen were primarily concerned with converting the Native Americans to Christianity, and they thought that the oppressive and exploitative behavior of the conquistadors made this task more difficult.

In 1542, Bartolomé de las Casas, a Spanish historian and Dominican friar, made a direct appeal to the Spanish Crown to abolish the *encomiendas,*

[3] For a public choice perspective on the *encomienda* system in the Americas, see Ronald Batchelder and Nicolas Sanchez, "The Encomienda and the Optimizing Imperialist: An Interpretation of Spanish Imperialism in the Americas," *Public Choice* 156 (2013), 45–60, p. 46.

arguing that they were a "mortal sin." Charles was persuaded by his argument and issued the New Laws of the Indies, which forbade the inheritance of *encomiendas*. The settlers were furious at this attack on their privileges and in Peru, they assassinated the viceroy in retaliation. In Mexico, the viceroy "prudently ignored the New Laws." P.E.B. Coy writes, however, that the laws "were the beginning of the end for the *encomiendas*, which now fell into the hands of the Crown as they became vacant and were thenceforth ruled by government officials or were sold by the government as land."[4]

The situation in the Spanish colonies changed radically in the mid-1540s. A huge silver deposit was discovered in Potosí in modern Bolivia in 1545, and the following year another great deposit was found in Zacatecas, 400 miles north of Mexico City. Other major discoveries were soon made in northern Mexico.

As the mining industry developed, the mine owners wanted a freer flow of labor to the mines and mining settlements, and hence they joined the church in opposing the conquistadors' policy toward the Native Americans. Philip II came to the throne in 1555 and supported the churchmen because he too did not want the conquistadors to become feudal lords. He regularized the administrative system, in the ways discussed in Chapter 8.

Philip II understandably focused his attention on the acquisition of silver. He allowed all inhabitants, including Native Americans, to engage freely in silver mining. He declared that everything under the ground was his property, and he gave everyone the right to prospect and to mine for silver without the permission of the owner of the surface land. If the mine stood idle for four months, another person could claim it.

Philip's only meaningful demand was that the miners give him 20% (the *quinto*) of the value of the silver they obtained. This was quickly reduced to 10%, the *diezmo* in Mexico, but not in South America.[5] The result in Mexico was "an army of individuals, ranging from lowly Indian to Spanish grandee ... scattered in all directions, through thousands of square miles of mountain vastnesses."[6] The higher tax in Peru reflected the concentration of the silver on one high mountain and, hence, the lesser need for prospecting.

4 P.E.B. Coy, "Justice for the Indian in Eighteenth Century Mexico," *American Journal of Legal History* 12 (1968), 41–9.

5 Peter Bakewell, "Mining in Colonial Spanish America," in Leslie Bethell, ed., *Cambridge History of Latin America*, Vol. 2 (Cambridge: Cambridge University Press, 1984), 105–52, p. 134.

6 Walter Howe, *The Mining Guild of New Spain and Its Tribunal General, 1770–1821* (Cambridge, MA: Harvard University Press, 1949), pp. 2–4 and 19.

Philip created two types of government controls on mining. One was the establishment of a state monopoly on the sale of mercury, a vital element in efficient silver refining. While Madrid made a profit on mercury sales, the primary purpose of the monopoly was to keep the government informed about the amount of mercury that each person was buying. This told the government the approximate amount of silver he was producing and should present for taxation.

Philip II placed treasury offices at the major mines to collect the 20% tax in Peru and the 10% tax in Mexico. Silver was then to be delivered to the state mint. In Peru, the mint was located in Lima (and later in Potosí), while in Mexico it was in Mexico City.

The second type of control imposed by Philip II was a set of draconian rules on the delivery of silver to Europe that were designed to prevent smuggling. The natural route to deliver silver to Europe from Potosí in the Andes passed through what is now northern and central Argentina to Buenos Aires and then to the sea. The king feared that this route would be difficult to police, and he ordered that it not be used.

Instead, silver from Bolivia had to be sent 1,100 miles westward to Lima on the Pacific Coast, then taken north to the Panamanian isthmus, carried across land to the port of Portobello on the Caribbean shore, and then shipped to Spain. The goods from Spain destined for Lima and Potosí had to follow the reverse path. Even trade with the Pampas area of the future Argentina could not pass through the Atlantic port of Buenos Aires, but instead had to go through Lima, 2,700 miles away on the Pacific coast.

In Mexico, silver destined for Europe had to be taken to Mexico City and then to Veracruz, the single port that could be used for trade with Spain. The most promising potential harbor for two-way trade between Spain and the northern mines was located at modern Tampico, but the route from the mines to Tampico did not go through Mexico City. Hence Spain forbade the construction of a port or even a town at that spot. Mexican silver intended for China could be taken only to Acapulco and then shipped to Manila in the Spanish colony of the Philippines.

Inside Spain, the trade with the colonies was supposed to go solely through the port of Seville and was to be handled only by the merchants of the city's foreign trade monopoly (*consulado*). Philip insisted on the use of annual armed convoys to and from the New World to secure the safe passage of the silver. Favorable trade winds from Panama and Veracruz to Iberia converged at Cuba, and the convoys from Veracruz and Lima followed their separate paths to Havana and then traveled together to Seville.

These restrictive trade rules are much emphasized by the scholarly literature, but they were less important than those on the sale of mercury in ensuring that the king received his *diezmo* and *quinto*. The trade rules were aimed more at the 80% or 90% of the silver that was legally left in private hands. As has been seen, Philip imposed a 15% to 17% tariff on private silver imported into Spain, and this was the silver that he feared would be smuggled to Europe to avoid the import tax. This, in fact, occurred in the 1600s under his successors.

Philip encouraged the mine owners to set up a company town around their mines and to supply it with the necessities of life. Native Americans produced most of the latter and supplied them either through a tax paid in goods or in money. The owners often set up ranches, raising mules and cattle to supply themselves with the huge quantity of mules, candle tallow, and leather belts that were essential in the operation of the mines and refineries. As a by-product, beef became extraordinarily cheap and plentiful.

So long as the immigrants to Spanish America were establishing themselves and devoting all their energy to prospecting, they only needed simple goods and supplies. The few necessary consumer goods and the equipment and tools needed for the mines could be brought on the ships returning to Mexico to pick up silver.

As the colony became more prosperous, however, an increasing number of colonists had the money to satisfy their desire for luxury and semi-luxury European goods. These goods had to be imported, and this created the fundamental problem that was already discussed in the previous chapter: since silver was of extremely high value for its size, it required relatively few ships to bring it from the Americas back to Spain. The consumers' goods needed by the colonists required a much larger fleet.

The obvious solution in Spanish America was to produce bulky agricultural commodities as other European powers were doing or were to do. This was not really possible at first when immigrants were obsessed with the potential riches of a major silver or gold strike, but policy should have changed in the 1570s and 1580s.

The most obvious exportable commodity was sugar, which was an extremely profitable crop that Portugal had begun growing in Brazil in the 1540s. Cuba had perfect soil and climate for tobacco and sugar, as did the Spanish island of Jamaica and the part of Hispaniola that became Haiti. Yet in the 1600s, Spain left sugar exports exclusively to England and France.

The best bulky exportable crops in Mexico and Central America were cacao (the base for chocolate), indigo, and dyewood. The most obvious item to ship from Mexico proper was the dyewood trees (*palo de tinte*) that grew naturally around the port of Campeche on the upper Yucatán and in what is now Belize. Campeche was on the normal route between Veracruz and Havana, and Belize was accessible. The dyewood trees produced a very valuable dye, but they usually were carried to Europe as trees or, more rarely, pulp. Hence they were quite bulky and would require a number of ships that could carry consumer goods to Veracruz on the return trip.

English smugglers demonstrated that the large-scale export of dyewood trees from England and Belize was quite profitable. Indeed, dyewood was so important that in 1763 Britain insisted on the future Belize as its prize following its victory in the Seven Years' War. It was named British Honduras. Naturally the British ships carried consumer goods on the return trip, and these were smuggled into Mexico and Central America.

Dyewoods were only one example of the products that the English and Dutch smuggled from Spanish America in the late 1500s and especially the 1600s. Cacao was perhaps the largest item exported, but a wide variety of goods were taken. Once England, France, and the Netherlands acquired colonies, the voyage became short enough that the smugglers did not even need full holds when they returned to their home island with silver and with gold from South America.

In the 1600s, smugglers came almost completely to dominate the empire's trade with Europe. As Henry Kamen wrote, "we may overthrow the idea that the trade system operating in the New World [during this period] consisted of a dominant official trade and a secondary informal one consisting of contraband":[7]

> The incapacity of the official Spanish trade system to minister to the needs of the empire was both flagrant and notorious. Without smuggling the Spanish colonies would have collapsed.... The evolution of an "informal economy" of smuggling was a logical consequence of the inexistence [of a formal economy] – it would be pointless to call it a "breakdown" for it had never reached the point of functioning properly.... The population was inevitably forced to buy goods from any other available suppliers.

The result was inevitable once Madrid decided not to develop commodity exports in the Caribbean islands and northern South America. The Europeans, first of all, wanted silver, and it was smuggled in huge amounts, far more than it would have been in conjunction with regularized legal trade.

Industry and commerce developed in the southern United States only after World War II because the South had not learned the skills or developed the infrastructure that the North possessed because of its trade with the Caribbean. If Spain had developed commodity production in the Caribbean, the slaves surely would have received supplies from the

[7] Kamen, *Empire*, p. 472.

mainland. The colonists there would have begun to learn a "capitalist culture" as well. The central unexplored question in Spanish American economic history is why this did not occur.

The Non-Decision on Commodity Production

Scholars face two main problems in comparing English and Spanish colonial policy in the 1500s and 1600s. One is to explain the events that took place. The other is to explain events that did not take place, but seemingly should have. The latter problem is particularly great in the failure of Spain to develop commodity exports. Sometimes non-decisions are explained by the failure of policymakers to consider options, but in this case, the Spanish kings had successful models from the beginning.

The most obvious export commodity from the Spanish Empire was sugar produced in the Caribbean. In the 1550s, Portugal quickly became a large-scale sugar producer in Brazil and showed that producing sugar there was highly profitable.[8] The climate and soil of the Spanish Islands were even better suited for sugar production. It would have been easy to solve the transportation problem by establishing the plantations in Cuba and sending the sugar back on convoys with silver.[9]

According to John Parry, "Portuguese emigrants ... took to life in the Tropics, even the humid and lowland Tropics, with the determination and the enthusiasm of pioneers proud of a new home." Sugar was so valuable that the Portuguese carried it to Lisbon by armed convoy. Even then Elizabeth I found it profitable to attack the sugar ships with pirates. Parry reported that Portugal "employed far more ships than the trade between Spain and the Spanish [America], and probably rivaled that trade in the value of total cargoes."[10]

[8] For a discussion of the elasticity of demand for sugar, see John McCusker, *Rum and the American Revolution: The Rum Trade and the Balance of Payments of the Thirteen Continental Colonies* (New York: Garland, 1989), p. 33; J. C. Drummond and Anne Wibraham, *The Englishman's Food: Five Centuries of English Diet* (London: Jonathan Cape, 1939), pp. 116–77 and 203–5; Eddy Slots, "The Expansion of the Sugar Market in Western Europe," in Stuart Schwartz, ed., *Tropical Babylons: Sugar and the Making of the Atlantic World, 1450–1680* (Chapel Hill: University of North Carolina Press, 2000), 237–88; Sidney Mintz, *Sweetness and Power: The Place of Sugar in Modern History* (New York: Viking, 1985).

[9] George Hunte, *Jamaica* (London: B.T. Batsford, 1976), p. 65: Herbert Klein, *Slavery in the Americas: A Comparative Study of Virginia and Cuba* (Oxford: Oxford University Press, 1967).

[10] J. H. Parry, *Trade and Dominion: The European Oversea Empires in the Eighteenth Century* (London: Phoenix Press, 1971), pp. 32–3. See Gilberto Freyre, *The Portuguese and the*

It would have seemed natural for Philip II to pour his income from silver into building a fleet to defend and expand his source of income in the New World. That was the policy followed by English rulers as different as Charles I, Cromwell, and Charles II from the 1630s into the 1680s. Philip II, a Hapsburg ruler, preferred to spend his silver earnings on wars in Central Europe and the Mediterranean and on the suppression of a revolution in the Low Countries.

Then Philip II and his successors increased the incentives for Europeans and the colonists to engage in smuggling by imposing a high tariff on the export of private silver. The Spanish kings received an immediate 10% of the silver mined in Mexico and 20% of that mined in South America. That left most silver in the hands of the colonists themselves. A modern reader would assume that this silver was simply money that the colonists could spend without paying any additional tax upon it. If they used it to purchase European consumer goods, the king could have raised his tax revenue simply by placing a tariff on the European goods sent to the colonies.

But for whatever reason, Philip II did not adopt that policy. He charged a 17% tariff on the private silver sent to Spain and a similar tariff on goods sent to the colonies. In addition, the Spanish merchants were necessary middlemen if foreign ships were not allowed to sail to colonial ports, and they took advantage of their position to charge high commissions on European consumer goods sent to the colonies. As a result, both the Europeans who wanted to acquire silver and the colonists who wanted to buy consumer goods with their silver had to pay a very high price for it. Hence both had a strong self-interest in obtaining it in other ways.

Nevertheless, Philip had other options. The Low Countries were part of Spain's semi-empire in Europe, and the great port of Antwerp remained Spanish even when revolution broke out. In 1580, Philip became king of Portugal as the person next in line to the throne. The fleets both in the Low Countries and Portugal were not only a means of transportation but were capable of serving as an armed naval force. Earl Hamilton notes that after Portugal became part of Spain, the combined Spanish-Portuguese fleet was triple the size of the English fleet in 1585.[11]

Tropics (Lisbon: International Congress of the History of Discoverers, 1961). For the development of sugar in Brazil, see Stuart Schwartz, *Sugar Plantations in the Formation of Brazilian Society: Bahia, 1550–1835* (Cambridge: Cambridge University Press, 1985). See also Schwartz, *Tropical Babylons*.

11 Earl Hamilton, "Revisions in Economic History: VIII. The Decline of Spain," *Economic History Review* 8 (1938), 168–79, p. 168.

In addition, a policy of allowing Portugal and the Low Countries access to the profits of the New World should have given both of them a powerful incentive to maintain their ties with Spain. Elizabeth was freezing the Dutch out of English trade as she built her own fleet, and Portugal's sugar ships were threatened by privateers. Neither the Low Countries nor Portugal had the population for large-scale settlements in the New World, but, as we have seen, England relied on African slaves for its labor force in sugar production in the Caribbean islands and had a very small white population there. If Spain had wanted to develop the lower Mississippi River valley with Europeans, it had access to a large number of Catholic immigrants from its semi-empire in Naples and Sicily.

When Spain took over Portugal in 1580, its growers must have sought permission to have sugar plantations in the Spanish Caribbean islands. In addition, Europe could increasingly afford chocolate, and cacao had a huge and growing demand. It was produced in a number of locales in Spanish America, especially Venezuela. The bulky dyewood trees in Mexico yielded an extremely valuable dye. All the products could have filled the holds on the return ships.

In practice, Philip did not give either the Portuguese or the Dutch access to the Spanish-American empire, even a section of an island such as Cuba and Santo Domingo, that they could develop and use as a port. Scholars often say that Philip II was so obsessed with the danger of silver smuggling that he feared to have commodities grown and shipped to Spain. His successors in the 1600s even moved to outlaw the growth of such commodities.

This interpretation may, in fact, be accurate, but the Spanish kings should have understood one basic fact. The colonists were going to insist on European goods, and if Spain did not provide them legally, others were going to provide them illegally. Illegally imported consumer goods would be bought with illegally exported silver.

So it proved to be. For example, as we will see, Britain was to be allowed to harvest the dyewood trees in Mexico and modern Belize illegally – and naturally to carry consumer goods westward in the process. They used other commodities from Central America and South America. As a result, an immense amount of silver was to flow in illegal trade from Mexico and South America to Europe.

Philip and his successors followed an immigration policy that further prevented non-Spanish entry into the colonial market. This policy was the diametric opposite from that of England. The English consciously reserved each colony for the proprietor of a different religion in the 1600s, but even then, people from all countries were essentially free to emigrate, at least to the mainland colonies where huge amounts of land were available. An increasing number of slaves were also brought from Africa to the English colonies.

The Castilian king, by contrast, strove to prevent diversity. The immigrants were supposed to be Catholics from Spain, normally Castile. Even the many Jews and Moors who had been converted to Catholicism in the 1490s were not allowed. Non-Spaniards, including people from Portugal after it supposedly became as attached to Spain as Aragon was, were forbidden to come to the New World. England pushed its dissidents to emigrate to the colonies and exiled criminals there, but Spain did neither.

Obviously the Crown could not enforce all these restrictions, and a number of immigrants came with prohibited backgrounds they did not acknowledge. Nevertheless, the number of immigrants was much smaller than in the English colonies.

Scholars explain this immigration policy by noting that Spanish colonists could employ large numbers of Native Americans and did not need as many immigrants. To a considerable extent, this explanation is correct, but it takes for granted the strange Spanish decision to develop only the extraction of silver and supporting economic sectors. Nearly all the relatively few Native Americans in the Caribbean died after the arrival of the Spaniards or intermarried with the colonists. Either Europeans or African slaves were needed to grow crops.

Perhaps Philip's policy can be explained by over-optimism about his ability to conquer the English with an armada. He had been married to the Catholic Mary Tudor from 1554 to 1558 and had been king of England in that period. He may have overestimated the Catholic opposition to Elizabeth. Then after the failure of the Spanish Armada in 1588, Philip was in his 60s and, like Elizabeth at the same time, may not have wanted to embark upon a major new venture.

Nevertheless, Philip's successors certainly should have had a commodity-export policy, especially after Charles I of England showed its value in the 1620s – and even more after the end of the Thirty Years' War in 1648 and the English and French discovery of the profitability of sugar production in the Caribbean.

The expansion of the fleet by Elizabeth I, Charles I, and Cromwell made Spanish ship construction even more important. Yet the Spanish kings of the 1600s even discouraged the construction of the private merchant ships that would have been required for commodity production in the colonies. Hamilton reported that "by the middle of the seventeenth century [Spain did not have] enough fishermen ... to equip a fleet" and that by the end of the period "five sixths of the cargoes of the outbound fleets" were controlled by foreigners.[12] The reason is not clear. Perhaps, the Seville merchants were profiting under the smuggling regime. Since they apparently were the ones being taxed for naval expenses, perhaps the kings had lost all control of Seville and had no independent source of funding. There is much research to be done.

Whatever the cause, Spain could do nothing when the Dutch began plundering the Brazilian coast in 1604 and seizing a long stretch of it in 1630. Having received no benefits from incorporation into Spain, the Portuguese merchants in 1640 led an independence movement. Madrid put up no resistance. The smuggling increased dramatically when England, France, and Holland began to colonize the New World in the 1620s and 1630s. This program required a rapid expansion in the merchant fleet. In 1663, the English merchant fleet weighed 90,000 tons, and this rose to around 180,000 tons in 1690 and 260,000 tons in 1701.[13]

The English, French, and Dutch now had ports in the area to use as bases for their smugglers. The English policy of providing basic goods for the Caribbean slaves from New England and then South Carolina was by necessity limited to crops and products that could be produced in those climates. The ships of the English smugglers could acquire commodities that could be produced in southern climates, take them to Barbados and Jamaica, and then pick up sugar to deliver to England. In England, they could acquire the desired consumer goods and take them to Spanish America to complete the triangular trade. The smugglers seldom landed in hidden coves of Spanish America or off distant beaches. The ships came to ports such as Buenos Aires in modern-day Argentina, and they dealt openly with local officials at all levels who charged their own "customs duties" for their own use.

Spain's failure to develop a fleet or use those of its European semi-colonies meant that a commodity export policy or an expansion of immigration was impossible. Indeed, Philip II's son, Philip III, went further. Philip III vigorously tried to attack smuggling by forbidding the production of items that had previously been smuggled.

[12] Guadalupe Chocano, "Decadencia del poder naval e imperio marítimo español desde el siglo XVII," in Enriqueta Vila Vilar and Allan Kuethe, eds., *Relaciones de poder y comercio colonial: Nuevas perspectives* (España: Concejo Superior de Investigaciones Científicas, 2004), pp. 993–1031; Hamilton, "Revisions in Economic History," pp. 168–79. For the decline in shipping, he quotes Clarence Haring, *Trade and Navigation between Spain and the Indies in the Time of the Hapsburgs* (Cambridge, MA: Harvard University Press, 1918), pp. 113, 122, 213–15.

[13] Abbott Payson Usher, "The Growth of English Shipping, 1572–1922," *Quarterly Journal of Economics* 42 (1928), 465–78, p. 467.

The classic example of the new policy is found in Santo Domingo. It had exported 50,000 hides a year around 1580, but beginning in 1605, Philip III forced settlers on the northern shore of the island to abandon their homes in order to end their contraband trade. This was the abandoned land that France occupied in 1625 and turned into a major sugar producer, the future Haiti. Yet when the northern settlers were forced to settle near the capital, they were not encouraged to form plantations or ranches there.[14]

Similarly, for ten years, the farmers of Venezuela were forbidden to grow tobacco even though it had a good market in Europe. Venezuela was also not allowed to export cacao to Europe. Planters in the Kingdom of Quito (modern Ecuador) tried to create cacao plantations to satisfy the growing demand of Mexico, but this was declared illegal.[15]

In an attempt to stop the illegal transmission of Peruvian silver through Acapulco to purchase Chinese silk, porcelain, and other goods, Philip III in 1616 tore down the long-time Mexican Pacific port of Huatulco, and in 1631 he made trade between Mexico and the Viceroyalty of Peru illegal. The great harbor of Acapulco was limited to a fort and a tiny village that had economic activity only when the legal fleets arrived.

The dramatic impact of these actions and inactions can be seen in the official statistics about trade between Spain and Spanish America. The combined total of exports plus imports between Spain and New Spain and reached a peak in 1605, with 29,435 tons of trade.[16] By 1630, this number had fallen to 14,648, and 20 years later, it stood at 9,080 tons. The amount of trade remained within a fairly stable range of 3,000 to 7,500 tons a year until the end of the century. Trade with South America followed a similar pattern.[17]

14 Kenneth Andrews, *The Spanish Caribbean: Trade and Plunder, 1530–1630* (New Haven, CT: Yale University Press, 1978), pp. 12–3.

15 See John Leddy Phelan, *The Kingdom of Quito in the Seventeenth Century: Bureaucratic Politics in the Spanish Empire* (Madison: University of Wisconsin Press, 1967), p. 17.

16 Having a measure of the value of merchandise traded would be ideal, but data constraints mean that unfortunately we only have measures of the average tonnage of merchant ships that sailed between Spain and the Indies. García-Baquero González notes that the total tonnage is not equivalent to tonnage in terms of capacity and argues that while the tonnage statistics are the best we have, they are "not an exceptionally good measure of trade trends." A. García-Baquero González, "Andalusia and the Crisis of the Indies Trade, 1610–1720," in I.A.A. Thompson and Bartolomé Yun Casalilla, eds., *The Castilian Crisis of the Seventeenth Century: New Perspectives on the Economic and Social History of Seventeenth-Century Spain* (Cambridge: Cambridge University Press, 1994), pp. 115–35.

17 Ibid., pp. 116–18, especially the graph on p. 117. Lutgardo García Fuentes, *El Comercio Español con America (1650–1700)* (Seville: Escuela de Estudios Hispanos-Americanos de Seville, 1980).

It is difficult to explain the actions of Philip's successors, except by citing incompetence or depression. Perhaps they were making a rational decision that they did not have the government capability to collect customs duties from Portuguese and Dutch ships, or to prevent the seizure of an island in a declaration of independence by foreign settlers.

The question of importance for building a market and state in Mexico is the impact on Mexico of the decline in official trade. The first question is the effect on the Mexican economy in the 1600s. Some scholars believe it led to a depression while others think that it forced the colonists to produce a greater variety of goods for themselves and thereby develop their economy. The second question is whether the "free market" smuggling contributed to the development of a more entrepreneurial merchant class inside Mexico. If it did not, why was this the case? We will discuss this in Chapter 8.

The Bourbon Reforms inside Spain and the Transition to a Minimally Effective State

Scholars who survey English history are struck by the slow pace of development, but they still have the sense of persistent movement forward toward a modern economic and political system. It seems astonishing that a century passed between Henry VIII's creation of a navy and England's first serious colonization program under Charles I. But it is also fairly astonishing that long-distance trade with the colonies was the first in which the king did not use foreign merchant guilds. Moreover, it seems strange that the man who introduced this innovation was so rigid in his actions at home that he provoked a successful Civil War and was beheaded.

A similar gradual development occurred in Spain and its relationship with its colonies in the century after the lack of effective control in the 1600s. When the French Bourbons consolidated their control in the first decades of the 1700s, they introduced the kind of "political centralization" (in Acemoglu and Robinson's words) or "minimally effective state" (in our words) that the early Tudors had introduced in England nearly two centuries before.

Only the first half of the evolution of Spain to a fully effective state occurred in the period before this book comes to an end. Upon reflection, we think it most useful to discuss it within the framework of the change in controls over the colonies, and especially Mexico. This simultaneous examination of homeland and colony permits us to see policy at the end of the colonial period in a more sophisticated manner than often occurs. What is frequently seen as increased Spanish repression in the late colonial period is actually a reflection of changes within Spain itself that are usually seen in far more positive terms in countries such as England. Not by coincidence, the Spanish king who began introducing free trade in the colonies was also the man who created a more effective bureaucracy and simultaneously supported the spread of rational-legal (Enlightenment) values.

No doubt, the court politics of the 1600s in Spain obscured a gradual improvement of the bureaucracy, but the political system was so moribund that foreigners were able to intervene to decide the Spanish succession. What is unclear is whether the transition to a minimally effective state would have occurred in Spain in the early 1700s without the seizure of the throne by the French Bourbons who introduced French values and practices.

In the War of Spanish Succession from 1700 to 1715, international coalitions led by France and the Hapsburg Empire supported different contenders to succeed Charles II. The candidate of the French Bourbons, Philip V, quickly won in Castile, but he did not gain control of Aragon and Valencia until 1707 and Catalonia until 1715.[18]

Philip V brought his closest advisers from France, and he was determined to replace the old elite with Spaniards more congenial to his way of thinking. Philip used a traditional technique to accomplish this goal: the replacement of the councils dominated by aristocrats with a cabinet council (*despacho*) and with four secretariats (ministries): State, Justice, War, and Navy and Colonial Affairs. He staffed these bodies with university-educated bureaucrats who had occupied secondary positions in the previous century.[19]

The formation of the secretariats had a significance that went beyond a change in personnel. They had the task of drafting and reviewing all legislation. In the words of Jaime Vicens Vives, "for the first time in the history of Spanish administration there were specialized persons held directly responsible to the king."[20]

The Bourbon monarchs also began the long process of trying to centralize the fiscal administrative system. The Hapsburg kings had appointed a weak representative in the regional capitals, but Philip V tried to move toward the French prefect system by appointing *intendants* with stronger financial,

[18] Henry Kamen, *The War of Succession in Spain, 1700–1715* (Bloomington: Indiana University Press, 1969); and David Francis, *The First Peninsular War, 1702–1713* (London: Ernest Benn, 1975). The foreigners exited the war in the Treaty of Utrecht in 1713, a fact that leads to different dating of the war by historians.

[19] John Lynch, *Bourbon Spain, 1700–1808* (Oxford: Basil Blackwell, 1989), pp. 60–1 and 99.

[20] Jaime Vicens Vives, *An Economic History of Spain* (Princeton, NJ: Princeton University Press, 1969), pp. 476–7.

administrative, and military powers. Philip V largely backed away from this reform, but his son, Ferdinand VI, would return to it in mid-century.[21]

More fundamental constitutional change was required in the Confederation of Aragon. The Confederation had had its own parliament, laws, taxes, and language during the 1500s and 1600s. Philip abolished the autonomous political institutions of Aragon and divided the area into districts, each headed by an *intendant* who served as its military governor. For the first time, the national government acquired the right to impose taxes in the Confederation. The Castilian language became the official language of Spain, and the Catalonian language could no longer be used in courts of law or in any official business. Tariffs between the various kingdoms were ended.[22]

The Spanish Catholic Church had censored the Enlightenment views of Paris and even considered the French Catholic Church "heretical." As a 17-year-old king from Paris, Philip V thought the Spanish Catholic Church was much too rigid. He quietly introduced looser censorship and even tolerated Benito Feyjoo, the most radical and populist dissident who argued for the adoption of foreign ideas and scientific inquiry. In 1750, Ferdinand VI officially embraced Feyjoo.

In the 1600s, Madrid's power over the regions and colonies had weakened, and at the same time the Crown had lost much control of the Catholic Church. In the Concordant of 1753, Ferdinand reestablished control over the church in a move that had ideological as well as financial consequences. The pope renounced the large payments he received from the Spanish church and conceded the king's unlimited right to appoint bishops.[23] Then in 1767, Ferdinand's son Charles III decided to expel the Jesuits and thereby transform the universities that they controlled and staffed.

The progress under Philip V, who ruled from 1700 to 1746, was slow, and this is usually attributed to his depression. Yet reform often is slow. So it was in England from 1540 to 1600 except in the development of the navy and merchant fleet, and there the private sector was given a major role in ship construction. The transformation of values, habits, and assumptions

21 Lynch, *Bourbon Spain*, pp. 102–4. Philip V did retain military *intendants* in nine provinces in which troops were stationed. Henry Kamen, "The Establishment of *Intendants* in Early Bourbon Spain," in Henry Kamen, *Crisis and Change in Early Modern Spain* (Aldershot, UK; Variorum, 1993), XIV, pp. 1–13.

22 Lynch, *Bourbon Spain*, pp. 116–23.

23 William Callahan, *Church, Politics, and Society in Early Modern Spain* (Cambridge, MA: Harvard University Press, 1984), pp. 39–41. See Helen Rawlings, *Church, Religion, and Society in Early Modern Spain* (New York: Palgrave, 2002), p. 53.

requires generational change – and, indeed, change across multiple generations. The early Bourbon kings had to work with personnel whose attitudes and skills were shaped in the Hapsburg era, and the elite of Aragon had to be treated with special care because they had been accustomed to almost full autonomy.

Stanley and Barbara Stein state that in 1750, Spain still had "a fragile (nominally 'absolutist') state and porous empire" with a "fractured territorial entity." This, they say, was reflected in the nature of the bureaucracy: "The patterns of recruitment and advancement… reinforced regional bureaucratic 'dynasties' closely attuned to local interest groups."[24]

Ferdinand VI (1746–1759) supposedly was like Philip V in having a phlegmatic and depressive personality, but even if this is true, Spain still made major progress during his 13 years in office. He was the first to unite the armies and navies of Castile and Aragon, and beginning in 1750, he expanded what we would call the defense industries that produced ships and materiel for the military.[25] The creation of a national flag was postponed until 1785, almost surely out of fear that such a symbol would be divisive.[26]

Ferdinand put special emphasis on administrative and economic modernization. Since the Mesta had become a less reliable instrument of royal rule in 1600s, the Crown came to rely largely on tax farmers to collect taxes on wool. In 1749, Ferdinand VI decided that the administrative system had become efficient enough to end this type of tax farming, but in practice, the change only occurred gradually.[27]

Ferdinand's reforms clearly were only a first step. If the regime was to establish uniform real tax rates across the country, it needed to have better information about national income. It began making more demands on the localities for information. The localities resisted, but Ferdinand also strengthened his power over the provinces. He succeeded in appointing French-like provincial governors called *intendants* on a permanent basis all across Castile as well as Aragon.[28]

The appointment of *intendants* had another long-term impact that is not apparent on the surface. Because of their military roles, the *intendants* often

[24] Stein and Stein, *Apogee of Empire*, pp. 24 and 28.

[25] Vicens Vives, *An Economic History of Spain*, pp. 529–30.

[26] Stanley Stein and Barbara Stein, *Silver, Trade, and War: Spain and America in the Making of Early Modern Europe* (Baltimore, MD: Johns Hopkins University Press, 2000), p. 232.

[27] Carla Rahn Phillips, "The Spanish Wool Trade, 1500–1780," *Journal of Economic History* 42 (1982), 775–95. See in particular pp. 784 and 789.

[28] For the complaints in Cadiz about the collection of statistics, see Stanley Stein and Barbara Stein, *Apogee of Empire: Spain and New Spain in the Age of Charles III, 1759–1789* (Baltimore, MD: Johns Hopkins University Press, 2003), pp. 18–20.

were selected from the ranks of military officers and not only from Castile. Their backgrounds were very different from those of the officials trained in Jesuit universities. The same change was to occur in Spanish America in the last quarter of the 1700s when *intendants* were introduced there as well.

Charles III (1759–1788) pushed his father's reforms far more vigorously. He had ruled Naples and Sicily for 24 years before coming to the throne in Spain, and he had earned the reputation of being a reformer. Charles III brought many top advisers from Naples to Spain to help him reform Spain. The most notable was his minister of Finance and War, the Marquis of Esquilache. Esquilache, as we will see below, would be a key figure in the reforms in Spanish America.

Charles began with a measure that symbolized his determination to modernize the country: the physical transformation of Madrid, a city of 150,000. Madrid had poorly lit streets onto which people threw garbage and human waste from their windows. Pigs wandered loose. The city, Anthony Hull asserts, resembled London in the Stuart period.[29] Charles III ordered an expensive paving of Madrid's streets and prohibited the disposal of garbage and refuse on the streets.

Charles III also launched a frontal attack on the bureaucracy. The upwardly mobile bureaucrats of 1700 had been used to undermine the old Hapsburg officials, but their successors had become the status quo officials as of 1759. As has been seen, the Jesuits had established a network of private colleges, and former kings had recruited the bureaucracy from the graduates of these colleges. Almost immediately, however, Charles III began to demand that those who had not graduated from Jesuit colleges be given preference in government appointments.[30]

Then, in 1767, Charles expelled all the Jesuits from Spain and Spanish America: 5,000 in Spain itself and 4,000 in the New World.[31] Charles also used the powers of appointment won by Ferdinand VI to replace the elite of the Catholic Church with more modern and pliant bishops.[32] The expulsion of the Jesuits meant the expulsion of the professors and staff of the elite Jesuit colleges, and the new personnel were forced to introduce a new

[29] Anthony Hull, *Charles III and the Revival of Spain* (Washington, DC: University Press of America, 1980), p. 107.

[30] David Ringrose, *Madrid and the Spanish Economy 1560–1850* (Berkeley: University of California Press, 1983), p. 366.

[31] For Mexico, D. A. Brading, *Church and State in Bourbon Mexico: The Diocese of Michoacán, 1749–1810* (Cambridge: Cambridge University Press, 1994), pp. 3–19.

[32] Richard Herr, *Eighteenth Century Revolution in Spain* (Princeton, NJ: Princeton University Press, 1958), p. 33.

curriculum based more on science. Mark Burkholder and Lyman Johnson describe the results – and, no doubt, the intention – of policy in Mexico, but their words also apply to Spain:[33]

> The expulsion of the Jesuits [in 1767] deprived New Spain and Peru of their prominent educators [and thus] removed the foremost advocates of scholastic thought. [This] facilitated the widespread introduction of a more modern approach to knowledge. By the close of the 18th century, skepticism of authority, observation of nature, experimentation, and analysis based on inductive reasoning had transformed the intellectual milieu of the colonies.

The attack on the church was also designed to change the intellectual atmosphere of Spain in a more rational-legal (Enlightenment, in more conventional language) direction.[34] While the pre-Bourbon monarchs largely legitimated their rule by associating themselves with religion, the pro-Crown intellectuals of the Bourbon regime naturally emphasized more secular functions of the state. The expansion of state power and the promotion of economic growth to increase both popular well-being and revenue were prominent among them. All this implied a powerful monarch who must act in a restrained manner.[35]

Of course, the establishment of the early stages of a rational-legal system in England required two centuries from 1485 to 1688. There is no reason to think that Spain could have made the transition from the personalistic regime of the Hapsburgs much more quickly. Indeed, it was not completed by the time of Napoleon's overthrow of the Bourbon regime in 1808.

From our perspective, the most important early policy of Charles III was a major economic liberalization inside Spain. The city-state councils long exerted control over crop deliveries to their own cities, and this had required them to restrict the sale of crops outside the area in order to guarantee supplies for their own citizens. For example, prior to the second half of the 1700s, olive oil from Seville could not be shipped without permission more than approximately 15 to 20 miles from the city.[36]

Suppliers were given a monopoly in delivering crops to Madrid and in collecting taxes on them. At least in the larger cities, the guilds – for example, the famous Five Major Guilds of Madrid – were deeply involved in the

[33] Mark Burkholder and Lyman Johnson, *Colonial Latin America*, 6th ed. (New York: Oxford University Press, 2008), pp. 323–8; Brading, *Church and State in Bourbon Mexico*, pp. 12–15.

[34] Herr, *Eighteenth Century Revolution in Spain*, pp. 37–41; see p. 39 for Ferdinand VI.

[35] Gabriel Paquette, *Enlightenment, Governance, and Reform in Spain and Its Empire* (New York: Palgrave, 2008), pp. 57–74.

[36] Ringrose, *Madrid and the Spanish Economy*, p. 305.

process.[37] Price controls were required to prevent anyone from undercutting the monopoly prices of the guilds that also were collecting taxes. The sales tax was a major national tax, and it was incorporated in the contracts and subsidies as direct add-ons or as a hidden part of the price.

The weakening of the state-created economic monopolies and guilds – and, therefore, also the mechanism by which taxes were collected – took place in the months before Charles III ascended to the throne. For the first time, anyone was able to bring grain freely into Madrid for sale. Price controls on the sale of wheat and other commodities were gradually loosened, but as in England in the 1500s and 1600s, the process was haphazard, inconsistent, and subject to reversal. Indeed, the uncertain rain supply on the plateau often resulted in temporary government action. Nevertheless, if time is measured in decades, change did move forward. The decline in the guilds of Madrid led to their disappearance in the 1800s.[38]

As mentioned repeatedly, Charles III of Spain was similar to Charles I of England in two respects that are crucial for this book. Both acted as increasingly authoritarian rulers and tried to tighten their control over the policy process. Yet, both introduced major economic liberalization. The important change for this book involves foreign trade. Charles I permitted virtually free trade within the Atlantic empire, although not between the empire and foreign countries. Charles III changed his policy more gradually, but, as we will see later in this chapter, his ultimate goal clearly was the English model.

When Charles III died in 1788, the French Revolution that overthrew the French Bourbons was only one year in the future and the beheading of the French king and queen only five years away. Charles III was succeeded by his son, Charles IV, who was an extremely weak and passive king. All power flowed to the queen and her favorite consort, who became prime minister. After the beheading of Louis XVI in 1793, the prime minister focused almost exclusively on an ill-advised war against France. In order to fight the war, the regime engaged in desperate attempts to raise money, including in the colonies. Then in 1808, Napoleon Bonaparte overthrew the Bourbons and installed his brother as king.

In a sense, it is fortunate that this book ends its discussion of Spain in the early 1800s. Scholars can only guess what would have occurred had

37 The Cinco Gremios was a big tax farmer; see Stein and Stein, *Apogee of Empire*, p. 20; See Miguel Capella Martínez and Antonio Malilla Tascón, *Los Cinco Gremios Mayores de Madrid. Estudio crítico-histórico* (Madrid: Camera de Comercio de Madrid, 1957).

38 David Ringrose has written about the irregular changes on a detailed basis. See Ringrose, *Madrid and the Spanish Economy*, pp. 150–4 for changing regulations on wheat and pp. 154–63 for other commodities. For the slow decline of guilds, see pp. 95, 98, and 131.

there not been the disruption caused by the French Revolution and then in 1808 by Napoleon's short-lived appointment of his brother as king of Spain. England in the 1500s had a "disruption" with 13 years of forgotten monarchs between Henry VIII and Elizabeth I that had little lasting impact. It is hard to judge the impact of the more serious disruption in Spain from 1787 until 1814.

The Bourbon Reforms in Mexico: An Overview

When the Bourbon Philip V came to power in 1700, he quickly showed that one of his major goals was to restore Madrid's loss of control over its colonies. He signaled his intentions at the beginning of his reign when he combined naval and colonial administration into a single Ministry of the Indies and the Navy. He built three new shipyards, but in 1720, the Spanish navy still had a total displacement of only 22,000 tons, while the British navy had 174,000 tons, the Dutch 79,000 tons, and the French 48,000.[39]

By 1740, Philip V had increased the navies of Spain and its French allies to 91,000 tons displacement each, and the fleets of the two allies combined were only 7% smaller than the British. Britain launched a major building program as it went to war with France in the 1750s, and by 1760 it had a fleet that was 22% larger than the fleets of Spain and France together. By 1770, however, Ferdinand VI and Charles III had once again created a larger combined navy than England.[40]

Even before the navy was built, Philip used semi-authorized privateers – the *guarda costas* – to combat smuggling.[41] They, and the growing fleet, were successful enough to have provoked the Anglo-Spanish War of 1727–1729 and the so-called War of Jenkins' Ear in 1739.

The Bourbons also reversed their policy toward commodities in Mexico – notably cochineal and indigo, and then dyewood. Only smugglers exported these products after the first quarter of the 1600s, and the Bourbons were

[39] Displacement is a measure of volume, the weight of the water that is displaced by a ship that is fully loaded. Jan Glete, *Navies and Nations: Warships, Navies and State Building in Europe and America, 1500–1860* (Stockholm: Almquist and Wiksell International, 1993), pp. 256–8. Philip V had the goal of regaining control not only of Spanish America but also of Italy.

[40] See the table in Carlos Marichal, *Bankruptcy of Empire: Mexican Silver and the Wars between Spain, Britain, and France, 1760–1810* (New York: Cambridge University Press, 2007), p. 24. The figures are drawn from Glete, *Navies and Nations*, pp. 256–7, 263, and 271.

[41] Richard Pares, *War and Trade in the West Indies, 1739–1763* (London: Frank Cass, 1963), pp. 14–28.

eager to end this smuggling. The mere reappearance of official statistics would seem to testify to their growing success by the 1730s.[42]

Madrid was particular concerned about smuggling from the area of modern Colombia and Venezuela that produced gold and a number of commodities, especially cacao. In 1828, six months after the truce in the Anglo-Spanish War, Madrid created a monopoly trading company, the Caracas Company. Its purpose was to attack the large-scale smuggling in the area.[43]

The Caracas Company was given the right to export a number of commodities, most importantly cacao from Venezuela. It was also charged with the responsibility of increasing production. In exchange for its monopoly profits, it not only collected taxes for the Crown but also served as a coast guard that fought smugglers along the coast between Venezuela and the port of Cartagena in modern Colombia.[44] Yet, even though it was monopoly, it was a signal of freer trade to come because it was a Basque company based in the northern ports, not in Seville.

At this time, Spain also began liberalizing its trade rules. The flotillas were replaced by individual ships, although not initially those bound for Mexico. This meant that owners registered with the Spanish authorities and therefore, were required to pay customs duties individually. They increasingly were allowed to sail from cities other than Cadiz. The Bourbons, for example, allowed ships to sail directly to Chile.

The Spanish kings also moved toward accepting the direct illegal trade between the Potosí silver mine in Bolivia and the Atlantic as the first step in controlling it. Britain was allowed to export more raw hides through Buenos Aires, and the Spanish permitted the city to become an important administrative and commercial center. Its population grew from 8,908 in 1720 to 22,551 in 1770 (the same as New York City at the time).[45] In 1776 Madrid carved a new Río de la Plata viceroyalty, centered on Buenos Aires, out of the Peru viceroyalty. Modern Bolivia was included within it. Silver now officially flowed east.

[42] Between 1703 and 1716, the Spanish were finally able to expel the British settlers from Laguna de Terminos in the Bay of Campeche and held that area from then on. Information based on a conversation with Terry Rugeley, one of the foremost historians of the Yucatán.

[43] For a detailed discussion of the smuggling and the reasons for it, see Lance Grahn, *Political Economy of Smuggling: Regional Informal Economies in Early Bourbon New Granada* (Boulder, CO: Westview Press, 1997).

[44] R. D. Hussey, *The Caracas Company, 1728–1788* (Cambridge, MA: Harvard University Press, 1934), pp. 60–2 and 87.

[45] David Rock, *Argentina from Spanish Colonization to the Falkland War, 1561–1987* (Berkeley: University of California Press, 1987), pp. 43 and 64; Samuel Amaral, "Rural

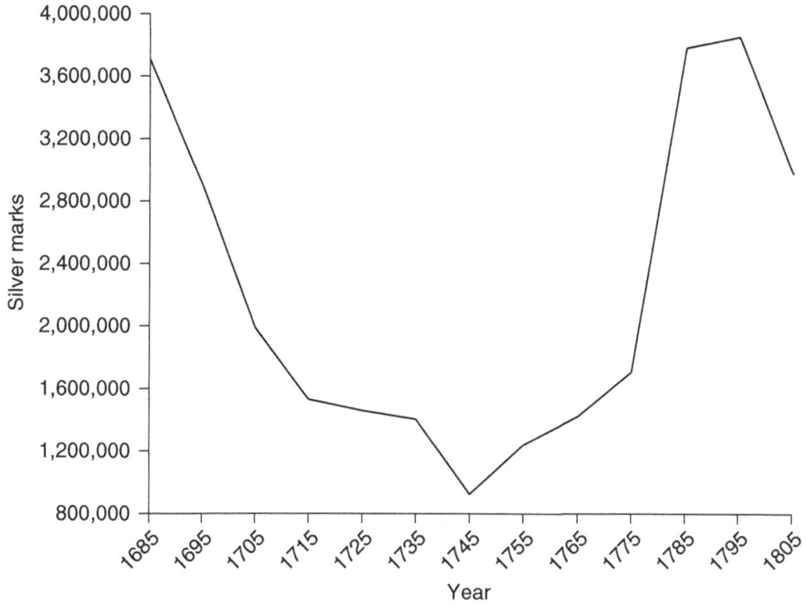

Figure 5.1. Reported Silver Production in Bolivia, in silver marks.
Source: Herbert Klein, *A Concise History of Bolivia,* 2nd ed. (Cambridge: Cambridge University Press, 2011), p. 304. Klein presents average annual data by decade (1680–1689, 1690–1699, and so on) and uses a multiplier of 5.2 to convert pesos corrientes into silver marks. We multiply the average data by 10 so it represents production over each decade. Note that for legibility reasons, the years listed on the x-axis above represent the mid-point of each decade (for example, 1685 represents the decade 1680–1689).

The policy had an important impact on Mexico. Since the Bourbons could not control the smuggling of silver from Bolivia in the first half of the 1700s, they limited investment in and the delivery of mercury to the Bolivian mines, and diverted them to Mexico where the controls were tighter.[46] As a result, Mexican silver production began to increase steadily and substantially, but the Bolivian production was allowed to fall every decade until the 1750s. When the authorities gained more confidence in their ability to control smuggling, Bolivian production tripled in a few decades.

Figures 5.1 and 5.2 show the evolution of the reported silver production in Bolivia and Mexico for the 1700s. It is striking how much Bolivian

Production and Labour in Late Colonial Buenos Aires," *Journal of Latin American Studies* 19 (1987), 235–78, p. 237; Jonathan Brown, "Outpost to Entrepôt: Trade and Commerce at Colonial Buenos Aires," in Stanley Ross and Thomas McGann, eds., *Buenos Aires: Four Hundred Years* (Austin: University of Texas Press, 1982), pp. 5–6.

46 Brown, "The Spanish Mercury Trade," in Ross and McGann, *Buenos Aires,* pp. 146 and 139.

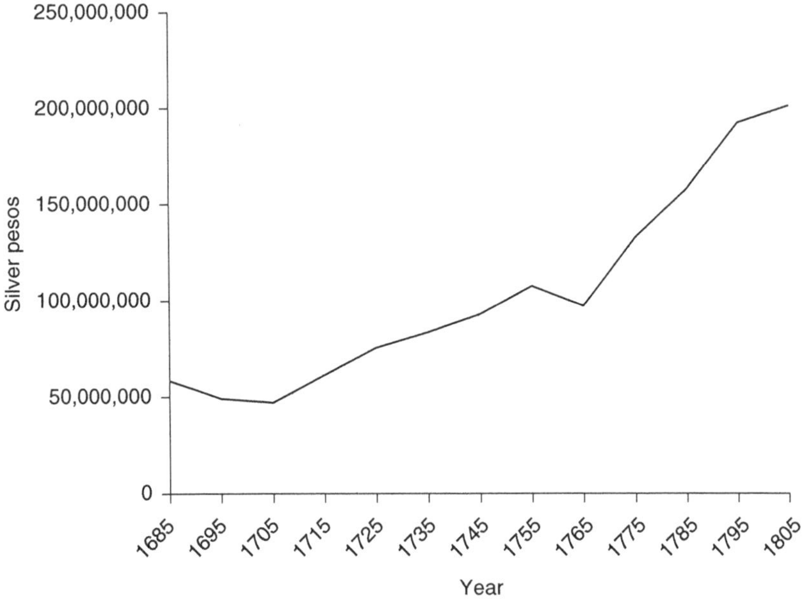

Figure 5.2. Reported Silver Production in Mexico, in silver pesos.
Source: Kendall Brown, "The Spanish Imperial Mercury Trade and the American Mining Expansion under the Bourbon Monarchy," in Kenneth Andrien and Lyman Johnson, eds., *The Political Economy of Spanish America in the Age of Revolution, 1750–1850* (Albuquerque: University of New Mexico Press, 1994), 137–69, p. 139. Note that for legibility reasons, the years listed on the x-axis above represent the mid-point of each decade (for example 1685 represents the decade 1681–1690).

production was allowed to fall from the 1690s (3.7 million marks) to the 1740s (900,000 marks) and how rapidly it rose to 3.9 million marks in the 1790s. Except for the decade of the 1760s, when Cuba was captured by the British, Mexican production rose steadily from 49.1 million pesos in the 1690s to 192.4 in the 1790s.

Charles III came to power in 1759 with a clear intention of reforming both Spain and the colonies in a major way. Three of his measures in Latin America are most emphasized by Latin American historians: a concerted effort to raise tax revenue, an effort to centralize the administrative structure with the appointment of *intendants*, and the appointment of *peninsulares* (officials from Spain) to replace local colonial officials in a number of key posts.

It is possible to interpret these measures as a concerted effort to exploit and repress Mexico, and Latin American historians often do so. We think that this is a distortion of what Charles III was doing. He was following the same policy in Mexico that he was in Spain. It seems clear that he was influenced by the great progress in Britain since 1668 and felt that Spain must move along the same path.

The reforms of Charles III in Mexico in the second half of the 1700s should also be seen in broad perspective. Charles III was only 43 years old when he came to power, and he clearly had the type of long-term perspective that Mancur Olson hoped to see in stationary bandits. He seems to have understood that the best way to increase tax revenues over time is to increase the amount of goods that are produced. Charles ordered his chief reform agent in Mexico, José de Gálvez, to increase production as a way to increase revenue. The *intendants* were given the same responsibility when they were introduced.

Gálvez naturally focused on the mining industry. A number of policies were taken to increase silver production, including fiscal measures – notably the reduction of the price of mercury from 82.5 pesos after 1617 to 60.2 in 1767 and to 41 in 1778.[47] David Brading points to the decision to encourage investment in old mines by forgiving the 10% royal silver tax from the mine up to the level of the investment.[48] The Valenciana mine in Guanajuato became the largest silver mine in Latin American history, and its growth was based on what Bakewell reports to have been "immense capital investment" in the period from 1780 to 1810.[49]

Charles III also sharply increased the production of export commodities. For example, the number of rawhides exported from Río de la Plata was reported to be in the 150,000 range in the 1760s, but to have reached 447,000 a year in the period from 1779 to 1784 and 743,000 a year from 1793 to 1796. The production of indigo in Guatemala from 1775 to 1799 far exceeded that in South Carolina. The production of cochineal in Oaxaca and gold in Colombia rose in a similar fashion.[50]

Nevertheless, there remained a key difference – perhaps *the* key difference – between the mainland American colonies and the mainland Mexican

[47] Bakewell, "Mining in Colonial Spanish America," p. 122. David Brading and Harry Cross, "Colonial Silver Mining: Mexico and Peru," *Hispanic American Historical Review* 52 (1972), 545–79, p. 562.

[48] David A. Brading, "Mexican Silver Mining in the Eighteenth Century," *Hispanic American Historical Review* 50 (1970), 665–81.

[49] Bakewell, "Mining in Colonial Spanish America," p. 147.

[50] Amaral, "Rural Production and Labour," p. 237. Troy Floyd, "The Guatemalan Merchants, the Government, and the Provincianos, 1750–1800," *Hispanic-American Historical Review* 41 (1961), 90–110, p. 91; David McCreery, "Indigo Commodity-Chains in the Spanish and British Empires, 1560–1860," in Steven Topik, Carlos Marichal, and Zephyr Frank, eds., *From Silver to Cocaine: Latin American Commodity Chains and the Building of the World Economy, 1500–2000* (Durham, NC: Duke University Press, 2006), 53–75.

colony: England developed sugar-producing islands with slave labor in the Caribbean, and permitted free trade between the mainland American colonies and the island ones. Spain did not.

The commercial tradition in the American mainland colonies – and the very large colonial merchant fleet – came from their free market trade with the Caribbean, domestic and foreign, in "non-enumerated" goods. Spain turned its islands into major sugar producers only in the 1800s when it lost its silver revenue. If it had done this in the 1600s and first half of the 1700s, Mexico would likely have had a major fleet and complex commercial staff. It did not have the time to develop one between 1795 and 1808.

Chile shows what might have been. Santiago was located at a height of 1,700 feet, only some 50 miles from the sea. It essentially was a city-state like London that could gradually expand. It had a port that connected it with Lima, Peru, but its location meant that Lima was on the direct line of trade northward that went by Chilean mines. It also was well positioned for its unofficial trade around the Horn or across the mountains to Buenos Aires. We would argue that it is not a coincidence that Chile was to be a major success story in South America.[51]

Charles's policies showed that he realized Spain was not yet ready for the same measures that England was taking in the 1770s, but that he first needed the steps that England had taken in the 1500s and early 1600s. In our terms he was building a minimally effective state – in Daron Acemoglu and James Robinson's terms a "centralized state." This is what he was doing in Mexico as well.

Administrative and Tax Reforms

The administrative system inside Mexico is discussed in Chapter 8. Suffice it to say here that, unlike England with a governor in each small city-state, Spain had had only two grossly understaffed viceroys. As in Spain, the dominant unit in the political system was the city-state, and the dominant organ in the city-state was its council, called a *cabildo* in Mexico.

Except in remote areas, there were no officials at the American state level who could coordinate the separate lines of command emanating from Mexico City and/or with the family-dominated city-states. Indeed the

51 Jerry Hough and Robin Grier, "The Hidalgo Rebellion and the Problem of Order: The Comparative Lessons of Chile and the United States," *Latin Americanist* 54 (2010), 59–80.

bureaucrats integrated themselves into the existing social order by marrying the daughters of the elite.

The indigenous villages were supervised by a network of non-professional, unpaid *alcaldes mayores* who had bought their office and who made their living largely by engaging in monopoly trade with the villages and by making loans to be secured by the coming harvest. Hence the *alcaldes mayores* were largely immune from viceroy pressure and were primarily interested in enriching themselves. Since the *alcaldes mayores* also served as judicial officials in the provinces, there was a desperate need for a separation of their executive, judicial, and business functions.

Charles III slowly began to modernize this system. He stopped the sale of offices and created a provincial tax bureaucracy staffed by 24 heads of provincial tax offices.[52] Gálvez also radically reorganized the customs office of Veracruz, where he changed personnel, achieving what his biographer called a "complete triumph."[53]

Charles's father had already begun to phase out tax farming gradually. In 1775, 24% of sales tax revenue still came from tax farming and 22% was collected by the *encabezado* route. This was "a quota to each territorial unit (city, town, or county).... Then it was the unit's business to collect it and deliver the pre-determined lump sum to the state in due time."[54]

The phasing out of tax farming, especially of the type found in Spain and Spanish America, must be accompanied by the imposition and collection of more direct taxes. Such taxes were introduced. A new tobacco monopoly was especially lucrative. There was a sharp increase in tax revenue under the Bourbon period, especially in the last half-century.[55] The cause of this

52 J. H. Parry, *The Sale of Public Office in the Spanish Indies under the Hapsburgs* (Berkeley: University of California Press, 1953).

53 Priestley has a long section on the opposition to this plan, the "legislative process," and the issues on customs collection in the debate that is very illuminating. Herbert Priestley, *José de Gálvez: Visitor General of New Spain, 1765–1771* (Berkeley: University of California Press, 1916), p. 208.

54 The statistics are from Ernest Sánchez Santiró, "La hacienda reformada: la centralización de la renta de *alcabalas* en Nueva España (1754–1781)," in Ernest Sánchez Santiró, Luis Jaúregui y Antonio Ibarra (coordinadores), *Finanzas y política en el mundo iberoamericano: del antiguo régimen a las naciones independientes, 1754–1850* (Mexico: UNAM, 2001), p. 149; Gabriel Tortella and Francisco Comín, "Fiscal and Monetary Institutions in Spain (1600–1900)," in Michael Bordo and Roberto Cortés Conde, eds., *Transferring Wealth and Power from the Old to the New World Monetary and Fiscal Institutions in the Seventeenth through the Nineteenth Centuries* (Cambridge: Cambridge University Press, 2001), p. 143.

55 Herbert Klein, *The American Finances of the Spanish Empire: Royal Income and Expenditures in Colonial Mexico, Peru, and Bolivia, 1680–1809* (Albuquerque: University of New Mexico Press, 1998), p. 75. For an extremely detailed discussion of the variety of taxes, see Priestley, *José de Gálvez*, pp. 312–90.

increase in revenue – or, rather, the relative weight of the causes – is difficult to judge. Thus, the increase in silver and commodity production, and the general development of the economy that accompanied it, naturally produced a great deal of revenue. Tax farming is less efficient and more subject to abuse than truly professional tax collection based on fixed rules. It is a good second-best solution at a stage when professional tax collection is administratively impossible, but it disappears in the middle stages of political development for a good reason.

When tax farming is abolished and tax revenue begins to rise, an outsider cannot judge the real source of the added revenue. One possibility is that more money was being extracted from the population. The opposite possibility is that the population paid much the same amount of taxes but the ruler received the excess taxes that the tax farmer was collecting. All factors were involved in Mexico, but we have no way of knowing the precise mixture.

The administrative reform that is most emphasized by American colonial historians is the introduction of governors (*intendants*), but this change occurred very gradually and really was not fully institutionalized in 1808, especially in Mexico. *Intendants* were first appointed in Spain, and then they were extended step-by-step to Spanish America over the next quarter of a century.

The first *intendants* were created in Cuba in 1764 and the next in 1778 in the newly organized Río de la Plata Viceroyalty: a total of eight, four in Upper Peru (largely modern Bolivia) and four in modern Argentina.[56] The system was finally extended to the core of Mexico in 1786.[57]

Historians of Mexico emphasize the introduction of the *intendants* and the logical corollary of transforming the "county-level" *alcaldes mayores* into the direct subordinates of the *intendants* (the sub-delegates). The difficulty was that Madrid remained conflicted. A centralized viceroyalty would be more efficient, but such a viceroy might be too powerful to control.

The *alcaldes mayores* system of taxation through monopoly prices and loan interest was controversial. It was obviously inefficient, and some said it exploited the Native Americans. Others thought the Native Americans

[56] Allan Kuethe, *Cuba, 1753–1815: Crown, Military, and Society* (Knoxville: University of Tennessee Press, 1986), pp. 68–74. The Cuban intendancy, unlike Spain's, had no judicial or police function. Lillian Estelle Fisher, *The Intendant System in Spanish America* (Berkeley: University of California Press, 1929).

[57] John Leiby, *Colonial Bureaucrats and the Mexican Economy: Growth of a Patrimonial State, 1763–1821* (New York: P. Lang, 1986); John Lynch, *Spanish Colonial Administration, 1782–1810: The Intendant System in the Viceroyalty of the Río de la Plata* (London: University of London Press, 1958); John Fisher, *Government and Society in Colonial Peru: The Intendant System, 1784–1814* (London: University of London Press, 1970).

were relatively satisfied and noted that, unlike in South America, there had never been major Native American unrest in Mexico. They feared that a transformation of the old arrangements might be destabilizing.[58]

The result was continual compromise and experimentation with different patterns of administrative subordination. Yet another set of laws redefining the powers of the *intendants* and sub-delegates was passed in 1803, and no fully established administrative system existed when Napoleon Bonaparte overthrew the Bourbon monarchy in 1808.

This is a crucial fact to understand when we think about the Mexican war of independence and post-independent Mexico. Historians can create the impression that the introduction of the *intendants* by Charles III and his successors left the Mexicans with an overly centralized administrative system. Instead, the system was never really institutionalized, and, as a result, it was easily swept away in 1810. Mexico did not become independent in 1821 with a strong bureaucratic system, but with administrative anarchy outside the area in and around Mexico City.

A second part of Charles III's plan to modernize the administrative system was to appoint administrators sent from Spain (the *peninsulares*) to replace the local officials in key posts. The first obvious purpose of the appointment of *peninsulares* was to reduce the power of the leading members of the local elite who had long dominated the respective city-states. The latter naturally treated the reform as an effort to impose dictatorial control on Mexico.

Yet, correctly or not, Charles must have believed that the Mexican elite, especially the provincial elite, was far less affected by the development of Enlightenment (rational-legal) values that had been occurring in Spain. He must have seen Spanish professionals as representatives of the Enlightenment needed to transform the colony. At the same time he tried to make the colonial office in Madrid more professional. Throughout the Hapsburg period, it had been staffed by men without experience in Spanish America. Now experience became important.

Nevertheless, the fact that the new officials were allowed to integrate into the elite society suggests that the purpose was not to replace that elite so much as to change its values. The Jesuits were expelled from Mexico at

[58] For an article that draws heavily on the arguments of the opponents of the *alcaldes mayores*, see Robert Patch, "Imperial Politics and Local Economy in Colonial Central America, 1670–1779," *Past and Present* 143 (1994), 77–107. For a book that largely accepts the arguments of those who supported the system, see Jeremy Baskes, *Indians, Merchants, and Markets: A Reinterpretation of the Repartimiento and Spanish-Indian Economic Relations in Colonial Oaxaca, 1750–1821* (Stanford, CA: Stanford University Press, 2000). For an intermediate position, see Brian Hamnett, *Politics and Trade in Southern Mexico, 1750–1821* (Cambridge: Cambridge University Press, 1971).

the same time they were expelled from Spain. As in Spain, the Jesuits controlled the elite colleges and had trained almost the entire educated elite. Now they lost their positions, and the staff and curriculum became much more secular.

As we have seen, the effort to construct a professional bureaucracy and inculcate rational-legal values in a population is a long process. We dated its beginnings in England roughly with Henry VII and Henry VIII in the first half of the 1500s. This was the initiation of what we call a minimally effective process. The process passed a tipping point in the first half of the 1700s. This was the time when the Bourbons really began the process, and Charles III came to the throne in 1759 a half century later. Mexican independence came another half century later.

As we discuss in Chapter 8, the overthrow of the French Bourbons threw the Spanish Bourbons into disarray and led them into unwise decisions about engaging in war against France. Then when Napoleon overthrew the Spanish king in 1808, over a decade of chaos occurred in Mexico. Surely much professionalization and value change had occurred, but much was also lost. An effective government was not rebuilt in Mexico until the 1870s.

Trade Liberalization

The final reform of Charles III is even more important for our purposes. This was a liberalization of trade. England began liberalizing trade under the Stuarts in the early 1600s for several reasons. The fleet was becoming strong enough to protect commerce. The state had become strong enough to collect tariffs without using monopoly organizations. The English economy was becoming too large and complex, and merchants, shippers, and tradesmen too numerous to be controlled and taxed by monopoly guilds, both foreign and domestic. Spain and its colonies were undergoing a similar change in the second half of the 1700s.

Charles III formed a commission of commercial specialists that reported on March 14, 1765. Its first recommendation was to end both the monopoly of trade with Cadiz and the practice of requiring ships to go in convoys or to be registered.[59] The commission also recommended the revision of customs duties that it believed to be counterproductive. The commission favored the calculation of duties on the basis of value and not of volume, the development of export agricultural crops, the reduction of duties on private gold and silver, the importation of more slaves into

[59] This paragraph and the next one are based on Priestley, *José de Gálvez*.

the colonies (and on Spanish ships), and greater protection for Spanish manufactured goods.

Cuba had been lost to England in 1762 during the Seven Years' War. When it was restored to Spain the next year, Charles gave Havana wider access to ports in Spain and the Caribbean. For the first time, eight Spanish ports besides Cadiz were permitted to trade freely with Havana. The ships were also permitted to sail directly between Havana and the Caribbean islands of Santo Domingo, Puerto Rico, Trinidad, and Margarita. Then in 1770, ships from the multiple ports were allowed to trade directly with Campeche and Merida in a largely successful effort to push the British out of the smuggling of dyewood in the region. In 1774, ships from these cities were given the right to go through Havana.

The opening of Havana to nine Spanish ports and four Caribbean ones introduced a system of free trade into the Caribbean Islands similar to what Charles II of England had introduced nearly 150 years earlier. Yet the open ports did not include the mainland areas adjacent to the Caribbean, notably modern Mexico, Venezuela, and the port of Cartagena. Then on October 12, 1778 – the date deliberately chosen to correspond with Columbus's discovery of America – Charles III introduced the principle of free trade to Chile and to the viceroyalties of Peru and Río de la Plata.

Free trade was not extended to Venezuela in order to protect the monopoly of the Caracas Company, nor extended to the heart of New Spain because of its importance. The Caracas Company was abolished in 1786, and free trade was finally extended to New Spain and Venezuela in 1789. From 1793 to 1795, the Crown authorized new *consulados* in Caracas, Guatemala City, Buenos Aires, Havana, Cartagena, Santiago de Chile, and even Veracruz and Guadalajara in Mexico.

Unfortunately, trade was seriously disrupted by the almost continuous war after 1793. Indeed, except for several years of peace from 1802 to 1804, trade between Spain and its colonies virtually ended. In desperation, Spain legalized trade between the Spanish colonies and Spain by neutral ships that could pass through the blockade. In practice, this primarily meant American ships. American shippers and merchants were happy to have legal access to Spanish colonial ports, and trade between the United States and nearby Mexico was more profitable than the long voyage to Spain. The result was predictable.

Nevertheless, the Spanish example clearly demonstrates that the combination of authoritarianism and free trade under Charles I of England was not a chance or unnatural development. The creation of an effective market is dependent on an effective state. Most basically, building a naval and merchant marine capability clearly is dependent on the ability to raise taxes. Development economists understand that the inability of modern developing countries to tax effectively has negative consequences. Some, however, have difficulty in assimilating that this implies a need for a stronger government vis-à-vis the economy, not a weaker one.

In our cases, the development of a centralized governmental power in the Tudor period was indispensable for a decentralization of decisions to the marketplace. Elizabeth not only had a small naval "ministry," but also the deliberate industrial policy of promoting the manufacture of cheap cannons for merchant ships. She had to persuade investors it was safe and profitable for them to invest in merchant ships. Economists and historians of England often take these facts for granted. The failure of Spain to do the same thing at the same time dramatically shows that the growing effectiveness of the Tudor policy and administrative process was a pre-condition for the policy.

6

A Dominant Coalition in Transition

England and the Rise of the Merchant – Navy Alliance after 1600

Thus far, England and Spain have been excellent case studies for a two-country comparison of the development of the market and state. The origins of the current Spanish and English states can be dated to the same time – 1038 and 1066, respectively. Both areas featured some 200 years of fairly chaotic conflict between warlords before England began to develop into a more coherent city-state in the late 1200s. In Castile, however, the early chaotic stage persisted until 1485. Another 200 years or so were required for England and Spain to institute what Daron Acemoglu and James Robinson call a centralized state – really the first semblance of an effective centralized state. This happened in the 1530s in England and the early 1700s in Spain.

Several key questions arise. First, why did the process take so incredibly long in the "successful" case of England? Second, why did it take 200 years longer in the case of Spain – which in turn was more successful than much of southern and Eastern Europe? Third, what were the mechanisms that made the development of an effective market dependent on the evolution to a more effective state?

The minimally effective states of England of the 1530s and Spain of the early 1700s then each took some two centuries from these dates to evolve toward what we called a fully effective state and market. A comparison of the English and Spanish transition is also highly illuminating because they were very different from each other. England had three major regime changes in the 1640s, 1660, and 1688, but was quite stable in the 1700s and remained that way.

Spain was reasonably stable for the first century after the establishment of Bourbon rule, but not in the 150 years after 1800. In Spain, the army remained powerful well into the 1900s, and the creation of a republic in 1931 produced a highly radicalized political situation. Another military coup occurred in 1936 and was followed by the 40-year rule of General Francisco Franco. Then in 1975, Spain quickly became a modern European state and economy. England had nothing like this.

We, alas, do not have the time and space to explore the extremely complex Spanish evolution from the early 1800s until the mid-1900s, and this is most unfortunate. The evolution to an effective state and market in Alexander Gerschenkron's "late industrializers" in southern and Eastern Europe has not been seriously studied from a development point of view. It is a subject that cries out for more study, because it is highly relevant for the still later industrializers of Asia, Latin America, and Africa.

Our inability to examine the transition of Spain to a truly effective government does, however, have one major advantage. We can give twice as much attention to this transition in England. The evolution of England always occupied the central place in the American debate about European evolution, and Douglass North and Barry Weingast's 1989 article, "Constitutions and Commitment," brought it even more to the fore in American economics.[1] Since Mancur Olson developed his collective action analysis of the state in response to this article, we always gave it major attention.

Unbeknownst to the vast majority of American economists, the English debate in 1988 and 1989 on the 300th anniversary of the Glorious Revolution featured multiple positions. The Whig position espoused by North and Weingast got little support. In the words of Steven Pincus and James Robinson, "scholars across the ideological and methodological spectrum have chimed in a single voice [that] the Revolution of 1688 … was [not] one of innovation."[2]

The major book published in the United States at the time of the 300th anniversary was John Brewer's *The Sinews of Power: War, Money, and the English State, 1688–1783*. Like "Constitutions and Commitment," *The Sinews of Power* dealt with the 1700s, not the 1600s. But while North and Weingast focused on the development of private financial bodies and property rights, Brewer concentrated on the growing complexity of the bureaucracy and its role in government. Brewer labeled Britain in the 1700s a "fiscal-military state" and described a policy process that featured increasingly complex

1 Douglass North and Barry Weingast, "Constitutions and Commitment: The Evolution of Institutions Governing Public Choice in Seventeenth Century England," *Journal of Economic History* 49 (1989), 803–32.

2 Steven C.A. Pincus and James A. Robinson, "What Really Happened during the Glorious Revolution?" in Sebastian Galiani and Itai Sened, eds., *Institutions, Property Rights, and Economic Growth: The Legacy of Douglass North* (Cambridge: Cambridge University Press, 2014), p. 192.

bureaucracies, multiple interest groups linked with them, and parliamentary specialists. *The Sinews of Power* has been highly respected as a descriptive analysis and frequently cited, but its broader implications have been ignored.[3]

We had always expected that the difference in the theses of *The Sinews of Power* and "Constitutions and Commitment" would be a central focus of our analysis of England in the 1600s and 1700s. This is especially the case because Brewer's interpretation is more congenial for scholars with a collective action approach. Then, however, North's two most recent books – *Violence and Social Orders* in 2009 and *In the Shadow of Violence* in 2013 – implied, but did not explore, a major change in his analysis of the meaning of the Glorious Revolution.

North and Weingast had explicitly argued in "Constitutions and Commitment" that representative institutions were a crucial political precondition for economic growth and marketization. As North and his co-authors stated in the 2013 preface to *In the Shadow of Violence*, the 2009 *Violence and Social Orders* was really dedicated to "explaining how modern political and economic orders emerged in the nineteenth century," including in England, France, and the United States.[4]

In their 2013 preface, North and his co-authors acknowledged that "less central to our focus [in *Violence and Social Orders*] was the 'second development problem,' that of the development of societies from fragile natural states [through basic natural states] to more mature ones." This second (really first) development problem involved the evolution of "natural states [which must] control the problem of violence by granting privileges and policy benefits to members of the elite capable of provoking violence." This, of course, included military commanders and rulers who controlled them. It is only as society evolves from a basic natural state to a mature natural state and an open access order that democratic elections become safe.

North's new focus on the dominant coalition and the role of the military implied a major change in the timing of the transition from the basic state to the mature natural state in England. The 2009 *Violence and Social Orders* indicated that the transition occurred in the 1600s, but the 2013 *In the Search of Violence* listed Mexico as a basic natural state in the 1980s and

[3] Tim Harris, *Restoration: Charles II and His Kingdoms, 1660–1685* (London: Penguin Books, 2006), pp. 9–10; John Brewer, *The Sinews of Power: War, Money, and the English State, 1688–1783* (New York: Knopf, 1989).

[4] Douglass North, John Joseph Wallis, and Barry Weingast, "Preface" to the paperback edition, *Violence and Social Orders: A Conceptual Framework for Interpreting Recorded History* (New York: Cambridge University Press, 2013), p. xi.

a mature natural state only in the 1990s. Surely England of the 1600s and early 1700s was not remotely as advanced economically and politically as Mexico in the 1980s.[5]

On the surface, it would seem that England became a mature natural state (essentially what we call a truly effective state) in the second half of the 1700s and became a reasonably open access society with the Reform Act of 1832.[6] If so, the analysis of *In the Shadow of Violence* about controlling violence through rents to elites (prominently including the military) certainly should apply to England of the 1600s and much of the 1700s.

In neither of their 2013 writings do North and his co-authors say anything about England of the time of the Glorious Revolution in 1688. Nevertheless, they begin their preface to *Violence and Social Orders* by referring to political philosophers such as John Locke, James Madison, and Alexander Hamilton. These philosophers, North and his co-authors say, "were not trying ... to help societies make the transition from natural states to open access orders."

Instead, they were "trying to solve the second development problem: how to improve the natural states in which they lived given the confines of the natural state logic where politics inherently tended to corrupt economics."[7] That clearly says that England in the 1600s was far from the transition to an open access society, but had the character and problems of modern developing societies. The arguments of "Constitutions and Commitment" and *In the Shadow of Violence* can be partially reconciled with great difficulty, but not in a way that was discussed in 1989. There are three obvious tensions between the two arguments.

First, *Violence and Social Orders* and *In the Shadow of Violence* argue that the control of violence is a pre-condition for economic growth. Yet the 1600s were a period of unquestioned economic progress, but also a time of great violence and three fundamental regime changes. Why was England able to combine economic progress with great violence?

Second, the 1700s featured even more economic progress. In "Constitutions and Commitment," North and Weingast attribute the progress to the credible commitment of the wealthy in Parliament to pay high taxes in exchange for being given a veto on taxes and the budget. Yet the analysis in *Violence and Social Orders* surely suggests that the dominant coalition of the 1600s and 1700s could have pushed a policy of economic growth without a strong Parliament.

[5] Douglass North, John Joseph Wallis, Steven Webb, and Barry Weingast, *In the Shadow of Violence* (New York: Cambridge University Press, 2009).

[6] North et al., "Preface" to the paperback edition," *Violence and Social Orders*, p. xi.

[7] Ibid., pp. x–xi.

Third, "the wealthy" of "Constitutions and Commitment" are undifferentiated, and, in practice, Parliament was dominated by the rural elite until 1832. They had refused to provide taxes to finance Charles I's navy, which the merchants wanted. A transition from a rural-based to an urban-based dominant coalition was obviously taking place in the 1600s and 1700s in England, and the dominant coalition of 1688 and afterward was more favorable to Brewer's fiscal-military state. By the mid-1770s, the dominant collation seemed to center on the merchants, the navy allied with it, the financial elite, the developing state bureaucracy, and the growing manufacturing sector.

This book has emphasized the development of the navy and armed merchant fleet under the Tudors, Charles I, and the Puritans. We have also emphasized that the naval officers and the merchants were close allies in the era of armed sailing ships. Indeed, to some extent they were the same men, and inevitably they played an increasingly important role in English politics. This interpretation is, of course, quite congenial to Mancur Olson's collective action theory and his emphasis on the importance of those who "can organize the greatest capacity for violence."[8]

Whatever the role of the navy in 1688 (and it certainly was great from 1660 to 1685), it gradually ended during the transition of England to a mature natural state in the mid-1750s. Nevertheless, a century passed from the first half of the 1600s to the first half of the 1700s. That is a very long period indeed, and it confirms North's thesis that the development process is extremely prolonged. Moreover, the stable England that the navy left in place featured a major role for merchants. This alliance likely is the main explanation for the greater stability of systems in which the navy rather than the army, is the dominant military force.

The Evolution toward a Market Economy and a Rational-Legal Worldview in the 1600s

The original purpose of this book was to develop a theory of change that integrated Douglass North's emphasis on the importance of "informal institutions" with Max Weber's and Mancur Olson's analysis. Since the 1600s featured evolution toward rational-legal norms and three regime changes that were fought out over religious issues, we obviously should begin this chapter with North's analysis of these developments. Alas, this is quite impossible because North never discussed them.

[8] Mancur Olson, "Dictatorship, Democracy, and Development," *American Political Science Review* 87 (1993), 567–76, p. 568.

Indeed, North and Weingast do not even mention religion in "Constitutions and Commitment," except for a brief statement that says they do not discuss religion. This seems strange on the surface, especially for a scholar who emphasizes values, ideas, and ideologies. A major English historian of the Civil War, Conrad Russell, argued that "the bitterest issues of the 1630s [leading to the civil war] were religious" and that "the clearest division between the two sides [during the civil war itself] seems to be religious and cultural."[9]

These religious conflicts had enormous breadth as well as intensity. They involved Catholics and Protestants, different Protestant groups, and (as the witch trials indicate) Christianity and the persistent pagan religions of the villages.[10] The Stuarts based each American colony on adherents of one of the warring religions of the 1600s, and hence the English religious conflict became ingrained in the colonial legacy.

Surprisingly, North's failure to discuss informal values in "Constitutions and Commitment" has been typical of all his historical work. He never has been concerned about the general role of informal institutions in human behavior but has focused on one basic argument: the spontaneous market of Friedrich Hayek is impossible unless self-interest is restrained by the appropriate norms and other informal institutions.

North consistently argued that these norms take a long time to develop and were not deeply enough ingrained in the developing countries to permit a modern market economy. Yet he never has discussed the role of ideologies, ideas, or systems of norms that were antithetical to the market or to a tolerant democracy.

In fact, peasants with traditional village values and customs often react violently when they come into contact with the alien values of the city. They often are attracted to populist leaders of political and religious movements – for example, communist, fascist, nationalist, and fundamentalist religions – who appeal to their anxieties and provoke them to major violence. Clearly those concerned with controlling violence in modern developing countries cannot ignore such dangerous informal institutions. That is why North and his co-authors now warn against premature elections.

9 North and Weingast, "Constitutions and Constituents," p. 805; Conrad Russell, *The Crisis of Parliaments: English History 1509–1660* (Oxford: Oxford University Press, 1971), pp. 313 and 343.

10 Margaret Alice Murray emphasized the persistence of pagan religion in Europe and the Catholic attack on them in the late 1400s. She claimed that the most heavily pagan areas became the strongest supporters of Protestantism and hypothesized a connection. Margaret Alice Murray, *The God of the Witches* (London: S. Low and Marston, 1933).

Without any question, the values and norms in England in the 1600s and 1700s were slowly evolving toward those that Max Weber thought inherent in modern urban society. This was especially so among the educated population in the larger cities. The values and norms in London were quite mixed both in 1600 and 1700, but on balance they were unquestionably more rational-legal in 1700 than in 1600.

Most educated Americans know little about London of 1600, except through the plays of William Shakespeare. These plays bracket the transition from Elizabeth to James I in 1603 – *Romeo and Juliet* (1594), *Merchant of Venice* (1596), *Hamlet* (1600), and *Macbeth* (1605) – and they reflect a rich and secular way of thinking among those who went to the theater. A line of the 1591 *Henry VI, Part II* showed clearly that lawyers and the law had become prominent enough to provoke resentment: "The first thing we do, let's kill all the lawyers."

As we have seen, however, Christopher Hill correctly described a much more traditional higher politics under James I. In Hill's words, James "was still expected to 'live of his own,' to finance government from crown lands, feudal dues, and the customs: no distinction was drawn between the public and private capacity of the king." Hill described the government of George I quite differently:[11]

> By 1714 Protestant dissent was legally tolerated: the Church could no longer burn, the state no longer tortured.... After 1701 judges could be removed only by address of both Houses of Parliament.... By 1714 politics had become a rational inquiry, discussed in terms of utility, experience, common sense, no longer in terms of Divine Right, texts, and antiquarian research.

Of course, the Elizabethan Age was only a midpoint in the long evolution toward the 1700s when rational-legal values became predominant, at least among the more educated population. The process clearly began at least in the Age of Discoveries, which textbooks on the history of Western civilization all describe as a watershed in the breakup of the medieval worldview. The Age of Discoveries did not mean simply the discovery of the New World but also the rediscovery of Greece and Rome, the transition to realism in art over the 1400s, the new developments in science, and the rise of a more realistic attitude in political theory.

It is striking how many key events in European history occurred in a very narrow time framework, apparently as the culmination of a long and broad process. They included Columbus's voyage to the Americas (1492), Vasco da

[11] Christopher Hill, *The Century of Revolution, 1603–1714* (New York: W. W. Norton, 1961), pp. 1–4.

Gama's return from his trip around the Cape of Good Hope to India (1499), the completion of a century of growing realism in Italian art (Leónardo da Vinci's *Mona Lisa* in 1507, Raphael's famous Florentine paintings from 1504 to 1508, and Michelangelo's Sistine Chapel in 1512), Nicolas Copernicus's heliocentric theory (1514, although published later), and Machiavelli's writing of *The Prince* (1513). The Reformation began with Luther in 1517.

Like Joseph Schumpeter, R.H. Tawney dated the origins of capitalism to the 1400s. He called the Age of Discovery "neither a happy accident nor the fruit of the disinterested curiosity of science" but contended that it was the product of "the economic energy [of the 1400s] in which it had been born."[12]

The Age of Discoveries is seldom integrated into thinking about the timing of marketization and the development of a rational-legal government and economy, but one fact is certain: whatever impact the Age of Discoveries had on the transformation of traditional values, this transformation came to fruition only after George I came to power in 1714 – over two centuries in the future.

The 1600s were part of that evolution, most obviously in "the scientific revolution." It began early in the 1600s, really in the 1590s. Kepler and Galileo revolutionized the view of the heavens, especially after Galileo's invention of the telescope of 1609. In England at the same time, Francis Bacon began his serious writings attacking the Aristotelian method and defending the inductive method. His writings became very influential after his death in 1626, and the process continued. In 1665, Isaac Newton began his work on calculus, and in 1687 he published his laws of motion.[13]

Yet evolution was very slow. The Salem trials, for example, occurred in 1692 and 1693 – that is, after the Glorious Revolution. Salem was a major port in the free trade with the Caribbean at that time, and many claim the Puritans were a major force in marketization.

The feverish rhetoric of the Civil War and of the anti-Puritan struggle remained a part of the political process well after 1714. Paranoid thinking about popish plots was strong in the governments of George I and George II, especially in Sir Robert Walpole, the great British prime minister from 1721 to 1742. Bernard Bailyn follows Walpole's biographer, J.H. Plumb, in seeing Walpole as a reflection of England itself at the time. In Bailyn's words,

[12] R.H. Tawney, *Religion and the Rise of Capitalism* (New York: Harcourt, Brace, 1926), p. 69.

[13] Charles Webster, *The Great Instauration: Science, Medicine, and Reform, 1626–1660* (London: Duckworth, 1975).

"Hogarth not Gainsborough was its true depicter."[14] Thomas Gainsborough (1727–1788) was a painter of elite portraits and peaceful landscapes, while William Hogarth (1697–1764) was a satirical painter who focused on politics, the economic elite, and immorality.

American revolutionaries were more influenced by the Whigs in their political thinking than the Walpole establishment. The Whigs were even more suspicious than those in the establishment. This continued after 1787. A major historian, Richard Hofstadter, focused on the paranoid thinking in the United States both before and after the colonial period. The mass immigration of Catholics in the 1830s and 1840s produced the Know Nothing movement in the 1850s. The Know Nothings, historians agree, destroyed the Whig Party and contributed in a major way to the Civil War.[15]

Indeed, we should not forget, "modern" for Weber meant Germany of the late 19th century in which he grew up. Alas, its rational-legal values did not preclude the existence of other "ascriptive" values and perceptions that intensified during the 1920s and produced the Third Reich in the 1930s.

Religion and Socioeconomic Turmoil in the 1600s

The Reformation was a complex political revolution as well as a religious one. First, of course, it occurred at the time of the creation of the nation-states, the codification of official state languages, and the rise of government-sponsored nationalism. Religion was deeply involved in the creation of the nation-state. At a minimum, support for the Reformation could be depicted as opposition to a foreign pope in a way that exploited the existing xenophobia.[16]

The Reformation was also a revolt against Latin. Latin was used in church services, government documents, and long-distance trade. As the size of bureaucracies and commerce grew, the number of people who had to know Latin became impossibly large, and Gutenberg's invention of the printing

[14] Bernard Bailyn, *The Origins of American Politics* (New York: Knopf, 1968), pp. 15, 34, 38–9, and 53. J.H. Plumb, *Sir Robert Walpole: The King's Minister*, Vol. 2 (London: Allen Lane, 1972), p. 41.

[15] Richard Hofstadter, *The Paranoid Style in American Politics and Other Essays* (New York: Knopf, 1965). Also see David Brion Davis, *The Slave Power Conspiracy and the Paranoid Style* (Baton Rouge: Louisiana University Press, 1970), and William Gienapp, *The Origins of the Republican Party, 1952–1956* (New York: Oxford University Press, 1987).

[16] Lien Bich Luu, "'Taking the Bread Out of Our Mouths': Xenophobia in Early Modern Europe," *Immigrants and Minorities* 19 (2000), 1–22.

press around 1439 created the prospect of mass literacy. A standardized vernacular language was needed, and rulers knew that "the translation of the bible into the vernacular and the substitution of a vernacular for a Latin ritual in church enormously increased the homogeneity of the national cultures."[17]

By 1600, the Reformation had also become involved in international relations. In England, the pro-Catholic Stuarts usually wanted better relations with Catholic Spain and Catholic France. The Protestants who overthrew the Stuarts in 1688 selected the strongly Protestant Dutch ruler, William of Orange, and then the strongly Protestant Hanover rulers. Both were already at war against France.[18]

Most important of all, the battles of the Reformation were closely associated with the enormous strains of industrialization. Most economists only know about the relationship of the Reformation to the economy from Max Weber's *The Protestant Ethic and the Spirit of Capitalism*. According to Weber, the spirit of capitalism derived in large part from Calvinism. Weber focused on Calvin's doctrine that everything was totally pre-determined by God, even the fate of individuals after death. He tried to explain how this doctrine of absolute predestination could lead to a compulsion to work and save.

Weber's most famous critic, R.H. Tawney, raised the fundamental question: why would people choose to accept such a frightening religion and an awful God who would damn people to eternal salvation or eternal damnation independent of their good or bad behavior on Earth? Tawney argued that Weber had reversed cause and effect.

Tawney emphasized the practical side of Calvinism, especially its "frank recognition of the necessity of capital, credit and banking, [and] large-scale commerce and finance." In Tawney's words, the Calvinists "broke with the tradition, which [regarded] a preoccupation with economic interests 'beyond what is necessary for subsistence' as reprehensible [and] had stigmatized the middleman as a parasite and the usurper as a thief."[19]

[17] Lawrence Stone, *The Past and the Present Revisited* (London: Routledge and Kegan Paul, 1987), p. 103.

[18] The war in which William of Orange was engaged is called the Nine Years' War (1688–1697) in English history. John Wolf, *The Emergence of the Great Powers, 1685–1715* (New York: Harper and Row, 1962); John Childs, *The Nine Years' War and the British Army* (Manchester: Manchester University Press, 1991).

[19] R.H. Tawney, *Religion and the Rise of Capitalism* (New Brunswick, NJ: Transaction, 1998), pp. 104–5.

Tawney thought Calvinism was adopted by those who already had the capitalist spirit. In his words, "Calvin, with all his rigor, accepted the main institutions of a commercial civilization, and supplied a creed to the classes which were to dominate the future."[20] By implication, Calvin even said that phenomena such as interest rates and profits were pre-determined by God.

In this view, England did not become entrepreneurial because it became Calvinist. Instead, Calvinism became an important force in England because England already had a substantial number of people who were entrepreneurial. Tawney thought that they embraced Calvinism as a legitimating ideology in Marx's sense of the word. Similarly, Spain did not fail to develop economically because Catholicism retarded growth but because Spanish capitalism had not yet produced enough entrepreneurs to overcome conservative opposition.

Tawney drew a sharp contrast between the views of John Calvin and Martin Luther. Tawney saw Luther as the spokesman for the counterrevolution against capitalism and the development of rational-legal values. He cited Luther's *Long Sermon on Usury* in 1520 and his *On Trade and Usury* in 1524 as proof that Luther's attack on a corrupt Catholic Church in 1517 was part of a general attack on commerce and capitalism. According to Tawney, Luther "dismissed the commercial developments of the last two centuries as a relapse into paganism.... International trade, banking and credit, capitalist industry, the whole complex of economic forces ... seem to him to belong in the very essence to the kingdom of darkness which the Christian will shun."

Tawney quoted Luther to document his argument:[21]

> The exploitation of the Church by the Papacy, and the exploitation of the peasant and the craftsman by the capitalist, are thus two horns of the beast which sits on the seven hills. Both are essentially pagan, and the sword which will slay both is the same. It is the religion of the Gospel.

We have cited Tawney's classic work on the Reformation for several reasons. First, Tawney's work is, in fact, classic. Too many modern American economists accept Weber's *The Protestant Ethic and the Spirit of Capitalism* uncritically and do not reflect sufficiently on the question of cause and effect. They need exposure to a broader interpretation that focuses first on economic conditions.

20 Ibid., p. 94.

21 Ibid., pp. 94–5.

Second, Tawney is certainly right that the 1500s and 1600s in rapidly developing northern Europe were a time of enormous social and economic conflict. Some people embraced the change under way, while others thought it was the devil's work (satanic, in the word of the Ayatollah Khomeini). This difference became associated with religion, and the overlap of religious and socioeconomic conflict led to an intensification of both. The same is true in the developing world today, and Tawney is invaluable in focusing our attention on the nature of communism and radicalism in the contemporary developing world.[22]

But what does this mean for England? Calvin became a force in Geneva in 1536 when the Protestant Reformation had already begun in England. Henry VIII's Reformation had little to do with theology or with emotional appeals that legitimized either urbanization or the reaction against it. Lutheranism never became a major force in England.

How then does the English Civil War fit within Tawney's analysis of the Reformation? The answer, is that religion, politics, and legitimizing ideologies are extremely complex. They are always contradictory, as are mental images, belief systems, and sets of values. Those with different self-interests naturally gravitate to those features of ideologies and religions that further their interests. Changes in technology, in the structure of the economy, and other aspects of the environment affect the distribution of interests. Indeed, as Joel Mokyr argues in a highly nuanced discussion, there are many reasons to de-emphasize persistence and incorporate an evolutionary model of cultural change into a general theory of change.[23]

Tawney illustrated this argument in a point that he made about Calvin. He noted that Calvin was criticizing "not the accumulation of riches, but their misuse for the purposes of self-indulgence or ostentation."[24] In the mid-1550s, this was a useful part of an effective ideology for the new entrepreneurial class to use against the conspicuous consumption of the old rural elite, the Catholic Church, and the monopoly guilds.

[22] Hough argued that Karl Marx's claim that the modern cultural "superstructure" served the economic needs of the ruling class was a major part of Communism's appeal – but at the early stages of industrialization, not the end of capitalism as he thought. For instance, Lenin appealed to similar emotions that Khomeini did in Iran in the 1970s and that Tawney described in England in the 1600s. Both were provoked by the movement of peasants to the city and their belief that modern values were Satanic. Jerry F. Hough, *Russia and the West: Gorbachev and the Politics of Reform* (New York: Simon and Schuster, 1988).

[23] Joel Mokyr, "Culture, Institutions, and Modern Growth," in Sebastian Galiani and Itai Sened, eds., *Institutions, Property Rights, and Economic Growth: The Legacy of Douglass North* (Cambridge: Cambridge University Press, 2014), pp. 153–61.

[24] Tawney, *Religion and the Rise of Capitalism*, p. 105.

The criticism of self-indulgence and ostentation continued to serve this function for the rising urban elite and for the gentry in the 1600s, but the urban elite themselves increasingly lived an opulent and ostentatious life. This was easily visible to the mass of peasants coming into London who witnessed this life, and Calvin could be turned against the Calvinists. Luther and Calvin originally may have represented opposite responses to the drastic socioeconomic change under way, but the illiterate peasants moving into the city absolutely did not like a religion of the ostentatious and opulent elite that said the poor were predestined to eternal damnation and should be treated that way during life.

The preachers of new sects naturally focused on the themes in Calvinism that would win them non-elite support. English historians often put "Puritan" in quotation marks when discussing the Puritan Revolution, because of the great diversity of views hidden by the term. The Civil War was a Puritan revolution and a parliamentary overthrow of the king only in an ambiguous sense. The Puritans in Parliament were largely a mixed and moderate lot, but they in turn were overthrown by more radical Puritans – really members of sects – in the New Model Army. The moderates had economic views closer to Tawney's Calvinists, but the sect preachers were closer to Luther in their appeals.

James I and the Dominant Coalition in Transition

James I (1603–1625) was a transitional figure. He was the most legitimate heir by genealogical descent, and his succession is largely taken for granted. Since he followed a policy of trying to accommodate everyone, his reign featured little drama and few accomplishments. Scholarly attention quickly shifts to his son and grandsons, who ruled through far more eventful times.

Nevertheless, James's accession to power deserves more attention. His mother, Mary Queen of Scots, was the real legitimate heir to Elizabeth, but she was executed to prevent her assumption of power. James obviously also would been denied the throne if he had been objectionable. Instead, the elite pressured Elizabeth to name him, despite her reluctance.

Several factors are likely to have been crucial in James's selection. First, like the kings chosen after the Glorious Revolution of 1688, James was a middle-aged foreign king who continued to rule his home country as well as England. In 1603 James had been the king of Scotland for 36 years and had exercised full power for 20 years after coming of age. The elite may have thought the Tudors had been real autocrats and had not been controlled by any dominant coalition. They may have thought that a foreign king would be more accommodating. If so, they judged James well because that is how he ruled.[25]

Second, James I had a personal background that made him particularly well-suited to reduce the religious tension of the 1500s. His mother was a martyred Catholic, but he had been raised as a Protestant and married a Protestant wife. Scotland had an established Calvinist (Presbyterian) Church, and James was, of course, the head of that church. At the same time, he was extremely eager for an alliance with Spain, and he wanted it to be cemented by his son's marriage to a Catholic Spanish princess. He was willing to facilitate this marriage with a more tolerant policy toward domestic Catholics.

In fact, James was to handle religious conflict in England skillfully. He commissioned the authorized Church of England translation of the Bible, which was to be called the King James Bible. The top churchmen whom James appointed usually had a Puritan approach. "All James's archbishops drew their divinity from John Calvin's Geneva, as did James himself, and the university establishments were largely Calvinist."[26] Yet they were moderate Calvinists. Presbyterians opposed strong bishops or even the very existence of bishops, and the rural elite, who generally controlled the county and parish churchmen, were particularly attracted to Calvinism for this reason. They saw James's bishops as a sign that he would not intervene to limit their autonomy.

James I, like Elizabeth, kept the church under strict control. Bishops "were royal nominees, economically and socially weak." David Loades even describes the church as being in "the degrading and indefensible position of a department of state for ecclesiastic affairs." Bishops comprised one-third of the members of the House of Lords, and they normally voted with the king.[27]

Nevertheless, the truly important changes during the reigns of James I and Charles I occurred in the socioeconomic realm. The 1600s were unquestionably a period of real economic progress in England. "It is astonishing to reflect on [the century's] achievements," Mark Kishlansky asserts

[25] For a discussion of the similar outside king in medieval Genoa, see Avner Greif, *Institutions and the Path to the Modern Economy: Lessons from Medieval Trade* (Cambridge: Cambridge University Press, 2006).

[26] Derek Hirst, *England in Conflict 1603–1660: Kingdom, Community, Commonwealth* (New York: Oxford University Press, 1999), p. 38.

[27] Davis Loades, *Politics and Nation: England 1450–1660*, 5th ed. (Oxford: Blackwell, 1999), pp. 287–8.

in opening a five-page introduction to his book on England in the 17th century.[28] Population estimates for the period are quite imprecise, but the population grew from, perhaps, two million in 1500 to over five million in 1650. London's population increased from 50,000 people in 1500 to 200,000 in 1600, 400,000–450,000 in 1650, and 550,000 in 1700.[29] These figures are not exact, but they convey a sense of the scale of what was happening.

The land shortage that produced the migration of peasants into London also resulted in substantial emigration to Northern Ireland (Ulster) and the New World. The population of the New World colonies rose from zero in 1600 to 490,000 in 1710. Two-thirds of the colonial population (330,000) was located on the mainland and a third in the Caribbean colonies. Whites comprised nearly 65% of the colonial population (315,000 people), and 75% of the blacks (135,000 of 180,000) lived in the Caribbean.[30]

A major improvement in agricultural productivity was clearly needed for such a rapid growth in population. Robert Brenner argues that colonial trade in the 1600s and early 1700s was less the cause of English growth than the "continuing growth in the home market produced by higher agricultural productivity."[31] He notes that in 1520 "about 76 percent of the population was involved in agriculture, [while] by 1700 only about 55 percent was so occupied."

The sharp rise in population played a major role in England's evolution toward a more modern society. Monopoly guilds were so universal in the early stages of development in Europe that they must have served important needs. In particular, they must have been the best way for rulers to collect taxes, adjudicate contract disputes, build infrastructure, and perform policing duties at a time when they were not able to build a functioning bureaucracy. The monopoly profits of the guilds included a hidden "sales tax" to finance these "government" activities.

[28] Mark Kishlansky, *A Monarchy Transformed: Britain 1603–1714* (London: Penguin Books, 1997), pp. 1–5.

[29] For a discussion of the growth population and the estimates in the literature of the scholar who puts greatest emphasis on this factor in provoking the civil war, see Jack Goldstone, *Revolution and Rebellion in the Early Modern World* (Berkeley: University of California Press, 1991), pp. 21–37 and 83–92; E. A. Wrigley and R. S. Schofield, *The Population History of England: 1541–1871: A Reconstruction* (Cambridge, MA: Harvard University Press, 1981).

[30] Jack Greene, *Pursuits of Happiness: The Social Development of Early Modern British Colonies and the Formation of American Culture* (Chapel Hill: University of North Carolina Press, 1988), pp. 178–9.

[31] Robert Brenner, *Merchants and Revolution: Commercial Change, Political Conflict, and London's Overseas Traders, 1550–1653* (Princeton, NJ: Princeton University Press, 1993), p. 44. The emphasis is Brenner's.

When the number of guilds and guild members was small, the king could control guild leaders through personalistic methods and the latter could control their members in the same way. This was especially true of London where the guilds tended to overlap with ward boundaries. Most of the members of the London city council were guild leaders and had the power to pass necessary laws. They were highly responsive to the king and thus helped him solve collective action problems in the city-state.

The phasing out of guilds also occurred at fairly predictable times in European development. Hence this too must have been a response to changing conditions. Again, London was typical, as was Madrid at the end of the 1700s. In the 1600s the increasing population of London required a growth in the number of grocers, carpenters, tailors, and so forth, and this made the domestic guilds increasingly unwieldy. London had long had a "second economy" of illegal traders not in the guilds, and their numbers grew rapidly. The problem became particularly great as people began to move beyond the city walls and were more difficult to control.

But what did the rise in the population of London and the decline of the domestic guilds mean for the "dominant coalition" of *Violence and Social Orders* and *In the Shadow of Violence*? In 1500, England was a rural society that had armed regional warlords, a capital of 50,000 people, strong domestic and foreign trade guilds, and an export economy without a navy or oceangoing fleet. The dominant coalition was composed of the warlords, the Merchant Adventurers foreign trade guild, and the London domestic guilds.

In 1750, England had a capital with some 650,000 people, New World colonies with two million people, and an English navy and merchant fleet that ruled the waves and made these colonies possible. The rural elite no longer had military forces, while the state bureaucracy, the financiers, the manufacturers, and the interest groups from broader groups in London were still not a powerful force. The 1600s were a century when the old power structure had been destroyed and the new one had not yet been consolidated.

The reigns of James I and Charles I from 1603 until 1642 took place in the midst of this development, and they seem best understood in the framework of North's concept of a dominant coalition. The Parliament rested on the rural elites, but now with checks and balances between the lords in their House in Parliament and the gentry in the House of Commons. Yet the lords had lost much of their military power, and the gentry no longer had military experience. Indeed, Lawrence Stone argued that "the crucial victories of the Crown over the nobility were won between about 1570 and 1620" – that is, substantially within the 20-year reign of James I.[32]

The domestic guilds had lost much of their power, and the old Manufacturers Adventurers monopoly guild, while still economically important in European trade, had lost most of its political power. Indeed, the London city council was now dominated by the East India Company and the Levant Company. From 1600 to 1625, 50 of the 140 aldermen were associated with the Merchant Adventurers, but in 1640, almost half of the 26 were associated with the Levant Company or the East India Company.[33]

The members of merchant guilds trading with Asia played an important part in providing revenue for the monarch by collecting customs and making loans, but they had relatively few ships – and they were usually away on a long voyage. They had little independent social and political support within England itself. The king himself had no standing army to give him a real monopoly of force.

Elizabeth I had begun the process of creating a new urban-based elite with her promotion of an oceangoing merchant fleet. This fleet continued to grow under James I, but James did not have a serious colonization program that would require a larger merchant fleet. Charles I, by contrast, was strongly dedicated to colonization and hence promoted the expansion of both the navy and the merchant fleet.

Under both James and Charles, the merchant-naval elite remained virtually alone as members of the urban elite, and the merchants engaged in Asian trade had disproportionate political power within it. The merchants were the main financiers, the state bureaucrats were few in number and had little power, and the manufacturers were only beginning to grow in strength.

In controlling London, James I had relied on the Establishment merchants of the East India and Levant companies as his loyal servants in the city council and as his main source of loans. He ruled the country as a whole through the court. Elizabeth had relied on a small number of families and played them off against each other.[34] By contrast, James drew a broad range of nobles into court politics. He bestowed lavish gifts and

[32] Lawrence Stone, *The Crisis of the Aristocracy, 1558–1641*, abridged edition (London: Oxford Press, 1967), p. 133.

[33] Brenner, *Merchants and Revolution*, pp. 51–82. For the aldermen, see p. 82.

[34] For a good sense of this in a detailed and enjoyable discussion of the creation of Shakespeare's Globe Theater toward the end of Elizabeth's reign, see Christopher Laoutaris, *Shakespeare and the Countess* (London: Penguin Books, 2014). See also David Loades, *The Cecils: Privilege and Power behind the Throne* (London: National Archives, 2007).

concessions on a range of elite figures. While many focus on the negative aspects of such behavior, Lawrence Stone sees the policy of involving the nobles in court politics as a device to distract them from the violence to which they had become accustomed. As has been noted, James's churchmen were moderates.

The political system at the end of James's reign in 1625 was more or less in equilibrium, one that might have evolved peacefully in the 1600s to a system with religious toleration and with growing power for an urban-based coalition – as, indeed, was finally to be achieved after 1688. The growing state military force – the navy – had an economically profitable coalition with the merchants and was quite happy with the moderate authoritarian regimes of James I, Charles II, and those who ruled from 1688 to 1832.

Of course, if the equilibrium were to be maintained, government policy would have to evolve gradually to reflect the evolving balance of power. So too would the structure of government. The bureaucracy would have to grow, and the power of Parliament would have to increase as the malapportionment in favor of the rural elite was ended and the urban elites drawn into it. The process could well be gradual, but James's successors could not rely so heavily on the rural elite or rely so heavily on the small Asian segment of the merchant-naval alliance.

Moreover, future kings would have to continue James I's balancing act with religious emotions. The expansion of London's population from 200,000 in 1600 to over 500,000 in 1700 would increase social tensions and the attraction of newcomers to Luther-like appeals.[35] The Thirty Years' War in Europe from 1618 to 1639 took on the character of a religious war between Catholicism and Protestantism and would strengthen suspicions inside England. Since the fading rural military power had not been replaced by a standing army, there was little to control violence if it broke out.

Charles I, the Dominant Coalition, and the Civil War of the 1640s

As Mancur Olson emphasized, rulers matter. Even in calmer times, stability depends on a ruler with a monopoly of force who has the ability to persuade and negotiate with others to solve the major collective action problems and persuade others to accept policies. In times of tension and conflict when the dominant coalition is in transition, a country needs an especially skilled ruler.

[35] The importance of rapid population growth is the major theme of Goldstone, *Revolution and Rebellion in the Early Modern World.*

Unfortunately, Charles I was not such a king, and he chose a policy that exacerbated tensions rather than reduced them. The result was Civil War.

The causes and nature of the English Civil War have long been a subject of great controversy. Historians always have conflicting interpretations of major historical events, but the debate about the English Civil War is peculiar. None of the major interpretations is really convincing.

The Whig historians saw the Civil War as a key event in the long struggle of English society against tyranny. The struggle, they said, was finally completed in the Glorious Revolution of 1688. Yet the Civil War and the Glorious Revolution were 40 years apart and any linear connection between them seems strained. Moreover, the victors in the Civil War overthrew Parliament as well as the king. We will argue that the Glorious Revolution was a repudiation of the Civil War and an embrace of the Restoration agreement. After Parliament was restored in 1660, it repeatedly voted in favor of sharp increases in taxes over a 30-year period, even though it received none of the supposedly crucial guarantees of the written constitution of 1689. The Whigs ignored this real mystery.

In the 20th century, the second popular interpretation of the Civil War was Karl Marx's. Marx thought the Civil War, maybe together with the Glorious Revolution, was England's bourgeois revolution. Yet he defined the bourgeoisie as the owners of the means of production and saw the merchants as parasites. If the bourgeois revolution occurred in the 1640s, then the restored Charles II must have represented the bourgeoisie. If the bourgeois revolution occurred in 1688, then it gave power to the rural elite in Parliament, and it was bourgeois only if the gentry are the bourgeoisie. Even that interpretation ignores the House of Lords.

The third major interpretation of the Civil War emphasized religion. England had been Catholic in the 1530s, and the conflicts of the 1640s only involved different types of Protestant groups that had been formed since 1530. The leading actors all called themselves Puritans, but they ranged from James I's establishment churchmen to untrained preachers who used the most extremist populist language in appealing to the lower classes. These different religious groups surely gained support from different types of people for reasons other than abstract theological differences. It would seem vital to explore and explain the reasons for the different religions.

The fourth major interpretation of the Civil War – the dominant revisionist theory of the last third of the 20th century – was that of Conrad Russell. Russell did not see England as revolutionary in the 1630s but believed the Civil War was the unexpected result of unnecessary and ill-considered decisions on all sides. Russell's opinion is widely accepted, at least in part, and we find it largely convincing. Yet the theory does nothing to explain why the period from the 1630s to the 1690s was so transforming. In fact, some kind of urban-led "revolution" occurred, whatever its cause, character, or timing.

To a political scientist with a collective action approach, the explanation for the Civil War should start with Charles I. James I knew from his mother's execution and his own selection that "the divine right of kings" should not be taken too seriously. Charles I, by contrast, seemed to think he had a right to have an authoritarian regime such as was being consolidated in France. He did not seem to realize this required a standing army that he did not have.

In 2014, Steven Pincus and James Robinson criticized North and Weingast's argument in "Constitutions and Commitment" that the Revolution Settlement introduced new principles into the English "constitution." We are sympathetic to this argument. James I acted as if he believed the elite had made a pact with him. Charles I then violated it and was beheaded. Charles II acted as if the elite, this time supported by naval force, had made a similar pact with him. James II inexplicably made the same mistake as his father.[36]

If England had still had the regional military forces of the medieval period, then Charles I would have provoked little alarm. In actuality, as Russell phrased it, the "peers had no armies [and] Charles did not need to worry if they sulked in their tents."[37] But this also meant that the peers did have the forces of peers to defend him in a crisis and that they would be frightened if he organized a force to defend himself.

Many scholars, including North and Weingast, emphasize financial issues as the central factor in Charles's conflict with Parliament, but these issues should not be exaggerated. By the 1630s Charles had had a decade to increase his income from the growing Eastern and Atlantic colonial trade. Annual customs duties increased from 300,000 pounds at the beginning of the 1630s to 500,000 pounds at the end. This made Charles independent of Parliament if he did not become involved in war until his colonial revenue grew still further.[38]

When Russell argued that religious issues were central before and during the Civil War, he was right about their role in creating the deep suspicions

[36] For a list of the precursors of the provisions of the Revolution Settlement, see Pincus and Robinson, "What Really Happened during the Glorious Revolution?," pp. 194–201.

[37] Russell, *The Crisis of Parliaments*, p. 320.

[38] Hirst, *England in Conflict 1603–1660*, pp. 140–3.

associated with the war. In a number of ways Charles I created the strong impression that he was a hidden Catholic. He married a strongly Catholic French princess and allowed her to worship in a public way and to be active in English politics. In the colonies, Charles took land from Virginia – a colony named for the Protestant Elizabeth – and made it a sanctuary for Catholics. He called it Maryland, officially after his Catholic wife but also, many suspected, after his Catholic grandmother whom Elizabeth had executed.

Charles also appointed a number of Catholics, open or secret, to high positions. They included the lord treasurer from 1628 to 1635, chancellor of the exchequer from 1629 to 1642, one of the secretaries of state from 1632 to 1640, and a number of officials in ranks just below them. These Catholics, Gerald Aylmer argued, "were important primarily because of the psychological effect which their presence had on the more militant, Puritan-inclined Protestants."[39]

Moreover, Charles I openly transformed the personnel and appearance of the Church of England that he headed. While his father's bishops were moderate and tolerant Calvinists, Charles wanted a Church of England that was "profoundly different from James's."[40] He replaced James's bishops with men who usually are called Armininians or Laudians. They emphasized authority, ceremony, and ritual, while their theology de-emphasized predestination.

In these respects, Arminianism was close enough to Catholicism to strengthen the suspicion that Charles I was a hidden Catholic. Charles's policy provoked a highly negative reaction from two different religious groups at opposite ends of the spectrum – James I's old religious establishment and evangelical preachers who were trying to gain lower-class support for new and more radical sects.

Property owners with land that Henry VIII or Elizabeth had seized from the Catholic Church feared that a restored church would demand it back. The rural lords and gentry also feared that a centralized Catholic Church would appoint bishops who would deprive them of control of the local parishes. The political class also feared that Charles might be attracted to the French and Spanish Catholic Church, as well as their autocratic political systems.

39 G. E. Aylmer, *The King's Servants: The Civil Service of Charles I, 1625–1647* (London: R & K Paul, 1961), p. 357.

40 Quote from Conrad Russell, *The Fall of the British Monarchies, 1637–1642* (Oxford: Oxford University Press, 1991), pp. 14–15.

The action that precipitated the Civil War was Charles's arbitrary – and quite unnecessary – decision to impose a common prayer book in Scotland in 1637. As King of Scotland, Charles thought this was within his right, but he inspired little loyalty in Scotland. A Scottish army invaded England in the summer of 1640, and it met little resistance in the northern part of England and quickly occupied the area. The borderland English had long been deeply suspicious of London, sympathized with the Scottish attack on Charles's authoritarianism, and sometimes even cooperated with it.[41]

As Conrad Russell emphasizes, the fears aroused by the king's arbitrary decisions on the Scottish prayer book were intensified because all issues of English politics were interconnected. In Russell's words, "If Charles could introduce a new liturgy simply by proclamation, then he could issue a new religion, or a new tax, or anything he chose by proclamation."[42]

Olson argued that the ruler is the person who "can organize the greatest capacity for violence."[43] The real problem from the 1630s to 1660s was that no one in England really had such a capacity that was organized. That really was the definition of the Civil War. Even Oliver Cromwell, who came to control an army, did not control most of the navy after its revolt in 1648.

At the beginning, the Scots could easily have been repelled if the king had had even a minimal standing army or had been able to assemble a fairly small military force. He had to call a session of Parliament to obtain financing, but members of Parliament were afraid that if they built a significant army, he would turn it against them. This same fear about the formation of a small military force to meet a legitimate need arose continually in the future. As a result, legitimate issues could not be solved.

The same fears about the army were to plague the Parliament. It too had no military force, and it could not control the commander of any new army it created. In 1640, relatively radical parliamentary leaders were able to take advantage of the military vacuum and the radical mood of lower-class Londoners to stimulate street action against its enemies. In May 1641, such mob action in frightened the king into accepting the execution of his top lieutenant, Thomas Stratford.

The navy was the most powerful military force in England, especially because it was allied with the armed merchant fleet. It often is said to have

[41] For a discussion of this attitude toward London and its impact on the colonies and then the United States when the Borderland British emigrated to the New World, see David Hackett Fischer, *Albion's Seed: Four British Folkways in America* (New York: Oxford University Press, 1989).

[42] Russell, *The Crisis of Parliaments*; Kishlansky, *A Monarchy Transformed*, pp. 145, 110.

[43] Olson, "Dictatorship, Democracy, and Development," p. 568.

supported Parliament from the beginning. Conrad Russell reports that naval support not only was "a crucial obstacle to [Charles's] attempts to get foreign help" but also "could be used regularly to relieve sieges of ports, or to move food and artillery." Russell asserts that "it is arguable" that "the Earl of Warwick, who commanded the fleet on Parliament's behalf ... contributed as much to Parliament's ultimate victory as any land commander."[44] Oliver Cromwell was a land commander.

The problem is that Warwick and other important merchants discussed in the literature were among the Puritan founders of the Massachusetts Bay Colony in 1630 and the Providence Island [Nassau shipping] Company which was "the 'cover' organization" for the Puritan Opposition in the colonies.[45] Naturally they opposed the king who had essentially exiled them.

Yet the other merchants – the guilds in European and Asian trade and the important merchants in the tobacco and sugar trade – had far different views, and their fleets were far larger. Most of the Navy should have been allied with the Europe-oriented guilds. What is most unclear is why the Puritans could overcome the much larger naval forces of the guilds and the Anglicans dealing with the tobacco colonies.

One suspects that Parliament's early ability to mobilize radicals in the streets of London was crucial. Mobs that could force the king to execute his chief lieutenant could also harass merchants and shippers who supported the king. Indeed, Warwick's crucial action is said to have been the mobilization of 2,000 seamen. These surely were seamen in London who were protesting not being paid. If merchants and shippers wanted to use the port of London, they may well have had to support Parliament or at least not oppose it.

Some English historians, especially ones in recent years, see the Civil War resting on genuine revolutionary pressure in the streets. Older scholars were more inclined to see the demonstrations being directed more against desired targets by leading members of Parliament, at least through a selective enforcement of the laws against looting. Whether the violence was spontaneous or directed, moderates in Parliament and the elite became increasingly worried. As a result, support for the king rose in the city in August and September of 1641.

[44] Russell, *The Crisis of Parliaments*, p. 352; Hirst, *England in Conflict, 1603–1660*, p. 201.

[45] Loades, *Politics and Nation*, p. 338; Sean Kelsey, "Rich, Robert, Second Earl of Warwick (1587–1658), Colonial Promoter and Naval Officer," in Colin Matthew and Brian Harrison, eds., *Oxford Dictionary of National Biography* (Oxford: Oxford University Press, 2004), online edition.

Then a revolt in Ireland against England – one in which the seizure of property was a major factor – raised the old fears about Catholicism and the king's possible use of an army raised to fight the rebellion. A city election in December 1641 brought radicals to power in the London city council, and the city government created a Committee of Safety composed of radicals who created and oversaw a citizen's militia.[46]

In early 1642, the king fled the city, first to the suburbs and then to York, and finally to Oxford. A real Civil War ensued. Parliament created regional armies that rested on the old source of military power in the past – the forces of the rural elite. Out of the first 20 colonels of these armies, 10 were peers and four were knights and baronets.[47]

The peers, however, did not have the same military power as in the past, and the gentry did not have the military experience of their ancestors. The local elites were quite willing to pay for troops to protect themselves when the Scots or the king's forces were in their region, but otherwise they usually were content to be free riders and let others do the fighting.

The result was military stalemate, but one in which no political agreement with the king seemed possible. The Parliament now felt it necessary to organize a national army – the New Model Army.[48] Oliver Cromwell used this army to defeat the king's forces, and the king fled to the Scots.

Once the war was over, however, the problems of the Parliament only intensified. Charles would not agree to an acceptable compromise, but Parliament had few options if it did not remove the king. Yet those in the New Model Army and the streets of London were more radical than most of the parliamentary leaders and a removal of the king might legitimate more extreme actions.

Parliament naturally wanted to disband the New Model Army, but a familiar problem arose. Parliament had not raised enough money to pay the troops. The members of the Army were owed three million pounds in back wages, a huge sum in comparison with the one million total annual income that the king received before the war. The radical soldiers demanded back pay before the army was disbanded.[49]

Without an ambitious leader in a key position of power within the army, the soldiers would have had no option but to return to civilian life

[46] Valerie Pearl, *London and the Outbreak of the Puritan Revolution: City Government and National Politics, 1625–43* (Oxford: Oxford University Press, 1961), pp. 127–59.

[47] Russell, *The Crisis of Parliaments*, p. 346.

[48] Mark Kishlansky, *The Rise of the New Model Army* (Cambridge: Cambridge University Press, 1979).

[49] Hirst, *England in Conflict 1603–1660*, p. 234.

and engage in various legal and illegal activities. But the soldiers did have such a leader in Oliver Cromwell. Everyone agrees that Cromwell was a first-class commander, but his political intentions remain controversial. A scholar is reminded of George Washington, a man who always insisted that he did not want power but who skillfully acted in a manner that brought him ultimate power.[50]

The period from late 1646 to late 1648 was characterized by disorder unnecessary for us to describe. The Parliament could not raise the money to pay the arrears of the New Model Army or others who demanded their claims not be forgotten. The army captured the king in June 1647, and in the spring of 1648, the Scots and royalists – now supported by the navy – launched what is called the Second Civil War.

When they were defeated, a large number of ships fled to Holland, essentially to become privateers. The army moved quickly in December 1648 to expel the moderates from the Parliament and to establish the so-called Rump. The next month, they tried Charles I, executed him, and abolished the monarchy.

A commonwealth, scarcely more orderly than the previous period for the same reasons, existed from 1649 to 1653 when Cromwell overthrew the Rump Parliament. He established what he called a Protectorate, but what was in reality a military dictatorship based on a divided army and a disgruntled navy. Cromwell had but five years to live, and he too accomplished little. The Puritan dictatorship ended with the restoration of Charles II to the throne in April 1660.

It is difficult to know how to characterize the dominant coalition or coalitions of the 1640s and 1650s. Modern military dictatorships usually begin with a strong, well-administered army, but the Puritan Army was not that. It won because its opponents' military forces were even weaker. The rural elite was excluded from power when their members of Parliament were dismissed. The navy was allied with the merchants of London and was highly suspicious of the New Model Army. It seems like a very weak dominant coalition, and this may well be the reason it fell so easily in 1660.

When Oliver Cromwell died, he was succeeded by his son Richard, who clearly did not have the personal qualities needed to control the chaotic situation, and he was forced out after eight months in office.[51] The army generals who overthrew him agreed on the need for a regime in which the

[50] For George Washington, see Chapter 9.

[51] Godfrey Davies, *The Restoration of Charles II, 1658–60* (Oxford: Oxford University Press, 1955), pp. 29–44, 72–85.

army was dominant, but they then engaged in a fierce power struggle in which they continued to be plagued with the old problem of how to pay the troops.

The situation deteriorated rapidly. After crushing a royalist uprising in late August, General John Lambert returned to London and on October 13 overthrew both the Rump Parliament and the commander of the army. The commander of the English 6,000-man army in Scotland, George Monck, was a longtime adversary of Lambert, and the two moved quickly toward battle. Order disintegrated in London as its elite feared the Lambert coup, and the capital and a number of lesser cities became increasingly disorderly. On December 3, a particularly dangerous full-scale rebellion broke out in Portsmouth.

The navy too was divided on a number of issues, but, as in 1648, it was united on the issues of army dominance and the financing of the navy. At the beginning of 1658, total government revenue was around one million pounds and debts were 714,000 pounds.[52] By the summer of 1659, the navy had received no money since September.[53] The admiral in charge of the Channel fleet, John Lawson, decided to end the confusion with a full-scale coup. On December 14 he sailed his fleet up the Thames and blockaded the city. By December 24, the generals had capitulated, and the Rump re-opened on December 26.[54]

On January 1, 1660, Monck began his march from Scotland to London with his 6,000-man army and entered the city on February 5 without any resistance. In the words of Conrad Russell, he was the "commander of the last paid and disciplined force left [and] he could do what he liked."[55] Indeed, Monck himself was the son of a prominent merchant and had headed the navy for a few years in the past. It is highly likely that he had informal understandings with the navy before he marched.

Within a week, Monck had demanded that the Rump readmit the other members of Parliament, a group known to favor a restoration of the Stuarts. He worked with the leading pro-royalist admiral, Edward Montagu, to organize the return of Charles II. Lawson, although a supporter of a republic,

52 Bernard Capp, *Cromwell's Navy: The Fleet and the English Revolution* (Oxford: Oxford University Press, 1989), p. 341.

53 N.A.M. Rodger, *The Command of the Ocean: Naval History of Britain, 1649–1815* (New York: W.W. Norton, 2005), p. 37.

54 For Monck, see Ted Jamison Jr., *George Monck and the Restoration: Victor without Bloodshed* (Fort Worth, TX: Texas Christian University Press, 1975). For the navy coup, see Capp, *Cromwell's Navy*, 331–401, especially pp. 344–50.

55 Russell, *The Crisis of Parliaments*, p. 396.

acceded and joined the other two. Charles arrived on May 29 on Montagu's ship. We have an insider's view of the final steps because Samuel Pepys was Montagu's aide and began his diary at this time.

The Central Role of the Restoration

In "Constitutions and Commitment," North and Weingast adopted the argument of John Locke and the Whig historians that the Revolution Settlement of 1689 rested on the principle of the consent of the governed, especially in the realm of taxation.[56] In their view, the members of the elite – "the wealthy" – were given a veto over laws, taxes, and the budget in Parliament, and this made them amenable to a sharp increase in the state debt to finance a new war and the taxes needed to service it.

North and Weingast supported their argument by pointing to a subsequent decline of interest rates on state loans despite a sharp growth in the size of the national debt.[57] This, they said, showed that the lenders were reassured by the new constitutional rules that the government would not default – that Parliament would be willing to levy taxes in order to make interest payments and redeem the bonds.

New Institutional economists have widely accepted the thesis of "Constitutions and Commitment," but many others have been skeptical. One reason is that the pattern of interest rates does not correspond to North and Weingast's thesis. As Nathan Sussman and Yishay Yafeh point out, "the four decades following the Glorious Revolution can be characterized as a period of a high and fluctuating cost of capital rather than an era of permanently low interest rates." The 40 years to which Sussman and Yafeh refer extended from 1688 to 1728.[58]

North and Weingast would have been on sounder ground if they had simply pointed to the continuing explosion of national debt and the taxes

56 Locke's work was entitled *Two Treatises of Government.* Its argument was developed in the 1670s for use in gaining support for a new Whig Party that was formed to organize opposition to the growing support for Charles II. The *Two Treatises* was then published in 1689 to legitimate the Glorious Revolution. See Richard Ashcraft, *Revolutionary Politics and Locke's Two Treatises of Government* (Princeton, NJ: Princeton University Press, 1986).

57 North and Weingast, "Constitutions and Commitment," p. 822

58 Nathan Sussman and Yishay Yafeh, "Institutional Reforms, Financial Development and Sovereign Debt: Britain 1690–1790," *Journal of Economic History* 66 (2006), 906–35, p. 921. For a very recent collection of articles that make this and other criticisms, see D'Maris Coffman, Adrian Leonard, and Larry Neal, eds., *Questioning Credible Commitment: Perspectives on the Rise of Financial Capitalism* (Cambridge: Cambridge University Press, 2013).

to service it. The debt was one million pounds in 1688, 14 million in 1700, 36.2 million in 1714, and 54 million in 1720.[59]

Nevertheless, the problem with "Constitutions and Commitments" goes deeper: what occurs after an event is not necessarily caused by it. Lenders seemingly should not have found a parliamentary veto reassuring. Until the Reform Act of 1832, 150 years after the Glorious Revolution, Parliament was dominated by the rural elite. The rural elite had refused to fund Charles I's building of a navy in the 1630s, and they had been frightened by every attempt by Charles to build an army to control the Scots or Irish during the Civil War. Indeed, Peter Lindert concluded that the dominant forces in Parliament in the 1700s had an anti-growth bias.[60]

Why should lenders have now trusted Parliament to raise taxes to pay for the war that William of Orange's selection in 1688 automatically guaranteed? Why should Parliament welcome William's "invasion" with 20,000 troops when George Monck's 6,000 troops had seemed so decisive in 1659? Why would the rural Parliament see its interests served by Britain being at war with France for 51 of the 95 years after 1688? Why should they be expected to vote for an army of 116,000 men in the 1689–1697 war, 136,000 in the 1702–1713 period, 113,000 from 1739 to 1748, and 168,000 from 1756 to 1763? The increase in military expenditures was the greatest cause of the huge increase in debt and taxes.[61]

North and Weingast recognize that they present no explanation for the Glorious Revolution: "Our discussion of the events prior to the Glorious Revolution (1603 to 1688) simply characterizes this period; it does not model or explain it." The more logical explanation for the results of the Revolution is that the forces that produced it were also responsible for the developments afterward.[62]

If North and Weingast had written their 1989 article 25 years later, they surely would have asked about the changes in England's dominant coalition that occurred between the late 1630s and the late 1680s that explained the policy of the 1700s. We think that is the right question. For all the issues in the phrase "bourgeois revolution," Marx surely pointed in the correct direction. The 1600s somehow featured an urban-based revolution and a transition to an urban-based dominant coalition.

[59] North and Weingast, "Constitutions and Commitment," p. 822.

[60] Peter Lindert, "Voice and Growth: Was Churchill Right?" *Journal of Economic History* 63 (2003), 315–50, pp. 330 and 340.

[61] Brewer, *The Sinews of Power*, p. 30.

[62] North and Weingast, "Constitutions and Commitment," p. 804, n. 1.

Given the armed nature of the conflict from the 1640s to 1660, it seems likely that the authors of *In the Shadow of Violence* would suspect that the military were prominent members of the coalition. If so, the obvious core member of the coalition was the merchant-navy alliance. The English army was kept under strict control after the Restoration of 1660. In the 1680s, it had only 15,000 troops, fewer than in 1475. The Spanish army had 70,000 troops, the Dutch 110,000, the French 120,000, the Swedish 63,000 and the Russian 130,000.[63] James was expanding it rapidly, but that only increased the fears about him and the determination of the navy to act as it did in 1648 and 1659.

Anyone thinking afresh about England's dominant coalitions in the 1600s does not instinctively focus on 1688. The first natural question is the character of the Dominant Coalition that arose at the end of the Civil War, not 40 years later. This is particularly so because most of the key developments attributed to the Glorious Revolution actually began with the Restoration.

First, Charles II did act in a restrained manner, surely the result of a clear pact made with him in 1660. There must have been a Dominant Coalition in place in a sense that was less true during the reigns of Henry VIII and Elizabeth I. Second, Parliament began to increase taxes very sharply in 1660 – and without any increase in its powers such as occurred in 1689. Patrick O'Brien and Philip Hunt's graphs of revenue and direct taxes from 1500 to 1800 show no change of trend in 1688. Third, the increase in the power of the executive also began in 1660. Since the additional revenue during the Restoration was not used for war, it was spent on hiring more government employees and improving government operations. The government also had more people to collect taxes, and improvement in the tax-collecting machinery had a circular effect. Tax farming was abolished, and this led to more revenue to hire more government collectors.

Stephen Baxter reports that the Treasury's formal powers did not change between 1660 and 1702, but it "gained control over other branches of the government by the simple means of using these powers every day or at least every week."[64] The effort to improve the administrative system extended into every realm. Alison Olson notes that "the second half of the Restoration era saw the most far-reaching attempts to reform and re-organize colonial administration ever undertaken by the British government in the seventeenth and eighteenth centuries."[65]

63 Brewer, *The Sinews of Power*, p. 8. Brewer relies on Geoffrey Parker.

64 Stephen Baxter, *The Development of the Treasury, 1660–1702* (Longmans, Green, 1957), pp. 3–4 and 167.

65 Alison Gilbert Olson, *Anglo-American Politics 1600–1775* (New York: Oxford University Press, 1973), p. 57.

Our focus on 1660 is not unique to us. The title of Alan Houston and Steve Pincus's *A Nation Transformed: England after the Restoration* points to 1660 as a breaking point, while John Brewer explicitly states this was so: "the change from the 1660s to the 1760s seems greater than those either from the 1650s to the 1750s or from the 1680s to the 1780s."[66]

What had happened in 1659–1660? The Parliament no longer was excluded from the policy process as it had since the rise of the army. It still overrepresented the rural elite, but it seemed to have little of the power it had in the 1630s, let alone that which it had tried to win from Charles I. Policy seemed responsive to urban forces.

Those who benefited directly from the policies of the Restoration were the urban elite. London had been disrupted for two decades. The London elite and even the broader educated population must have had a sense that the country needed a strong government to maintain law and order and much higher taxes to ensure that soldiers and sailors would not be driven to revolt simply because they had not been paid. Indeed, the need to pay the sailors was a key talking point in the arguments over increasing taxes, and it was a quiet reminder of the power of those who commanded the ships.

More directly, the merchants and nascent manufacturing classes wanted economic growth, while the military wanted the ability to wage war. The army was cut back in size, but the merchant fleet thrived with the colonial growth. The navy generally shared in this prosperity. A reader of the diary written from 1660 to 1669 by Samuel Pepys, Chief Secretary of the Admiralty, shows how those like himself quickly became wealthy.[67] A person looking for those who "can organize the greatest capacity for violence" and had the ability to overthrow the king surely would look at the navy and its merchant allies.

The Glorious Revolution

Anyone with the foregoing view of the Restoration has no difficulty accepting the traditional interpretation of the character of the Glorious Revolution. In that view, the Glorious Revolution simply reflected the elite reaction to James II's extremely foolish attempt to establish an authoritarian regime

[66] Alan Houston and Steve Pincus, eds., *A Nation Transformed: England after the Restoration* (New York: Cambridge University Press, 2001); Brewer, *The Sinews of Power*, p. xiv. In 2009, Pincus emphasizes 1688 as a turning point, but only in the institutional role of Parliament, not in the principles of government or policy. Steve Pincus, *1688: The First Modern Revolution* (New Haven, CT: Yale University Press, 2009).

[67] C. S. Knighton, *Pepys and the Navy* (Stroud, UK: Sutton, 2003), pp. 50–3, 77, 80, and 93.

based on the French Catholic model. This interpretation has been challenged to a partial extent by some younger American historians who now emphasize social forces, but the pattern of mass reaction seems to suggest that it followed rather than preceded the elite.[68]

Our only addendum to the traditional view would be to emphasize that the merchants had the major military force of the country behind them, both their own and that of the navy. Paradoxically, the very inaction of the military showed its power. On the surface, the Glorious Revolution was not glorious at all. William of Orange landed with 20,000 troops and forced the king to flee – the only foreign conquest of England since 1066. Beneath the surface, however, William had demanded and received assurance that his "invading forces" would not be opposed by the English army and navy. The navy did not try to engage the troop ships on the English Channel. The army's loyalty was never tested, but James fled because he believed it would not fight.

But what were the consequences of the revolution? Here we basically agree with Steven Pincus and James Robinson: "The Glorious Revolution was not significant because it was a change in the de jure rules, but it was important in helping to cement a change in the distribution of power in the country." We agree with them that the Revolution "did lead to a significant shift in power and authority to Parliament."[69]

Yet Pincus and Robinson disagree specifically with North and Weingast about the nature of the "parliamentary interests" that won in the Glorious Revolution. North and Weingast argued that the parliamentary classes agreed to "restrictions on the state's ability to manipulate rules to the advantages of itself" and agreed to "limited economic intervention." Pincus and Robinson are clearly right that the victors followed the opposite course.[70]

Some may not like John Brewer's phrase, "the fiscal-military state," but it surely points to the basic nature of the England of the 1700s. Many would see the state actively pursuing an industrial policy of promoting manufacturing through protectionism and repeated war. Without any question, however, tax revenues soared. Patrick O'Brien calculates that they rose by 18 times between 1688 and 1815, while gross national product only tripled. The

[68] See Pincus, *1688: The First Modern Revolution* for this interpretation. Pincus presents an excellent survey of the debate on 1688 in Britain both in 1988 and the earlier decades and centuries in pp. 3–29 of this book.

[69] Pincus and Robinson, "What Really Happened during the Glorious Revolution," pp. 220 and 217.

[70] North and Weingast, "Constitutions and Commitment," pp. 829, 808.

Crown was able to introduce a bewildering combination of different kinds of internal land and excise taxes – and, in 1799, the first income tax.[71]

J.H. Plumb gave his standard book on the years of transformation the title of *The Growth of Political Stability in England: 1675–1725*. This expressed his conviction that stability was not fully established until nearly 40 years after the revolution. Plumb attributes much of this early instability to the weakness of the monarchs and the strength of Parliament. Parliament had no natural leader or party discipline, and it often intervened in the political process in a disorderly fashion.

These years of parliamentary strength were, incidentally, the period when Sussman and Yafeh find that interest rates remained high. Yet, from the very beginning, N.A.M. Rodger reports, the generosity of Commons toward the Navy "astonished" contemporary observers.[72] Even under William III in the 1680s, Parliament was not able to prevent spending from growing "as never before." Brewer concludes that after 1703, the treasury control of financial legislation "was almost never checked by parliamentary opposition."[73]

George I was particularly eager to develop a strong executive branch and bring Parliament under control. He created a dominant Court Treasury party by using various types of patronage and payments that often were distributed through the Treasury Department. As a result, in Plumb's words, "the development of oligarchy and the growth of the executive [in the first years of George I] was to achieve the subjugation of the legislature that the Stuarts had frequently attempted but never achieved."[74]

Adam Smith's analysis of the Hanover monarchs in his 1776 *The Wealth of Nations* made the same point about the power of Parliament quite flatly. The king, Smith wrote, was an authoritarian ruler who had brought

[71] Patrick O'Brien, "Inseparable Connections, Trade, Economy, Fiscal State, and the Expansion of Empire, 1688–1815," in P.J. Marshall, ed., *The Oxford History of the British Empire*, Vol. 2: *The Eighteenth Century* (Oxford: Oxford University Press, 1998), 53–77, p. 68. Some impression of the multiplicity of taxes can be gained from pp. 67–70 of the article. O'Brien and Philip Hunt estimate that the taxes available at the time of the American Revolution were 11 times larger than those available to Charles I, who really began colonization in the mid-1620s. Patrick O'Brien and Philip Hunt, "England, 1485–1815," in Richard Bonney, ed., *The Rise of the Fiscal State in Europe, c.1200–1815* (Oxford: Oxford University Press, 1999), 53–100, pp. 57–8. For a graph of revenues and per capita revenues, see pp. 56 and 64. For a graph of customs revenues (by far the greatest source of tax revenue from 1275 to 1485), see W.M. Ormrod, "England in the Middle Ages," in Richard Bonney, ed., *The Rise of the Fiscal State in Europe, c. 1200–1815* (Oxford: Oxford University Press, 1999), 19–52, p. 33.

[72] Rodger, *Command of the Ocean*, p. 182.

[73] Brewer, *The Sinews of Power*, pp. 149, 151–2.

[74] Plumb, *The Growth of Political Stability in England*, p. 49.

Parliament under control. Smith wrote about the royal "system of management" (bribery) of Parliament. One of Smith's arguments for making the colonies independent was that the multitude of colonial legislatures made the king's "system of management" in London too expensive and hence not cost-effective. Smith simply took for granted that this would be a convincing argument to this audience, prominently including the king and his advisers.[75]

Plumb's dating of the change in London corresponds to the pattern of politics found by Alison Olson in the colonies. Between 1688 and 1714, colonial parties (or factions) had enjoyed a "comfortable, informal working relationship" with their counterparts in Parliament and used them to obtain decisions that they wanted. The rise of the Court Treasury Party meant that by the 1730s the colonies no longer gave much attention to Parliament. Rather, they turned to the executive, and the "ministerial factions were ... decisively linked with colonial factions."[76]

John Brewer's emphasis on the growth in power of the executive, not the legislature, follows the analysis of J.H. Plumb and Adam Smith. The broad British economic historians such as Patrick O'Brien and Stephan Epstein are far closer to Brewer's views in 1989 than to North and Weingast's. They see the increased ability of Britain to collect taxes as the result of the creation of a stronger government and administrative structure rather than the consent of Parliament.[77]

Modern historians disagree on the structure of power within the executive during the Hanover dynasty. Clearly England had what historians used to call "a liberal [restrained] authoritarian state," but the differences of interpretation center on the relative power of the king, the rising figure of the prime minister, the cabinet, and the bureaucracy. Historians agree that Parliament as a broader legislative institution lost power to the executive branch, however defined. Nobles often served as high officials, probably because they had the executive experience of managing their estates and local government, but while in office, they derived their power from the rapidly growing bureaucracy they led.

From this perspective, the Glorious Revolution did not give the rural elite the dominant power to veto measures that they opposed. The rural elite

[75] Smith, *The Wealth of Nations*, p. 785.

[76] Olson, *Anglo-American Politics*, pp. 76, 106–8, 136, and 155.

[77] For Brewer's long and detailed discussion of taxes and debts, see Brewer, *The Sinews of War*, pp. 88–134; Patrick O'Brien, "Inseparable Connections"; Stephan Epstein, *Freedom and Growth: The Rise of States and Markets in Europe, 1300–1750* (London: Routledge, 2000).

and its Parliament had been ostentatiously excluded from the dominant coalition during the Civil War and only partially restored under Charles II. Now, we think, they were simply being readmitted as a junior partner to ensure that the agricultural interests of a predominantly rural country were taken into account.

Yet we believe that Parliament did not represent the interests of the rural wealthy, but those with the greatest power in 1660 and 1686. Why do we agree with Pincus and Robinson that 1688 featured "a significant shift in power and authority to Parliament"? In our opinion the phrase needs to be understood more in process than policy terms. We agree with Brewer's summary statement in 2014: "Parliamentary approval was necessary for government to work at all.... [It] meant that policy matters were discussed in an extremely sophisticated (if self-centered) way."[78]

Brewer is not concerned about the locus of power in the executive, but about the nature of the policy process and the need for mechanisms to ensure that a broad variety of information be brought to bear. He thinks that the mere holding of annual sessions and the demand that Parliament approve all laws and the budget guaranteed that this process would occur, at least if those who dominated the system desired. This is discussed in the next section.

Parliament, Bureaucratic Specialization of Labor, and the Policy Process

Max Weber rightly argued that the essence of the transition to modern society, including a modern market, is the introduction of rule through universal and impersonal rules. Paul Aligica and Peter Boettke report that even scholars of the "spontaneous order" school believe the pursuit of individual self-interest in economic life is not productive unless it takes place "within a given system of rules."[79] Douglass North agrees and says such a system of rules is not part of the law of nature but must be embodied in a network of laws that protect property rights in government courts.

Yet because American economists give little attention to Weber, they have not absorbed the meaning of his analysis for economic development. They usually follow Adam Smith in focusing on the lingering harmful effects of guilds, other monopoly organizations, and monopoly grants in

[78] John Brewer e-mail to Jerry Hough, February 14, 2014.

[79] Paul Dragos Aligica and Peter J. Boettke, *Challenging Institutional Analysis and Development: The Bloomington School* (London: Routledge, 2009), p. 30.

the mid-1700s, and they treat the end of such behavior as de-regulation. We quite agree about the desirability of the changes that Smith advocated, but de-regulation is a misleading word to describe them. Smith did not concentrate his attack on rules and regulations, but on various types of individual and personalistic subsidies or protection from market competition.

In fact, the network of rules and regulations must increase during marketization, not decrease. There cannot be a rule by rules without rules. A London of 850,000 people in 1776 could not be governed through monopoly guilds that set prices and wages and that resolved disputes over contracts. The number of people in each of these businesses simply became too large. Even a mercantilist state increasingly had to utilize a market, at least in most of the economy.

In the process, property and property rights, which have always existed, become more complex. Even serfs living on land "owned" by the lords had had customary rights in the houses in which they lived and the land they farmed, but property rights became far more complicated as the economy developed and increased in size.

Think of the personalistic credit provided to merchants and shippers who created tobacco plantations in Virginia. Much of it was provided by friends and relatives. Banks developed only in the late 1700s, and the simplest banks have far more complex property rights than those that might exist for an agreement between individuals. Bank depositors have property rights. The banks have property rights in their loans but so do the borrowers. There must be complex rules on foreclosure and bankruptcy. Bank owners have complex property rights if they are members of a partnership, different ones if they are stockowners. If such property rights are to be protected, the maintenance of "law and order" must go well beyond police protection of houses and stores from thieves.

Yet property rights cannot be protected in the courts unless there are laws to be enforced that protect these rights. The transition toward a modern society in the 1700s required not only the impartial enforcement of law but also the creation of law. Dan Bogart and Gary Richardson, for instance, reported that between 1600 and 1815 Parliament passed 3,335 Acts about real estate property inheritance, 3,682 about enclosure questions, and 1,682 about roads. Analogous developments had to take place across the spectrum.[80]

[80] Dan Bogart and Gary Richardson, "Parliament, Property Rights, and Public Goods in England, 1600–1815," University of California-Irvine, Working Paper, 2010, pp. 31 and 35. Also see Dan Bogart and Gary Richardson, "Property Rights and Parliament in Industrializing Britain," *Journal of Law and Economics* 54 (May 2011), 241–74.

The question of which rules and regulations are desirable is a highly controversial subject. What is important for us is that these controversies must be resolved. While scholars such as Bogart and Richardson have created datasets that list laws and regulations, they say little about how laws, rules, and regulations are enacted.

In John Brewer's view, the main role of Parliament after 1689 was not the right of veto on taxes. Indeed, he presents evidence of the subservience of Parliament in the financial realm. Instead, Brewer emphasizes the consequence of the formalization of ways in which the budget, tax codes, and laws were drafted. A range of interests was drawn in and allowed to participate in the process to try to influence the outcome.

As John Brewer believes, it is impossible for technical laws and rules to be drafted by untrained members of Parliament during unstructured parliamentary debates. Rules and regulations may be amended during debates, but they must begin as specialized drafts of some sort. Some rules and regulations may come from common law precedents and some from the codes of the commercial courts, but the drafts of laws protecting new, complex property rights have to come from bureaucrats, law firms, interest groups, or members of Parliament with specialized knowledge.[81]

Brewer is known for his thesis that the British government became a "fiscal-military state, complete with large armies and navies, industrious administrators, high taxes and huge debts."[82] Nevertheless, a person interested in the development of a rational-legal society is most attracted to his seldom-cited concluding chapter titled "The Politics of Information: Public Knowledge and Private Interest" in *The Sinews of Power: War, Money, and the English State, 1688–1783.*

During the Restoration, the political system did not have the institutional base needed for a regularized policy process. Disclosing the contents of parliamentary debates was a treasonable offense, and this restricted the amount of public participation in debate on the issues. Interest groups had to function through personalized access to the court.

All of this changed in the early 1700s. A parliament that met annually and had to pass all laws or taxes might or might not have great influence on the content of these decisions. At a minimum, however, Parliament had to have detailed debates and specialized deputies who knew the details of

[81] Sheila Lambert, *Bills and Acts: Legislative Procedure in Eighteenth-Century England* (Cambridge: Cambridge University Press, 1971). For the evolution, see Lucy Sutherland, "The Merchant Law of England," in Lucy Sutherland, *Politics and Finances in the Eighteenth Century* (London: Hambledon Press, 1984), 9–36.

[82] Brewer, *The Sinews of Power*, p. 250.

different policy areas. More important, lawmakers needed precise information that could stand challenges from all sides.

The bureaucracy was particularly important in producing increasingly specialized documents for the legislative and, therefore, the policy process. In an e-mail written three decades after publication of his book, Brewer recalled his own experience in the archives: "Anyone who has read the T1 class of documents, which is basically the chronologically configured inbox of the Treasury will be astonished at the volume and sophistication of the materials produced by other government departments and by interested actors in civil society." In *Sinews of Power*, Brewer simply alluded to the volume of detailed information in this file as he listed other agencies with similar files: the customs commissioners, the Excise, the Navy Board, and the Board of Trade.[83]

Brewer also emphasizes the changes that occurred in the interest group system during the evolution of the executive and Parliament in the 1700s. In a day of monopoly guilds and palace politics, the interest groups were seeking – and obtaining – access to the king and court, and this access tended to be personalistic. Edward III might assemble merchants to obtain information about the detailed implications of tariff changes, but the interest groups were basically engaged in what we now call "rent-seeking."[84]

Interest groups obviously continued rent-seeking in the 1700s – and today. Yet, as Brewer notes, many specialized interest groups, including economic ones, formed to gain access to the political process in a way that was impossible in a day of court politics. Each group came to include persons and sub-groups whose own interests were varied, and the interest group leaders had to negotiate among their members.

Each interest group pushed for more information from government, and each examined every bill to discover the implications for its members. In the process, the interest groups played an informational role for government as well as for themselves and the public. As Michael Kammen and Alison Olson emphasize, the colonists were a major player in this activity in the 1700s.[85]

[83] John Brewer e-mail to Jerry Hough, February 14, 2014; Brewer, *The Sinews of Power*, p. 221.

[84] Robert Ekelund Jr. and Robert Tollison, *Politicized Economies: Monarchy, Monopoly, and Mercantilism* (College Station: Texas A & M University Press, 1997).

[85] Brewer, *The Sinews of Power*, pp. 231–49; Michael Kammen, *Empire and Interest: The American Colonies and the Politics of Mercantilism* (Philadelphia: Lippincott, 1970); Alison G. Olson, *Making the Empire Work: London and American Interest Groups, 1690–1790* (Cambridge, MA: Harvard University Press, 1992).

We do not have the space to analyze this process as a whole, but we will concentrate briefly on one factor that economists usually neglect but that Max Weber emphasized: the increasing importance of the bureaucracy. Its size rose sharply after the Glorious Revolution of 1688. The number of full-time fiscal employees alone went from 2,524 in 1690 to 4,780 in 1708, 6,497 in 1726, and 7,525 in 1770.[86]

The bureaucrats were not undifferentiated agents of the ruler, but they began to specialize on different problems and acquire different types of knowledge. They had to be organized into specialized bureaus. Brewer rightly emphasized that long careers and internal promotion within a bureaucratic unit produced specialized knowledge and identification with that unit.[87]

Yet such bureaucratic specialization of knowledge requires officials, coordinating bodies, and commissions that can bring this information together in the policy process. Coordinating bodies must be created, and ministries become more complex entities. The British system of government, unlike the American, developed a real cabinet and came to need a prime minister.

This evolution took an enormous length of time. As we saw in Chapter 4, Geoffrey Elton argued that Henry VIII's chief minister in the 1530s, Thomas Cromwell, regularized the ministerial system, but more recently, historians argue that Cromwell was only a part of a long and gradual process.[88] They have tended to say that Elton minimizes the length of time needed for such a bureaucratic system to develop.

The Treasury began effective supervision of other ministries only in the 1670s and 1680s, and this process took decades to evolve. This key ministry remained subordinated only to the king after 1688, not Parliament. The great political figure of the period from 1721 to 1742, Robert Walpole, is considered the first de facto prime minister, but no such post existed at the time.

It is important to take great care when we use formal models to discuss phenomena such as the king's and Parliament's oversight of ministries in the 1690s. In the 1690s, even the Treasury did not have actual oversight

86 Brewer, *The Sinews of Power*, p. 66.

87 Ibid., pp. 79–85.

88 Geoffrey Elton, *The Tudor Revolution in Government Administration: Changes in the Reign of Henry VIII* (Cambridge: Cambridge University Press, 1953); Christopher Coleman and David Starkey, eds., *Revolution Reassessed: Revisions in the History of Tudor Government and Administration* (Oxford: Clarendon Press, 1986), especially Coleman's introduction and conclusion on pp. 1–12 and 199–208.

over the ministries, and neither Parliament nor the ministries really were institutionalized bodies. Overly precise and abstract formal models often totally obscure the importance of time and the ambiguities in relations and assumptions about government structure as they evolve over decades and centuries. They fail to illuminate why the gradual change takes immense periods of time.[89]

We have already noted Stephen Baxter's argument that after the Restoration, the Treasury Department slowly began to exercise the powers it already had. But as Baxter noted, the process was circular: "If these powers were to be in constant use, a natural consequence would be the development of a professional staff at the executive level."[90] By "professional," Baxter meant officials with specialized knowledge and a sense of professionalism.

Again, we should not exaggerate. A great deal of pursuit of private interests and outright veniality continued to exist. Brewer documents much of it himself. The literature on the colonies describes it in detail. When Stanley Katz asked rhetorically why the first four governors of the colony of New York under the Hanover dynasty sought these posts, he responded that "the answer is simple: they hoped to improve their fortunes in America."

Katz emphasized a number of sources of income for colonial governors: fees for land grants, other fees, "gifts" and "gratuities" in exchange for "his favor," retention of the money allocated for salaries and clothing for soldiers not hired in peacetime, profits on supply contracts, and profits on land speculation. Surely the English bureaucracy was not that different, but it and the colonial administration were still not the worse in Europe.

Both *The Sinews of Power* and *Violence and Social Orders* document the progress that the navy made in becoming a much more effective fighting force in the mid-1700s.[91] Indeed, that was part of the process by which the navy left broader politics and became a purely professional organization. By the 1770s, Brewer says, the navy had no role in politics at all.[92]

The rise of a professional bureaucratic system is also, we argue, a crucial element in developing constraints in the policy process. In the 20th-century USSR, Stalin's behavior clearly showed that a professional bureaucracy does

[89] See Gary Cox, "War, Moral Hazard, and Ministerial Responsibility; England after the Glorious Revolution," *Journal of Economic History* 71(2011), 133–61.

[90] Baxter, *The Development of the British Treasury*, p. 176.

[91] North et al., *Violence and Social Orders*.

[92] Brewer, *The Sinews of Power*, pp. 70–79; Stanley Katz, *Newcastle's New York: Anglo-American Politics, 1732–1753* (Cambridge, MA: Harvard University Press, 1968), p. 28. General information is summarized on pp. 28–31, and especially in footnote 24 on pp. 29–30. John Brewer e-mail to Jerry Hough, February 14, 2014.

not guarantee limitations on the arbitrary power of rulers. Yet we agree with Weber that such a bureaucracy is a pre-condition for the development of rational-legal constraints on governmental and military officials.

Indeed, there is a political logic to the link between greater bureaucratic specialization of labor and the development of restraints on the ruler. A small-scale warlord in the countryside can plausibly think he knows as much about every policy question as any of his lieutenants or subjects. Modern rulers, by contrast, realize that specialized officials inside and outside government know more than they do about multiple issues. Baxter notes that this was true of English monarchs after 1660: "the business of Treasury [gradually] became too complicated for the sovereign to grasp or control and the office assumed a measure of independence."[93]

In conclusion, we would reemphasize that this book does not deal with the modern Western countries, but development economists must never mistake the ideal world of their models even for the reality of the modern West. The British administrative system, both at home and the colonies, was far from Weber's ideal-type.

Development economists should not forget, however, that such behavior was not incompatible with the Industrial Revolution. Indeed, America in the 19th century also featured a great deal of corruption that did not prevent a century of growth. Rather, development economists should look at the real experience of Britain of the 1700s and the United States of the 1800s and strive to help the developing countries achieve that kind of success.

That involved making the executive more efficient, improving the sophistication of the policy processes, developing the financial system and the protection of property rights that North and Weingast emphasized in "Constitutions and Commitment," and moving toward the pluralist dominant coalition of public and private elites. Indeed, dominant coalitions do not disappear in modern societies. They simply become, it is to be hoped, more pluralist and open and more subject to majority wishes expressed in democratic elections. Many countries assumed to be democratic do not, alas, justify this hope.

[93] Baxter, *The Development of the Treasury*, p. 4.

7

The English Colonies

It is difficult for modern Americans to develop a complex understanding of the English colonies. The first problem is generic to the history of all former colonies: historians naturally want to study the colonial antecedents of the independent country as it emerged from the empire. Yet the British did not even speak of the American colonies collectively until the 1730s, and then they had in mind all of their American colonies, not just those that became the United States.

Indeed, in the 1600s the Caribbean colonies were economically and strategically far more valuable to England than the mainland colonies. Moreover, the Caribbean colonies were actually more integrated with the mainland colonies than the mainland colonies (or at least regions) were with each other. A free-market trade economy was created in New England and then in New York and Pennsylvania in order to supply food and materials to the slaves of Barbados and Jamaica.

A second problem in understanding the colonies is that the elite of a post-independence country is naturally more interested in legitimating the new country than in exploring embarrassing aspects of the colonial past. Jamestown was the first permanent English settlement in the New World, 13 years before Plymouth, and it was vastly more important to London than Plymouth. Yet the Thanksgiving holiday focused on Plymouth because acknowledging, let alone celebrating, the real reason for colonization – the introduction of slave-produced tobacco –would have been awkward.

Other distortions in colonial history were introduced for more specific political reasons. During the first half of the 20th century, the European Americans called themselves "races," and they could feel as strongly about American policy toward their homelands as modern Cuban Americans feel about policy toward Cuba. This had a disastrous impact on American foreign policy and domestic politics in World War I, the interwar period, and then in the period of the post–World War II settlement in Europe. McCarthyism was basically an attack of the German Americans and Irish Americans on the British Americans and Jewish Americans that resulted from this conflict.[1]

As a result, the American elite emerged from World War II determined to end the conflict between Britain and Germany in order to prevent the reemergence of the ethnic conflict in America. A number of steps were taken, both consciously and unconsciously, to end the central identification of European Americans with individual "races" and to replace it with a common consciousness of being "white."[2]

One technique used to achieve the goal of a common "racial" identification among European Americans was to make the discussion of the historical differences among the white "races" virtually taboo. The image of the colonists as people with a common set of values was created as a golden past to which America should return. The origins of the colonies in the English Civil War of the 1640s and the resulting deep religious conflict in the colonial period are facts to be avoided.

The policy of ending the conflict in Europe and ending the conflict among European Americans was successful. Even the memory that race in the North was once defined by cultural differences rather than color of skin has disappeared. Other results, however, have been more negative. The American experience with handling religious conflict in the Constitutional Convention and afterward that is highly relevant for the advice to be given developing countries has rarely been learned by Americans working in the development process, even though it is highly relevant.

The intellectual climate of the postwar period naturally led economists to assume that common values were part of the colonial legacy that was important in American economic growth. In actuality, the rapid transition in the 1750s from isolated city-state colonies based on mutually hostile religions created enormous problems of governance in the new United States that had to integrate them into a single country.

In 1787, the Founding Fathers tried to solve this problem by creating a confederate government in the domestic sphere (but not foreign policy). This government had a number of features almost never recognized by

[1] See Jerry F. Hough, *Changing Party Coalitions: The Strange Red State-Blue State Alignment* (New York: Algora Press, 2006), chaps. 4 and 5, and Jerry F. Hough, *American Domestic Politics and the Cold War: Ending the Civil War in Europe, 1930–1960* (unpublished book manuscript).

[2] See Matthew Jacobson, *Whiteness of a Different Color: European Immigrants and the Alchemy of Race* (Cambridge, MA: Harvard University Press, 1998), pp. 1, 4, 9, and 247.

educated Americans: (1) the denial to the central government of a role in economic policy other than the tariff, (2) decentralization of military and taxing power to the state level, and (3) a veto for the slave states built into the Constitution. Even then the Constitutional Convention that produced this result required a "velvet" military coup by George Washington, an obvious fact completely absent from the literature. We discuss this in Chapter 9.

The acceptance of the myths that Americans originally had common origins and that they formed a federal government has two serious consequences for readers of this book. First, Americans seem to have little awareness of the extremely slow pace of the creation of an effective government in their own country. The essence of the Constitution was to guarantee the South the right to treat its slaves as it wanted. Until Franklin Roosevelt forced an informal change in the Constitution in 1937 – 150 years after the Constitutional Convention – it was even unconstitutional for the United States Congress to pass the Social Security law. It still required another quarter of a century to end the right of the South to treat its former slaves as it wanted. Only in 1964 was segregation outlawed and only in 1965 was a law passed that fully enforced the Fifteenth Amendment that supposedly guaranteed blacks the right to vote. That is nearly 200 years after 1776. The United States has little reason to complain about the slow pace of change in modern developing countries.

Second, the myths about the colonial and revolutionary period heritage have greatly complicated the understanding of the reasons for American economic and political success. Those Mexicans who were politically relevant in 1821 were much more united in their values than the Americans of that time. Mexico also had a political system with power decentralized to the city-state level. They too had great difficulty in developing a central government that controlled the regions. Why then did the federalism of Mexico prove to be far more ineffective than that in the United States? Why did Mexico become virtually anarchic for much of the 60-year period after the Hidalgo rebellion of 1810? That is the subject of this chapter and the next three.

The Deliberately Disunited English Colonies

The first fact to assimilate about the English colonial system in the Atlantic is that there never were 13 colonies. The varying number of English colonies in modern Canada (usually one or two) and the six Caribbean island colonies with governors were as much "American colonies" as those on the mainland.

The second fact is that London deliberately created colonies in a way that made the development of a sense of community among the colonists quite difficult. Each of the colonies was based on a different religion from the English religious wars of the 1500s and 1600s. New England was given to the Puritans, Pennsylvania to the Quakers, and Maryland to the Catholics. Virginia, the Caribbean colonies, and the Carolinas were Anglican. New York was a Dutch colony with Dutch religions, and it remained so after it was conquered by England in 1664.

London always wanted to keep these diverse colonies separated from each other. The Puritans who founded Plymouth were forbidden to settle closer than 200 miles from the Anglican colony of Jamestown. As the empire increased in size, this general policy was continued, and the chief colonial officer from 1720 to 1760, the Duke of Newcastle, supported it as a conscious policy. By this time, many proposed the appointment of a supergovernor to coordinate the activities of an empire approaching a population of two million. Newcastle explicitly rejected the suggestion on the grounds that this might bring the colonies together and facilitate joint action against Britain.

Newcastle spoke explicitly of "the ill Consequences to be apprehended from uniting too closely the [mainland] Colonies with each other; an independency upon the Country being to be apprehended from Such an Union."[3] He wanted to strengthen the hub-like relationships of the individual colonies with London and prevent the development of horizontal relationships among them. He may well have been articulating a policy that existed throughout the 1600s.

Charles I began colonization by giving Barbados, Maryland, Massachusetts, and Virginia to proprietors of different religions. The New England colonies that broke away from Massachusetts remained Puritan or offshoots from Puritanism. The Puritan regime added no colonies except Jamaica in the Caribbean in 1655. Charles II followed the pattern of his father. He concentrated on creating mainland colonies that would fill in all of the coastal territory from New Hampshire to the Savannah River.[4] He formed Carolina (modern South Carolina and North Carolina together) in 1663, New York and New Jersey in 1664, and Pennsylvania in 1681. In 1679, Charles II resolved a simmering dispute between settlers in New Hampshire and Boston by breaking New Hampshire off Massachusetts as a separate colony.

3 Quoted in James Henretta, *"Salutary Neglect:" Colonial Administration under the Duke of Newcastle* (Princeton, NJ: Princeton University Press, 1972), pp. 341 and 337.

4 The Savannah River is on the border between modern South Carolina and Georgia.

Charles II, like his father, had mixed motives in creating these colonies. The territory of Carolina was huge, but the colony really was limited to Charleston (then Charles Town) and the surrounding territory in what is now coastal South Carolina. The founders of Carolina came from Barbados, and the purpose of the colony was to supplement New England in supplying food and other necessities for the rapidly growing number of slaves in the Caribbean, especially because of the acquisition of Jamaica in 1655.[5] Carolina, like Jamaica and other Caribbean Islands, was Anglican.

Charles II's goal in establishing New York was to capture the Dutch New Netherlands and close the main Dutch base for smuggling. He fully achieved this goal, but New York was given no important economic role until after 1688. In practice, it remained a Dutch colony whose inhabitants overwhelmingly spoke Dutch and who still used the Dutch legal code. Only the new English king in 1688, the Dutch William of Orange, made it a priority to integrate New York with the other colonies and develop it economically.

New Jersey had been part of New Netherlands but was ethnically and religiously diverse. Charles detached it from New York in 1664 and, indeed, divided it into East Jersey and West Jersey from 1674 to 1702.[6] Historians generally say that this action was motivated by a desire to make a gift to two political supporters, but Charles also probably wanted to discourage the Dutch from migrating south. New Jersey never became important. Its capital, Newark, was at the mouth of the Hudson and too close to New York City to be a significant independent port.

The last major colony formed by Charles II was Pennsylvania in 1681, 17 years after New Jersey. It was a natural and even inevitable colony for economic reasons, but, like Massachusetts, its character was determined by political considerations. The most important dissident religious group during the reign of Charles II was the Quakers. They even refused to bow to the monarch or to pay the tithe to support the Anglican Church.

An important Quaker leader was William Penn, the son of an admiral of the same name who had conquered Jamaica and then played an important role in restoring Charles to the throne. At least partly out of gratitude to Penn's father but also to have a debt to him canceled, Charles did not repress his son, but gave him a colony to which he could remove many of the troublesome Quakers from England. The colony was named for

[5] Leila Sellers, *Charleston Business on the Eve of the American Revolution* (Chapel Hill: University of North Carolina Press, 1934), pp. 49–51.

[6] The history of the division of New Jersey and then its reunification is complicated and is not germane for our purposes.

Admiral Penn.[7] Charles was perhaps thinking of Pennsylvania and New York as his father had thought of Massachusetts – a place of exile. Like New York, Pennsylvania was economically unimportant until the second decade of the 1700s.

Despite the diversity of the mainland colonies, however, they had certain features in common. Each was centered on a coastal port or on a large river not far from the coast. The east coast of North America contained a substantial number of rivers that emptied into the Atlantic, and their lower valleys contained the best land in the area. Proprietors naturally wanted their colony to be centered along such a river.

The proprietors put their capitals near the mouths of these rivers so that they would be in a position to control trade between their colony and the rest of the empire. London also placed a governor in each of those ports. As the colonists expanded and moved inland, they naturally sought out the good land along the river. This facilitated the flow of crops to the market.

Most of the colonial capitals were located directly on the coast at the point where a major river reached the sea: from north to south, New Hampshire (Portsmouth), Massachusetts (Boston), Rhode Island (Newport), New York (New York City), New Jersey (Newark), South Carolina (Charles Town), and Georgia (Savannah). After 1701, the coastal New Haven was co-capital of Connecticut.

In the other cases, the capital was on a river or bay that provided nearby and direct access to the sea: Connecticut (Hartford), Delaware (Wilmington), Pennsylvania (Philadelphia), North Carolina (New Bern), and Maryland (Baltimore). In the case of Virginia, the great port of Norfolk on the Atlantic was considered too vulnerable to Spanish attack. The capital stayed in Jamestown, 50 miles up the river, for most of the 1600s until it was moved to the very small town of Williamsburg a few miles downstream.

Since the colonists usually migrated inland up a river or its feeder rivers rather than along the coast, the colonies tended to remain quite separate from each other and also insular in their religious and cultural views. The religious differences remained paramount not only because of the intensity of the emotions of the religious wars of the 1600s, but also because the different religions were largely based in different regions in England that had varying cultural backgrounds before the Reformation.[8]

7 Lucie Street, *An Uncommon Sailor: A Portrait of Admiral Sir William Penn: English Naval Supremacy* (New York: St. Martin's Press, 1988).

8 The result was expressed in the subtitle of one of the great books on American history: David Hackett Fischer, *Albion's Seed: Four British Folkways in America* (New York: Oxford University Press, 1989).

The result was what Newcastle wanted. Charles Andrews, one of the best colonial historians of the past, argued that the colonies, or at least the regions, remained "far apart [both] geographically and mentally" from each other in 1750. They had little contact by land and also little by sea except for merchants. Colonists talked about going "abroad" when they visited another colony. Andrews concluded that "few barriers had been removed" by the time of the American Revolution.[9]

This separateness was expressed in the absence of an "American" self-identification. The "national identity" of the educated population was based on their particular colony, while less-educated people identified either with the colony, a territorial sub-unit within it, or their religion. George Washington called Virginia his "country" until just before the Revolution, and Thomas Jefferson late in his life said that he still thought of himself as a Virginian, not an American. The misnamed Civil War really was, as southern historians long claimed, the War Between the States, with nearly half the states rejecting American identity.

Richard Merritt did a content analysis of the colonial press prior to the Revolution to see how reporters casually referred to the colonies as a whole in their articles. The colonists, it turned out, were very slow in thinking of themselves as Americans. Merritt found that prior to 1763, local writers in the colonial press almost always used terms such as "colonies," "His Majesty's subjects," and "His Majesty's colonists" to describe the inhabitants of the thirteen colonies.

Paradoxically, the English first felt the need to refer to the American colonies as a collective unit. By 1740, writers of articles in the colonial press with British datelines referred to the land as "America" more often than with phrases such as "the colonies," and by 1768 they used "Americans" to refer to the people more often than "colonists" or "his Majesty's subjects." In articles with datelines in the colonies, references to "America" as a place overtook other references only in 1763 and references to "Americans" predominated only in 1773.

Nevertheless, Andrews was right in mentioning 1750 when he spoke of the separateness of the colonies. Changes had been occurring in the first part of the century that meant the end of the old colonial system. One was a growth in population that resulted in migration westward and the destruction of the old city-state as a political unit. The total population of the United States had risen from 250,000 in 1700 to 1,170,000 in 1750 and

[9] Charles Andrews, *The Colonial Period of American History*, Vol. 4 (New York: Yale University Press, 1938), pp. 413–4.

Table 7.1 *Population of the British colonies in 1710, by regions*

	White	Black	Total
New England	112,509	2,585	115,094
Mid-Atlantic	63,314	6,218	69,532
Chesapeake	89,959	31,063	121,022
Lower South	21,003	5,000	26,003
Caribbean	27,461	133,800	161,261
Total	314,246	178,666	492,912

Source: Susan Carter, Scott Sigmund Gartner, Michael Haines, and Alan Olmstead, eds., *Historical Statistics of the United States; Earliest Times to the Present*, Millennial Edition, (New York: Cambridge University Press, 2006), Vol. 5, p. 78.

2,500,000 in 1750. As the population grew, the land along the coast was increasingly settled, and a network of roads was created.

At first, the number of colonists remained small and the colonial economies quite simple. When the first wave of colonization ended around 1650, the English mainland colonies contained 40,000 whites, 25,000 in New England alone.[10] In 1700, the total white population was 223,000, 91,000 of them in New England. The white population of New York, Pennsylvania, and New Jersey totaled only 47,000, and one-third of them were Dutch-speaking farmers living on the Hudson River and not really part of the empire. (See Table 7.1 for the population of the British colonies in 1710, by regions.)

Another crucial change in the middle 1700s was in the character of immigration. For all their mutual religious hostility, the immigrants of the 1600s were overwhelmingly ethnic English. After Scotland was annexed in 1707 and a rebellion resulted, George I allowed (or encouraged) a large number of Protestant Scots from Scotland and Northern Ireland to go to the colonies. The coastal land was now basically occupied, and the new immigrants were almost all sent to Philadelphia. They moved to the interior of Pennsylvania. Their children and new immigrants moved to eastern Maryland, then Virginia, and finally the Carolinas. Just before the Revolution, they were beginning to move to what is now Kentucky and Tennessee.

10 Bernard Bailyn, *The New England Merchants in the Seventeenth Century* (Cambridge, MA: Harvard University Press, 1953), pp. 16 and 23. On the drying up of immigration, see Winthrop, *Journals*, Vol. 2, p. 31; Alison Games, *Migration and the Origins of the English Atlantic World* (Cambridge, MA: Harvard University Press, 1999); Charles McLean Andrews, *Colonial Self-Government, 1652–1689* (New York: Harper, 1904), p. 7.

A new Scottish colony in the interior would not, however, have a port on the Atlantic and would have been difficult to control. It eventually would have looked toward the Mississippi River and the port of New Orleans, then under the control of Spain. Hence, George I had the land they settled remain part of an existing colony.

In addition, the new migration ensured that the interior – and, therefore, the colony – would become ethnically and religiously mixed. George I was a German king, and he encouraged a large number of German immigrants to come to the colonies and intermix with the Scots and Protestant Irish in the West. Presumably he thought they would be loyal to a German-speaking king. In addition, the children of the coastal ethnic English who sought cheap land naturally also migrated west. The ancestors of Abraham Lincoln were among them.

As a result, the percentage of the population with non-English roots became quite high in a number of colonies. An official study in the late 1920s estimated that 65% of Pennsylvanians in 1790 were non-English, and a later recalculation put the figure at 80%. The figures are between 30% and 65% in the southern states, and much higher in the interior.[11]

In 1774, John Adams testified to the result of this policy in terms that supported Andrews's conclusion. When he passed through New York on his way to the first Continental Colony in Philadelphia, Adams wrote in his diary of a blunt warning by Philip Livingston of the powerful Livingston family and a brother-in-law of John Jay. "[Livingston] says if England should turn us adrift we should instantly go to civil Wars among ourselves to determine which Colony should govern all the rest. Seems to dread New England.... Hints were thrown out ... of the Goths and Vandalls."[12]

When Adams reached the First Continental Congress in 1774, he wrote to his wife that the delegates were "fifty Gentlemen meeting together, all Strangers, [who] are not acquainted with Each others Language, Ideas,

[11] The estimates refer to 1790 because the names of all those counted in the first U.S. census of that year have been used in very sophisticated ways to try to estimate ethnic backgrounds. The original effort was needed to calculate the ethnic quotas for the 1924 immigration law, and any bias was in the direction of increasing the percentage of the number of English. For the revision, see Forrest McDonald and Ellen Shapiro McDonald, "The Ethnic Origins of the American People, 1790," *William and Mary Quarterly*, 2 (1980), pp. 180 and 198. For the calculation of the national origins quotas, see Margo J. Anderson, *The American Census: A Social History* (New Haven, CT: Yale University Press, 1988), pp. 144–9.

[12] Diary entry of August 22, 1774. L.N. Butterfield, ed., *Diary and Autobiography of John Adams* (Cambridge, MA: Harvard University Press, 1962), Vol. 2, p. 107.

Views, Designs. They are therefore jealous of each other – fearfull, timid, skittish."[13]

Later in life, Adams looked back at the Revolution and pointed to an English desire to create an Anglican bishopric as a major cause. In Adams's words, "the apprehension of Episcopacy contributed … as much as any other cause, to arouse the attention not only of the inquiring mind, but of the common people, and urge them to close thinking on the constitutional authority of parliament over the colonies."[14]

As discussed in Chapter 9, an explosive factor was the increasing conversion of the merchants and other elite of Boston to the Church of England. The status of the Puritan (Congregational) ministers declined in the city but remained strong in the small towns. The historian Carl Bridenbaugh reported that the Congregational ministers preached incessantly against "the terrible threat of episcopacy. They had made the word *bishop* stand for everything hateful in the Yankee past."[15]

This raises a series of questions to which we will return later. How did such diverse people unite in a revolution? How did states based on colonies with no experience with colonial governance create a country that remained stable for 75 years and returned quickly to stable growth after a terrible Civil War?

The Governance of the Colonial City-States Prior to 1750

By 1740 the structure of the mainland colonies was very similar to that of the Articles of Confederation prior to 1787, at least if Canadian colonies are excluded. Indeed, a map of 1740 would be familiar to a modern American except in one key respect: boundaries often extended to the west, sometimes to the Mississippi River, in an ill-defined and often overlapping manner. They could include land beyond the Appalachian Mountains claimed by France and land in the south claimed by Spain. For this reason, the boundaries of 1740 contained the seeds of war not only with France and Spain, but also between the colonies when they became independent.

13 John Adams to Abigail Adams, September 25, 1774, in Paul Smith, ed., *Letters of Delegates to Congress, 1774–1789*, Vol. 1 (Washington, DC: Library of Congress, 1976), p. 99.

14 This, according to Adams, was "a fact as certain as any in the history of North America." Quoted in Carl Bridenbaugh, *Mitre and Spectre* (New York: Oxford University Press, 1962), pp. 55–6, 233.

15 Bridenbaugh, *Mitre and Spectre*, p. 190. This point had been emphasized much earlier by Alice Baldwin, *The New England Clergy and the American Revolution* (Durham, NC: Duke University Press, 1928), pp. xi–xiii, 3–12, 90–92, and Alice Baldwin, "Sowers of Sedition: The Political Theories of Some of the New Left Presbyterian Clergy of Virginia and North Carolina," *William and Mary Quarterly* 5 (1948), 52–76.

Yet, despite the impression created by the map of the English mainland colonies in 1740 of a huge British empire in North America, the real empire was actually tiny as late as 1740. Since settlers had not moved more than 100 to 200 miles from the coast, the map of the settled mainland British empire south of Nova Scotia looked like Chile, but with only one-half of its north-south length.

Until 1750, the main political unit both in the English and Spanish colonies was the city-state, but they were quite different in the two empires. Until the late 1700s, the Spanish viceroy did not even send a representative with any overall authority into the city-states or even larger regions. The city-state in Mexico had little formal political structure until the very end of the colonial period, and the heads of the leading families ruled them through informal negotiation. The city-states did not have a formal governmental structure, a formal system of laws, or any significant military force with which to exercise their will.

Each English colony, by contrast, had an English governor stationed within it and a formal government structure and legal code. It had an assembly whose members were elected by the population – or, rather, by the propertied white males. The assembly initiated all legislation. Scholars have traditionally emphasized the importance of the elected assembly, but a scholar comparing the Spanish and English colonies is also struck by the presence of a governor in the English colonies.

The English colony also had a Governor's Council that had similarities with the House of Lords or the Mexican *audiencia*. Its members were officials who either held their position ex officio or through appointment by the governor. The Council served as a continuous advisory body for the governor and also as a Supreme Court. It could veto the laws of the Assembly. The courts decided cases on the basis of English common law.

There were differences in detail in governing structure from colony to colony and from time to time, but those interested in these details need to examine the work of an older generation.[16] Until 1750, however, the assemblies were usually dominated by a few families. In the words of John Shy,[17]

> A small minority of families [controlled the assembly] in every colony, from New England to Georgia, often descended from the first settlers of the colony,

[16] The details of colonial politics differed. See, for example, the 15 volumes of Lawrence H. Gipson, *The British Empire before the American Revolution* (Caldwell, IN: Caxton Printers, 1936 1970). See also Andrews, *The Colonial Period*.

[17] John Shy, "The American Colonies in War and Revolution," in P. J. Marshall, ed., *The Oxford History of the British Empire*, Vol. 2: *The Eighteenth Century* (Oxford: Oxford University Press, 1998), 300–24, p. 309.

more affluent, better educated, well known, experienced in governing, and intermarried. This colonial elite had managed their numerous, mobile, fecund, contentious, and increasingly diverse and dispersed constituents not by means of armed force, of which there was virtually none, but by consent and accommodation.

The colonial assemblies did not have much military force except on the frontiers, but they had little other need for it. Everyone knew that if something extraordinary occurred, London could (and often did) intervene militarily – as they were forced to do in the French and Indian War. Memories of this war remained an important symbol a decade later. In 1775, George Washington was making a powerful statement when he wore his uniform as head of the Virginia militia in the French and Indian War to the Second Continental Congress in Philadelphia in 1775.

The relationship between the assembly and the governor could become quite acrimonious in some colonies, and in some the formal powers of the governor were restricted. Newcastle once described his colonial policy as one of "benign neglect" and some scholars have taken him at his word. They have called his policy ineffective and saw the colonies as being largely autonomous and the governors powerless.

The policy actually was quite different. Newcastle acted as if he were deliberately creating a system of checks and balances between the governor and assembly in each colony. In the words of Alison Olson,[18]

> American loyalty [cannot] be explained away as purely ceremonial by arguing that the colonists enjoyed de facto autonomy within the empire and paid little attention to British authority. Quite to the contrary, Americans sent provincial laws to England for review, accepted governors and councilors appointed in England, paid customs duties, generally obeyed the Navigation Acts, and contributed men and money to imperial conflicts. By eighteenth-century standards theirs was not a bad record of compliance.

In understanding London's control over the colonies, we must remember the fundamental change that was taking place in the British political system of this time. The system of governance was becoming less personalistic and more regularized. It relied less on commands and individual decision making and more on the devolution of authority to a network

[18] Alison Olson, *Making the Empire Work: London and American Interest Groups, 1690–1790* (Cambridge, MA: Harvard University Press, 1992), p. 1. For more on the legal powers, see Bernard Bailyn, *The Origins of American Politics* (New York: Knopf, 1968), pp. 66–70.

of more specialized officials in the executive, legislature, and interest groups. That should have affected the way the colonies were controlled, and it did.

If the neoclassical model is examined with perspective as a coordinating mechanism, it is based on the assumption that societal control of economic decisions and the protection of property rights are best exercised not through issuing direct commands, but through establishing rules and incentives that guide the pursuit of self-interest in desired directions.

The same is true in the political sphere. Sometimes commands are necessary, but wise rulers – even "absolute" dictators – rule through incentives as much as possible. They defer to those with more specialized knowledge than themselves in the belief that this will produce more sophisticated policy and more economic growth.

What this means, however, is that the system of control becomes more complex and differentiated. This was reflected in colonial administration as well as governance at home. The colonial economy rested on trade, and an increasing number of middle-level officials in London were involved in the regulation of colonial trade. Since each colony focused on the production of goods that were exported either to Great Britain or the Caribbean, the colonial elite wanted the assistance of the departments and officials in London who could facilitate this trade. The governors were in a position to intervene to support either specific commercial projects or laws wanted by the colonial elite as a whole.

This created a set of incentives for the local elite to act in a manner to court the governor and London. That is one reason that merchants and those surrounding them were converting to the Church of England in the non-Anglican colonies. This reflected self-interest more than theology. But the process showed that the governor and his leading lieutenants were becoming an inherent part of the colonial elite who were all located in the same small town as the governor.

The assemblies were elected by property holders in a colony that was 95% rural. As elections in the northern colonies became more democratic, the representatives had to take populist positions to appeal to the farmers who owned property. The division between the "governor's party" and the rural-based assemblies became increasingly intense. In a famous line, Carl Becker wrote a century ago of the struggle for home rule being a struggle for who would rule at home. Marc Egnal found a division within the cities between members of the elite who had interest in the interior and those who did not.[19] Bernard Bailyn, the top colonial historian of his generation, summarized the resulting situation well:

> Politics in America was therefore profoundly different from politics in England in that it operated at two levels, the level of the provincial governments and the level of the central government at "home"; and it was the latter – more distant, less palpable, and less predictable – that was the more important.... By the mid-eighteenth century a stable pattern of informal communications had emerged, linking political forces in England capable of overturning decisions taken in the colonies by the resident executive.

Alison Olson explored in detail how the colonial interest groups became integrated with their London counterparts.[20] London wanted to increase revenue from tobacco and sugar and hoped to achieve it through a stable and productive environment. The integration of the British governor with the colonial economic elite also had the advantage of giving the governor the incentive to develop commerce. The governor, if appointed from Britain, usually returned home enriched after his tour of duty, but lower officials and governors who lived in the colonies before their appointment normally became integrated into the colonial elite and shared a long-term interest in colonial prosperity.[21]

The Economic Integration of the Mainland Colonies

The great paradox of the English colonies was that they were kept separate from each other politically and religiously, but their economies became intimately connected after the 1650s. Except for colonial historians, and often not even them, Americans focus on the thirteen colonies as they came to exist in the mid-1750s. They also differentiate sharply between the economies of the North and South. These assumptions within the educated elite have affected the thinking of comparative economists about the development of the market in the United States in unfortunate directions.

The entire economy of the North, the South, and the Caribbean in the second half of the 1600s was tightly integrated to promote the

[19] Carl Becker, *The History of Political Parties in the Province of New York, 1760–1776* (Madison: University of Wisconsin, 1909), p. 20; Marc Egnal, *A Mighty Empire: The Origins of the American Revolution* (Ithaca, NY: Cornell University Press, 1988).

[20] Bailyn, *The Origins of American Politics*, p. 92; Olson, *Making the Empire Work.*

[21] Stanley Katz, *Newcastle's New York: Anglo-American Politics, 1732–1753* (Cambridge, MA: Harvard University Press, 1968), p. 159.

production of tobacco and particularly sugar. The production of both grew rapidly from 1650 to the American Revolution. Virginia and Maryland naturally continued to concentrate on tobacco production. Tobacco exports grew from 249,000 pounds per year in the period 1699–1791 to 560,000 pounds per year in 1752–1754. Eighty-five percent was re-exported by Britain to Europe by the time of the Revolution. Yet tobacco, unlike sugarcane, can be profitably grown on small fields owned by a single farmer, and much tobacco was grown without the use of slaves.[22]

Legally, colonial ships could carry the tobacco to London, but Norfolk and Baltimore never developed a shipping fleet or even a foreign merchant community. One frequent explanation is that the merchants there lacked the closer ties with the financial community in London that provided the needed credit for developing such a fleet. Even more important may have been the practice of re-exporting virtually all tobacco to Europe and relying on continent-produced consumer goods to supply the colonies. This three-way trade had complexities that English merchants were better able to handle.

Because of the failure of a merchant class to develop, tobacco production had far less impact on the development of the American economy and market in the 1800s than might have been expected. The slave economy in the Caribbean was far more important. From the 1640s until the 1710s, the developing economy of the North was centered on two tiny islands in the Caribbean to an extent that is hard to imagine today. The most important components were Barbados, which was only one-seventh the size of Rhode Island, and Jamaica, which was three-quarters of the size of Connecticut.

In 1710, the English Caribbean colonies as a whole contained only 27,000 whites, while the mainland colonies collectively had 287,000. Yet, as we have seen, the Caribbean islands in 1700 provided 9% of the total value of imports to Britain, and the mainland colonies provided 8%.[23] Sugar production in the English Caribbean increased from 8,176 tons in 1663 to

[22] For a discussion of tobacco production in the Cuban context, see M. Moreno Fraginals, *The Sugarmill: The Socioeconomic Complex of Sugar in Cuba, 1760–1860* (New York: Monthly Review, 1976), 20–5.

[23] J.H. Parry, *The Age of Reconnaissance: Discovery, Exploration, and Settlement, 1450–1650* (London: Littlehampton Book Services, 1963), p. 223; J.H. Parry, *Trade and Dominion: The European Overseas Empires in the Eighteenth Century* (London: Weidenfeld and Nicolson, 1971), p. 48.

97,000 tons in 1775, and the number of Caribbean slaves rose from 134,000 in 1710 to 313,000 in 1760.[24]

In the second half of the 1600s, the economy of New England increasingly focused on supplying food and necessary items for the Caribbean slaves. As late as 1710, the population of all the Mid-Atlantic colonies was only half that of New England, and, except for trade with Montreal and the Iroquois along the Hudson River, the colonists in the mid-Atlantic areas were farmers producing for themselves.

Then, as the number of slaves in the Caribbean increased, the North had to be developed to provide for them. In 1663, Charles II had given a group of Barbados planters a charter to found the colony of Carolina – really South Carolina centered on Charles Town (Charleston). It supplemented New England in supplying the Caribbean islands at a time when the newly acquired Jamaica had to be developed.

As a result, the core of northern commerce continued to be directed toward the Caribbean. A major reason for the development of the ports of New York City and Philadelphia was the need to expand shipments to the Caribbean to bring food and other supplies to the large and growing population of slaves there.[25]

Despite having only 10% of the whites of the mainland colonies, the Caribbean Islands had about 134,000 slaves compared with 31,000 in the Chesapeake colonies, 9,000 in the North and mid-Atlantic, and 5,000 in the lower South (Carolina). The Caribbean slaves had to be provided for; however, the islands had too little land to divert the acreage that would be needed for agriculture away from the more profitable sugarcane production, and they lacked the inexpensive work force necessary to grow food crops.

Several developments of fundamental importance occurred in the colonies between 1700 and 1776. First, of course, England – Great Britain after 1707 – changed from a country with continual conflict and three regime changes in the 1600s into a country with a truly effective government and market, as well as an increasingly rational-legal set of values and habits.

[24] Jacob Price, "The Imperial Economy, 1700–1776," in P. J. Marshall, ed., *The Oxford History of the British Empire*, Vol. 2: *The Eighteenth Century* (Oxford: Oxford University Press, 1998), pp. 81, 85, and 100. An excellent detailed discussion of the changes in enumerated crops of the 1700s is found in Adam Smith, *The Wealth of Nations* (New York: Bantam Dell, 2003), pp. 731–6.

[25] Jack Greene, *Pursuits of Happiness: The Social Development of Early Modern British Colonies and the Formation of American Culture* (Chapel Hill: University of North Carolina Press, 1988), pp. 178–9.

Table 7.2. *The white population of the colonies, 1650–1770*

Colony	1650	1680	1700
Massachusetts	13,800	39,600	55,100
Other New England States	5,700	28,400	36,000
New York	3,600	8,600	16,900
New Jersey	–	3,200	13,200
Pennsylvania	–	700	17,500
Delaware	200	1,000	2,300
Virginia	18,300	40,600	42,200
Maryland	4,200	16,300	26,400
N. Carolina	–	5,200	10,300
S. Carolina	–	1,000	3,300

Source: Susan Carter et al., *Historical Statistics of the United States,* p. 652.

Indeed, the experience of operating a growing colonial system with a rapidly expanding free market trade was a valuable part of the learning process.

Second, the population of the mainland colonies grew rapidly in size. The most important source of the increase was high natural growth because of the percentage of infants who survived into adulthood. In addition, some 300,000 immigrants came to the English colonies in the 1700s – over 100,000 more people than the total white population in 1690. Table 7.2 illustrates what was happening on a state-by-state basis.

The great majority of immigrants were non-English: perhaps 150,000 Scots and Protestant Irish, 85,000 Germans, 20,000 Welsh, and 10,000 French.[26] A substantial percentage of the ethnic English were exiled convicts. The coastal areas and the lower river valleys were becoming well populated, and hence most of the immigrants and children of those living on the coast went inland to seek cheaper land.

They moved gradually from the interior to the center of Pennsylvania and then into western Maryland, Virginia, and the Carolinas. They reached Virginia in the 1740s, and the first job of George Washington was to survey land for the non-English immigrants as they began arriving. At that time he described them as "a Parcel of Barbarian's and an Uncooth Set of People."[27]

26 Aaron Fogleman, "Immigration, German Immigration, and 18th-Century America," in Eberhard Reichmann, LaVern Rippley, and Jorg Nagler, eds., *Emigration and Settlement Patterns of German Communities in North America* (Indianapolis, IN: Max Kade German-American Center, 1995), pp. 4–5.

27 Warren Hofstra, "'A Parcel of Barbarian's and an Uncooth Set of People': Settlers and Settlements of the Shenandoah Valley," in Warren Hofstra, *George Washington and the Virginia Backcountry* (Madison, WI: Madison House, 1998), pp. 87–114.

As the population of the colonies increased and expanded geographically, the economies of the mainland colonies became more complex. Trade among the main colonies, except that involved in the triangular trade with the Caribbean, was relatively unimportant when the colonists were few in number and lived far apart in small city-states. The expanding mainland population inevitably produced a sharp increase in the amount of trade among the mainland colonies. This at least meant a decline in the relative importance of the trade to the Caribbean. Additionally, the direct trade of colonial shippers with the European continent increased by mid-century. Demand for grain in Europe began to outstrip local supply, and as the price of grain rose, the mainland colonies began to produce it for export, including to Europe.

The growing amount of trade among the mainland colonies had a series of consequences. Most of the trade was conducted by oceangoing ships rather than by land, and this created powerful incentives for the merchants of the different colonies to integrate with each other. They began promoting intermarriage among their children in order to develop the trust that would make multilateral trade easier to conduct. This too was a factor in the increasing conversion to the Church of England among merchants in the non-Anglican colonies of New England, New York, and Pennsylvania.

Also, the expansion of the population and internal trade produced an increasing amount of specialization of the economy. Even in the 1600s, this specialization had begun to occur in the small cities of New England. Molasses was imported primarily into Boston and Newport, and rum was produced in those areas. Salem was the fishing and fish-curing center of New England, and fish-curing required salt. So Salem began to ship timber to salt-producing islands such as the British Barbados and the Dutch Bonaire, returning with cargoes of salt.[28] In the 1760s, the whaling industry began to grow rapidly, and New Bedford specialized in the production of whaling oil. Rhode Island also took part in that activity.

Of course, New England and coastal Virginia were always climatically different and their economies would have been different under any system. Then the addition of the more tropical South Carolina added to the diversity.

[28] Richard Pares, *Yankees and Creoles: The Trade between North America and the West Indies before the American Revolution* (Cambridge, MA: Harvard University Press, 1956), p. 104.

The transportation system was also growing as the population increased. The roads between Norfolk, Baltimore, Philadelphia, New York City, and Boston were continually being improved, and this reduced the time required for coaches to travel between these cities. Better roads contributed further to the economic integration of North and South.

All the colonies from the North to the South were affected by the increase in population. New England received few immigrants in the 1700s other than some quietly from Quebec, but natural growth increased its population from 91,000 in 1700 to 525,000 in 1770.

Although migration to the west relieved the pressure on coastal land to the south of New York, as we will see in Chapter 9, the British forbade migration from overcrowded New England into central New York. Moreover, the Dutch along the Hudson River were extremely hostile toward New Englanders who wanted to move into the Hudson Valley.[29]

The inability of New Englanders to migrate westward increased the incentive for them to move into the cities. By 1770, New England had ten cities with more than 4,000 people, all located on the sea or on a river a short distance from the sea. In 1770, these ports contained 65,000 people, nearly 12% of the total population of New England compared with less than 5% urban population in the other colonies.

New York remained little more than a Dutch-speaking agricultural community in the 1600s. As mentioned earlier, the Dutch legal code was left in place, and Dutch merchants continued to speak Dutch. All this made New York City a good "neutral" intermediary trading point between the English-speaking colonies to the South, the French in Montreal, and the Iroquois Indians, but it made the city very alien to London investors and led them to ignore it.

The Dutch merchants in New York City, although not the other Dutch settlements, had long felt a need to assimilate to the English culture in order to trade effectively in the other colonies, including in the Caribbean, but real change occurred only when the Dutch William of Orange came to power in England in 1689; he wanted New York to become a normal member of the colonial system. He encouraged English investment in New York and pressured authorities in New York to integrate the colony into the English colonial system.

An early key step was the replacement of the Dutch legal code with the English common law. The desire to ensure that lawyers were familiar with

[29] Washington Irving's story of Ichabod Crane and the headless horseman, "The Legend of Sleepy Hollow," dealt with this resistance against a Puritan schoolteacher who dared to court Dutch women.

the English legal codes led New York to become the first state in which lawyers formed a bar association. The need to change from a Dutch legal system to the English law as a sign of loyalty seemed to ingrain the legal system more deeply there than elsewhere in the colonies.[30]

As the internal New York population and grain production increased, New York City grew to a population of 25,000 in 1775, compared with 16,000 in Boston. Nevertheless, the city did not become the great port of the future until Americans moved to the Midwest and the Erie Canal was opened in 1825.

In the 1700s, Philadelphia became America's largest and most important city, growing to 35,000 people in 1775. The great turning point in Pennsylvania's history occurred when London decided to make Philadelphia the entry point for nearly all of the 300,000 immigrants coming to America. Twenty-five percent of Philadelphia's population was involved in work connected with the port, and some immigrants stayed to do the unskilled labor required in it.

Most immigrants moved inland first to the Lancaster area of Pennsylvania and then to the Susquehanna River. The current Amish community is a remnant of one of the early German settlements in that area. Pennsylvania was the best colony for producing grain, and the increasing settlement of the interior contributed to a rapid increase in the amount of grain produced.

Since grain remained a non-enumerated crop, Philadelphia merchants could ship it legally to any locale in the world, including non-English ports in Europe. The literature on Spanish America repeatedly mentions ships from Philadelphia that violated Spanish law to smuggle grain to colonies such as Venezuela, Chile, and even the Pampas of the future Argentina. After mid-century, Philadelphia merchants began to use their own ships to transport their grain across the Atlantic.

Toward the end of the colonial period, tobacco was beginning to leach the minerals from the soil, leaving the land too impoverished to continue to grow it, and large-scale production of cotton would not be possible until Eli Whitney invented the cotton gin in 1793. Hence, the rise in grain prices led an increasing number of larger planters and small farmers alike to replace tobacco with grain production. They included both George Washington and Thomas Jefferson. Virginia and Maryland came to export from two

[30] Michael Kammen, *Colonial New York: A History* (New York, Scribner's, 1975), pp. 128–9; Cathy Matson, *Merchants and Empire: Trading in Colonial New York* (Baltimore, MD: Johns Hopkins University Press, 1997).

to three million bushels of grain or grain equivalent a year, enough to feed 390,000 people by European standards.[31]

Carolina was another colony that underwent major changes in the 1700s. Until George I became king in 1714, Carolina was little more than the area around Charles Town that produced basic items for Barbados and Jamaica. George I turned it into a commodity producer and exporter as well. This began with the production of rice. Rice production in South Carolina and Georgia rose from 5.8 million pounds per year in the 1715–1724 period to 72 million pounds in 1765–1774.

In 1748, George II offered South Carolina six pence a pound bounty to produce indigo. As we will see, Britain had been relying on smuggled indigo from Central America, but as the Bourbons consolidated their power, they largely ended this British smuggling. London had to obtain its indigo legally.[32]

Rice and indigo were designated as enumerated crops. Even though South Carolina had a merchant community and fleet already engaged in free trade with the Caribbean, the colonial shippers did not take rice and indigo to England. As with Chesapeake tobacco and Caribbean sugar, British ships took the rice and indigo to Britain on ships based in Britain.

As Charles Town became a commodity exporter, Carolina was divided in 1729, and the new North Carolina began to produce tar, pitch, and wood from pine trees to ship to the Caribbean from the port of New Bern. Economies also developed in the interior from Maryland to South Carolina. They began as subsistence farming, but as they developed, direct connection between the Appalachians and the southern colonial capitals of Charles Town, New Bern, and Norfolk proved physically quite difficult. As a result, a network of north-south roads was built in the interior that allowed much inland trade flow from the western Carolinas to the Potomac River in Virginia.

[31] Carville Earle, *Geographical Inquiry and American Historical Problems* (Stanford, CA: Stanford University Press, 1992), pp. 109–10; David Klingaman, "The Significance of Grain in the Development of the Tobacco Colonies," *Journal of Economic History* 29 (1969), 268–78.

[32] David Duncan Wallace, *The Life of Henry Laurens: With a Sketch of the Life of Lieutenant-Colonel John Laurens* (New York: G. P. Putnam's, 1915), pp. 22–4; Walter Fraser, *Charleston! Charleston! The History of a Southern City* (Columbia: University of South Carolina Press, 1989); A. Roger Ekirch, *"Poor Carolina": Politics and Society in Colonial North Carolina, 1729–1776* (Chapel Hill: University of North Carolina Press, 1981); Richard Waterhouse, *A New World Gentry: The Making of a Merchant and Planter Class in South Carolina, 1670–1770* (New York: Garland Press, 1989).

The migration beyond the mountains toward the fertile land of the Midwest was just beginning. It was a key step leading to the Revolution because The Royal Proclamation of 1763 that prohibited immigration beyond the Allegheny Mountains. This was especially explosive in New England, where land was scarce. The rapidly expanding number of young people wanted to be able to migrate into central New York. But British troops in Montreal allied with the Iroquois to prevent this migration. The Proclamation was also explosive in the South, but for a different reason. The migrants who wanted to go into modern Kentucky and Tennessee were able to so because of the absence of British troops. Yet they occupied territory owned by eastern landowners and destroyed their property rights. Those affected included George Washington, the largest landowner in the West.[33]

The Development of a Capitalist Culture in the Colonies

A book that covers 1,000 years and four countries has costs as well as benefits. One of the costs is that we do not have the time or space to explore such a subtle and hard-to-document phenomenon as the evolution of a country toward a more rational-legal capitalist culture.

The development of a merchant class and culture is especially important. An earlier generation of historians was interested in the major merchant families who were an important factor in colonial politics as revolutionaries or counter-revolutionaries. The revolutionary period, however, was 125 years after the first development of trade in New England and occurred at a time when the leading merchants were moving into the Anglican Church and developing close ties with England.[34]

The merchants in the 1600s were very different from those of the mid-1700s. When they began trading with the Caribbean islands nearly a half-century before the Glorious Revolution of 1688, they had to develop extremely entrepreneurial skills. Since little money was available in the colonies, the trade with the Caribbean at first was literally "trade" – barter exchange. So long as the goods in the trade were in the non-enumerated category (and even sugar and molasses was considered non-enumerated), the trade was conducted on a purely free market basis and prices were determined by market forces.

[33] Marc Egnal, "The Economic Development of the Thirteen Continental Colonies, 1720 to 1775," *William and Mary Quarterly: A Magazine of Early American History* (1975): 192–222, p. 205.

[34] The classic study is Arthur Schlesinger Sr., *The Colonial Merchants and the American Revolution* (New York: Columbia University Press, 1918).

If the mainland shippers wanted to trade with the Caribbean colonies, they often had to play the role of creditor for the goods they sold. They might take contracts for molasses not yet produced – indeed, not always simply the next crop, but at times the crop after. Yet the New England shippers did not want to return home with empty holds. They took payment in whatever they could obtain, even if the goods were of doubtful value. Many of them were partial shipments.

New England merchants then had to become involved in retail trade at home to dispose of their "payments." They found land one of the only stable forms of investment, and this led them into vertical integration. They bought timberland and sawmills; they raised horses and cattle. As a result, they developed a flexibility and set of abilities that were to be invaluable.[35]

New England also moved into large-scale shipbuilding. After the English Civil War began, New Englanders were forced to build their own ships if they were to fish off Newfoundland and trade with the Caribbean. After the Restoration, Charles II even subsidized New England shipbuilding. By 1674, two-thirds of the oceangoing ships built in Massachusetts of 100 tons or more were subsidized. In 1730, one-sixth of the entire English merchant fleet had been built in Massachusetts, and this proportion rose to at least one-third of the British fleet in 1775. Ship captains carrying goods to the Caribbean or England often were told to sell the ship itself if they received an attractive offer.[36]

London's policy on shipbuilding was one more dramatic piece of evidence that the promotion of manufacturing was not the driving force of its colonial policy. The kings clearly were not simply – or mainly – focused on promoting manufacturing in England. Even the English shipbuilding industry was not protected from the more economical producers in the colonies. The kings were interested in high customs revenues. London wanted tobacco and sugar to be produced at the lowest cost so as to maximize their sale abroad and leave the largest possible margin between cost and market price – and thus allow the highest level of customs duties that could be imposed without reducing competitiveness.

Recently, historians have begun to look more closely at the entire merchant community, especially in the important ports of the 1700s, Philadelphia and New York. They have discovered merchants of a variety of

[35] Bailyn, *The New England Merchants*, pp. 98–104; Pares, *Yankees and Creoles*, pp. 73–8 and 92–138; Richard Johnson, *Adjustment to Empire, New England Colonies, 1675–1715* (New Brunswick, NJ: Rutgers University Press, 1981).

[36] Joseph Goldenberg, *Shipbuilding in Colonial America* (Charlottesville: University Press of Virginia, 1976), pp. 53 and 125.

types and degrees of importance. A young man in Philadelphia who had the necessary recommendations might receive goods from a British manufacturer on credit as a trial. An upwardly mobile retail merchant might enter export-import wholesale trade simply by buying his own ship and engaging in trade with the Caribbean himself.[37]

It is this broader merchant class that began to develop a commercial culture that permeated the major cities, that permitted the American colonies to retain a commercial culture even though many of the leading merchants either fled during the American Revolution or were driven out.

Virginia and Maryland played a very different role in international trade from that of New England, New York City, and Philadelphia. Ships came from England and usually London to pick up the tobacco that Virginia and Maryland produced, as trade with Great Britain was conducted almost exclusively in British ships. In New England, New York City, and Philadelphia, merchants and shippers normally operated with ships owned by the colonists.

Virginia's use of British ships was scarcely surprising at the beginning, since the planters had to rely on credit to get their indebted servants and basic products from England, and they had no money to acquire ships even if they so desired. More surprising, this pattern never changed. Even as the planters became affluent, neither they nor their children ever acquired ships. Hence they never were able to engage in trade with England, with the Caribbean, or even with other mainland colonies.

The destinations of British ships in 1769 showed the relationship of commodity trade and trade patterns. Of 672 ships sent from Britain to the New World, 330 went to Virginia and Maryland and 140 to South Carolina. The other colonies received far fewer: New England – 47; Pennsylvania – 35; North Carolina – 34; New York – 30; Georgia – 24, and Florida – 12.[38]

As a result, the Chesapeake never developed a foreign trade merchant class in the traditional sense of the term. Unlike medieval London, Norfolk did not even develop a merchant community dominated by foreign merchants – or in this case, merchants from England. It developed no merchant community at all. The ships came to Norfolk and Baltimore with consumer goods, unloaded them, picked up tobacco, and returned home.

The detailed histories of Virginia often mention "merchant-planters" and create the impression that the colony did, indeed, have a merchant class.

[37] Thomas Doerflinger, *A Vigorous Spirit of Enterprise: Merchants and Economic Development in Revolutionary Philadelphia* (Chapel Hill: University of North Carolina Press, 1986).

[38] Sellers, *Charleston Business*, p. 9.

In one sense this was true, but the term "merchant-planter" was used for a real reason. The merchants were planters, not real foreign trade merchants dealing with foreign merchants. They were middlemen between the English merchants and the smaller farmers who grew tobacco.

England, let alone the colonies, did not have an institutionalized private banking system in the 1700s. A financial system, like a state, must evolve very slowly from a personalized, private system into a bureaucratized one. Just as the state had to develop through the creation of informal and imperfect mechanisms (for example, private collection of taxes and private merchant naval fleets), banks and the trust on which they rested also had to emerge in a more informal manner.

A crucial fact about tobacco production and sales was that the planter and private farmer alike were not paid for their tobacco until it was sold in Europe. Since 85% of the tobacco was re-exported to Europe and sold there, it could take a year before the money (or bill of sale) reached the grower. Few had the resources to go through an entire growing season before they received payment for the previous year's crop. Credit became a key part of the production process.

The major planters received credit from the London merchant. This is a major explanation that historians give for the failure of colonists to participate in the transportation of commodities to Britain, whether these were Virginia tobacco or South Carolina indigo and rice. The London merchants, it is said, had access to credit in London, but the colonists did not.

Of course, this fails to explain why Philadelphia shippers found it possible to engage in long-distance trade in grain. Perhaps the financial system in the North was better developed, especially by the mid-1750s. Perhaps the re-exporting of tobacco virtually required English merchants to handle it. Perhaps the economic imperatives of feeding slaves made quick payment more important in the South. And perhaps the British government installed political barriers to colonial involvement in the shipment of commodities because of a fear that colonial shippers could more easily evade taxes.

The explanation is not important. In fact, the planters did want credit, and the English merchants did provide it. Since the owners of small farms were, of course, much closer to the subsistence line, they needed credit too. The English merchants did not want to deal with small lots of tobacco or small loans to cover the payments. They delegated both tasks to the planters. George Washington made much of his income at Mount Vernon not from the crops he sold, but from the interest he received as a lender.

While the South did not develop a merchant class dealing with Europe, the lower South did have one that dealt with the Caribbean. The pattern was repeated with the export of rice and indigo from South Carolina, even though the colony continued to use their own ships in dealing with the Caribbean.

Nevertheless, even the southern merchant-planters were developing business skills and habits. They dealt with the commission representatives of the British merchants, who usually were called "factors." The following succinct description of the work of the factors in South Carolina applies to Virginia as well:[39]

> The Charleston factor was not only a merchant but a banker and broker as well. In his character as merchant, he sold merchandise sent out to him by the British firms and bought rice, indigo, deerskins, naval stores, and other produce for his British correspondents; in his character as financier, he managed the fiscal system and controlled the financial life of the [rural areas]. The Charleston factor derived his importance from his connection with the British merchants, who gave him a year's credit for merchandise, paid him a commission (usually five percent) for selling merchandise and buying rice and indigo, and furnished him in the bill of exchange a medium by which he could purchase cargoes in any part of the world with which he was allowed to trade.

Planters often persuaded the London merchants to allow their sons to serve as their factors as a kind of apprenticeship. Indeed, the sons sometimes even served in London for a year or two as part of the experience.

The Expansion to the West and the Transformation of the Colonial Political System

While the map of the English mainland colonies in 1740 creates the impression of a huge British empire in North America, this totally distorts the reality of the time. Settlers had not moved more than 100 to 200 miles from the coast, and they were divided into small city-states with their own British governor and an elite-dominated assembly. This city-state system of the first century of the English empire was, however, doomed by the rapid increase in population and territory in the mid-1700s. The colonies, like London in the 1300s and 1400s, had been effectively governed city-states that were culturally and religiously homogenous. The movement to the West changed that, even in a small state such as Massachusetts.

[39] Sellers, *Charleston Business*, p. 49. The discussion of the Charleston factor in this book extends over two chapters and is extremely detailed and sophisticated.

North Carolina in its modern boundaries is 8% larger in area than England and 7% smaller than England and Wales together. In the colonial period, Virginia contained Kentucky and West Virginia, and the three together were twice the size of England. North Carolina contained modern Tennessee. Kentucky and Tennessee extended to the Mississippi River. The river was 900 miles west of Norfolk, Virginia, more than twice the distance between London and Edinburgh.

Even if the colonists ended their migration at the Mississippi River, they would inhabit an area larger than Western Europe excluding Scandinavia.[40] In 1821, the year of Mexican independence, Missouri was admitted to the Union, the first state west of the Mississippi. That made the United States roughly the same size as modern Mexico. At a minimum, this expansion would require a major change in the administrative system. The old coastal colonies surely would have to be divided, and the creation of a colony-wide governor and assembly was inevitable.

The real structure of political power in the colonies would also have to change. As we have seen, the governors gained informal political influence because of their contact with elites whose interests centered on commerce. Indeed, the merchants of the North had converted to the same church as the governors. It was not a coincidence that in the first party system after 1787, the merchants of the North and the South were united in the same Federalist Party.

The colonial assemblies would also change. Those of the city-states had been controlled by the elite in and near the port-capital. Now with suffrage based on property, political power in a country that was 95% rural would have to shift to the interior. The old assemblies dominated by the elite in the coastal ports would have to give equitable representation to the interior and become much more democratic, or else they would risk the secession of the western part of the colonies.

Perhaps even more important, the colonists in the interior became increasingly different in character from those along the coast. The colonists of the 1600s were divided by intensely emotional differences of a religious character, but, excluding the Dutch population in New York, the great bulk of the colonists were ethnically English. The small groups and individuals who were not English or Dutch were so scattered that they assimilated quickly with the English in the area where they lived.[41]

[40] We are defining Western Europe to include the Benelux countries, Denmark, France, Germany, Great Britain, Ireland, Italy, Portugal, Spain, and Switzerland.

[41] Scholars who tried to determine the ethnicity of names in the 1790 census discovered that one-quarter of those in New England appeared by their nature to be English but

In the 1700s, however, those fleeing the overcrowded English countryside did not leave the country but found jobs in the rapidly growing city of London. For this reason, few ethnic English, other than exiled criminals, came to the colonies at this time. From 1700 to 1775, more than 80% of the 300,000 immigrants to the colonies – some 80,000 more than the total white population in the colonies in 1700 – were not ethnically English.

Even more important politically, a disproportionate number of the 18th-century immigrants came in the period just before the American Revolution. Bernard Bailyn puts the number of white immigrants between 1760 and the Revolution at around 140,000. Aaron Fogleman later estimated that only 125,000 whites arrived during these 15 years, but he thought that 71,000 white immigrants came in the 10 years prior to 1760. That is, Fogleman believed that the colonies received a total of 196,000 immigrants from 1750 to 1775.[42]

By either estimate, the number of immigrants in the 25 years before the Revolution was very large. Bailyn's 140,000 immigrants between 1760 and 1775 is 11% of the white population of 1760, and Fogleman's 196,000 from 1750 to 1775 is 21% of the white population of 1750. These figures do not include the children of recent immigrants who were born in the colonies and who were considered "foreign" by the coastal population. Almost all immigrants went south of New England, an area in which only 585,000 whites lived in 1750. Fogleman's figure of 196,000 is 34% of that number.

Unlike other groups from the English Civil War, the Scottish and Protestant Irish were not given their own colony, but moved instead into the inland areas of Quaker Pennsylvania and later into western Maryland, Virginia, North Carolina, and South Carolina, all of them dominated economically and politically by Anglicans on the coast.[43]

Perhaps because a German Hanover king ruled England, the Germans seemed not to have been anti-London. Nevertheless, they caused fears about the dominance of the English language. In 1753, even the urbane

were almost never found in England. They obviously included many assimilated Native Americans and French Canadians who changed their name and religion as they quietly moved south.

42 Fogleman, "Immigration, German Immigration, and 18th-Century America," pp. 4–5. Bernard Bailyn, *Voyagers to the West: A Passage in the Peopling of America on the Eve of the Revolution* (New York: Knopf, 1986).

43 For the culture of the Borderland English, Lowland Scots, and Protestant Irish and its roots in Britain – and the difference from the culture of the New England Puritans, Pennsylvania Quakers, and southern coastal Anglicans and their roots in England, see David Hackett Fischer, *Albion's Seed: Four British Folkways in America* (New York: Oxford University Press, 1989).

and sophisticated Benjamin Franklin wrote that "unless the stream of their importation could be turned to other colonies ... they will soon so outnumber us that all the advantages we have will not be able to preserve our language, and even our government will become precarious."[44]

The more numerous, and more dangerous, non-English immigrants were the Scots, the Protestant Irish from Ulster (people predominantly of lowland Scottish origin), and the Welsh. They comprised some 175,000 of the 300,000 immigrants to the United States from 1700 to 1775. All were deeply involved in the English Civil War, and all had intensely anti-London and anti-Anglican feelings. They were even more hostile to the Puritans because of the nature of the war that Oliver Cromwell conducted in Scotland and Ireland during the Civil War.

As a result, an East-West political and cultural bifurcation was developing in the 1760s along with an economic one. One group of modern historians has argued that the coastal elite was becoming increasingly a part of the English cultural world. They have talked about "the integrated nature of the early modern [English] Atlantic world" in cultural terms. In the words of David Hancock:[45]

> What fascinates one group of scholars are the connections agents forged in building the foundational information, distribution, and financial institutions.... What intrigues these scholars is the decentralized nature of the emerging Atlantic economies, and the coordination of agent-based, nonhierarchical production, distribution, and consumption activities.

This thesis would have been quite congenial to older generations of historians, but only in a quite literal sense of the word "Atlantic": the integration of the colonial elite on the Atlantic coast with London. But the older generation also insisted that this created a growing cultural and political division between the coastal elite and the interior.

While some modern American historians see a united British group at the time of the American Revolution, Robert Kelley's view is far more persuasive, in our opinion:[46]

> [The British peoples] had brought with them to the New World ancient ethnic identities that were almost tribal in nature. Each of the colonies' separate peoples had

44 "Letter to Peter Collinson" in H.W. Brands, *The First American: The Life and Times of Benjamin Franklin* (New York: Doubleday, 2000), p. 217.

45 David Hancock, "Rethinking the Economy of British America," in Cathy Matson, ed., *The Economy of Early America; Historical Perspectives and New Directions* (University Park: Pennsylvania State University Press, 2006), p. 87.

46 Robert Kelley, *The Cultural Pattern in American Politics: The First Century* (New York: Knopf, 1979), pp. 34–5.

a firm conviction, rooted in bloody ancestral memories, that certain other peoples were their folk enemies to be battled at every opportunity.

> Within the British Isles, the English, Scots, Irish, and Welsh had been at each other's throats, literally and figuratively.... The English millions regarded [the] much less numerous ethnic outgroups in Scotland, Wales, and Ireland as crude, hill country tribes – in one sense comic, in another contemptible. In their turn, the Scots, Welsh, and Irish thought the wealthy and self-important English arrogant and domineering.

Carl Becker argued that the non-English groups and Borderland English in the West saw the differences among themselves or among the colonies as less important than that in their own colony between themselves and those who lived to the east. They identified themselves as "Westerners":[47]

> To the Scotch-Irish or German dweller in the Shenandoah Valley, it mattered little whether he lived north or south of an imaginary or disputed [Mason-Dixon] line that divided Maryland from Pennsylvania.
>
> Before the Revolution opened, the western imagination had conjured up the specter of a corrupt and effete "East": land of money-changers and self-styled aristocrats and a pliant clergy, the haunt of lawyers and hanger-ons, proper dwelling place of "servants" and the beaten slave: a land of cities, scorning the provincial West and bent on exploiting its laborious and upright people. And who could doubt that men who bought their clothes in London would readily crook the knee to kings?

Not surprisingly, the non-English migrants with such views produced major anxiety among the coastal elite. George Washington was one of the members of the Virginia elite who knew the most about the West. Washington had a very low opinion of the Westerners in the 1750s, but in 1784 (only three years before the Constitutional Convention), he still referred to them as "foreign emigrants, who can have no particular predilection for us" and who might become "as unconnected with us, indeed more so, than we are with South America."[48] The anti-Anglican views in the West could cause severe conflicts in colonial legislatures such as Virginia whenever issues involving the established Anglican Church arose.[49]

The political impact of the conversion of the elite to the Anglican Church was particularly great in New England because of the Puritans' hostility toward the Anglican Church and the king in England. The growing

47 Carl Becker, *Beginnings of the American People* (Boston, MA: Houghton Mifflin., 1915), pp. 184 and 183.

48 "To Jacob Reed," November 3, 1784, in W.W. Abbot and Dorothy Twohig, *The Papers of George Washington, Confederation Series* (Charlottesville: University Press of Virginia, 1992), Vol. 2, p. 121.

49 Bernhard Knollenberg, *Origin of the American Revolution: 1759–1766*, rev. ed. (New York: Free Press, 1961), p. 49.

conversion of the elite lowered the status of the Congregational ministers, the longtime intellectual elite of the colonies, although they remained dominant in the interior. The result was the politicization discussed earlier of the issue of the appointment of an Anglican bishop in the colonies.

All of this posed a major problem for George III. The colonies had changed fundamentally since George II came to power in 1727. It is unclear how much the king understood about the colonies, and he may have attributed the problems to the defiant nature of the colonists rather than to a fundamental transformation in the basic economic, social, and political conditions. At a minimum, George III never seems to have thought through a coherent policy. That lack of policy – and its consequences – will be discussed in Chapter 9.

8

Colonial Mexico

American economists recently have shown little interest in early Spanish development. Spain is barely mentioned either in Daron Acemoglu and James Robinson's *Why Nations Fail,* or in the two books of Douglass North et al., but many comparative scholars have retained the old explanations for Mexico's slow economic progress. Acemoglu and Robinson are typical. Because of their lack of attention to Spain, perhaps they have not absorbed the new conventional wisdom of historians that Spain created their centralized (minimally effective) government much later than England.[1]

As we have documented in previous chapters, England had an effective state and a reasonably well-developed market economy by the mid-1700s, and mainland English colonies had much the same kind of state and market as in England in the 1600s and 1700s. Indeed, the colonial elite had learned how to operate within constitutional restraints. They not only had absorbed the values of the Glorious Revolution – indeed, the rather extreme version of them espoused by the opposition Whigs – but also had begun to operate a semi-democratic system within constraints imposed by London. Despite slavery, the colonies never had guilds and had more of a market economy than the homeland. Even the South had a market economy outside the labor sector of a small plantation system. The plantation owners themselves were almost always responding to market forces.

1 Daron Acemoglu and James Robinson, *Why Nations Fail: The Origins of Power, Prosperity, and Poverty* (New York: Crown Business, 2012); Douglass North, John Joseph Wallis, and Barry Weingast, *Violence and Social Orders: A Conceptual Framework for Interpreting Recorded History* (New York: Cambridge University Press, 2009); Douglass North, John Joseph Wallis, Steven Webb, and Barry Webb, eds., *In the Shadow of Violence: Politics, Economics, and the Problems of Development* (Cambridge: Cambridge University Press, 2013).

Mexico too reflected the slow development of Spain and Philip II's failed attempt to impose rigid controls on the city-states inside Spain. In the 1600s, the return to court politics in Spain had led to a collapse of control over the colonies, while the gradual strengthening of Bourbon authority in the homeland in the 1700s was accompanied by a similar development in the colonies. Latin American specialists often think Charles III was obsessed with repressing and exploiting the colonies, but, in fact, he was introducing the same reforms inside Spain itself.

There was, however, one major difference between Spain and its colonies. Until the Bourbon period, the Spanish city-states had their own military power, but the kings feared that the viceroys or Latin American city-states might use military force to declare independence and seize the silver mines. Hence the authorities in Mexico had little military force except on the far northern borders.

As time passed, Madrid's concern about military force might have faded somewhat. As American settlers moved westward and southward, their migration would likely have produced fear both in Madrid and Mexico City that would draw the two together. The Mexicans would not want independence without Spanish protection, and Spain would want to create a major defense force to deter the United States. It was Napoleon's unexpected overthrow of the Spanish government in 1808 that left the unarmed Mexican authorities entirely unequipped to handle the chaos produced by the Hidalgo rebellion of 1810 and the post-independence aftermath.

Nevertheless, as discussed in the next two chapters, there remains a major mystery about the different fates of the United States and Mexico in the first decades after independence. However weak the central Mexican government apparatus may have been in 1800, it certainly was stronger than the non-existent central government in the English colonies at the end of the colonial period.

Moreover, despite the weakness of the colonial administrative system in Mexico, all roads in the country literally led to Mexico City. It was taken for granted that the capital was the political, economic, and cultural center of the country. Despite all the chaos and even anarchy for 60 years after 1810, Mexico never had a meaningful separatist movement except in distant regions like the Yucatán and Texas. The United States had no center of any type, and the colonies were so divided that the capital had to be built on empty land halfway between the southernmost and northernmost state capitals.

Why then did the United States remain so stable during the War of Independence and for another three-quarters of a century? In the next chapter, we explain the stability in the United States by English colonial policy. Historians emphasize the importance of the semi-democratic assemblies, and they were, in fact, important in helping to bring the growing interior of each state into the political process. Yet it was even more important that the states had, in fact, been states in North's definition of the term when they were colonies. Within the framework of London's overall control, they had control of local taxation and military forces. They retained these military forces and powers of taxation after independence and even had to strengthen them during the period of the Articles of Confederation.

Recently, historians have concentrated on demonstrating that Spain did not have a centralized, bureaucratic system either at home or in its colonies. We agree, but we think it is necessary to go a step further. A key issue was not so much lack of a solid administrative structure under the viceroy, but the lack of any structure at all below him. Power was located in what we call city-states, but, in fact, these units did not have a state. They were ruled informally by families without significant military forces or a formal tax-collecting system. Charles III was wise to start building an administrative system with *intendants,* but the system was far from completed in 1808 and disintegrated during the War of Independence.

This chapter concentrates on two aspects of colonial Mexico. One is the colony's peculiar semi-market economy. The other is the informal kind of political system that existed. In the early 1700s Mexico remained roughly at the stage of economic and political development of England in the 1500s. Mexico had developed a market economy based on illegal smuggling, which should have produced a strong entrepreneurial spirit and a good understanding of market trade, at least inside the colony. A smuggling economy did not, however, have a growing system of laws, rules, and regulations that were enforced in the judicial system.

This illustrates a great paradox in the work of Douglass North and other New Institutionalists about Latin America. The Spanish colonial system actually presents real evidence that supports North's main scholarly contribution. As North said, it is important to have property rights that are internalized in people's consciousness and unconsciousness, embodied in multi-volume codes of laws and regulations, and enforced by impartial courts and professional bureaucracies. Mexico did not have such a structure because of its smugglers' economy. This is the point New Institutionalists should emphasize, not the old mistaken stereotypes about a centralized bureaucratic system and a conservative Spanish culture.

The Development of the Mining Industry and an Indigenous Labor Force

From the beginning, the Mexican colony faced two fundamentally different problems from the English colonies. First, Mexico had an export product that was very valuable, had a low volume-to-value ratio, and was easy to steal and smuggle. The administrative problem of maintaining law and order was, therefore, more challenging than in the English colonies.

Second, unlike the English colonies, Mexico had a huge indigenous population that could be used as a labor force. Spain had no reason to adopt the English policy of encouraging large numbers of white immigrants or slaves unless it wanted to develop the lower Mississippi River valley, the Gulf Coast of the future United States, the Caribbean islands, and/or areas including the Pampas in South America.

The size of the indigenous population in the future Mexico at the time of the Spanish conquest is a highly controversial subject, and most current estimates range from 10 million to 25 million. In 1976, a geographer, William Denevan, reflected the higher estimates of the University of California-Berkeley of the 1950s and put the number of Native Americans in Mexico at 21.4 million. A major modern historian of Mexico, Mark Burkholder, is closer to the estimates of his generation with a figure of 10 to 12 million.[2]

Estimates of the number of the Native Americans in Spanish America in 1500 are highly politicized, because the difference between that figure and the more reliable figures of later years represents the number of deaths that can be attributed to colonization. The higher the original estimates, the higher the number of deaths. Yet, precisely for this reason, the size of the original estimates of the indigenous population is not directly relevant for a student of the evolution of the Mexican economy.

The important fact for us is that scholars more or less agree on the number of Native Americans in Mexico once the economy began to develop in the second half of the 1500s. The typhoid epidemic of 1546–1548 was a crisis that served to reduce the indigenous population sharply and focus thinking on labor policy. Most scholars believe that only 2.5 to 3 million Native

2 William Denevan, ed., *The Native Population of the Americas in 1492* (Madison: University of Wisconsin Press, 1976), p. 291. Denevan also estimated an original 5.6 million Native Americans in Central America, 5.9 million in the Caribbean, and 20 million in Spanish South America. Mark Burkholder, "An Empire beyond Compare," in William Beezley and Michael Meyer, eds., *The Oxford History of Mexico* (Oxford: Oxford University Press, 2000), 111–42, p. 127.

Americans remained in 1568. That that number fell to 1.5 million to 2 million in 1697, and finally to a low of 300,000 to 400,000 in the mid-1600s.[3]

To be sure, these later numbers are also uncertain because of the difficulty of knowing how many Native Americans actually lived in the more remote regions. Moreover, the labeling of the children of mixed parents (*mestizo* children) is quite ambiguous. Those who lived with their mother in the villages were probably called indigenous, while those who lived with their father often – and perhaps usually – were called whites. The label of "white" became even more widespread with further intermarriage in the second and third generations. Especially in the later years, the number of Native Americans who "disappeared" because they were labeled *mestizo* or white – a benign outcome – may have been substantial, but it is unknown.

Nevertheless, without any question, the decline in the indigenous population even between 1560 and 1660 was so great that the Spanish in the colonies at this time began to worry about labor shortages in the growing urban sector. In the early *encomienda* system, the conquistadors procured vegetables, fruits, crafts, and other products from Native Americans living on their own land, but the opposition of the mining community led to replacement of this practice by a system of tribute called *repartimiento*.

The tribute was direct taxation on the village that took two forms – first, the delivery of concrete goods, and second, a quota of people who would work temporarily in the Spanish agricultural and mining sectors. Over time, the concrete goods were often replaced by cash earned in free market sales in peasant farmers' markets. A new governmental office, the *alcaldes mayores*, was established not only to collect the physical tribute, but also to assign labor quotas to the villages and to allocate the persons provided by the villages to different claimants, urban and rural.[4]

As silver mining in the north began to expand, however, the *repartimiento* recruitment of labor also proved unsatisfactory. The area around Mexico City and to the south had adequate rainfall and was heavily populated before the arrival of the Spanish. Hence *repartimiento* recruitment worked reasonably well in the areas around Mexico City and to the south.

The *repartimiento* worked far less well in the north where the major silver mines were located. Mexico was drier in the north and progressively

[3] Jonathan Israel, *Race, Class, and Politics in Colonial Mexico, 1610–1670* (New York: Oxford University Press, 1975), pp. 26–7. For the typhoid epidemic of 1546–1548, see Brian Owensby, *Empire of Law and Indian Justice in Colonial Mexico* (Stanford, CA: Stanford University Press, 2008), p. 15.

[4] J. H. Parry, *The Spanish Theory of Empire in the Sixteenth Century* (Cambridge: Cambridge University Press, 1940), pp. 8–9.

turned into real desert land. These areas were inhabited by a small number of nomadic Native Americans whom the Aztecs had not been able to conquer. Hence, new temporary workers would have to be brought to the mines from the south.

From one perspective, the importation of labor from the south was a plus. Those near Mexico City had had long contact with Spaniards, had learned some basic Spanish, and had probably developed more immunity to the new European and African diseases. Young *mestizos* were ideal. Yet the newcomers would have to learn mine-oriented skills, and employers did not want them replaced regularly by those without these skills.

All of these factors gave the Spanish a strong reason to create incentives that would attract and keep the most skilled indigenous workers. This meant a fairly rapid transition toward a wage economy and a relatively free labor market. Scholars have vigorously debated the extent to which this continued in the 1600s. This is a subject to which we turn in a later section.

The Illusion of a Centralized Bureaucratic System and the Central Role of the City-State

On paper at least, the Spanish colonial system seemed highly centralized, and the viceroys were supposedly the all-powerful representatives of the absolutist kings in the colonies. This is not how things worked on the ground. Philip II came to power shortly after the great silver discoveries at Potosí in Peru and Zacatecas in Mexico in 1545 and 1546, respectively, and he was the first king to start constructing a real administrative system. However, he really focused only on the delivery of silver to Spain, and his successors in the 1600s did not consolidate his system but instead, let it disintegrate.

The Council of the Indies in Madrid had the responsibility of drafting the laws and decrees for the colonies, but until the Bourbon period, the Council was composed of lawyers with no colonial experience. It issued a great multiplicity of laws, but many of them were largely ignored. The colonists from the beginning used the phrase "I obey, but do not comply" to "simultaneously demonstrate respect for the royal authority while asserting the inapplicability of royal orders in this instance."[5]

[5] John Elliott, *Empires of the Atlantic World: Britain and Spain in America 1492–1830* (New Haven, CT: Yale University Press, 2007), p. 132. Elliott goes on to explain that "Spanish theories of the state allowed for different levels of resistance … [and that] … the first and most fundamental was articulated first by the Basques and then embedded in medieval Castilian law; that of obeying but not complying."

London had a separate governor in each of its small city-state colonies, but Spain's entire empire in the Americas had only two viceroys until the early 1700s. The New Spain viceroyalty contained modern Mexico, much of North America, Venezuela, the Caribbean Islands, the Philippines, and all of Central America except modern Panama. Even in the 1600s it nominally included most of the future United States except the Atlantic coastline and the French areas north of the Ohio River. The Viceroyalty of Peru contained all the rest of Spanish South America plus modern Panama.

Centralized administration of a large territory requires ministries that can provide the leader with policy advice and administrative oversight of the provinces. Centralized control must rest on well-staffed bureaucratic lines of command that converge on a strong official at the top and that are integrated by a strong figure at key territorial levels. The Hapsburg colonial system had neither. The viceroy also had no significant military forces at his command, probably because Madrid feared loss of the silver mines.

The central economic regions of the viceroyalty also had no broad provincial officials until the gradual creation of the *intendant* system between 1762 until 1786. Even then, the kings wavered on whether to give the viceroy and/or the *intendants* full authority over the tax organs. The kings long had established governors in peripheral areas such as Chile, Guatemala (Central America), Florida, and the Philippines, but, while formally subordinated to the viceroy, they were largely autonomous and reported to Madrid.

The viceroys had little more than their personal staff as administrative staff. There really was no executive branch. The *Audiencia* was a Supreme Court that considered appeals from local courts and determined the constitutionality of the viceroy's actions. It also was supposed to supervise the *alcaldes mayores* in the provinces and to serve as the viceroy's cabinet in some ill-defined way. The justices of the *Audiencia* (the *oidores*) were given lifetime appointments so they could function independently.

The Hapsburg colonial system featured three major hierarchies. One consisted of the *alcaldes mayores* in some 150 to 200 mini-provinces of modern Mexico. The *alcalde mayor* had a strange combination of judicial and administrative functions. He served as the chief judicial officer in the district and also the tax collector in the Native American villages. In addition, he chaired the sessions of the city-state councils (the *cabildos*), but had no administrative authority within the city.

The second hierarchy was the state tax-collecting hierarchy (*Real Hacienda*) for the Spanish sector of the Mexican economy, but the exact nature of its role is unclear. Tax farmers collected much of the tax money, and some was little more than lump sums from the city-states – tribute in the sense we meant in our discussion of Spain. In a country without banks or checks, someone had to collect the tax money for the king and guard it. Perhaps they did little else.

The third hierarchy was the Catholic Church. The church collected taxes from the haciendas on wheat and maize through the tithe, and two-ninths of the proceeds went to the Crown. In addition, the church also financed and administered "governmental" institutions such as hospitals, schools, poorhouses, and insane asylums.[6] Haring called the Catholic Church "in a very real sense another branch of government."[7]

With the possible exception of the church, the administrative organs were grossly understaffed. David Brading notes that even in the late 1700s, "the Spanish Crown depended on a mere handful of officials to govern its American empire." He reports that "in New Spain the entire judicial bureaucracy, for example, the salaried members of the *Audiencia* of Mexico and Guadalajara, numbered about 30 persons." Besides the court of audit, the treasuries "did not employ more than 60 men above the level of mere clerks." The colonies had no real military forces besides "frontier patrols and the port guards."[8]

The hierarchies in the core regions were subordinated to the viceroy but also independent from him in many ways. The justices of the *Audiencia* were selected by the king and had lifetime tenure. The tax collectors were formally appointed by the king instead of the viceroy, but they became even more independent of the viceroy when they had to purchase their offices after 1633. The *alcaldes mayores* also had to buy their offices. The viceroy

6 D.A. Brading, *Church and State in Bourbon Mexico: The Diocese of Michoacan, 1749–1810* (Cambridge: Cambridge University Press, 1994), p. 181; J. Lloyd Mecham, *Church and State in Latin America: A History of Politico-Ecclesiastical Relations*, revised edition (Chapel Hill: University of North Carolina Press, 1966), pp. 9–11 and 12–28; Clarence Haring, *The Spanish Empire in America* (New York: Oxford University Press, 1947), pp. 178–82.

7 Haring, *The Spanish Empire*, p. 182. For a similar view, see Brian Hamnett, *The Mexican Bureaucracy before the Bourbon Reforms, 1700–1770: A Study in the Limitations of Absolutism* (Glasgow: University of Glasgow, 1979), p. 1.

8 D.A. Brading, "Government and Elite in Late Colonial Mexico," *Hispanic American Historical Review* 53 (1973), 389–414, pp. 399–400. For the tiny bureaucracy inside Guatemala (actually all of Central America), see Robert Patch, "Imperial Politics and Local Economy in Colonial Central America, 1670–1779," *Past and Present* 143 (1994), 77–107, p. 81. In the late 1600s, the entire area had 24 officials, a number that had only increased to 27 a century later.

had the authority to appoint middle-level church officials, but he deferred to the advice of the archbishop.[9]

For these reasons, Clarence Haring argued that the "Spanish imperial government was one of checks and balances" and that it was deliberately designed to limit the viceroy's power.[10] Charles Petrie, a biographer of Charles III agrees, stating that the king had established a "system of checks and balances calculated not so much to produce good government in the colonies as to prevent any tendency to break away from Spain."[11]

As in Spain, the real power in the regions was exercised by the elite in the city-states – formally at least through its council, the *cabildo*. The *cabildo* was a setting in which the leading families negotiated the political and financial decisions of the city-state.

Brian Loveman's description of the work of the city-state council in Santiago, Chile, applies to Mexico as well. In his words, "public policy in colonial Chile left no room for the free competitive marketplace":[12]

> The *cabildo* regulated the quality and price of all manufactured services, and commodities, including such items as bread, tools, clothing, and fish. As soon as brick-making took on a commercial character, the *cabildo* decreed official prices and established a fine of ten pesos in addition to forfeiture of goods sold in excess of these prices.... Adjustments took place as business interests or consumers pressured the municipal officers.

Spanish America, like Spain itself, still needed corporate institutions such as guilds that were slowly being phased out in England in the 1600s (and were never introduced in the English colonies created at that time). One reason that price controls on basic agricultural crops needed to be tighter in Mexico was that the unreliability of rain periodically produced sharp and politically dangerous price increases. John Fisher characterized the orga-

[9] Burkholder, "An Empire beyond Compare," pp. 121–3. For the details of the purchase of offices, see J. H. Parry, *The Sale of Public Offices in the Spanish Indies under the Hapsburgs* (Berkeley: University of California Press 1953). The best description of the collection houses (*cajas*) is John J. TePaske and Herbert Klein, "Introduction," *The Royal Treasuries of the Spanish Empire in America*, Vol. 1: *Peru* (Durham, NC: Duke University Press, 1982), pp. vii–xiii.

[10] Haring, *The Spanish Empire*, p. 122. For another scholar who strongly supports Haring, see John Leddy Phelan, "Authority and Flexibility in the Spanish Imperial Bureaucracy," in Mark Burkholder, ed., *Administrators of Empire* (Aldershot: Ashgate, 1998), 1–20, p. 17.

[11] Charles Petrie, *King Charles III of Spain: An Enlightened Despot* (London: Constable, 1971), p. 92.

[12] Brian Loveman, *Chile: The Legacy of Hispanic Capitalism*, 3rd ed. (New York: Oxford University Press, 2001), p. 78. For a similar description of the role of the Lima *cabildo*, see John Preston Moore, *The Cabildo in Peru under the Bourbons: A Study in the Decline and

nization of production as one that centered on "a guild structure which conformed to the medieval European tradition":[13]

> Within most cities in [Spanish] America the production of goods such as shoes, leatherware, candles, cheerots, alcoholic beverages, and similar products was carefully regulated by municipal ordinances which sought to establish a balance between supply and demand, and regulated both working pressures and progression within guilds.

The leading families of the *cabildo* certainly coordinated the activities of the local officials of the three major hierarchies of the colony, but the cabildo had no legal authority over them. At times the *cabildo* was the leading tax farmer of the sales tax in the region. In Mexico City, these taxes were farmed by the *consulado* in 82 of the 135 years that taxes were farmed, but at other times, they were farmed by the *cabildo* or sometimes collected by royal authorities.[14]

Since the viceroy lacked the military force to crush a rebellion, the kings also did not want significant military forces at the regional level that might be used to seize control of the mines. The *cabildos* had militias, but they never seemed to have much substance. A German mining engineer who went to the great South American silver city of Potosí in 1790 provided a dramatic example. Only a decade before, the nearby wealthy town of Oruro was sacked and most of the Spanish residents were killed in a massive Indian rebellion. The engineer wrote with disbelief about the "defense" militia that had been created in Potosí to deal with a second Indian uprising: "only five hundred men, of a most wretched appearance, without uniforms, and without cannon, and of whom one half parade with wooden muskets."[15]

Mexico was little different. The most astonishing fact about the 1810 Hidalgo uprising that sacked the great mining city of Guanajuato is that a

Resurgence of Local Government in the Audiencia of Lima (Durham, NC: Duke University Press, 1966), pp. 66–87.

[13] John Fisher, *The Economic Aspects of Spanish Imperialism in America, 1492–1810* (Liverpool: Liverpool Press, 1988), pp. 107–8.

[14] One suspects that the *cabildo* was the farmer in provincial cities on a more permanent basis, and in any case the *cabildos* provided "numerous loans and gifts to a chronically embarrassed exchequer." Nevertheless, the variation in tax collection even in Mexico City suggests the need for extreme caution in making broad generalizations. Robert Sidney Smith, "Sales Taxes in New Spain, 1575–1770," *Hispanic American Historical Review* 28 (1948), 2–37, pp. 6 and 13.

[15] Anthony Helms, *Travels from Buenos Ayres, by Potosí, to Lima*, 2nd ed. (London: Richard Phillips, 1807), p. 46.

relatively few thousand troops suppressed Hidalgo's forces several months later. Yet such troops were not available to defend Guanajuato at the beginning, even with two weeks' notice.

The lack of military force had an important consequence that often is overlooked in the discussion of the Spanish system as a repressive authoritarian system. The government officials had to exercise care in economic policy in order to keep the resentment of white colonists, *mestizos*, and Native Americans under control.

The Debate about Mexican Economic Development in the 1600s

The 1600s – which included the reigns of Philip III's successors, Philip IV and Charles II – were not a prosperous period in Spain, and it is absolutely clear that the country did not experience the type of economic development seen in England during that period. The question is the kind of impact that this had on Mexican economic development.

The debate about the Mexican economy in the 1600s has implicitly focused on the meaning of the decline in official trade between Spain and New Spain at that time. As we have seen, official trade between Spain and New Spain reached a peak in 1605 when exports and imports combined totaled 29,435 tons of trade. By 1650, this number had fallen to 9,080 tons, and it remained within a range of 3,000 to 7,500 tons a year until the end of the century.[16]

In the mid-20th century, scholars who characterized the Spanish economy in negative terms also had a negative view of Mexico in the 1600s. The title of Woodrow Borah's *New Spain's Century of Depression* typified this perspective. One of Borah's colleagues, Lesley Simpson, wrote of a "shrinking economy" in Mexico from about 1590 to 1700.[17]

Another famous scholar of mid-century, Francois Chevalier, contended that "in the early decades of the seventeenth century the silver boom collapsed, smothering in its passage the first stirrings of a barely nascent capitalism." With the mines "half-deserted" and trade having "come virtually to

[16] A. García-Baquero González, "Andalusia and the Crisis of the Indies Trade, 1610–1720," in I.A.A. Thompson and Bartolomé Yun Casalilla, eds., *The Castilian Crisis of the Seventeenth Century: New Perspectives on the Economic and Social History of Seventeenth-Century Spain* (Cambridge: Cambridge University Press, 1994), 115–35.

[17] Woodrow Wilson Borah, *New Spain's Century of Depression* (Berkeley: University of California Press, 1951); Lesley Simpson, "Foreword," in Francois Chevalier, *Land and Society in Colonial Mexico: The Great Hacienda* (Berkeley: University of California Press, 1963), pp. v, vii, and viii.

a halt," Chevalier thought that those who had accumulated wealth poured it into estates (haciendas) and made themselves self-sufficient.[18]

From 1969 onward, as scholars developed a more positive view of the Spanish economy in the 1600s, they also began to see Mexico differently. In 1969, John Lynch argued that the lessened trade with Spain meant that Mexico "appropriated more of their own production and employed their capital in their own administration, defense and investment." Richard Boyer agreed. He argued that the weakening of Madrid's control over its colonies and the replacement of most legal trade with Europe by smuggling gave New Spain an "increasing latitude to act for and by itself." He thought that Mexico City featured "vitality which reflected the economic transition of New Spain."[19]

Without any doubt, the massive decline in official trade was accompanied by a massive increase in the amount of smuggling. The combination effectively ended the rigid trade rules of Philip II that modern comparative scholars grossly over-emphasize when they attribute poor Latin American economic growth to colonial rules. These rules had increasingly been circumvented after the 1550s, but they collapsed over a century when the population and the need for crops meant a vast increase in violations of the rules.

The question, of course, is the impact of smuggling on the Mexican economy. Naturally, few statistics can be collected on the amount of goods being smuggled, and hence the archives contain fragmentary data at best. Since scholars prefer to work on the periods with archival data, the years from 1620 to 1700 became what Leslie Simpson in 1953 called "the forgotten century." Fifty years later, Murdo MacLeod reported that the gap between our knowledge about the 1600s and that about the late 1700s had widened.[20]

There is one item about the Mexican economy on which statistics are available – the amount of silver reported to authorities for taxation. The Spanish sector of the Mexican economy grew rapidly after 1550 as the amount of registered silver production rose from 25 million pesos (a physical measure of weight) in the decade from 1561 to 1570 to a high of 53 million in the decade from 1611 to 1620.[21]

18 Chevalier, *Land and Society*, pp. 309–12.

19 John Lynch, *Spain under the Hapsburgs* (Oxford: B. Blackwell, 1969), p. 195; Richard Boyer, "Mexico in the 17th Century: Transition of a Colonial Society," *Hispanic-American Historical Review* 57 (1977), 454–78, pp. 456–7.

20 Lesley Simpson, "Mexico's Forgotten Century," *Pacific Historical Review* 22 (1953), 113–21; Murdo MacLeod, "A New Introduction: More than Three Decades of Writing on Spanish Central America, 1973–2006," in Murdo MacLeod, *Spanish Central America: A Socioeconomic History, 1520–1720* (Austin: University of Texas Press, 2007), pp. xi–iv.

21 Burkholder, "An Empire beyond Compare," p. 130.

The level of reported silver production in the 1600s varied greatly from year to year because of war-related uncertainties in the delivery of mercury needed for efficient smelting.[22] In general terms, however, reported Mexican silver production fell by a third from 53 million pesos in the 1611–1620 period to 34 million pesos in the decade from 1641 to 1650. Then by the 1680s, it recovered to the 60-million peso level. The figures on the next two decades declined somewhat because of the wars of the period.[23]

We do have highly unreliable statistics on silver smuggling. Scholars looking at European records have found that Europe was receiving much more silver than was officially leaving Spanish America. Clearly, China was also receiving a large amount of untaxed silver as well. The estimates of official and unofficial production and exports vary greatly, but Mark Burkholder estimates that in some decades, over 50% of the silver sent to Europe was shipped illegally.[24]

The amount of silver that never was reported to authorities and then was exported can never be known. The primary source of illegal exports, however, was surely the 90% silver that remained in private Mexican hands after the 10% tax had been paid.[25] Either explanation has favorable implications for the economy. If production was higher than reported, this clearly had positive effects, and if private persons were freed of the tax of 15% to 17% of exported silver or imported goods, this increased their purchasing power.[26]

It is likely that the decline in official shipping and reported silver production in the second quarter of the 1600s resulted from disruptions in

[22] Fisher, *The Economic Aspects of Spanish Imperialism*, p. 101. Zacatecas, for example, suffered "persistent" shortages of mercury.

[23] Burkholder, "An Empire beyond Compare," p. 130.

[24] Eric Hamilton, *American Treasure and the Price Revolution in Spain*, 1501–1650 (Cambridge, MA: Harvard University Press, 1934), p. 37; Stanley Stein and Barbara Stein, *Silver, Trade, and War: Spain and America in the Making of Early Modern Europe* (Baltimore, MD: Johns Hopkins University Press, 2000), pp. 23–6. Burkholder, "An Empire beyond Compare," p. 130.

[25] Some producers smelted their silver without mercury when they could not obtain the metal. Others obtained mercury smuggled from Peru. Still others bribed tax collectors or other officials to allow them to under-report production. Peter Bakewell, *Silver Mining and Society in Colonial Mexico, Zacatecas 1546–1700* (Cambridge, MA: Cambridge University Press, 1972), pp. 169–70, 177–8.

[26] Clarence Henry Haring, *Trade and Navigation between Spain and the Indies in the Time of the Hapsburgs* (Cambridge, MA: Harvard University Press, 1918), pp. 83–6; Lynch, *Spain under the Hapsburgs*, pp. 163–9. For the debate, see Carlos Marichal, "Mexican Cochineal and the European Demand for American Dyes, 1550–1850," in Steven Topik, Carlos Marichal, and Zephyr Frank, eds., *From Silver to Cocaine: Latin American Commodity Chains and the Building of the World Economy, 1500–2000* (Durham, NC: Duke University Press, 2006), 53–75, pp. 34–9.

shipments because of the Thirty Years' War, especially in mercury shipments. If so, this surely was reflected in some kind of downturn during that period.[27] European smuggling did not really soar until English, French, and Dutch colonization of the Caribbean provided the necessary island bases for the smugglers. The English acquisition of Jamaica in 1655 was particularly important.

Other crucial questions in the debate about the Mexican economy in the 1600s involve agriculture, cattle ranching, manufacturing, and domestic trade. The expansion of the hacienda sector cited by Chevalier does not logically lead to a conclusion of economic decline, especially since property relationships changed in the 1620s and 1630s. In Spain, grazing lands had been considered common property, and this principle was naturally adopted in cattle ranching in Mexico, especially in the vast and semi-arid lands near the northern mines. But as the area was pacified and the herds multiplied in size, the cattle owners naturally wanted to establish their title to what had been common grounds. In English terms, they wanted enclosure.

Another group of Spaniards wanted title to land in central Mexico. The huge number of Native American deaths in the 1500s and first half of the 1600s left much land untilled, and Spaniards wanted to use it for smaller sheep and cattle ranches. Since the king charged a fee for land titles, he was inclined to "enclose the Mexican commons" or let existing estates absorb the abandoned lands.

But what were the consequences of this movement toward the establishment of firm individual property rights? Those with a neo-Marxist approach usually interpret the enclosure movement in England as an exploitation of peasants, a theft of their land. Those with a neoclassical approach believe that the clearly defined property rights of the enclosure were crucial for the establishment of a market economy.

Chevalier, Borah, and Simpson essentially took the anti-enclosure argument about England and used it in somewhat different terms in Mexico. They were saying that in the depressed economic conditions, Spain permitted the mining elite to use the enclosure policy to recreate the *encomiendas* in less rigid form. In this view, the Native Americans were not formally tied to the estates but were effectively rendered immobile by debts to the landlords and to the merchant–*alcaldes mayores* partnership.

[27] Richard Morrisey, "Cattle Raising in New Spain" (PhD dissertation, University of California-Berkeley, 1949); Richard Salvucci, *Textiles and Capitalism in Mexico: An Economic History of the Obrajes, 1539–1840* (Princeton, NJ: Princeton University Press, 1987).

The positive view of an enclosure movement has not been represented in the debates about the 1600s. It has been politically very difficult to praise the strengthening of property rights in New Spain in the commons or unregistered land because the peasants were Native Americans. The New Institutionalists who might be expected to have emphasized property rights followed North's reliance on the negative Borah-Simpson-Chevalier literature on Spain and its colonies. This meant that they never even thought to look at its premises.

Finally, the Mexican and Central American economies featured the production of several types of dyes that were exported: indigo from Guatemala, dyewoods from Campeche in Mexico and the current area of Belize, and cochineal from Oaxaca in Mexico. The cochineal exports were especially valuable: 9% of the value of the silver exports.[28] In 1600, Spain was importing some 250,000 to 300,000 pounds of cochineal from Mexico legally, but a leading scholar says that there was "massive smuggling" of the dye at that time.[29]

The export of these items came to be dominated by English, Dutch, and French smugglers after the 1620s.[30] Recent articles on cochineal and indigo "document" the fact most clearly in a negative manner. They provide statistics on the production of these items in the late 1500s and the mid-1700s, but none on the 1600s because no statistics exist.[31]

Whatever cochineal and indigo smuggling took place, however, made a direct contribution to the Mexican economy. Foreign ships picked up the product in the Villahermosa area on the Gulf of Mexico, but it continued to be produced in the western and southern parts of the country. It and

[28] Murdo MacLeod, "Spain and America: The Atlantic Trade, 1492–1700," in Leslie Bethell, ed., *Cambridge History of Latin America,* Vol. 1: *Colonial Latin America* (Cambridge: Cambridge University Press, 1985), p. 355; Raymond Lee, "American Cochineal in Europe Commerce, 1526–1625," *Journal of Modern History* 23 (1951), 205–24.

[29] Marichal, "Mexican Cochineal," in Steven Topik, Carlos Marichal, and Zephyr Frank, eds., *From Silver to Cocaine: Latin American Commodity Chains and the Building of the World Economy, 1500–2000* (Durham, NC: Duke University Press, 2006), 78–84.

[30] MacLeod, *Spanish Central America*, pp. 348–56 and 368–70; Richard Pares, *War and Trade in the West Indies* (London: F. Cass, 1963), pp. 101–2. For more on the valuable dyewood trees (*palo de tinte*) in the Yucatán and the territory of modern Belize, see Nancy Farriss, *Maya Society under Colonial Rule: The Collective Enterprise of Survival* (Princeton, NJ: Princeton University Press, 1984), pp. 36–7 and 417, n. 23, and William David Setzekorn, *A Profile of the New Nation of Belize, formerly British Honduras* (Athens: Ohio University Press, 1981), 132–50.

[31] David McCreery, "Indigo Commodity-Chains in the Spanish and British Empires, 1560–1860," in Steven Topik, Carlos Marichal, and Zephyr Frank, eds., *From Silver to Cocaine: Latin American Commodity Chains and the Building of the World Economy, 1500–2000* (Durham, NC: Duke University Press, 2006), 53–75; and Marichal, "Mexican Cochineal."

domestic transportation remained in the same type of Mexican hands in the western and southern part of the colonies who had handled it in the 1500s. By contrast, the British smuggling of dyewoods produced in Campeche was largely a loss to the Mexican economy except for the employment of Mayan labor and the bribing of Mexican officials.

The real question is whether the shift to smuggling was accompanied by a decline in production or a continuing increase. Scholars disagree, but Raymond Lee, a long-respected specialist on cochineal, argued that the production of cochineal was demand-driven and that demand remained high for 250 years.[32] One thing we do know is that European demand for dyewood increased dramatically after 1660 when the Dutch invented a way to extract the dye in such a way that it infused color much more quickly in fabric.

The behavior of Great Britain strongly suggests that the same was true of indigo. India had had a dominant position in the indigo market but lost it during the 1600s. As we have seen, South Carolina did not produce much indigo for the 75 years after it was settled in 1560, but it became a major producer of indigo when South Carolinians responded to a British subsidy for its production. Some region of the world was providing the world with indigo in the 1600s and early 1700s, and that region had to be Central America. The bounty to South Carolina indicates when the Bourbon attack on smuggling in the 1700s became effective.

The real issues about the 1600s, especially the second half of the century, center on the service and trade sectors. The recovery in reported mining production should have affected much of the rest of the economy, and the increase in smuggling by the other European colonists should have produced a growing trade network inside Mexico. The size of the indigenous population was finally beginning to grow again, and, even more important, the integration of the growing *mestizo* population into the Spanish sector of the economy should have translated into higher productivity. All of this should have led to a rapid increase in the production and export of commodities and to an increasing complexity in the rest of the agricultural production in the second half of the 1600s.

This, of course, is a subject on which official statistics are extremely weak. Nevertheless, the measurement of the changes in gross domestic product (GDP) is not important for this book. The central issue for us is what was happening in the social structure of Mexico. The next section discusses that subject.

[32] Carlos Marichal agrees that the production of cochineal was demand-driven and that it remained high. Lee, "American Cochineal," pp. 205, 212–4, 219, and 224; Marichal, "Mexican Cochineal," p. 78.

The Mystery of the Evolution of Mexican Society in the 1600s

It is likely that Mexico suffered economic difficulties in the second quarter of the 1600s. The severe conflict in Europe at the time would have affected smuggling as well as official trade. Mexico almost surely recovered in the second of the half-century, but the question for us is the effect of the large-scale smuggling and the virtual loss of Spanish control of the life of the colony in the underlying Mexican economic and political system.

In practice, although not for inherently logical reasons, the scholarly debate about the colonial Mexican structure became linked in the 20th century with the debate about economic development. Woodrow Borah and Francois Chevalier, we have seen, thought that the future Mexico suffered an economic depression in the 1600s. More important for our purposes, however, they saw this depression linked with the creation of a feudal society that took the dynamism out of the system. Chevalier believed that the landlords did not have a capitalist mentality dedicated to the maximization of profit but only yearned "to eliminate rivals and hold sway over an entire region."[33]

In this view, a "dangerous feudalism" was based on "norms of conduct [which] were set by a raw nobility of landed gentry – norms which have persisted to this day." Lesley Simpson thought that officialdom came to reflect these new norms: "undistinguished bureaucrats in church and state were slowly molding public life into a suffocating routine, and corruption, nepotism, and time-serving make the records of the day dismal reading."[34]

The scholars who disagreed with Borah and Chevalier on the course of Mexican economic development in the 1600s also generally disagreed with them on the course of social development. While most did their research on the 1700s, many explicitly attacked Chevalier and Borah in a way that showed they thought their conclusions applied to the 1600s as well. They believed, in their language, that Mexico was developing capitalism and had been for some time.

Eric Van Young best expressed this view. The haciendas and ranches, he thought in 1981, were capitalist enterprises in which the "peasants" had really become proletarianized in a market economy. James Lockhart agreed and reported in 1983 that "recent studies of Spanish American rural estates

[33] Chevalier, *Land and Society*, pp. 308–14.

[34] Simpson, "Foreword," pp. v, vii, and viii.

often reach very different conclusions [from Chevalier]."[35] In 2006, John Coatsworth looked back 25 years and agreed fully with the thesis that Van Young expressed 25 years previously: "Haciendas *were* businesses, markets *did* work, indebted peons owed an average of only two months' wages and were *not* fixed to the earth."[36]

The analysis of the scholars of the 1970s and 1980s implied that the Mexican society never could have been as rigid as Chevalier and Borah believed. They argued that the establishment of peonage was difficult because of the supply-and-demand relationship in the labor sector. They believed that the immense number of indigenous deaths created a labor shortage that required the introduction of wage and other incentives. They saw the acceptance of *mestizos* and even their frequent identification as whites as providing relatively easy upward mobility of peasants into urban occupations. The labor shortage was even greater in the 1600s than the 1700s, and hacienda owners should have been forced to respond to market pressures even more than in the 1700s. If so, any type of semi-feudal system was difficult to maintain.

This skeptical view of "feudalism" on the estates naturally extended to the urban sector as well. Those who denied an economic depression in the 1600s saw the smuggling-based economy as entrepreneurial and the rising merchant class as the crucial element in this sector. Scholars did recognize that the economy rested on personalistic ties, but they saw the family ties between those in agriculture, mining, trade, the church (the main rural bank), and the government not as a sign of social stagnation, but as an effort to promote comprehensive enrichment. This was especially so since these ties were strengthened by deliberate strategies of intermarriage.

What we do know about New Spain officials makes it difficult to see them as Simpson's "undistinguished bureaucrats [who] were slowly molding public life into a suffocating routine, and corruption, nepotism, and time-serving." The officials often seem more like businessmen. The extension of family ties into credit, trade, government, and the church does not suggest an estate owner who was living the static life of a conservative estate owner. He surely was trying to help the businesses of his children.

[35] James Lockhart, *Early Latin America: A History of Colonial Spanish America and Brazil* (Cambridge, MA: Cambridge University Press, 1983), p. 440.

[36] John Coatsworth, "Foreword," and Erik Van Young, "Introduction to the Twenty-Fifth Anniversary Edition," in Eric Van Young, *Hacienda and Market in Eighteenth-Century Mexico: The Rural Economy of the Guadalajara Region, 1675–1820*, 2nd ed. (Lanham: Rowman and Littlefield, 2006), pp. xviii and 344.

Moreover, it undoubtedly is necessary to take a multi-generational perspective. The sons and sons-in-law who were placed in other sectors of the economy had their own sons and daughters who had to be placed. Downward social mobility surely occurred, but the pressure to maintain family power and position had economic implications. In the process, the Mexican elite became increasingly complex and diverse in the 1600s. This, we think, was one of the pre-conditions for the progress made under the Bourbons in the 1700s.

The official about whom scholars know the most is the *alcalde mayor* who collected taxes from the indigenous population. The *alcaldes mayores* had a small salary, at least around 1600, but had to pay a deputy, a constable, and an interpreter.[37] The *alcaldes mayores* had to pay the king the taxes due him (the "tribute" from the Native Americans) even before they themselves collected them. Thus, they had to obtain money, and one way or another, they had to engage in regular business activity.[38]

In practice, the *alcaldes mayores* usually received a large loan from a merchant (the *aviador*) and built working relations with the indigenous village leaders. The merchant would loan the *alcalde mayor* the money to pay the tax, and in return he would receive a monopoly or near-monopoly position in providing goods to the villages. The Native Americans were offered money on credit, and they repaid these loans with the product they were delivering as part of the tribute.

The *alcaldes mayores* in some way shared in the business profits. The two men could recoup their investment in any way that seemed best to them. The easiest way was to use their monopoly position in selling urban goods to the villages to set the prices so they would cover their earlier tax payment and leave themselves a profit.

As we will see, scholars disagree on whether this business was unduly exploitative, but the role seems far more entrepreneurial than suffocating time serving. More information is available about remote areas such as the Yucatán, and it indicates that their officials were even more entrepreneurial. The relationship between the *alcalde mayor* and the village chiefs had a similar character and came to be featured by economic exchange more than tax collection in the traditional sense.

Yet the *alcalde mayor* and his *aviador* knew that if the level of resentment reached an explosive level, they would be the first to be killed. They

[37] James Lockhart, *Nahuas and Spaniards: Postconquest Central Mexican History and Philology* (Stanford, CA: Stanford University Press, 1991), pp. 218–9.

[38] Patch, "Imperial Politics," pp. 86–7.

could – and, no doubt, did – adjust the prices to the ability of the Native Americans to pay, an ability that at least in part must have been influenced by the amount of rainfall in a particular year. Since the *alcalde mayor* chaired the *cabildo* sessions, he could report about the mood of the villages to the urban elite and also observe and assess the mood of the urban population. The priests of the Catholic Church took confessions, and this gave another member of the local elite a sense of what people were thinking.

Urban officials had the same problems as the *alcaldes mayores*, and their "salaries" too were based on some kind of legitimate or illegitimate activity. The city that has been the subject of the best American book – Zacatecas, studied by Peter Bakewell – had a *corregidor* rather than an *alcalde mayor*. The *corregidor* in Zacatecas received a salary of 1,630 pesos a year; but the person in this position did not deal with the indigenous population and hence had no possibility of profiting from trade with them. When the Crown started selling the post after 1670, however, the required "donation" for a ten-year appointment was 10,000 pesos. The post of *corregidor* was obviously lucrative for reasons that are not well documented.[39]

All this economic activity, even if personalistic and often illegal, led scholars in the 1980s and 1990s to the conclusion that "colonial Mexico ... is no longer viewed primarily as a source of Spanish silver; it is also seen as the center of a large trading region that included the Caribbean and extended south to Peru and west to the Philippines. The society that emerged out of the chaos of the conquest period was diverse, healthy, remarkably stable, and expansionist to boot."[40]

To repeat, the consensus about this view may well be stronger for the mid- and late-1700s than for the 1600s and the first half of the 1700s. This is not for us to judge, and it is also not important for our purposes. To the extent that scholars are describing a society that required several centuries to develop, that does not shake our judgment or that of Douglass North about time and development, but reinforces it. No one says that Spain in the 1600s had the same type of evolution toward (but only toward) the rational-legal norms and practices that was occurring in England in the late 1600s and especially the first half of the 1700s.

As we discuss at the end of this chapter, rational-legal norms (usually called Enlightenment norms in Spain and Mexico) clearly began to develop in Spain

[39] For more on the relationship of the *cabildo* and *corregidor* in Zacatecas, see Bakewell, *Silver Mining and Society*, pp. 81–113.

[40] Elinor G. K. Melville, *A Plague of Sheep: Environmental Consequences of the Conquest of Mexico* (Cambridge: Cambridge University Press, 1994), p. 10.

under the Bourbons and some progress had been made by 1760. No doubt, some such evolution had begun in the larger cities by the late 1600s. Mexico may have lagged somewhat, but Mexico City and Veracruz were dominated by merchants, and they were exposed to the changes occurring in Spain.

In assessing the Mexican economy during the 1600s, we should also remember that smuggling is market activity and that it can be more conducive to growth than monopoly trade. It requires a commercial network of suppliers and importers, a network that consists almost entirely of local personnel. Corruption can be a kind of taxation, and if the income is not simply transferred abroad, the smuggling and corruption should have a multiplier effect within the economy.

The politics of the Mexico City *consulado* in the early 1740s suggested the structure and consequences of that trade, both legal and illegal, at that time. The *consulado* was so divided between contentious factions that the regime had to intervene. These divisions probably reflected differences among those engaged in legal trade with Seville and Caracas and those engaged in smuggling. As Spain brought the smuggling under control, the groups engaged in it had to become part of the *consulado*. They brought their differing perspectives, ethnic and social characteristics, and interests with them.

The combination of legal and illegal trade within Mexico was developing a commercial culture. The legal cacao trade with Venezuela was marked by a complexity in the credit system that is closer to the trade of tobacco in Virginia than our usual stereotypes about the *consulados*. The rule was established that one-third of the space on ships from Caracas to Veracruz was reserved for Caracas merchants, one-third for hacienda owners, and one-third for the captain. Those who wanted cash immediately for their cacao sold it to the merchants, while those who could wait and take a risk generally found it more profitable to retain ownership and sell it on the Mexican market. If all merchants could join a *consulado* and compete, the phrase "*consulado* monopoly" can hide a great deal of market activity.[41]

The Bourbon Regime in Mexico: The Expansion of the Merchant Class and Trade

The Bourbon kings who came to power in the early 1700s had notable success in establishing control over the colonies and promoting their economic development. In an index in which 100 represents the number of

[41] Robert Ferry, *The Colonial Elite of Early Caracas: Formation and Crisis, 1567–1767* (Berkeley: University of California Press, 1989), p. 295.

tons of goods shipped between Cadiz and the colonies from 1691 to 1700, the number fell to 53.1 from 1701 to 1710 as a result of the war. It rose to 162.3 in the decade from 1731 to 1740, 318.9 from 1751 to 1760, and 402 from 1761 to 1777.[42] During this period, an increasing number of ships were allowed to sail from other ports, and hence the real increase in official trade was greater. This not only increased the income of the Spanish government, but also was of real importance in the economic development of the New World.

The first concerted effort of the Bourbons to improve the Mexican economy was naturally directed toward increasing silver production. As we have seen in Chapter 5, the Bourbons deprived Bolivia of investment and mercury sales and concentrated them on Mexico. Silver production in Mexico showed relatively steady growth from the 1660s under the Hapsburgs through the 1800s under the Bourbons. Some scholars believe this shows the change from the Hapsburg to the Bourbon regime in 1700s had little impact on the level of production.[43] We find this unconvincing.

We think the decline from the 1620s to the 1660s largely resulted from the turmoil of the Seven Years' War and the recovery largely from a return to normalcy. From this perspective, silver production in Mexico was on a plateau during the 1600s, and the Bourbons deserve credit for most of the increase that began in the 1710s.

The Bourbons took a number of steps to encourage silver production besides increasing the delivery of mercury. As miners had to follow the veins deeper into the earth, they needed soaring amounts of investment. They formed working partnerships and then turned to different types of private lenders. In the first half-century of the 1700s, special silver banks (*Bancos de Plata*) were formed to serve the mining industry.[44]

Another change involved the mint. The Hapsburgs had forced all employees to purchase their offices and live on commissions. In 1733, the Bourbons ended this "privatization," and over the next two years they turned the mint into a standard governmental operation with a professional administrative staff. Improved machinery was introduced to produce almost perfect coins in large quantity.

[42] Fisher, *The Economic Aspects of Spanish Imperialism.*

[43] See Richard Garner, "Long-Term Silver Mining Trends in Spanish America: A Comparative Analysis of Peru and Mexico," in Peter Bakewell, ed., *Mines of Silver and Gold in the Americas* (Aldershot: Variorum, 1997), pp. 227–36.

[44] Walter Howe, *The Mining Guild of New Spain and Its Tribunal General, 1770–1825* (Cambridge, MA: Harvard University Press, 1949), pp. 13–5.

Madrid hoped that Spanish silver coins would become the most reliable medium of exchange in the world so that foreigners, including smugglers, would demand them and use them abroad. They hoped this would guarantee the silver would have to be taken to the mint and reported.[45] All this happened.

While the statistics on Mexican silver production are reasonably good, the trends in the rest of the economy are much more obscure. Even though the mining sector only constituted 7% of Mexican GDP by the end of the century, the supplies that the sector required and the wealth that it generated clearly had a major impact on the rest of the economy. Nevertheless, the scale and even the nature of that impact are difficult to judge. The basic problem is that no one can know the base figure because of the smuggling that occurred in the 1600s and much of the 1700s.

The lack of good statistics on the production and export of Mexico's chief commodities – cochineal, dyewood, and indigo – is the best evidence of the relative absence of legal trade. The foreign ships that came to the east coast of Mexico to collect commodities and silver brought consumer goods, which Mexican merchants had to distribute throughout the colony. The contracts could not be enforced in court, but, of course, officials at all levels knew exactly what was going on. They were receiving the same goods as everyone else, and they were, no doubt, collecting various kinds of formal and informal "taxes."

A number of signs indicate that the authorities ended much of the foreign smuggling by the 1730s. The decision of Britain to subsidize indigo production in South Carolina is one of the clearest indicators. So, too in a way, are the Anglo-Spanish War of 1727–1729 and the so-called War of Jenkins' Ear in 1739 as the English reacted to the harassment of their ships.

For most of the 1700s, however, the Bourbons were concerned only with foreign smuggling, which basically was limited to the Atlantic. They did not re-legalize trade between Lima and New Spain until 1774, but the illegal trade must have risen rapidly as the Spanish American economies improved. They must not have wanted to waste resources on customs collectors on trade they thought they could tax indirectly. In this they were following the English model on trade between the mainland and Caribbean colonies.

[45] Howe, *The Mining Guild*, pp. 13–15. Similar steps were taken in gold mining in South America. In the 1750s the use of gold dust was prohibited in merchant trade, and then in the 1770s investment in the industry was promoted. Both produced marked jumps in the reported level of production. Ann Twinam, *Miners, Merchants, and Farmers in Colonial Colombia* (Austin: University of Texas Press, 1982), pp. 30, 33, and 36.

The same forces that transformed the English commercial system of 1500 over the next two centuries were also at work on the system inside Mexico in the 1700s: the strengthening of the state and the growing complexity of the economy. The great wholesale merchants of Mexico City, the *almaceneros*, could no longer control all internal trade simply because the volume was becoming too large. As in England under Elizabeth, the rise in smuggling in Spanish America in the 1600s and the 1730s attracted a substantial number of merchants and shippers, some members of the establishment and some not.

The illegal merchants who replaced the illegal market trade of the past with legal trade during the 1700s began to transform the *consulados*. By the mid-1750s the *consulado* was becoming too large and complex for the old type of monopoly. According to John Kicza, the merchants regularly formed consortiums and interest groups on the basis of consanguinity, affinity, and compatible economic interest.

The most important division among the Mexican merchants was between the ethnic Spanish merchants with their roots in Seville and the Basques with their roots in the northern ports. Not surprisingly, the Basques wanted to trade with the northern ports while the ethnic Spanish were more content with Seville. The situation became so tense that in 1742 the viceroy ordered the *consulado* members to be divided into two parties, the Basques and the Montaneses, with the major posts to be alternated between them on an annual basis.[46]

The other great division must have been between those engaged in Atlantic and Pacific trade. The foreigners had operated primarily in the Atlantic, and legal Mexican merchants and shippers must have filled the vacuum. The major Basque merchant family that came to be an important force in the trade with South America when it became legal in 1774 likely was an important force in that trade when it was illegal. The major question that we cannot answer is how many of the ships were based in Lima and how many in Mexico.

In the late 1700s, the opening of Havana to nine Spanish ports and five Caribbean ones introduced a system of free trade into the Caribbean Islands

[46] John Kicza, *Colonial Entrepreneurs: Families and Business in Bourbon Mexico City* (Albuquerque: University of New Mexico Press, 1983), pp. 51–2; D.A. Brading, *Miners and Merchants in Bourbon Mexico, 1763–1810* (Cambridge: Cambridge University Press, 1971), p. 107; John Kicza, "Mexican Merchants and Their Links to Spain, 1750–1850," in Kenneth J. Andrien and Lyman L. Johnson, eds., *The Political Economy of Spanish America in the Age of Revolution, 1750–1850* (Albuquerque: University of New Mexico Press, 1994), pp. 115–36.

similar to what Charles II of England had introduced nearly 150 years earlier. It had a major impact on Mexico. In the period before 1770, some dozen ships a year left Campeche and none arrived in the period between 1758 and 1770. In 1802, 960 arrived and departed.

Much of the increase in exports from Campeche consisted of cattle products – meat, hides, and tallow – but it is not clear how much this reflected an increase in trade and how much an increase in registered trade. The number using the port surely was much higher prior to legalization than reported.[47]

In 1789, free trade was finally extended to New Spain and Venezuela. In 1794, a new *consulado* was formed in Veracruz. As Barbara and Stanley Stein caution, however, Spain had only 2,835 merchant ships in 1788 compared with 13,827 for England.[48] Nevertheless, the Steins treat the creation of the Veracruz consulado in 1794 as a particularly important development, because it also transformed the politics of New Spain.

The Mexico City *consulado*, as we have seen, featured many cleavages in the commercial realm, but it was a basically united interest group on questions such as maintaining Mexico City's monopoly in the distribution of goods to the interior. The interests of Veracruz were very different, and the new *consulado* advanced them vigorously. Since the interests of Veracruz often coincided with those of the interior, the Steins believed that the Veracruz *consulado* had great potential power:[49]

> Not content with handling commodity exports like silver and dyestuffs, the [Veracruz merchants] as developmentalist offspring of the metropole's *proyectistas* promoted new exportables such as flour and sugar, along with items needed by Barcelona's late-developing textile industry, raw cotton and yarn, silk and flax.
>
> The major thrust of Veracruz's independents, however, was their design to capitalize on their port's geographical position so as to transform it into a coastal entrepôt attracting merchants of the interior seeking to bypass the added freight costs, warehousing, commission fees, and customs and sale taxes of Mexico City wholesalers and their *consulado*. Small wonder that Veracruz independents sponsored improvements in portworks, accommodations for muleteers and their *recuas*,

[47] The military commander, who saw himself as the major figure in illegal trade, found himself in severe conflict with *cabildo* on the issue. Robert Patch, "The Bourbon Reforms, City Councils, and the Struggle for Power in Yucatán, 1770–1796," in Jaime Rodríguez O., *Mexico in the Age of Democratic Revolutions, 1750–1850* (Boulder, CO: Lynne Rienner, 1994), pp. 58–59; Robert Patch, *Maya and Spaniard in Yucatán, 1648–1812* (Stanford, CA: Stanford University Press, 1993).

[48] Barbara Stein and Stanley Stein, *Edge of Crisis: War and Trade in the Spanish Atlantic, 1789–1808* (Baltimore, MD: Johns Hopkins University Press, 2009), p. 24.

[49] Stein and Stein, *Edge of Crisis*, p. 143.

road and bridge construction and maintenance, public infrastructure studiously neglected by the capital's merchant body.

Unfortunately, from the perspective of independent Mexico, the development of the Veracruz *consulado* came too late – or, perhaps instead, independence came too early. The road network was somewhat improved in the years before independence, but the year of 1789 in which semi-free trade was introduced into Mexico was also the year of the French Revolution against the French Bourbons. Fifteen years of war between the execution of Louis XVI in 1793 and Napoleon's overthrow of the Bourbons in 1808 resulted in much higher emergency taxation in New Spain. The amount of capital that remained for infrastructure and other investment was sharply reduced.

In principle, the de facto legalization of trade between Mexican ports and the United States during the war with France should have been highly beneficial to the development of a commercial culture in Mexico. It was, in fact, advantageous, but the benefits were limited by the fact that Mexico had few ships on the east coast to use in trade with either the United States or any other country. The end of the Napoleonic wars surely would have led to a transformation of Mexican commerce, but Napoleon's overthrow of the Spanish king in 1808 brought that prospect to an end.

The Social Situation in Mexico at the End of the Colonial Period

It is difficult to characterize Mexican societal development at the time of Napoleon's coup d'état in 1808 in Madrid. One reason is simply the natural ambiguity of the early stages of the transition to a rational-legal society and the difficulty of describing and documenting it. As we have emphasized, the English administrative system only gradually became much more professional and competent from the early 1500s under Henry VIII until the system that emerged in the late 1700s.

Even though the period of Restoration from 1660 to 1688 seems like a major watershed in England, Samuel Pepys's diary shows the great mixture of "modern" and "pre-modern" practices that characterized the English bureaucracy at that time. So does the corruption among the British governors in America in the 1700s. Spain and Mexico were undergoing the same kind of very gradual change at the end of the 1700s, but it is harder to document in the English-language literature.

In 1994, as has been noted, a scholar wrote that "the (Mexican) society that emerged out of the chaos of the conquest period was diverse, healthy, remarkably stable,and expansionist to boot."[50]

These views were cited in our discussion of the late 1600s and they surely are more accurate when applied to the Mexico of 1800. The Hapsburgs had governed by means of a crude personalistic system that was incompatible with an effective market. The first two Bourbon kings made a concerted effort to replace the Hapsburg values with the Enlightenment values of their native France. Charles III accelerated the process.

Mark Burkholder and Lyman Johnson strongly emphasize the change that occurred, especially after the expulsion of the Jesuits from both Spain and the colonies. Burkholder and Johnson believe the Jesuits were expelled in order to change the intellectual atmosphere of the bureaucracy, especially in the colleges where they trained the elite. Burkholder and Johnson saw the effort as quite successful. "By the close of the eighteenth century, skepticism of authority, observation of nature, experimentation, and analysis based on inductive reasoning had transformed the intellectual milieu of the colonies."[51]

Murdo MacLeod agrees, speculating that American scholars came to devote more research to the period after 1759 not simply because of the greater availability of data. He finds a more rational skeptical analysis in the documents of the late 1700s that he thinks makes modern scholars more comfortable in working in them.[52]

In their 2009 book, Barbara and Stanley Stein, both of whom had long held a pessimistic dependency view of Mexican development, presented a more favorable view of the Spanish bureaucratic system at the end of the 1700s – one close to Burkholder and Johnson's. In a section entitled "The Civil Service: The Vanguard of Change," they wrote:[53]

> In general the civil service attracted intellectuals (far more than did the eighteenth-century religious establishment), many of them economists (proyectistas), political commentators, critics (usually safely anonymous), and literary figures. An expanding civil service afforded steady (usually underpaid) employment, retirement benefits, perquisites, and status.

A classic way for a ruler to control a system dominated by elite families and professional bureaucrats is to create representative bodies to which

[50] Melville, *A Plague of Sheep*, p. 10.

[51] Mark Burkholder and Lyman Johnson, *Colonial Latin America*, 6th ed. (New York: Oxford University Press, 2008), pp. 323–8.

[52] MacLeod, "A New Introduction," p. xiii.

[53] Stein and Stein, *Edge of Crisis*, pp. 19–20.

other social groups have access. This had happened in England when the Tudors strengthened the relative role of the House of Commons dominated by the gentry in order to weaken the House of Lords and the lords.

Madrid, which liked checks and balances to limit the viceroys in the colonies, remained torn in the late 1700s on whether to subordinate the *intendants* and tax officials to the viceroy. Surely the Crown foresaw a growth in the strength of the *cabildos* to limit the *intendants* in the same way. Indeed, Mark Burkholder and Lyman Johnson report the *cabildos* of the new provincial capitals were already gaining greater power:[54]

> In the provincial capitals ... typically the intendant sought to revitalize a city council by enlarging its membership, often by recruiting prominent, long-resident peninsulars of the city, raising its revenues, and making a variety of improvements in public services. Improved roads and bridges, street lights, and better sanitation and water supplies increased civil pride. With the limitations on the employment of native sons in a number of other government institutions, the cabildos increasingly became the primary political arena for local grievances in many parts of the Spanish Empire.

The Spanish kings were clearly studying the experience of England in North America. Indeed, Elliott notes that in the 1760s, "Madrid wanted to see Spain's American possessions transformed into British-style 'colonies,' a rich source of staple products and a market for its goods."[55] As they fitfully sought to create a system of checks and balances between the viceroy, the *intendants*, and the tax collectors, they must have looked at the way in which the Duke of Newcastle used the governors and assemblies to do that.

Without question, the values and habits of Mexicans in 1810 reflected Bourbon New Spain more than those of the Hapsburgs of more than 100 years in the past. The question is how much they reflected the changes introduced by Charles III. Charles III began his efforts to introduce Enlightenment attitudes 60 years before independence. Anyone under 61 years of age in 1821 was born after 1769, and most Mexicans under 40 were born to parents who had been small children in 1759. Two full generations had been raised entirely in that Mexico, and they should have been affected by that exposure. Values, at least among the educated in the large cities, had had a long time to evolve.

In short, the colonial legacy to independent Mexico is very difficult to judge. Charles III's administrative reforms were never really institutionalized. The wartime measures that began in 1793 disrupted the

54 Burkholder and Johnson, *Colonial Latin America*, pp. 323–8.
55 Elliott, *Empires of the Atlantic*, p. 303.

development of a more professional system of taxation and the building of infrastructure. Burkholder and Johnson argue that the role of the *cabildos* was being strengthened, but this had not been formalized as it was in the English colonies.

A single road connected Mexico City with Veracruz, but "road" is a generous characterization. As late as 1800, the famous geographer Alexander von Humboldt describes this main artery as "frequently nothing but a narrow and crooked path and is one of the most difficult in all America." A top provincial official wrote that it never was cared for or repaired.[56] It was not until 1823 that Tampico, which would become an important Atlantic port, was re-opened after being destroyed by pirates in 1683.[57]

Change in norms, habits, and assumptions take a long time. The transition from traditional to rational-legal values was a long process in England. Value change is not likely to have been much more rapid in Mexico. Burkholder and Johnson's conclusions about values in Mexico City may be right, but the provinces and the church must have been different from the salons of the capital. Indeed, Will Fowler argues that the Hidalgo rebellion of 1810 was "a reactionary clerical backlash against the liberal and enlightenment Bourbon reforms."[58]

There are scholars such as Alan Knight who still see Mexico of 1821 as feudal, but Brian Hamnett is more typical in writing of a society in transition and the coexistence of "traditional and modern practices":[59]

> New Spain became a society in which the decisive element was not so much the landowner as such (who, of course, remained socially predominant) but the merchant-financier with accumulated capital ... at his disposal. Traditional and modern practices coexisted among the merchant-financiers. Matrimony and personal ties continued to be the principal means of solidifying business interests. Nephews, other relatives, "compadres," and friends formed broad networks of interest over a

[56] Alexander Von Humboldt, *Political Essay on the Kingdom of New Spain* (Norman: University of Oklahoma Press, 1988), p. 205. The provincial official is quoted in Stanley Stein and Barbara Stein, *Apogee of Empire: Spain and New Spain in the Age of Charles III, 1759–1789* (Baltimore, MD: Johns Hopkins University Press, 2003), p. 251. See also Joel Roberts Poinsett, *Notes on Mexico Made in the Autumn of 1822* (New York: Frederick A. Praeger, 1969), p. 16.

[57] Carmen Galicia Patino, *Comercio y comerciantes en Tampico, 1823–1850* (Ciudad Victoria, Tam: El Colegio de Tamaulipas, 2003).

[58] Will Fowler, *Mexico in the Age of Proposals, 1821–1853* (Westport, CT: Greenwood Press, 1998), p. 13.

[59] Alan Knight, *Mexico: A Colonial History* (Cambridge: Cambridge University Press, 2002); Brian Hamnett, *A Concise History of Mexico*, 2nd ed. (Cambridge: Cambridge University Press, 2006), p. 81.

wide geographical area from the capital cities into the countryside and through the span of economic activities.

We particularly agree with Hamnett's emphasis upon the merchant-financiers and his argument that "the key relationship at the top levels of colonial society was between the central bureaucratic organs and the mercantile-financial elite."[60] Madrid judged the viceroy primarily by his success in getting silver to Spain, while the Mexico City elite judged him by his ability to keep them supplied with luxury goods. Those two facts should have made the merchants the focus of the viceroy's attention. Cattle and sheep – and those who raised them – simply did not have the central role in New Spain that sheep had in Spain or cattle in independent Argentina.

What we can say for certain is that Mexico was changing. By the mid-19th century, several more new generations would have come to the fore, and they surely would have been more modern. The bureaucracy would have become more institutionalized and professional. In addition, Spain likely would have promoted the construction of better transportation, including the new railroads, because of the threat of the United States, but also the growing commercial opportunities along the Gulf Coast and the Mississippi River.

In particular, the development of Cuba as a major sugar producer in the 1800s should have developed commerce in Mexico as the English production of sugar in the Caribbean did in New England. A half-century of free trade would have developed a more deeply rooted legal commercial culture.

As we discuss in the next two chapters on American and Mexican independence, the major difference between the United States and Mexico after independence was the level of the development of government structure at the provincial level. The year of 1821 was the year of Mexican independence and of the admission of Missouri into the United States. The United States was essentially the same size as Mexico, if we exclude the territory that Mexico was to lose to the United States in the 1840s. The central government was weak in both the United States and Mexico, and the dominant unit in both was the state and city-state, respectively. Yet the United States was stable in the 1820s and 1830s and prospered, while Mexico was in chaos and in an economic depression.

We examine this divergence in the next two chapters, but in a preliminary way, we express our strong belief that the difference was not due to the

[60] Hamnett, *A Concise History of Mexico*, p. 81.

absence of democratic legislatures or excessive bureaucratic control. Many non-democratic, centralized systems are quite stable and prosperous. The problem, we argue, is that the American states were real "states" with a governing structure, military power, and an ability to tax. The Mexican city-states had no formal provincial governing structure except the *intendants* that disintegrated. The provincial elite had almost no military power at all or taxing ability in 1808. That was the legacy that was so lethal to Mexico for a half-century after 1821.

9

The Collective Action Problems of the Formation of the United States

Revolutionaries naturally claim they represent the people against the repressors. They treat their revolution as coming from below and describe their constitutions as social contracts that express the public will. The textbook analyses of the American Revolution and the Constitutional Convention are typical. More sophisticated scholarly analysis normally follows a different path. Societies undergo a variety of economic, technological, structural, and social changes, and these inevitably create pressure for political change as well. Such pressure eventually has an impact.

Normally, political change comes through evolution – or, perhaps, through some type of military coup that is not accompanied by mass revolutionary activity. Unfortunately, when revolution does occur, scholars often do not distinguish between the causes of the revolution and the pressures for evolutionary change.

Scholarly analysis of the American Revolution often shows this confusion of evolution and revolution. In Chapters 4, 6, and 7, we pointed to a number of basic changes that were taking place both in the colonies and in London around 1750. The population and territory of the colonies were becoming too large to be ruled through the old city-states. The colonial economies were becoming so complex and interconnected that some kind of coordinating government mechanism was needed. London had pressing financial needs and was finally acquiring the ability to collect taxes in the colonies.

Major political changes had to take place, but they did not have to take the form of the American Revolution, the War of Independence, and the Constitutional Convention – let alone any successful revolution, War of Independence, or stable political system afterward. Home rule within the empire or the formation of two relatively loose independent federations seemed far more likely.

A collective action theorist must ask why pressures for evolutionary change sometimes produce revolutions, despite the great collective action problems faced by popular uprisings. Moreover, the Constitutional Convention resulted in a very weak central government with virtually no military force or taxing ability. This leads to the question, How did such an American government maintain a Union of slave and non-slave states for 70 years and then quickly restore order after the Civil War?

Those who conducted the American Revolution faced a particularly large number of collective action problems. The British had tried to create an empire of quite separate and mutually hostile colonies, and they had, by all appearances, succeeded. The colonists did not even think of themselves as Americans in the 1750s, and relatively few did in the 1760s. Washington pleaded for an American identity in his Farewell Address as president, but even Thomas Jefferson said at the end of his life that he always thought of himself as a Virginian.

There was little contact between politicians of different colonies, or at least politicians of non-adjacent colonies. As we have seen, John Adams reported that the delegates to the First Continental Congress in 1774 were "fifty Gentlemen meeting together, all Strangers, [who] are not acquainted with Each others Language, Ideas, Views, Designs. They are therefore jealous of each other – fearfull, timid, skittish."[1]

When the colonies resisted George III's harsh reaction to the Boston Tea Party of December 1773, they were defending their independence as individual colonies, not calling for a colony-wide government. When they formed the Articles of Confederation, the government had no chief executive. The Congress was based on the principle of one state-one vote, and unanimous agreement was required for any important matter.

The financing of the war was one such question that required unanimous assent. Mancur Olson could have written a book with his only examples coming from Washington's wartime correspondence about the free rider problems he faced. Even after the war, Washington wrote angrily about "the darling Sovereignties of the States individually."[2]

1 Charles Andrews, *The Colonial Period of American History*, Vol. 4 (New York: Yale University Press, 1938), pp. 413–14; John Adams to Abigail Adams, September 25, 1774, in Paul Smith, ed., *Letters of Delegates to Congress, 1774–1789*, Vol. 1 (Washington, DC: Library of Congress, 1976), p. 99.

2 "To Henry Knox," February 3, 1787, in W. W. Abbot and Dorothy Twohig, eds., *The Papers of George Washington, Confederation Series*, Vol. 5 (Charlottesville: University Press of Virginia, 1992), p. 9.

Yet when John Adams and a majority in Congress wanted Washington to step down in the fall and winter of 1777–1778, they could not achieve their collective goal. Instead, Adams was exiled to France for the remainder of the war. The Constitutional Convention was an unconstitutional overthrow of the constitution – the Articles of Confederation – that many states did not want to attend. How did all this happen?

Politics is always complex and multi-faceted. Yet when we explained key events in English history, we often pointed to developments that lent support to Mancur Olson's emphasis on the ability to "organize the greatest capacity for violence." So it was, we argue, with the formative years of the American state.

George Washington really was the father of his country, in that he was the linchpin in solving the seemingly unsolvable collective action problems of the formative years. Congress could not remove him in 1777–1778 because he moved his troops to Valley Forge near the Congress and was able to force it to exile John Adams to France and John Hancock and Sam Adams to Boston. His continued retention of the loyalty of the officer corps was crucial in 1787.

But the Constitution that Washington wanted did not establish a standing army at the federal level. How then was stability maintained? Many believe that America was stable because it was a federal state. We generally agree but think that the language is not precise. America did not have a federal government in the domestic policy sphere, but a confederate one. The states really were states. Like the feudal lords, they were the ones with a "comparative advantage in violence, extending over a geographic area whose boundaries are determined by its power to tax constituents."[3] They were the ones who really maintained stability.

Nevertheless, we argue that Mancur Olson's theory of collective action must still be supplemented by the work of Douglass North. As we noted earlier, Jean Jacques Rousseau made a famous statement in *The Social Contract*: "The strongest is never strong enough to be always the master, unless he transforms strength into right, and obedience into duty." As North wrote, rulers have shown Rousseau is right by the "immense amount of resources [they have] invested throughout history in attempting to convince individuals about the justice or injustice of their position."[4]

[3] Douglass North, *Structure and Change in Economic History* (New York: W. W. Norton, 1981), p. 21.

[4] Ibid., pp. 54 and 51.

George Washington's words and actions are consistent with Rousseau's point. As we document through Washington's own correspondence to his closest political aides (e.g., James Madison), Washington used a quite credible threat of a military coup to achieve the Constitutional Convention and the Constitution that he wanted. He made the threat credible not only by what he said, but by scheduling the Constitutional Convention at the precise time and place when the meeting of the military officers loyal to him was being held.

Washington told his chief aides he knew the Convention was an illegal overthrow of the Articles of Confederation but that it was necessary. "That which takes the shortest course to obtain [a strong government], will, in my opinion, under present circumstances, be found best. Otherwise, like a house on fire, whilst the most regular mode of extinguishing it is contending for, the building is reduced to ashes."[5]

Yet even though the Constitutional Convention and the Constitution ultimately rested on might, Washington's letters to his aides show an obsession with timing so that he would turn might into right even before he came into power. Washington wanted the reluctant states to believe that his constitutional rule was the better option because they had had some influence on the provisions of the Constitution. He also wanted a stable government that would protect the South from the more populous North after his death.

Policies of George III and the Grievances of the Colonists

In recent decades scholars have seen the American Revolution as originating almost exclusively in the cities – which in colonial America meant a handful of coastal ports. This means they have emphasized either issues of taxation, which had little impact except on the merchants and the intellectual professions, and/or conceptions about republicanism and representation present only among intellectuals. The argument would be strengthened if they added the resentment of artisans of competition from cheap British goods, but it still would be insufficient.

The paradox of the American Revolution is that the colonies were not being repressed at all except by the short-term Coercive Acts of 1774 provoked by the Boston Tea Party. The Massachusetts colonists actually threw British tea into the harbor because protests were dying down. They hoped a desperate act taken might provoke a reaction and renew protests, and

5 "To Henry Knox," February 3, 1787, *Papers of George Washington*, pp. 8–9.

they succeeded beyond their organizers' wildest dreams. The colonists were already repudiating the extremism of the Tea Party when news arrived of George III's overreaction.

Since the demonstrations took place in the port cities on issues related to taxation, most historians – and even more so, scholars who are not historians – have focused on this issue as the most important in the Revolution. In fact, the explanation does not really make much sense when examined closely.

Without question, George III did face financial problems and needed to raise revenue. Because of the French and Indian Wars, the national debt had risen from 72 million pounds in 1755 to 130 million pounds in 1764.[6] George had good reason to believe that the colonists should contribute to the payment of the debts for a war that seemed to benefit them so much. Moreover, London for the first time was gaining the ability to collect taxes in the colonies themselves.

The king had a strong case to make to the colonists. He could say that they had greatly benefited from the French and Indian War because it allowed them to occupy the rich former French land between the Appalachian Mountains and the Mississippi River. Migration toward the Mississippi would raise defense costs as the colonies faced the Native Americans in the Midwest, the French who controlled the land west of the Mississippi River, and the Spanish who were in charge of New Orleans at the mouth of the Mississippi. The colonists would want to take their crops down the Mississippi River and would be tempted to cross the rich land along the western bank. All this would require defense expenditures that the colonists should pay.

The colonial politicians agreed in principle that the colonies should be taxed for defense. The question was how. London had established a link between taxes and representation when Scotland was forced to join England in 1707. The Scots received relatively few members of Parliament, but also paid lower taxes than the English. The American colonists naturally argued that they too should not have to pay taxes without representation.

As a practical matter, however, Scotland was very different from the mainland colonies. Scotland had 1,250,000 people in 1750 and 1.6 million in 1800. The American colonies had 1.2 million people in 1750, and this figure would grow to 5.3 million in 1800. The colonies were growing much more rapidly than England, and the demographic balance between England

6 Edmund Morgan and Helen Morgan, *The Stamp Act Crisis: Prologue to Revolution* (Chapel Hill: University of North Carolina Press, 1953), p. 21.

and its colonies was changing radically. In 1700, the mainland colonies of the future United States had 5% of the English population, but by 1770 this was 36%.[7]

No formula would produce significant revenue in the New World without a level of colonial representation that no one in Britain wanted. The obvious solution was some kind of colony-wide assembly that voted a collective payment of taxes. Some kind of limited self-rule would solve the representation problem.

George III never took a step in that direction. Instead, he tried to impose the stamp tax used in Great Britain on the colonies. This was a stamp that was placed on all printed material, from government documents to business contracts to books and newspapers. The Stamp Tax was a reasonable tax to extend to the colonies, but it was a terrible tax from a political perspective. It was paid only by the talking class who had the issue of representation to talk about. It led to a political explosion, and the king repealed it.

Rulers often make mistakes, and the results are seldom disastrous, because policy is subsequently modified. The strange – and ultimately disastrous – fact about George III was that he never seemed to learn from his mistakes. Instead, he kept imposing small taxes and then reducing them to insignificant amounts in the face of protests. He wanted a tax that symbolized his right to tax, even though it raised almost no money. The tax only annoyed the colonists. The king's last attempt was a 1773 tax on tea that actually lowered the total tax but benefited the East India Company at a cost to colonial merchants.

The truly disastrous policy of the king – and it really seems the fundamental cause of the revolution – was the Royal Proclamation of 1763 that destroyed his one strong argument for colonial taxation. It forbade colonists from crossing the Appalachian Mountains and settling central and western New York, western Pennsylvania, and all the new land in the Midwest acquired from France. The Royal Proclamation made sense immediately after the end of the war when London needed to organize an administrative system in the huge new territory, but George III never repealed it.

The colonists had assumed, quite accurately, that the French and Indian War had been fought over the issue of their migration to the west. If an

[7] The English figures and general points are from Jacob Price, "The Imperial Economy, 1700–1776," in P. J. Marshall, ed., *Oxford History of the British Empire, 18th Century*, Vol. 2 (Oxford: Oxford University Press, 2001), p. 100. Price rightly includes Nova Scotia among the mainland colonies, and we have adjusted his figures to those found in the latest *Historical Statistics of the United States* that are limited to colonies that entered into the United States. Carter et al., *The Historical Statistics of the United States* (New York: Cambridge University Press, 2006).

acceptable form of taxation could be found, they were willing to help pay for the war and the defense of the territory that was acquired.

But if the colonists could not go beyond the Appalachian Mountains into the French lands, the argument for higher taxes made no sense whatsoever and instead seemed like offensive taunting – a symbol of the king's intention to oppress them. George III came to power in 1759 and had been in power for 16 years in 1775. The American colonists may have thought that he was following Charles's path of strengthening Madrid's control over its colonies at the time.

This is what Clarence Alvord meant a century ago when he said that "two series of events, one eastern and one western" converged to produce an explosion on the eve of the revolution."[8] To a political scientist, it seems wrong to treat the events as being of equal political weight, let alone to emphasize the eastern events with an urban-centered explanation of the American Revolution.

The powerful forces along the coast simply did not want revolution. The merchants were, of course, glad to promote urban unrest against tax increases, but their life centered on the coastal community. They had a vital interest in remaining within the imperial trading zone. After all, if the United States became independent, it became a foreign country with no right to trade with the Caribbean and Canada.

When the situation became politically dangerous, even Boston merchants abandoned support for the tax protests.[9] The New York and Charles Town merchants and elite were always conservative, while the Quaker elite did not want to be involved but had a bias in favor of the status quo.

The ruling planters of the South were not seriously affected by the taxes, and they had little patience with the illegal attack of the Boston Tea Party on property rights. They shared Adam Smith's condemnation of the action on the same grounds. The one surviving letter of George Washington on the subject shows what his foremost biographer calls "positive detachment":[10]

> The Stamp Act imposed on the Colonies by the Parliament of Great Britain expresses the conversation of the speculative part of the Colonists, who look upon this constitutional method of taxation as a direful attack upon their liberties, and loudly

[8] Clarence Walworth Alvord, *The Mississippi Valley in British Politics*, Vol. 2 (Cleveland, OH: Arthur H. Clark Company, 1917), p. 250.

[9] Arthur Schlesinger Sr., *The Colonial Merchants and the American Revolution* (New York: Columbia University Press, 1918).

[10] Douglas Southall Freeman, *George Washington: Planter and Patriot*, Vol. 3 (New York: Charles Scribner's Sons, 1951).

exclaim against the violation; what may be the result of this and some other (and I think, I may add ill-judged) measures, I will not undertake to determine.

While contemporary historians focus on the elected colonial assemblies, which were located in the capital, they do not face the fundamental problem that the legislators were not elected in the capital but in the countryside. The colonies were 95% rural, and the voters were small rural property holders, notably farmers. The deputies in the colonial assemblies had to appeal to their constituents, and their political positions somehow must have reflected constituent grievances. This poses a major problem for an urban-centered interpretation of the Revolution.

Greater attention to the Royal Proclamation of 1763 shifts attention to the electoral base of the Revolution and to the mixed and highly improbable alliance between Anglican slave-owning planters in Virginia and small Puritan farmers in Massachusetts that underlay it. British troops in Montreal prevented the movement of ethnic English colonists from overcrowded New England into central and western New York. This turned Puritan New England into the most revolutionary region.

Yet the Proclamation of 1763 was not enforced in the South where the "foreign emigrants" were moving beyond the Appalachians. Thus, the Proclamation only destroyed the property rights of those who could not collect rents on their western lands. Not by coincidence, George Washington was the country's leading owner of land in the West.

In New England, the resentment and suspicion – even paranoia – produced by London's policy was intensified by a growing conversion of the urban elite to the Anglican Church. As we have seen, this lowered the status of the Congregational ministers, the longtime intellectual elite of the colonies, but they retained a dominant position in the interior. The Congregational ministers preached incessantly against "the terrible threat of episcopacy," and the agitation of the Anglicans for an Anglican bishop became an explosive political issue.

Those who attacked Charles I's conception of the Anglican Church in the 1630 and 1640s generally depicted it as the Catholic Church without a foreign pope. This view was naturally transmitted to the colonies. For this reason, the issue of the Anglican bishop became even more emotional in 1774 when London passed the Quebec Act at the same time as the Coercive Acts. The Quebec Act permitted the Catholic Church to function in Quebec (Canada) and moved the border of Quebec south and west to include the Midwest north of the Ohio River. This allowed agitators to say that the king had the intention of imposing Anglican-Catholic rule on all the mainland colonies.

The Collective Action Problems of Establishing American Independence

It remains a mystery that George III kept making mistakes in his colonial policy over a 10-year period. A rational explanation would be that he never believed the colonies could solve the collective action problems they faced in uniting against him. They were too divided by different economic interests, religious beliefs, and conceptions of property rights. Moreover, they had too strong a need for access to the Caribbean market and would be denied entry if they became foreigners.

The American revolutionaries did, in fact, have a multiplicity of collective action problems. Had the colonists not overcome them, as would have been the case without French assistance, historians naturally would have concluded that the problems were insuperable. It seems most improbable that they overcame them and carried out a successful revolution.

The Collective Action Problems of Colonial Cooperation and the French Solution

The classic collective action obstacle to a successful mass revolution is that an individual cost-benefit calculation makes it irrational for average individuals to participate in a revolution. This was not, however, a problem because the American Revolution was not a mass revolution and did not even arise from a mass demand for independence. The revolutionaries were the leaders of the colonial assemblies.

Unless England would intervene with overwhelming force, the colonial legislatures were the real state in the colonies. They were the ones who controlled military force and taxation. As a result, the individuals with the most severe collective action problems were the opponents of independence. When the police will not defend people and their property, and when the ruling officials provide ideological cover for violence, even persons who are quite indifferent about independence have the incentive to seize homes and stores and/or loot them.

In the past, historians estimated that 80,000 to 100,000 "Tories" voluntarily or involuntarily left the colonies and lost their property in the American Revolution, but Maya Jasanoff recently conducted a painstaking examination of the data and put the number at 60,000 whites plus 15,000 of their slaves.[11]

[11] Maya Jasanoff, *Liberty's Exiles: American Loyalists in the Revolutionary World* (New York: Knopf, 2011), pp. 351–8.

Robert Palmer estimated that five times more people per thousand were exiled in the American Revolution than in the French and that an equal amount of property was expropriated even though France was 10 times larger. Palmer's numbers were based on the old estimates of the number of Tories and should be reduced somewhat, but they still are quite large.[12]

Nevertheless, while the loyalists had collective action problems vis-à-vis the revolutionaries, the legislatures had serious collective action problems in cooperating with each other. The first was how to unite in collective action against the British when the assemblies wanted their own independence, not a powerful United States government. The second arose when the war for independence became irrevocable. How should the costs be divided among themselves? The third was how to ensure that the commanding general of the new Continental Army did not use that army against the state legislatures as Cromwell had against Parliament.

The first revolutionary act of the colonial legislatures was military assistance to Massachusetts during the British siege after the clash at Lexington and Concord in April 1775. The collective action explanation is probably found in a corollary of rational actor analysis seldom mentioned in the literature: politics involves a great deal of posturing. If politicians assume that their opponents are posturing, they may respond by posturing themselves on the assumption that nothing will happen. They may hope for benefits without cost. Many unexpected revolutions and civil wars begin precisely in this way.

Since George III had always backed off from his tax proposals in the face of determined colonial resistance, many colonists probably thought he would do the same thing if the colonies showed determined resistance to the Coercive Acts against Massachusetts. When the assemblies provided armed assistance to Massachusetts, they knew they were quite willing to compromise and to reimburse the East India Company for the tea destroyed in the Tea Party. They were willing to help Britain with its tax revenue problem in exchange for some kind of home rule. Both sides miscalculated the other's response.

The explanation for the solution of the collective action problem of dividing the financial costs of a prolonged war is quite simple: the colonial legislatures never really solved it. When enemy troops were nearby (for example, at Lexington and Concord), the small militia units easily solved

[12] Robert Palmer, *The Age of the Democratic Revolution: A Political History of Europe and America, 1760–1800*, Vol. 1 (Princeton, NJ: Princeton University Press, 1959), p. 188.

their collective action problems and performed extremely well in defending their home territory. When enemy troops were a threat to a state, its assembly appropriated substantial funds.

But when British troops moved away from a state, the legislatures' self-interest in being a free rider became much stronger. New England actively participated at the beginning of the war because the main military action was in Massachusetts and the nearby Hudson Valley. Then it virtually withdrew from the war after 1777 when British troops moved south. The states did not appropriate enough money to sustain the Continental Army until the battle of Yorktown in September and October 1781. They did even less in the period between Yorktown and the peace settlement in 1783.

How then did the Continental Army survive? First, George Washington conducted a low-cost war in which he never engaged British troops in set battle. Instead, he harassed them in skirmishes that minimized his loss of troops and his financial expenses.

The small size of the Continental Army gave Washington the option of living off the land. For example, when the New Jersey legislature once refused to appropriate the funds to feed the troops stationed in the state, Washington simply told them that he was going to seize the food. Washington's major biographer reported that "the magistrates responded promptly and with both patriotism and intelligence."[13] Similarly when Washington was at Valley Forge for the winter of 1777–1778, he simply took the local food that his soldiers needed.[14]

Second, France provided covert aid from the beginning, and a formal alliance resulted in greater support. As John Dull pointed out, the Declaration of Independence was "largely a foreign-policy statement" to allow a formal alliance with France.[15] Once American forces defeated a major British army at Sarasota in October 1777, Britain decided to offer home rule, but France responded by offering a full alliance. There was an additional, unacknowledged reason to accept the French offer. Home rule would require

[13] Douglas Southall Freeman, *George Washington: A Biography*, Vol. 5 (New York: Charles Scribner's Sons, 1952), p. 145.

[14] John Buchanan, *The Road to Valley Forge: How Washington Built the Army that Won the Revolution* (Hoboken, NJ: John Wiley, 2004), p. 287. Later when Washington was in North Carolina, the top smuggler in New Bern is reported to have "lent" a large sum to Washington's army that he must have known would not be repaid. That is, the smuggler surely forgave payment for goods he was supplying the troops because he would not be paid in any case. Mary Stanley Hessel, *Profile of a Patriot: Revolutionary War Privateer* (New Bern, NC: Bagg and Griffin, 1983), pp. 75–80.

[15] Jonathan Dull, *A Diplomatic History of the American Revolution* (New Haven, CT: Yale University Press, 1985), p. 52.

the return of expropriated property to the Tories. Many such as Sam Adams had moved into fine abandoned homes.

The war dragged on for four more years after the September 1777 victory at Saratoga. Ultimately France decided to move from financial aid to direct military intervention in 1781 in one last attempt to end the war. France paid the entire 1781 salary of the Continental Army, sent 10,000 French troops to fight in the decisive battle at Yorktown, and used its ships to lay siege to General Cornwallis's troops and force him to surrender. If the 1781 effort had failed and the French had withdrawn support, Congress almost surely would have had to negotiate home rule.[16]

The Unsuccessful Efforts to Control George Washington

The collective action problem of controlling George Washington is, of course, never discussed in the textbooks and is mentioned only obliquely in most monographs. Yet it unquestionably was on the minds of colonial leaders. Dave Palmer emphasizes a little-discussed aspect of the Constitutional Convention,[17]

> The ghost participating in the Constitutional Convention was Oliver Cromwell.... The delegates in debates very carefully avoided referring to any [live person] by name.... But historic figures were fair game. Cromwell led the list of men whose names surfaced most often.... The ghost of Oliver Cromwell brought long shivers – and an abiding determination never to permit its reincarnation.

Like Oliver Cromwell, George Washington controlled the army of the legislature. Both men were to complain bitterly about non-payment of the army's salaries. Washington became increasingly insistent after the war on the failure of Congress to make good on its promise to pay officers back payment after the war.

Washington tried to create the impression that he was above the fray, but a former aide, Gouverneur Morris, spoke quite differently about the general at his funeral in 1799. Washington's widow and friends were in attendance, and it is unlikely Morris would have made the following statement unless it was true:[18]

16 For the events leading to Yorktown, see Barbara Tuchman, *The First Salute* (New York: Knopf, 1988).

17 Dave Palmer, *1794: America, Its Army, and the Birth of the Nation* (Novato, CA: Presidio Press, 1994), pp. 54–8, 94, and 103.

18 Gouverneur Morris, *An Oration upon the Death of General Washington* (New York: John Firman, 1800), p. 4. John Marshall wrote the first biography based on Washington's papers, and he made the same point.

> Heaven ... had given [him] the tumultuous passions which accompany greatness, and frequently tarnish its lustre. With them was his first contest and his first victory was over himself.... Calmness of manner and of conduct distinguished him through life. Yet, those who have seen him strongly moved, will bear witness that his wrath was terrible; they have seen boiling in his bosom, passion almost too mighty for man; yet, when just bursting into act, that strong passion was controuled by his stronger mind.

In 1799, Morris and everyone else knew that Washington had kept his emotions under control and had been an extremely restrained leader. This was not widely known in 1776.

George Washington was an Anglican vestryman from Virginia who aroused special fears in New England. The editor of the first edition of his complete works found that Washington had the old "Cavalier-Roundhead prejudice" – that is, the 17th-century Anglican attitude toward Puritans.[19] In 1775, Washington wrote another Virginian with contempt about those from Massachusetts under his command. There is, he said, "an unaccountable kind of stupidity in the lower class of these people which believe me prevails but too generally among the Officers of the Massachusetts part of the Army, who are ne(ar)ly of the same Kidney with the Privates."[20] It seems likely he let his attitude show in public, too.

At first, the Congress tried to control Washington by denying him the power to appoint generals and by retaining this power for itself – or, rather, for the respective states. As early as July 1775, John Adams wrote that it was "against every proper Rule and Principle" that Washington be allowed to appoint his quartermaster general and other top commissary officers: "As these officers are Checks upon the General, and he a Check upon them: there ought not to be too much connection between them." In fact, Washington's quartermaster general became a leading member of the 1777 conspiracy to replace him with Adams's favorite general, Horatio Gates. It is not hard to imagine who selected him.[21]

States also controlled the appointment of line officers, and each had a quota of generals proportionate to the number of troops that it contributed.

[19] John Fitzpatrick, *George Washington Himself* (Indianapolis, IN: Bobbs-Merrill, 1933), p. 335.

[20] "To Richard Henry Lee," August 29, 1775, in W. W. Abbot, ed., *The Papers of George Washington, Revolutionary War Series*, Vol. 1 (Charlottesville: University Press of Virginia, 1985), p. 372.

[21] E. Wayne Carp, *To Starve the Army at Pleasure: Continental Army Administration and American Political Culture* (Chapel Hill: University of North Carolina Press, 1984), pp. 21 and 25; Kenneth Rossum, *Thomas Mifflin and the Politics of the American Revolution* (Chapel Hill: University of North Carolina Press, 1952).

Benedict Arnold was the best general in the war, but at first Washington could not promote him to major general because Arnold's state (Connecticut) had filled its quota. Then when Arnold was promoted, Washington could not give him a top command post if an earlier-promoted general was to serve under him.[22]

Nevertheless, Congress also desired to control Washington – even to remove him – for another reason. In the spring of 1776, France told the Americans that an alliance was conditional on the appointment of one of its top generals to replace Washington. New England's representatives in France, Arthur Lee and Silas Deane, both supported this demand, and Washington knew of their position. He had to suspect – perhaps even know – that they were speaking for important New England politicians.[23]

By the fall of 1776, Deane began offering commissions to high French officers who then were attached to the leading American generals to control them. The Marquis de Lafayette, a family friend of the top French general, was assigned to Washington, and Thomas Conway was assigned to Washington's main rival, Horatio Gates.[24] When Gates defeated the British at Saratoga in October 1777 shortly after Washington lost at Philadelphia, Washington's opponents moved forcefully against him with Gates and Conway as willing partners.[25]

Congress transformed the War Board of the Congress into a military command organization superior to Washington. It quickly replaced Washington's allies with Gates's men and named Gates head of the board.

[22] "To John Hancock," May 12 1777, in *The Papers of George Washington*, Vol. 9, pp. 396–8. See also pp. 349 and 368–9.

[23] See the letters in Friedrich Kapp, *The Life of John Kalb: Major-General in the Revolutionary War* (New York: Henry Holt, 1884), pp. 94–7, 127, and 131. For a letter by Deane supporting Broglie and a discussion of earlier historians who had not found the letter "politic to discuss," see Francis Wharton, *The Revolutionary Diplomatic Correspondence of the United States*, Vol. 2 (Washington, DC: Government Printing Office, 1889), pp. 218–21. Letters from Washington to John Hancock, May 18, 1776, and May 19, 1776, mentioning "matters of intelligence of the most interesting nature" may refer to this. *The Papers of George Washington*, Vol. 4, pp. 333–4 and 341. Also see Louise Dunbar, *A Study of "Monarchical" Tendencies in the United States from 1776 to 1801* (Urbana: University of Illinois Press, 1923), pp. 26–37.

[24] For the debate on the subject of Lafayette's real role, see Louis Gottschalk, *Lafayette Comes to America* (Chicago: University of Chicago Press 1935), pp. 149–52. Lafayette obviously knew why he was sent, but he may have decided that since Thomas Conway was linked with Horatio Gates, his own best option was to bind himself to Washington.

[25] Dunbar, *A Study of "Monarchical" Tendencies*, pp. 34–5; Paul David Nelson, *General Horatio Gates: A Biography* (Baton Rouge: Louisiana State University Press, 1976), pp. 48–9 and 58–62. Samuel White Patterson, *Horatio Gates: Defender of American Liberties* (New York: Columbia University Press, 1947), pp. 48–50, 63, and 64.

Conway was appointed inspector general, a post responsible to Congress and not Washington. The decision to place a War Board dominated by a hostile Gates over Washington was made by a Congress in which each state had a single vote. Congress took the anti-Washington decisions over a three-month period, and members of Congress understood their meaning and the significance of the issue. A majority of states clearly supported the action.

Many modern historians are loath to acknowledge a serious effort by John Adams and Congress to remove Washington, especially one based on Anglican-Puritan antagonisms. Hence, they seldom discuss the implications of the votes in Congress. Historians early in the 20th century felt freer to discuss ethnic and religious tensions among European-Americans both in colonial and modern times. It may even be they also knew, in the words of Paul David Nelson, that "this military controversy reflected deep divisions among congressmen about the very nature of the Revolution."[26]

The actual events are, however, quite visible, and they cast a clearly defined shadow. This was the winter when Washington stationed his troops at Valley Forge, a politically strategic locale close to the Congress that was trying to humiliate him into resigning. After his arrival at Valley Forge on December 1777, Congress could not even deny him supplies because he lived off the land. This "self-supply" dramatized Washington's willingness to use extra-legal measures to stay in office.

The standoff was resolved when the leader of the opposition, John Adams, was exiled as envoy to Paris. The motion about Adams was introduced in Congress by 24-year-old Gouverneur Morris, a close ally of Washington. Adams was "flabbergasted" at the decision to send him to France and resisted mightily. He later wrote in a letter that "he had as many thoughts of a Voyage to the Moon as to France."[27] Despite his pleas, Adams was forced to sail across the wintry Atlantic into exile in Paris for the duration of the war.[28] He continually agitated to return but was not allowed to do so.

[26] Nelson, *General Horatio Gates*, p. 61. Jonathan Rossie, *The Politics of Command in the American Revolution* (Syracuse: Syracuse University Press, 1975). For a succinct summary of events that reflects the general modern disbelief about a concerted effort against Washington, see Buchanan, *The Road to Valley Forge*, pp. 290–302.

[27] James Hutson, *John Adams and the Diplomacy of the American Revolution* (Lexington: University Press of Kentucky, 1980), p. 34. "Flabbergasted" is Hutson's word, and he is the one who quotes the Adams letter. See also Page Smith, *John Adams*, Vol. 1 (Garden City, NY: Doubleday, 1962), pp. 349–53.

[28] David McCullough's biography of Adams reports that no one wanted to sail across the North Atlantic in winter, all the more so because of the danger of capture by the British. He provides a graphic description of the hardships of the trip. He does not mention the

The struggle over control of the Continental Army and George Washington's victory had profound consequences. In revolutions, radicals often defeat the moderates who launched the revolution and thereby transform it, but Washington's defeat of the radicals prevented any such a development in the United States. Moreover, the continued loyalty of these officers to Washington enabled him to call a Constitutional Convention and overthrow the Articles of Confederation.

The structure of military power that emerged during the revolution and continued in place afterward was the main reason that the new United States did not have the chaos or near-chaos that most countries (for example, Mexico) experience during a Civil War or War of Independence. In the United States, the states remained real states with control over the militia and taxation unless British troops were in control. This made them quite stable, except when war was actually raging. Washington had the military force to maintain cohesion at the national level and prevent conflict among the states.

The Collective Action Problems of George III

Ultimately, when a conflict reaches the stage of military action, the victory belongs to the side best able to "organize the greatest capacity for violence." Or, actually, it belongs to the side that best organizes and maintains the means of violence at its disposal. In the case of the American Revolution, the side with the greatest capacity for violence was obviously Great Britain. It had driven France off the American continent in 1763. France was delighted to use limited means to drive Britain from its colonies south of the Great Lakes, but it did not want to renew a war against a determined Great Britain.

Nevertheless, rulers on both sides should wage war on the basis of a cost-benefit analysis. The problems of collective action should make impossible a revolution against a ruler who maintains a comparative advantage in violence and has the willingness to use it. The word "willingness" points to the key cost-benefit decision of the stronger.

Indeed, this view of revolution was not invented by collective action theorists. The philosopher Hannah Arendt wrote that "no revolution is even possible where the authority of the body politic is truly intact, and this means, under modern conditions, where the armed forces can be trusted to obey the civil authorities." Theda Skocpol, a famous sociologist of revolutions,

reason for the trip or Adams's concrete actions against Washington. David McCullough, *John Adams* (New York: Simon and Schuster, 2001), pp. 175–88.

agreed that a regime can always remain stable "if its coercive organization remains coherent and effective."[29]

In the 1930s, Crane Brinton, a top historian of the American and the three major European revolutions – the English, French, and Russian – made a classic statement on the subject. In Brinton's words, "It is almost safe to say that no government is likely to be overthrown until it loses the ability to make adequate use of its military and police powers."[30] Brinton attached special importance to the loss of a belief at the top that maintaining the status quo was worth the loss of life it would require:[31]

> When numerous and influential members of [a ruling class] begin to believe that they hold power unjustly, or that all men are brothers, equal in the eyes of eternal justice, or that the beliefs they were brought up on are silly, or that "after us the deluge," they are not likely to resist successfully any serious attacks on their social, economic, and political power.... When those of them who hold positions of power [do] use force, they [use] it sporadically and inefficiently.

Of course, these explanations of revolution "from above" cannot totally ignore the pressures "from below." A sense of illegitimacy among those in power does not develop in a vacuum but can be affected by the intensity of popular discontent or the abandonment by the intellectuals. This is particularly true when those in the streets are the children and grandchildren of those who must give the order to shoot.[32] Even soldiers may be reluctant to fire upon demonstrators whose grievances, ethnicity, or religion they share.

Without question, there was pressure from below in the American colonies from 1765 to 1776 and then during the War of Independence. Indeed, since the chief revolutionaries were the legislators of the colonial assemblies located in the capital, they had to be responsive to the grievances and emotions of their voters.

29 Hannah Arendt, *On Revolution* (New York: Viking Press, 1963), p. 112; Theda Skocpol, *States and Social Revolutions: A Comparative Analysis of France, Russia, and China* (Cambridge: Cambridge University Press, 1979), p. 32.

30 Crane Brinton, *The Anatomy of Revolution* (New York: W.W. Norton, 1938), p. 289. On pp. 110–11, Brinton had tentatively suggested an even more extreme hypothesis that included the word "ever." Specifically, he wrote that "No government has ever fallen before revolutionists until it has lost control over its armed forces or lost the ability to use them effectively; and conversely ... no revolutionists have ever succeeded until they have got a predominance of effective armed force on their side."

31 Brinton, *The Anatomy of Revolution*, pp. 64–5. Mikhail Gorbachev and the collapse of the Soviet Union can be analyzed precisely in these terms. See Jerry F. Hough, *Democratization and Revolution in the USSR, 1985–1991* (Washington, DC: Brookings Institution, 1997).

32 Jerry F. Hough, "The Logic of Collective Action and the Pattern of Revolutionary Behavior," *Journal of Soviet Nationalities* 2 (1990), 46–59.

Brinton's emphasis on the loss of self-confidence of a ruler and ruling elite naturally fits the American situation well, because it was one of the cases in his book. The only reasonable explanation for the Royal Proclamation of 1763 was that George III was not confident of his ability to control a colonial empire that extended to the Mississippi River.

Indeed, in 1763, the cabinet approved a Board of Trade Report that expressed a fear of the possible economic and political independence of colonists living in the West. The cabinet recommended that colonists be prohibited from settling beyond the Appalachians and that the area be left a vast Native American reserve as it had been under the French. George III must have retained this fear even as colonists began migrating into the future Kentucky and Tennessee in the 1770s.

But George III did not feel confident enough about his policies to use sufficient military power to impose them in a ruthless manner against the colonies. For nearly a decade, George III had repeatedly retreated in the face of colonial opposition before overreacting to the Boston Tea Party. He never stationed enough troops in Kentucky and Tennessee to stop the migration of colonists. And after the Continental Army was formed, he never acted as if he believed that the control of the colonies was worth the bloodshed that would make victory certain.

George III was right, in that it was irrational to use maximum force in the colonies, all the more so if he did not think he could control the West afterward. As is so often the case, Adam Smith provides an excellent insight into elite thinking in London at the time. *The Wealth of Nations* presented two strong reasons to give independence to the colonies.

The first reason was royal revenue. Smith stated that the sole purpose of colonization was to provide a market for British manufactured goods and thereby increase the revenue from the increased production. This argument was not historically accurate, but Smith was trying to persuade the king that he was wrong in opposing an expansion of the American market.

The second reason Smith gave to the king involved a foreign policy that extended beyond a short-term alliance with France:[33]

> Great Britain would not only be immediately free from the whole annual expence of the peace establishment of the colonies, but might settle with them such a treaty of commerce as would effectually secure to her a free trade, more advantageous to the great body of the people, though less so to the merchants, than the monopoly which she at present enjoys.

[33] Adam Smith, *The Wealth of Nations* (New York: Bantam Dell, 2003), p. 783.

By thus parting good friends, the natural affection of the colonies to the mother country, which, perhaps, our late dissensions have well nigh extinguished, would quickly revive. It might dispose them not only to respect, for whole centuries together, that treaty of commerce which they had concluded with us at parting, but to favour us in war as well as in trade, and, instead of turbulent and factious subjects, to become our most faithful, affectionate, and generous allies.

Nowhere else in *The Wealth of Nations* were Smith's predictions more accurate than those in the second paragraph about the foreign policy the United States would follow, even in the distant 20th century.

Obviously George III did not agree with Smith in 1775 and 1776. Even when he decided to recognize American independence in 1781, he delayed a commerce treaty that would re-open his Caribbean colonies to American shippers. He agreed only in 1794 when a new war with France forced him to accept the Jay Treaty that gave the colonists access to the other British colonies, including Canada, which they had lost when they became a foreign country for Britain. Britain waited 70 years before following Smith's advice to end grain tariffs.

Yet Smith's views seemed to have been widely enough accepted within London's elite to undercut the king's willingness to apply the force needed to crush the Revolution. When colonial forces defeated General John Burgoyne in the Battle of Saratoga in October 1777, George III agreed to offer the colonists home rule. At the same time, he signaled approval of Smith – and implicitly his idea – by naming him the tax collector in Edinburgh. The offer of home rule was rejected, but the offer could never really be withdrawn as the basis for a postwar settlement. Draconian repression of the colonists would be even more unthinkable if the purpose was to give them home rule.

The Collective Action Problems of Convening the Constitutional Convention

Nearly all historians depict the Constitutional Convention as a social contract. The country – or at least the broad elite – supposedly decided to create a new stronger government when they realized the government of the Articles of Confederation was ineffective. A collective action theorist would, however, instinctively doubt that such an important change could take place by a simple voluntary collective decision to come to Philadelphia.

This doubt is especially strong since many states feared George Washington as chief executive and commander in chief of the military. In fact, when Washington had used his chief aides, James Madison and

Alexander Hamilton, to call a similar convention at Annapolis, Maryland the previous September, only twelve delegates from five states had come.

Despite this widespread fear of George Washington as commander in chief, the crucial figure missing from almost all discussion of the Constitutional Convention and its origins is George Washington.[34] However, Washington actually was the key figure in the whole process. The states knew that Washington retained the loyalty of the officer corps, and many states feared his army more than they did the British. This is why so many were reluctant to create a government with a chief executive and commander in chief.

The issue came to a head in the winter of 1782–1783, when the officers apparently came close to a rebellion in March 1783 in the so-called Newburgh Conspiracy. Washington quelled it, if quelled is the right word.[35] In reality, Washington only called on the officers at Newburgh to be patient since Congress by its nature is forced to act deliberately. He declared that Congress would offer "compleat justice" to the officers and pledged "in the most unequivocal manner, to exert whatever ability I am possessed of, in your favor."[36] He did not specify what he would do if Congress did not provide "compleat justice."

Washington's control of the "instruments of violence" was, we argue, the crucial fact in the 1780s. Nevertheless, he provides a superb example of the way in which a wise man with full control of an area's dominant military forces still tries to create legitimacy for a drastic action before he takes it.

After the Newburgh rebellion, Washington undertook a four-year campaign during which he not only allowed pressure to build, but also increased it himself. The process began in April 1783 when word arrived in the United States that a peace agreement had been reached in Paris. In the next month Washington formed the Society of the Cincinnati, an organization of former officers. Washington became its president, and his most trusted military aide, Henry Knox, its organizational officer.

This created great concern. Cincinnatus had been a general who returned to civilian life after a war only to be given political power despite his desires.

[34] For the almost total failure of a major scholar to mention him in a 40-page chapter, see Jack Rakove, *The Beginnings of National Politics: An Interpretative History of the Constitutional Convention* (New York: Knopf, 1979), 360–399.

[35] The origins and details of the "conspiracy" remain murky and controversial. See Richard Kohn, "The Inside History of the Newburgh Conspiracy: America and the Coup d'Etat," *William and Mary Quarterly* 27 (1970), 187–220; Merrill Jensen, *The New Nation: A New History of the United States during the Confederation 1781–1789* (New York: Knopf, 1950), 54–84.

[36] "To the Officers of the Army," March 15, 1783, Fitzpatrick, *The Writings of George Washington*, Vol. 26, pp. 222–7.

John Jay, soon to become secretary for Foreign Affairs, stated privately that "if the Society of the Cincinnati did take well in the United States, he [Jay] should not care whether the Revolution has succeeded or not." Washington himself reported that New England was alarmed.[37]

The peace treaty obligated the United States to repay pre-revolutionary debts to private English citizens – in practice, merchants and Loyalists. Congress had no independent source of revenue, and the states refused to appropriate money for the purpose. In response, the British refused to evacuate 10 forts on the American side of the border until the debt was paid. The forts were used to provide covert aid to the Native Americans.

Washington was outraged. In June 1783, he sent each governor an uncompromising and threatening "Circular to State Governments." The United States must have, he said, "an indissoluble Union of the States under one Federal Head," "a sacred regard to Public Justice," and "the adoption of a proper Peace Establishment." By "peace establishment," Washington meant "the Militia of the Union" with uniform structure, discipline, and arms in all states. By "public justice," he meant fulfillment of the promise to pay creditors (mainly the foreign debt promised in the peace treaty) and to pay the officers and the soldiers. If any state would refuse to comply with the requisitions of funds, he said, it "will be responsible for all the consequences."[38]

Washington relinquished command of the troops in December 1783, but he continued to speak out. In January 1784, he wrote of "the jealous and contracted temper which seems to prevail in some of the States" and "the present unsettled and deranged state of public Affairs." He professed optimism that "the good sense of the People will ultimately get the better of their prejudices ... though ... not so soon as one would wish."[39]

By 1786, Washington felt that the point had arrived at which action was possible. In January 1786, James Madison began pushing for a convention in Annapolis in September to discuss a change in the Articles of Confederation. In the minds of modern Americans, Madison and

[37] For Cincinnatus, see Michael Hillyard, *Cincinnatus and the Citizen-Servant Ideal: The Roman Legend's Life, Times, and Legacy* (Philadelphia: Xlibris, 2001). For a summary of the Society and the attitude toward it, see North Callahan, *Henry Knox: George Washington's General* (New York: Rinehart, 1958), pp. 210–226. The Jay quote is on p. 229. For Washington's awareness of New England's views, see "To Nathaniel Greene," in *The Papers of George Washington*, Vol. 1, p. 236.

[38] "Circular to the States," June 8, 1783, Fitzpatrick, *The Writings of George Washington*, pp. 483–96. The threatening quote is on p. 490.

[39] "To John Trumbull, Jr.," January 5, 1784, in *The Papers of George Washington*, Vol. 1, pp. 12–13.

Alexander Hamilton are giants who stride across the 1780s and 1790s. In fact, Hamilton became Washington's political aide for the North during the Revolutionary War and Madison his chief political aide for the South around 1781. They were quite young – Hamilton was 24 years old in 1781 and Madison was 30.

In short, everyone knew that Madison and Hamilton spoke for Washington and that Washington really was calling the convention in Annapolis. On March 16, 1786, Secretary for Foreign Affairs John Jay wrote Washington to plead to him with "fervor … to favor your country with your counsels" on the forthcoming Annapolis convention and revision of the Articles of Confederation. Washington said he agreed "perfectly" that "there are errors in our National Government which call for correction; loudly I will add." But then he expressed doubt that, tactically at least, "the remedies are at hand":[40]

> My fear is that the people are not sufficiently misled to retract from error.… That it is necessary to revise, and amend the articles of Confederation, I entertain no Doubt.… Something must be done, or the fabrick must fall. It certainly is tottering! Ignorance & design are difficult to combat. Out of these proceed illiberality, improper jealousies, and a train of evils which oftentimes, in republican governments, must be sorely felt before they can be removed.

When Jay asserted in late June that "our affairs seem to lead to some crisis – some Revolution," Washington replied: "your sentiments, that our affairs are drawing rapidly to a crisis, accord with my own." Washington denounced the states in harsh terms: "If you tell the Legislatures they have violated the treaty of peace and invaded the prerogatives of the confederacy they will laugh in your face." Washington then talked about a coup in the indirect way he loved:[41]

> It is much to be feared, as you observe, that the better kind of people being disgusted with the circumstances will have their minds prepared for any revolution whatever.… I am told that even respectable characters speak of a monarchical form of government without horror. From thinking proceeds speaking, thence to acting is often but a single step. But how irrevocable & tremendous! … Would to God that wise measures may be taken in time to avert the consequences we have but too much reason to apprehend.… I frankly acknowledge I cannot feel myself an unconcerned spectator.

40 "From John Jay," March 16, 1786, and "To John Jay," May 18, 1786. *The Papers of George Washington*, Vol. 3, p. 601, and Vol. 4, pp. 55–6 and 131.

41 "From John Jay," June 27, 1786, and "To John Jay," August 15, 1786, in *The Papers of George Washington*, Vol. 4, pp. 131 and 212–13.

Hamilton and Madison echoed these fears about monarchy in early 1787.[42]

Naturally Washington ended his letter with the pious statement that no one cared what he thought and that he could not become involved. Yet no one was talking about a return of George III. There was only one potential "monarch" on the scene. When only twelve delegates appeared at the Annapolis convention, Madison and Hamilton almost immediately called for another convention, this time in Philadelphia in May 1787.

The meaning of the place and time that Madison and Hamilton – and implicitly Washington – chose for the Philadelphia convention could not have been clearer. The Society of the Cincinnati was scheduled to hold its convention in Philadelphia in May 1787. These were the retired officers who had been damning Congress for years and calling for a military coup. Unless the proposed constitutional convention took "wise measures in time," Washington was clearly signaling there would be "consequences we have but too much reason to apprehend."

Over the next six months Washington repeatedly asserted he would not attend the convention, and many historians take these statements seriously – much too seriously, we think. Madison and Hamilton continued to refer to the danger of monarchy, and Washington's letters to his chief military aide, the 37-year-old Secretary for War Henry Knox, became increasingly insistent.

Constitutional amendments to the Articles of Confederation required a unanimous vote of the states. On February 3, 1787, Washington recognized this in a letter to Knox when he insisted that the Articles must be altered by extra-constitutional means:[43]

> The legality of this [Philadelphia] Convention I do not mean to discuss – nor how problematical the issue of it may be. That powers are wanting, none can deny. Through what medium they are to be derived, will, like other matters, engage public attention. That which takes the shortest course to obtain them, will, in my opinion, under present circumstances, be found best. Otherwise, like a house on fire, whilst the most regular mode of extinguishing it is contending for, the building is reduced to ashes….
>
> However constitutionally it may be for Congress to point out the defects of the federal System, I am strongly inclined to believe that it would not be found the most efficatious channel for the recommendation, more especially the alterations, to flow – for reasons too obvious to enumerate.

Washington's earlier-cited scorn for "the darling Sovereignties of the States individually" is found in this letter to Knox. Three weeks later, Washington

42 Dunbar, *A Study of "Monarchical Tendencies."*

43 "To Henry Knox," February 3, 1787, *The Papers of George Washington*, Vol. 5, pp. 8–9.

wrote to Knox that "our Affairs ... seem really, to be approaching to some awful crisis. God only knows what the result will be. It shall be my part to hope for the best." But he also explained to Knox his general views on the importance of political timing: "It is among the evils, and perhaps is not the smallest, of democratical governments, that the people must *feel*, before they will *see*. When this happens, they are roused to action."[44] Earlier in this letter of March 8th, Washington told Knox that "I wish to see [the convention in Philadelphia] tried." But then he hinted at the reason:

> After which if the present government is not efficient, conviction of the propriety of a change will disseminate through every rank and class of people [and it] may be brought about in peace. Till which [time], however necessary it may appear in the eyes of the more discerning, my opinion is, that it cannot be effected without great contention and much confusion.

On the same day, Washington sent almost the identical letter to one of his favorite former aides, David Humphreys.[45] Humphreys was serving as head of the Connecticut militia and obviously was keeping New England politicians informed about Washington's thinking. In his letters to Knox and Humphreys, Washington did not explicitly specify the kind of change whose propriety would be accepted if a new constitution were not adopted. Yet the only change that was possible if the convention failed was a coup. This letter made clear Washington's conviction that, in such an eventuality, it would be accepted without unrest or great contention.

At the end of March, when Washington had predictably announced his decision to attend the convention, he made the point with total clarity to his closest aide, James Madison. This time, however, he warned that he was talking about a "monarchical government" – that is, a military coup – [but] the period is not arrived for adopting the change without shaking the Peace of this Country to its foundation." Then Washington decisively informed Madison about the consequences of a failure of the Convention:[46]

> A thorough reform of the present system is indispensable ... and with hand and heart I hope the business will be essayed in a full Convention.... [If] after this essay is made if the system proves inefficient, conviction of the necessity of a change will be dissiminated among all classes of the People – Then and not till then, in my opinion can it be attempted without involving all the evils of civil discord.

[44] "To Henry Knox," February 25, 1787, and "To Henry Knox," March 8, 1787, in *The Papers of George Washington*, Vol. 5, pp. 52 and 74.

[45] "To David Humphreys," March 8, 1787, *The Papers of George Washington*, Vol. 5, pp. 72–3.

[46] "To James Madison," March 31, 1787, in *The Papers of George Washington*, Vol. 5, p. 115.

"Not till then" was a convention that would begin in five weeks!

These communications of Washington to his closest aides over a number of months are vitally important for our understanding of the Constitutional Convention and Washington's role. Washington still preferred to legitimize the kind of government he wanted by wrapping it in civilian form and by letting the states choose between "consent" and an open military coup. He did not want to set the precedent for a military coup by a northern president after he was gone.

Washington's aides knew from private conversation what he was thinking, and his letters to them really were providing them with talking points on a month-to-month basis that they should use with others. No other example can better illuminate the way in which changes in values and "consent" can arise from the perception of what is inevitable or nearly inevitable.

Anyone who emphasizes "negotiations" or "consent" must understand the general applicability of this specific point about Washington. The "consent" or the outcome of negotiations does not simply emerge spontaneously nor is it the result of a disinterested discussion of the common good. No political system, economic system, or political leader is absolutely ideal in anyone's eyes. Instead, people always "consent" to the lesser evil as they perceive it, and the task of great leaders is not limited to defending their own proposal. It also entails convincing people to think – and, as Washington put it, to "feel" – that other alternatives are worse.

The U.S. Constitution of 1787 and the Reestablishment of a Confederate Government

When scholars try to explain the economic and political success of the United States in the 18th and 19th centuries, they almost always point to its federal structure as a major factor. We fully agree that federalism was crucial in promoting political stability and economic growth in the United States, but this begs the question as to why it was successful in the United States, and not in Mexico in the 1800s.

The answer is far from obvious. The colonists had gained no experience in operating a federal system during the colonial period. London did not create either a federal or confederate system – but only separate colonies, each with its own governor. Indeed, even as the colonies began stretching to the Mississippi River and had a population of 2.5 million people, the Hanover kings made a deliberate decision not to appoint a super-governor or colony-wide assembly to oversee and coordinate the governors or assemblies of the individual assemblies. As has been seen, the Duke of Newcastle flatly rejected this proposal on the grounds that the colonists would gain a sense of common interests and would learn to work together.

As a result, the colonial politicians never gained any experience of negotiating and working together with each other to accomplish common goals until the illegal Continental Congresses of 1774 and 1775. They had no opportunity to develop mutual trust, and the strong mutual suspicions of George Washington and John Adams toward each other were the natural result. They were far from unique.

What then was the essence of American federalism that was established by the Constitution and the reasons it made such a positive contribution to American development? In Chapters 4 and 7, we hinted at a key, if paradoxical, reason: the lack of any colonial experience with federalism. Instead, the colonial politicians learned how to run strong states, to use the word with which they labeled themselves in 1776. The colonies had their individual legislatures, taxing power, and military forces. The states retained this system of governance in the dozen years of the Articles of Confederation, but without the constraints imposed by London.

The Constitution that was created in 1787 basically retained this system. George Washington controlled the Constitutional Convention and he had two goals. The first was to create a national government with a chief executive who had a dominant role in foreign and defense policy and a modicum of independent funding to support this goal. The second was to create a government that would deny the more populous North the power to impose its will on the South after he was gone.

Washington knew that his own control of the military prevented any danger from the North while he was alive, and he wanted a Constitution that would protect the South in the future. As a person with a keen instinctive understanding of the problems of collective action, he began with the two points emphasized by Olson – and by North in his definition of the state: control of the military and control of the taxes to finance the military.

The key decision of the Constitutional Convention was to decentralize military power to the state level. The state militias that existed during the colonial period, the Revolution, and the 1780s were to remain the dominant military force after 1787. Madison repeatedly denounced a standing army at the Convention, and he spoke for Washington. A large standing army might be commanded by some future northern general.

The Bill of Rights dramatically showed the importance of this measure. The First Amendment prohibited either section from imposing its religion on the other. The Second Amendment, and it was the second in importance, guaranteed that the states could retain "a well-regulated Militia." The next section of the amendment gave the reason: such a militia was "necessary to the security of a free State." "State" was used only to refer to the states and not to the nation as a whole.

The Constitution did make the president commander in chief of the army, but his central military power was the right to call the militias "into the actual Service of the United States" and to command those who were mobilized. Ultimately, however, the states made the decision about whether to permit their militias to be mobilized. After the Gulf States declared independence in 1860, the states of the upper South made the key decision when they refused to let Lincoln mobilize their militias.

The second measure was the decentralization of taxing power to the state level – or, rather, to leave it at the state level. The federal government was given little more than the tariff. The tariff provided 90% of federal revenues for nearly a century, and the revenues were not enough to have a significant standing army or even navy. When the Congress tried to pass an income tax in the late 1800s, the Supreme Court declared it unconstitutional. A constitutional amendment (the Sixteenth) was needed to legalize an income tax. The United States had an active industrial policy and some social welfare – but only at the state level.

The third measure to protect the South was the creation of a very weak central government in the domestic sphere. We agree with Alexander von Humboldt's argument that the Constitution established a confederation in the domestic sphere. Indeed, the main domestic question the federal government could decide was tariff rates. It really was foreign economic policy. When the South tried to justify its fear of Abraham Lincoln, the only threatening power it could find was his ability to appoint postmasters in the South. The danger, the southern leaders said, was that northern postmasters might let abolitionists send propaganda through the southern mails!

Washington had Madison structure the new federal government in a way that would protect the South if the distribution of military and taxing power made the Constitution effective. The basic problem was that the North had a much larger white population, and even the three-fifths credit for southern slaves left this majority in place. The North also had one more state under the Articles of Confederation: 7 to 6. Hence the so-called Great Compromise of having one house based on population and the other based on an equal number of senators from each state would leave the North with a majority in both houses.

When other English, white-dominated colonies became independent, they instituted the British parliamentary system with majority rule, but the American Founders introduced a system of checks and balances that went far beyond the restraints that a modern American can even imagine. The checks and balances were designed to give the South a veto on all legislation and the election of the president.

The most basic fact about the Constitution was a seemingly innocuous unwritten provision that could not be acknowledged publicly. There would be an even number of slave and non-slave states. Least of all could it be mentioned in *The Federalist Papers* that were written to promote ratification in New York, one of the states harmed by the equal-state rule.

The decision on the equal number of slave and non-slave states arose from a crisis in the Congress in 1776. The Articles of Confederation had 13 states and only six of them retained slavery. In 1786 a crisis erupted in the Congress over a commercial treaty with Spain that the North wanted. The West and most of the South wanted to make the treaty conditional upon the opening of the Mississippi River, but they lost 7 to 5 in the Congress, with Delaware abstaining. The southern states knew this could always happen with an uneven number of states. The delegates to the convention agreed to begin with 12 states in 1789 and raise the number to 16 almost immediately.[47]

The peculiar decision to give the vice president a deciding vote in the Senate in case of a tie was also based on the informal agreement about having an equal number of slave and non-slave states. The problem with the veto in the Senate was that a southern senator might be absent and an anti-South law might be passed. When the missing senator returned, a bill reversing the law would fail on a tie vote. But a vice president could cast the deciding vote to overturn the offending law. So long as the president and vice president were from different sections, each section had a "presidential" veto, one in the White House and the other in the evenly divided Senate.

Obviously the number of states would not remain at 16, and until 1850, northern and southern states were essentially admitted as a pair. They were not admitted at exactly the same time, but the balance was always restored before a presidential election that might be competitive. The Congress had to approve the constitution of any new state. Each was required to be a republic and to have its own militia. In practice, this combination meant that the governors would be commanders of the states' militias.

47 When the new Congress opened in 1789, the original northern states were Connecticut, Massachusetts, New Hampshire, New Jersey, New York, and Pennsylvania. The slave states were Delaware, Georgia, Maryland, North Carolina, South Carolina, and Virginia. The new northern states were Rhode Island, and the new southern states were Kentucky and Tennessee.

But a key provision in the Constitution was whether slavery was permitted or not. This was the question that made the free soil issue so explosive. If slave-holders could not bring slaves into the territory, its inhabitants were scarcely likely to legalize slavery in the Constitution. Then the admission process for Kansas in 1850s showed that competing constitutions were also possible.

Of course, the real potential danger both to the South and the North was posed by the president as commander in chief. If he had sufficient military power at his disposal, he could simply overthrow the Congress. The dispersal of military force to the states was some protection, but a president could mobilize the militias of his section of states to use against the other. That is precisely what Lincoln did in 1861.

The natural solution to this problem was to have a sectional veto in the selection of the president. Indeed, the natural solution was to have the Congress select the president and to require that both houses concur in his election. This would automatically introduce the sectional veto that existed within the Senate and should ensure that the president would be a moderate. The losing section could demand the vice president as the price for its agreement.

That was precisely what the delegates of the Congress wanted, but George Washington did not wish to be elected by the Congress. He said it would be undignified, but surely he feared he would have to defer to the Congress in his first term if he wanted a second and perhaps a third term. The conflict between the preferences of George Washington and the delegates made presidential selection the most contentious subject at the convention. The question was discussed repeatedly, and a total of 32 votes was taken. The delegates reached a decision seven different times, only to reconsider and usually revise it. The election of the president by Congress was approved on July 17 and then again on August 24. As late as August 31, this method was still included in the draft constitution.[48]

When Washington would not change his mind, the Convention chose the Electoral College as the alternative. Each state would be given a set amount of Electors regardless of the number of votes cast in the state election. Each elector would be given two votes, and the candidate with the most votes would be the president if he were named by a majority of the electors. The man with the second most would be vice president.

The slave states were allocated members of the House of Representatives on the basis of their free population and three-fifths of their slaves. Since

[48] Richard McCormick, *The Presidential Game: The Origins of American Presidential Politics* (Oxford: Oxford University Press, 1982), p. 17.

each state received an elector for each representative and senator, the slave states would also receive presidential electors that reflected three-fifths of the number of their slaves even though the slaves could not vote. The senatorial electors would naturally reflect the equal number of slave and non-slave states.

The North still had a majority in the Electoral College, a 73 to 66 majority in the first two competitive elections in 1796 and 1800. The North might well insist on a northern president as the successor to the southerner George Washington, and it had the power to elect one if it voted for a single candidate.

Madison did not record the delegates' thinking about the solution to this problem, but the result made their calculations clear. If no one obtained a majority of the electors, a runoff would be held in the House of Representatives among the five candidates who received the most Electoral College votes. Each state would have one vote, whatever the number of its representatives. With an equal number of slave and non-slave states, the North and the South would have an equal number of the votes in the presidential runoff.

Obviously the delegates were trying to ensure the southern veto in an indirect manner, but they needed to ensure that no candidate obtained a majority in the Electoral College. They assumed no parties would form, and they demanded that all states elect their electors on the same date and in their own state capitals. That is, the electors never could meet in a "college" in the national capital and have what Hamilton called a cabal – in this case a meeting at which northern delegates could negotiate among themselves about the candidate who would receive all their votes.

The states were allowed to choose the method of selecting electors, but the Founders did not expect that any method would produce a majority in the country as a whole. The fact that five candidates were to be in the runoff may mean that the delegates anticipated the outcome that occurred in 1824: each sub-section had its own candidate and then had to negotiate in the House.

On the surface, a brilliant solution had been found to the problem created by Washington when he refused to be elected by the Congress. Washington himself would be unanimously elected in the Electoral College, but his successors would be elected in the Congress either in the formation of a consensus ticket at the outset or in the runoff. In either case, his successors would have to receive the endorsement of both the North and the South.

Unfortunately, however, the assumption that no one would receive a majority in the Electoral College did not take into account the collective action problem that had been created. America was not organized politically by section. The North and South had no government units or officials with the mechanism to compel electors to vote for a variety of candidates or to provide selective side payments that would induce them to do so. The sections could not prevent the formation of a two-party system that would almost surely guarantee the election of the president within the Electoral College itself.

The political units with the power to compel action and to raise tax revenue for selective side payments were the states, and two sets of state officials had their interests adversely affected by the runoff.

The first were the officials of the populous states such as New York that received the same one vote in the House runoff as Delaware. Candidates wanting to win the vote of the one Delaware representative had a smaller payoff to make, than if they sought a majority of the New York representatives. New York officials did not like that.

The second group of powerful state officials who were disadvantaged by the House runoff included the governors and the senators. They were far more significant than the lowly representatives. If the issue were decided in the Electoral College itself, benefits such as cabinet offices could go to the governors and senators, and especially to those in states with a large number of Electoral College votes.

The issue came to a head in the first competitive election in 1796. The leading candidate of the South, Thomas Jefferson, knew that his rival, Alexander Hamilton, would control a majority of the state delegations of the House in the runoff and would use his control to elect John Adams. Jefferson could not win unless he (or really his chief ally, James Madison) organized a party – the Republicans – that would secure a majority in the Electoral College. In response, Hamilton organized a party for Adams – the Federalists.

In fact, only two elections were to be decided in the Electoral College. The first was an accident. The two parties had to have their electors vote for two candidates so they would elect the vice president, but if the two candidates received the same number of votes, there would be no winner. That happened in 1800 when Jefferson and his running mate, Aaron Burr, each received a majority but an equal number of votes. The problem was solved with the Twelfth Amendment that separated the presidential and vice-presidential elections.

The second House runoff occurred in 1824 when the parties had dissolved in the Era of Good Feelings and each micro-section supported a different candidate. Instead of a calm deliberation as the

Founders seemingly expected, the negotiations were emotional. General Andrew Jackson explained his defeat in highly polemical terms, and the governors and senators moved quickly to reestablish a two-party system.

But why did the two-party competition not threaten the South and destabilize the political system? Several factors were important. One is that southern politicians such as Jefferson, Madison, and Andrew Jackson realized that they had to win several "battleground states" in the North – notably Pennsylvania and New York – in order to win a majority in the Electoral College. They could not succeed on economic issues but were able to appeal to a large number of the non-English population on ethnic and religious issues. As a result, southerners occupied the presidency for 48 of the first 60 years after 1789 and felt no threat from the North.[49]

The submergence of the issue of unfair slave-holder competition to free farmers was most fortunate for political stability. So too was the reassurance to the South of an equal number of slave and non-slave states in the Senate. The balance of states was ended in 1850, and the issue of slave versus free farming became central in the "Free Soil" issue of the 1850s. The result was the Civil War.

The Mystery of American and Mexican Federalism

It is clear that federalism – really, confederation – was a key factor in the maintenance of political stability, order, and economic growth in the United States, but no one attributes these results to the federalism that was introduced in Mexico. There is an obvious reason. Mexico had major disorder and meager economic growth from 1821 to 1870, and after 1870, power was concentrated in Mexico City.

In one key respect, it is, of course, bizarre to talk about the success of American federalism. The United States had a long Civil War that cost some 600,000 lives. The section of George Washington, James Madison, and Thomas Jefferson rejected America national identity, demanded independence, and was kept in the Union only by military force. What went wrong, and what are the implications?

First, we need to emphasize once more the importance of time. The United States survived for 85 years from 1776 to 1861 under its two confederate central governments. That is a very long time. If India were to follow

[49] See Jerry F. Hough, *Changing Party Coalitions: The Strange Red State-Blue State Alignment* (New York: Algora, 2006).

the American path and have such a devastating Civil War 85 years after independence, it would take place in 2032. Then within a decade after the end of the war, the United States returned to the earlier accommodation between the two sections. For 75 years after 1876, the North essentially allowed the South to treat the blacks as they wanted, barring only the right to buy and sell them.

During the period when American federalism was stable, the United States began to industrialize in 1817, and around 1843 it reached what W. W. Rostow called the "takeoff period." By 1861 the country had solidified its control of the territory stretching to the Pacific Coast, and it had a fully secure position vis-à-vis other nations. The Civil War brought no interruption in the period of rapid growth.

With the exception of the Civil War period, the Constitution worked much as the Founders wanted throughout the 19th century. The federal government could impose no important decision on the states, and the autonomy of the South was guaranteed even when it no longer had an equal number of states. The southern veto in the Senate was restored through a filibuster rule that allowed the South to block any measure that affected its vital interests. The northern-dominated Supreme Court found implausible excuses to nullify the Fourteenth and Fifteenth Amendments that had been intended to guarantee the civil rights and the right to vote for the slaves.

Unlike the situation today, however, the filibuster rested on an informal understanding that it could be used only when the vital interests of the South were affected, not on every policy issue. This informal understanding itself rested on the formal power of the North to change the filibuster rule by a majority vote. Thus the North was basically as autonomous as the South. No one from a Confederate state became president until Lyndon Johnson in 1963. Jimmy Carter in 1976 was the first such president to be elected on his own. In addition, the South informally agreed to support whatever foreign policy the northern president of either party wanted.

These informal understandings were an important element in the stability of the American system. Yet, in our opinion, this was not really the key to the success of American federalism. In the real world, the government in Mexico City had as little power until 1870 as the government in Washington, DC, had until 1870.

The key factor in the success of American federalism, we argue, was the solid nature of the governments of the states. We agree with George Washington's criticism of the Articles of Confederation. The new country needed a chief executive, a common foreign and foreign economic policy, an independent source of funding for the national government, and an end to conflicting territorial claims beyond the Appalachian Mountains.[50] Yet the 11 years of the Articles of Confederation played a quite positive role in American history. This period permitted independent colonies to consolidate themselves into real independent state governments.

In short, the name of the new country was half right. The word "United" was nothing but a pious hope. Nevertheless, the word "States" had real meaning. The states came close to meeting Douglass North's definition of a state as a government with a predominance of military force and the ability to tax within the territory it controlled. The states themselves often approximated the size of England, but their governments ruled quite effectively.

Unlike the federal government, each state had a political elite that met Joseph Schumpeter's prerequisite for a stable democracy or semi-democracy: "a social stratum, itself a product of a severely selective process, that takes to politics as a matter of course" and that has "traditions that embody experience … a professional code and … a common fund of views";[51] the political elite of each state constituted such a stratum.

The United States did not, as many think, develop its economy on the basis of a completely laissez-faire policy. Even leaving aside the high federal tariff of the 19th century and other federal actions, the real American government was at the state level. The states had an active economic role in the 19th century. They helped build canals and railroads, drafted complex legal codes and regulations, created an excellent state education system, and even provided some social welfare measures.

Of course, bad went with the good. The amount of rent-seeking and corruption was enormous, but this was true almost exclusively at the state level where the key economic decisions were being made. When a historian wrote of the politicians of the 1840s and 1850s as "the plundering generation," he was referring primarily to the state politicians.[52]

North et al. advocate the toleration of rent-seeking – corruption – by key members of the political, economic, and military elite in order to produce the political stability that is necessary for economic growth. We agree. Yet, as will be seen, the Mexican provincial governments also had high levels of

50 Onuf is right that the last-named problem was perhaps the most important of all.

51 Joseph Schumpeter, *Capitalism, Socialism, and Democracy* (New York: Harper & Brothers, 1942), pp. 290–1.

52 Mark Summers, *The Plundering Generation: Corruption and the Crisis of the Union, 1849–1867* (New York: Oxford University Press, 1987). The phrase is a play on the phrase "the blundering generation" that was applied by those who thought the Civil War was unnecessary.

corruption, but it was not associated with any positive economic contributions, at least for the first 50 years of independence.

Why was Mexican federalism so very different from federalism in the United States? The answer to this question is discussed in detail in the next chapter, but Lloyd Mecham made the important point about Mexico: "the normal process of federation was reversed.... Instead of the national state being created by the local states, as in the United States, the local states were created by the national representative body." Mecham concluded that Mexico had only "pseudo-federalism."[53]

Although Mexico City had little power over the provinces, power was not decentralized to provincial governments. The latter had little power either. Power was dispersed among warlords and militia bands who had no real ability to form coherent provincial governments that could maintain the kind of order needed for a well-functioning economy. There were no such provincial governments that could pass legislation that mattered or raise revenue to pay foreign debts. It was independent Mexico's lack of real provincial governments (or a centralized national government with effective bureaucracies) and the presence of such provincial governments in the United States that was the key difference.

In conclusion, let us repeat a point from the introduction. This book ends before our four cases introduced meaningful democracy, and it is not the place for a serious analysis of the various questions associated with democracy. A few of the northern states were becoming reasonably democratic by the end of the 1700s, at least for white males, but the central government was far from having a meaningful democracy. Our point about the southern veto in the Senate, which is quite fresh, indicates that that government was even less democratic than most scholars believe.

This is not the place to discuss the evolution of democracy in America in the 1800s. Nevertheless, we agree with North et al. that "the World Bank's attempts to transform countries into 'open access orders' typically yield more violence than development."[54] We would like to end this chapter by adding that the American experience should be cited to support their position.

Other than the presence of slavery, the experience of the United States is never mentioned in a negative manner in discussing the relevance of that

[53] J. Lloyd Mecham, "The Origins of Federalism in Mexico," *Hispanic American Historical Review* 18 (1938), 164–82. The quote is on p. 164.

[54] These, it may be remembered, are David Laitin's words in his blurb on the back cover of the paperback edition of North, Douglass, John Joseph Wallis, Steven Webb, and Barry Webb, eds., *In the Shadow of Violence: Politics, Economics, and the Problems of Development* (Cambridge: Cambridge University Press, 2013).

experience for developing nations. The American financial experience is cited in distorted terms, and the positive role of American corruption is not mentioned. The decentralization of military power to the regional level in the Second Amendment is never openly discussed as a possible political solution in civil wars in areas such as the Middle East.

The implications of the American experience with democratization are also never mentioned at all, and non-specialists are not even aware of the American experience. Before it became politically necessary to attribute the Civil War almost entirely to the moral outrage of slavery, an earlier generation treated the Civil War as the accidental result of a series of unfortunate decisions by a "blundering generation" of politicians. Probably the best historian of the Civil War in the second half of the 20th century, David H. Donald, was an exception who retained the older view. He believed that the basic cause of the Civil War was an "excess of democracy" – that is democratization.[55]

Donald's emphasizes the major democratization that occurred in the United States from the 1820s through the 1840s. The states had control of voting rules, and they gradually moved in a more democratic direction after 1776. Universal white male suffrage was introduced everywhere during the half century after 1787. By the late 1820s, presidential electors were popularly elected everywhere except in South Carolina, and real political parties were being formed to mobilize voters to go to the polls. By the 1840 presidential election, 80% of white males went to the polls, and this figure remained in the 70% to 80% range until the Civil War.

Democratization did not seriously threaten the stability of the states since the politicians of the various states chose the pace and manner in which they introduced their own rules. Democratization did, however, have a disastrous impact at the national level. The early stages of industrialization and urbanization always create anxiety, and this anxiety was especially high in the United States because the new cities were disproportionately built by Catholic immigrants and the new factories were staffed by them.

The Catholics flocked to the Democratic Party. If the Whigs had adopted an anti-Catholic position and embraced the South and the seizure of Mexican territory as necessary to expand to the Pacific, they likely would have been the dominant political party in the United States for decades. Instead, the

[55] David Herbert Donald, *An Excess of Democracy: The American Civil War and the Social Process* (Oxford: Clarendon, 1960), esp. pp. 17 and 22. Reprinted in David Herbert Donald, *Lincoln Reconsidered: Essays on the Civil War Era*, 3rd ed. (New York: Vintage, 2001), 44–62. In a letter to me on August 15, 1997, Professor Donald asserted he was "delighted to learn" the essay was remembered and that "I still think that (with some modifications perhaps) it has validity." He reaffirmed the point in an e-mail of November 12, 2005.

Whigs courted the Catholic immigrants, and the Protestant voters swung strongly to a new anti-Catholic Know-Nothing Party. As a result, the Whig Party collapsed, and it was replaced by a new Republican Party that adopted an anti-Catholic position and made a quite demagogic and inaccurate claim that the slave-holders wanted to take over North. Included in this claim was the charge that the South dominated by the Democratic Party wanted to incorporate the 7 million Mexican Catholics into a United States that numbered some 18 million whites.

This is not the place to discuss American history in the 1840s and 1850s, but one point is worth making about the construction of constraints on government. The Founding Fathers' generation occupied the presidency from 1789 to 1829 and was dedicated to sectional accommodation. The next generation, which rose in the wake of the War of 1812, was led by men such as Henry Clay, Martin Van Buren, and Daniel Webster. They too were dedicated to accommodation and constraint.

Yet the Henry Clay generation was moving into its 60s in the 1840s without any understanding of the anxieties produced by immigration and industrialization or any understanding of the mass democracy that produced an 80% turnout in the 1840 presidential election. They were the ones who, as a result, badly handled the Catholic immigrant issue. The new generation – for example, Jefferson Davis (born 1808), Stephen Douglas (1813), and Abraham Lincoln (1808) – had come of age in the democratization of the late 1830s. They were highly skilled in making populist appeals that won votes, but they had little experience in accommodative politics.

The incentives of democracy in their own respective section led the politicians of the new generation in directions that undercut feelings of sectional trust. In responding to the disaster that occurred, the generation that came to power after the Civil War sharply reduced the democratic elements in the elections and reemphasized sectional accommodation. The point of crucial importance for this book, however, is that the most solid constraints can be quite ephemeral. Those constrained by them inevitably die. Unless the constraints have been thoroughly instilled in rising generations and in all parts of the political strata, a quite stable situation can explode in a terrible civil war.

10

The Collective Action Problems of the Formation of Mexico

The Mexican war of independence – really the first Mexican revolution – began in 1810, 35 years after the onset of the American Revolution. Large parts of the colony quickly degenerated into general disorder, anarchy, and economic collapse. Other than in some subsistence regions, only Mexico City and the valley of Mexico remained stable. The economic sectors based directly or indirectly on mining and foreign trade income fell into deep depression. After the declaration of independence in 1821, order and economic growth were very slow to be restored.

Of course, serious revolutions and immediate post-revolutionary periods can often have this nature. Chile was to be the most successful of the areas of the Spanish Empire, but in the 1820s it too had a very troubled decade, with multiple changes in constitutions. In 1829, however, Chile had a military-based conservative coup that introduced basic stability and produced economic growth for the rest of the century. Mexico too had a conservative military coup in 1829 that seemingly should have ended the period of severe disorder and stagnation. It did not. The question is why.

Scholars do not agree about the exact pattern of Mexican economic performance from 1810 to 1870. As Richard Salvucci argues, the subsistence peasant economy outside of the large cities continued much as it had in the colonial period.[1] Nevertheless, the Spanish sector seriously declined from 1810 to 1825, and it recovered slowly at best until 1870.

In broader perspective, the performance of Mexico was even worse. Its economy did not experience the economic growth that other industrializing countries were enjoying in that period. In 1820, serious railroad construction was just beginning in the United States, and rail lines were quickly extended

1 Richard Salvucci, *Textiles and Capitalism in Mexico: An Economic History of the Obrajes, 1539–1840* (Princeton, NJ: Princeton University Press, 1987), pp. 234–6.

toward the Mississippi River and to the South. The first transcontinental railroad in the United States was completed in 1869. A railroad from the mines to the sea was completed in Chile in 1851, but the railroad from the Mexican plateau to Veracruz was not finished until 1873.[2]

Silver production was the core sector in the Mexican economy, and it was extremely slow to recover from the revolutionary period. Jaime Rodríguez O. estimates that total silver production (not coinage) averaged 9.2 million pesos annually from 1825 to 1829, about 11.4 million from 1830 to 1839, and 12.4 million from 1840 to 1844. Strangely, it rose to 15.6 million from 1845 to 1849, the years of the war with the United States. Yet production did not reach colonial levels until the late 1880s.[3]

The mining sector itself constituted only a relatively small percent of GDP, but agriculture, industry, and trade were intimately connected with it. For example, the sale of mules declined from millions in the late colonial period to thousands in 1850.[4] Cattle were raised primarily for leather and tallow that was to be used by the mines and refineries. The economy of Mexico City rested on foreign trade, and silver was almost the only export product. After the default of 1827, no one would give loans for imports.

How then do we explain the 50 years of economic stagnation from the 1820s to the 1870s? Or rather, how do we explain the stagnation from the 1830s to the 1870s? We agree with Douglass North that the maintenance of order during the American war of independence and afterward was a crucial pre-condition for its economic and political development in the 19th century.[5] We agree that the American federal system was crucial in maintaining this order. We also agree that the level of disorder in Mexico in much of the 19th century seriously retarded its economic and political development, but we strongly disagree with his explanation of the reasons for this disorder.

North, as would be expected, attributes the difference in the two countries to values – the existence of common values in the United States and conflicting values in Mexico. "The beliefs underlying the institutions

[2] John Coatsworth, "Indispensable Railroads in a Backward Economy: The Case of Mexico," *Journal of Economic History* 39 (1979), 939–60.

[3] Jaime E. Rodríguez O., "Down from Colonialism: Mexico's Nineteenth-Century Crisis," in Jaime E. Rodríguez O., ed., *The Mexican and Mexican-American Experience in the Nineteenth Century* (Tempe: Bilingual Press, 1989), pp. 10, 13.

[4] Rodríguez O., "Down from Colonialism," pp. 8, 20.

[5] Douglass North, William Summerhill, and Barry Weingast, "Order, Disorder and Economic Change: Latin America vs. North America," in Bruce Bueno de Mesquita and Hilton Root, eds., *Governing for Prosperity* (New Haven, CT: Yale University Press, 2000), 17–58.

promulgated by the Spanish Crown have provided two centuries of instability, turmoil, personal exchange, and limited development." In a recent statement on the subject, he concluded that the personalistic values left by Spain meant "there was no shared belief system about the role of government, the state, corporate privilege, and citizen."[6]

As is clear from the previous chapters, we believe it is ahistorical to speak of common values about government, state, and citizen in the 1700s and 1800s in a United States so divided by religion, ethnicity, and mutual suspicion. We would also emphasize the drastically different conceptions of property rights in slaves. The solution in 1787, we have seen, was to have a central government so weak that it could not interfere in the real governments – those of the states. Yet even this did not prevent a Civil War in 1861 that killed more than 600,000.

Even after the Civil War, the North-South conflict was "solved" by allowing southern whites to deny blacks the right to vote and to institute a strictly regulated economy that denied the business community and blacks the right to engage in market relations with each other in an impersonal manner. Only in 1964 – 100 years after the Civil War and nearly 200 years after the American Revolution – did Congress pass a law that outlawed segregation and required a free market in the South. Only in 1965 did Congress enforce the 15th Amendment passed 100 years previously that "guaranteed" blacks the right to vote.

As for Mexico, we agree that Mexicans did not have a system of values that would sustain a stable democracy. But the question is why Mexico had such prolonged disorder. Personalistic relations and corporate institutions are quite compatible with patrimonial authoritarian states that maintain order. Spain, after all, maintained order in Mexico for nearly 300 years, and it had a most imperfect authoritarian state for a large part of that period.

Even though both the American and Mexican colonies had strong city-states, Mexicans had looked to Mexico City economically, politically, and intellectually for 300 years and the colonists had a basic national identity. The Spaniards in Mexico had a common culture, language, and, religion. As

[6] Douglass North, *Understanding the Process of Change* (Princeton, NJ: Princeton University Press, 2005), pp. 112–15. This chapter is a summary of North, Summerhill, and Weingast. "Order, Disorder and Economic Change." There is an evolution from the working paper of the article to the article to North's chapter in his book. The working paper, like North's chapter, emphasizes what seem to be North and Weingast's views on shared values. The article emphasizes more the personalistic, corporate character of Mexico and implies the importance of rational-legal views. This seems to reflect the view of Summerhill, a historian on Latin America whose belief in the importance of government has often been cited in this book.

the Native Americans moved into the Spanish sector of the economy, they became *mestizos* and mostly accepted integration as the path to a better life. Mexico seemed ideally suited to have an authoritarian form of federalism that was quite orderly and experienced reasonable growth. The question is why this did not occur for so long.

We cited Chile several times in this chapter for different reasons. But, as Alan Knight emphasized in a private conversation, Chile was a country that was just as imbued with Spanish values as Mexico – indeed, more so since its much smaller indigenous population had a far smaller role in its culture. Moreover, Chilean creoles had the usual conflicts found throughout Latin America: conservatives versus liberals, pro-clerical versus anti-clerical conservatives, Castilian conservatives versus Basque conservatives, mining interests in the north versus landed interests in the center.[7]

As we discussed at the end of the previous chapter, we think the best way to explain the greater political order in the 19th-century United States is to ask why an effective federal system was created in the United States after the War of Independence, but not in Mexico. This chapter is a detailed counterpart to the previous one. We have already examined how the collective action problems of maintaining order were solved in a new United States that seemingly would be difficult to govern. In this chapter, we ask why they were not solved in Mexico.

A large part of the answer, we suggest, is that the United States had highly effective provincial governments in which the political elites in the original city-state colonies had developed Joseph Schumpeter's "social stratum that takes to politics as a matter of course" and that has "traditions that embody experience … a professional code and … a common fund of views."[8] The United States continued to have these "informal institutions" as the settled areas of the states expanded and as the population moved west to establish new states.

The Mexican colonial elite also had well-developed norms of governance based on informal, personalistic negotiations, but the important word is "informal," not personalistic. Early patrimonial bureaucracies are also infused with personalistic values, but the very experience of working within them can create the condition for a slow evolution toward more rational-legal norms. This happened in Spain of the 1700s.

[7] A detailed discussion of the political events of the decades after independence is found in Simon Collier and William Sater, *A History of Chile, 1808–2002* (Cambridge: Cambridge University Press, 2004).

[8] Joseph Schumpeter, *Capitalism, Socialism, and Democracy* (New York: Harpers and Brothers, 1942), pp. 290–1.

Such an evolution also was occurring in Mexico in the 1700s, but the revolution of 1810 destroyed the nascent Bourbon bureaucracy. Much of Mexico was returned to pre-state conditions, but without the stable warlords of medieval England or the more unstable ones of medieval Castile. Only when Porfirio Díaz came to power in 1870 was Mexico able to re-establish the kind of orderly rule it had had at the end of the Bourbon period. A key reason was that by 1870, a stable-enough political structure had been created in the Mexican regions for it to have real dominant coalitions of the type North et al. have in mind.

The Hidalgo and Morelos Rebellions and Their Aftermath

The Mexican war of independence was atypical in a number of ways. For starters, revolutionary movements usually are strongest in the capital and other large cities, but there was no hint of an independence movement in such cities in Mexico. The central areas of Mexico City, the Valley of Mexico, Puebla, and the environs of Puebla were unusually peaceful throughout the entire violent revolutionary period from 1810 to 1821. Instead, independence was proclaimed by the leader of a loose coalition of regional generals, who then conquered the capital.

On the surface, the non-revolutionary attitude in the capital seems strange. While the English urban colonists strongly benefited from their access to the British and Caribbean markets, the Mexican colonists gained little from access to the Spanish market. Silver was easy to transport and would be accepted anywhere in the world. The merchant and political classes were located in Mexico City and should have benefited the most from independence.

Two factors were likely decisive. First, while the American Revolution brought the mainland colonies together into a natural mainland trading area, independence in Spanish America certainly would create separate countries. The natural trading area of Mexico included Peru, Venezuela, and the Caribbean Islands. It would be destroyed unless the vast empire became independent more or less simultaneously. The Spanish American colonies had no recognized leaders who could negotiate collective independence.

Second, the Mexican elite feared the United States. In 1763, France had to cede to lands west of the Mississippi River to Spain, but in 1800 Spain ceded this territory back to Napoleon. Spain probably hoped Napoleon would defend this area and adjacent Spanish lands against the United States, but instead, he sold it to the United States in the Louisiana Purchase in 1803.

The territory that made up the Louisiana Purchase was a geographically unnatural area without ports on the Pacific Ocean, and it was obvious that the United States would want access to the ocean. Indeed, when Jefferson sent Lewis and Clark to explore the Louisiana Purchase in 1803, he had them continue their voyage to the mouth of the Columbia River on the Pacific. The three great ports on the Pacific were Puget Sound, San Francisco Bay, and San Diego Bay. The latter two were part of New Spain. Since American settlers were not showing any respect for the property rights of Native Americans, they undoubtedly would have the same attitude about poorly defended Mexican Pacific ports, and perhaps even the Mexican mines to the south. The Americans might be more afraid to seize land from Spain.

The misnamed Mexican War of Independence began unexpectedly in Spain in early May 1808. In mid-March, Charles IV of Spain was forced to abdicate in favor of his son, Ferdinand VII, and six weeks later, Napoleon forced the Bourbons to abdicate in favor of his brother, Joséph Bonaparte. Napoleon then imprisoned both of the Bourbon kings. Anti-French juntas arose in several Spanish cities, notably in Seville.

The Latin American elites could not have any rational idea about how best to respond. They could not judge the relative strength of the forces of Joséph Bonaparte and the juntas inside Spain until 1810. They could not know the ultimate outcome of the war between Napoleon and Great Britain. Then, unlike in the other areas of the Empire, top *peninsulares* under a leading member of the *consulado*, Gabriel de Yermo, entered the palace in September 1808 with a group of 300 *consulado* guards and clerks and arrested the viceroy, José de Iturrigaray.

Two facts about the overthrow of the viceroy are crucial for us. First, a handful of *consulado* guards were enough to overthrow a viceroy, and two small regiments potentially were a decisive military force. The conspirators charged that Iturrigaray was uniting with the *cabildos* to seek independence, but since the viceroy had called two regiments headed by friends to the capital, the other *peninsulares* probably feared a military coup.

Second, the victors did not organize a strong military force to maintain order but sent the small military units of the capital far into interior as if they were a major danger. Hence the new government had as little military force at its disposal as the viceroy. The city-states also remained virtually unarmed.

In January 1810, the Central Junta of Seville collapsed and was reconstituted as a protectorate (the Regency Council) in the British-controlled port of Cádiz. Now the Spanish Americans had to make choices. The British-protected Regency Council called for Spanish American representation in a new Spanish *Cortes* (parliament), and the colonies had to decide whether to send them. Revolutions were attempted in a number of viceroyalties in South America in the political instability that ensued.

Once again, Mexico was atypical. A few members of the middle-level elite in the Bajío, north of Mexico City, were planning anti-regime action when the conspiracy was betrayed.[9] On September 16, 1810, one of them, the priest Miguel Hidalgo in Dolores (now Dolores-Hidalgo) summoned his parishioners and called on them to march against the *peninsulares*. Over the next six weeks, Hidalgo led his growing number of followers from town to town in the central Bajío. They sacked almost every town that they entered, as well as the haciendas between them. Many Creoles and *peninsulares* alike were killed.[10]

On September 26, Hidalgo was on the outskirts of Mexico's second largest city, Guanajuato with its 60,000 people and the country's greatest silver mine. On September 28, when Guanajuato refused to surrender, Hidalgo's forces captured and plundered both the city and the mine. Some 300 officials and well-to-do individuals were killed. In addition, Hidalgo's men gratuitously destroyed the machinery at the mines and burned the silver refineries.

After Iturrigaray was overthrown in 1808, the new viceroy had sent Félix Calleja, one of the best commanders in New Spain, to command forces in the city of San Luis Potosí. The city is over 250 miles north of Mexico City, and Calleja really was responsible for the control of the non-pacified Native Americans to the north, including in Texas.[11] Yet when Hidalgo's rebellion broke out 125 miles to the south, Calleja told the capital that he possessed no mobilized units even at the company level.

Guanajuato was located in an excellent defensive position and was less than a two-day ride to San Luis Potosí to the north.[12] Obviously Guanajuato also had no effective defensive forces. Even with 10 days'

9 The word "Bajío" means lowlands and it refers to a highly fertile region of Mexico that encompasses parts of modern-daỳ states Guanajuato, Querétaro, Aguascalientes, and Jalisco.

10 Hugh Hamill Jr., *The Hidalgo Revolt* (Gainesville: University of Florida Press, 1966), pp. 135–50 and 180–202. The map of Hidalgo's route is printed just before the title page. Robert Scheina, *Latin America's Wars: The Age of the Caudillo, 1791–1899* (Washington: Brassey's, 2003), Vol. I, p. 73.

11 Calleja's wife lived in the city and was a member of the wealthiest family in the region. Modern visitors can now dine in her and Calleja's luxurious home in the central square of the city.

12 The strong defensive position of Guanajuato and the ease of reaching it from San Luis Potosí are emphasized by an American diplomat in 1822. Joel Roberts Poinsett, *Notes on Mexico Made in the Autumn of 1822* (New York: Frederick A. Praeger, 1969), p. 154.

notice, Calleja did nothing to defend Guanajuato, and he refused to act for seven weeks.[13] He seemingly should have been able to organize a significant militia and even a regiment after a relatively short time. Yet he did nothing. It is possible, perhaps even probable, that Calleja wanted to keep his troops close to home to protect his property and that of his wife and her family. Hidalgo was allowed to inflict enormous devastation on the Bajío for four months.

At the end of October, Hidalgo decided to march on Mexico City, which had no real armed forces. The viceroy managed to mobilize an ill-prepared militia of some 1,300 to 2,500 soldiers to defend the city against Hidalgo's tens of thousands of men. On November 3, Hidalgo decided to retreat and on November 7 he encountered a more professional militia unit organized by Calleja.[14] Again, many of Hidalgo's men dispersed in disorder.

Hidalgo retreated once more into the Bajío, where he spent the months of November and December attacking a series of towns. Then in January 1811, Calleja defeated him decisively just east of Guadalajara. This time Hidalgo's forces of some 40,000 men occupied a defensive position, and Calleja, now with 7,000 men, had to attack. Yet, Hidalgo's forces ran once more and his rebellion was over. Hidalgo fled to north where he was captured and executed.

Hidalgo's forces are often described as a "rebel army" or "rebel horde," but we think the latter is probably more accurate. In the words of Hugh Thomas, they were "an unruly mob of Indians and peasants, with stones, with sticks, with crude lances, without organization of any kind.... Mixed with the half-naked, hungry hordes were countless women dressed in rags.... There were whole families.... It was like the ancient Aztec migrations."[15]

Scholars refer to 20,000, 40,000, or 60,000 Hidalgo troops in various battles, but this hides the nature of the "troops." An official's report certainly suggested that Thomas's "hungry hordes" were no longer hungry after the looting of haciendas began: "The Indians walked carrying their children, sheep, quarters of beef, and [as evidence of the plundering they do] they bear doors, tables, chairs, and even beams on their shoulders."[16]

[13] Christon Archer, "'La Causa Buena': The Counterinsurgency Army of New Spain and the Ten Years' War," in Jaime Rodríguez O., *The Independence of Mexico and the Creation of the New Nation* (Los Angeles: UCLA Publications, 1989), p. 87. For a series of communications between Calleja and the viceroy, see pp. 87–91 of the Archer chapter.

[14] For the response in the capital, see Timothy Anna, *The Fall of the Royal Government in Mexico City* (Lincoln: University of Nebraska Press, 1978), pp. 70–3.

[15] Hugh Thomas, *Conquest of Mexico* (New York: Pimlico, 2004), p. 185.

[16] Hamill, *The Hidalgo Revolt*, pp. 135–7.

No one could carry quarters of beef, doors, and beams for the hundreds of miles that Hidalgo covered nor would anyone desire to do so. Clearly most of Hidalgo's followers in one place returned to their homes with their booty and were replaced by those in the next villages and towns through which Hidalgo passed. Timothy Anna believes 2 million people became involved between mid-September 1808 and mid-January 1809. Others consider this figure excessive, but the number was very large.[17]

The uncertainty about how to label Hidalgo's men extends to the events of the whole period. Scholars use a wide variety of words to describe the "war of independence": rebellion, insurgency, uprising, revolution, insurrection, guerrilla war, Civil War, or simply the period of anarchy and banditry. Mexican troops never had to fight a major Spanish army, and the "royalist" generals leading the "counterinsurgency armies" seemed mainly to be seeking their own wealth and power. The confusion in language reflects the multi-sided character of events.

In mid-October, Hidalgo had given another priest, José Morelos, the responsibility for organizing an army in the south.[18] For four years, Morelos dominated a large region that included the cities of Oaxaca and the road from Taxco to Acapulco. He made an effort to establish a constitutional regime and launched unsuccessful campaigns against both the Bajío and the region of Puebla, but they failed.

Scholars devote much attention to the reasons for the Hidalgo and Morelos insurgencies. At one extreme, some refer to a virtual Marxist revolution against the elite ("one of the greatest guerilla insurgencies in modern history"), while those at the other extreme attribute events to "a reactionary clerical backlash against the liberal and enlightened Bourbon reforms of the second half of the eighteenth century."[19]

The motivations ascribed to the participants include religious fervor and a social resentment, both of them expressed in the slaughter at Guanajuato and elsewhere. Others see a desire for booty as the primary motivation. Hidalgo succeeded only in the indigenous anti-Aztec Otomi region in the Bajío. Morelos succeeded only in the non-Aztec areas to the southwest of the capital. Both leaders utterly failed in the Aztec valley in the center, and resentment toward Mexico City and its Aztec-based *mestizo*s may have

[17] Anna, *The Fall of the Royal Government*, p. 65.

[18] Wilbert Timmons, *Morelos: Priest, Soldier, Statesman of Mexico* (El Paso: Texas Western College Press, 1963), pp. 42 and 44.

[19] Christon Archer, "La Causa Buena," pp. 102–7. Will Fowler, *Mexico in the Age of Proposals, 1821–1853* (Westport, CT: Greenwood Press, 1998), p. 13.

been involved. The participants both on the whole and as individuals almost certainly had mixed motivations.

Morelos finally was captured and executed in December 1815. Most see that event as ending the period of major organized resistance, but it did not end the violence. Christon Archer argues there was "no lull" in what he calls a "guerilla war" after 1815, but most scholars seem to agree more with Hamnett, who argues that "without effective direction by a coordinated political leadership and without constraint by a regular army force, the guerilla war rapidly degenerated into little more than brigandage, a plague on the countryside."[20]

While Eric Van Young emphasizes the religious motivations and inherent peasant grievances behind the instability, he also discusses the "selective side payments" that went on during the war:[21]

> Whether one chooses to regard the gains from looting as direct wages, compensatory payments for normally depressed wage-earning levels, compensation for high risk behavior, windfall income, or a combination of all of these, there certainly was a great deal of it during the period.... Insurgent bands frequently moved across the countryside like plagues of locusts, alternately fighting with royalist forces; robbing obviously Spanish travelers (both creole and European), sacking haciendas, homes, stores, and whole towns; then fleeing to attack and loot again another day.

Of course, there were different types of bands. Many were based in small towns and simply attacked travelers on a nearby road before fading back into the mountains or the civilian population. Others were merchants trading with both sides and often with illegally procured goods. Mule drivers and would-be mule drivers were especially active participants. Brigands would attack mule trains carrying mercury for the silver mines, throw the mercury away, and keep only the mules.[22]

The process had a circular character. The indigenous villages continued to engage in subsistence farming, but with diminished demand in the local towns for their market crops. Yet the disorder made economic reconstruction in the Spanish sector virtually impossible. The poor seized land and/or the fruits of still-functioning farms to survive. This in turn further reduced the chance of an economic recovery that would increase the possibility of peasants finding employment.

[20] Brian Hamnett, *Roots of Insurgency: Mexican Regions, 1750–1824* (Cambridge: Cambridge University Press, 1986), p. 59.

[21] Eric Van Young, *The Other Rebellion: Popular Violence, Ideology, and the Mexican Struggle for Independence, 1810–1821* (Stanford, CA: Stanford University Press, 2001), p. 89.

[22] María Eugenia Romero Sotelo, *Minería y Guerra: La economía de Nueva España, 1810–1821* (Mexico: El Colegio de Mexico, 1997), pp. 63–5.

Order was gradually, if intermittently, restored by the techniques that have always been used to create order in pre-state conditions. Roving bandits might offer protection to those passing along a road or to various haciendas or businesses (protection that, of course, included immunity against attacks by themselves). If bandits succeeded in driving off other bandits, they might be offered permanent employment in the security apparatus of a city or town. The more successful might become the boss of a small town or city and offer fealty to a more powerful commander.

Other successful militia leaders might occupy an abandoned hacienda or drive off its owners. The future dictator Santa Anna became the owner of a large estate in this way, and he was typical of important military commanders. Santa Anna reportedly "gave" abandoned haciendas to other rebels to end their struggle. He more likely was recognizing the legitimacy of their conquest in order to draw them into his military and political machine. These are all among the tortuous ways in which a multiplicity of roving bandits evolves toward a system with a single stationary bandit who provides enough protection to promote economic growth.

The "Royalist Army" Rebels

The simplified version of the Mexican War of Independence depicts a struggle between rebels and royalist army commanders, but in reality this is a false dichotomy. Except for the foremost political rebels, the rebels and the loyalists were not that different. The striking fact about the Hidalgo rebellion is the enormous amount of damage that Hidalgo's primitively armed "troops" were able to do over a four-month period to the country's richest agricultural area, its second largest city, and its greatest mine. There was no royal army or even effective royal regiment to suppress them during this period.

No such army was ever created. Throughout 1811, Félix Calleja continued to command the major group of troops charged with trying to regain control of the Bajío and the mining areas north of it: the Army of the Center. This army was a ragtag group of 4,000 to 5,000 troops. By contrast, the three-day battle at Gettysburg in the U.S. Civil War involved 90,000 Union troops and 70,000 Confederate troops, all grouped in normal army units.

At the end of 1811, Calleja was called back to Mexico City to join the fight against José Morelos in the Puebla area, and he remained in the central region. In March 1813, Calleja was appointed viceroy and began to develop what is often called a counterinsurgency strategy.[23] Once again, however, the language is misleading. Part of the counterinsurgency strategy was to pressure hacienda owners, mine owners, and other economic leaders to form (and finance) their own defense units that might include some 50 men. Those who had not fled had surely already done this.

Calleja then divided the territory of modern Mexico into districts and appointed a military commander to deal with the militias within each. The military units concentrated on the larger bands and gradually succeeded in dispersing most of them. But as Hamnett wrote, "Calleja's emphasis on the regionalization of the counterinsurgency unintentionally contributed to the creation of military satrapies in the provinces."[24] Indeed, rebel groups apparently could move from one district to another as a safe haven, confident that a pursuing commander could not follow.

The only question about Hamnett's statement is whether the consequences of Calleja's policy were unintended, or at least unanticipated. When Calleja appointed commanders of army groups, of intendancies, or of city-states, he may have simply legitimized commanders who were already in the field. Whatever the basis for their selection, commanders could not rely on the central government for salaries, supplies, and equipment.

Doris Ladd presents a good deal of evidence that Calleja was thinking of a powerful role for himself after the war. He may well have thought that if he controlled Mexico City, his base in the mining areas, and Veracruz, the other regional military commanders would have to become governors through whom he could rule after the war.[25]

In any case, the formal structure of the counterinsurgency forces should not mislead us. Calleja did not command an army with headquarters in Mexico City. He simply did not have the financial resources to fund either a centralized army or a decentralized one. When he called on Creoles to join volunteer units, he received the response that a collective action theorist would expect.[26]

[23] Christon Archer, "Years of Decision: Félix Calleja and the Strategy to End the Revolution of New Spain," in Christon Archer, ed., *The Birth of Modern Mexico* (Wilmington, DE: Scholarly Resources, 2003).

[24] Brian Hamnett, "Royalist Counterinsurgency and the Continuity of Rebellion: Guanajuato and Michoacán, 1813–1820," *Hispanic American Historical Review* 62 (1982), 19–48. For the quotations, see pp. 46 and 48.

[25] Doris Ladd, *Mexican Nobility at Independence, 1780–1826* (Austin: University of Texas Press, 1976).

[26] Christon Archer, "Where Did All the Royalists Go? New Light on the Military Collapse of New Spain, 1810–1822," in Jaime E. Rodríguez O., ed., *The Mexican and Mexican-American Experience in the Nineteenth Century* (Tempe, AZ: Bilingual Press, 1989), pp. 27–8.

Calleja told the "royalist" officers that they must be self-financing. They should "solicit" support from local inhabitants and seize merchandise in military operations against rebels. Calleja instructed the commanders to give some of the seized material to the soldiers in lieu of salary. The city-states were instructed to tax themselves to help supply the armies, but the commanders usually did not wait for the taxes to be paid in some regularized way. The war was even more disorganized and led to the booty-based "rule" that the Castilian kings had before 1262.

Calleja surely would have preferred a professional army, but he had no choice. He simply did not have the necessary funding. The tax revenues of the Central Treasury fell precipitously. The center collected 28 million pesos at the high point in 1809, but the receipts fell to 18 million pesos in 1810, 13.5 in 1811, and 8.7 million in 1813. They remained essentially at 9 to 10 million pesos from 1813 to 1817 – the last year of the war for which data are available.[27]

The first reason for the decline in central revenue is that the regional treasuries were not sending the money they collected to Mexico City: "Most of these, formerly shipped to Mexico [City]," John TePaske reports, "now went to pay military salaries locally."[28] This language is too clinical. American state governments paid salaries to militia members in the American War of Independence, but this did not happen in Mexico. Mexican commanders simply took the money. They distributed it or kept it as they saw fit.

Since the commanders were acting in a semi-legal manner, we are left with little documentation. Fortunately, however, one of the royalist commanders, Agustín de Iturbide, seized control of Mexico City in 1821 and declared independence. This led scholars to explore for more information about his path to power. While Iturbide may not have been fully typical, other commanders used similar techniques to a greater or lesser degree.

Iturbide was the son of an important landlord and son-in-law of the *intendant* of Valladolid (the current city of Morelia). When the first rebellious militias arose in 1810, each town tried to organize some defense under a local commander. Because of his upbringing and access to local financial resources, he was able to organize a force that was more successful than most.

When Calleja was transferred to Mexico City, Iturbide first became the commander of the troops in the town that was a gateway to Guanajuato and

[27] Ladd, *Mexican Nobility at Independence*, pp. 4–5.

[28] John Jay TePaske, "The Financial Disintegration of the Royal Government of Mexico during the Epoch of Independence," in Jaime Rodríguez O., *The Independence of Mexico and the Creation of the New Nation* (Los Angeles: UCLA Publications, 1989), pp. 67–8.

then of all the troops in the Bajío area surrounding Guanajuato. Iturbide replaced Calleja as the commander of the Army of the Center in the Bajío and gained a reputation both for ruthlessness in suppressing rebels and for his dedication to self-enrichment. He allegedly took 1.6 million pesos from the Guanajuato treasury.[29]

One of the chief responsibilities of the royalist commanders was to protect trade within their respective regions. They could demand a percentage of the proceeds, but in practice, they could also ally with a particular merchant and deny protection to competing merchants. Indeed, one of the accusations made against Iturbide was that he was such a merchant himself. He even had his own stores in which he sold goods that he was "protecting." This role was so important that Doris Ladd called the commanders "merchant-generals."[30]

From the perspective of local residents, "royalist" commanders and units were often not that different from their "rebel" counterparts. When rebels were the most threatening nearby force, a town would make protection payments to them to avoid being sacked. This led such town officials to be called "pro-insurgent." If larger royalist forces arrived, their commannders would "collect taxes" that had not been paid during insurgent occupation, and the town would become "pro-royalist." This pattern was so typical that a phrase arose to describe it: "*voltaron caras*" ("they change faces or loyalties").[31]

By the spring of 1814, Napoleon was facing defeat in Europe and Ferdinand VII was restored to power in Spain. When the capture of Morelos in December 1815 ended any chance of popular rebellion, Ferdinand removed the two commanders who were capable of a military coup, Calleja and Iturbide. Calleja was replaced as viceroy and recalled to Spain, while Iturbide was removed as head of the Army of the Center on grounds of corruption. He resided in the capital, reportedly living a dissolute life.

The years from 1816 through 1820 are the period in the War of Independence about which we have the least information. Nearly all the major rebel and militia gangs were defeated except for the band of Vicente Guerrero in the South. The viceroy who replaced Calleja in September 1816, Juan Apodaca, followed a policy of pacification through offers of amnesty and the incorporation of former militia leaders into the political structure.

29 William Robertson, *Iturbide of Mexico* (Durham, NC: Duke University, 1952).

30 Ladd, *Mexican Nobility*, p. 116.

31 James William Taylor, "Socio-Economic Instability and the Revolution for Mexican Independence in the Province of Guanajuato" (Ph.D. dissertation, University of New Mexico, 1976), p. 278.

When Ferdinand VIII returned to power, he created two officials at the intendancy level to reestablish an administrative system. One, the *intendant*, was placed in charge of financial affairs, while the other – the political chief (*jefe político*) – supervised other administrative matters. In addition, *cabildos* in towns and Native American villages performed governmental functions, and those in the capitals of the intendancies developed informal relations with the *intendant*.

Although the armies seemingly should have created the conditions for a more stable regional system of governance at the provincial level, there were numerous reasons that the situation improved so slowly.

First, despite some lessening of violence, solid regional governments were not formed. The relationship of the *jefe políticos*, *intendant*s, and capital *cabildos* was not well defined, and the major royalist commanders had districts whose borders did not correspond to those of the intendancies. The situation was politically quite unstable.

Second, the Mexican regional *caudillos* had the same problems as the stationary bandits of medieval England and Spain.[32] A stationary bandit who is powerful enough to protect a town or estate against other militia leaders can extract regular income from it. But the extraction of revenues from a more complex economy, especially one that is dependent on long-distance trade, requires a more regularized system of tax collection – the set of institutions that we usually call a state. Efficient modern commerce depends on a transportation network and on financial organs that can provide secure credit and investment.

Third, the economy of the capital and many of the provinces was dependent on trade between the mines and Veracruz. The mining economy had been devastated, and Mexico City never really controlled Veracruz and the roads between the plateau and the coast. The "royal commanders" near the mines continued to appropriate resources for their own use. Mexico City was left without a reliable source of income, other than in areas around the capital. Without foreign trade, this income was only large enough to finance activities in the central region.

Fourth, the commanders of the royalist "armies," let alone the official governmental organs, did not have control of their regions in the way that the word *caudillo* usually connotes. The regional economies of the future Mexico were too integrated with each other and also with the world economy to be self-sufficient. Hence most of the *caudillos* had the same problem as the authorities of the capital: their income was too dependent on

[32] *Caudillo* means leader or political boss in Spanish.

long-distance commerce that was disrupted. They had to form tenuous coalitions ("make deals" is a more accurate expression) with leaders of lesser militia leaders and with local estate owners who had their own private forces. They had to worry about the rise of new militia leaders in towns or areas under their nominal control.

One minor commander on whom we have information for the period after 1816 is Santa Anna, the future dictator of Mexico. Santa Anna was only 16 years old in 1810 and came from a semi-elite family in the commercial city of Xalapa, which is located between Veracruz and Puebla. He was an excellent commander and was given four villages along the Veracruz coast that he ruled in a "military-autocratic" manner. The villages were a source of taxation for his men and he appointed four friends to govern them. He let other rebels have control of abandoned haciendas in exchange for their making "tax" payments. Yet Santa Anna clearly had plans for a greater role in politics and he was not the only commander with such ambitions.

The Royalist Commanders and the Proclamation of Independence

Except in the Morelos rebellion, the word "independence" was never mentioned in the Mexican War of Independence. In 1812, the British-protected Regency Council adopted a constitution with a constitutional monarch and a parliament (*Cortes*). The Constitution treated Spanish America as an inherent part of Spain itself by granting each of the 10 Spanish American colonies representation – the four viceroyalties and six captaincy-generals.[33]

The Constitution of 1812 had little real meaning in Spain. When Napoleon was defeated in 1813–1814 and Ferdinand VII was restored to power, he repudiated the constitution and dissolved the *Cortes*. In practice, the colonies were essentially autonomous, and Ferdinand was too preoccupied with matters at home to try to reestablish real control over them.

In late 1819, Ferdinand finally decided to assemble troops to impose Spanish control on Buenos Aires and restore the flow of rawhides and Potosí silver to Spain. When he tried to send troops in 1820, however, the troops rebelled and refused to go. Their leader, Rafael del Riego, marched with his troops against Ferdinand, and in response, Ferdinand accepted the Constitution of 1812 that turned him into a constitutional king. In practice, Ferdinand was placed under house arrest.

[33] Nettie Lee Benson, ed., *Mexico and the Spanish Cortes* (Austin: University of Texas Press, 1966).

The restoration of the Constitution of 1812 had a dramatic impact on Mexico. Now that Napoleon was gone and Ferdinand had been removed from power, Spain seemed incapable of organizing a military attack. The provisions of the Constitution now seemed to have real meaning. The viceroyalty was abolished, and the Provincial Deputation of New Spain represented the smaller Kingdom of New Spain (the core of modern Mexico). This Provincial Deputation had seven provinces: Mexico, Puebla, Michoacán, Oaxaca, San Luis Potosí, Tlaxcala, and Querétaro.[34]

While the *Cortes* wanted to retain the colonies in the New World, it began the decisive movement toward Mexican independence by calling for two sets of elections in the second half of 1820. One was for deputies to represent the colonies in the *Cortes* in Spain. The new *Cortes*, like that of 1812, gave representation to administrative territories, not to districts based on more or less equal numbers of people. Each area would have a Provincial Deputation of from five to seven members. Seven of these areas would become part of the future independent Mexico.[35]

An overwhelming percentage of the population was located in the two areas: the Mexico [City area] Deputation and to some extent New Galicia (Guadalajara). Naturally, the people in populous central Mexico complained about the inequality of the representation, and each of the territories that had been ruled by an *intendant* claimed the right to have their own Provincial Deputation. The *Cortes* gradually acceded to these demands. The number of Provincial Deputations rose from 7 in November 1820 to 14 by the end of 1821 to 18 in November 1822 to 23 by December 1823.[36]

The second set of local elections ordered by the *Cortes* was to choose representatives in newly created *ayuntamientos* (the new name of *cabildos*) in more than 1,000 city-states. Small towns and Native American villages always had had *cabildos*, but in practice, they had been subordinated to the *cabildos* of larger city-states or to the *alcaldes mayores* who collected taxes from the indigenous villages. Charles III's establishment of intendancies had given added power to the large cities that became their capitals, and

[34] A brief summary is found in Jaime Rodríguez O., "The Transition from Colony to Nation: New Spain, 1820–1821," in Jaime Rodríguez O., *Mexico in the Age of Democratic Revolutions* (Boulder, CO: Lynne Rienner, 1994), pp. 100–101, footnote 8.

[35] Nettie Lee Benson, "Spain's Contribution to Federalism in Mexico," in Thomas Cotner, ed., *Essays in Mexican History* (Austin: University of Texas Press, 1958), p 94.

[36] For the number of deputations and maps of their boundaries at each date, see Nettie Lee Benson, *The Provincial Deputation in Mexico: Harbinger of Provincial Autonomy, Independence, and Federalism* (Austin: University of Texas Press, 1992), pp. 21, 31, 51, and 59.

the *cabildos* of these capital cities seemed ready to evolve into provincial legislatures.

Now any town with 1,000 people could form an independent *ayuntamiento* and rule the area surrounding it. The *cabildo* elections had been formalistic in character, but *ayuntamientos* had no hereditary members. The Native Americans and *mestizos* were granted the right to vote in the elections.[37] The *ayuntamiento* elections varied greatly in their character. Some were dominated by the old elite and others by anti-elite members, but the crucial fact was that the *ayuntamientos* of the smaller towns and villages were largely autonomous from those located in the *intendant* capitals.

In short, the local government reform of the *Cortes* reversed the evolution of governmental power that had occurred in the last quarter of a century before the overthrow of Charles IV. Instead of trying to end a decade of political disorder by re-creating strong governmental units at the provincial level (roughly the equivalent of the American state), the *Cortes* promoted a decentralization of power to county-like units too small to collect taxes in a nation-state economy and to govern effectively.

Conflict between the *ayuntamientos* of the small towns and the appointed and elected officials of the intendancy capitals was inevitable. This conflict was intensified by the decision to have the Provincial Deputations elected indirectly by the *ayuntamientos*. Obviously the *ayuntamientos* in the smaller areas were more numerous than those in larger cities, and, therefore, they had the dominant role in selecting the Provincial Deputations. The final step to total governmental disorder at the provincial level was the decision in February 1823 to transform the Provincial Deputations into the provincial government.

Finally, of course, there were the royalist commanders and the various lower commanders more or less associated with them. If Mexico was moving from a decade of violence to a more normal political life, then the structure of the military and the financing of the military needed to be regularized as well. So long as Ferdinand VII was in power, the city-states were required to pay a war tax to support the local royalist troops. The concentration of power in intendancy capitals made it easier for the commanders to enforce this requirement.

The decentralization of regional power complicated the collection of money by the military. When the Constitution was restored, the local authorities often stopped their payments. The newly elected *ayuntamientos* formally reaffirmed this policy and forbade the commanders from forming militias.[38]

[37] Rodríguez O., "The Transition from Colony to Nation," p. 104.

[38] Santa Anna's villages were among those who took this step.

The movement to Mexican independence began in November 1820 when Viceroy Juan Apodaca appointed Augustín Iturbide commander of the 3,000-man southern army and gave him the responsibility of ending the rebellion of Vicente Guerrero. Iturbide was also allowed – or, perhaps had to be allowed – to add a 1,300-man regiment from the Bajío that was loyal to him personally. The appointment of Iturbide never has been convincingly explained. He was the commander most likely to lead a pro-independence military coup, and even before leaving Mexico City, he began hinting about independence with increasing frankness. Iturbide began his march southward in December 1820 and soon began reaching out to the rebel leader with offers of cooperation.[39]

On February 24, 1821, only several months after he re-entered the military fray, Iturbide proclaimed his plan – the so-called Plan of Iguala that was expressed in the title he gave his forces: the Army of the Three Guarantees (Roman Catholicism, unity, and independence). Roman Catholicism became the state religion, a repudiation of the *Cortes*' anti-church position. "Unity" pledged equality for all citizens including *peninsulares*, Native Americans, blacks, and those of mixed origins. The independent country would be a constitutional monarchy. The throne was to be offered to Ferdinand or, if he rejected it, to one of his sons.

The plan's provision about the constitutional monarchy was wholly unrealistic or disingenuous. Neither Ferdinand nor the *Cortes* wanted the king or one of his sons to be in Mexico City legitimizing an independent Mexico. The likely purpose of the provision was to create a presumption about the form of government to be created when the Spaniards predictably refused.

Nothing was said in the plan about who would be the head of the army, let alone who might be chosen as the constitutional monarch from within Mexico. Nevertheless, Iturbide declared in a proclamation that "at the head of a valiant and resolute army, I have proclaimed Mexican independence," and there was no doubt about who was the dominant figure in the drive for independence. Most scholars believe that Iturbide was determined from the first to rule Mexico – and not as a constitutional monarch.[40]

Without any doubt, Iturbide had a clear conception about how to build a force that would ultimately overthrow the government in Mexico City. He knew that the soldiers of his own army required a salary, and he acquired the money ruthlessly. For instance, he seized 500,000 pesos of

[39] Robertson, *Iturbide*.

[40] Ibid., p. 75.

silver that merchants sent to Acapulco to pay for goods arriving from the Philippines. He then seized the goods themselves to obtain the proceeds from their sale.

When Iturbide issued the Plan of Iguala, he was removed from commander of the Army of the South and was left only with his own regiment of 1,300 men. He needed a coalition, and he began by forming an alliance with Guerrero. Iturbide gained the rebel's agreement to the Plan of Iguala by promising him continued control of his own armed militia and territory, an area with the economic base of cochineal production and with control of the road to Acapulco. Iturbide combined his men and Guerrero's and marched into the Bajío. As he roamed the area, he gave the commanders in the recalcitrant towns and cities the choice of being sacked or joining his cause.

Iturbide's basic technique with the royalist generals of the interior was the same one he used with Guerrero. He tried to negotiate alliances with what Will Fowler called "the strongmen ... the chieftains ... the caudillos of the War of Independence."[41] The most important was Anastasio Bustamante, the commander of the 6,000-man Army of the Center. Bustamente had fought in the area of the Bajío and the mines from 1810 onward and knew Iturbide well.

We do not know the precise offers that Iturbide made to the various commanders, but they almost surely contained the major assurance given to Guerrero: continued command of the forces in their base areas and recognition of their ability to raise funds for their army and themselves in the familiar informal ways. But Iturbide could also use other inducements as well. For example, an imprisoned rebel, Nicholas Bravo, was offered the return of his family's land.

The word *caudillo* often is used to refer to the major regional commanders, but it can be misleading at this stage if it conveys a sense of stability that did not exist. Commanders or would-be commanders often fought with each other to acquire a territory that they could control, but not in the sense that they had the power to collect regularized taxes if they won. They hardly had the power to form any kind of coalition on which a meaningful government could rest.

Santa Anna is the best-known example of a regional commander. In 1821, he was 27 years old and became the protégé of a genuinely pro-royalist governor of Veracruz. When the governor tried to expand his power to the west, he used Santa Anna to fight an Iturbide ally, the *caudillo* of the Puebla

[41] Will Fowler, *Santa Anna of Mexico* (Lincoln: University of Nebraska, 2007), p. xviii.

area. Instead, Santa Anna was persuaded to join Iturbide and, as a reward, was given control of the town of Xalapa, the city where he had grown up. He tried to use Xalapa as a base to defeat his former royalist mentor and to conquer Veracruz. When he failed, Iturbide tried to remove him, but instead, Santa Anna formed a coalition that forced out Iturbide. Similar patterns of conflict occurred throughout Mexico on a lesser level, both before independence and afterward.

The final step to independence began when a new Captain General and Superior Political Chief (the new title for "viceroy"), Juan O'Donoju, arrived in July 1821. Under the new Constitution, he had authority only over the area of the provincial deputation in Mexico City.[42] Within two weeks, O'Donoju decided that independence was inevitable. On August 23, he and Iturbide met in Córdoba, halfway between Puebla and Veracruz. The next day they signed a treaty that recognized Mexican independence and essentially followed the provisions of the Plan of Iguala. On September 27, Iturbide and O'Donoju marched into Mexico City with their troops and declared independence on September 28.[43]

The interim structure of government and the relationship between Iturbide and O'Donoju were left totally ambiguous. When O'Donoju died a few days after the declaration of independence, apparently of natural causes, Iturbide was left in complete control of the government. Yet within two years he was deposed and the disorder continued.

The Failure of the Iturbide Regime

Whatever the causes of the long-term political disorder and economic difficulties in Mexico, the answer surely must begin with an explanation of why the leader who achieved Mexican independence with a military coup was unable to consolidate a stable authoritarian regime in a country with an authoritarian political tradition.

42 When O'Donoju was appointed on February 14, 1821, the Mexico deputation included much of the core of modern Mexico, but then on May 8, it was divided into many parts. It is not clear if O'Donoju retained his original jurisdiction and whether it was reduced to the area around Mexico City. He died before really assuming his office, and the issue was never clarified. Benson, "Spain's Contribution," pp. 94 and 96–7.

43 Conservatives considered September 27 to be Mexico's independence day, but over the last century, a regime eager to emphasize the indigenous roots of modern Mexico has celebrated September 16, 1812, the day of the beginning of the Hidalgo rebellion, as independence day. Samuel Brunk, *Heroes and Hero Cults in Latin America* (Austin: University of Texas Press, 2006).

Under the new regime, a Regency Council was made the chief executive body, and Iturbide was named as its de facto head. Iturbide was appointed commander of chief of the army and given the right to appoint all officers at the level of brigadier and above. He divided the country into six military districts and appointed six captain-generals to head them – in practice, the key commanders in his coalition. The number of provincial governments was much higher, and, hence, the captain-generals did not have regional governments to use as their instruments of rule.

Although the historian John Lynch calls Iturbide a military dictator, this is true only in the sense that Iturbide's power was based on the military.[44] Iturbide was not commanding a real army or even leading a coherent coalition of commanders. In the words of Brian Hamnett:[45]

> One cannot precisely speak of the army [of 1823] as if it were a unified body, a monolith. It was, on the contrary, a very complex aggregation of autonomous bands directed by ambitious military politicians who frequently had a clientele to satisfy.

In November 1821, the Regency called for the election of a Constituent Assembly to draft a constitution. Yet when the Assembly met in January 1822, it immediately assumed the functions of a congress and never tried to draft a constitution. It acted as if it were the legitimate legislature and government. Since the flawed indirect electoral system was used, the smaller towns were overrepresented, but the main problem is that the deputies were disproportionately the types of liberal intellectuals who would be attracted to the writing of constitutions. They did not have the experience best suited for a legislative congress.

Iturbide accepted the broader role of the Assembly, but he insisted on his right to occupy the dominant symbolic and political positions within it. The result was an intense conflict between him and the congressional leaders. In February 1822, the Congress declared that it, not the monarch, was sovereign, but in May, Iturbide had himself declared the emperor. In doing so, he claimed, he was responding to popular demand. The "popular

[44] John Lynch, *The Spanish American Revolutions, 1808–1826*, 2nd ed. (New York: W.W. Norton, 1986), pp. 323–35.

[45] Brian Hamnett, "Factores regionales en la desintegración del regimen colonial en la Nueva España; El federalismo de 1823–1824," in Inge Buisson, Kahle, Günter, König, Hans-Joachim, and Horst Pietschmann, eds., *Problemas de la formación del estado y de la nación en Hispanoamérica* (Bonn: Internations, 1984). Quoted in Timothy Anna, *The Mexican Empire of Iturbide* (Lincoln: University of Nebraska Press, 1990), p. 171; William DePalo, *The Mexican National Army, 1822–1852* (College Station: Texas A&M Press, 1997), pp. 24–6 and 183, note 4; Frank Samponaro, "The Political Role of the Army in Mexico, 1821–1847" (Ph.D. dissertation, State University of New York-Stony Brook, 1971).

demand" was represented in the streets of Mexico City by the troops of Iturbide's old 1,300-man regiment.

The financial situation in Mexico was rapidly deteriorating, and the government could not collect the revenue needed to cover its expenses. In 1822, the government had revenue of 9.3 million pesos and expenses of 13.5 million. The sources of the revenue are obscure, but scholars write of attempts, often successful, to secure voluntary loans and then forced loans. There are reports of the seizure of money from the *consulado*, the church, and charitable institutions. The forms and amount of "taxation" by regional commanders seem unknown.

The revenue went primarily toward military and civilian salaries. In the words of Frank Samponaro, "important army commanders were absolutely opposed in principle to any substantial cut in the size of the forces under their command." One reason was that when a soldier deserted, he often was kept on the rolls, and the commander simply kept for himself the salary that was appropriated for the missing soldier.[46] It is unclear how much revenue the regional commanders remitted to the capital, but it likely was small, except in the case of commanders in the center.

On October 28, 1822, the Ministry of Finance announced that paper money would be issued to fill the shortfall. Several days later, Iturbide dissolved the Congress and created the Junta Nacional Instituyente as the top policy body. In December, the government said that four million pesos of paper money would be issued and that paper must be used to pay one-third of civilian and military salaries.[47] Timothy Anna writes that by January 1823 "the paper money was wreaking havoc everywhere."[48]

Iturbide's downfall began scarcely a month later. Spanish loyalists occupied the fort at Veracruz that had been the collection point for customs duties. When Iturbide tried to relieve Santa Anna of his duties, Santa Anna responded by launching a revolt against Iturbide. Santa Anna called for the creation of a republic, and on December 6, he issued a manifesto (the Plan of Veracruz) that annulled all of Iturbide's acts and called for the restoration of the Congress.

The general whom Iturbide sent to suppress the rebellion failed to do so, but again we should not think of clashes of professional armies. Mexican "armies" contained some 2,000 to 3,000 troops who lived off the land. The

46 Samponaro, "The Political Role," pp. 35 and 64.

47 The figures of 9.3 and 13.5 come from Alamán, a leading politician and historian of the period. Anna, *The Mexican Empire of Iturbide*, pp. 131–3.

48 Ibid., p. 162.

majority of people in Veracruz supported Santa Anna, Will Fowler reports, because they were "convinced that [the opposing general's] troops would pillage the city if they were allowed in."[49] When Santa Anna led his troops into San Luis Potosí to spread his revolt, he himself acted precisely in the way that the people of Veracruz feared.

After three months of stalemate, the generals whom Iturbide had sent to suppress Santa Anna called a truce, and on February 1, 1823, these generals issued a manifesto opposing Iturbide called the Plan of Casa Mata. Santa Anna signed it the next day. Like the Plan of Veracruz, the Plan of Casa Mata called for a return of power to the Congress. But, as Nettie Benson emphasized, it contained a crucial clause: "the provincial deputations ... shall be the one to administer affairs" until a new regime was established."[50]

The clause about the provincial deputations was a concession to Santa Anna, who was supported by the Veracruz provincial deputation but opposed by the local government. Nevertheless, it had broad significance. After independence, the provincial deputations were usually controlled by the liberals who opposed Iturbide and wanted a federal republic. They accepted the Plan of Casa Mata, as did the local military commanders.

Santa Anna's small army, which moved irregularly through the country winning military support, was not opposed by significant force. On February 1, 1823, after less than a year and a half in power, Iturbide and Santa Anna met, and Iturbide agreed to reconvene the Congress, abdicate, and go into exile. Benson argued that the provinces were "virtually autonomous" by March 1823.[51]

Why had Iturbide failed so completely in such a short period? When a "military dictator" falls after little more than a year in office, short-term collective action problems are likely the reason. Such an explanation seems especially probable when the dictator's successors suffer the same fate. Indeed, there were more than 50 presidents between 1822 and 1847 and 36 changes of president between May 1833 and August 1855.[52] The vast

[49] Fowler, *Santa Anna of Mexico*, p. 65.

[50] The plan is found in its entirety in Nettie Lee Benson, "The Plan of Casa Mata," *Hispanic American Historical Review* 25 (1945), 45–56, pp. 49–50.

[51] Iturbide left on May 11, 1823, and the Congress subsequently passed a death sentence on him if he returned. The following year, conservatives persuaded him to return. He was executed on July 19, 1824, five days after landing in Mexico. Anna, *The Mexican Empire of Iturbide*, p. 169; Benson, "The Plan of Casa Mata," p. 55.

[52] Likewise, Mexico had 112 finance ministers in the period from 1830 to 1863. D. C. M. Platt, "Dependency in Nineteenth-Century Latin America: An Historian Objects," *Latin American Research Review* 15 (1980), 113–30, p. 118.

majority were military officers. As one historian expressed it succinctly, the country "constantly teetered between simple chaos and unmitigated anarchy."[53]

The major reason for Iturbide's fall is that he did not have the means to pay the troops. On November 2, two days after Iturbide dissolved the Congress, he gave an interview to Joel Poinsett, President James Monroe's personal representative in Mexico. Poinsett was not impressed either by the emperor's talents or by the stability of his regime:[54]

> [Iturbide] has attached the officers and soldiers to his person, and so long as he possesses the means of paying and rewarding them, so long he will maintain himself on the throne; when these fail he will be precipitated from it.

Poinsett added that "it is a maxim of history ... that a government not founded on public opinion, but established and supported by corruption and violence, cannot exist without ample means to pay the soldiery, and to maintain pensioners and partisans." This maxim, he said, will "probably be again illustrated by this example [of Iturbide]." In fact, Iturbide did not have the means to pay the troops, and this would have caused difficulties for much more legitimate rulers.

Nevertheless, Poinsett's explanation simply begs the question of why Iturbide and his commanders did not collect sufficient taxes. It is easy to understand why tax collection was difficult at the end of the war, but not why so catastrophically little was collected afterward.

One reason for the low tax collection is that the economy remained deeply depressed. The coinage of silver, which fell from 24.7 million pesos in 1809 to 7.7 million pesos in 1812, rose to 9.6 million pesos in 1815 and 1816, and averaged 12.0 million from 1818 through 1820. After a temporary drop to 7.6 million in 1821, the coinage remained around 10 million pesos in 1822 and 1823 – below the level of 1818 to 1820.[55] Other parts of the Spanish economy also were slow to recover during this period.

A second reason for the collapse of regularized tax revenue was the abolition or sharp reduction of the level of taxes that was imposed on the population. Barbara Tenenbaum reports that Iturbide abolished the "royal tenth" on silver, lowered total taxes on silver to 3%, reduced import taxes from

[53] Enrique Krauze, *Mexico: Biography of Power: A History of Modern Mexico* (New York: HarperCollins, 1997), p. 133; Michael Meyer and William Sherman, *The Course of Mexican History*, 5th ed. (New York: Oxford University Press, 1995), p. 324.

[54] Poinsett, *Notes on Mexico*, p. 68.

[55] Rodríguez O., "Down from Colonialism," p. 10.

36.5% to 25% and the *alcabala* tax from 10% to 6%, and ended the 10% tax on goods leaving Mexico City.[56]

Tenenbaum suggests that the reduction in the level of taxes resulted from a deliberate decision to adopt the standard liberal economic advice in Europe: the stimulation of production and investment by cutting taxes. She says that "modern economists would praise Iturbide for his sound strategy for promoting national recovery."[57] A political scientist seriously doubts that Iturbide was influenced by the standard thinking of liberal economists. Most likely, he found himself unable to collect the taxes and was simply happy to be told by some liberals in the Congress that by necessity, he was following the best European advice.

In any case, if economists of either of that time or the present time believe Iturbide had a "sound strategy for promoting national recovery," they are quite mistaken. As has been seen, Adam Smith's convincing case for free-market measures in 1776 was dependent on the ability of the king to collect taxes on manufacturers. Iturbide certainly did not have any ability to collect any sophisticated taxes in 1821.

If Iturbide was to have any chance in the 1820s, and he may not have, he needed to focus on a few simple, "second-best" alternatives: (1) Maintain silver production at least at its 1820 level by any practicable combination of force, state-directed policies, and market-oriented measures. (2) Concentrate troops on guarding convoys on the core transportation routes between the mines and Veracruz. (3) Keep the port of Veracruz open. (4) Replace the failed government tax system with taxes easy to collect with regularized tax farming by the guilds (including the *consulados*) and the Mining Tribunal. In fact, Iturbide accomplished none of these goals and probably did not have the capacity to do so. The guilds were essentially abolished from 1820 to 1824, the *consulados* in 1824, and the Mining Tribunal in 1826.[58]

The Failure of the Constitution of 1824

After the overthrow of Iturbide in 1823, the victors moved quickly to introduce the Constitution of 1824. The constitution created a president and

[56] Barbara Tenenbaum, *The Politics of Penury: Debts and Taxes in Mexico, 1821–1856* (Albuquerque: University of New Mexico Press, 1986), p. 18.

[57] Ibid., p. 18.

[58] Stanley Green, *The Mexican Republic: The First Decade, 1823–1832* (Pittsburgh, PA: University of Pittsburgh Press, 1987), pp. 113–15. For the *consulados*, see Brian Hamnett, "Mercantile Rivalry and Peninsular Division: The *Consulados* of New Spain and the Impact of the Bourbon Reforms, 1780–1824," *Ibero-Amerikanisches Archiv* 2 (1976), 273–305.

vice president elected for four years, a Congress, and a Supreme Court. The country was divided into 19 states, each with its own elected governor, legislature, and judiciary. The unpopulated north was divided into four territories.[59] The country was called the United Mexican States and was proclaimed a federal republic. Indeed, the Mexican president was elected directly by the state legislatures, and each state had one vote, regardless of population.[60]

Unfortunately, the Mexican Constitution was drafted and approved by those elected in the unrepresentative elections of 1820 and 1821. The state officials were selected in the same system of indirect elections that brought the Provincial Deputations to power and that overrepresented the *ayuntamientos* of the smaller towns and villages. The states, like those of the original provinces of the Provincial Deputations, had very different population levels.

Of course, the American states also had unequal population, and the less populous states had a veto in the Senate and in the House of Representatives runoff in which the president was expected to be elected. In 1787, however, each of the least populous American states was geographically, economically, and religiously similar to a more populous one with similar interests and values. The two together were represented in proper proportion to their joint population. Hence, the population differences were less politically important.[61]

In Mexico, by contrast, the least populous states were almost all on the northern and southern periphery, while the more populous states, especially if we exclude the Mayan Yucatán, were in the prosperous core of the country. The 10 central states from San Luis Potosí and Zacatecas southward to Oaxaca contained 4.5 million people, while the 13 peripheral states had a population of 1.7 million; 1.1 million if Yucatán is excluded.[62]

As a result, the one state-one vote in the Mexican presidential election could produce a result resented by those in the core of the country. The first two elected presidents were rebels in the Civil War: Guadalupe Victoria and

[59] For the number of deputations and maps of their boundaries at each time, see Benson, *The Provincial Deputation*, pp. 21, 31, 51, and 59.

[60] Actually, each legislature had two votes, and the candidate with the most votes became president and the runner-up become vice president.

[61] This is no longer true. The least populous states are concentrated in the Mountain, Prairie, and Southern regions and are overwhelmingly rural. The 21 most rural states have 21% of the population, the same as California, New York, and Illinois. The latter have six senators and the former 42 – enough to veto any legislation in the Senate, and, therefore, the Congress.

[62] Green, *The Mexican Republic*, pp. 54–5. The map is on p. 46.

Vicente Guerrero. Victoria had come from Durango in the far north and had fought in the area around Veracruz. Guerrero, as has been seen, came from the area southwest of Mexico City. Both of these men naturally had an anti–Mexico City perspective. They disproportionately received their votes from the state legislatures in more outlying areas.

The most important difference between the United States and Mexico, however, did not involve the structure of the central government but the character of the state governments. The American colonial and state political elite had the experience, the tax revenue, and the military force to govern. After 1776, they had ruled independently for 11 years under the Articles of Confederation. Farmers owned their own land and had rifles to control brigands who might interfere with the transportation of their goods to market. This also limited the ability of brigands to interfere with the movement of people.

Mexico was quite different. Mexican provinces had been informally ruled for 250 years by elite families through *cabildos* that had little governmental apparatus to collect taxes and maintain security. The creation of territories (intendancies) analogous in size and population to American states eventually was producing a more effective provincial system, but Madrid kept experimenting with the structure. The *intendants* had not become well rooted or even well defined by 1810. Moreover, the chief "crop" of the economy – silver – was very valuable, and villagers had an incentive to attack those carrying it rather than to defend them.

After 1810, the just-emerging system of provincial government was destroyed not only by the disorder inside Mexico but also by the series of constitutional and unconstitutional changes that occurred in Spain from 1808 into the early 1820s. The changes that the Spanish *Cortes* introduced when it was restored to power in 1820 were particularly destructive.

The Mexican deputies were not experienced politicians, and they were primarily interested in weakening the power both of provincial officials appointed by Ferdinand VII and the provincial elite associated with these officials. The provincial officials and elite were located in the intendancy capital, and the expansion in the power of the small towns and villages came at the expense of these capitals. The new Provincial Deputations, which basically represented the outlying small towns, were certain to come into conflict with the *ayuntamientos* of the provincial capitals.

More important, nothing was done to strengthen the executive branch in the provinces. As a result, the laws of the newly elected officials in the central or provincial legislatures could not have any real effect. Indeed, the name "deputations" correctly implied representative responsibilities, not governing ones. The powerful military officials also had no significant bureaucracy through which to rule. We have already cited Lloyd Mecham's important point: "the normal process of federation was reversed.... Instead of the national state being created by the local states, as in the United States, the local states were created by the national representative body."[63]

In 1824, the Congress tried to introduce order into the system of taxation. The state governments were given the right to collect a series of taxes and to control some specific sources of income while the national government was given others. The states received the taxes on sales (the *alcabala*), gold and silver, and pulque (the most popular hard liquor). The states were allowed – really, expected – to impose a new income tax equal to three days' salary. The states were supposed to raise a total of 7.4 million pesos in revenue, 3.1 million of it from the income tax.[64]

The main source of direct income for the national government was a 15% tariff on all imports. The national government also obtained the revenue from the tobacco, gunpowder, and salt monopolies. It was estimated that in the first year the national government would collect taxes worth 7.5 million pesos. In addition, the states as a whole were supposed to transmit 3.1 million pesos to the national treasury, the exact amount of the income tax. In effect, the income tax was a national tax that the states were obligated to collect. It was projected that 44% of national revenue was to come from the tariffs and 29% from the state income tax.

On the surface, this tax structure seems to be strong evidence of a centralized federal system. Yet it would be naïve to believe that the states were likely to submit half the taxes they collected to the national government unless compelled to do so. The experience of the U.S. Articles of Confederation with far fewer obligations certainly suggested otherwise. The Mexican tax structure implied that the central government would have a strong army financed in large part by the tax assessment received from the state governments. Precisely for this reason, the state governments had a powerful incentive not to remit taxes to the central government.

In fact, the 1824 congressional decisions and projections had no relationship to reality. Pro-Spanish forces continued to control the fort at the entrance to the Veracruz harbor, and the harbor was formally closed from 1823 to 1825. This meant that neither Spain nor the Mexican government

[63] J. Lloyd Mecham, "The Origins of Federalism in Mexico," *Hispanic American Historical Review* 18 (1938), 164–82. The quote is on 164.

[64] This figure and those in the next two paragraphs come from Tenenbaum, *The Politics of Penury*, pp. 22–9.

collected any tariffs in Veracruz, and that those in control of the fort and of the area (essentially Santa Anna and Guadalupe Victoria) profited personally from the smuggling that occurred. Some tariffs were collected at other ports, but the national government did not have a customs service that was even semi-effective.

When the state legislatures elected the first president in 1824, they chose the decentralizing rebel, Guadalupe Victoria, as president. Another former rebel, Nicholas Bravo, became the vice president. The Mexicans immediately obtained a loan from British banks on onerous terms: $8 million in cash in exchange for 30-year bonds that had a face value of $16 million when repaid. Mexico had to pay 5% interest on the $16 million. The terms of a second loan in 1825 were somewhat better, but Mexico still received only $12 million for 6% bonds valued at $16 million.[65] British investors also put money into silver mines.

The entire financial program assumed a rapid increase in the production of silver and of the industrial, agricultural, and animal products used in the mining communities. This was the pre-condition for the sharp increase in foreign trade on which national tax collection depended. As in the 1600s, it is not clear how much silver was actually exported, but officially it was around 10 million pesos in 1820 and 1821 each and 9.3 million in 1822. Official exports fell to 3.4 million in 1823, 6.5 million in 1824, 3.7 million in 1825, and 5.9 million in 1826. They returned to the 9.7 million level in 1827.[66]

Only when Veracruz was re-opened in 1826 did customs receipts climb from 6.5 to 9 million pesos, still below the 1820 and 1821 level. Moreover, one-third of this money was pledged to pay the interest on the British loans. The tobacco monopoly, which produced over 6 million pesos income a year in the late 1700s, was predicted to produce 2.5 million pesos a year in the 1820s. The figure reached 50% of the predicted amount in only one year between 1824 and 1833. The states never paid the national treasury as much as 50% of their general assessment, and much of that surely remained in the states to pay the soldiers there.[67] That is, it was a bookkeeping transfer.

The result was a financial disaster. The annual colonial tax receipts had averaged 20 million pesos from 1785 to 1789 and then, together with loans and supplements, had risen to 58.8 million pesos in the wartime year of 1808. By contrast, only some 11 to 12 million pesos were collected in a

[65] Ibid., pp. 21–22.
[66] Green, *The Mexican Republic*, p. 131.
[67] Tenenbaum, *The Politics of Penury*, pp. 22, 27–28.

normal year between 1825 and 1834. The total amount of military salaries was much higher in the 1820s and 1830s than in the colonial period, and the Victoria government had to use the proceeds from the foreign loans to pay them.

Mexico had to default on its British loans in 1827 because of lack of funds. Now the government had to turn to domestic lenders. It had a policy of expelling all Spaniards, but it allowed those who made large financial contributions to remain. It obtained loans from Creoles by offering extremely high rates for extremely short-term loans.

Victoria's strategy was successful enough in the short run to ensure that he was the only president in the first 30 years of Mexican independence who served his entire term in office. The exhaustion of the foreign loans meant, however, that his successor, Vicente Guerrero, could not use the same financial strategy.

Beginning in May, Guerrero's minister of finance, Lorenzo Zavala, introduced a vigorous policy of balancing the budget. He raised taxes on the income and property of the wealthy, cut the salaries and pensions of civilian and military personnel, and called for a forced loan of $2.8 million from the states. Zavala was compelled to resign around November 1, and on December 4, General Anastasio Bustamante overthrew Guerrero. The announced purpose was to establish a strong central government and army, but the regime soon repealed Zavala's taxes.[68] The conservatives gradually moved toward the replacement of the 1824 Constitution with the centralist documents of the constitutions of 1836 and 1843.

Chile and the Explanation for the Failed Mexican State

Scholars have put forth many explanations for Mexico's poor performance prior to 1870. John Coatsworth, for example, thought the increase in silver production in the late Bourbon period was simply the result of inefficient government subsidies. He believed that "the mining industry was so sick that it can be doubted whether the industry's decline had anything to do with the insurgency at all."[69]

Coatsworth's interpretation is not, however, totally convincing since many were willing to invest in Mexican mining early in the century. More

[68] Margaret Henson, *Lorenzo de Zavala: The Pragmatic Idealist* (Fort Worth: Texas Christian University Press, 1996).

[69] John Coatsworth, "The Mexican Mining Industry in the Eighteenth Century," in Peter Bakewell, ed., *Mines of Silver and Gold in the Americas* (Aldershot: Varorium 1997), pp. 280 and 264.

important, much sustained growth – for example, China's for over three decades – has been based on various kinds of subsidies. For whatever reason, Mexican silver production – and investment in it – rose to colonial levels toward the end of the century even though commodity prices collapsed in 1873 and 1893.[70]

Since serious economic recovery started in 1871, most economists focus on the period after that and only have an introductory chapter that summarizes the reasons for Mexican economic difficulties prior to that time. Unfortunately, these reasons are often broad, long-term factors: the lack of adequate domestic investment sources for modernization, a poor transportation system (the poor roads inherited from the colonial period and the failure to build railroads), the lack of a strong domestic market to absorb domestic production, and a large peasantry that was poor, ill-educated, largely non-Spanish in ethnicity, and deeply resentful about its social position.[71]

The problem with these explanations is that they emphasize factors that are found in almost all countries at a low level of development. Some such countries remain relatively stagnant for a prolonged period, while others begin the slow process of economic development and a few develop quite rapidly. We need to understand how these obstacles were overcome – or why they were not – at a specific time in a specific place.

[70] Coatsworth deflates the silver production with data on maize prices, but the crucial issue for silver was its exchange value on the world market. John Fisher, *The Economic Aspects of Spanish Imperialism in America, 1492–1810* (Liverpool: Liverpool University Press, 1997), p. 188; Tom Cassidy, *British Capital and the Mexican Silver Industry, 1820–1850* (Cambridge: Cambridge University Press, 1975); Richard Salvucci, *Politics, Markets, and Mexico's London Debt* (New York: Cambridge University Press, 2009).

[71] For arguments about the devastating economic effects of the War of Independence, see Enrique Cárdenas, "A Macroeconomic Interpretation in Nineteenth-Century Mexico," in Stephen Haber, ed., *How Latin America Fell Behind: Essays on the Economic Histories of Brazil and Mexico* (Stanford, CA: Stanford University Press, 1997). For a discussion of how capital markets were slow to develop in Mexico, see Carlos Marichal, "Obstacles to the Development of Capital Markets in Nineteenth Century Mexico," in the same book. Herrera Canales shows how trading markets, especially of mercury, were disrupted in the 19th century. Inés Herrera Canales, "Mercurio para refiner la plata Mexicana en el siglo XIX," *Historia Mexicana* 40 (1990), 27–51. Stephen Haber provides an excellent discussion of the effect of geography on the creation of a unified market in the country. Stephen Haber, "Assessing the Obstacles to Industrialization: The Mexican Economy 1830–1940," *Journal of Latin American Studies* 24 (1992), 1–32. Last, for more on the political uncertainty and brigandage that took place both during and after the War of Independence, see Paul Vanderwood, *Disorder and Progress: Bandits, Police, and Mexican Development* (Lincoln: University of Nebraska Press, 1981) and Hilarie Heath, "British Merchant Houses in Mexico, 1821–1860: Conforming Business Practices and Ethics," *Hispanic American Historical Review* 73 (1993), 261–90.

North emphasizes that the control of violence is necessary for economic growth, and North's earlier article with Summerhill and Weingast explains the difference in the economic performance of the United States and Mexico in these terms. North and Weingast in particular think that in Mexico, the lack of a "shared belief system about the role of government, the state, corporate privilege, and citizen" was crucial, an argument with which we are in disagreement.[72]

A really thorough explanation of the reasons for the instability and economic problems of Mexico requires a comparison with all or most of the countries that emerged from the Spanish Empire – a comparison that looks at the physical endowments, their colonial history, their difference in physical and ethnic endowments, and the policies their rulers followed in their early post-independence period. That is for another book.

Unfortunately, we do not have the time and space for a proper comparison, but Chile in the 1810s and 1820s provides a useful contrast.[73] Chile had inherited the same Spanish culture as Mexico, and it had an actual war with royalist troops from Peru from 1813 to 1817. Until 1830, Chile had more constitutional instability than Mexico: five liberal constitutions (1812, 1812, 1822, 1823, and 1828), punctuated by short-lived military dictatorships and coups and revolts. France and Britain did not recognize Chile until 1830 and 1831, respectively, because it was so unstable.

Yet Chile was one of the more successful Spanish-American regimes in the 19th and 20th centuries. Per capita income in Chile rose from $694 in 1820 to $1,290 in 1870. This 86% increase was identical with Great Britain's and only slightly less than the 95% increase in the United States.[74] This was before Chile conquered the guano-rich areas of Bolivia in 1879 and achieved further economic growth by exploiting it.

In 1829, Chile had a military-based conservative coup that introduced basic stability for decades. Chile's government was nominally elected, but it was what a noted Chilean historian called a conservative "autocratic republic." Chile attracted a substantial amount of British capital investment to modernize its silver mines and to build a number of railroads.[75]

[72] North, *Understanding the Process of Change*, pp. 112–15.

[73] The following paragraphs are a summary of Jerry Hough and Robin Grier, "The Hidalgo Rebellion and the Problem of Order: The Comparative Lessons of Chile and the United States," *Latin Americanist* 54 (2010), 59–80.

[74] Angus Maddison, Historical Statistics of the World Economy: 1-2008 AD (http://www.ggdc.net/MADDISON/oriindex.htm).

[75] Luis Galdames, *A History of Chile* (Chapel Hill: University of North Carolina Press, 1941), chap. 9; Leland Pederson, *The Mining Industry of the Norte Chico, Chile* (Evanston, IL: Northwestern University, 1966), 187–225.

The Bustamente military coup d'état in Mexico, also conducted in 1829, seemingly should have had a similar result, but it did not. While economic progress was made at certain times and places in the four decades from 1830 to 1870, it was uneven at best. It is particularly difficult to calculate Mexican GDP during this politically turbulent period, but at a minimum, Mexico had a stagnant economy over a period when many other countries – including the United States, Argentina, and Chile – did very well.

Why did Mexico not follow Chile's path? Why did it acquire a ruler like Porfirio Díaz only in 1870, not in 1830? Díaz's government was far from fully effective, let alone morally ideal, but it achieved impressive economic growth. The Chilean rulers after 1830 and, indeed, the English kings from Henry VII in 1485 to Charles II in the 1660s and 1670s, were similar to Díaz in all three respects.

One major difference between Mexico and Chile was the same as that between Spain and England – one of size. Chile, for all its north-south length, had a small and well-run city-state on the Santiago-Valparaiso axis both before and after independence. So long as that city-state had a navy based in Valparaiso – and it did – it could easily control the northern mine owners unless its navy was weaker than the Peruvian one. The mine owners had to export their product by sea, and the issue with Peru was decided in the early 1820s.

Order could and did break down in Chile, but it was restored without enormous difficulty. Modern Mexico, however, is the size of Western Europe, and the distances between the mines, Mexico City, and the ports were quite great. In short, Mexican geography created enormous problems.

Second, as we have seen in England in 1660 and 1688, the concentration of military power in the navy instead of the army, typical in a city-state based on a port, makes the restoration of order less difficult. If a large army is effective, this must be because it rests on a well-functioning military bureaucracy. As Samuel Huntington said, the army is one of the first effective bureaucracies to arise in a developing country – one of the first with rational-legal values, especially in the military realm. Indeed, for this reason, Huntington thought a military dictatorship could be an effective engine of development. In any case, this is a reason that military dictatorships often do emerge.

The dependence of an effective large army on an effective system of taxation means, however, that it is far less stable than a navy capable of piracy and trade. Once order breaks down in a large area because the police and army disintegrate, the disorder can easily feed on itself. A failed state at its extreme is anarchy, and Dennis Mueller, as may be recalled, argued that "in an anarchic environment, the independent choices of both individuals can be expected to lead both to adopt the dominant stealing strategy."[76]

Even if most people are restrained from choosing the stealing strategy by ethical considerations, they may be driven to that strategy in order to meet what they consider their higher ethical duty to feed their families. Hence, when tax collection and then the army collapse, this can create a circular process that is quite difficult to solve when production depends on transportation that has also collapsed because of the disorder.

The American states did not have a large standing army, but they did raise taxes and could mobilize a militia and pay its salary. As we have seen, nearly all of Spanish America was very different. The viceroys did not have significant military force at their disposal, and the provincial authorities did not have meaningful militias. The "armies" in the War of Independence usually contained no more than a few thousand men. The good ones were like Iturbide's 1,300-man regiment from his home area. The regional generals of his coalition after independence usually were similar in their core, reliable units.

This fact is a central explanation not only of Iturbide's tenuous control on power but also that of his successors. Most of the presidents from the 1820s to 1860 were military generals. Michael Costeloe counts 15 such generals.[77] The disparity between the number of generals and the number of presidents indicates that some generals held the presidency more than once. The most noted general, Santa Anna, was president 11 times.

It is surprising that none of these generals could establish a solid military dictatorship, at least in the central city-state. But this did not occur until Benito Juárez came to power in 1867, and he faced a competing president and disorder outside the capital.

Only Porfirio Díaz established a moderately effective but basically non-repressive military dictatorship and basic order (the so-called *pax Porfiriana*) 60 years after 1810. Even that regime collapsed in the Mexican Revolution of 1910 when he mishandled the succession. The revolutionary turmoil extended into the 1920s before a stable state was established.

When most authors try to explain the instability after 1824, they focus on the weakness of the legislature and the political struggles within the

[76] Dennis Mueller, *Public Choice II* (Cambridge: Cambridge University Press, 1989), pp. 9–10.

[77] Michael Costeloe, *The Central Republic in Mexico, 1835–1846* (Cambridge: Cambridge University Press, 1993).

top political elite. Few explore the executive branch, the provinces, and the military forces in the provinces.

The liberals of the time charged that men like Santa Anna were tyrants, but from a comparative perspective, the really surprising fact about Santa Anna is that he was not a tyrant. He never really made an effort to consolidate power even though he essentially was the *caudillo* in control of the key port of Veracruz. This seemingly should have given him the power to become a permanent national leader. Since he controlled customs collection, he seemingly had the interest of Mancur Olson's classic stationary bandit to promote economic growth and increase customs collection, as this would maximize his illegal as well as legal income.

In fact, the behavior of the politically oriented generals appears peculiar. Michael Costeloe points to a very strange phenomenon. Hundreds of coup attempts (*pronunciamentos*) were made against both the central government and state governments. Of course, such military coups often occur in developing countries, but if a group of commanders is involved in a coup, the victors often engage in a brutal and lethal struggle among themselves for a few years. Then, however, the eventual winner usually has a prolonged reign, far longer than the eight years of two American presidential terms. This did not happen until the success of Benito Juárez in mid-century and then only partially in the country as a whole.

The reason for the usual pattern in military coups throughout world history is clear. A military coup normally is a high-risk affair that can result in assassination or execution for treason. A successful coup usually is followed by a thorough and often violent purging of supporters of the old regime. Since all generals in a collective military coup feel highly vulnerable, they often take violent action against their collaborators for defensive reasons, if nothing else.

Except with the early presidency of Vicente Guerrero, this did not happen in Mexico.[78] In the words of a contemporary cited by Michael Costeloe, "The rebellions are speculations in which one risks nothing and can gain a lot." Costeloe concluded, "Throughout all the turmoil, there was a remarkable degree of human continuity in the sense that the people involved did not change.... Rebel military and civilians lived to fight another day and mostly did so."[79]

[78] Vicente Guerrero was the only president to be executed, and many suspect that this anomaly was partly because of his ethnicity – a black-*mestizo* mix. Theodore G. Vincent, *The Legacy of Vicente Guerrero: Mexico's First Black Indian President* (Gainesville: University of Florida Press, 2001).

[79] Costeloe, *The Central Republic*, pp. 7, 27.

The group of generals who ruled Mexico from 1821 into the 1850s and served more than a year were, with one exception, born between 1780 and 1794 and had been commanders during the War of Independence. Many think that this fact was crucial, that there was an esprit de corps and camaraderie among them that led to mutual tolerance. Yet such personal relations exist in other revolutions, coups, and Wars of Independence, but this seldom prevents those involved from using violence against one another.

We have several hypotheses for the deviation of Mexico from the normal pattern and for the change in the 1860s. We suspect that it was not camaraderie but continued personal and personalistic control of regional military force that prevented any president, even Santa Anna, from bringing the other regional *caudillo*s under control. Santa Anna himself seemed to feel safer in Veracruz, and even there, he preferred a low-visibility profile.

Another factor was that no administrative structure existed outside through which a victorious general could introduce enough firm control to create the order necessary for investment and the reliable collection of taxes. Hence the normal incentive to obtain increased revenue from control of increasing economic growth was very weak.

Many explain the change that occurred with Juárez and then Díaz by the demographic facts of life. A cohort born between 1780 and 1794 was entering its 60s and 70s in the 1850s and 1860s. Change was inevitable. Benito Juárez was born in 1806 and Porfirio Díaz in 1830, and they were not part of the generation of generals from the War of Independence.

Nevertheless, the aging of the American cohort of top politicians born in the 1780s did not lead to peaceful change, but to the Civil War. Given the general instability in Mexico for decades, the disappearance of the close-knit cohort from the War of Independence also seemed likely to promote further destabilization, not the opposite.

Our primary explanation for the stability that emerged from the generational change in Mexico flows from our basic explanation for the difference in outcome of federalism in the United States and the federalism in Mexico. We have emphasized the lack of correspondence between the borders of intendancies, military districts, and *ayuntamientos* – and, therefore, the impossibility of creating effective executive branches of government in the Mexican provinces. This problem gradually disappeared over time.

After independence, the state boundaries were stable, and their chief executives were formally elected governors. The *caudillo*s or their lieutenants normally became governors, but the post became more regularized and an administrative structure gradually formed and matured. The government came to have meaningful governmental instruments of rule, and the *caudillo* himself created a more stable military force under his control.

The result was reflected in the title of one of the well-known books about Juárez and Díaz: *Juárez and Díaz: Machine Politics in Mexico*. The author of the book, Laurens Ballard Perry, described in detail the operation of that machine politics and the system of alliances that could be made among those functioning within it.[80]

We will, however, end with a point that we first made at the beginning of Chapter 2 about pre-states. Stable coalitions must rest on specialized elites or leaders who rest on a stable base of power, either a solid military unit or a civilian structure that has a reliable corporate or bureaucratized base. England before Henry III really did not have that character nor did Spain before Queen Isabella. A failed state like Mexico after 1810 had an even less stable base for any but short-term alliances. The necessary state structure developed in Mexico in the mid-1800s, but real stability depended on the formal coalition institutionalized in the 1920s and 1930s in the PRI (Partido Revolucionario Institucional, or Institutional Revolutionary Party).

[80] Laurens Ballard Perry, *Juárez and Díaz: Machine Politics in Mexico* (DeKalb: Northern Illinois University Press, 1978), p. 28.

11

The Implications for Development Theory

This book has focused in great detail on the economic and political development of Europe and its implications for a theory of change that is useful for the development community today. In an ultimate sense the book originated in the early 1990s with the excessive optimism about the transition from communism and the speed of transformation of Latin America. The book project itself was born in the aftermath of the optimism of the Iraq War about the possibility of rapid democratization, an optimism that remained quite alive at the time of the Arab Spring, years after we began.

We were drawn to the work of Douglass North because he was a prominent economist in the 1990s who was skeptical about the promised speed of reform in the communist world and Latin America. We especially liked his stark statement when he accepted the Nobel Prize in Economics in 1993: "Neoclassical theory is simply an inappropriate tool to analyze and prescribe policies that will induce development." The theory, he said, rests on "two basic erroneous assumptions" – one that "institutions do not matter" and the other that "time does not matter."[1]

North did not follow the Old Institutionalists in defining institutions as government organs, but he used the word to mean "a human construct of rules, norms, conventions, and ways of doing things that define the framework of human interaction."[2] When we began this project, North's argument about institutions had already had a major impact on development economists. Hence, we decided to focus on "time." Why did development

1 Douglass North, "Epilogue: Economic Performance through Time," in Lee Alston, Thrainn Eggertsson, and Douglass North, eds., *Empirical Studies in Institutional Change* (Cambridge: Cambridge University Press, 1996), p. 343.

2 Douglass North, *Understanding the Process of Economic Change* (Princeton, NJ: Princeton University Press, 2005), p. 11.

take so long, perhaps 400 years as North said or centuries and millennia as Oliver Williamson said?

Since 1993, North has consistently and explicitly recognized that he had not been able to produce a theory of developmental change. Critics went further and charged that, in the words of three leading New Institutionalists in 2014, "some aspects of current institutional theory make change seem almost impossible."[3] The purpose of this book was to introduce dynamism into North's work and contribute to a theory of change.

We were convinced that North's insights about norms, values, and habits were invaluable but needed to be supplemented by insights from other disciplines. We thought that the work of the sociologist Max Weber and the de facto political scientist Mancur Olson were the most useful such major figures for our purpose.

In recent years, most broad books on development have focused on the steps to democratization and their impact on economic development, but as North says, this evolution is largely limited to the last 10% of the development process. Little democratization occurred during the centuries we were examining, and hence we were focusing on the first 90% of the process – what North was to call the second development problem (really the first). In the language of Daron Acemoglu and James Robinson, our concern was with the 500 years of English development before the "political centralization" of the Tudors in the early 1500s and the 200 years afterward.[4]

We essentially began with the opening sentence of the most famous book of the leading development theorist of the 1960s, Samuel Huntington: "The most important political distinction among countries concerns not their form of government but their degree of government." In this book written a half century ago, the strongly anti-communist Huntington continued:[5]

> The United States, Great Britain, and the Soviet Union have different forms of government, but in all three systems the government governs.... [In this respect, their], political systems ... differ significantly from the governments which exist in many, if not most of the modernizing countries of Asia, Africa, or Latin America.... The political community [often] is fragmented against itself.... [P]olitical institutions

[3] Claude Menard and Mary Shirley, "The Contribution of Douglass North to New Institutional Economics," p. 28, and John Joseph Wallis, "Persistence and Change in Institutions: The Evolution of Douglass North," p. 48, in Sebastian Galiani and Itai Sened, eds., *Institutions, Property Rights, and Economic Growth* (Cambridge: Cambridge University Press, 2014).

[4] Daron Acemoglu and James Robinson, *Why Nations Fail: The Origins of Power, Prosperity, and Poverty* (New York: Crown, 2012), pp. 83–7.

[5] Samuel Huntington, *Political Order in Changing Societies* (New Haven, CT: Yale University Press, 1968), pp. 1–2.

have little power, less majesty, and no resiliency.... In many cases, governments simply do not govern.

Interestingly, many of Huntington's cases of 50 years ago are still in the headlines today because of their continued difficulties in governing. This book demonstrates that progress was also very slow in Europe and that the transition from what we call a pre-state to an early state, a minimally effective state, and a truly effective state, let alone to a real democracy, was tortuous indeed.

This book was based on the conviction that a theory of change should begin with three core assumptions. First, North's analysis of informal institutions must be enriched. North focuses only on the crucial need for norms and belief systems that underpin a modern market, but he does not specify their content. More important, he never discusses the old values and ethical norms that must be replaced or new values and belief systems that may arise to hinder the development of the market or democracy.

North's 1989 article "Constitutions and Commitment" that he coauthored with Barry Weingast is typical. It has the subtitle of "The Evolution of Institutions Governing Public Choice in Seventeenth Century England" but it does not mention religion even though the three great violent regime changes of the century – the Civil War, the Restoration, and the Glorious Revolution – were all centered on religious conflict. The summary articles in *In the Shadow of Violence* on the developing world do not mention religious fundamentalism as a contributor to violence.

We believe that Max Weber's distinction between the values and norms of the village and those of modern society provides a vital supplement to North on this point. The peasants with the traditional values of the village often react with anxiety, fear, and outright hostility to the "satanic" values of the educated elites they meet when they come to the city.

In our discussion of this point, we looked at England in the 1600s. It was also true of the French Revolution, the Revolution of 1848 in central Europe that provoked Marx's *The Communist Manifesto* (his proletariat were peasant newcomers to the city), the Russian Revolution, the Chinese Revolution, and the Iranian Revolution. We are inclined to agree that the Hidalgo rebellion in 1810 in Mexico was substantially "a reactionary clerical backlash against the liberal and enlightened Bourbon reforms of the second half of the eighteenth century."[6]

[6] Will Fowler, *Mexico in the Age of Proposals, 1821–1853* (Westport, CT: Greenwood Press, 1998), p. 13.

Second, a theory of change must emphasize the crucial importance of building an effective state as a pre-condition of building an effective market. The central reason for the extreme optimism of the Washington consensus in the 1990s about the Soviet Union and Latin America was well expressed in 1977 by the chairman of the US Federal Reserve Board Alan Greenspan: "Some supposed [that] the dismantling of the central planning function in an economy [would] automatically establish a free market entrepreneurial system."[7]

Greenspan certainly is not a proponent of a strong government in the normal sense of that phrase, but he understands that a modern market of laws and rules is created by government and is enforced by government. Progress is dependent on introducing impersonal laws, regulations, and norms to replace personalistic subsidies, tax farming, concessions, monopoly guilds, trust built on family ties and intermarriage, and so forth. Specific regulations clearly can become counterproductive and should be changed or repealed, but de-regulation cannot occur until regulations exist. Americans say they have a rule of law, but it is more accurate to say rule of laws.

A well-functioning modern market is little more than the combination of the network of laws and rules that create the incentives to which economic actors respond and the trust the government creates that they will be enforced impartially. An obvious conclusion follows. The immediate reason that the development process is so long is the length of time needed to develop an effective set of laws and rules and the government on which they depend.

We believe that the place to start is with Max Weber – this time with his argument that professional bureaucracies both in government (including the military) and in the private sector (prominently including the business corporation) are the defining feature of modern society.

While most scholars have focused on the problem of "society" controlling the ruler, we think that the first problem – and it takes centuries to solve – is the acquisition by rulers of the ability to control their so-called agents. These are, first of all, the military and the tax collectors who are needed to consolidate a regime in a larger territory and to strip the warlords of the troops that prevent the formation of an effective state.

Third, the fundamental changes involved in development are at every step injurious to the interests of powerful forces who benefit from the status quo. Their resistance cannot be overcome simply by persuading them

7 Alan Greenspan, *The Embrace of Free Markets* (Washington, DC: Woodrow Wilson International Center for Scholars, 1997), p. 2.

that broader societal interests are served by their agreeing to sacrifice their interests and power. We think Robert Bates is right in emphasizing "the basic insight … that coercion can be socially productive."[8]

We build on the work of Mancur Olson to make this point. Olson was one of North's major rivals and developed his theory of the origins and nature of the state in response to North and Weingast's 1989 "Constitutions and Commitment." He vigorously denied that any kind of social contract can form or maintain a state. Instead he asserted that the pre-democratic ruler is the man who "can best organize a capacity for violence."

From our perspective, the most useful aspect of Olson's work was that he did not simply present his thesis but constructed a model to justify it. He followed James Buchanan in arguing that those in the political and economic sphere must have the same basic human motivation. Like Buchanan, Olson began for heuristic reasons with the assumption of narrow individual self-interest in the neoclassical economic model. He applied this assumption to individual participants in the political process, including governmental officials.

Olson demonstrated that this assumption alone leads to the conclusion that narrow self-interest normally makes it irrational for people to take part in large-scale collective actions to achieve goals that they themselves want to be achieved. This certainly includes mass participation in action to overthrow a dictator or to protect a constitutional order.

Olson's point also includes the observance by rulers or military commanders of constitutional rules and obedience by officials of the ruler's commands. A self-interested person should be a "free rider" and pursue self-interest even to the point of carrying out a military coup or accepting bribes or engaging in outright theft. Only compulsion and selective side payments make participation rational.

But if this is true, a crucial element in development must be the collection of revenue to pay the necessary side payments (salaries) to induce the military and civilian officers to participate in the collective action of government and follow the rules of the game. As Margaret Levi emphasizes, "it is costly to use coercion to enforce compliance" and rulers need to establish various types of incentives to achieve "quasi-voluntary compliance."[9] Yet even in the United States, the payment of taxes requires compulsion.

[8] Robert Bates, "The New Institutionalism," in Sebastian Galiani and Itai Sened, eds., *Institutions, Property Rights, and Economic Growth: The Legacy of Douglass North* (Cambridge: Cambridge University Press, 2014), 50–65.

[9] Margaret Levi, *Of Rule and Revenue* (Berkeley: University of California Press, 1988), pp. 50 and 52.

This means that we must look to the ruler, not some amorphous dominant coalition or social contract, to take the actions that promote change. Olson argued that the desire to maximize tax revenue gives rulers a powerful incentive to promote the economic growth that increases revenue and to restrain themselves if that promotes growth. Not all rulers do this, but we have seen many examples in pre-industrial England and Spain of such action.

Our research design was based on the conviction that it is impossible to understand why development takes so long unless we examine the history of several comparable countries over many hundreds of years. We were determined to cut beneath the deeply embedded mythology which surrounds all regimes and always emphasizes the consent of the governed.

Mancur Olson's assumptions often, in fact, did illuminate the factors that were driving development in unexpected ways in our four countries. In England, the added "taxes" at times of medieval wars actually were a contribution, not always voluntary, to a collective effort to obtain booty abroad. In Castile prior to 1262, this was so open, and the king so weak, that this contribution was not even called a tax. Similarly, the military (the navy and the armed merchant ships) played a major, even decisive, role in the three regime changes in the turbulent 1600s.

Since American economists naturally know best the mythology of the colonial and revolutionary period in the United States, they may not recognize the severity of the religious conflicts before, during, and after the revolutionary period and the lack of a common American identity until the very eve of the Revolution. Hence they might not appreciate this factor in the developing world.

In Spain, Franco's myths about a centralized Spain hid the fact that Castile had no state at all before 1480 and an extremely weak one before the Bourbon overthrow of the Hapsburgs in 1700. This had an inevitable impact on the ability of Spain to control its distant colonies in the 1500s and 1600s. As a result, we supported William Summerhill's conclusion that "the old association of centralization with negative [economic] outcomes has ... been turned on its head."[10]

Since many of the assumptions of American economists about Spain and Spanish America rest on a historical literature that was superseded after

[10] William Summerhill, "Fiscal Bargains, Political Institutions, and Economic Performance," *Hispanic-American Historical Review* 88 (2008), 219–33, pp. 221 and 227. See also Alejandra Irigoin and Regina Grafe, "Bargaining for Absolutism: A Spanish Path to Nation-State and Empire Building," *Hispanic-American Historical Review*, in the same issue, pp. 173–4.

Franco's death, this finding has major implications for those economists. On this question, comparative work does, in fact, reaffirm our major theses and those of Acemoglu and Robinson about the importance of their "political centralization."

Finally our work unexpectedly proves of great use to economists working on the most important "developing country" that of Europe. After we began this study, the crisis over the euro and the attempt of the European Community to use an undemocratic European state to impose permanent severe budgetary constraints on the democratically elected governments of the periphery has led to an optimism about the nascent European state that far transcends the optimism of the Washington consensus.

Those thinking about, and working on, building a European state and market should understand that that state began barely 70 years ago. A surprising amount has been done in those years, and the formation of a European state certainly should not take the 400 years posited by Douglass North. Nevertheless, in our terms the European state is still in its pre-state phase.

It will take a long time before the European state is effective enough to impose its will on democratic states whose peoples are suffering. The nationalism associated with national currencies would make the austerity politically easier to tolerate. The issue that must be pondered is whether a benign nationalism needs to be encouraged to prevent one that is far from benign. Europeans need to read about the Europe of this book, even the "good" England that was culturally far more united than the present-day nation-states of Europe.

The Importance of Time

The first conclusion of this book is that England and Spain confirm our underlying hypothesis: European development took a very long time. Of course, as anyone who has examined the historical record even superficially already knows, this was, indeed, a simple hypothesis to confirm. Our purpose in emphasizing this basic point was to get the reader to understand – really, to feel – just how long the process takes. This is crucial if we are to overcome an inevitable desire to have unrealistic expectations today.

We have tried to increase realism by comparing the country that was most successful and had the "good culture" with the one that supposedly was quite different. Even in England nearly 500 years passed between the Norman Conquest in 1066 and the creation of a minimally effective state in the 1530s. It took another 200 years to build a truly effective state in the first half of the 1750s.

The evolution toward constitutional democracy took even longer. The Magna Carta signed by King John in 1212 was disregarded by his son Henry III in a civil war in which he conquered London. The Glorious Revolution of 1688 was still more than 400 years in the future, and it followed 175 years of the most authoritarian rulers in English history. That is as long as the time between the presidency of Andrew Jackson and the present. The first true electoral system in England was established in 1832, and universal suffrage was introduced 50 years later.

Our central question was why English development was so slow and why Spanish and Mexican development was even slower. Acemoglu and Robinson begin their book *Why Nations Fail* with a comparison of the stark differences between the two cities of Nogales, one in the United States and the other across a purely artificial border in Mexico. They explain the difference by "the way [their different] institutions, both economic and political, shape the incentives of businesses, individuals, and politicians."[11]

Few would disagree with this general explanation. But what is the nature of that difference, and what explains it? Acemoglu and Robinson explain the difference between the two cities by the presence of inclusive institutions in the American Nogales and extractive institutions in the Mexican. These terms are similar to North's open-access and limitedaccess orders.

Acemoglu and Robinson's analysis sometimes seems to imply that the difference among developing countries is a matter of political choice and that any country could be a Botswana, their prime example of success.[12] While they recognize the importance of inertia, we believe that this argument does not fully take into account North's warning about time.

Acemoglu and Robinson's book title, *Why Nations Fail*, is drawn from the phrase "failed state" that is widely used in political science. We would argue, however, that most developing nations are not failing. Instead, their market economies and democratic institutions are being created. As in Europe, the process takes hundreds of years.

One of our key explanations for the faster development of England than Castile was the difference in the size of their territory. England began as the city-state of London in the late 1200s. The warlord of London still required 200 years to seize effective control of England in 1485. Only 220 years later did he acquire Scotland, 400 miles away. When Alfonso X captured Cadiz

[11] Acemoglu and Robinson, *Why Nations Fail*, pp. 83–7.

[12] Ibid., pp. 83–7.

in 1262, his realm stretched 600 miles from there to the wool-exporting northern ports on the Bay of Biscay.

It is interesting that the East Asian tigers (Singapore, Hong Kong, Taiwan, and South Korea) are all small countries. One of the most successful, Taiwan, is only slightly larger than Massachusetts and Rhode Island combined, while South Korea is the same size as Indiana. Vietnam is three-and-ahalf times larger than South Korea, Thailand five times larger, Myanmar and Afghanistan seven times. The latter two countries are the size of Texas, but with far more difficult terrain.

A small country such as Botswana with less than 1 million people in 1980 and 2 million people today can make rapid progress. Or at least this is true if it is dominated by a small elite from a single tribal group that is allied with a powerful foreign diamond cartel and that then uses a near-monopoly one-party system like the Mexican PRI to suppress other ethnic groups. Elections in such a country do not mean, however, that it has an open-access society.

A country such as Mexico with the size of Western Europe and 70 million people in 1980 and 123 million in 2014 is a different matter altogether. If seen in the perspective of European development and that of many other developing countries, Mexico has actually done quite well since the 1970s.

The political system in Mexico has undergone a major transformation. We agree with Douglass North that whatever language is used, Mexico made the transition from a basic limited-access state in 1980 to a mature limited one in the 1990s. Rule by the monopoly PRI was replaced by a competitive party system in which the PRI lost presidential elections in 2000 and 2006 to a pro-business party.

Then in 2012 the PRI won a competitive presidential election with Enrique Peña Nieto, an attractive candidate who promised major reform. Surprisingly, he delivered on his promises even though their final results can, of course, only be judged in the future. Peña Nieto invited foreigners to invest in the nationalized oil industry, and he challenged the powerful trade unions in reforming the education system. The old PRI had "privatized" the nationalized telephone industry but allowed an insider to create a near-monopoly on its foundation. Now Peña Nieto has passed legislation to open up the telecommunications industry.

These reforms are a continuation of the longtime opening of the economy to outsiders, including foreigners. This began before the introduction of the North American Free Trade Agreement (NAFTA) in 1993, but NAFTA accelerated the process. It is estimated that NAFTA increased foreign direct

Table 11.1. *Mexican economic development, 1980–2010*

	GDP*	Per capita GDP	Total tax revenue (as a % of GDP)
1980	337	2,763	14.8
1985	477	2,369	15.5
1990	612	5,993	15.8
1995	752	7,986	15.2
2000	1,065	10,339	16.9
2005	1,297	12,017	18.1
2010	1,565	14,667	18.9

* GDP is adjusted for purchasing power parity and is measured in hundreds of millions of current international dollars.
Source: World Bank, *World Development Indicators, 2014,* retrieved June 6, 2014. Total tax revenue as a percentage of GDP is from OECD, *Combined Revenue Statistics, Comparative Tables*, OECD Tax Statistics, retrieved June 6, 2014. http://stats.oecd.org/Index.aspx?DataSetCode=REV.

investment by 70%. By 2013, the World Bank Ease of Starting a Business Index listed Mexico as ranking 48 of 185 countries. In 2004, it took an average of 58 days to start a business and 9 government procedures. By 2012, those numbers had fallen to 6 days and 6 procedures.[13]

As Table 11.1 shows, the Mexican government's ability to collect taxes rose substantially. Tax revenue as a percentage of GDP increased from 14.8% in 1980 to 18.9% in 2010. It rose to 19.5% in 2011. Indeed, the increase is even better than it seems on the surface. Approximately 40% of tax revenue in 1980 was a near-100% tax on the nationalized petroleum industry, but oil production has fallen sharply in recent years and oil tax revenue is now only about a third of the total. The percentage of taxes from the citizenry and foreigners has risen to fill that gap.

The Mexican economy also did quite well in concrete quantitative terms. It is by no means clear that border cities such as Nogales, Tijuana, and Juarez are the best indicators of the progress in the modern urban areas in the center of the country. For a long time, the debt crisis of 1982 and the "tequila crisis" of 1994 loomed large in investors' eyes. Yet the United States had the Panic of 1837, the Panic of 1857, the Panic of 1873, and the Panic of 1893, and these downturns did little to prevent the 19th century from being a century of stunning economic success.

[13] World Bank, "Doing Business – Measuring Business Regulations – World Bank Group," *Doing Business*, 2014. Retrieved 2014-06-06.

The same is true of the last 40 years of Mexican history. The numbers in Table 11.1 show little long-term effect of the financial crises of the 1980s and 1990s or even of 2008. Per capita GDP was $14,273 in 2008. It dropped but 2.2% to $13,954 in 2009, and had risen to $16,246 in 2012.

Of course, 30 years is a substantial period of time, and Mexican GDP per capita income and tax collection are still behind the rich countries. Corruption continues to exist. Yet we insist that these problems be seen in light of the experience of the advanced countries. The medieval English kings had to use unpaid or underpaid officials, merchants, domestic guilds, clerics, and so forth to perform various government functions and to "pay" them through allowing them to make economic gains.

This continued in the 1500s and 1600s in England. N.A.M. Rodger emphasizes the deep involvement of the navy in various legal and illegal trade activities in the 1500s and 1600s, and Samuel Pepys's diary dramatically illustrates the "corruption" in the 1660s in the elite naval bureaucracy. In the 1700s, men sought the post of colonial governors in order to make their fortune. America is famous for the Robber Barons the end of 1800s, but the "plundering generation" in the mid-1800s was no different.

Tax collection is a major problem throughout the developing world. Even though foreign trade was the economic activity that English monarchs taxed most successfully, it still took them an extremely long time to create a professional system of taxation in this sphere. And since a tax on foreign trade was the easiest to impose, it shows how difficult was the overall process of taxation.

In the 1300s, the English kings collected export taxes largely through an alliance with the most powerful armed fleet in Europe, that of the Hanseatic League. English monopoly guilds were also deeply involved. In Castile, when looting ended with the conquest of the south, the king immediately created the Mesta to collect more "export taxes" on the wool being sheared from the migrating sheep before it was sent to northern Europe.

In England of the 1500s, the Hanseatic League had faded, and Henry VIII in 1540 did not have an armed merchant fleet large enough to overcome Spanish resistance and settle the New World. Much of his revenue came from seizure of the land of the abbeys.

By 1580, Elizabeth was able to increase the size of the merchant fleet and to develop a state with the capacity to tax smugglers and pirates who illegally obtained goods, preferably silver from Spain and its colonies. By the 1620s, when Charles I came to power, England had become a country with the administrative ability to permit free entry of all English subjects into trade within the Atlantic empire.

When the Caribbean Islands began producing sugar, the mainland English colonists could be allowed to engage in multi-faceted free trade with the Caribbean colonists because this trade could be taxed indirectly. Supplies for Caribbean slaves permitted a greater number of slaves and the production of greater amounts of sugar. The sugar could be taxed in England. Only in the 1760s could the kings collect taxes in the colonies effectively even though the monarchs were actively promoting the effort.

Spain followed a less linear course. Isabella began in 1480 with monopoly trade guilds, including the Mesta. Yet, 100 years later, Philip could not prevent the merchants from trading illegally with the English ships of Elizabeth I, and in the 1600s his successors lost virtually all their ability to tax colonial trade. In the 1700s, the Bourbons quickly regained control of their monopoly guilds, but only at the end of the century were they able to move toward the establishment of colonial free trade of the type that Charles I of England had been able to establish more than 150 years previously. The Spanish were only developing the ability to tax it.

Development economists can draw two major lessons. First, they cannot expect the speed of improvement that they would like or their superiors in the government might expect. The time from 1570 to 1620 seems insignificant in retrospect, but it is longer than a person's career. The year 1620 was still a century and a half from the time when Adam Smith wrote. When North cautioned that we must be patient, he meant *very* patient.

Second, the various developing countries today have varying levels of governmental capacity that place them at different points along these ill-defined English and Spanish lines of development. Per capita GDP numbers is one of the most easily available indicators of the level of development for a wide range of countries. Per capita GDP in Mexico, for example, is similar to that in Turkey but is somewhat below Chile, Argentina, and Uruguay. It is somewhat above Brazil and Venezuela, but has five times the per capita GDP of Bolivia and 12 times that of Haiti.

With the exception of South Africa, most sub-Saharan African countries became independent in the 1960s with minimally effective or maybe early truly effective governments in the capital areas, but they were pre-states outside the capital. They have made progress in 50 years, but Robert Bates, one of the most prominent American political scientists working on Africa, entitled his 2008 summary book *When Things Fell Apart: State Failure in Late-Century Africa.*[14]

[14] Robert Bates, *When Things Fell Apart: State Failure in Late-Century Africa.* (New York: Cambridge University Press, 2008).

Some sub-Saharan countries (for example, the Democratic Republic of the Congo) have per capita figures distorted by a mineral-producing sector with little impact on the population as a whole, but Haiti's per capita figure is close to that of most of sub-Saharan Africa. Indeed, Haiti is not far from the median level.

Like Latin America, Asia has countries with enormous variation in development. South Korea has a per capita GDP more or less equal to the EU average, while Taiwan is above that average. Both have democratic political systems, while several Asian countries in the headlines are as poor as Haiti or only slightly above it. The East Asian countries with large Chinese populations and/or strong US economic support for foreign policy reasons have done extremely well, but the strong cultural and political ties of the Philippines with the United States had little positive impact on that country's economy. The per capita GDP of the Philippines is on the level of Nicaragua and Honduras. Except for Tunisia, that of the Arab Spring countries is less than half that of Mexico.[15]

India is the major anomaly. Its per capita income is quite low and it has a population that is only 31% urban. A very substantial number of Indians are illiterate. Yet it has had a stable democracy for nearly 70 years. The most obvious explanation is that India meets three of Schumpeter's prerequisites of democracy to be discussed in the next section: an integrated and experienced political stratum, a strong bureaucracy, and a government whose range of decisions is fairly limited. In our terms, this means that it has an unusually strong state for its level of development, the result surely of the fact that England began to build its state in the 1600s.

With this enormous range of levels of economic development, it would be wrong to assume that the same policy advice is appropriate to all of them. Indeed, as important as it is to absorb Dani Rodrik's argument about "second-best institutions," it would be wrong to suppose that there is a single set of second-best (or third-best) institutions to introduce at particular times. Instead, as Rodrik insists, there are many "recipes."[16]

There is no realistic way to describe such a range of experiences, both historically and at the present, without positing different stages of development. North acknowledged this in 2009 when he created four categories of development: the limited natural state (or limitedaccess order), a basic state, a mature state, and an openaccess order. The fundamental practical

[15] World Bank, "Doing Business."

[16] Dani Rodrik, "Second-Best Institutions," *American Economic Review: Papers and Proceedings*, 98 (2008), 100–104; Dani Rodrik, *One Economics, Many Reforms: Globalization, Institutions, and Economic Growth* (Princeton, NJ: Princeton University Press, 2007).

problem with this division is that he dates the basic state in England to the period from 1066 into the mid-1700s. That is, it included 85% to 90% of the process before the democratization of 1832! Such a period simply must be subdivided if any meaningful theory of change is to be developed.

This book concentrates only on the change within that 85% to 90% of the development process. We subdivide it into four stages: pre-state, early state, minimally effective state, and beginnings of a truly effective state. Some scholars may think that this is too close to the old modernization theory. We do not apologize except to express our regrets that we wish we knew how to define the categories more precisely or how to subdivide such prolonged periods as 200 years.

The sine qua non of any sophisticated theory of change that contains elements of modernization theory or even stages of any kind is to avoid any implication of inevitability. In this book we emphasize the near-anarchy in Castile for two centuries after the late 1200s and in Mexico from 1810 to 1870. We recognize the relative stagnation of England of the 1400s and Spain of the 1600s. We understand that if Britain had strongly supported the Confederacy in 1861, the history of the United States would have been very different and quite likely the history of Europe and England itself.

Yet, as we have stated several times, the greatest defect of the research design of this book is that all four cases in our study were successes even though Spain and Mexico do not have that appearance from a "short-term" perspective of 200 years. We understand full well that the great success stories of the medieval period – the Italian city-states – never made the transition to modern nation-states, and except for Rome, became minor pawns.

We know that Poland was the great power of Eastern Europe until it fell into near anarchy in the mid-1660s and then was partitioned in 1772 and ceased to exist as a nation-state until 1918. Even then it was not recreated in response to popular pressure but by a decision by foreigners at the Versailles Conference.

Indeed, we are much impressed by the almostforgotten monumental work of Arnold Toynbee on the rise and fall of civilizations.[17] The Pharaohs, the Romans, the Greeks, and the Mayans – as well as a number of their counterparts in Asia – had quite effective governments for their time, but when they collapsed, the areas that they ruled did not recover for a very long time. Indeed, they are areas today that lag behind their counterparts.

[17] Arnold Toynbee, *A Study of History*, Vols. 1–12 (London: Oxford University Press, 1948–1961). A revised and abridged version in one volume with the same name and publisher was produced in 1972.

Our book begins with small warlords in England and Christian Spain around AD 800. At that time, Baghdad was the richest city in the world and may have contained nearly a million people. Yet in 1258 – almost exactly the same time when Henry III gained control of London in 1265 and Alfonso X conquered Cadiz in 1262 – the Mongols destroyed Baghdad. By the seventeenth century it had a mere 20,000 people, a figure that had only risen to 100,000 in 1800. In 1917, Baghdad had 200,000 people, and 80,000 of them were Jews. This shows how few Arabs had come there by that time. Only in 1921 did the British create the puppet state of Iraq with Baghdad as a capital.[18]

This point is necessary for modern Westerners to understand as well. Modern Western industrial society has only lasted for some 200 to 400 years, a very short period in comparison with other great civilizations. The plague killed as much as half the population in many European countries, and it is not difficult to imagine some technological calamity that would be just as devastating and that could have more lasting effects than the plague.

In a way, the examples of Spain and Mexico raise a particularly interesting question in this respect. The United States did not begin industrialization until 40 years after the American Revolution, but it had no problem catching up with Britain over a reasonable number of decades. Since Spain and Mexico were much less developed in the 1770s, it is not surprising that the independent Mexico continued to lag behind the United States.

On the surface, the more surprising fact is that Mexico was so far behind Spain in the 1990s. Spain, after all, had quite troubled transition from the creation of a minimally effective government in the early 1770s to a democratic, freemarket country in 1975. The military had been periodically involved in Spanish politics until the creation of the republic in 1931. The republic had experienced severe clashes among extremists until it was overthrown by a military coup d'état in 1936. Three years of bitter Civil War followed and then nearly 40 years of military rule under Francisco Franco. But when Franco died, Spain rapidly became a typical member of the European Community.

However one wants to characterize the progress of Mexico, it certainly does not yet compare with that of Spain. The question is why. We suspect

[18] Phebe Marr, *The Modern History of Iraq* (Boulder, CO: Westview, 1985), p. 21; Nessim Rejwan, *The Jews of Iraq: 3000 Years of History and Culture* (London: Weidenfeld and Nicolson, 1985), pp. 210–11.

that the answer is to be found in the "lost" 60 years between 1810 and 1870 when much of Mexico outside of the central capital area often had little state at all. We believe that Mexico will become a fairly modern state by mid-century or shortly afterward, but not in five or ten years.

Values, Dominant Coalitions, and Collective Action Theory

We began this research project with a strong conviction that Douglass North was right that institutions and time had to be taken into account in thinking about economic development. Since a large school of "New Institutionalists" had already risen in response to this appeal, we focused on North's demand that time be taken into account.

We believed that the fact that the New Institutionalists had yet to develop a theory of change meant that North's insights must be integrated with those of leading theorists from other disciplines in order to make progress. We thought Max Weber and Mancur Olson were two such theorists.

In focusing on the outside theorists, we took for granted that we did not have to give a great deal of attention to informal institutions themselves. As we went through North's writings and voluminous correspondence from the late 1970s until the mid-1990s, however, we discovered that informal institutions played a broader role in a theory of change than North suggested.

We knew that North did not emphasize the values that had to be overcome as the new ones necessary for an effective market emerged, but we discovered that he never mentioned any informal institution that had a negative impact on economic development. When North began to emphasize violence in his most recent two books, this remained true. The phrase "informal institutions" is not even mentioned in the theoretical chapters of *In the Shadow of Violence*.

Yet all development specialists and, indeed, everyone who even superficially follows political events in the developing world know that "negative" norms, ideas, and ideologies have a major role in the development process and are a major source of violence. Today, policymakers are absorbed with the anti-Western, anti-secular values and attitudes held by radical Muslims and their attraction to a broad swath of the population. Yet the conflicts between Sunni and Shiite radicals are even more explosive, and those between Muslim radicals and Muslim moderates are also extremely important.

Muslim fundamentalism is hardly a unique phenomenon. Religious conflict has been a persistent part of human history. In England in the mid-1600s, many Puritans or at least members of sects in the 1600s were religious fundamentalists. Religious conflicts were strong both in the English colonies and the post-independence United States because each colony was deliberately given to a representative of one of warring religions in the English Civil War when the United States was first colonized. Ethnic and national differences have, of course, also been a persistent source of conflict and violence and often are especially intense because they usually overlap with religious and other cultural differences.

Max Weber offers an important clue to a major reason that such conflict in values is a major source of violence in the developing world. The values of the village emphasize personalistic ethical norms, family-oriented obligations, and relatively fixed social positions. These values almost always have a religious base. Political authorities who are to be given the unquestioning obedience owed to a traditional father, but the rulers in turn are restrained by the expectation that they will show a sense of paternal responsibility.

When rural migrants arrive in the city, they face a largely secular, socially mobile, educated, professional elite who promote impersonal ethical norms and non-ascriptive norms even at the ethnic (clan) level. Cities such as Baghdad and Teheran are far removed from Weber's ideal type, but they are still different enough from the village to produce a combination of anxiety, uncertainty, and even revulsion. Demagogues arise who appeal to these feelings.

As Jack Goldstone emphasized, the danger of destabilization becomes especially great in the fairly long period when the migration from rural areas is at its height. Thus, London grew from approximately 75,000 people in 1550 to the 350,000–400,000 level in 1650 – a fivefold increase. It was near the 600,000 level in 1750, but that was less than a twofold increase in a century. Jack Goldstone argued that this may have been a major factor both in the great instability in the 1640s and in the ability of the elite to introduce peace after 1688.[19]

From Goldstone's perspective, it is clear why the Middle East has been so violence-dominated during the first half of the 20th century. The population of the key cities has been soaring since 1950: Baghdad from 580,000 in 1950 to 6.2 million in 2014, Cairo from 2.4 million

[19] Jack Goldstone, *Revolution and Rebellion in the Early Modern World* (Berkeley: University of California Press, 1991).

to 12.7, Teheran from 1 million to 8.1, and Istanbul from 1.1 million to 11.8.

One should remember the Nasser revolution in 1952 in Egypt and then the pan-Arab nationalist movement he led, the military coup by Saddam Hussein and his group in 1958, and, of course, the revolution in Iran in 1978. The Turkish military introduced multi-party democracy in 1945 but was powerful behind the scenes until 2010 and had coups in 1960, 1971, and 1980. Yet if Goldstone looked at the slowing rate of population growth from 1990 to 2010, he might well wonder if the Middle East will transition to the kind of restrained authoritarian rule that emerged in England after 1688.

A major reason that religious and ethnic differences have a particular tendency to produce violence during the transition from rural to urban society is that the conflict of values is usually reinforced by economic resentments. When the economic elite is associated with one religion or culture and the migrants to the city are associated with another, economic grievances and non-economic differences can intensify each other. This was true of the Catholics in Quebec and Ireland as they migrated into the Protestant cities. It is true of Shiite peasants moving into Sunni-dominated cities.

But, in addition, the economic elite and/or non-elite can gravitate toward a new religion or identity, and this can produce a real potential for violence. We discussed the conversion of the elite merchants of the non-Anglican colonies to the Church of England in the 1700s and the explosive reaction of the rural non-Anglican poor to this development. John Adams, it will be recalled, called the reaction in Massachusetts the most important cause of the American Revolution in that colony.

We dealt with this phenomenon most fully in our discussion of R.H. Tawney's analysis of the rise of Calvinism and Lutheranism in the 1500s and 1600s. Tawney argued that people who favored industrial and commercial development frequently found Calvinism attractive, while those who were threatened by the economic change responded to Luther's denunciation of commercial activity. Lutheranism never established itself in England, but Puritan sects arose in the 1630s and 1640s that had a similar orientation. We pointed to this as a central cause of the violence in the English Civil War.

We observe analogous developments in many different settings. The conflict between the ethnic Vietnamese (identified as the "Buddhists" at the time) and the ethnic Chinese, especially those in Saigon, was a central factor in the internal South Vietnamese revolution and was intensified by the status of the Chinese as the economic elite in the city. While the Sunnis are usually the economic elite in the Muslim world, the situation is reversed in Syria where the elite are the Alawite Shiites.

One could go on and on. Indeed, a major reason that communism was so attractive at the early stages of industrialization was because Marxist-Leninists characterized the Western culture of the local educated elite, like that in the West, as the "superstructure" that served the economic interests of bourgeois ruling class. In the developing world, this argument was especially effective because it became combined with nationalism by Lenin's charge that the local ruling class served the interests of Western "imperialists." They were said to be profiting from the economic suppression of the colony or semi-colony. Those who thought Western culture was satanic were given a strong emotional reason to overthrow the local economic elite.

Yet as one of North's early close collaborators, Margaret Levi, noted, "North does not acknowledge that ideology also may intensify or confirm self-interested behavior." Indeed, "he ... explicitly states that he is not concerned ... with ideology when it merely justifies self-interested behavior."[20] The neglect of the conflicts produced by the fear of Western values that peasants encounter as they migrate to the cities prevents an understanding of a major source of violence in the development process. The refusal to look at the frequent connection between self-interest and religious or ethnic differences is even more damaging.

Such a neglect of the relationship of religion or ideology and self-interest may lead to fundamental errors in American foreign policy. We did not understand the attitudes of the Vietnamese toward the Chinese economic elite in Saigon. We may not understand the attitude of the Pashtun toward the Iranian Farsi speakers in Kabul or a central army they create. And, of course, it makes it very difficult for economists and even historians to have Tawney's understanding of the conflicts and violence in 17th-century Europe. But it does explain why North and his co-authors are right in cautioning against premature democratization.

The argument remains one-sided. In many countries, the systemic pressures for long-term violence and anti-market activity are kept under control. Even the English and American civil wars did not disrupt a basically healthy, if prolonged, course of development.

As we have seen, many prominent theorists of revolution focus not on the role of pressure from below but on rulers who lack the skill to control turbulent social forces or the self-confidence to do so. Charles I of England is an example of a ruler with the lack of the necessary skill on the eve of the Civil War, and George III of a ruler with the lack of determination. Just as the English navy brought an end to the violence of the 1650s without the

[20] Levi, *Of Rule and Revenue*, pp. 51–2, including n. 6 on p. 51.

creation of an army dictatorship, so the American northern elite ended the turmoil from 1840 to 1875 by reducing sharply the level of democracy that existed in the 1840s and 1850s.

As we look at the control of violence during the middle stages of development from this perspective, Douglass North's concept of a dominant coalition is an extremely useful addition to a development theory. Like his earlier work, however, North's discussion of a dominant coalition has a very abstract character. By definition, every pre-democratic political system has a dominant coalition, and most political scientists think this is true of democracies as well.

The concept of dominant coalition becomes a useful part of a theory of change only if the nature of its membership is specified. For us, the crucial point is the nature of the change in the membership of the dominant coalition during the course of economic development. The dominant coalitions within England prior to 1500 and in Spain prior to 1700 were primarily based on the warlords of the various regions. The dominant coalition of an early industrial state includes merchants, manufacturers, a professional military, an independent financial elite, the government bureaucracy, and a more collective agricultural group often represented in the legislature. The dominant coalition of an advanced democracy is even more pluralistic, including within the military.

The first major problem in the transition from an effective rural-centered dominant coalition to an effective urban-centered one is the length of time that it usually takes. In this book the problem is best illustrated by the case of England in the 1500s and 1600s. Henry VII began disarming the warlords in 1485, but they were not fully disarmed until the early 1600s. Even then they retained considerable power in the court politics of the king and in the Parliament.

During this long period only one powerful member of the new urban-centered coalition was acquiring real political strength: the alliance of the armed merchant fleet and navy that Henry VIII began to build in the first decades of the 1500s and that was not really completed until the 1650s during Oliver Cromwell's dictatorship. Colonization was crucial in leading the monarchs to understand how much tax revenue could be generated and how non-guild merchants could be given an incentive to build oceangoing ships that would also serve as the king's navy. In the process, the navy-armed merchant alliance exercised decisive power in 1660 and 1688.

From this perspective, the ultimate cause of the English Civil War was the dangerous combination that is often found in the developing world.

The reign of Charles I was marked by high anxiety about economic change in London, a city that grew from 75,000 to nearly 400,000 in the century after 1550 at the same time that the old dominant coalition had largely disappeared and a new urban dominant coalition had not yet become strong enough, especially since Parliament was making London an unsafe port for anyone openly supporting the king.

Neither the king nor the Parliament had an army that could suppress even the minor levels of violence at the beginning of the 1640s, and the situation spun out of control. The navy was divided, and the radical-led mob violence made it too unsafe for its merchant allies to resist the radicals if they wanted to sail into London. The Parliament had to create a new army under Oliver Cromwell, but it did not have enough tax revenue to pay the salaries of the soldiers and sailors. The result was predictable.

In our opinion, the second major problem with the concept of a dominant coalition is that it is treated as a social contract, although one among the top elite rather than society as a whole. In North's model the members of the coalition, all with an ability to promote violence, somehow manage voluntarily and peacefully to negotiate a distribution of rent. Then by common agreement they peacefully maintain that distribution without even a ruler to negotiate their differences, let alone to enforce the distribution with his military forces and considerable control of side payments.

Mancur Olson and anyone attracted to his collective action approach would be extremely skeptical about the stability of any such social contract. After all, the participants in the coalition, according to North's argument, all have the ability to organize violence. We agree with Dennis Mueller that the self-interest of the neoclassical model leads actors "in an anarchic environment … to adopt the dominant stealing strategy."[21] The incentive for members of the dominant coalition to try to overturn the distribution of rent is enormous. We agree with Douglass North that restraining norms had not developed by this time.

In short, although North recognizes the importance of violence and of selective side payments in his recent work, the government officials are largely absent as more than vague recipients of rent. The military does not play a useful role in suppressing violence or protecting liberty and property rights, and there is no sense of the dilemmas posed by the fact that the military also is a major danger to liberty and property rights.

[21] Dennis Mueller, *Public Choice II* (Cambridge: Cambridge University Press, 1989), pp. 9–10.

In his two new books, North and his co-authors defend the concept of dominant coalition by contrasting it to a singleactor analysis of the state. This criticism seems aimed at the stationary bandit image of North's major rival, Mancur Olson. North is clearly right that the stationary bandit is a single actor, but Olson was playing a familiar heuristic game. Like John Locke and Karl Marx, Olson developed an oversimplified model of the origins of a state in order to illustrate his argument about the nature of the modern state.

It seems clear that Mancur Olson would have agreed that his focus on a single stationary bandit had to be expanded as society became more complex, that even the original stationary bandit would have needed some kind of coalition of lieutenants as he expanded the territory he was ruling. The more complex the state and the more specialized the knowledge of his lieutenants or their employees, the more the ruler had to become more of a chairman of a board. Olson would have strongly agreed with North's new insistence that "rent" (Olson would have said "selective side payments") is one of the elements necessary to hold a dominant coalition together.

Yet Olson also argued that a stable society depends on a strong figure with a preponderance of military force to organize the coalition. The inclusion of a monopoly of military power in the definition of a state does not have an abstract meaning. It means that an area has a ruler who controls that monopoly, appoints the key military and bureaucratic members of the coalition, coordinates its activities, and uses rewards and the threat of punishment to hold it together.

Olson would likely have agreed with our emphasis on the great difficulty – and the absolute centrality – in solving the collective action problems of controlling large military and tax-collecting bureaucracies. In our opinion, the central reason for the extremely slow transition to an effective market and state is the great difficulty that the ruler or coalition members who head bureaucratic organizations have in establishing control over their so-called "agents."

In conclusion, however, we would like to emphasize that the flaws in the concept of a dominant coalition are those of omission. We must recognize that a ruler is needed to solve the collective action problems of a dominant coalition and that military is necessary to curb violence. For our purposes it is even more important to understand that the transition from a coalition based on regional warlords to one based on a professional and restrained modern military takes a very long time. The overlap of this transition with the prolonged period of movement of anxious and frightened peasants into the city makes the danger of violence during the development process especially great.

Thinking Seriously about Democratization and the Creation of an Effective State and Market

Many broad books written by economists on economic and political development focus on the process of democratization. The reason, as North and his co-authors acknowledged in the 2013 preface of their 2009 *Violence and Orders*, is that they implicitly are focusing on developing countries in the last 50 to 100 years of their development. North believes, as do Acemoglu and Robinson, that careful democratization is necessary in such countries. We quite agree.

However, we argue that persons thinking about the development process must always have "time" foremost in their minds. The introduction of democracy in England, although still without universal suffrage, can reasonably be dated to the Reform Act of 1832. The mid-1750s were the period 75 years prior to the Reform Act – that is, the period of the consolidation of what we call a truly effective state, the period that North calls the mature state and one increasingly on the threshold stage. No one has ever thought that the Glorious Revolution of 1688 introduced democracy into England, but many must be reminded that it took place 150 years before the Reform Act of 1832.

This book has said very little about democracy. The most obvious reason is that it did not exist in any of our four countries in the period this book covers. It is true that representative institutions did exist these countries throughout most of our period, including Spain and its colonies. Yet the book is already long, and we were focusing on the need for the development of the state as a pre-condition for economic growth and the creation of a market, not the early precursors to democracy.

We think that the creation of a stable democracy – not just the forms of democracy – is quite difficult, even more so than the building of an effective state. We very much like the discussion of the conditions for success of the democratic method of the great economist, Joseph Schumpeter, in *Capitalism, Socialism, and Democracy.* Schumpeter listed four preconditions:[22]

(1) a [political] stratum ... with traditions that embody experience, with a professional code and with a common fund of views
(2) [an] effective range of political decision [that is not] be extended too far

[22] Joseph Schumpeter, *Capitalism, Socialism, and Democracy* (New York: Harper and Brothers, 1942), pp. 290–6.

(3) the services of a well-trained bureaucracy of good standing and tradition, endowed with a strong sense of duty and a no less strong *esprit de corps.*

(4) electorates and parliaments [that are on] an intellectual and moral level high enough to be proof against the offerings of the crook and the crank, or else men who are neither will be driven into the ways of both.

We believe that this analysis is particularly sophisticated, especially if combined with data on per capita income, education, and other social indicators. The really important point for this book, however, is the date of *Capitalism, Socialism, and Democracy*'s publication. Schumpeter was an Austrian who had taught in Germany before coming to the United States in 1932. His book was published in 1942, and he was implicitly writing about the failure of democracy in the large countries across continental Europe and many of the small countries. It is most unclear that democracy would have been stable in much of Europe after World War II without American troops there.

We are talking about Western Europe, not even Eastern Europe, nearly 250 years after the Glorious Revolution! If continental Europe of the 1920s and 1930s did not have the prerequisites for democracy, what should we say about the developing world, especially Asia, Africa, and the lessdeveloped countries of Latin America today? India at least has the needed political stratum and bureaucracy, but it still remains to be proved that it has the necessary popular attitudes if there is an economic crisis. Nevertheless, many poor countries in Africa and South Asia certainly do not meet Schumpeter's prerequisites, and that includes the Arab Spring middle-income countries.

For us, the most useful recent contribution to an analysis of democratization in Europe is Acemoglu and Robinson's point that "a lack of, or weak, political centralization" is not only a major "barrier to the spread of industry," but also a prerequisite for the creation of inclusive political institutions. We agree, but Acemoglu and Robinson date the political centralization in England to the first decades of the 1500s. The Reform Act of 1832 was 300 years in the future, and the Glorious Revolution was exactly midway.

As North and his co-authors recognized in the 2013 preface of their 2009 *Violence and Social Orders*, the book focused on the transition to a more or less modern democracy and freemarket economy after the establishment of a truly effective state. It gave less attention to what they called "the second development problem" – the multi-hundred-year transition prior to the final stage. Their 2013 *In the Shadow of Violence* was devoted to an examination of this latter problem within the contemporary developing world.[23]

Our book was always devoted to an examination of this "second development problem," but within England, Spain, and its colonies. We agreed with Samuel Huntington that the central problem during this long transition is that "in many cases, governments simply do not govern" – or govern in an extremely ineffective or minimally effective manner.

From the beginning we had agreed with North's recent books that control of violence was the central problem in state formation – that the default option was not dictatorship, but anarchy. We had engaged in detailed historical research to explore the consequences of our collective action approach and to confirm whether it was useful.

The approach was even more useful than we thought. We were convinced that it was necessary to focus less exclusively on the problem of controlling the ruler and to concentrate more on the rulers' problem of ending the military decentralization of power to regional warlords and creating and controlling the bureaucracies needed to do this – first of all, the military and tax-collecting ones.

The collective action problems in accomplishing this goal were dramatically illustrated in the large territory of Spain and the inability of supposedly strong rulers to create even an early state for 500 years after the "kingdom" was created. England was no better except in the city-state of London.

Olson led us to believe that compulsion and the collection of the funds needed for selective side payments were crucial, but we were still surprised at the scale of that role and the way it was accomplished in the early centuries. The extra "taxation" of the warlords by both the English and Castilian kings was basically inducing them to share in the loot, the essential purpose of wars. The armament of merchant ships made them a major military and political instrument, and the creation of the London city-state depended on the king's alliance with the owners of the most powerful "navy" of Europe, the fleet of the Hanseatic League.

We were not aware, however, of the length of time it took both English and Spanish monarchs to disarm the local warlords. Even more important, we had not expected the intimate alliance of the navy and merchants and the importance of this alliance in 1660 and 1688. Hough had long understood from his work in the primary sources that George Washington had

[23] Douglass North, John Joseph Wallis, and Barry Weingast, "Preface to the Paperback Edition," *Violence and Social Orders: A Conceptual Framework for Interpreting Recorded History* (New York: Cambridge University Press, 2009), p. xii.

used his control of the army to exile John Adams to France in early 1778. Then a decade later Washington used his control of the retired officers to convene and control the Constitutional Convention through his two young political aides, James Madison and Alexander Hamilton.

Yet, although we were aware that Douglass North and other economists had exaggerated the degree of centralization in Spain and the colonies, we did not suspect Madrid's almost total lack of control of its colonies in the 1600s, even over the shipment of silver in that time. Neither of us realized that Mexico did not have provincial governments that controlled military force until the 1860s, while the United States did – and the difference was vital.

Perhaps more important for those in the development community, the extremely detailed historical work that was central to our research design allowed us to learn – and present – many of the techniques that rulers used to raise money before they had a well-functioning tax system. These included joint looting, structuring of government organs to permit the use of personalistic techniques of control, granting privileged access to those such as the merchants of the Hanseatic League or Genoa, the use of tax farmers, and "taxation" through demands that infrastructure be constructed, supplies be provided to the king and his entourage, and so forth.

Our concentration on the realm of foreign trade allowed us to watch the progressive evolution to more effective techniques of taxation over literally hundreds of years. We learned that merchant guilds did not result primarily from merchant pressure imposed on monarchs but instead were the monarchs' instruments of taxation if he could only control them. This was also true of the Spanish sheep-grower guild (the Mesta) in the "foreign trade" of wool to Flanders on the backs of the sheep migrating to the northern plateau.

Perhaps our greatest surprise was to discover that Charles I of England, who was beheaded for his authoritarianism, was the king who really started colonization of the Americas in 1623 and who introduced free trade within the Atlantic empire. Charles III of Spain was also an authoritarian king, but he was using the growing ability of the administrative system to begin introducing the same system in the Spanish empire 150 years later.

Since we were concentrating on the enormous length of time it takes rulers to consolidate control over their "agents," we did not examine the evolution of representative institutions in our four cases in any detail, but the developing nations and development scholars surely can learn from that experience as well. The role and power of those bodies in European countries have varied over time. As in the United States, the evolution of legislative bodies has not been linear. Parliament was stronger in the 1400s than it was in the 1500s and less accommodating in the 1620s and 1630s than after 1660 and even after 1688.

The important lesson of Chapter 6 is that legislative bodies can play quite different roles than simply approving or vetoing proposals of the monarch, including in the realm of taxation. We learned that J.H. Plumb, one of the foremost British historians of the period, concluded that George I achieved "the subjugation of the legislature that the Stuarts had frequently attempted but never achieved."[24] Adam Smith expressed the same opinion.

Yet we concur with John Brewer that the agreements of 1689 played a hugely important role in Britain in the 1700s. But that role centered on forcing the political process to become more sophisticated. The increasingly specialized knowledge of bureaucrats and the particular concerns of interest groups had to be represented in the policy process and brought to bear on multi-faceted decisions being made. Indeed, the rules of the post-1688 Parliament compelled bureaucratic specialization to be increased.

The power of the Spanish *Cortes* varied as much in both directions. The Spanish *Cortes* in the 1500s and 1600s actually seems to be more powerful than the British Parliament of the 1700s on tax questions because it directly represented regional warlords in their tax negotiations with the center.

Yet the *Cortes* seemingly did not ever meet to discuss policy decisions, let alone to help draft decisions by the kings. The Spanish kings themselves did not have a great reservoir of specialized knowledge until the 1700s. In the second half of the 1500s, Philip II of Spain seemed to make decisions without taking into account their implications for decisions in related fields. Such lack of integration of policymaking was much more difficult in Britain of the 1700s.

For that reason it was not unnatural that the *Cortes* could be abolished under the Bourbons. Once the warlords were being disarmed, the *Cortes* had no reason to exist. If it had already been discussing policy, it might have been kept by the Bourbons for its informational purposes. Development specialists need to look at the policy-relevant roles of Parliament, especially after 1688, for a model.

This is not the place to discuss the enormous micro-variations in the power and role of representative bodies. Indeed, they need not even be elected. When we think of what may be decades of building inclusive insti-

[24] J.H. Plumb, *The Growth of Political Stability in England: 1675–1725* (London: Macmillan, 1967).

tutions, we should not see them only as free elections that, as North says, can be highly dangerous if Schumpeter's pre-conditions are not met.

We can never, however, improve the analysis unless we become more precise in our conceptualization. From the 1930s through the 1950s, the debates on the New Deal and the protection of black rights led to sophisticated distinctions about the definition of majority rights and federalism. In particular, it was understood that Americans wanted "constitutional democracy" with a distinction between the majority rule of the word "democracy" and the limitations on the majority of the word "constitutional."

Much of that distinction has been lost, especially among economists. James Buchanan, who strongly opposed majority rule and who even wanted tax rates to be constitutional in nature and almost impossible to change, still called himself a democrat. He was, he said, "an individualist, a constitutionalist, a contractarian, a democrat" and asserted that these are "terms that mean essentially the same thing to me."[25] In fact, these words have quite opposing meanings, and those must be reflected in debates about development.

Buchanan was more direct and honest than most, but in an extreme form he spoke for many. He correctly understood that the majority will want some redistribution of wealth and some protection against market forces and that a system with majority rule will limit the efficiency promised by the neoclassical model.

As we emphasize the "constitutional" part of constitutional democracy, we must not forget the "democratic" element. If this book had been extended beyond 1800, we would have agreed with North and his co-authors that premature free elections are crucial to stability. But we also agree that free elections are vital in a modern market economy because the absence of elections that give real power to the majority eventually leads to political instability when the population is educated.

There are countless examples of this fact. The Reform Act of 1832 was a response to the fear among the elite created by the French Revolution of 1830. The further democratization of the second half of the 19th century was a response to the Revolution of 1848 and the fear was that the alternative was the revolution Karl Marx predicted at the time. Franklin Roosevelt's democratization of the United States in the 1930s was partly a response to the fear that the population would support Huey Long or another demagogue if changes were not made.

[25] James Buchanan, *The Limits of Freedom: Between Anarchy and Leviathan* (Chicago: University of Chicago Press, 1978), p. 7.

Last, while it may seem counterintuitive to think of the European Union as a developing state, it is just that in many ways, and the lessons from this book are applicable to it as well. Those trying to avoid a partial disintegration of the Euro zone have understood that the alternative to national currencies as a means of austerity is an austerity program that eventually requires strict budgetary limits. These limits are to be imposed by unelected European officials upon countries in the periphery that have democratically elected officials.

The sharp rise in the nationalist vote in the 2014 elections to the European parliament is a warning of the possible consequences. In the long run, a European state must be democratic, but such a state must have an integrated tax system, social benefits, uniform regulations, and so forth. The northern members understandably do not want the members of the periphery to have the majority of the votes in such elections. More basically, however, it takes time to build a state, even with the experience and attitudes found in Western Europe.

In short, it is not merely development economists dealing with Asia, Africa, and Latin America who must look at the development of European states and markets prior to 1800. The "development economists" dealing with the European Union need also to reexamine their own past. The building of the European state and market began nearly 70 years ago, and those at that time would not believe the progress that has been made. But 70 years is a rather short time in the framework of the time required both in Europe and the developing world. The development process is, indeed, a long one, and time matters.

References

Abbot, W. W., ed., *The Papers of George Washington, Revolutionary War Series*, Vol. 1 (Charlottesville: University Press of Virginia, 1985).

Abbot, W.W. and Dorothy Twohig, *The Papers of George Washington, Confederation Series*, (Charlottesville: University Press of Virginia, 1992).

Abu-Lughod, Janet, *Before European Hegemony: The World System A.D. 1250–1350* (New York: Oxford University Press, 1989).

Acemoglu, Daron, Simon Johnson, and James Robinson, "The Colonial Origins of Comparative Development: An Empirical Investigation," *American Economic Review* 91(2001), 1369–1401.

"Reversal of Fortune: Geography and Institutions in the Making of the Modern World Income Distribution," *Quarterly Journal of Economics* 117 (2002), 1231–94.

Acemoglu, Daron and James Robinson, *Why Nations Fail: The Origins of Power, Prosperity, and Poverty* (New York: Crown Business, 2012).

Aligica, Paul Dragos and Peter Boettke, *Challenging Institutional Analysis and Development: The Bloomington School* (London: Routledge, 2009).

Allen, Paul, *Philip III and the Pax Hispanica, 1598–1621: The Failure of Grand Strategy* (New Haven, CT: Yale University Press, 2000).

Almond, Gabriel and Sidney Verba, *Civic Culture: Political Attitudes and Democracy in Five Nations* (Princeton, NJ: Princeton University Press, 1963).

Alvord, Clarence Walworth, *The Mississippi Valley in British Politics*, Vol. 2 (Cleveland, OH: Arthur H. Clark, 1917).

Amaral, Samuel, "Rural Production and Labour in Late Colonial Buenos Aires," *Journal of Latin American Studies* 19 (1987), 235–78.

Andersen, Gary and Robert Tollison, "Morality and Monopoly: The Constitutional Political Economy of Religious Rules," *Cato Journal* 12 (1992), 373–92.

Andrews, Charles McLean, *Colonial Self-Government, 1652–1689* (New York: Harper, 1904).

Andrews, Charles, *The Colonial Period of American History: England's Commercial and Colonial Policy*, Vol. 4 (New Haven, CT: Yale University Press, 1938).

Andrews, Kenneth, *Elizabethan Privateering 1583–1603* (Cambridge: Cambridge University Press, 1964).

Drake's Voyages: A Re-Assessment of Their Place in Elizabethan Maritime Expansion (New York: Scribner, 1967).

The Spanish Caribbean: Trade and Plunder, 1530–1630 (New Haven, CT: Yale University Press, 1978).
Trade, Plunder, and Settlement: Maritime Enterprise and the Genesis of the British Empire (Cambridge: Cambridge University Press, 1984).
Anna, Timothy, *The Fall of the Royal Government in Mexico City* (Lincoln: University of Nebraska Press, 1978).
The Mexican Empire of Iturbide (Lincoln: University of Nebraska Press, 1990).
Archer, Christon, "'La Causa Buena:' The Counterinsurgency Army of New Spain and the Ten Years" War," in Jaime Rodríguez O., ed., *The Independence of Mexico and the Creation of the New Nation* (Los Angeles: UCLA Publications, 1989), 88–108.
"Where Did All the Royalists Go? New Light on the Military Collapse of New Spain, 1810–1822," in Jaime E. Rodríguez O., ed., *The Mexican and Mexican-American Experience in the 19th Century* (Tempe, AZ: Bilingual Press, 1989), 37–8.
"Years of Decision: Felix Calleja and the Strategy to End the Revolution of New Spain," in Christon Archer, ed., *The Birth of Modern Mexico* (Wilmington, DE: Scholarly Resources, 2003).
Arendt, Hannah, *On Revolution* (New York: Viking Press, 1963).
Ashcraft, Richard, *Revolutionary Politics and Locke's Two Treatises of Government* (Princeton, NJ: Princeton University Press, 1986).
Ashton, Robert, *The City and the Court, 1603–1643* (Cambridge: Cambridge University Press, 1979).
Aubet, Maria-Eugenia, *The Phoenicians and the West: Politics, Colonies, and Trade* (Cambridge: Cambridge University Press, 2001).
Axelrod, Robert, *The Evolution of Cooperation* (New York: Basic Books, 1984).
Aylmer, G. E., *The King's Servants: The Civil Service of Charles I, 1625–1647* (London: Routledge and Kegan Paul, 1961).
The Crown's Servants, Government and Civil Servants under Charles II, 1660–1685 (Oxford: Oxford University Press, 2002).
Bailyn, Bernard, *The New England Merchants in the Seventeenth Century* (Cambridge, MA: Harvard University Press, 1953).
The Origins of American Politics (New York: Knopf, 1968).
Bakewell, Peter, *Silver Mining and Society in Colonial Mexico, Zacatecas 1546–1700* (Cambridge, MA: Cambridge University Press, 1972).
"Mining in Colonial Spanish America," in Leslie Bethell, ed., *Cambridge History of Latin America*, Vol. 2 (Cambridge: Cambridge University Press, 1984), 105–52.
Baldwin, Alice, *The New England Clergy and the American Revolution* (Durham, NC: Duke University, 1928).
"Sowers of Sedition: The Political Theories of Some of the New Left Presbyterian Clergy of Virginia and North Carolina," *William and Mary Quarterly* 5 (1948), 52–76.
Barton, Simon, *Aristocracy in the Twelfth Century León and Castile* (Cambridge: Cambridge University Press, 2002).
Baskes, Jeremy, *Indians, Merchants, and Markets: A Reinterpretation of the Repartimiento and Spanish-Indian Economic Relations in Colonial Oaxaca, 1750–1821* (Stanford, CA: Stanford University Press, 2000).
Batchelder, Ronald and Nicolas Sanchez, "The Encomienda and the Optimizing Imperialist: An Interpretation of Spanish Imperialism in the Americas," *Public Choice* 156 (2013), 45–60.

Bates, Robert, "The Preservation of Order in Stateless Societies: A Reinterpretation of Evans-Pritchard's *The Nuer*," in Robert Bates, *Essays on the Political Economy of Rural Africa* (Berkeley: University of California Press, 1983), 7–20.

When Things Fell Apart: State Failure in Late-Century Africa (New York: Cambridge University Press, 2008).

Prosperity & Violence: The Political Economy of Development, 2nd ed. (New York: W. W. Norton, 2010).

Baugh, Daniel, *British Naval Administration in the Age of Walpole* (Princeton, NJ: Princeton University Press, 1966).

Bautier, R. H., *The Economic Development of Medieval Europe* (New York: Harcourt, Brace and Jovanovich, 1971).

Baxter, Stephen, *The Development of the Treasury, 1660–1702* (New York: Longmans, Green, 1957).

Beardwood, Alice, *Alien Merchants in England 1350–1377: Their Legal and Economic Position* (Cambridge, MA: Medieval Academy of America, 1931).

Becker, Carl, *The History of Political Parties in the Province of New York, 1760–1776* (Madison: University of Wisconsin, 1909).

Beginnings of the American People (Boston, MA: Houghton Mifflin, 1915).

Beer, George, *The Old Colonial System, 1660–1754* (New York: Macmillan, 1933).

Bell, Adrian, Chris Brook, and Paul R. Dryburgh, *The English Wool Market, c. 1230–1327* (Cambridge: Cambridge University Press, 2007).

Bennett, Charles, *Laudonniere & Fort Caroline: History and Documents* (Gainesville: University of Florida Press, 1964).

Benson, Nettie Lee, "The Plan of Casa Mata," *Hispanic American Historical Review* 25 (1945), 45–56.

"Spain's Contribution to Federalism in Mexico," in Thomas Cotner, ed., *Essays in Mexican History* (Austin: University of Texas Press, 1958), 90–103.

Benson, Nettie Lee, ed., *Mexico and the Spanish Cortes* (Austin: University of Texas Press, 1966).

Benson, Nettie Lee, *The Provincial Deputation in Mexico: Harbinger of Provincial Autonomy, Independence, and Federalism* (Austin: University of Texas Press, 1992).

Berman, Eli and David Laitin, "Religion, Terrorism, and Public Goods: Testing the Club Model," *Journal of Public Economics* 92 (2008), 1942–67.

Bethell, Leslie, ed., *Cambridge History of Latin America*, Vol. 2 (Cambridge: Cambridge University Press, 1984).

Bishko, Charles, "The Castilian as Plainsman: The Medieval Ranching Frontier in La Mancha and Extremadura," in Archibald Lewis and Thomas McGann, eds., *The New World Looks at Its History* (Austin: University of Texas Press, 1963), 47–69.

Bisson, Douglas, *The Merchant Adventurers of England: Company and the Crown, 1474–1564* (Newark: University of Delaware Press, 1993).

Black, J. B., *The Reign of Elizabeth, 1558–1603*, 2nd ed. (Oxford: Clarendon Press, 1949).

Blair, Peter Hunter, *Roman Britain and Early England, 55 B.C.– A.D. 871* (New York: W.W. Norton, 1963).

Bogart, Dan and Gary Richardson, "Parliament, Property Rights, and Public Goods in England, 1600–1815," University of California-Irvine, Working Paper, 2010.

"Property Rights and Parliament in Industrializing Britain," *Journal of Law and Economics* 54 (2011), 241–74.
Boone, Marc and Marysa Demoor, eds., *Charles V in Context* (Ghent: Ghent University, 2003).
Borah, Woodrow Wilson, *New Spain's Century of Depression* (Berkeley: University of California Press, 1951).
Boyajian, James, *Portuguese Bankers at the Court of Spain, 1626–1650* (New Brunswick, NJ: Rutgers University Press, 1983).
Boyer, Richard, "Mexico in the 17th Century: Transition of a Colonial Society," *Hispanic-American Historical Review* 57 (1977), 454–78.
Braddick, Michael, *State Formation in Early Modern England, c. 1550–1700* (Cambridge: Cambridge University, 2000).
Brading, David A., "Mexican Silver Mining in the Eighteenth Century," *Hispanic American Historical Review* 50 (1970), 665–81.
Miners and Merchants in Bourbon Mexico, 1763–1810 (Cambridge: University Press, 1971).
"Government and Elite in Late Colonial Mexico," *Hispanic American Historical Review* 53 (1973), 389–414.
Church and State in Bourbon Mexico: The Diocese of Michoacán, 1749–1810 (Cambridge: Cambridge University Press, 1994).
Brading, David A. and Harry Cross, "Colonial Silver Mining: Mexico and Peru," *Hispanic American Historical Review* 52 (1972), 545–79.
Brands, H. W., *The First American: The Life and Times of Benjamin Franklin* (New York: Doubleday, 2000).
Brennan, Geoffrey and James Buchanan, *The Reason of Rules: Constitutional Political Economy* (Cambridge: Cambridge University Press, 1985).
Brenner, Robert, *Merchants and Revolution: Commercial Change, Political Conflict, and London's Overseas Traders, 1550–1653* (Princeton, NJ: Princeton University Press, 1993).
Brewer, John, *The Sinews of Power: War, Money, and the English State, 1688–1783* (Cambridge, MA: Harvard University Press, 1990).
Bridenbaugh, Carl, *Mitre and Spectre* (New York: Oxford University Press, 1962).
Brinton, Crane, *The Anatomy of Revolution* (New York: W. W. Norton, 1938).
Brown, Jonathan, "Outpost to Entrepôt: Trade and Commerce at Colonial Buenos Aires," in Stanley Ross and Thomas McGann, eds., *Buenos Aires: Four Hundred Years* (Austin: University of Texas Press, 1982), 3–17.
Brown, Kendall, "The Spanish Imperial Mercury Trade and the American Mining Expansion under the Bourbon Monarchy," in Kenneth Andrien and Lyman Johnson, eds., *The Political Economy of Spanish America in the Age of Revolution, 1750–1850* (Albuquerque: University of New Mexico Press, 1994), 137–69.
Brunk, Samuel, *Heroes and Hero Cults in Latin America* (Austin: University of Texas Press, 2006).
Buchanan, James, *Freedom in Constitutional Contract: Perspectives of a Political Economist* (College Station: Texas A and M University Press, 1977).
The Limits of Freedom: Between Anarchy and Leviathan (Chicago: University of Chicago Press, 1978).
Constitutional Economics (Oxford: Blackwell, 1991).

Economics From the Outside In: 'Better than Plowing' and Beyond (College Station: Texas A and M Press, 2007).

Buchanan, James and Gordon Tullock, *The Calculus of Consent: Logical Foundations of Constitutional Democracy* (Ann Arbor: University of Michigan Press, 1965).

Buchanan, John, *The Road to Valley Forge: How Washington Built the Army that Won the Revolution* (Hoboken, NJ: John Wiley, 2004).

Burgon, John William, *The Life and Times of Thomas Gresham* (London: Robert Jennings, 1839). https://archive.org/stream/lifetimesofsirth01burguoft#page/n9/mode/2up.

Burkholder, Mark, "An Empire beyond Compare," in William Beezley and Michael Meyer, eds., *The Oxford History of Mexico* (Oxford: Oxford University Press, 2000), 111–42.

Burkholder, Mark and Lyman Johnson, *Colonial Latin America*, 6th ed. (New York: Oxford University Press, 2008).

Burns, Robert, *Islam under the Crusaders: Colonial Survival in the Thirteenth Century Kingdom of Valencia* (Princeton, NJ: Princeton University Press, 1973).

Butterfield, L. N., ed., *Diary and Autobiography of John Adams* (Cambridge, MA: Harvard University Press, 1962).

Caldwell, Bruce, *Hayek's Challenge: An Intellectual Biography of F. A. Hayek* (Chicago: University of Chicago Press, 2004).

Callahan, North, *Henry Knox: George Washington's General* (New York: Rinehart, 1958).

Callahan, William, *Church, Politics, and Society in Early Modern Spain* (Cambridge, MA: Harvard University Press, 1984).

Cantor, Norman, *The Civilization of the Middle Ages* (New York: HarperCollins, 1993).

Capella Martínez, Miguel and Antonio Malilla Tascón, *Los Cinco Gremios Mayores de Madrid. Estudio crítico-histórico* (Madrid: Camera de Comercio de Madrid, 1957).

Capp, Bernard, *Cromwell's Navy: The Fleet and the English Revolution, 1648–1660* (Oxford: Oxford University Press, 1989).

Cárdenas, Enrique, "A Macroeconomic Interpretation in Nineteenth-Century Mexico," in Stephen Haber, ed., *How Latin America Fell Behind: Essays on the Economic Histories of Brazil and Mexico* (Stanford, CA: Stanford University Press, 1997), 65–92.

Carp, E. Wayne, *To Starve the Army at Pleasure: Continental Army Administration and American Political Culture* (Chapel Hill: University of North Carolina Press, 1984).

Carpenter, David, *The Struggle for Mastery: History of Britain, 1066–1284* (Oxford: Oxford University Press, 2003).

Carter, Susan, Scott Sigmund Gartner, Michael Haines, and Alan Olmstead, eds., *Historical Statistics of the United States; Earliest Times to the Present*, Millennial Edition, Vol. 5 (New York: Cambridge University Press, 2006).

Carus-Wilson, E. M., *Medieval Merchant Ventures: Collected Studies* (London: Metheum, 1954).

Casey, James, *Early Modern Spain: A Social History* (London: Routledge, 1999).

Cassidy, Tom, *British Capital and the Mexican Silver Industry, 1820–1850* (Cambridge: Cambridge University Press, 1975).

Catlos, Brian, *The Victors and the Vanquished: Christians and Muslims of Catalonia and Aragon, 1050–1300* (Cambridge: Cambridge University Press, 2004).

Chatterton, E. Keble, *King's Cutters and Smugglers: The Revenue Service and the War against Smuggling* (Philadelphia, PA: J. B. Lippincott, 1912).
Chauduri, K. N., *The English East India Company: The Study of an Early Joint-Stock Company 1600–1640* (London: Frank Cass, 1965).
Childs, John, *The Nine Years" War and the British Army* (Manchester: Manchester University Press, 1991).
Chocano, Guadelupe, "Decadencia del poder naval e imperio marítimo español desde el siglo XVII," in Enriqueta Vila Vilar and Allan Kuethe, eds., *Relaciones de poder y comercio colonial: Nuevas perspectives* (España: Consejo Superior de Investigaciones Científicas, 2004), 993–1031.
Chrimes, S. B., *Lancastrians, Yorkists, and Henry VII* (London: Macmillan, 1964).
Clark, Dora Mae, *The Rise of the British Treasury: Colonial Administration in the 18th Century* (New Haven, CT: Yale University Press, 1960).
Clark, Gregory, "The Political Foundations of Modern Economic Growth: Britain 1540–1800," *Journal of Interdisciplinary History* 26 (1996), 563–88.
Coatsworth, John, "Indispensable Railroads in a Backward Economy: The Case of Mexico," *Journal of Economic History* 39 (1979), 939–60.
"The Mexican Mining Industry in the Eighteenth Century," in Peter Bakewell, ed., *Mines of Silver and Gold in the Americas* (Aldershot, UK: Varorium, 1997).
"Foreword to the Twenty-Fifth Anniversary Edition," in Eric Van Young, *Hacienda and Market in Eighteenth-Century Mexico: The Rural Economy of the Guadalajara Region, 1675–1820*, 2nd ed. (Lanham, MD: Rowman and Littlefield, 2006).
Coffman, D'Maris, Adrian Leonard, and Larry Neal, eds., *Questioning Credible Commitment: Perspectives on the Rise of Financial Capitalism* (Cambridge: Cambridge University Press, 2013).
Coleman, Christopher and David Starkey, eds., *Revolution Reassessed: Revisions in the History of Tudor Government and Administration* (Oxford: Clarendon Press, 1986).
Collier, Simon and William Sater, *A History of Chile, 1808–2002* (Cambridge: Cambridge University Press, 2004).
Connor, Walker, "Nation-Building or Nation-Destroying?" *World Politics* 24 (1972), 319–55.
Costeloe, Michael, *The Central Republic in Mexico, 1835–1846* (Cambridge: Cambridge University Press, 1993).
Cox, Gary, "War, Moral Hazard, and Ministerial Responsibility; England after the Glorious Revolution," *Journal of Economic History* 71 (2011), 133–61.
Coy, P. E. B., "Justice for the Indian in Eighteenth Century Mexico," *American Journal of Legal History* 12 (1968), 41–9.
Craven, Wesley Frank, *Dissolution of the Virginia Company: The Failure of a Colonial Experiment* (New York: Oxford University Press, 1932).
Southern Colonies in the Seventeenth Century, 1607–1689 (Baton Rouge: Louisiana State University Press, 1949).
Creach, Jerome, *Joshua: Interpretation* (Louisville, KY: John Knox Press, 2003).
Croft, J. Pauline, ed., *The Spanish Company* (London: London Record Company, 1973).
Cross, Claire, *Church and People: England 1450–1660*, 2nd ed. (Oxford: Blackwell, 1999).
Cunningham, Sean, *Henry VII* (Oxford: Routledge, 2007).

Cust, Richard, *Charles I and the Aristocracy, 1625–1642* (Cambridge: Cambridge University Press, 2013).

Davies, J. D., *Gentlemen and Tarpaulins: The Officers and Men of the Restoration Navy* (Oxford: Oxford University Press, 1991).

Davies, Godfrey, *The Restoration of Charles II, 1658–60* (London: Oxford University Press, 1955).

Davis, David Brion, *The Slave Power Conspiracy and the Paranoid Style* (Baton Rouge: Louisiana University Press, 1970).

de Forteza, Patricio, Norah Ramos, and María Estela Gonzalez de Fauve, "Desplazamientos de la corte castellana: Notas para su estudio," *Estudios de historia de España* 3 (1990), 29–50.

Del Carmen Carlé, Maria, *Del Concejo Medieval Castellano-Leones* (Buenos Aires: Instituto de Historia de España, 1968).

Denevan, William, ed., *The Native Population of the Americas in 1492* (Madison: University of Wisconsin Press, 1976).

DePalo, William, *The Mexican National Army, 1822–1852* (College Station: Texas A and M Press, 1997).

Diago Hernando, Máximo, "El papel de los linajes en las estructuras de gobierno urbano en Castilla y en el Imperio alemán durante los siglos bajomedievales," *En la España medieval* 20 (1997), 143–78.

Dickerson, Oliver, *The Navigation Acts and the American Revolution* (Philadelphia: University of Pennsylvania Press, 1951).

Di Palma, Giuseppi, *To Craft Democracies: An Essay on Democratic Strategies* (Berkeley: University of California Press, 1990).

Dobson, Richard Barrie, ed., *The Church, Politics, and Patronage in the Fifteenth Century* (Gloucester: A. Sutton, 1984).

Dobson, Richard Barrie, *Durham Priory 1400–1450*, Vol. 6. (Cambridge: Cambridge University Press, 2005).

Dollinger, Philippe, *The German Hansa* (New York: Macmillan, 1970).

Domínguez Ortiz, Antonio, *The Golden Age of Spain, 1516–1659* (Worthing: Littlehampton Book Services, 1971).

Donald, David Herbert, *An Excess of Democracy: The American Civil War and the Social Process* (Oxford: Clarendon Press, 1960).

Lincoln Reconsidered: Essays on the Civil War Era, 3rd ed. (New York: Vintage, 2001).

Dougherty, Martin, *A Dark History: Vikings: Raiders, Pillagers, and Traders–The Truth Revealed* (New York: Metro Books, 2013).

Drelichman, Mauricio, "License to Till: The Privileges of the Spanish Mesta as a Case of Second-Best Institutions," *Explorations in Economic History* 46 (2009), 220–40.

Drummond, J. C. and Anne Wibraham, *The Englishman's Food: A History of Five Centuries of English Diet* (London: J. Cape, 1939).

Dull, Jonathan, *A Diplomatic History of the American Revolution* (New Haven, CT: Yale University Press, 1985).

Dunbar, Louise, *A Study of 'Monarchical' Tendencies in the United States from 1776 to 1801* (Urbana: University of Illinois, 1923).

Duverger, Maurice, *Political Parties: Their Organization and Activities in the Modern State* (London: Methuen, 1962).

Egerton, H. E., ed., *A Short History of British Colonial Policy*, 3rd ed. (London: Metheun, 1910).
Egnal, Marc, "The Economic Development of the Thirteen Continental Colonies, 1720 to 1775," *William and Mary Quarterly: A Magazine of Early American History* 32 (1975): 192–222.
A Mighty Empire: The Origins of the American Revolution (Ithaca, NY: Cornell University Press, 1988).
Ekelund, Robert and Robert Tollison, *Politicized Economies: Monarchy, Monopolies, and Mercantilism* (College Station: Texas A and M Press, 1997).
Ekelund, Robert, D. R. Street, and Robert Tollison, "Rent Seeking and Property Rights Assignments as a Process: The Mesta Cartel of Medieval - Mercantile Spain," *Journal of European Economic History* (Spring 1997), 9–35.
Elliott, John, *The Revolt of the Catalans: A Study in the Decline of Spain, 1598–1640* (Cambridge: Cambridge University Press, 1963).
Imperial Spain, 1469–1716 (New York: St. Martin's Press, 1964).
Empires of the Atlantic World: Britain and Spain in America 1492–1830 (New Haven, CT: Yale University Press, 2007).
Elton, Geoffrey, *The Tudor Revolution in Government: Administrative Changes in the Reign of Henry VIII* (Cambridge: Cambridge University Press, 1953).
Reform and Reformation, England, 1509–1558 (Cambridge, MA: Harvard University Press, 1977).
Engerman, Stanley and Kenneth Sokoloff, "Factor Endowments, Institutions, and Differential Paths of Growth among New World Economies," in Stephen Haber, ed., *How Latin America Fell Behind: Essays on the Economic Histories of Brazil and Mexico, 1800–1914* (Palo Alto, CA: Stanford University Press, 1997), 260–304.
Epstein, Stephan, *Freedom and Growth: The Rise of States and Markets in Europe, 1300–1750* (London: Routledge, 2000).
Ertman, Thomas, *Birth of the Leviathan; Building States and Regimes in Medieval and Early Modern Europe* (Cambridge: Cambridge University Press, 1997).
Estow, Clara, "The Economic Development of the Order of Calatrava, 1158–1366," *Speculum* 57 (1982), 267–91.
Ekwall, Eilert, *Studies on the Population of Medieval London* (Stockholm: Almquist and Wiksell, 1956).
Fagan, Brian, *The Little Ice Age: How Climate Made History, 1300–1850* (New York: Basic Books, 2000).
Farriss, Nancy, *Maya Society under Colonial Rule: The Collective Enterprise of Survival* (Princeton, NJ: Princeton University Press, 1984).
Fernández Albaladejo, Pablo, "Cities and the State in Spain," *Theory and Society* 18 (1989), 721–31.
Fernea, Elizabeth Warnock and Robert Fernea, *The Arab World: Forty Years of Change* (New York: Doubleday, 1997).
Fernea, Robert, *Shaykh and Effendi: Changing Patterns of Authority among the El Shabana of Southern Iraq* (Cambridge, MA: Harvard University Press, 1970).
Feros, Antonio, *Kingship and Favouritism in the Spain of Philip III, 1598–1621* (Cambridge: Cambridge University Press, 2000).
Ferry, Robert, *The Colonial Elite of Early Caracas: Formation and Crisis, 1567–1767* (Berkeley: University of California Press, 1989).

Finlay, Roger, *Population and Metropolis: The Demography of London, 1580–1650* (Cambridge: Cambridge University Press, 1981).
Fischer, David Hackett, *Albion's Seed: Four British Folkways in America* (New York: Oxford University Press, 1989).
Fisher, John, *Government and Society in Colonial Peru: The Intendant System, 1784–1814* (London: University of London Press, 1970).
The Economic Aspects of Spanish Imperialism in America, 1492–1810 (Liverpool: Liverpool University Press, 1997).
Fisher, Lillian Estelle *The Intendant System in Spanish America* (Berkeley: University of California Press, 1929).
Fitzpatrick, John, *George Washington Himself* (Indianapolis, IN: Bobbs-Merrill, 1933).
Fletcher, Richard, *The Episcopate in the Kingdom of Leon in the Twelfth Century* (Oxford: Oxford University Press, 1978).
The Quest for El Cid (London: Hutchinson, 1989).
"The Early Middle Ages 700–1250," in Raymond Carr, ed., *Spain: A History* (New York: Oxford University, 2001).
Floyd, Troy, "The Guatemalan Merchants, the Government, and the Provincianos, 1750–1800," *Hispanic-American Historical Review* 41 (1961), 90–110.
Fogleman, Aaron, "Immigration, German Immigration, and 18th-Century America," in Eberhard Reichmann, LaVern Rippley, and Jorg Nagler, eds., *Emigration and Settlement Patterns of German Communities in North America* (Indianapolis, IN: Max Kade German-American Center, 1995), 87–103.
Fowler, Will, *Mexico in the Age of Proposals, 1821–1853* (Westport, CT: Greenwood Press, 1998).
Santa Anna of Mexico (Lincoln: University of Nebraska, 2007).
Francis, David, *The First Peninsular War, 1702–1713* (London: Ernest Benn, 1975).
Freeman, Douglas Southall, *George Washington: A Biography*, Vol. 5 (New York: Charles Scribner's Sons, 1952).
Freedom, Douglas Southall, *George Washington: Planter and Patriot*, Vol. 3 (New York: Charles Scribner's Sons, 1951).
Freyre, Gilberto, *The Portuguese and the Tropics* (Lisbon: International Congress of the History of Discoverers, 1961).
Fryde, E. B., *William de la Pole, Merchant and King's Banker* (London: Hambledon Press, 1998).
Galdames, Luis, *A History of Chile* (Chapel Hill: University of North Carolina, 1941).
Galicia Patino, Carmen, *Comercio y comerciantes en Tampico, 1823–1850* (Ciudad Victoria, Tam: El Colegio de Tamaulipas, 2003).
Gallup, John and Jeffrey Sachs, "Agriculture, Climate, and Technology: Why Are the Tropics Falling Behind?" *American Journal of Agricultural Economics* 82 (2000), 731–7.
Games, Alison, *Migration and the Origins of the English Atlantic World* (Cambridge, MA: Harvard University Press, 1999).
García-Baquero González, A., "Andalusia and the Crisis of the Indies Trade, 1610–1720," in I. A. A. Thompson and Bartolomé Yun Casalilla, eds., *The Castilian Crisis of the Seventeenth Century: New Perspectives on the Economic and Social History of Seventeenth-Century Spain* (Cambridge: Cambridge University Press, 1994), 115–35.

García Fuentes, Lutgardo, *El Comercio Español con America (1650–1700)* (Seville: Escuela de Estudios Hispanos-Americanos de Seville, 1980).
Garner, Richard, "Long-Term Silver Mining Trends in Spanish America: A Comparative Analysis of Peru and Mexico," in Peter Bakewell, ed., *Mines of Silver and Gold in the Americas* (Aldershot, UK: Variorum, 1997), 227–36.
Gelabert Gonzáles, Juan Eloy, "La evolución de la monarquía hispánica entre 1598 y 1650: Asientos de Felipe III y Felipe IV," *Studia histórica, Historia moderna* 18 (1998), 265–97.
Gemie, Sharif, *A Concise History of Galicia* (Cardiff: University of Wales Press, 2006).
Gienapp, William, *The Origins of the Republican Party, 1952–1956* (New York: Oxford University Press, 1987).
Gillingham, John, *The Wars of the Roses: Peace and Conflict in Fifteenth-Century England* (London: Weidenfeld and Nicolson, 1981).
"The Early Middle Ages (1066–1290)," in Kenneth Morgan, ed., *The Oxford History of Britain*, rev. ed. (Oxford: Oxford University Press, 2001), 120–91.
Gipson, Lawrence, *The British Empire before the American Revolution* (Caldwell, IN: Caxton Printers, 1936–1970).
Glete, Jan, *Navies and Nations: Warships, Navies and State Building in Europe and America, 1500–1860* (Stockholm: Almquist and Wiksell International, 1993).
Glick, Thomas, *Islamic and Christian Spain in the Early Middle Ages* (Princeton, NJ: Princeton University Press, 1979).
Glubb, John, *A Short History of the Arab Peoples* (New York: Stein and Day, 1969).
Goldenberg, Joseph, *Shipbuilding in Colonial America* (Charlottesville: University Press of Virginia, 1976).
Goldstone, Jack, *Revolution and Rebellion in the Early Modern World* (Berkeley: University of California Press, 1991).
González Jiménez, Manuel, "Frontier and Settlement in the Kingdom of Castile (1085–1350)," in Robert Bartlett and Angus MacKay, eds., *Medieval Frontier Societies* (Oxford: Clarendon Press, 1989), 70–3.
Goodman, Anthony and Anthony Tuck, eds., *War and Border Societies in the Middle Ages* (London: Routledge, 1992).
Gottschalk, Louis, *Lafayette Comes to America* (Chicago: University of Chicago Press 1935).
Grafe, Regina, *Distant Tyranny: Markets, Power, and Backwardness in Spain, 1650–1800* (Princeton, NJ: Princeton University Press, 2012).
Grahn, Lance, *Political Economy of Smuggling: Regional Informal Economies in Early Bourbon New Granada* (Boulder, CO: Westview Press, 1997).
Green, Stanley, *The Mexican Republic: The First Decade, 1823–1832* (Pittsburgh, PA: University of Pittsburgh Press, 1987).
Greene, Jack, *Pursuits of Happiness: The Social Development of Early Modern British Colonies and the Formation of American Culture* (Chapel Hill: University of North Carolina Press, 1988).
Greenspan, Alan, *The Embrace of Free Markets* (Washington, DC: Woodrow Wilson International Center for Scholars, 1997).
Greif, Avner, *Institutions and the Path to the Modern Economy: Lessons from Medieval Trade* (Cambridge: Cambridge University Press, 2006).

Grier, Kevin and Robin Grier, "Only Income Diverges: A Neo-Classical Anomaly," *Journal of Development Economics* 84 (2007), 25–45.
Grier, Robin, "The Effect of Religion on Economic Development: A Cross-National Study of 63 Former Colonies," *Kyklos* 50 (1997), 47–62.
"Colonial Legacies and Economic Growth," *Public Choice* 98 (1999), 317–35.
"Losing Ground: Economic Growth in Latin America from 1955–1999," *Southern Economic Journal* 74 (2007), 177–203.
Grindle, Merillee, "Good Enough Governance: Poverty Reduction and Reform in Developing Countries," *Governance: An International Journal of Policy, Administration and Institutions* 17 (2004), 525–48.
Haber, Stephen, "Assessing the Obstacles to Industrialization: The Mexican Economy 1830–1940," *Journal of Latin American Studies* 24 (1992), 1–32.
Hamill, Hugh Jr., *The Hidalgo Revolt* (Gainesville: University of Florida Press, 1966).
Hamilton, Earl, "Revisions in Economic History: VIII. The Decline of Spain," *Economic History Review* 8 (1938), 168–79.
Hamilton, Eric, *American Treasure and the Price Revolution in Spain,* 1501-650 (Cambridge, MA: Harvard University Press, 1934).
Hamnett, Brian, *Politics and Trade in Southern Mexico, 1750–1821* (Cambridge: Cambridge University Press, 1971).
"Mercantile Rivalry and Peninsular Division: The Consulados of New Spain and the Impact of the Bourbon Reforms, 1780–1824," *Ibero-Amerikanisches Archiv,* 2 (1976), 273–305.
The Mexican Bureaucracy Before the Bourbon Reforms, 1700–1770: A Study in the Limitations of Absolutism (Glasgow: University of Glasgow, 1979).
"Royalist Counterinsurgency and the Continuity of Rebellion: Guanajuato and Michoacán, 1813–1820," *Hispanic American Historical Review* 62 (1982), 19–48.
"Factores regionales en la desintegración del regimen colonial en la Nueva España; El federalismo de 1823–1824," in Inge Buisson, Günter Kahle, Hans-Joachim König, and Horst Pietschmann, eds., *Problemas de la formación del estado y de la nación en Hispanoamérica* (Bonn: Internations, 1984).
Roots of Insurgency: Mexican Regions, 1750–1824 (Cambridge: Cambridge University Press, 1986).
A Concise History of Mexico, 2nd ed. (Cambridge: Cambridge University Press, 2006).
Hancock, David, "Rethinking the Economy of British America," in Cathy Matson, ed., *The Economy of Early America; Historical Perspectives and New Directions* (University Park: Pennsylvania State University Press, 2006), 71–106.
Haring, Clarence Henry, *Trade and Navigation between Spain and the Indies in the Time of the Hapsburgs* (Cambridge, MA: Harvard University Press, 1918).
The Spanish Empire in America (New York: Oxford University Press, 1947).
Harriss, G. L., *Shaping the Nation: England, 1360–1461* (Oxford: Clarendon Press, 2005).
Harris, Tim, *Restoration: Charles II and His Kingdoms, 1660–1685* (London: Penguin Books, 2006)
Hayek, Friedrich, *Law, Legislation, and Liberty* (Chicago: University of Chicago Press, 1973).

Heath, Hilarie, "British Merchant Houses in Mexico, 1821–1860: Conforming Business Practices and Ethics," *Hispanic American Historical Review* 73 (1993), 261–90.

Helms, Anthony, *Travels from Buenos Ayres, by Potosí, to Lima*, 2nd ed. (London: Richard Phillips, 1807).

Henning, Basil, ed., *The House of Commons, 1660–1690*, Vol. 7 (Woodbridge, UK: Boydell and Brewer, 1983).

Henretta, James, *"Salutary Neglect": Colonial Administration under the Duke of Newcastle* (Princeton, NJ: Princeton University Press, 1972).

Henshall, Nicholas, *The Myth of Absolutism: Change and Continuity in Early Modern European Monarchy* (New York: Longman, 1992).

Henson, Margaret, *Lorenzo de Zavala: The Pragmatic Idealist* (Fort Worth: Texas Christian University Press, 1996).

Herr, Richard, *Eighteenth Century Revolution in Spain* (Princeton, NJ: Princeton University Press, 1958).

Rural Change and Royal Finances in Spain at the End of the Old Regime (Berkeley: University of California Press, 1989).

Herrera Canales, Inés, "Mercurio para refiner la plata Mexicana en el siglo XIX," *Historia Mexicana* 40 (1990), 27–51.

Hessel, Mary Stanley, *Profile of a Patriot: Revolutionary War Privateer* (New Bern, NC: Bagg and Griffin, 1983).

Heston, Alan, Robert Summers, and Bettina Aten, Penn World Tables, Version 7.0, Center for International Comparisons of Production, Income and Prices at the University of Pennsylvania, 2011. http://econ.unpenn.edu/.

Hill, Christopher, *The Century of Revolution, 1603–1714* (New York: W. W. Norton, 1961).

Hillgarth, J. N., *The Spanish Kingdoms, 1250–1516*, Vol. 2 (Oxford: Clarendon Press, 1978).

Hillyard, Michael, *Cincinnatus and the Citizen-Servant Ideal: The Roman Legend's Life, Times, and Legacy* (Philadelphia: Xlibris, 2001).

Hirst, Derek, *England in Conflict 1603–1660: Kingdom, Community, Commonwealth* (London: Bloomsbury Academic Press, 1999).

Hofstadter, Richard, *The Paranoid Style in American Politics and Other Essays* (New York: Knopf, 1965).

Holt, J. C., "The Origins and Audience of the Ballads of Robin Hood," in Stephen Knight, ed., *Robin Hood: An Anthology of Scholarship and Criticism* (Woodbridge, UK: D. S. Brewer, 1999), 211–32.

Hotchkiss, George, "Introduction," in John Wheeler, *A Treatise of Commerce* (New York: New York University Press, 1931).

Hough, Jerry F., *Russia and the West: Gorbachev and the Politics of Reform* (New York: Simon and Schuster, 1988).

"The Logic of Collective Action and the Pattern of Revolutionary Behavior," *Journal of Soviet Nationalities* 1 (1990), 34–65.

Democratization and Revolution in the USSR, 1985–1991 (Washington, DC: Brookings Institution Press, 1997).

The Logic of Economic Reform in Russia (Washington, DC: Brookings Institution Press, 2001).

Changing Party Coalitions: The Strange Red State-Blue State Alignment (New York: Algora, 2006).

Hough, Jerry and Robin Grier, "The Hidalgo Rebellion and the Problem of Order: The Comparative Lessons of Chile and the United States," *Latin Americanist* 54 (2010), 59–80.

Houston, Alan and Steve Pincus, eds., *A Nation Transformed: England after the Restoration* (Cambridge: Cambridge University Press, 2001).

Howarth, David, *British Sea Power: How Britain Became Sovereign of the Seas* (London: Collins, 1974).

Howe, Walter, *The Mining Guild of New Spain and Its Tribunal General, 1770–1825* (Cambridge, MA: Harvard University Press, 1949).

Hughes, Jonathan R. T., "Douglass North as Teacher," in Roger Ramsom, Richard Sutch, and Gary Walton, eds., *Explorations in the New Economic History: Essays in Honor of Douglass C. North* (New York: Academic Press, 1982), 4–5.

Hull, Anthony, *Charles III and the Revival of Spain* (Washington, DC: University Press of America, 1980).

Hunte, George, *Jamaica* (London: B. T. Batsford, 1976).

Hunter, Joseph, "Robin Hood," in Stephen Knight, ed., *Robin Hood: An Anthology of Scholarship and Criticism* (Woodbridge, UK: D. S. Brewer, 1999), 187–96.

Huntington, Samuel, *Political Order in Changing Societies* (New Haven, CT: Yale University Press, 1968).

Hussey, R. D., *The Caracas Company, 1728–1788* (Cambridge, MA: Harvard University Press, 1934).

Hutson, James, *John Adams and the Diplomacy of the American Revolution* (Lexington: University Press of Kentucky, 1980).

Irigoin, Alejandra and Regina Grafe, "Bargaining for Absolutism: A Spanish Path to Nation-State and Empire Building," *Hispanic-American Historical Review* 88 (2008), 173–209.

Israel, Jonathan, *Race, Class, and Politics in Colonial Mexico, 1610–1670* (New York: Oxford University Press, 1975).

Jacob, E. F., *The Fifteenth Century, 1399–1485* (Oxford: Oxford University Press, 1961).

Jacobson, Matthew, *Whiteness of a Different Color: European Immigrants and the Alchemy of Race* (Cambridge, MA: Harvard University Press, 1998).

Jakiela, Pamela, "Using Economic Experiments to Measure Informal Institutions," in Sebastian Galiani and Itai Sened, eds., *Institutions, Property Rights, and Economic Growth: The Legacy of Douglass North* (Cambridge: Cambridge University Press, 2014), 248–65.

Jamison, Jr., Ted, *George Monck and the Restoration: Victor without Bloodshed* (Fort Worth: Texas Christian University Press, 1975).

Jasanoff, Maya, *Liberty's Exiles: American Loyalists in the Revolutionary World* (New York: Knopf, 2011).

Jensen, Merrill, *The New Nation: A New History of the United States during the Confederation 1781–1789* (New York: Knopf, 1950).

Johnson, William Fletcher, *The History of Cuba*, Vol. 2 (New York: B. F. Buck, 1920).

Jones, J. R., *The Revolution of 1688 in England* (London: Wiedenfeld and Nicolson, 1972).

Kaeuper, Richard, *Bankers to the Crown: The Riccardi of Luca and Edward I* (Princeton, NJ: Princeton University Press, 1973).

Kamen, Henry, *The War of Succession in Spain, 1710–1715* (London: Weidenfeld and Nicolson, 1969).

"The Establishment of Intendants in Early Bourbon Spain," in Henry Kamen, *Crisis and Change in Early Modern Spain* (Aldershot, UK; Variorum, 1993), 1–13.

The Spanish Inquisition: A Historical Revision (New Haven, CT: Yale University Press, 1998).

Empire: How Spain Became a World Power: 1492–1763 (New York: Harper Perennial, 2004).

Kammen, Michael, *Empire and Interest: The American Colonies and the Politics of Mercantilism* (Philadelphia, Lippincott, 1970).

Colonial New York: A History (New York, Scribner's, 1975).

Kapp, Friedrich, *The Life of John Kalb: Major-General in the Revolutionary War* (New York: Henry Holt, 1884).

Katz, Stanley, *Newcastle's New York: Anglo-American Politics, 1732–1753* (Cambridge, MA: Harvard University Press, 1968).

Kicza, John, *Colonial Entrepreneurs: Families and Business in Bourbon Mexico City* (Albuquerque: University of New Mexico Press, 1983).

Kelley, Robert, *The Cultural Pattern in American Politics: The First Century* (New York: Knopf, 1979).

Kelsey, Sean, "Rich, Robert, Second Earl of Warwick (1587–1658), Colonial Promoter and Naval Officer," in Colin Matthew and Brian Harrison, eds., *Oxford Dictionary of National Biography*, Oxford University Press, 2004, online edition [http://www.oxforddnb.com/view/article/23494, accessed 14 May 2014].

Kennedy, Donald, "The English Naval Revolt of 1648," *English Historical Review* 77 (1962), 247–56.

Kennedy, William, *English Taxation, 1640–1799: An Essay on Policy and Opinion* (London: G. Bell, 1913).

Kicza, John, "Mexican Merchants and Their Links to Spain, 1750–1850," in Kenneth Andrien and Lyman Johnson, eds., *The Political Economy of Spanish America in the Age of Revolution, 1750–1850* (Albuquerque: University of New Mexico Press, 1994), 115–36.

Kishlansky, Mark, *The Rise of the New Model Army* (Cambridge: Cambridge University Press, 1979).

Parliamentary Selection: Social and Political Choice in Early Modern England (Cambridge: Cambridge University Press, 1986).

A Monarchy Transformed: Britain, 1603–1714 (London: Penguin, 1997).

Klein, Herbert, *Slavery in the Americas: A Comparative Study of Virginia and Cuba* (Oxford: Oxford University Press, 1967).

The American Finances of the Spanish Empire: Royal Income and Expenditures in Colonial Mexico, Peru, and Bolivia, 1680–1809 (Albuquerque: University of New Mexico Press, 1998).

A Concise History of Bolivia, 2nd ed. (Cambridge: Cambridge University Press, 2011).

Klein, Julius, *The Mesta: A Study in Spanish Economic History, 1273–1836* (Cambridge, MA: Harvard University Press, 1920).

Klingaman, David, "The Significance of Grain in the Development of the Tobacco Colonies," *Journal of Economic History* 29 (1969), 268–78.

Knighton, C. S., *Pepys and the Navy* (Stroud, UK: Sutton Publishing, 2003).
Knollenberg, Bernhard, *Origin of the American Revolution: 1759–1766*, rev. ed. (New York: Free Press, 1961).
Knowles, David, *The Religious Orders in England*, Vols. 1 and 2 (Cambridge: Cambridge University Press, 1979).
Kohn, Richard, "The Inside History of the Newburgh Conspiracy: America and the Coup d'Etat," *William and Mary Quarterly* 27 (1970), 187–220.
Kowaleski, Maryanne, "Warfare, Shipping, and Crown Patronage: The Impact of the Hundred Years War on the Port Towns of Medieval England," in Lawrin Armstrong, Ivana Elbl, and Martin Elbe, eds., *Money, Markets, and Trade in Late Medieval Europe: Essays in Honour of John H. Munro* (Leiden: Brill, 2007).
Krauze, Enrique, *Mexico: Biography of Power: A History of Modern Mexico* (New York: HarperCollins, 1997).
Kuethe, Allan. *Cuba, 1753–1815: Crown, Military, and Society* (Knoxville: University of Tennessee Press, 1986).
Kupperman, Karen Ordahl, "The Puzzle of the American Climate in the Early Colonial Period," *American Historical Review* 87 (1982), 1262–89.
Labarge, Margaret, *Gascony, England's First Colony, 1204–1453* (London: H. Hamilton, 1980).
Lachmann, Richard, "Greed and Contingency: State Fiscal Crises and Imperial Failure in Early Modern Europe," *American Journal of Sociology* 115 (2009), 39–73.
Ladd, Doris, *Mexican Nobility at Independence, 1780–1826* (Austin, TX: University of Texas Press, 1976).
Ladero Quesada, Miguel-Ángel, "Monarquía y ciudades de realengo en Castilla siglos XII a XV," *Anuario de estudios medievales* 24 (1994), 719–74.
"Los primeros pasos de la alcabala castellana, de Alfonso X a Pedro I," *Anuario de estudios medievales* 22 (1992), 785–802.
"Castile in the Middle Ages," in Richard Bonney, ed., *The Rise of the Fiscal State in Europe, c. 1200–1815* (Oxford: Oxford University Press, 1999).
Lambert, Sheila, *Bills and Acts: Legislative Procedure in Eighteenth-Century England* (Cambridge: Cambridge University Press, 1971).
Lane, Frederic, *Venice and History* (Baltimore. MD: Johns Hopkins University Press, 1966).
Lane, Robert, *Political Ideology: Why the Common Man Believes What He Does* (New York: Free Press of Glencoe, 1962).
Laoutaris, Christopher, *Shakespeare and the Countess* (London: Penguin Books, 2014).
Lee, Raymond, "American Cochineal in Europe Commerce, 1526–1625," *Journal of Modern History* 23 (1951), 205–24.
Leiby, John, *Colonial Bureaucrats and the Mexican Economy: Growth of a Patrimonial State, 1763–1821* (New York: P. Lang, 1986).
Levi, Margaret, *Of Rule and Revenue* (Berkeley: University of California Press, 1988).
"A Model, a Method, and a Map: Rational Choice in Comparative and Historical Analysis," in Mark Irving Lichbach and Alan Zuckerman, eds., *Comparative Politics: Rationality, Culture, and Structure* (Cambridge: Cambridge University Press, 1997).
"Death and Taxes: Extractive Equality and the Development of Democratic Institutions," in Ian Shapiro and Casiano Hacker-Cordón, eds., *Democracy's Values* (Cambridge: Cambridge University Press, 1999), 112–31.

Lewis, James, "Anglo-American Entrepreneurs in Havana: The Background and Significance of the Expulsion of 1784–1785," in Jacques Barbier and Allan Kuethe, eds., *The North American Role in the Spanish Imperial Economy, 1760–1819* (Manchester: Manchester University Press, 1984), 112–26.

Lewis, Archibald, "Mediterranean Maritime Commerce, A. D. 300–1000. Shipping and Trade," in Archibald Lewis, *The Sea and Medieval Civilizations: Collected Studies* (London: Variorum Reprints, 1978), 172–191.

Lewis, Archibald and Timothy Runyan, *European Naval and Maritime History, 300–1500* (Bloomington: Indiana University Press, 1985).

Lindert, Peter, "Voice and Growth: Was Churchill Right?" *Journal of Economic History* 63 (2003), 315-50.

Linehan, Peter, "The Economics of Episcopal Politics: The Cautionary Tale of Bishop Severo Pérez," in Peter Linehan, *The Processes of Politics and the Rule of Law: Studies on the Iberian Kingdoms and Papal Rome in the Middle Ages* (Aldershot, UK: Varorium, 2002).

Spain, 1157–1300: A Partible Inheritance (Oxford: Blackwell, 2008).

Lipset, Seymour Martin, *Political Man: The Social Bases of Politics* (Garden City, NY: Doubleday, 1960).

Lipson, Ephraim, *The Economic History of England*, Vols. 1 and 2 (London: A and C Black, 1956).

Lloyd, T. H., *The English Wool Trade in the Middle Ages* (Cambridge: Cambridge University Press, 2005).

Loades, David, *The Tudor Navy: An Administrative, Political, and Military History* (Leicester, UK: Scolar Press, 1992).

Politics and Nation, England 1450–1660, 5th ed. (Oxford: Blackwell, 1999).

England's Maritime Empire: Seapower, Commerce, and Policy, 1490–1690, Turning Points (Harlow, UK: Longman, 2000).

The Cecils: Privilege and Power behind the Throne (London: National Archives, 2008).

Lockhart, James, *Nahuas and Spaniards: Postconquest Central Mexican History and Philology* (Stanford, CA: Stanford University Press, 1991).

Lockhart, James and Stuart Schwartz, *Early Latin America: A History of Colonial Spanish America and Brazil* (Cambridge: Cambridge University Press, 1983).

Lomax, Derek, *Reconquest of Spain* (London: Longman, 1978).

Loveman, Brian, *Chile: The Legacy of Hispanic Capitalism*, 3rd ed. (New York: Oxford University Press, 2001).

Lunenfeld, Marvin, *Council of Santa Hermandad: A Study of the Pacification Forces of Ferdinand and Isabella* (Miami, FL: University of Miami Press, 1970).

Luu, Lien Bich, "'Taking the Bread Out of Our Mouths:' Xenophobia in Early Modern Europe," *Immigrants and Minorities* 19 (2000), 1–22.

Lynch, John, *Spanish Colonial Administration, 1782–1810: The Intendant System in the Viceroyalty of the Río de la Plata* (London: University of London Press, 1958).

Spain under the Hapsburgs (Oxford: B. Blackwell, 1969).

The Spanish American Revolutions, 1808–1826, 2nd ed. (New York: W.W. Norton, 1986).

Bourbon Spain, 1700–1808 (Oxford: Basil Blackwell, 1989).

Lyons, John, Louis Cain, and Samuel Willington Jr., eds., *Reflections on the Cliometrics Revolution: Conversations with Economic Historians* (London: Routledge, 2008).

MacKay, Angus, *Spain in the Middle Ages, from Frontier to Empire, 1000–1500* (New York: St. Martin's Press, 1977).

"A Pluralist Society: Modern Spain," in John Elliott, ed., *The Spanish World: Civilization and Empire: Europe and the Americas, Past and Present* (New York: Harry N. Abrams, 1991), 35–56.

Mackay, Ruth, *The Limits of Royal Authority: Resistance and Obedience in Seventeenth Century Castile* (Cambridge: Cambridge University Press, 1999).

MacLeod, Murdo, "Spain and America: The Atlantic Trade, 1492–1700," in Leslie Bethell, ed., *Cambridge History of Latin America*, Vol. 1: *Colonial Latin America* (Cambridge: Cambridge University Press, 1985), 341–88.

"A New Introduction: More Than Three Decades of Writing in Spanish Central America, 1973–2006," in Murdo MacLeod, *Spanish Central America: A Socioeconomic History, 1520–1720* (Austin, TX: University of Texas Press, 2007), xi.

Maddison, Angus, Historical Statistics of the World Economy: 1-2008 AD (http://www.ggdc.net/MADDISON/oriindex.htm).

Maltby, William, *The Reign of Charles V* (New York: Palgrave, 2002).

Mannheim, Karl, *Ideology and Utopia: An Introduction to the Sociology of Knowledge* (New York: Harcourt, Brace, 1936).

Marichal, Carlos, "Obstacles to the Development of Capital Markets in 19th Century Mexico," in Stephen Haber, ed., *How Latin America Fell Behind: Essays on the Economic Histories of Brazil and Mexico* (Stanford, CA: Stanford University Press, 1997), 118–45.

"Mexican Cochineal and the European Demand for American Dyes," Steven Topik, Carlos Marichal, and Zephyr Frank, eds., *From Silver to Cocaine: Latin American Commodity Chains and the Building of the World Economy, 1500–2000* (Durham, NC: Duke University Press, 2006), 76–92.

Marichal, Carlos. *Bankruptcy of Empire: Mexican Silver and the Wars between Spain, Britain, and France, 1760–1810* (New York: Cambridge University Press, 2007).

Marr, Phebe, *The Modern History of Iraq* (Boulder, CO: Westview, 1985).

Masschaele, James, "Toll and Trade in Medieval England," in Lawrin Armstrong, Ivana Elbl, and Martin Elbl, eds., *Money, Market and Trade in Late Medieval Europe: Essays in Honour of John H. A. Munro* (Leiden: Brill, 2007), 146–78.

Mathias, Peter, "Risk, Credit, and Kinship in Early Modern Enterprise," in John McCusker and Kenneth Morgan, eds., *Early Modern Atlantic Economy* (Cambridge: Cambridge University Press, 2000), 1–35.

McArthur, John and Jeffrey Sachs, "Institutions and Geography: Comment on Acemoglu, Johnson and Robinson (2000)," NBER Working Paper No. 8114, 2001.

McCormick, Richard, *The Presidential Game: The Origins of American Presidential Politics* (Oxford: Oxford University Press, 1982).

McCreery, David, "Indigo Commodity-Chains in the Spanish and British Empires, 1560–1860," in Steven Topik, Carlos Marichal, and Zephyr Frank, eds., *From Silver to Cocaine: Latin American Commodity Chains and the Building of the World Economy, 1500–2000* (Durham, NC: Duke University Press, 2006), 53–75.

McCullough, David, *John Adams* (New York: Simon and Schuster, 2001).

McCusker, John, *Rum and the American Revolution: The Rum Trade and the Balance of Payments of the Thirteen Continental Colonies* (New York: Garland, 1989).

McHardy, A. K., "Clerical Taxation in the Fifteenth Century: The Clergy as Agents of the Crown," in Barrie Dobson, ed., *The Church, Politics, and Patronage in the Fifteenth Century* (Gloucester, UK: Alan Sutton, 1984), 169–70.

McKisack, May, *The Fourteenth Century, 1307–1399* (Oxford: Clarendon Press, 1959).

Mecham, J. Lloyd, "The Origins of Federalism in Mexico," *Hispanic American Historical Review* 18 (1938), 164–82.

Church and State in Latin America: A History of Politico-Ecclesiastical Relations, rev. ed. (Chapel Hill: University of North Carolina Press, 1966).

Melville, Elinor G. K., *A Plague of Sheep: Environmental Consequences of the Conquest of Mexico* (Cambridge: Cambridge University Press, 1994).

Merriman, Roger, *The Rise of the Spanish Empire in the Old World and in the New*, Vol. 1 (New York: Macmillan, 1918).

Merritt, Richard, *Symbols of American Community* (New Haven, CT: Yale University Press, 1966).

Meyer, Michael and William Sherman, *The Course of Mexican History*, 5th ed.(New York: Oxford University Press, 1995).

Milgrom, Paul, Douglass North, and Barry Weingast, "The Role of Institutions in the Revival of Trade: The Law Merchant, Private Judges, and the Champagne Fairs," *Economics and Politics* 2 (1990), 1–23.

Mintz, Sidney, *Sweetness and Power: The Place of Sugar in Modern History* (New York: Viking, 1985).

Mokyr, Joel, "Culture, Institutions, and Modern Growth," in Sebastian Galiani and Itai Sened, eds., *Institutions, Property Rights, and Economic Growth: The Legacy of Douglass North* (Cambridge: Cambridge University Press, 2014), 151–91.

Moore, John Preston, *The Cabildo in Peru under the Bourbons: A Study in the Decline and Resurgence of Local Government in the Audiencia of Lima* (Durham, NC: Duke University Press, 1966).

Morgan, Edmund and Helen Morgan, *The Stamp Act Crisis: Prologue to Revolution* (Chapel Hill: University of North Carolina Press, 1953).

Morris, Gouverneur, *An Oration upon the Death of General Washington* (New York: John Firman, 1800).

Morrisey, Richard, "Cattle Raising in New Spain" (PhD dissertation, University of California–Berkeley, 1949).

Mueller, Dennis, *Public Choice II* (Cambridge: Cambridge University Press, 1989).

Müller, Christian, "The Methodology of Contractarianism in Economics," *Public Choice* 113 (2002), 465–83.

Munger, Michael, "Coercion, the State, and Obligations of Citizenship, *Public Choice* 152 (2012), 415–21.

Murray, Margaret Alice, *The God of the Witches* (London: S. Low and Marston, 1933).

Myers, A. R., *London in the Age of Chaucer* (Norman: University of Oklahoma Press. 1988).

Nader, Helen, *The Mendoza Family in the Spanish Renaissance, 1350 to 1550* (New Brunswick, NJ: Rutgers University Press, 1979).

Liberty in Absolutist Spain: The Hapsburg Sale of Towns, 1516–1700 (Baltimore: Johns Hopkins University Press, 1990).

Nelson, Paul David, *General Horatio Gates: A Biography* (Baton Rouge: Louisiana State University Press, 1976).

Netanyahu, Benzoin, *The Origins of the Inquisition in Fifteenth Century Spain* (New York: Random House, 1995).

Newhall, Richard Ager, *The English Conquest of Normandy 1416–1424: A Study in Fifteenth Century Warfare* (Brasted, UK: Russell and Russell, 1971).

Nightingale, Pamela, "Knights and Merchant Trade, Politics and the Gentry in Late Medieval England," in Pamela Nightingale, *Trade, Money, and Power in Medieval England* (Aldershot, UK: Ashgate, 2007), 36–62.

Trade, Money, and Power in Medieval England (Aldershot. UK: Ashgate, 2007).

North, Douglass, *Structure and Change in Economic History* (New York: W. W. Norton, 1981).

"Institutions and Economic Growth: An Historical Introduction," *World Development* 17 (1989), 1319–32.

Institutions, Institutional Change and Economic Performance (Cambridge: Cambridge University Press, 1990).

"Economic Performance through Time," *American Economic Review* 84 (1994), 359–68.

The Contribution of the New Institutional Economics to an Understanding of the Transition Problem (Helsinki: UNU World Institute for Development Economics, 1997).

"Response to Geddes and Keohane," in James Alt, Margaret Levi, and Elinor Ostrom, eds., *Competition and Cooperation: Conversations with Nobelists about Economics and Political Science* (New York: Russell Sage Foundation, 1999).

Understanding the Process of Economic Change (Princeton, NJ: Princeton University Press, 2005).

North, Douglass, William Summerhill, and Barry Weingast, "Order, Disorder and Economic Change: Latin America vs. North America," in Bruce Bueno de Mesquita and Hilton Root, eds., *Governing for Prosperity* (New Haven, CT: Yale University Press, 2000), 17–58.

North, Douglass and Robert Paul Thomas, *The Rise of the Western World: A New Economic History* (Cambridge: Cambridge University Press, 1973).

North, Douglass, John Joseph Wallis, and Barry Weingast, *Violence and Social Orders: A Conceptual Framework for Interpreting Recorded History* (New York: Cambridge University Press, 2009).

North, Douglass, John Joseph Wallis, Steven Webb, and Barry Webb, eds., *In the Shadow of Violence: Politics, Economics, and the Problems of Development* (Cambridge: Cambridge University Press, 2013).

North, Douglass and Barry Weingast, "Constitutions and Commitment: The Evolution of Institutions Governing Public Choice in Seventeenth Century England," *Journal of Economic History* 49 (1989), 803–32.

Norton, Leslie, "The Dangers of Lessons Unheeded: Interview with Joseph Stiglitz," *Barrons*, March 21, 2011, p. 40.

Nugent, Jeffrey and Nicolas Sanchez, "The Efficiency of the Mesta: A Parable," *Explorations in Economic History* 26 (1989), 261–84.

Nunn, Nathan, "Historical Legacies: A Model Linking Africa's Past to Its Current Underdevelopment," *Journal of Development Economics* 83 (2007), 157–75.

"The Long-Term Effects of Africa's Slave Trades," *Quarterly Journal of Economics* 123 (2008), 139–76.

Nunn, Nathan and Diego Puga, "Ruggedness: The Blessing of Bad Geography in Africa," *Review of Economics and Statistics* 94 (2012), 20–36.
O'Brien, Patrick, "Inseparable Connections, Trade, Economy, Fiscal State, and the Expansion of Empire, 1688–1815," in P. J. Marshall, ed., *The Oxford History of the British Empire*, Vol. 2: *The Eighteenth Century* (Oxford: Oxford University Press, 1998), 53–77.
O'Brien, Patrick and Philip Hunt, "England, 1485–1815," in Richard Bonney, ed., *The Rise of the Fiscal State in Europe, c. 1200–1815* (Oxford: Oxford University Press, 1999), 53–100.
O'Callaghan, Joseph, *The Spanish Military Order of Calatrava and Its Affiliates* (London: Variorum, 1975).
Olson, Alison, *Anglo-American Politics 1600–1775* (New York: Oxford University Press, 1973).
Making the Empire Work: London and American Interest Groups, 1690–1790 (Cambridge, MA: Harvard University Press, 1992).
Olson, Mancur, *The Logic of Collective Action: Public Goods and the Theory of Groups* (Cambridge, MA: Harvard University Press, 1965).
The Rise and Decline of Nations: Economic Growth, Stagflation, and Social Rigidity (New Haven, CT: Yale University Press, 1982).
"The Logic of Collective Action in Soviet-Type Societies," *Journal of Soviet Nationalities* 1 (1990), 8–27.
"Dictatorship, Democracy, and Development," *American Political Science Review* 87 (1993), 567–76.
Power and Prosperity: Outgrowing Communist and Capitalist Dictatorships (New York: Basic Books, 2000).
Ormrod, W. M., *The Reign of Edward III: Crown and Political Society in England, 1327–1377* (New Haven, CT: Yale University Press, 1990).
"England in the Middle Ages," in Richard Bonney, ed., *The Rise of the Fiscal State in Europe, c.1200–1815* (Oxford: Oxford University Press, 1999), 19–52.
Owen, David and Tracy Strong, "Introduction," in David Owen and Tracy Strong, eds., *Max Weber: The Vocation Lectures* (Indianapolis, IN: Hackett, 2004).
Owensby, Brian, *Empire of Law and Indian Justice in Colonial Mexico* (Stanford, CA: Stanford University Press, 2008).
Palmer, Robert, *The Age of the Democratic Revolution: A Political History of Europe and America, 1760–1800*, Vol. 1 (Princeton, NJ: Princeton University Press, 1959).
Palmer, Dave, *1794: America, Its Army, and the Birth of the Nation* (Novato, CA: Presidio Press, 1994).
Pantin, William Abel, *The English Church in the Fourteenth Century: Based on the Birkbeck Lectures, 1948* (Cambridge: Cambridge University Press, 2010).
Paquette, Gabriel, *Enlightenment, Governance, and Reform in Spain and Its Empire* (New York: Palgrave, 2008).
Pares, Richard, *War and Trade in the West Indies, 1739–1763* (London: Frank Cass, 1963).
Parry, J. H., *The Sale of Public Offices in the Spanish Indies under the Hapsburgs* (Berkeley: University of California Press, 1953).
The Age of Reconnaissance: Discovery, Exploration, and Settlement, 1450–1650 (London: Littlehampton Book Services, 1963).

Trade and Dominion: The European Overseas Empires in the Eighteenth Century (London: Phoenix Press, 1971).

Patch, Robert, *Maya and Spaniard in Yucatán, 1648–1812* (Stanford, CA: Stanford University Press, 1993).

"The Bourbon Reforms, City Councils, and the Struggle for Power in Yucatán, 1770–1796," in Jaime Rodríguez O., *Mexico in the Age of Democratic Revolutions, 1750–1850* (Boulder, CO: Lynne Rienner, 1994).

"Imperial Politics and Local Economy in Colonial Central America, 1670–1779," *Past and Present* 143 (1994), 77–107.

Patterson, Samuel White, *Horatio Gates: Defender of American Liberties* (New York: Columbia University Press, 1947).

Pearl, Valerie, *London and the Outbreak of the Puritan Revolution: City Government and National Politics, 1625–43* (Oxford: Oxford University Press, 1961).

Pederson, Leland, *The Mining Industry of the Norte Chico, Chile* (Evanston, IL: Northwestern University Press, 1966).

Perry, Laurens Ballard, *Juárez and Díaz: Machine Politics in Mexico* (DeKalb: Northern Illinois University Press, 1978).

Petrie, Charles, *King Charles III of Spain: An Enlightened Despot* (London: Constable, 1971).

Phelan, John Leddy, *The Kingdom of Quito in the Seventeenth Century: Bureaucratic Politics in the Spanish Empire* (Madison: University of Wisconsin Press, 1967).

"Authority and Flexibility in the Spanish Imperial Bureaucracy," in Mark Burkholder, ed., *Administrators of Empire* (Aldershot, UK: Ashgate, 1998), 1–20.

Phillips, Carla Rahn, *Ciudad Real, 1500–1750: Growth, Crisis, and Readjustment in the Spanish Economy* (Cambridge, MA: Harvard University Press, 1979).

"The Spanish Wool Trade, 1500–1780," *Journal of Economic History* 42 (1982), 775–95.

Phillips, Carla Rahn and William Phillips Jr., *Spain's Golden Fleece: Wool Production and the Wool Trade from the Middle Ages to the Nineteenth Century* (Baltimore, MD: Johns Hopkins University Press, 1997).

Pincus, Steven C. A., *1688: The First Modern Revolution* (New Haven, CT: Yale University Press, 2009).

Pincus, Steven C. A. and James A. Robinson, "What Really Happened during the Glorious Revolution?" in Sebastian Galiani and Itai Sened, eds., *Institutions, Property Rights, and Economic Growth: The Legacy of Douglass North* (Cambridge: Cambridge University Press, 2014), 192–222.

Pirenne, Henri, *Economic and Social History of Medieval Europe* (New York: Harcourt, Brace, 1937).

Pike, Ruth, *Aristocrats and Traders: Southern Society in the Sixteenth Century* (Ithaca, NY: Cornell University Press, 1972).

Platt, D. C. M, "Dependency in Nineteenth-Century Latin America: An Historian Objects," *Latin American Research Review* 15 (1980), 113–30.

Plumb, J. H., *The Growth of Political Stability in England: 1675–1725* (London: Macmillan, 1967).

Sir Robert Walpole: The King's Minister, Vol. II (London: Allen Lane, 1972).

Poinsett, Joel Roberts, *Notes on Mexico Made in the Autumn of 1822* (New York: Frederick A. Praeger, 1969).

Pomeranz, Kenneth, *The Great Divergence: China, Europe, and the Making of the Modern World* (Princeton, NJ: Princeton University Press, 2000).

Pounds, Norman J. G., *An Economic History of Medieval Europe* (London: Longman, 1974).

Power, Eileen, *The Wool Trade in English Medieval History* (Oxford: Oxford University Press, 1965).

Powers, James, *A Society Organized for War: The Iberian Municipal Militias in the Central Middle Ages, 1000–1284* (Berkeley: University of California Press, 1988).

Prestwich, Michael, *Edward I*, 2nd ed. (New Haven, CT: Yale University Press, 1957).

War, Politics, and Finance under Edward I (London: Faber and Faber, 1972).

Price, Jacob, "Glasgow, the Tobacco Trade, and the Scottish Customs, 1707–1775: Some Commercial, Administrative, and Political Implications of the Union," in Jacob Price, *Overseas Trade and Traders: Essays on Some Commercial, Financial, and Political Challenges Facing British American Merchants* (Aldershot, UK: Variorum, 1996), Vol. 9, 1–36.

"The Imperial Economy, 1700–1776," in P. J. Marshall, ed., *Oxford History of the British Empire, 18th Century*, Vol. 2 (Oxford: Oxford University Press, 2001).

Priestley, Herbert, *José de Gálvez: Visitor General of New Spain, 1765–1771* (Berkeley: University of California Press, 1916).

Pritchett, Lant and Michael Woolcock, "Solutions When the Solution Is the Problem: Arraying the Disarray in Development," *World Development* 32 (2004), 191–212.

Pritchett, Lant and Frauke de Weijer, " Fragile States: Stuck in a Capability Trap?" Background Paper for World Development Report, 2011.

Quinn, David and A. N. Ryan, *England's Sea Empire, 1550–1642* (London: George Allen and Unwin, 1983).

Rakove, Jack, *The Beginnings of National Politics: An Interpretative History of the Constitutional Convention* (New York: Knopf, 1979).

Rawlings, Helen, *Church, Religion, and Society in Early Modern Spain* (New York: Palgrave, 2002).

Rawls, John, "Justice as Fairness: Political, Not Metaphysical," *Philosophy and Public Affairs* 14 (1985), 223–51.

Reilly, Bernard, *The Kingdom of Leon-Castilla under King Alfonso VI, 1065–1109* (Princeton, NJ: Princeton University Press, 1988).

The Medieval Spains (Cambridge: Cambridge University Press, 1993).

Rejwan, Nessim, *The Jews of Iraq: 3000 Years of History and Culture* (London: Weidenfeld and Nicolson, 1985).

Richardson, Glenn, *Renaissance Monarchy* (New York: Oxford University Press, 2002).

Ringrose, David, *Madrid and the Spanish Economy, 1560–1850* (Berkeley: University of California Press, 1983).

Spain, Europe, and the 'Spanish Miracle,' 1700–1900 (Cambridge: Cambridge University Press, 1998).

Robertson, William, *Iturbide of Mexico* (Durham, NC: Duke University, 1952).

Rock, David, *Argentina from Spanish Colonization to the Falkland War, 1561–1987* (Berkeley: University of California Press, 1987).

Rodger, Nicholas A. M., "Guns and Sails in the First Phase of English Colonization, 1500–1650," in Nicholas Canny, ed., *The Oxford History of the British Empire*, Vol. I:

The Origins of Empire: British Overseas Enterprise to the Close of the Seventeenth Century (Oxford: Oxford University Press, 1998).

The Safeguard of the Sea: A Naval History of Britain, 660–1649, Vol. 1 (New York: W.W. Norton, 1998).

The Command of the Ocean: Naval History of Britain, 1649–1815 (New York: W. W. Norton, 2005).

Rodríguez O., Jaime E., "Down from Colonialism: Mexico's Nineteenth-Century Crisis," in Jaime E. Rodríguez O., ed., *The Mexican and Mexican-American Experience in the 19th Century* (Tempe, AZ: Bilingual Press, 1989).

"The Transition from Colony to Nation: New Spain, 1820–1821," in Jaime Rodríguez O., ed., *Mexico in the Age of Democratic Revolutions* (Boulder, CO: Lynne Rienner, 1994).

Rodrik, Dani, *One Economics, Many Recipes: Globalization, Institutions, and Economic Growth* (Princeton, NJ: Princeton University Press, 2007).

"Second-Best Institutions," *American Economic Review: Papers and Proceedings* 98 (2008), 100–104.

Romero Sotelo, María Eugenia, *Minería y Guerra: La economía de Nueva España, 1810–1821* (Mexico City: El Colegio de Mexico, 1997).

Rondinelli, Dennis, *Development Projects as Policy Experiments: An Adaptive Approach to Development Administration* (New York: Routledge, 1993).

Rossie, Jonathan, *The Politics of Command in the American Revolution* (Syracuse, NY: Syracuse University Press, 1975).

Rossum, Kenneth, *Thomas Mifflin and the Politics of the American Revolution* (Chapel Hill: University of North Carolina Press, 1952).

Rostow, W. W., *The Stages of Economic Development: A Non-Communist Manifesto* (Cambridge: Cambridge University Press, 1960).

Rouge, Jean, *Ships and Fleets of the Ancient Mediterranean* (Middletown, CT: Wesleyan University Press, 1981).

Roux, Georges, *Ancient Iraq* (London: Penguin, 1980).

Rubin, Miri, *The Hollow Crown: A History of Britain in the Late Middle Ages* (London: Penguin Books, 2006).

Ruiz, Teofilo, *The City and the Realm: Burgos and Castile, 1080–1492* (Aldershot, UK: Ashgate, 1992).

Crisis and Continuity: Land and Town in Late Medieval Castile (Philadelphia: University of Pennsylvania Press, 1994).

Russell, Conrad, *The Crisis of Parliaments: English History 1509–1660* (Oxford: Oxford University Press, 1971).

Russell, Peter, *The English Intervention in Spain in the Time of Edward III and Richard II* (Oxford: Clarendon Press, 1955).

Saint-Saens, Alain, ed., *Young Charles V, 1500–1531* (New Orleans: University Press of the South, 2000).

Sachs, Jeffrey, "Tropical Underdevelopment," National Bureau of Economic Research Working Paper No. 8119, 2001.

"Government, Geography, and Growth: The True Drivers of Economic Growth," *Foreign Affairs* 91 (2012), 151.

Sachs, Jeffrey and Pia Malaney, "The Economic and Social Burden of Malaria," *Nature* 415 (2002), 680–85.

Sachs, Wolfgang, "The Rise and Decline of an Ideal," Wuppertal Institut für Klima, Umwelt, Energie (Orgs): Wuppertal Papers 108, 2000.

Salvucci, Richard, *Textiles and Capitalism in Mexico: An Economic History of the Obrajes, 1539–1840* (Princeton, NJ: Princeton University Press, 1987).

Politics, Markets, and Mexico's London Debt (New York: Cambridge University Press, 2009).

Samponaro, Frank, "The Political Role of the Army in Mexico, 1821–1847 (PhD dissertation, State University of New York-Stony Brook, 1971).

Sánchez Santiró, Ernest, "La hacienda reformada: la centralización de la renta de alcabalas en Nueva España (1754–1781)," in Ernest Sánchez Santiró, Luis Jaúregui y Antonio Ibarra (coordinadores), *Finanzas y política en el mundo iberoamericano: del antiguo régimen a las naciones independientes, 1754–1850* (Mexico City: UNAM, 2001).

Scheina, Robert, *Latin America's Wars: The Age of the Caudillo, 1791–1899* (Washington, DC: Brassey's, 2003).

Schlesinger, Arthur Sr., *The Colonial Merchants and the American Revolution* (New York: Columbia University Press, 1918).

Schumpeter, Joseph, *Capitalism, Socialism, and Democracy* (New York: Harpers and Brothers, 1942).

Schwartz, Stuart, *Sugar Plantations in the Formation of Brazilian Society: Bahia, 1550–1835* (Cambridge: Cambridge University Press, 1985).

Schwartz, Stuart, ed., *Tropical Babylons: Sugar and the Making of the Atlantic World, 1450–1680* (Chapel Hill: University of North Carolina Press, 2000).

Sellers, Leila, *Charleston Business on the Eve of the American Revolution* (Chapel Hill: University of North Carolina Press, 1934).

Setzekorn, William David, *A Profile of the New Nation of Belize, formerly British Honduras* (Athens: Ohio University Press, 1981).

Seward, Desmond, *The Monks of War: The Military Religious Orders* (London: Eyre Methuen, 1972).

Shy, John, "The American Colonies in War and Revolution," in P. J. Marshall, ed., *The Oxford History of the British Empire*, Vol. II: *The Eighteenth Century* (Oxford: Oxford University Press, 1993), 300–324.

Skaperdas, Stergio and Constantinose Syropoulous, "Gangs as Primitive States," in Gianluca Fiorentini and Sam Peltzman, eds., *The Economics of Organised Crime* (Cambridge: Cambridge University Press, 1995), 61–81.

Skocpol, Theda, *States and Social Revolutions: A Comparative Analysis of France, Russia, and China* (Cambridge: Cambridge University Press, 1979).

Shepsle, Kenneth, "The Rules of the Game: What Rules? What Games," in Sebastian Galiani and Itai Sened, eds., *Institutions, Property Rights, and Economic Growth: The Legacy of Douglass North* (Cambridge: Cambridge University Press, 2014), 66–83.

Simpson, Lesley, "Mexico's Forgotten Century," *Pacific Historical Review* 22 (1953), 113–21.

"Foreword," in Francois Chevalier, *Land and Society in Colonial Mexico: The Great Hacienda* (Berkeley: University of California Press, 1963).

Slots, Eddy, "The Expansion of the Sugar Market in Western Europe," in Stuart Schwartz, ed., *Tropical Babylons: Sugar and the Making of the Atlantic World, 1450–1680* (Chapel Hill: University of North Carolina Press, 2000), 237–88.

Smith, Adam, *The Wealth of Nations* (New York: Bantam Dell, 2003).
Smith, Robert Sidney, *The Spanish Guild Merchant: A History of the Consulado, 1250–1700* (Durham, NC: Duke University Press, 1940).
Smith, Robert Sidney "Sales Taxes in New Spain, 1575–1770," *Hispanic American Historical Review* 28 (1948), 2–37.
Smith, Page, *John Adams*, Vol. 1 (Garden City, NY: Doubleday, 1962).
Smith, Paul, ed., *Letters of Delegates to Congress, 1774–1789*, Vol. 1 (Washington, DC: Library of Congress, 1976).
Spencer, Andrew, *Nobility and Kingship in Medieval England, the Earls and Edward I, 1272–1307* (Cambridge: Cambridge University Press, 2013).
Stein, Barbara and Stanley Stein, *Edge of Crisis: War and Trade in the Spanish Atlantic, 1789–1808* (Baltimore: The John Hopkins University, 2009).
Stein, Stanley and Barbara Stein, *Silver, Trade, and War: Spain and America in the Making of Early Modern Europe* (Baltimore, MD: Johns Hopkins University Press, 2000).
Apogee of Empire: Spain and New Spain in the Age of Charles III, 1759–1789 (Baltimore, MD: Johns Hopkins University Press, 2003).
Stern, Philip and Carl Wennerlind, eds., *Mercantilism Reimagined: Political Economy in Early Modern Britain and Its Empire* (Oxford: Oxford University Press, 2013).
Stiglitz, Joseph and Arnold Heertje, eds., *The Economic Role of the State* (Oxford: Basil Blackwell, 1989).
Stone, Lawrence, *The Crisis of the Aristocracy, 1558–1641*, abridged ed. (London: Oxford University Press, 1967).
Street, Lucie, *An Uncommon Sailor: A Portrait of Admiral Sir William Penn: English Naval Supremacy* (New York: St. Martin's Press, 1988).
Summerhill, William, *Order against Progress: Government, Foreign Investment, and Railroads in Brazil, 1854–1913* (Stanford, CA: Stanford University Press, 2003).
"Fiscal Bargains, Political Institutions, and Economic Performance," *Hispanic-American Historical Review* 88 (2008), 219–33.
Summers, Mark, *The Plundering Generation: Corruption and the Crisis of the Union, 1849–1867* (New York: Oxford University Press, 1987).
Sussman, Nathan and Yishay Yafeh, "Institutional Reforms, Financial Development and Sovereign Debt: Britain 1690–1790," *Journal of Economic History* 66 (2006), 906–35.
Sutherland, Lucy, *Politics and Finances in the Eighteenth Century* (London: Hambledon Press, 1984).
Tanner, Norman, *The Church in Late Medieval Norwich: 1370–1532* (Toronto: PIMS, 1984).
Tawney, R. H., *Religion and the Rise of Capitalism* (New Brunswick, NJ: Transaction Publishers, 1998).
Taylor, James William, "Socio-Economic Instability and the Revolution for Mexican Independence in the Province of Guanajuato" (PhD dissertation, University of New Mexico, 1976).
Tenenbaum, Barbara, *The Politics of Penury: Debts and Taxes in Mexico, 1821–1856* (Albuquerque: University of New Mexico Press, 1986).
TePaske, John J., "Bullion Production in Mexico and Peru, 1546–1810," unpublished paper.

"The Financial Disintegration of the Royal Government of Mexico during the Epoch of Independence," in Jaime Rodríguez O., ed., *The Independence of Mexico and the Creation of the New Nation* (Los Angeles: UCLA Publications, 1989).

TePaske, John J. and Herbert Klein, "Introduction," *The Royal Treasuries of the Spanish Empire in America*, Vol. 1: *Peru* (Durham, NC: Duke University Press, 1982).

Thomas, Hugh, *Conquest of Mexico* (New York: Pimlico, 2004).

Thompson, I. A. A., "The Armada and Administrative Reform: The Spanish Council of War in the Reign of Philip II," *English Historical Review* 82 (1967), 698–725.

Thompson, I. A. A. and B. Yun Casalilla, "Introduction," in I. A. A. Thompson and Bartolomé Yun Casalilla, eds., *The Castilian Crisis of the Seventeenth Century: New Perspectives on the Economic and Social History of Seventeenth-Century Spain* (Cambridge: Cambridge University Press, 1994), 1–12.

Tilly, Charles, "Reflections on the History of European State-making," in Charles Tilly, ed., *The Formation of National States in Western Europe* (Princeton, NJ: Princeton University Press, 1975).

Timmons, Wilbert, *Morelos: Priest, Soldier, Statesman of Mexico* (El Paso: Texas Western College Press, 1963).

Tortella, Gabriel and Francisco Comín, "Fiscal and Monetary Institutions in Spain (1600–1900)," in Michael Bordo and Roberto Cortés Conde, eds., *Transferring Wealth and Power from the Old to the New World Monetary and Fiscal Institutions in the 17th through the 19th Centuries* (Cambridge: Cambridge University Press, 2001).

Tout, Thomas, *The English Civil Service in the Fourteenth Century* (Manchester: University of Manchester Press, 1916).

Toynbee, Arnold, *A Study of History*, Vols. 1–12 (London: Oxford University Press, 1948–1961).

Tuchman, Barbara, *The First Salute* (New York: Knopf, 1988).

Tuck, Anthony, *Crown and Nobility: England 1272–1461* (Blackwell, 1999).

Twinam, Ann, *Miners, Merchants, and Farmers in Colonial Colombia* (Austin: University of Texas Press, 1982).

Usher, Abbott Payson, "The Growth of English Shipping, 1572–1922," *Quarterly Journal of Economics* 42 (1928), 465–78.

Vanderwood, Paul, *Disorder and Progress: Bandits, Police, and Mexican Development* (Lincoln: University of Nebraska Press, 1981).

Van de Walle, Nicholas, "The Paths from Neopatrimonialism: Democracy and Clientelism in Africa Today," Cornell University, Center for International Studies, Working Paper No. 3-07, 2007.

Van Young, Eric, *The Other Rebellion: Popular Violence, Ideology, and the Mexican Struggle for Independence, 1810–1821* (Stanford, CA: Stanford University Press, 2001).

Van Young, Erik, "Introduction to the Twenty-Fifth Anniversary Edition," in Eric Van Young, *Hacienda and Market in Eighteenth-Century Mexico: The Rural Economy of the Guadalajara Region, 1675–1820*, 2nd ed. (Lanham, MD: Rowman and Littlefield, 2006), xviii and 344.

Vicens Vives, Jaime, *An Economic History of Spain* (Princeton, NJ: Princeton University Press, 1969).

Von Humboldt, Alexander, *Political Essay on the Kingdom of New Spain* (Norman: University of Oklahoma Press, 1988).
Wallis, John Joseph, "Answering Mary Shirley's Question, or What Can the World Bank Learn from American History?" in Stephen Haber, Douglass North, and Barry Weingast, eds., *Political Institutions and Financial Development* (Stanford, CA: Stanford University Press, 2008).
Walton, Gary and Roger Miller, *Economic Issues in American History* (New York: Harper and Row, 1978).
Waters, David, *The Art of Navigation in England in Elizabethan and Early Stuart Times* (New Haven, CT: Yale University Press, 1958).
Waugh, Scott, *England in the Reign of Edward III* (Cambridge: Cambridge University Press, 1991).
Weber, Max, *Economy and Society: An Outline of Interpretive Sociology*, edited by Guenther Roth and Claus Wittich (Berkeley: University of California Press, 1978).
Max Weber: Essays in Sociology (New York: Routledge, 2009).
Theory of Social and Economic Organization, trans. A. M. Henderson and Talcott Parsons (New York: Oxford University Press, 2009).
The Protestant Ethic and the Spirit of Capitalism (trans. Talcott Parsons) (London: Scribner, 2013).
Webster, Charles, *The Great Instauration: Science, Medicine, and Reform, 1626–1660* (London: Duckworth, 1975).
Weingast, Barry, "The Political Foundations of Democracy and the Rule of Law," *American Political Science Review* 91 (1997), 245–63.
Wharton, Francis, *The Revolutionary Diplomatic Correspondence of the United States*, Vol. 2 (Washington, DC: Government Printing Office, 1889).
Wicksell, Knut, "A New Principle of Just Taxation," in Richard Musgrave and Alan Peacock, eds., *Classics in the Theory of Public Finance* (London: Macmillan, 1958), 72–118.
Willan, T. S., *The Early History of the Russia Company, 1553–1603* (Manchester: Manchester University, 1968).
Williams, Ann, *Kingship and Government in Pre-Conquest England c. 500–1066* (London: Macmillan, 1999).
Williams, Gwyn, *Medieval London: From Commune to Capital* (London: Athlone, 1963).
Williams, Patrick, *The Great Favourite: Duke of Lerma and the Court and Government of Philip III of Spain, 1598–1621* (Manchester: Manchester University Press, 2006).
Williamson, Oliver, "Transaction Cost Economics," in Richard Schmalensee and Robert Willig, eds., *Handbook of Industrial Organization*, Vol. 3 (New York: Elsevier Science, 1989).
"The New Institutional Economics, Taking Stock, Looking Ahead," *Journal of Economic Literature* 38 (2000), 595–613.
Wilson, Charles, *England's Apprenticeship, 1603–17*, 2nd ed. (London: Longman, 1985).
Winthrop, John, *Journals* (Boston: Massachusetts Historical Society, 1947).
Wrigley, E. A. and R. S. Schofield, *The Population History of England: 1541–1871: A Reconstruction* (Cambridge, MA: Harvard University Press, 1981).

Wolf, John, *The Emergence of the Great Powers, 1685–1715* (New York: Harper and Row, 1962).
Wood, A. C., *A History of the Levant Company* (Oxford: Oxford University Press, 1935).
World Bank, *World Development Report 2009: Reshaping Economic Geography* (Washington, DC: World Bank, 2009).

Index